The **Rough Guide** to

Hong Kong
& Macau

written and researched by

Jules Brown and David Leffman

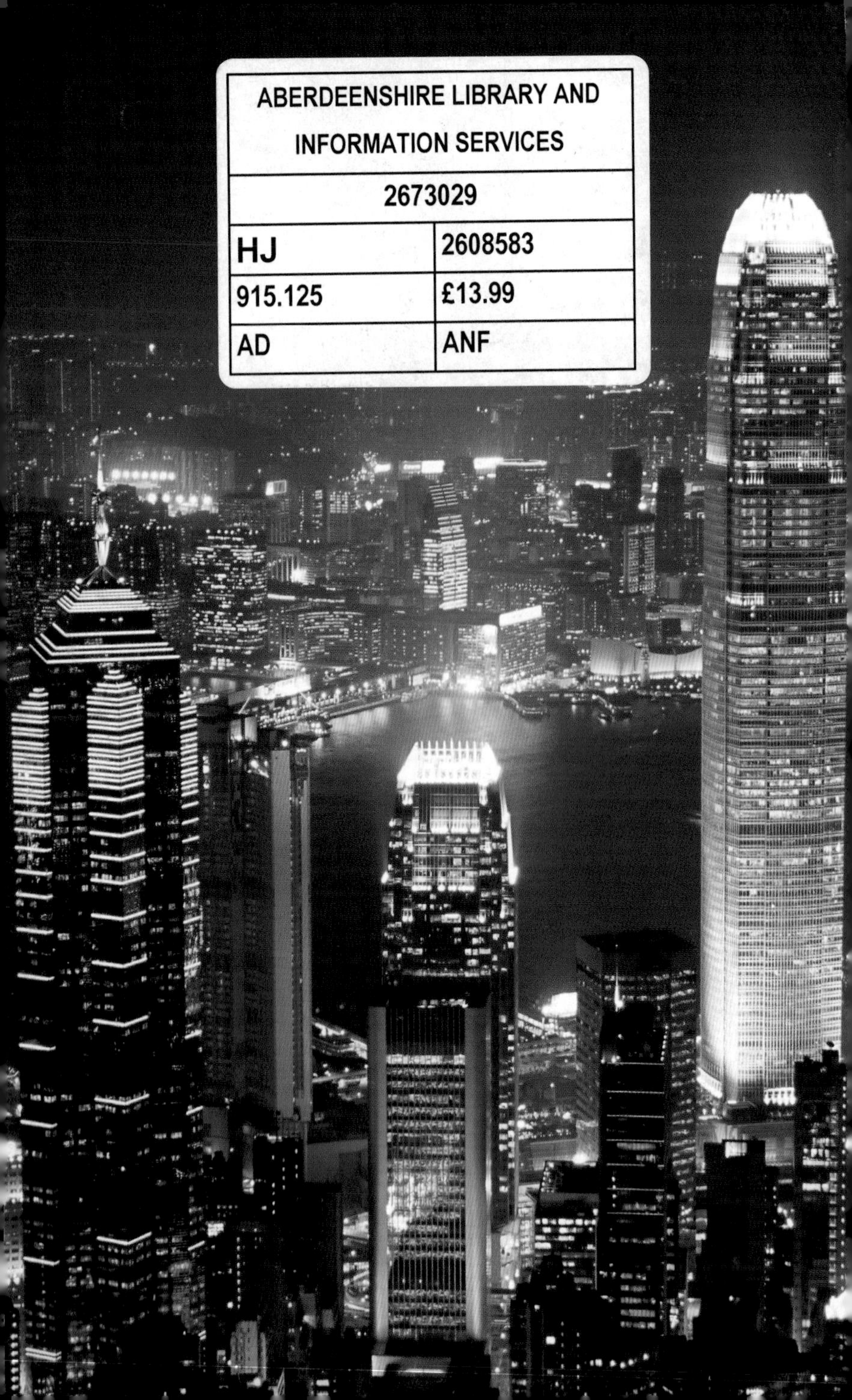

Contents

Architecture colour section following p.112

Cantonese cuisine colour section following p.208

Central Hong Kong Island **Colour maps** following p.352

◄◄ Golden dragon ◄ Hong Kong by night

Introduction to

Hong Kong
& Macau

Set 60km apart from each other across the Pearl River estuary, Hong Kong and Macau offer the visitor an exciting yet easy entry into the Chinese world. Colonies of Britain and Portugal respectively until they were returned to mainland China in the 1990s, today they are seeking to establish fresh identities for themselves under new administrations. While evidence of their colonial eras lingers in buildings, languages and high-tech infrastructure, the essentially Chinese heritage underpinning it all is becoming increasingly apparent.

In **Hong Kong**, the architecture is an engaging mix of styles, from the soaring towers of Central to traditional Chinese temples and villages; the markets and streetlife are compelling; while the shopping – if no longer the bargain it once was – is eclectic, ranging from open-air stalls to hi-tech malls. Hong Kong is also one of the best places in the world to eat **Chinese food** (and a good many other cuisines besides), while the former Western influence has left it a plentiful selection of bars and night-spots. Surprisingly, Hong Kong also boasts some beautiful **countryside**, featuring beaches, rugged hills and wild coastline warranting a day or two's exploration. If there's a downside to the place, it's that commercialism and consumption tend to dominate life, making it hard to engage with the day-to-day Chinese culture – though there's a range of well-presented museums and the usual run of cultural events you'd expect to find in any big city.

Smaller and more immediately attractive than its neighbour, **Macau** makes for an enjoyable side-trip from Hong Kong. Chinese life here is tempered by an almost Mediterranean influence, manifest in the ageing Catholic churches, hilltop fortresses and a grand seafront promenade. Like Hong Kong, Macau is ethnically Chinese; but while all the temples and festivals of southern China are reproduced here, they're not the main reason for a visit. Instead, Macau offers alternative attractions, especially **gambling**: this is the only place in the region where casinos are legalized, pulling in swarms of punters from Hong Kong and mainland China. Eating is another highlight: **Macanese food** is an exciting combination of Portuguese colonial cooking, with dishes and ingredients taken from Portugal itself, Goa, Brazil, Africa and China, washed down with cheap, imported Portuguese wine, port and brandy.

▶ *Dim sum in a teahouse*

Fact file

• The Special Administrative Region (SAR) of Hong Kong comprises a mainland peninsula and more than 260 islands on the southeastern tip of China, occupying a total **land area** of just under 1100 square kilometres. The region's **population** is approaching seven million, 95 percent of whom are Chinese in origin. Macau, 60km west of Hong Kong, consists of a peninsula and two islands, covering just over 25 square kilometres. Its population is roughly half a million, 96 percent of whom are of Chinese origin.

• Hong Kong's two official **languages** are Cantonese and English: Cantonese is the dominant everyday language, and English is the main business language. Macau's two official languages are Cantonese and Portuguese, although Portuguese is little used.

• The principal **religions** in Hong Kong are Taoism and Buddhism, with Confucianism also having a strong influence. Of the minority religions, 5 percent of the population are Protestant, 4 percent Catholic and 1 percent Muslim.

• Formerly European colonies, Hong Kong and Macau were both returned to Chinese sovereignty during the 1990s and are now **Special Administrative Regions (SARs)** of China, headed by locally selected chief executives, themselves approved by the mainland Chinese government.

What to see

Although Hong Kong is fairly compact – it's just 40km from the Chinese border in the north to the south coast of Hong Kong Island – and could be whizzed round in a few days, this small region packs in enough geographical and cultural diversity to fill weeks of exploration. **Hong Kong Island** itself is the heart of the territory, and houses the main business centre, known as **Central** – approaching here by Star Ferry across the harbour is one of the most thrilling city rides in the world. Central is where you'll find some of Hong Kong's most stunning contemporary landmarks, such as the Bank of China, the HSBC building and the IFC2 tower, which dominates the harbourfront skyline. However, traditional Chinese life is never very far away and the neighbouring districts are thick with Chinese herbalists, raucous markets, smoky temples and narrow lanes, all largely unchanged since colonial times. Everyone should make the effort to visit The Peak, whose 550-metre-high summit gives unsurpassed views – the precipitous tram ride up is another Hong Kong institution. East of Central, the districts of **Wan Chai** and **Causeway Bay** are well known for their shops, restaurants, bars

> Everyone should make the effort to visit The Peak, whose 550-metre-high summit gives unsurpassed views

and nightlife. The island's south side is characterized by its bays and beaches, with settlements such as **Aberdeen** and its floating restaurants; **Shek O**, with its white-sand beach; and **Stanley**, with its popular tourist market and restaurants aimed at foreign residents.

▲ Shopping street in Yau Ma Tei, Kowloon

Street addresses

Finding your way around Hong Kong isn't particularly difficult, though there are local peculiarities to be aware of. Addresses make great use of building names – often designated "Mansions" or "Plazas" – as well as street names and numbers, and usually specify whether the address is in Hong Kong (ie on Hong Kong Island) or Kowloon. Abbreviations to note are HK (Hong Kong Island), Kow (Kowloon) and NT (New Territories).

The shop or office numbering system follows this format: no. 803 means no. 3 on the 8th floor; 815 is no. 15 on the 8th floor; and so on. When written in English, floors are numbered in the British fashion (ie the bottom floor is the ground floor), but in Chinese they are numbered according to Chinese rules (ie the bottom floor is the first floor). Most abbreviations are straightforward: G/F is the ground floor and B indicates a basement level; M (mezzanine) and L (lobby) are also used.

In Macau, addresses are written in the Portuguese style: street name followed by number. Abbreviations you may come across are Av. or Avda. (Avenida), Est. (Estrada), Calç. (Calçada) and Pr. (Praça).

Across the harbour is the **Kowloon** peninsula and the districts of **Tsim Sha Tsui** and **Tsim Sha Tsui East**, home to some of Hong Kong's major museums and the vast shopping horizons along **Nathan Road**. Here, on Hong Kong's "Golden Mile", every consumer durable under the sun is traded, while the further north you head, the less recognizably Western and more Chinese the crowded grid of streets becomes. Noisy residential and shopping areas – in particular, **Yau Ma Tei** and **Mong Kok**, the latter one of the world's most densely populated neighbourhoods – host atmospheric markets devoted to items as diverse as goldfish, birds and jade.

When you tire of the city, the obvious escape is to one of the **outlying islands**, many of which are less than an hour away from Central by ferry. The southwestern group especially – **Lamma**, **Lantau**, **Cheung Chau** and **Peng Chau** – is popular with beach-goers and seafood connoisseurs, though hiking trails, the vast bronze Big Buddha and the Ngong Ping 360 cable-car ride provide other reasons to visit.

Further afield, the **New Territories** – the land between Kowloon and the Chinese border – feature modern, self-contained New Towns like **Sha Tin** and **Tai Po**, interesting for their civic-minded designs but also useful as access points for some surprisingly old villages and wild country parks. There's a lot of choice – especially if you're after a good hike – but if time is limited head straight for the **Sai Kung Peninsula** and its superb islands, bays and beaches.

Given Hong Kong's attractions, many visitors wonder if it's worth making the side-trip to **Macau**. The answer, emphatically, is yes: Macau's slower paced, historic atmosphere is the perfect antidote to Hong Kong's frenetic

downtown districts; tellingly, Macau's most famous landmark is the ruin of the seventeenth-century church of **São Paulo** rather than any bank. Other **colonial relics**, too, set the tone – the solid walls of Portuguese fortresses, the cracked facades of Catholic churches, dusty squares, old cemeteries and formal gardens. But change is afoot in Macau, with dramatic construction projects under way, which in recent years have turned the city from a sleepy backwater into a Las Vegas of the East: Macau has 29 **casinos** at present, a lure for millions of Hong Kongers and Mainland Chinese every year. It costs nothing just to look, however, and Macau also has its own offshore islands to visit – **Taipa** and **Coloane** – with some fine restaurants, beaches and colonial mansions.

When to go

H ong Kong and Macau's **subtropical climates** are broadly similar. Apart from a couple of months a year during which the weather is reliably good, for most of the time it's generally unpredictable, and often downright stormy. The heat is always made more oppressive by the **humidity**: you'll find your strength sapped if you try to do too much walking, and you'll need air-conditioning in your hotel room, or – at the very least – a fan. Macau does have the bonus of the cool breeze off the sea in summer, which makes nursing a beer on the waterfront a pleasant experience.

The best time is undoubtedly **autumn** (mid-Sept to mid-Dec), when the humidity is at its lowest and days are bright and warm. In **winter** (mid-Dec to Feb), things get noticeably cooler (you'll need a jacket), and though the skies often stay clear, there will be periods of wind and low cloud – don't expect reliable, broad views from The Peak at this time. Temperatures and humidity rise during **spring** (March–May), and while there can be beautiful warm days towards April, earlier in the season the skies usually stay grey and there are frequent showers and heavier rain. The **summer** (June to mid-Sept) is dramatically different: it's terribly hot and humid, and best avoided, if possible. If you do visit, you'll need an umbrella to keep off both the rain and the sun; raincoats are hot and aren't much use in heavy downpours.

The summer also sees the **typhoon season**, which lasts roughly from July to September. The word comes from the Cantonese *tai fung*, or "big wind", an Asian hurricane, and over the years typhoons whistling through Hong Kong have had a devastating effect – leaving scores of people dead and millions of dollars' worth of damage. A typhoon signal 3 means you should tie things down on balconies and rooftops, and some public facilities, such as swimming pools, will close. Once a typhoon is in full swing (after the no. 8 signal has been announced), planes will start to be diverted, local transport such as buses and cross-harbour ferries will stop

The best time to visit is undoubtedly autumn, when humidity is at its lowest and days are bright and warm

running, and you should stay indoors and away from exposed windows. Typhoon signal 10, known melodramatically as a "direct hit", is the strongest typhoon warning and means hurricanes of 118km per hour and upwards, with gusts of wind up to and above 220km per hour. Heavy rainstorms – which are not accompanied by the winds that characterize typhoons – can also be extremely disruptive, and businesses and transport links may close. Listen to the radio or TV to find out what's happening: weather signals for both typhoons and rainstorms are displayed as an icon on top of the pictures on local TV channels.

▶ Beach at Clearwater Bay in the New Territories

◄ Worshippers at the Wong Tai Sin Temple, Kowloon

The other factor to consider in deciding when to visit is the region's many **festivals**. If you can, try and coincide with the picturesque Mid-Autumn Festival in September/October when lanterns are lit and fireworks colour the sky, or June's Tuen Ng Festival to watch the dragon-boat races. Hong Kong's most important festival, however, is Chinese New Year, a two-week extravaganza of firework displays, lantern shows and eating – though many shops and businesses shut for the first three days, and accommodation can be hard to find.

Average daily temperatures and rainfall

Note that the figures below are averages. In summer, the temperature is regularly above 30°C, and the humidity over 90 percent. The winter is comparatively chilly, but the temperature rarely drops below 15°C.

	Jan	Feb	Mar	Apr	May	Jun	Jul	Aug	Sep	Oct	Nov	Dec
Average daily temperature												
Max/min (°C)	17/14	18/15	20/17	23/20	27/23	29/26	30/27	29/27	28/26	26/23	22/19	19/15
Max/min (°F)	63/57	64/59	68/63	73/68	81/73	84/79	86/81	84/81	82/79	79/73	72/66	66/59
Average rainfall												
(mm)	25	40	70	130	280	390	360	370	290	110	30	20

things not to miss

It's not possible to see everything that Hong Kong and Macau have to offer in one trip – and we don't suggest you try. What follows is a selective taste of the highlights: outstanding buildings, atmospheric markets, unforgettable views, glittering entertainment – as well as delicious things to eat and drink. All highlights have a page reference to take you straight into the Guide, where you can find out more.

01 Nan Lian Gardens Page **119** • This elegant reconstruction of a Tang dynasty garden provides an oasis of calm in the city.

02 **Hiking on the Sai Kung Peninsula** Page 155 • Explore the best of Hong Kong's outdoor scenery, with dozens of beautiful coastal headlands, seascapes, beaches and hills.

03 **Bird nest wholesale shops, Sheung Wan** Page 70 • Sheung Wan's traditional stores offer rare medicinal ingredients such as ginseng, crushed pearls, dried sea slugs and birds' nests.

04 **Pink dolphins** Page 177 • Spend a half-day on the sea off Lantau Island, tracking down these rare and endangered creatures, which are unique to Hong Kong.

05 Po Lin Monastery and the Big Buddha Page 174 •

The serene Tian Tin Buddha (or Big Buddha) on Lantau Island is the world's tallest outdoor, seated bronze Buddha, and weighs as much as a Jumbo Jet.

06 A tram ride up The Peak

Page **74** • Since 1888, The Peak tram has inched up the steep slopes behind Central to give visitors some of the most spectacular views in the region.

07 Lord Stow's Bakery, Coloane Page 286 •

The highlight of a visit to the quiet Macanese village of Coloane is sampling this bakery's superb *natas*, Portuguese custard tartlets.

08 Climbing at Lion Rock

Page **137** • Tremendous views over the New Town of Sha Tin reward climbers who conquer these dramatic rock faces.

09 Waterfront restaurants on Cheung Chau Island
Page 168 • Cheung Chau is best known for its seafood restaurants along the harbourfront. Sit by the water's edge and enjoy garlic-fried prawns, steamed scallops and fresh fish.

10 The ruins of São Paulo
Page 270 • All that's left of this magnificent Jesuit church built in Macau in 1602 is a flight of stone steps, and a facade carved with Christian symbols and Chinese characters.

11 Horseracing at Happy Valley
Page 84 • More than 23,000 race-goers pack the stands at each meeting to indulge in the only form of legal gambling in Hong Kong.

12 Tsang Tai Uk
Page 136 • A small but well-preserved traditional fortified village in Hong Kong's New Territories – just one of many similar settlements in Hong Kong built by the Hakka peoples.

13 **Tea at the Peninsula Hotel** Page **106** • High tea has been served in the lobby of the *Peninsula Hotel* in Tsim Sha Tsui to the strains of a string quartet since the 1920s; doilies and crumpets are still included.

14 **Watching tai chi in Kowloon Park** Page **108** • You'll have to get up early to catch the dawn tai chi artists run through their graceful slow-motion martial art.

15 **The Hong Kong Central skyline** Page **102** • Central's futuristic towers create one of Hong Kong's most memorable vistas, especially at night or seen from the Star Ferry ride across Victoria Harbour (see p.59).

16 A dim sum lunch Page

206 • Knuckle down with the locals in one of Hong Kong's many noisy *dim sum* restaurants, such as *Lin Heung Tea House* in Sheung Wan, and fill up on snack-sized portions of steamed dumplings, vegetables and barbecued meats.

17 Temple Street Night Market Page 111 • As well as stalls selling clothing, tack and tat, the night market is renowned for its street restaurants.

18 Grand Lisboa casino Page

274 • The Grand Lisboa casino is one of the most ostentatious in the whole of Macau, and its gold-plated windows are visible from any high point across the peninsula.

19 Largo do Senado

Page **267** • This beautifully cobbled square at the heart of old Macau is surrounded by antique Portuguese Baroque churches and government buildings.

Basics

Basics

Getting there

Hong Kong International Airport is one of the busiest in Asia, handling flights from all over the world; Macau's smaller airport has arrivals from a few Chinese cities and Southeast Asian countries. It's also possible to get to Hong Kong from Europe by train via Russia, Central Asia and China.

Airfares to Hong Kong and Macau are at their highest during the fortnight before Christmas, the fortnight before Chinese New Year (see p.34) and from mid-June to early October. The cheapest time to fly is in February (after Chinese New Year), May and November. You'll get the best deals by **booking online**, but, wherever you shop, also look out for **package tours** including accommodation and flights, either for Hong Kong and Macau alone or as part of a trip to China and other regions of Asia. Note that flying at weekends is generally more expensive; price ranges quoted below assume midweek travel. For information on how to get to Macau from Hong Kong, see p.265.

Flights to Hong Kong from the UK and Ireland

Direct flights to Hong Kong **from the UK** depart London Heathrow with British Airways, Cathay Pacific, Qantas, Air New Zealand and Virgin Atlantic. All charge between £400 low season and £800 in high season and take thirteen hours or so. Many European and Southeast Asian airlines also fly from London to Hong Kong via their home hubs (sometimes with a couple of other stops too). These flights cost roughly the same as nonstop services but can take much longer.

From **Ireland** your best bet is to connect at Heathrow or fly via another European hub with direct flights to Hong Kong such as Paris (Air France) or Amsterdam (Cathay Pacific).

Flights to Hong Kong from the US and Canada

Airlines flying direct daily from the North American continent's **west coast** to Hong Kong include Cathay Pacific (from LA and Vancouver), Singapore Airlines (San Francisco), Thai (LA), Air Canada (Vancouver) and United Airlines (LA). Flying time is approximately fourteen hours; fares range from US$800 in low season to US$1200 or more in high. Non-direct carriers from the above cities and Honolulu include Japan Airlines, Korean Air, Air China and EVA (via Taipei) and Thai Airways; **costs** can be lower at around US$700–1050, but the journey can take upwards of eighteen hours.

From the **east coast**, direct daily flights are with Cathay Pacific (from New York), United (New York and Chicago) and Air Canada (Toronto); flying time is about twenty hours and costs range between US$850 and US$1300 depending on season. Options involving a stopover include Thai (via Bangkok), Northwest (via Tokyo), Korea (Seoul) and Singapore (via Singapore); expect to spend 24 hours or more on the journey, and pay around US$900.

Flights to Hong Kong from Australia and New Zealand

Direct flights from Australia are covered by Cathay Pacific, which flies daily to Hong Kong from Sydney, Brisbane, Cairns and Perth; while Qantas flies from Sydney daily, and several times a week from Melbourne, Brisbane, Cairns and Perth. Fares range from AUS$1250 low-season to AUS$1600 in high; the journey takes 8–10 hours. **Indirect flights** are offered by just about every Southeast Asian carrier, but are not always cheaper than a low-season fare with Cathay Pacific.

Direct flights **from New Zealand** to Hong Kong are limited to Cathay and Air New Zealand (NZ$1600–2200; 11hr). Malaysia, Singapore and other carriers also fly via hub cities to Hong Kong, though not for substantially less money.

Flying to Hong Kong and Macau via Southeast Asia or China

If you are already in Southeast Asia, you'll find that the concept of no-frills **budget airlines** is just taking off in the region, with a couple of operators advertising seriously cheap tickets to both Hong Kong and Macau. The best deals are currently **from Bangkok** with Air Asia to Macau or Hong Kong (single fares from £49/US$70/AUS$110), or Orient Thai Airlines to Hong Kong (return fares from £100/US$140/AUS$220); and **from Kuala Lumpur** with Air Asia to Macau or Hong Kong, at just £36/US$52/AUS$82. Otherwise, Southeast Asia's major carriers all fly to Hong Kong at a reasonable cost from national capitals;

expect to pay upwards of £150/US$250/AUS$300 for a return ticket. Other airlines serving Macau include Air Macau (ⓦwww .airmacau.com.mo) with connections to Taipei, Shanghai, Beijing, Xiamen, Nanjing, Bangkok, Manila, Seoul and Tokyo; EVA Airways to Taipei and Kaohsiung; and Tiger Airways (ⓦwww.tigerairways.com) to Singapore.

From inside China, however, it's better not to fly direct to Hong Kong or Macau: it's considerably cheaper to aim for nearby Chinese airports at Guangzhou, Zhuhai or Shenzhen and make your way overland from there. For example, air fares from Beijing to Guangzhou with China Southern are around £130/US$200/AUS$310, instead of £200/US$315/AUS$480 to Hong Kong. Once in Guangzhou, a **train** to Hong Kong costs HK$185 and takes 2hr; or you can catch a **bus** for around half this. From Shenzhen or Zhuhai airports, you can catch direct buses

---

Six steps to a better kind of travel

At Rough Guides we are passionately committed to travel. We feel strongly that only through travelling do we truly come to understand the world we live in and the people we share it with – plus tourism has brought a great deal of **benefit** to developing economies around the world over the last few decades. But the extraordinary growth in tourism has also damaged some places irreparably, and of course **climate change** is exacerbated by most forms of transport, especially flying. This means that now more than ever it's important to **travel thoughtfully** and **responsibly**, with respect for the cultures you're visiting – not only to derive the most benefit from your trip but also to preserve the best bits of the planet for everyone to enjoy. At Rough Guides we feel there are six main areas in which you can make a difference:

- Consider what you're contributing to the **local economy**, and how much the services you use do the same, whether it's through employing local workers and guides or sourcing locally grown produce and local services.
- Consider the **environment** on holiday as well as at home. Water is scarce in many developing destinations, and the biodiversity of local flora and fauna can be adversely affected by tourism. Try to patronize businesses that take account of this.
- Travel with a purpose, not just to tick off experiences. Consider **spending longer** in a place, and getting to know it and its people.
- Give thought to how often you **fly**. Try to avoid short hops by air and more harmful night flights.
- Consider **alternatives to flying**, travelling instead by bus, train, boat and even by bike or on foot where possible.
- Make your trips "**climate neutral**" via a reputable carbon offset scheme. All Rough Guide flights are offset, and every year we donate money to a variety of charities devoted to combating the effects of climate change.

and ferries to Hong Kong or Macau, or cross the borders on foot.

Airlines, agents and operators

Online booking

Many airlines and discount travel websites offer you the opportunity to book your tickets, hotels and holiday packages online, cutting out the costs of agents and middlemen.

Ⓦ www.ctrip.com (in China)
Ⓦ www.ebookers.com (in UK), Ⓦ www.ebookers.ie (in Ireland)
Ⓦ www.expedia.com (in US), Ⓦ www.expedia.co.uk (in UK), Ⓦ www.expedia.ca (in Canada)
Ⓦ www.lastminute.com (UK and Australia)
Ⓦ www.opodo.co.uk (in UK)
Ⓦ www.orbitz.com (in US)
Ⓦ www.travelocity.com (in US), Ⓦ www.travelocity.co.uk (in UK), Ⓦ www.travelocity.ca (in Canada), Ⓦ www.travelocity.co.nz (in New Zealand)
Ⓦ www.travelonline.co.za (in South Africa)
Ⓦ www.zuji.com.au (in Australia)

Airlines

The main airlines serving Hong Kong are listed below. If you need to contact them while you're there they can be found in the Hong Kong Yellow Pages under "Air Line Companies"; for airport information check out Ⓦ www.hongkongairport.com or Ⓦ www.macau-airport.gov.mo.

Aeroflot Ⓦ www.aeroflot.com.
Air Asia Ⓦ www.airasia.com.
Air Canada Ⓦ www.aircanada.ca.
Air China Ⓦ www.airchina.com.
Air France Ⓦ www.airfrance.com.
Air New Zealand Ⓦ www.airnewzealand.com.
All Nippon Airways Ⓦ www.anaskyweb.com.
British Airways Ⓦ www.ba.com.
Cathay Pacific Ⓦ www.cathaypacific.com.
China Airlines Ⓦ www.china-airlines.com.
China Southern Ⓦ www.flychinasouthern.com.
Emirates Ⓦ www.emirates.com.
EVA Airways Ⓦ www.evaair.com.
Gulf Air Ⓦ www.gulfairco.com.
Japan Airlines Ⓦ www.japanair.com.
KLM Airlines Ⓦ www.klm.com.
Korean Air Ⓦ www.koreanair.com.
Lufthansa Ⓦ www.lufthansa.com.
Malaysia Airlines Ⓦ www.malaysiaairlines.com.

Orient Thai Ⓦ www.orient-thai.com.
Philippine Airlines Ⓦ www.philippineair.com.
Qantas Ⓦ www.qantas.co.uk.
Royal Brunei Ⓦ www.bruneiair.com.
SAA Ⓦ ww2.flysaa.com.
SAS (Scandinavian) Ⓦ www.flysas.com.
Singapore Airlines Ⓦ www.singaporeair.com.
Swiss Ⓦ www.swiss.com.
Thai Airways Ⓦ www.thaiair.com.
United Airlines Ⓦ www.united.com.
Virgin Atlantic Ⓦ www.virgin.com/atlantic.

Agents and operators

Abercrombie and Kent UK ☏ 0845/070 0610, Ⓦ www.abercrombiekent.co.uk; US ☏ 1-800/323-7308 or 630/954-2944, Ⓦ www.abercrombiekent.com; Australia ☏ 02/9241 3213; New Zealand ☏ 0800/441 638; Ⓦ www.abercrombiekent.com.au. Upmarket sightseeing tours of Hong Kong, with knowledgeable guides; also experienced in the overland rail routes to Hong Kong from Europe.
Absolute Travel US ☏ 1-800/736-8187, Ⓦ www.absoluteasia.com. Luxurious, in-depth tours of the SAR, including trips out to the New Territories and Macau.
Co-op Travel Care UK ☏ 0870/112 0085, Ⓦ www.co-operativetravel.co.uk.
CTS (China Travel Service) US ☏ 1-800/899-8618, Ⓦ www.chinatravelservice.com; Australia ☏ 02/9211 2633, Ⓦ www.chinatravel.com.au. Air tickets, visas, hotel bookings and tours by this major China-based tourist corporation.
CTS Horizons UK ☏ 020/7836 9911, Ⓦ www.ctshorizons.com. Chinese government-run tour operator offering umpteen China and Hong Kong tours.
Europe Train Tours US ☏ 1-800/551-2085 or ☏ 704/876-9081, Ⓦ www.etttours.com. Rail specialist which can organize travel on the Trans-Mongolian and Trans-Siberian expresses.
Flight Centre UK ☏ 0870/890 8099, Ⓦ www.flightcentre.co.uk; US ☏ 1-866/WORLD-51, Ⓦ www.flightcentre.us; Canada ☏ 1-888/WORLD-55, Ⓦ www.flightcentre.ca; Australia ☏ 13 31 33 or 02/9235 3522, Ⓦ www.flightcentre.com.au; New Zealand ☏ 0800 243 544 or 09/358 4310, Ⓦ www.flightcentre.co.nz.
International Gay & Lesbian Travel Association US ☏ 1-800/448-8550, Ⓦ www.iglta.org. Trade group with lists of gay-owned or gay-friendly travel agents and accommodation in Hong Kong.
Jade Travel UK ☏ 0870 898 8928, Ⓦ www.jadetravel.co.uk. Hong Kong company specializing in flights, hotels and sightseeing tours.

Overland by train

The **overland train route from London to Hong Kong** passes through Eastern Europe, Russia and Mongolia to China and Beijing, from where trains run south to the end of the line in Hong Kong. It's a satisfying – though exacting – journey (the route follows the **Trans-Siberian**, one of the world's classic train journeys, for much of its length), but it doesn't save you any money compared with flying. Prices for the Moscow–Beijing journey start at around £450/US$620/AUS$970 one-way for a bed in an intolerably uncomfortable four-berth "hard-sleeper" compartment – with fares at their highest (£550) between May and October – but for an extra £100/US$150/AUS$220 you can upgrade to a two-berth cabin and improve the chances of a comfortable night's sleep for the duration. Prepare for a very long haul: from London to Moscow takes two days, Moscow to Beijing five or six days depending on the route, and it's another 24 hour from there to Hong Kong.

If this doesn't put you off, you'll have to decide on the route and train you want to take – services are operated by both the Russians and the Chinese, either passing through, or bypassing, Mongolia (for which you need a separate visa). To sort it all out, talk to an experienced agent (see "Specialist operators" for your home country listed above), who can organize all tickets, visas and stopovers and can arrange a cheap flight back to London – you'll need to plan at least six weeks ahead.

Kuoni Travel UK ☎01306/742 002, ⊛www.kuoni .co.uk. Flexible package holidays combining a few nights in Hong Kong with multiple destinations in Southeast Asia, the Far East and Australia; good deals for families.

Magic Of The Orient UK ☎01293/537 700, ⊛www.magic-of-the-orient.com. Hong Kong and Southeast Asian tailor-made tours.

Maupintour US ☎1-800/255-4266 or 913/843-1211, ⊛www.maupintour.com. Lavish upmarket tours of Hong Kong, staying at the *Peninsula Hotel* and including cruises, beach trips and a concert.

North South Travel UK ☎01245/608 291, ⊛www.northsouthtravel.co.uk.

Pacific Delight Tours US ☎1-800/221-7179, ⊛www.pacificdelighttours.com. Offers a wide range of Hong Kong tours and packages, which can be combined with river cruises in mainland China.

Passport Travel Australia ☎03/9867 3888, ⊛www.travelcentre.com.au. Experienced Trans-Siberia booking agents; also tours and packages in China and Hong Kong.

Regent Holidays UK ☎0117/921 1711, ⊛www .regent-holidays.co.uk. Specialist agent for trans-Siberian and trans-Mongolian train tickets.

STA Travel UK ☎0870/1600 599, ⊛www .statravel.co.uk; US ☎1-800/329-9537; Canada ☎1-888/427-5639, ⊛www.statravel.com; Australia ☎1300/733 035 or 02/9212 1255, ⊛www.statravel.com.au; New Zealand ☎0508/782 872 or 09/309 9273, ⊛www .statravel.co.nz.

Sundowners Australia ☎03/9672 5300 or ☎1800/337 089, ⊛www.sundownerstravel.com. Specialists in overland rail travel, including the Trans-Siberian Express and the Silk Road.

Thomas Cook UK ☎0870/750 0512, ⊛www .thomascook.co.uk. Long established agent for package holidays, tours and cruises taking in Hong Kong as well as China and Southeast Asia.

Trailfinders UK ☎0845/0585 858, ⊛www .trailfinders.co.uk; Republic of Ireland ☎01/677 7888, ⊛www.trailfinders.ie; Australia ☎/9247 7666 or 1300/780 212, ⊛www.trailfinders.com.au.

Travel Bag UK ☎01/602 1904, ⊛www.travelbag .co.uk.

Travel Bound US ☎1-800/456-8656, ⊛www .booktravelbound.com. Good range of short-stay packages including air fare and accommodation, plus some local tours; most are extremely good value.

Twohigs Dublin ☎01/648 0800 or ⊛www .twohigs.com. Far East specialists.

usit NOW Republic of Ireland ☎01/602 1600, Northern Ireland ☎028/9032 7111; ⊛www.usit.ie.

Vantage Travel US ☎1-800/322-6677, ⊛www .vantagetravel.com. Specializes in group travel for seniors worldwide.

World Travel Centre Dublin ☎01/416 7007, ⊛www.worldtravel.ie. Specialists in flights and packages to the Far East.

Arrival

Hong Kong and Macau's main points of entry are their respective international airports, though you could also arrive at one of several train stations, ferry ports or – if you're on foot – border crossings. Whichever it is, you'll find plentiful public transport into the cities.

Hong Kong Airport

Hong Kong International Airport (@www .hongkongairport.com) is at Chek Lap Kok, Lantau Island, about 30km from the downtown area. The arrivals hall is wi-fi enabled, has foreign-exchange counters (with poor rates), an ATM hidden away in an alcove which accepts Visa cards but not bankcards with Cirrus/Maestro connections, and a left-luggage office. **The Hong Kong Hotels Association** (@www.hkha.org) can help you book a room, while the **Hong Kong Tourism Board** (@www.discoverhongkong .com) has several counters open daily 7am–11pm, along with helpful Airport Ambassadors wandering around the arrivals area to answer all questions.

The quickest way between the airport and the city is on the **Airport Express train** or AEL (every 10min 6am–12.45am). Carriages have air-conditioning and a reasonable amount of luggage space, but no toilets. **Tickets** are cheapest if bought from the customer service desk in the arrival hall, which always seems to offer some kind of discount on the full fare; or you can get them from automatic vending machines nearby. Note that you can also buy **Octopus cards** (see p.25) at the ticket desks, which you should definitely do if you're staying in Hong

Kong long enough to be using the transport system extensively. There are **three stops** on the Airport Express line: Tsing Yi (12min; HK$60), Kowloon in Tsim Sha Tsui (20min; HK$90) and Hong Kong Station in Central (23min, HK$100); return tickets (valid for 30 days) and child tickets are discounted. From Kowloon and Hong Kong stations, you can catch **free shuttle buses** to local hotels between about 6am and 11pm; you don't have to be staying at any of the hotels to use the service. Hong Kong Station is also linked to the Central MTR station on Hong Kong Island – it's a five-minute walk between the two.

A cheaper but less convenient alternative is to catch bus #S1 from the airport to **Tung Chung** (HK$4), and then use the MTR line (p.26) to reach the city or New Territories – it's about HK$23 from here into Kowloon.

The cheapest way of all from the airport into the city (and to most hotels) is by Airbus from outside the terminal. There are ten routes (some of which are detailed in the box p.24) with regular departures between 6am and midnight, and there's plenty of room for luggage. The airport customer-service counters sell tickets and give change; on the buses themselves you'll need to have the exact fare. The average journey time is about an hour. Brief English-language

In-town check-in

If you have a late flight out, one way to get rid of your luggage after leaving your hotel is to use the **in-town check-in** service, at either the Hong Kong Station in Central or Kowloon Station in Tsim Sha Tsui, which allows you to check in your luggage up to one day in advance of departure (check which airlines offer this service on the airport website). Deposit carry-on luggage that you don't want to lug around town for the rest of the day at **left luggage offices** at the stations (6am–1am). There are free shuttle buses from major hotels in Tsim Sha Tsui and on Hong Kong Island to Hong Kong Station and Kowloon Station.

announcements on board the buses tell you where to get off for the main hotels.

Taxis from the airport cost roughly HK$300 to Tsim Sha Tsui and about HK$350 to Hong Kong Island, so it's cheaper than taking the AEL for a group of four, though there may be extra charges for luggage and for tunnel tolls – on some tunnel trips the passenger pays the return charge too. **Rush-hour traffic** can slow down journey times considerably, particularly if you're using one of the cross-harbour tunnels to Hong Kong Island. Note that many major hotels offer **hotel buses** (around $120) and limos ($560) from the airport direct to their front doors; book at counters in the arrivals hall.

Those arriving **by helicopter** from Macau with East Asia Airlines will touch down on the helipad above the Macau Ferry Terminal (see box, p.265), where they'll clear customs.

Hong Kong cruise boat and ferry terminals

Ocean-going **cruise liners** stopping at Hong Kong dock at the Harbour City Ocean Terminal in downtown Tsim Sha Tsui, just a short walk from MTR stations and the Star Ferry across to Hong Kong Island.

Ferries **from China** originating at Zhuhai, Shenzhen, Zhaoqing and various riverside settlements between here and Guangzhou (Canton) terminate at the **China Ferry Terminal** on Canton Road, Tsim Sha Tsui, Kowloon. There are left-luggage lockers here (useful if you want to leave your bags somewhere while you look around Kowloon's extensive budget accommodation options) along with several ATMs; and it's a fifteen-minute walk to Tsim Sha Tsui MTR station on Nathan Road, though there are plenty of taxis too. Ferries **from Macau** either also arrive at the China Ferry Terminal, or at the **Macau Ferry Terminal** in the Shun Tak Centre, Connaught Rd, Sheung Wan, Hong Kong Island; here you'll find more lockers and ATMs, with the Sheung Wan MTR Station and bus terminus next door.

Hong Kong train and bus stations

Express trains from Guangzhou arrive at Hung Hom East Rail Station in Kowloon. From here, either catch a taxi from the rank outside; ride the East Rail to East Tsim Sha Tsui or Mong Kok for nearby accommodation; or exit south out of the station to the waterfront, where you can catch ferries across the harbour direct to the Wan Chai or Central Star Ferry piers.

Local trains **from Guangzhou** drop you in the Chinese city of Shenzhen, from where you walk across the border to Lo Wu on the Hong Kong side and pick up the East Rail Line to Kowloon: it's a fifty-minute ride, terminating again at East Tsim Sha Tsui Station.

It's also possible to arrive **by bus** from Guangzhou, Shenzhen, Zhuhai and other

---

Airbus routes

#A11 to North Point via Sheung Wan, Central, Admiralty and Wan Chai (daily 6am–midnight, every 15–25min; HK$40).

#A21 to Hung Hom East Rail Station via Mongkok, Yau Ma Tei, Jordan and Tsim Sha Tsui (daily 6am–midnight, every 10min; HK$33). Stops near all the hotels and guesthouses lining Nathan Road.

#A31 to the New Territories and Tsuen Wan (Discovery Park) via Tsuen Wan MTR Station (daily 6am–midnight, every 15–20min; HK$17). Travels via *Panda Hotel*.

#A35 to Mui Wo, Lantau Island (daily 6.30am–12.25am, at least hourly; HK$14, HK$23 at weekends and holidays).

#A41 to the New Territories and Sha Tin via Sha Tin KCR Station (daily 6am–midnight, every 15–20min; HK$20). Travels via *Regal Riverside* and *Royal Park*.

If your flight arrives after midnight or before 6am, you'll need a **night bus service**, which includes the #N11 to the Shun Tak Centre/Macau Ferry Terminal in Sheung Wan, Hong Kong Island (every 30min); the #N21 to the Tsim Sha Tsui Star Ferry pier, Kowloon (every 20min); and the #N35 to Mui Wo, Lantau Island (every 30min).

nearby Chinese cities, or direct from Shenzhen and Zhuai airports. Most services are run by the China Travel Service (CTS; see p.31 for their Hong Kong contact details) and stop along the way in Sheung Shui, Sha Tin and at Kowloon Tong MTR Station, before terminating at either Hung Hom Station or CTS branch offices in Mong Kok or Wan Chai.

Arrival in Macau

Macau International Airport is located at the eastern end of Taipa Island. From the airport, the airport bus #AP1 (MOP$3.30) runs across the Ponte Governador Bobre de Caravalho bridge and stops outside the Jetfoil Terminal before heading on to the *Hotel Lisboa* and the Portas do Cerco at the border.

Hong Kong **turbojets** and **catamarans** dock at the Jetfoil Terminal in the Porto Exterior, on the eastern side of the Macau peninsula. There are **money-exchange** office and ATMs here (though you don't need to exchange Hong Kong dollars as they're accepted everywhere in Macau), and a **left-luggage office** on the second floor of the terminal building (daily 6.30am–midnight) and 24-hour luggage lockers on the ground

and first floors. The terminal's ground floor **Visitor Information Centre** (8am–7pm) hands out maps and brochures.

From the Jetfoil Terminal, it takes around twenty minutes to **walk into central Macau**; otherwise, buses from the stops directly outside the terminal run into the centre, past several of the main hotels and out to Taipa and Coloane: #3, #3A, #10, #28A, #28B and #32 all go past the *Lisboa*; the #10 or #10A run to Largo do Senado; and the #28A goes on to Taipa Island. There are also plenty of taxis, which cost MOP$14–100 depending on your destination.

Ferries from Shekou (Shenzhen) dock at the Porto Interior on the west side of the peninsula, from where it's a short walk to the main avenue, Avenida de Almeida Ribeiro; bus #3A from here stops at Largo do Senado, the *Lisboa* and Jetfoil Terminal.

Crossing into Macau **from Zhuhai** lands you at either the Portas do Cerco (open 7am–midnight), from where bus #10 or #3 runs down to Avenida de Almeida Ribeiro; or on the Lotus Bridge (open 9am–5pm), between the islands of Taipa and Coloane – any north-bound bus will take you from here into central Macau.

Getting around

Both Hong Kong and Macau have excellent public transport systems and getting around is rarely a problem, even in relatively far-flung corners. Chinese characters for all sights mentioned in the text, along with some important streets, are given in boxes at the end of each chapter – use them if you're having trouble communicating on public transport or in asking directions on the street.

Transport in Hong Kong

Hong Kong's extensive network of trains, trams, buses and ferries is impressively integrated, reliable, cheap and easy to use – there's virtually nowhere in the SAR where public transport of some kind is more than a short walk away. You can pay for everything as you go, but it's far more

convenient – and slightly cheaper – to buy an **Octopus Card** (Ⓦwww.octopuscards .com), a rechargeable, stored-value ticket which works on all public trains, trams, buses, minibuses and ferries within the SAR (but not, for example, on trains into China or ferries to Macau, or private *kaido* ferries). They're available from train station service counters and Hong Kong New World First Ferry ticket offices, and can also be used like a debit card to buy goods in 7-Eleven stores and meals at *KFC Fairwood* and *Café de Coral* (including some branches of these in Macau and in Shenzhen, China). An adult Octopus card costs an initial HK$150, which includes a refundable HK$50 deposit (less HK$7 handling fee) and HK$100 usable value. When it runs out you simply add credit at machines in the MTR or over the counter at any 7-Eleven store. To **use** an Octopus Card, just pass it over the sensor pad on top of turnstiles; they'll work even if inside a wallet or in the pocket of a bag, as long as you get it close enough to the sensor.

If you're not going to be in Hong Kong very long, Octopus also offer various **Visitor Passes**, valid for different combinations of transport and for varying lengths of time; contact any Octopus retailer for current details.

Transport websites and Hong Kong Tourist Board offices can provide a heap of **information and timetables** for the city's public transport; you'll also find comprehensive bus, ferry and train routes marked in the *Hong Kong Guidebook* pocket atlas (see "Maps", p.46), with schedules – mostly in Chinese only – at the back.

The MTR

Hong Kong's **MTR** (Mass Transit Railway; ⓦ www.mtr.com.hk) comprises six interlinked lines from Lantau Island through Kowloon and along Hong Kong Island's North Shore (with a planned extension to Aberdeen, on southern Hong Kong Island) – see the colour map at the back of this book. The service is fast and efficient, with trains running every few minutes from 6am to 1am daily; you'll pay somewhere between HK$4 and HK$25 a ride depending on the distance covered, with bilingual ticket machines and customer service counters in all station concourses. Children under 12 pay half-price with a **Child Ticket**, also available from the machines. To **use the system**, you feed your ticket into the turnstile, walk through and pick it up on the other side. At the end of your journey,

the turnstile will retain your ticket as you exit. Avoid morning and evening **rush hours** (8–9.30am & 5.30–7pm), when horrendous crowds pile onto the escalators and trains.

Bilingual **MTR maps** are posted at all stations, and each train carriage also has maps of the specific line you're travelling on above the seats. Next-station announcements are made on trains in English, Cantonese and Mandarin Chinese. Note that most MTR stations have a handful of **exits**, each given a letter; these can be widely spaced so check with **locality maps** on station walls to make sure you take the correct one – details are given in the Guide where needed.

You're not allowed to eat, drink or smoke inside MTR stations or on trains. There are also **no toilets** on any of the station platforms. There's a fine of HK$100 if you're caught **travelling without a ticket** or Octopus Card debited for the journey.

The East Rail, West Rail, Ma On Shan and Airport Express lines

Four rail lines run through the New Territories, all of them managed by MTR (ⓦ www .mtr.com.hk): the **East Rail Line** between Tsim Sha Tsui and the border with China at Lo Wu and Lok Ma Chau (see p.30); the **West Rail Line** from Kowloon to Tuen Mun (see p.126); the **Ma On Shan Line** from Tai Wai to Wu Kai Sha (of limited interest for visitors); and the **Airport Express Line** from Hong Kong Island to the airport (see p.23). For **interchange stations** between these different lines and the MTR system, see the colour map at the back of this book.

The air-conditioned trains **operate** from around 5.30am to 1am and run every three to ten minutes; the ticketing and turnstile systems are the same as that on the MTR. **Fares** range from HK$3.50 to around HK$45; **children** under 3 travel free, those under 12 pay half-fare. There's a **first-class** compartment, staffed by a guard, for double the standard fare. You'll pay a HK$100 fine if caught travelling without a ticket, or travelling first-class with an ordinary ticket. Again, there's **no smoking** and no eating on board, but there are **toilets** on all the station concourses.

The Light Rail (LR)

The **Light Rail** (@www.mtr.com) is a tram-like network linking the major western New Territory towns of Yuen Long, Tin Shui Wai, Siu Hong and Tuen Mun with both their outlying suburbs and the West Rail Line. LR trains are electric, running alongside – and down the middle of – the New Territories' roads, and the system is zoned. Automatic ticket machines on the platforms tell you which zone your destination is in and how much it'll cost. Fares are around HK$4–6 per journey; feed your money in and wait for your ticket. Octopus Card users need to scan the "entry" or "exit" sensors on station platforms as they begin or end their journey respectively. Tourists are unlikely to use the Light Rail system except for trips to the Hong Kong Wetland Park (see p.134); see the colour map at the back of the book.

Buses

Double-decker buses are operated by Citybus-New World First Bus (@www .nwstbus.com.hk for schedule) and KMB (@www.kmb.hk), which between them cover just about every corner of Hong Kong Island, Kowloon and the New Territories. **Bus fares** range from HK$1.20 to around HK$35 a trip – the amount you have to pay is posted at most bus stops and on the buses as you get on. Scan your Octopus Card over the sensor or put the exact fare into the box by the driver (who is unlikely to speak English); there's no change given.

Most buses **run** from around 6am to midnight, marked at the front with the destination in English and Chinese, and a number. "K" after the number means that the bus links with a stop on the East Rail, West Rail or Ma On Shan lines; "M"-suffixed buses stop at an MTR station; buses with an "R" only run on Sundays and public holidays; and "X" buses are express buses with limited stops. **Night buses** operate from around midnight to 6am, and are prefixed with "N". Inside all buses, the name of the next stop is scrolled up in English and Chinese – the English doesn't stay up for very long though.

Minibuses

Hong Kong has two types of **minibuses**: those striped in **green** run along fixed routes between stops but can also be flagged down or set down anywhere along the way that vehicles are allowed to stop (so not, for example, on expressways); those striped in **red** run looser routes between set fixed points. You don't need them much around the downtown areas, but the green minibuses in particular come into their own for reaching outlying parts of the New Territories. Both types seat sixteen people and are not allowed to carry standing passengers, which is why they might ignore your frantic roadside waving or not allow you to board if the person ahead of you in the queue takes the last seat. Their destination is shown on a card on the front, usually in Chinese characters with a tiny English version. They charge HK$2–18, and you need the exact fare or to use an Octopus Card. To get off, shout *yau lok*, though you can say almost anything as long as you catch the driver's attention. **Hours of operation** are from around 6am until well after midnight on some routes; details for specific services are given in the Guide.

Trams

Archaic, double-decker **trams** (@www .hktramways.com) rattle along the north shore of Hong Kong Island, from Kennedy Town in the west to Shau Kei Wan in the east, via Western, Central, Admiralty, Wan Chai and Causeway Bay; some detour around Happy Valley and the racecourse. Not all trams run the full distance, so check the destination (marked in English) on the front and sides before you get on. From Central, east to Causeway Bay takes around forty minutes, to Shau Kei Wan around fifty minutes, and west to Kennedy Town around half an hour.

Climb aboard at the back. If you're staying on for a long journey, head upstairs for the views. Otherwise, start working your way through to the front and, when you get off, swipe your Octopus Card or drop the **flat fare** (HK$2 for adults, HK$1 for senior citizens and children) in the box by the driver: there's no change given. Trams operate from 6am to 1am, though services on some parts of the line finish earlier; avoid rush hours if you actually want to see out of the window.

Incidentally, the **Peak Tram** is not really a tram at all but a funicular railway, which climbs swiftly from the Lower Peak Tram Terminal on Garden Road to the Peak Tower on The Peak (with a couple of local commuter request stops on the way) – see p.74 for more details.

Ferries

On a clear day, the **cross-harbour ferries** provide unforgettable views of Hong Kong Island, with countless boats zipping across the harbour. Services are cheap, reliable and run every day of the week: the only days to watch out for are in **typhoon** season, when crossings sometimes become very choppy and can be suspended altogether. **Star Ferry** (ⓦ www.starferry.com.hk) operates the famous crossing between Tsim Sha Tsui and Central, along with other routes between Tsim Sha Tsui and Wan Chai (see p.59), and between Hung Hom and Wan Chai or Central – the last two useful if you've just arrived by train from China at Hung Hom station (see "Arrival", p.24). Ferries run every few minutes 6.30am–11.30pm, and **fares** cost between HK$1.70 and HK$6 depending on service and class; you pay in cash or use an Octopus Card.

The islands of **Lantau Lamma Cheung Chau** and **Peng Chau** are serviced by ferries from the **Outlying Island Ferry Piers** in Central, Hong Kong Island – see the "Outlying Islands" chapter, p.161, for more information. Other islands reached from elsewhere by public ferries and **kaido** – small boats – are covered separately in the Guide. On a public *kaido* (not chartered), you generally pay the HK$5–10 fare to the person operating the boat. If there's no regular service, you'll need to charter the whole boat – the text in this Guide tells you when it's necessary and roughly how much it will cost, but expect to haggle.

Taxis

Hong Kong's **taxis** are relatively cheap – many people treat them as a branch of public transport. You can flag them down in the street or pick one up at the ranks at major train stations and ferry terminals. Taxis

can't drop or pick up on yellow lines. Look for a red "For Hire" flag in the windscreen; at night the "Taxi" sign on the roof is lit. Make sure the driver turns the meter on when you get in (though rip-offs are rare).

On **Hong Kong Island and Kowloon**, taxis are red: minimum charge is HK$18 (for the first 2km) and then it's HK$1.50 for every 200m. In the **New Territories**, taxis are green and flag fall is HK$14.50; those on **Lantau** are pale blue and cost HK$13 to stop. You'll also have to pay HK$5 **extra** per piece of luggage that goes in the boot, as well as picking up any **tolls** (HK$5–15), such as for the Crossy-Harbour tunnels between Kowloon and Hong Kong Island. Drivers are allowed to charge you for the return toll, too, if they think they won't be able to get a customer for the journey back to the side you hired them on; if you're not happy with this, ask if it is going to happen before getting in. There's a yellow sign displayed in every cab outlining possible extra charges.

Taxis can be extremely hard to come by when it rains, during typhoons, on race days, after midnight and at driver changeover time (around 9.30am and again at 4pm). Many drivers don't speak English, although they'll know the names of major hotels – and they should have a card somewhere in the cab with major destinations listed in Chinese and English. Otherwise you'll need to have someone write down where you're going on a piece of paper to show to the driver. If you get really stuck, gesture to the driver to call his control centre on the two-way radio, and state your destination into the microphone. Someone there will translate.

Renting cars and bikes

Renting your own car in Hong Kong isn't a sensible idea. The public transport system is so good that it's rarely quicker to drive, and in any case one dose of rush-hour traffic would put you off driving forever. If you really need a car, out in the New Territories, say, or on Lantau, it's always cheaper just to take a taxi. If you're determined to rent, you'll pay from around $580 a day, $2600 a week, for the smallest available car. You need to be over 18 (21 or 25 with some firms), have been driving for at least a year and have a valid overseas driving licence (with which you can drive in Hong Kong for a year) or an international driving licence. Remember that you **drive on the left**. Agencies include: Avis, ⓦ www.avis .com.hk; or Hertz, ⓦ www.hertz.com. You can also hire a car and driver by the day or hour with Fung Hing Hire ⓣ 2572 0333, ⓦ www .funghingcar.com.hk, though it's not cheap. **Parking** can be a bit of a problem; finding a space in the centre is nigh impossible, and the multistorey car parks are generally expensive and located where you least want them. The biggest firm is Wilson (ⓦ www.wilsonparking .com.hk), which has 250 car parks spread all over Hong Kong – see website for locations. Charges are roughly $20 an hour.

Bike rental is more feasible, though again, not in crowded central Hong Kong or Kowloon. There are several places in the New Territories where it's fun: in particular, the cycle lanes around Sha Tin (see p.135) which stretch all the way along Tolo Harbour to Tai Po and then on to Tai Mei Tuk (Plover Cove). You can rent bikes on Sha Tin Rural Committee Rd and on the ground floor of Lucky Plaza in Sha Tin; around Tei Mei Tuk reservoir; and on Kwong Fuk Rd in Tai Po (see p.142); or around the train station in Tai Wai (see p.135). The less congested outlying islands are also excellent places to cycle: there are bikes for rent near the Mui Wo ferry pier on Lantau, on Cheung Chau and on the rather hilly Lamma Island just outside Yung Shue Wan. Expect to pay around HK$40–60 a day per bike.

Organized tours

There are a huge range of organized tours of Hong Kong, as well as day-trips beyond the city, including the following favourites:

Bengseng Travel Floor 3, Shun Tak Centre, 200 Connaught Rd, Sheung Wan ⓣ 2546 4022, ⓦ www .bengsengtravel.com. Macau specialists.

Detours Suite 17E, Neich Tower, 128 Gloucester Rd, Wan Chai ⓦ www.dukling.com. Charter the *Duk Ling*, the last authentic sailing junk in Hong Kong harbour for cruises, weddings and events; it takes 36 passengers and a day costs HK$18,000.

Gray Line Tours 5th Floor, Cheong Hing Building, 72 Nathan Rd, Tsim Sha Tsui ⓦ www.grayline.com.hk. An international organization whose Hong Kong arm runs predictable coach tours around the SAR (HK$320 upwards) plus longer trips to Macau and China.

Hong Kong Dolphinwatch Ltd 1528A Star House, Tsim Sha Tsui ⓣ 2984 1414, ⓦ www .hkdolphinwatch.com. Popular boat trips out to north Lantau waters to spot rare pink dolphins; half-day trip for HK$360.

Hong Kong Tourism Board ⓦ www .discoverhongkong.com (see p.51 for office contact details). Excellent range of tours, from 2hr harbour cruises (HK$230) or an evening's horse-racing in Happy Valley (from HK$690), to guided day-trips around Lantau (HK$580) or the entire New Territories (at HK$530 probably the best-value tour available in Hong Kong). They also offer informative free courses in tea or jewellery appreciation, tai chi, Cantonese opera and even cake making; each lasts an hour or two; sign up at least a day in advance.

Jason's Walks ⓦ www.jasonswalks.com. Guided walks around central Hong Kong and Macau led by noted local historian and author Jason Wordie. HK$280 per person, minimum of ten people; solo travellers might be allowed to join existing groups but you'll need to organize this in advance.

Jaspa's ⓦ www.jaspasjunk.com. Party cruises out to remote coast and island beaches, with as much food and drink as you can handle. You need at least fourteen people for a charter (maximum of forty) and it costs HK$600 a head.

Star Ferry ⓦ www.starferry.com.hk. Hour-long, day and night harbour cruises (HK$50–140). Book at Star Ferry piers.

Tip Top Tours Shop B126, 1/B, Regal Kowloon Hotel, 71 Mody Rd, Tsim Sha Tsui East ⓦ www .tiptoptours.com.hk. Range of culture-oriented day-trips around different parts of Hong Kong, the best of which is out to Cheung Chau Island (HK$340).

Traway Travel ⓣ 2527 2531, ⓦ www.traway.com .hk. Boat tour from Sai Kung Town to Tap Man Chau (p.146), via remote stretches of Sai Kung and Plover Cove country parks, including Lai Chi Wo village (see p.157). HK$480.

Walk Hong Kong ⓣ 9187 8641, ⓦ www .walkhongkong.com. Guided walking trips in English or German, from 3hr-long market or heritage tours (HK$400), to day-trips along hiking trails on Hong Kong Island, Lantau and the New Territories (around HK$700).

Watertours of Hong Kong Ltd 1023A, 10th Floor, Star House, Salisbury Rd, Tsim Sha Tsui ⓦ www .watertours.com.hk. Catch the sunset, the firing of the Noon Day Gun, the Symphony of Lights or enjoy a night cruise around Victoria Harbour with cocktails. HK$250–400.

Transport in Macau

You'll can feasibly **walk** around Macau's peninsula, though to reach Taipa and

Into mainland China

To enter China, you'll need a **visa**, which in Hong Kong are issued at the Consulate Department of the Chinese Ministry of Foreign Affairs building on Kennedy Road, in Central (Mon–Fri 9am–4pm); and in Macau through the CTS, Ave. do Dr. Rodrigo Rodrigues 223–225 ☎2870 0888, ⓦwww.cts.com.mo. However, it's cheaper and faster to arrange a visa through a **travel agency** or through your accommodation, many of which offer the service. **Fees** vary between around HK$200 and HK$600, according to whether you want a single-entry or double-entry, one-month, three-month, or six-month visa, and whether you want fast (same-day) processing or two to three days. Bring a passport photo with you. Agents can also arrange hotel accommodation and onward journeys to all major cities in China.

From Hong Kong

The simplest route into China **from Hong Kong** is by **direct train to Guangzhou** from Kowloon's Hung Hom Station to Guangzhou East Station; there are a dozen trains daily, and the trip takes under three hours (from about HK$185 one way). Trains are run by the MTR; you can check **timetables prices** and **book online** at ⓦwww.it3.mtr .com.hk, or buy tickets on the day at Hung Hom Station. As a cheaper alternative, ride the **East Rail Line** up to Lo Wu, cross into Shenzhen on foot and pick up one of the hourly trains to Guangzhou from there – in all, this costs around HK$110.

The other land route is by **bus**. The China Travel Service (☎2988 7888, ⓦwww .ctshk.com) runs frequent services to Shenzhen, Zhuhai and Guangzhou, and to Shenzhen and Zhuhai airports. The Guangzhou run takes about 3 hours 30 minutes and costs HK$150 one-way.

By **boat**, there are around six fast ferries daily to **Shenzhen** (Shekou) each from the Macau Ferry Terminal on Hong Kong Island, and from the China Ferry Terminal on Canton Road, Kowloon. Tickets cost HK$105–170 depending on class and time of day, and the crossing takes under an hour. Further departures from the China Ferry Terminal include to towns around the Pearl River Delta and to the scenic city of **Zhaoqing** in eastern Guangdong province.

Finally, you can **fly** from Hong Kong into all major Chinese cities on regional Chinese carriers. Note, however, that it's much cheaper to fly out of Shenzhen, Zhuhai or Guangzhou airports instead, even after you factor in transport to these places. All air tickets can be booked through any agent in Hong Kong.

Coloane and a couple of the more far-flung sights, you'll need transport. **Buses** run just about everywhere from 7am until 11pm daily; a few services stop after 6–8pm, though the short distances mean you shouldn't get stuck. **Fares** are low: MOP$2.50 for any single trip on the peninsula; MOP$3.30 from the peninsula to Taipa; MOP$4 to Coloane village; and MOP$5 to Hác Sá. You pay as you board with the exact fare; drivers don't give change.

The main **terminals** and bus stops are outside the Jetfoil Terminal; in front of the *Hotel Lisboa*; at Barra district in the southwest of the peninsula (near the Maritime Museum and A-Ma Temple); along Avenida de Almeida Ribeiro; at the border crossing with Zhuhai; and at Praça Ponte e

Horta. Details of individual buses are given in the Macau chapter where useful.

Taxis, pedicabs and car rental

Macau's **taxis** all have a flag fall of MOP$13, after which it's MOP$1.50 for every 250m, plus MOP$4 for each piece of luggage. There's a **surcharge** of MOP$5 for travelling from the peninsula to Coloane (but not back the other way), or for catching a taxi at the airport; and a MOP$2 surcharge for travelling between Taipa and Coloane. There are ranks outside all the main hotels and at various points throughout the enclave, but you can also flag them down on all the central main roads.

Outside the Jetfoil Terminal and the *Hotel Lisboa* you'll be accosted by the drivers of

Travel agencies in Hong Kong

The places below can help with travel to China, as well as flights to the rest of Southeast Asia and beyond. If you're looking for budget flights or tours, you should also check the classified sections of the *South China Morning Post* and *HK Magazine*. One word of warning: when making a booking don't hand any money over, even a deposit, until the ticket is confirmed. Many agents offer great deals, and ask for a holding deposit while they put you on a waiting list. You'll find out later that your agent couldn't get you a seat on the great deal but on a more expensive one instead. If you don't buy, then you lose your deposit.

China Travel Service (CTS; ⓦ www.ctshk.com), at least forty branches in Hong Kong. Extremely organized for China flights, accommodation, tour packages and visas, though not especially cheap. They also run direct buses to various places across the border, including Shenzhen airport and Guangzhou. Useful branches include: Ground Floor, CTS House, 78–83 Connaught Rd, Central ☎2853 3533; China Travel Building, Southorn Centre, 138 Hennessy Rd, Wan Chai ☎2832 3888; and 1st Floor, Alpha House, 27–33 Nathan Rd (entrance in Peking Rd), Tsim Sha Tsui ☎2315 7188.

Connaught Travel, 4th Floor, Chung Hing Commercial Building, 62 Connaught Rd, Central ☎2544 1531, ⓦ www.connaught-travel.com. Efficient, friendly and good air fare rates.

Shoestring Travel, 4th Floor, Alpha House, 27–33 Nathan Rd, Tsim Sha Tsui (entrance on Peking Rd) ☎2723 2306, ⓦ www.shoestringtravel.com.hk. Friendly and efficient place with flights, visas and bus tickets to China.

Time Travel, Block A, 16th Floor, Chungking Mansions, 40 Nathan Rd (☎2366 6222, ⓕ3583 1403). China visas and budget flights in Southeast Asia.

From Macau

From Macau, the quickest way to China is to cross the land border into Zhuhai, from where you can catch a bus to Guangzhou (MOP$65; 2hr). You can also book direct buses to Guangzhou with Macau's CTS for MOP$95, or **fly** to a dozen or so cities across China – though, as with air fares into China from Hong Kong, it's cheaper to fly to Chinese destinations from Zhuhai, Shenzhen or Guangzhou.

---

pedicabs – three-wheeled bicycle rickshaws. They're more suited for short tourist rides – say around the Praia Grande – than for serious getting around, since Macau's hills prevent any lengthy pedalling. You're supposed to bargain for rides, but expect to pay around MOP$40–50 for a short turn along the harbour and MOP$150 for an hour's sightseeing.

Renting a car doesn't make a lot of sense: it's easy to get around cheaply by public transport and on foot and also extremely difficult to find parking spaces in central Macau. If you still need to, Avis at the *Mandarin Oriental* (ⓦ www.avis.com.mo) rents out cars from MOP$700 for 24hr, and mini-mokes from MOP$450; rates include vehicle and third-party insurance (prices for all vehicles rise at weekends). You need to be at least 21, to have held a driving licence for two years and have an international driving licence. Remember to drive on the left.

Organized tours

Tour options are fairly limited in Macau, with the MGTO offering the best deals.

Gray Line Tours 179 Rua do Campo ☎2833 6611, ⓔ grayline@macau.ctm.net. Six-hour spin around the key sights from MOP$350.

Macau Government Tourist Office (MGTO) ⓦ www.macautourism.gov.mo (see p.51 for office locations). Guided tours of the city highlights, World Heritage Monuments, Taipa and Coloane islands, shopping opportunities or cuisine, from MOP$90.

New Sintra Tours 2nd Floor, Jetfoil Terminal ☎2872 8050, ⓦ www.estoril.com.mo. More coach tours with a local operator from MOP$350.

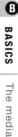

The media

Cantonese might be the language of the majority in Hong Kong, but there's also good English-language media coverage, including television and radio. In Macau, local newspapers and broadcasts are mainly in Cantonese and Portuguese.

Newspapers

There are four **English-language newspapers** published in Hong Kong. The *South China Morning Post* (www.scmp.com) gives the party line on the various problems besetting Hong Kong, and carries a daily "what's on" listings section. Its only rival is the *Standard* (www.thestandard.com.hk), which is aimed more at the business community but is occasionally very scathing about government shortcomings. The other two papers are the *Asian Wall Street Journal* (www.wsj-asia.com) and the *International Herald Tribune* (www.iht.com) – the first business-led, the second culled mostly from American newspapers. Another business journal worth getting hold of is the *Far Eastern Economic Review* (www.feer.com). Published in China, but widely available in Hong Kong, the *China Daily* (www.chinadaily.com.cn) makes interesting reading in an Alice-in-Wonderland kind of way – straight-down-the-line Beijing government propaganda. There are also over forty **Chinese newspapers** published daily in Hong Kong of various political hues, some with pro-China slants and others independentlyy minded. British, European and American newspapers are widely available, too, normally a couple of days late. Many bookshops and downtown newsstands stock a wide range of local and foreign magazines. For local listings magazines and free sheets, see p.225.

The *Macau Post* is **Macau's single English-language** paper, giving a desperately thin round-up of international headlines. You can also buy Hong Kong's newspapers in Macau, as well as imported copies of foreign newspapers, from the newspaper stands along the central *avenidas*.

Television and radio

In Hong Kong, every hotel and most guesthouses lay on TV and radio for their guests, and you'll be hard pushed to escape them in bars and restaurants – although what you'll get is likely to be quantity rather than quality.

Hong Kong's two TV broadcasters are **TVB** and **ATV**, who together provide an astoundingly dull selection of news, soaps, documentaries and dramas, many imported from the mainland and overseas. The presiding ethos is safe, uncontroversial family viewing with very little variety. Broadcasting is in Cantonese and English depending on the programme; there are also a few news programmes in Mandarin Chinese. There's a much better range of **pay TV** however, though of course not everywhere is connected. Other than horse racing and a few major international events, **sport** is not well covered – fans are better off trying one of the sport-oriented bars in Lan Kwai Fong or Wan Chai. **Radio** – with at least five English-language channels – is provided by Radio Television Hong Kong (RTHK; get frequencies or listen in online at www.rthk.org.hk). Full programme details for TV and radio are contained in the daily newspapers.

You can pick up Hong Kong's television stations in Macau, as well as some from mainland China; there's also a local station, Teledifusão de Macau (TdM), whose programmes are mostly in Cantonese and Portuguese, though a few are in English.

Festivals

Hong Kong and Macau's traditional Chinese festivals have roots going back hundreds (even thousands) of years, though today they're often more secular than religious. The biggest event by far is Chinese New Year, when both cities grind to a complete standstill as the population comes out on the street to celebrate; but even small festivals, perhaps focused on just one temple, can be exuberant affairs filled with noise, activity and gold and red decorations.

Not all festivals are public holidays, though bigger events can mean crowds on public transport, higher prices for certain services, and overwhelming swarms at festival venues. Note that Chinese festival dates are set using the **lunar calendar**, and so fall on different days, even different months, each year; for exact details contact the HKTB or MGTO. The box on the next page lists the best-known events, though individual temples might also hold minor celebrations for particular deities: for Kwun Yam (or Kun lam in Macau) on the 26th of the first lunar month, and the 19th of the second, sixth, ninth and eleventh lunar months; for the Dragon Mother on the 8th of the fifth month; and for Kwan Tai (Kwan Kung) on the 13th of the fifth month.

The **Christian calendar** also throws up a number of festivals celebrated in churches in both Hong Kong and Macau, such as New Year, Easter and Christmas. In addition, Macau also celebrates the **first day of Lent**, when an image of Christ is carried in procession from the church of Santo Agostinho to the Sé for an overnight vigil and then returned via the Stations of the Cross; and the **Procession of Our Lady of Fatima** (May 13), which moves from São Domingos church to the Penha chapel to commemorate a miracle in Fatima, Portugal, in 1913.

For a list of **public holidays**, see p.48.

For a list of traditional Chinese festivals, and details about celebrations in Hong Kong and Macau, see box on p.34.

Traditional Chinese festivals

The festivals below are dealt with **chronologically**, starting with the Chinese New Year.

Chinese New Year

The most important of all the festivals, **Chinese New Year** (called "Spring Festival" in Chinese) is celebrated for the first two weeks of the first lunar month (Jan or Feb). Decorations covered in Chinese characters for long life, wealth and happiness go up everywhere, and markets sell huge quantities of flowers, oranges, lanterns and sweets. **Lion dances**, with brightly coloured "pantomime" lions (roles performed by local martial arts teams), parade through the streets visiting businesses, whose owners provide them with cabbages; the Cantonese words for "cabbage" and "wealth" sound similar, and the whole dance is symbolic of chasing away bad luck and bringing prosperity for the forthcoming year.

Most of all, the festival is a **family affair**, when people clean their houses, settle debts, visit friends and relations, wear new clothes and generally ensure a fresh start for the year. Vast crowds descend on temples; married couples hand out red envelopes of money to their families; people on salaries get a bonus; and shop assistants and waiters are feasted by their employers. Particular **things to eat** at New Year include noodles (for longevity), fish (the Cantonese word sounds similar to that for "surplus") and dumplings (for wealth). To wish someone a "Happy New Year", you say *"kung hei fat choi"*. The biggest public spectacle is the tremendous, shattering **fireworks display** – held on Hong Kong's harbour and Macau's Lagos de Nam Van – designed to drive away evil spirits; with a **lantern festival** (Yuen Siu) held in public parks on the fifteenth day.

Ching Ming Festival

Held at the beginning of the third moon (early April), Ching Ming is a day when families visit **ancestral graves** to clean them. Incense and paper offerings are burnt, food (and drink) is left for the dead, prayers are recited and blessings sought for new generations. Extra public transport is laid on for trips to cemeteries, and in places the event can become one enormous scrum.

Tin Hau (A-Ma) Festival

Held on the 23rd day of the third lunar month (late April or May) in honour of the sea goddess Tin Hau (A-Ma), this is understandably one of the most important festivals in Hong Kong and Macau. Fishing boats are cleaned from stem to stern and decorated with flags and pennants as worshippers converge on Tin Hau temples to watch Cantonese opera, dances and parades and to offer fruit and pink dumplings as a mark of respect. The biggest events are at Joss House Bay in Clearwater Bay, Hong Kong (p.152) and Macau's A-Ma Temple (p.277), but any Tin Hau shrine is worth a visit.

Buddha's Birthday

A low-key event on the eighth day of the fourth lunar month (in May) when Buddha's statue is "bathed" in scented water. The Po Lin Monastery on Lantau, Hong Kong (p.174), is a good place to see the rites being performed.

Tam Kung Festival

Celebrated on the same day as Buddha's Birthday, this celebrates the maritime deity Tam Kung at his temples in Shau Kei Wan, Hong Kong Island (see p.87), and in Coloane, Macau (p.286).

Drunken Dragon Festival

Again falling on the eighth day of the fourth moon, this boisterous event is celebrated at Macau's Hong Kung Temple (p.272) and the Tam Kung Temple in

Hong Kong (p.87), and features a march of inebriated worshippers, martial arts displays and noise.

Tai Chiu (Cheung Chau Bun) Festival
A week-long extravaganza held on Cheung Chau Island, Hong Kong, in late April/ early May (starting on the same day as the Tam Kung Festival, above). See p.166 for more details. Expect the island and all transport there to be in a state of siege during festivities.

Tuen Ng (Dragon Boat) Festival
Celebrated on the fifth of the fifth lunar month (in June), the Tuen Ng Festival commemorates the virtuous Chinese official **Ch'u Yuen**, who committed suicide by drowning in 278 BC in protest against government corruption. The local people tried to save him in their boats, and having failed threw **rice dumplings** into the water as an offering to his ghost. The modern festival features **dragon boat races**, the narrow vessels crewed by up to eighty people; rice dumplings are also eaten. Check local press and tourist offices for event venues; most waterside towns hold races.

Birthday of Lo Pan
Held on the thirteenth day of the sixth lunar month (July), this festival honours the patron deity of builders, Lo Pan, at his temple in Kennedy Town, Hong Kong (p.73).

Maidens' Festival
Also known as the **Seven Sisters' Festival**, the Maidens' Festival falls on the seventh day of the seventh lunar month (August), when young girls and lovers burn incense and leave offerings of fruit and flowers. The festival is celebrated informally everywhere, but the most popular destinations for devotees are Lovers' Rock in Wan Chai (p.82) and Amah Rock near Tai Wai (p.137), both in Hong Kong.

Yue Lan Festival
Yue Lan, held on the fifteenth day of the seventh lunar month (Aug), is also known as the "**Festival of the Hungry Ghosts**", when ghosts are released from the underworld to roam the earth. It is considered an unlucky day, when accidents or sinister events can happen; people burn peace offerings in the form of paper models of food, cars, houses, money, furniture, etc, which the ghosts then take back to the underworld with them.

Mid-Autumn Festival
The Mid-Autumn Festival takes place on the fifteenth day of the eighth lunar month (Sept) and commemorates a fourteenth-century revolt against the Mongols, when the call to arms was written on pieces of paper, stuffed inside cakes and distributed to the population. People celebrate by eating wonderfully sickly **moon cakes** (*yuek beng*), full of preserved egg or sweet lotus paste, light **paper lanterns** and watch the moon rise; there are also public lantern displays in parks and, in Tai Hang, Hong Kong Island, a fire dragon dance (see p.86).

Cheung Yeung Festival
Celebrated on the ninth day of the ninth lunar month (Oct), the Cheung Yeung Festival relates to a tale from Han Dynasty times, when a soothsayer advised an old man to take his family to the mountains for 24 hours to avoid disaster. On his return, everyone else in the village had died. The same trip to high places is made today in remembrance, with people also using the opportunity to visit family graves.

Culture and etiquette

Hong Kong and Macau are cosmopolitan and sophisticated, with a strong streak of European culture overlying the Chinese one, and acceptable public behaviour is pretty much the same as wherever you've come from – possibly a little bit more conservative. The one big difference are the downtown crowds: though aggressive shoving and jostling is surprisingly rare, the sheer density of pedestrians, along with heat, humidity and – in tourist areas – pushy vendors trying to sell you fashion accessories, all test your temper, especially if you're in a hurry.

In general, the Chinese are less obsessed with **privacy** and their "personal space" than Westerners, and much more socially oriented – given Hong Kong and Macau's crowded living conditions, they have to be. Silence, loneliness and darkness are associated with death, so for most Chinese the ideal social occasion is spent with lots of other friends and family in noisy, informal and bright surroundings; hence the lively nature of most Chinese restaurants, parks, temples and festivals.

Local tastes in **clothing** lean towards smart-casual wear for any social occasion, with perhaps more rigorous dress standards at more exclusive venues and events. So no shorts, sandals or flip-flops if you're going for tea at the *Peninsula* and a jacket and tie if you're eating in an expense-account restaurant. For formal dinners, you'll need the penguin suit and tie rental services of Tuxe Top Co. Ltd, 1st Floor, 18 Hennessy Rd, Wan Chai ⊕2529 2179, ⓦwww.tuxetop.com (open daily 10am–7pm). If you're meeting someone formally for the first time, especially over business, an exchange of **name cards** might be expected; you give and receive cards with both hands (polite shop keepers do the same thing with your change), and it's good manners to read the card before tucking it away. **Shaking hands** is normal practice in both Hong Kong and Macau.

If you visit a Chinese house, it's expected that you'll bring a **gift** (for instance, imported spirits or wine, or some good tea), though it probably won't be opened in front of you. Thanks are sometimes perfunctory, as in Chinese culture you often express gratitude by actions rather than words – though in Hong Kong or Macau this is more down to personal choice nowadays.

In all but the more upmarket **restaurants**, expect to have to be more assertive than you're used to in order to attract staff's attention; Hong Kong's waiters are famously surly or dismissive – and insanely busy – so don't take abrupt service personally. For more on restaurant etiquette, see p.210. In **temples**, you'll find the Chinese respectful but in no way precious about their religion, and the atmosphere is always one of informality rather than hushed observance; just don't barge in front of people who are kowtowing to deities or point your camera around rudely – in fact, photography is **banned** in many temples. It's a similar situation with **festivals**, at which public involvement is often encouraged rather than frowned upon – play things by ear.

Smoking is now banned in most public places in Hong Kong, though not in Macau – see p.39 for more.

Travelling with children

The Chinese are very child-friendly people as a rule, and make a lot of fuss over both their own offspring and other people's. In addition, both Hong Kong and Macau have abundant attractions – parks, temples, festivals, food, shopping and tours – for keeping the little ones entertained (see p.258 for details).

The local **hazards** – outlined in the box below – are mostly a matter of common sense, with only a few things (like the weather and pollution levels) which are beyond your control. There are also plenty of supermarkets and chemists with English-speaking staff, where it's possible to find familiar brands of formula, nappies and child medicines.

Some **restaurants** – usually only Western ones – have child menus while others might allow you to order half portions; and having children in tow, especially young ones, might also secure you half-decent table service. Many of the better hotels offer **child-minding services**; public washrooms in urban shopping malls often have changing facilities. Don't **breast-feed** in public.

Hazards

- Hong Kong can be extremely hot and humid. Small children should wear a hat and suncream when outside, and drink plenty of liquids.

- Intense crowds, especially in downtown Hong Kong, can also be stressful – if not for the children themselves, then the adults trying to keep an eye on them. Give yourself plenty of time to get around and avoid rush hours.

- Pollution is a growing problem. Air contamination in urban areas makes them worth avoiding at peak times, particularly if your child is asthmatic. The seawater in many popular swimming spots may not be healthy for small children with no immunity to local bugs.

- Restaurant hygiene may also be an issue, particularly for children who are not used to Chinese food. Use your common sense when choosing where to eat.

- Keep a close eye on children when riding public transport. Tram rides on Hong Kong Island, the Peak Tram and the MTR are all exciting, but they're nearly always packed. Keep kids away from tram windows (there's no glass to stop them falling out), and from the edges of the cross-harbour ferries. It's easy to get separated in crowds, although it's very unlikely that anyone will try to abduct them.

- Don't encourage or allow children to play with animals found on the street. Rabies and bird flu are recurrent problems here, and if your child gets bitten or scratched by a stray kitten or bird, you're in for lengthy hospital visits.

Travel essentials

Costs

In Hong Kong, staying in hostels and dormitories and eating cheap Chinese meals at street stalls, and walking everywhere, you can survive – just – for HK$250/£23/EU$25/US$32 a day. Eat out more or go to better restaurants, take a taxi or two, have a drink in a bar, and you're looking at a minimum of HK$350/£32/EU$35/US$45 a day. If you upgrade to a room with en-suite facilities, eat three meals a day and travel around a fair amount, your daily expenses will exceed HK$600/£54/EU$60/US$77 – though if you're staying in any sort of hotel, this figure won't even cover your accommodation.

Living costs in **Macau** are 10–20 percent less than in Hong Kong: you'll pay slightly more for cheaper beds, but will get much better value in the larger hotels. Meals, too, are good value: wine and port is imported from Portugal and untaxed, and an excellent three-course Portuguese meal with wine and coffee can be had for as little as MOP$250. Transport costs are minimal, since you can walk to most places, though buses and taxis are in any case extremely cheap.

Crime and personal safety

Hong Kong and Macau are both relatively safe places for tourists, certainly compared

> In both Hong Kong and Macau, dial ☏999 for any emergency service (police, ambulance or fire).

with other Asian cities. The only real concern is the prevalence of **pickpockets**: the crowded streets, trains and buses are the ideal cover for them. Keep money and wallets in inside pockets, sling bags around your neck (not just over your shoulder) and pay attention when getting on and off packed public transport.

Hong Kong's MTR rail system is clean, well lit and well used at night. Taxis, too, are reliable, though it's still wise to use registered taxis from proper taxi ranks only. If it's late at night and you find yourself somewhere vaguely threatening, look purposeful, don't dawdle and stick to the main roads. If you are **held up and robbed** – an unlikely event, though a few hikers have been mugged in remote parts of the New Territories – hand over your money and *never* fight back.

More common problems are those associated with **drunkenness** in Hong Kong. If it's your scene, be careful in bars where the emphasis is on buying hugely expensive drinks for the "girls": if you get drunk and can't/won't pay, the bar gorilla will help you find your wallet. And unless you like shouting and fighting, try to avoid

Free things

Hong Kong and Macau might be relatively expensive places, but there are a number of **free things** to take advantage of while you're here. **In Hong Kong**, these include entry to all downtown parks, plus the Zooolgical and Botanical Gardens (p.65); the Edward Youde Aviary and the Museum of Teaware in Hong Kong Park (p.66); all government-run museums on Wednesdays; martial arts performances in Kowloon Park on Sunday afternoons (p.108); the ferry ride through Aberdeen Harbour to the *Jumbo* floating restaurant (p.90); Mong Kok's bird garden and markets (p.114); harbour views from Tsim Sha Tsui waterfront (p.102), the Bank of China tower (p.64) and Central Plaza (p.77); all beaches and hiking trails; and introductory cultural courses offered by the HKTB (p.247). You can also **camp for free** at any of the campgrounds run by the AFCD (p.197). **In Macau**, all the old forts, casinos and temples are free to enter – enough to keep you busy for a few days.

the bars when the sailors of various fleets hit the city.

Finally, **pedestrians** need to pay close attention when crossing roads in Hong Kong, even at designated crossings, as traffic takes no prisoners and will definitely not slow down or swerve to avoid you – hardly a day passes when the news doesn't feature a pedestrian death.

Police and offences

The **Hong Kong Police** are armed and wear olive or blue uniforms; English-speakers have a red swatch on their epaulettes. Probably the only contact you'll have with them is if you have something stolen, when you'll need to get a report for your insurance company. In this case, contact one of the police stations – headquarters is at Arsenal St, Wan Chai ☎2860 2000 (call this number and you'll be given the address and phone number of your nearest police station). For Crime Hotline and taxi complaints, call ☎2527 7177; for complaints against the police, call ☎2866 7700.

Macau Police wear a dark blue uniform in winter, and sky-blue shirts and navy blue trousers in summer. The main police station, where you should go in the event of any trouble, is at Av. Dr Rodrigo Rodrigues ☎2857 3333.

There are a few **offences** you might commit unwittingly. In Hong Kong, you're required to carry some form of **identification** at all times: residents need a special ID card, while visitors only need something with their photograph, such as passport or driving licence. As a Westerner you are unlikely to be stopped by police in the streets, though you might be involved in the occasional police raid on discos and clubs, when they're usually looking for illegal immigrants and drugs. They'll prevent anyone from leaving until they've taken down ID details.

Buying, selling or otherwise being involved with **drugs** in Hong Kong or Macau is extremely unwise. If you're caught in possession, no one is going to be sympathetic, least of all your consulate. Less seriously, **smoking** is prohibited in just about all public spaces in Hong Kong, including restaurants, bars, clubs, beaches and most public parks

(except designated areas); there are no such restrictions in Macau. **Littering or spitting** on the streets in Hong Kong carries an HK$1500 fine; and **topless bathing** on any of Hong Kong's or Macau's beaches is illegal.

Sexual harassment

Harassment is not common, and women travelling in Hong Kong and Macau are more likely to be hassled by foreign expats than by Chinese men. To minimize risks try to avoid travelling alone late at night on Hong Kong's MTR, or during rush hour when men might take advantage of the crush for a quick grope.

Organized crime: the Triads

Hong Kong and Macau's organized crime gangs, collectively known as **Triads**, are directly and indirectly responsible for the drug dealing, prostitution, corruption and major crime in the SARs. Needless to say, the average visitor won't come into contact with any of this, though drug addicts support their habit by pickpocketing and mugging, while shops and restaurants you visit may be supplied by a Triad-related company.

Electricity

In Hong Kong the current is 200V AC. Plugs are a mixture of round two or three pins, but the most common is the large three square-pinned socket used in the UK. Either way, a travel plug is useful, or you can buy adaptors at the night market, shops on the ground floor of Chungking Mansions, or many other similar places for $5–10. Most of Macau's electricity is supplied at 220V, although some buildings in the older parts of the city still use power at 110V. Plugs are the small three round-pin type.

Entry requirements and customs allowances

Citizens of the UK, Ireland, US, Canada, Australia, New Zealand and most European countries do not require a visa before arrival and can stay in Hong Kong or Macau for between thirty and ninety days, depending on nationality. Everyone else should consult the relevant Chinese Embassy, Consulate or High Commission in their country of origin for visa requirements (see below). Passports for all visitors must be valid for at least six months from the planned date of departure. Note too that though Hong Kong and Macau are technically part of China, you still need a separate visa to enter the Chinese mainland – see the "Into mainland China" box, p.30.

Chinese consulates and embassies

Australia 15 Coronation Drive, Yarralumla, ACT 2600 ☏02/6273 4780, ⓦau.china-embassy .org/eng. Also 539 Elizabeth St, Surry Hills, Sydney ☏02/9698 7929, and 77 Irving Rd, Toorak, Melbourne (visa & passport enquiries ☏03/9804 3683).
Canada 515 St Patrick's St, Ottawa, ON K1N 5H3 ☏613/789 3434, ⓦwww.chinaembassycanada .org. Also 240 St George St, Toronto, ON M5R 2P4 ☏416/964 7260; 3380 Granville St, Vancouver, BC V6H 3K3 ☏604/736 5188; 1011 6th Ave SW, #100 Calgary, Alberta T2P 0W1 ☏403/264 3322.
New Zealand 2–6 Glenmore St, Wellington ☏04/472 1382, ⓦwww.chinaembassy.org.nz. Also 588 Great South Rd, Greenland, Auckland ☏09/525 1588, ⓦwww.chinaconsulate.org.nz.
Republic of Ireland 40 Ailesbury Rd, Dublin 4 ☏053/1269 1707, ⓦie.china-embassy.org.
South Africa 965 Church St, Arcadia 0083, Pretoria ☏012/342 4194, ⓦwww.chinese-embassy.org.za.
UK 49–51 Portland Place, London W1B 1JL ☏020/7299 4049, ⓦwww.chinese-embassy.org .uk. Also Denison House, Denison Rd, Victoria Pk, Manchester M14 5RX ☏0161/224 7480.
USA 2300 Connecticut Ave NW, Washington DC 20008 ☏202/328 2500, ⓦwww.china-embassy .org. Also 520 12th Ave, New York, NY 10036 ☏212/330 7410; 100 W Erie St, Chicago, IL 60610 ☏312/803 0095; 3417 Montrose Blvd, Houston, TX 77006 ☏713/524 4311; 443 Shatto Place, Los Angeles, CA 90020 ☏213/807 8018.

Hong Kong

There shouldn't be any trouble with the **immigration officers** on arrival, all of whom speak English. You may be asked how long you intend to stay and, if it's a fairly lengthy period, for referees in Hong Kong and proof that you can support yourself without working, unless you have an employment visa (see p.45).

Given the length of time most people are allowed to stay in Hong Kong, you are unlikely to need to **extend your stay**. If you do, the simplest solution is to go to Macau for the weekend and come back, and nine times out of ten you'll just get another period stamped in your passport. If you want to ensure a longer stay, though, you'll need to apply for a visa in advance of your visit from the Immigration Department, as you will if you're intending to work in the territory. Allow at least six weeks for most visa applications.

If you're in trouble or lose your passport, or you want details of the visas necessary for travel on to neighbouring countries, consult the relevant **foreign consulate** in Hong Kong.

Foreign consulates and embassies

Australia 23rd Floor, Harbour Centre, 25 Harbour Rd, Wan Chai ☏2827 8881.
Canada 14th Floor, 1 Exchange Square, Central ☏2810 4321.
China 42 Kennedy Rd, Central ☏2106 6303.
India 16th Floor, United Centre, 95 Queensway, Admiralty ☏2528 4028.
Ireland 54th Floor, Bank of China Tower, 1 Garden Rd, Central ☏2527 4897.
Japan 46th Floor, One Exchange Square, Central ☏2522 1184.
Korea 5th Floor, Far East Finance Centre, 16 Harcourt Rd, Central ☏2529 4141.
Malaysia 24th Floor, Malaysia Building, 50 Gloucester Rd, Wan Chai ☏2821 0800.
New Zealand 6501 Central Plaza, 18 Harbour Rd, Wan Chai ☏2525 5044.
Philippines 14th Floor, United Centre, 95 Queensway, Admiralty ☏2823 8501.
Singapore 901–2 Tower 1, Admiralty Centre, Admiralty ☏2527 2212.
South Africa 2706 Great Eagle Centre, 23 Harbour Rd, Wan Chai ☏2577 3279.
Thailand 8th Floor, Fairmont House, 8 Cotton Tree Drive, Central ☏2521 6481.
UK 1 Supreme Court Rd, Admiralty ☏2901 3000.
US 26 Garden Rd, Central ☏2523 9011.
Vietnam 15th Floor, Great Smart Tower, 230 Wan Chai Rd, Wan Chai ☏2591 4510.

You're allowed to bring the following duty-free goods into Hong Kong: 60 cigarettes (or 50 cigars or 75g of tobacco) and 1 litre of alcoholic beverages. You can take most other things into Hong Kong with little difficulty. Prohibited items include all firearms and fireworks, and if you're caught carrying any kind of illegal drugs you can expect very tough treatment.

Macau

You'll barely notice the **customs officials** as you arrive in Macau, though there might be the odd spot check; there are no import restrictions as long as what you're bringing in is for personal use (except, of course, for illegal drugs or firearms).

Gay and lesbian travellers

Most people in Hong Kong and Macau are fairly tolerant of gay and lesbian issues, and – unless you make overt displays of affection in public – you shouldn't encounter any problems. For information on **Hong Kong**'s busy but low-profile gay scene – including listings for bars, clubs, spas and fitness centres, local organizations and counselling services – check GLB (W sqzm14.ust.hk /hkgay) or Utopia (W www.utopia-asia.com); the latter also has good information on the gay scene in various mainland Chinese cities. Gaystation (W www.gaystation.com.hk) is an internet radio station on gay and lesbian affairs which live-streams daily 11pm–midnight, with shows archived for listening at any time; and there's a round-the-clock **chat room** service. They also produce the Gaystation brochure, which you can find in the gay venues themselves, or Page One bookshop (see p.241). See the box on p.227 for a list of popular night-time venues; you'll also find a great listings page at W www.dragoncastle .net/hongkong.shtml. There's a helpline service, Horizons, open Tues and Thurs 7.30–10.30pm (T 2815 9268), or at W www .horizons.org.hk.

There's very little information available about **Macau's limited gay nightlife** – again, Utopia is your best bet for listings and events.

Health

No vaccinations are required to enter Hong Kong or Macau; but if you've been in an area infected with cholera or typhoid during the fourteen days before your arrival, you'll need certificates of vaccination against the two diseases. These requirements might change, so ask your doctor if you're unsure about what constitutes an infected area.

The region's population density, along with steamy summers and high levels of airborne pollution, mean that **respiratory infections** can be a problem in both Hong Kong and Macau. Generally, this is nothing more serious than you'll encounter at home, though the 2002 outbreak of pneumonia-like **SARS** (Severe Acute Respiratory Syndrome), which originated in southern China, killed three hundred people in Hong Kong. The event was short-lived – Hong Kong and Macau have been SARS-free since June 2003 – but the lessons have been taken seriously; you'll often see locals with colds wearing surgical face-masks in the streets. There have also been regular – but contained – outbreaks of potentially deadly **bird flu**, and outbreaks see the mass slaughter of ducks and chickens across the region. None of this is reason for paranoia, however, and Hong Kong and Macau remain safe places to visit for a short stay – see the "Medical Contacts" websites on p.43 for up-to-date information.

General **hygiene standards** are reasonable, though don't expect surgical cleanliness in cheaper hotel bathrooms or the smaller places to eat – the latter might just rinse their bowls and chopsticks with lukewarm water, or sometimes tea. Market-bought **fruit and vegetables** should be washed carefully, as many are grown in mainland China where pesticide and fertilizer use is uncontrolled. **Meat and fish** are often sold alive and cooked soon afterwards, which guarantees freshness, but locally-caught **shellfish** are all more or less contaminated – though today most seafood comes from cleaner seas around Australia, the Philippines and Indonesia. **Water** is safe to drink everywhere (except from old wells on some of Hong Kong's outlying islands), though bottled water always tastes nicer. If you come down with

---

For all **emergencies** in Hong Kong or Macau (ambulance, police, fire), dial T 999.

In **Hong Kong**, the St John's Ambulance Brigade runs a **free ambulance service**, on T 2576 6555 (Hong Kong Island), T 2713 5555 (Kowloon) or T 2639 2555 (New Territories).

In **Macau**, you can also call an ambulance on T 2857 7199.

stomach trouble, the best advice is not to eat anything for 24 hours, drink lots of water or weak tea and take it easy until you feel better. Once on the mend, start on unspiced foods like soup or noodles, though if you don't improve quickly, get medical advice.

Take summer heat seriously; temperatures rise well into the thirties and the humidity can be almost paralyzing. Prickly heat skin rashes can be countered by showering often, using talcum powder and wearing light cotton clothing. Make sure you drink plenty of water – at least a couple of litres daily in hot weather – especially if you're hiking. Wearing sunglasses and a hat is also a good idea during the summer.

While AIDS is not as prevalent as in some other Southeast Asian cities, don't contemplate unprotected sex, and if you have acupuncture, ensure that new needles are used.

Pharmacies

Pharmacies can advise on minor ailments and will prescribe basic medicines; they're all registered, and (in the centre of Hong Kong, less so in Macau) usually employ English-speakers. They are generally open daily 9am–6pm. Watsons is a big, Hong Kong-wide chain which stays open to 7pm or later, with branches in Macau, too, and stocks toiletries, contact-lens fluid and first-aid items. A number of products are available over the counter that are prescription-only in many Western countries, notably contraceptive pills and melatonin. Manning's sells more or less the same as Watson's, usually a fraction cheaper. Both have outlets everywhere.

In Macau, in addition to the two branches of Watsons (one in Largo do Senado next to the MGTO, and one on Rua de Santa Clara near the junction with Rua do Campo), the following pharmacies take it in turn to open for 24hr (details posted on the door in Chinese and Portuguese):

Farmácia Lap Kei Calç. do Gaio 3D ☎ 2859 0042.
Farmácia Nova Cidade Av. Barbosa, Centro Comercial ☎ 2823 5812.
Farmácia Popular Largo do Leal Senado 16 ☎ 2857 3739.
Farmácia Tsan Heng Av. de Almeida Ribeiro 215 ☎ 2857 2888.

Chinese medicine

If you're after treatment using Traditional Chinese Medicine (see box below), ask at your accommodation or the Hong Kong Tourism Board offices for recommended practitioners. Alternatively, you can try one of the many Chinese herbal medicine shops, found throughout Hong Kong and Macau, which are stacked from floor to ceiling with lotions, potions and dried herbs. The people in these shops are not likely to speak English, but if you can describe your ailment they'll prescribe and mix for you a herbal remedy. Note, however, that many Chinese herbal

Traditional Chinese Medicine

Traditional Chinese Medicine (TCM) works on the principle that, to function properly, there must be a healthy flow of chi (energy) around the body. According to Chinese beliefs, chi circulates along lines known as meridians, each of which originates in an organ and travels to the body's extremities. If the chi flow becomes irregular – through injury or illness – energy will pool in parts of the body and be absent in others, causing illness. TCM works on restoring the body's chi balance with acupuncture – where fine needles are inserted into key points along meridian lines to either increase or decrease chi flow – and by prescribing the patient brews made from combinations of medicinal herbs which help tonify and regulate energy in the body (even if they taste disgustingly bitter). Certain martial arts, such as tai chi, are also believed to be good for the health because they exercise the meridian system, thereby regulating the body's chi flow and preventing illness. Though there is considerable scepticism outside China as to TCM's effectiveness, there seems to be a case to be made for its use in certain chronic illnesses, to assist recovery after surgery, or simply to maintain good health.

prescriptions are not one-off cures but might need weekly follow-up visits, and that herbalists are not required to have formal training to set up shop – although many do.

Doctors and dentists

For a **doctor**, look in the local phone directories' Yellow Pages (under "Physicians and Surgeons" in Hong Kong; "*Medicos*" in Macau), or contact the reception desk in the larger hotels. Many doctors in Hong Kong have been trained overseas, but you should ask for one who speaks English. You'll have to **pay for a consultation** (around HK$400) and any medicines they prescribe; ask for a receipt for your insurance. If the medicine is not prescription-only, it's often cheaper to write down the name and pick it up from an ordinary chemist, rather than buy it from the surgery. It's cheaper to visit the nearest **local government clinic** (often with the words "Jockey Club" in the title, since that's who partly funds them): they stay open late, and you'll only pay a few dollars if you need a basic prescription or treatment at the casualty desk – though you may have to queue. All the clinics are listed in the Hong Kong phone books (at the beginning, in the Government directory).

Finally, both doctors and **dentists** are known as "doctor" in Hong Kong, so be sure you're not wasting your time at the wrong place. Having dental work done costs a lot, so if you possibly can, wait until you get home for treatment. If not, dentists are listed in the Yellow Pages under "Dental Practitioners", or contact the Hong Kong Dental Association (☎2528 5327, ⓦwww.hkda.org) for a list of qualified dentists. Treatment is expensive.

Hospitals

Hospital treatment is infinitely more expensive than seeing a doctor at upwards of HK$3000 a day (with $19,000 deposit) – unless you're a Hong Kong ID card holder in which case you pay $68 per day on a public ward – which makes it essential to have some form of medical insurance. Casualty visits are free, however, and hospitals in both territories have 24-hour casualty departments. Private hospitals are more expensive but the standard of care is higher.

Hospitals in Hong Kong

Canossa Hospital 1 Old Peak Rd, Hong Kong Island ☎2522 2181 (private).
Hong Kong Baptist Hospital 222 Waterloo Rd, Kowloon Tong ☎2339 8888 (private).
Matilda Hospital Suite 2601, 9 Queen's Rd, Central ☎2537 8500 (private).
Princess Margaret Hospital 2–10 Lai King Hill Rd, Lai Chi Kok, Kowloon ☎2990 1210.
Queen Elizabeth Hospital 30 Gascoigne Rd, Kowloon ☎2958 8888.
Queen Mary Hospital Pokfulam Rd, Hong Kong Island ☎2855 3838.

Hospitals in Macau

Centro Hospitalar Conde São Januário Calç. Visconde São Januário, Macau ☎2831 3731 (English-speaking).
Hospital Kiang Wu Est. Coelho do Amaral, Macau ☎2837 1333 (mostly Chinese-speaking).

Medical resources for travellers

ⓦ**www.cdc.gov/travel** US government travel advice, listing precautions, diseases and preventive measures by region.
ⓦ**www.fitfortravel.scot.nhs.uk** UK NHS website carrying information about travel-related diseases and how to avoid them.
ⓦ**www.gov.hk** The Hong Kong government website includes a health section outlining facilities and services.
ⓦ**www.istm.org** The website of the International Society for Travel Medicine, with a full list of clinics specializing in international travel health.
ⓦ**www.tripprep.com** Travel Health Online provides a comprehensive database of necessary vaccinations for most countries, as well as destination and medical service provider information.

In the UK and Ireland

Hospital for Tropical Diseases Travel Clinic 2nd Floor, Mortimer Market Centre, off Capper St, London WC1E 6JD ☎0845/155 5000 or 020/7387 4411, ⓦwww.thehtd.org. Mon–Fri 9am–5pm by appointment only.
MASTA (Medical Advisory Service for Travellers Abroad) ☎0870/606 2782, ⓦwww.masta.org. Call for the nearest one of 40 regional clinics.
Travel Medicine Services PO Box 254, 16 College St, Belfast 1 ☎028/9031 5220.

Tropical Medical Bureau Grafton Buildings, 34 Grafton St, Dublin 2 ☎1850/487 674, ⓦwww.tmb.ie.

In the US and Canada

CDC ☎1-800/311-3435, or ⓦwwwn.cdc.gov /travel. Official US government travel health site.
Canadian Society for International Health 1 Nicholas St, Suite 1105, Ottawa, ON K1N 7B7 ☎613/241-5785, ⓦwww.csih.org. Extensive list of travel health centres.
International Society for Travel Medicine ☎1-770/736-7060, ⓦwww.istm.org. Has a full list of travel health clinics.

Australia, New Zealand and South Africa

Travellers' Medical and Vaccination Centres ⓦwww.tmvc.com.au. Lists all Travellers Medical and Vaccination Centres throughout Australia, New Zealand and South Africa.

Insurance

Though Hong Kong and Macau are essentially safe places to travel, the cost of medical care alone makes taking out a travel-insurance policy worthwhile. Policies typically provide cover for loss of baggage, tickets and – up to a certain limit – cash or cheques, as well as cancellation or curtailment of your journey. Many policies can be chopped and changed to exclude coverage you don't need – for example, sickness and accident benefits can often be excluded or included at will. With medical coverage, ascertain whether benefits will be paid as treatment proceeds or only after return home, and whether there is a 24-hour medical emergency number. When securing baggage cover, make sure that the per-article limit – typically under £500/US$750 – will cover your most valuable possession. If you need to make a claim, you should keep receipts for medicines and medical treatment, and in the event you have anything stolen, you must obtain an official statement from the police.

Before paying for a new policy, however, check whether you are already covered: some all-risks **home insurance policies** may include your possessions when overseas; items purchased with a **credit card** might enjoy limited protection against loss or damage; and flights or holidays paid for with

a credit card might entail you to comprehensive travel insurance. **Private medical schemes** sometimes include partial overseas coverage, as do Canadian provincial health plans, while holders of official student/teacher/youth cards in Canada and the US are entitled to limited accident coverage and hospital in-patient benefits. **Students** will often find that their student health coverage extends during the vacations and for one term beyond the date of last enrolment.

Internet

For **free terminals** in Hong Kong, ask at your accommodation, head to any branch of the *Pacific Coffee Company* (for customers), or visit the Central Library, Causeway Bay (see p.84), which has 500 or more. If you carry a laptop, go to the library, airport, or many public buildings and cafés, for **free wi-fi** access. The British Council, 3 Supreme Court Rd, Admiralty, has a small internet café on the first floor. Otherwise, pay $15 an hour at Fresh Cyber Café, Shop 2, 1/F Tak Woo House, Wo On Lane, Central (near Lan Kwai Fong), and also at Flat C, 2/F, King Toa Building, 95–100 Lockhart Road, Wan Chai. There are also several netbars in the lower floors of Chungking Mansions, Nathan Road, Tsim Sha Tsui.

The best place in **Macau** is in the Tourist Office on Largo do Senado, where it's free though you might have to go on a waiting list as they only have two terminals. Otherwise, the UNESCO Centre on Alameda Dr Carlos d'Assumpção (south off Av. da Amizade near the Star World Casino) has six computers in its library on the second floor (daily except Tues noon–8pm; MOP$10 per hr); the entrance is a small glass door on the southeast side of the building. In addition, most of the upmarket hotels have business centres with pricey internet access.

Laundry

Most hotels offer (expensive) laundry services; guesthouses are usually cheaper. Otherwise, there are laundries in almost every back street, charging by the weight of your washing – around $30 for a bagfull – and taking a couple of hours. Most laundries also offer dry cleaning, which can take a day or two.

Left luggage

You can usually leave luggage at your guest-house or hotel, but they might charge for the service and security is seldom good. Storage lockers at the airport, Airport Express stations, the China-Hong Kong Ferry Terminal (Kowloon), Hung Hom train station (Kowloon) and Shun Tak Centre (Sheung Wan) cost around $90 per day. In Macau, you can leave luggage at the ferry terminal (in lockers or at the left luggage office).

Libraries

The main **English-language** library in Hong Kong is the twelve-floor Central Library at 66 Causeway Rd, facing Victoria Park in Causeway Bay (ⓦwww.hkpl.gov.hk; Mon–Tues & Thurs–Sat 10am–9pm, Wed 1–9pm, Sun 10am–6pm). The library boasts computers, internet access on every floor, an exhibition gallery, a toy library, stacks of comfortable sofas, 450,000 million publications for lending, a reference library and over 4000 periodicals and newspapers. Without a Hong Kong ID card and proof of address, you can borrow books by showing your passport and paying a $130 deposit for each book, with a maximum of six books. Check the website for locations of 66 other public libraries around Hong Kong, which you can use in the same way. There's also a small library with British newspapers and magazines at the British Council, 3 Supreme Court Rd, Admiralty ☎2913 5100, ⓦwww.britishcouncil.org.hk (Mon–Fri noon–8.00pm, Sat 10.30am–5.30pm).

Living in Hong Kong and Macau

Hong Kong and Macau have always been full of expats working and living in the SARs, though these days things are more controlled than they were under colonial rule. Nowadays, all foreigners seeking work must already have obtained a work visa before arriving, and these are only issued with copious supporting documentation from locally based firms. It is possible to study here, but the cost of living doesn't make it an attractive proposition unless you're being sponsored: it's far cheaper to study Cantonese or other Chinese

languages, for example, over the border in mainland China.

Finding work

Before you start looking for work in **Hong Kong**, remember that you're up against a well-educated, multilingual local population who are themselves facing increasing unemployment in the face of cheaper labour conditions on the Chinese mainland. The government also imposes stringent conditions on recruiting from abroad – employers have to show that the job cannot be done by a local. Likely openings are for skilled and specialized work, usually requiring fluency in English and/or other languages. **Teaching English** is your best bet; to get a job with an official language school you'll need a degree and a TEFL qualification, while for government and international schools you'll need an officially recognized teaching qualification from your home country. For details on what you'll need to apply for a **work visa**, contact the Hong Kong Immigration Department (ⓦwww.immd.gov.hk).

In **Macau**, your options are far more limited – about the only employers regularly needing staff are the **casinos**, and applications usually outnumber available jobs by a factor of ten. Macau's Department of Human Resources' website (ⓦwww.grh.gov.mo/en/legislations.html) outlines the requirements for working in Macau.

Useful websites

An idea of the sorts of jobs available in Hong Kong (including TEFL) can be gleaned from the "classifieds" section of the *South China Morning Post* (ⓦwww.scmp.com) or Asia Expat (ⓦwww.asiaexpat.com) – which also has a Macau section; and from job websites such as ⓦwww.jobmarket.com.hk or ⓦwww.monster.com.hk. Going Global (ⓦwww.goinglobal.com) also includes a Hong Kong-specific guide for finding work in the SAR, with further web resources.

Lost property

Police ☎2860 2000; **trains**, offices at Admiralty Station, Tai Wai Station and Siu Hong Station (daily 8am–8pm, ☎2861 0020).

To recover items left in **taxis**, call ☎ 187 2920, although you'll pay a steep fee up front – even then, they don't have a very good record for finding anything.

Mail

Post offices throughout **Hong Kong** are open Monday to Friday 9.30am to 5pm and Saturday 9.30am to 1pm. The main GPO building, at 2 Connaught Place, Central, by the Star Ferry on Hong Kong Island, and the main post office at 10 Middle Rd in Tsim Sha Tsui stay open longer – Monday to Saturday 8am to 6pm and Sunday 9am to 2pm. Letters sent **poste restante** will go to the GPO building on Connaught Place (collection Mon–Sat 8am–6pm) – take your passport along when you go to collect them. Letters and cards sent via airmail take three days to a week to reach Britain or North America. **Surface mail** is slower, taking weeks rather than days; rates are listed in a leaflet available from post offices.

If you're sending **parcels** home, they'll have to conform with packaging regulations. Either take your unwrapped parcel along to a main post office – together with your own brown paper and tape – and follow their instructions, or buy one of their cardboard boxes. The post office will have the relevant forms to **insure** your parcels, as well as the **customs declaration** that must be filled in for all goods sent abroad by post. Your parcel will go by surface mail unless you specify otherwise – the price obviously increases the bigger the parcel and the further it has to go.

The main post office in **Macau** is on Largo do Senado, just off Avenida de Almeida Ribeiro (Mon–Fri 9am–6pm, Sat 9am–1pm), and is where the **poste restante** mail is sent. There's also a post office at the Jetfoil Terminal (Mon–Sat 10am–7pm). Otherwise, little booths all over Macau sell **stamps** (*selos* in Portuguese), as do the larger hotels, and there are post offices on Taipa and Coloane. Letters and cards sent from Macau to Europe and North America take around the same time as from Hong Kong – between five days and a week.

Maps

In **Hong Kong**, the HKTB hands out free maps of the downtown, covering Sheung Wan to Causeway Bay, and Kowloon as far north as Mong Kok (with additional little inserts for popular places like Stanley, Sha Tin and Sham Shui Po). For further explorations, pick up the pocket-sized, bilingual Hong Kong Guidebook, a **street directory** available from any bookshop (HK$60). It covers all of Hong Kong's built-up areas in detail, with buildings, some sights and all transport routes included. It's less useful for country areas and islands, though main hiking trails, campsites and the like are marked. At the back you'll find rail maps along with bus, minibus and ferry schedules (though some are in Chinese only).

For any serious **hiking** in Hong Kong, you'll need the *Countryside Series*, five maps published by the Survey and Mapping Office which cover rural Hong Kong in good detail – each costs HK$62. You can buy them from the Map Publications Centre, 23/F, North Point Government Offices, 333 Java Rd, North Point, Hong Kong Island (Quarry Bay MTR Station, Exit C); the GPO, G/F, 2 Connaught Place, Hong Kong Island; the Map Publications Centre, 382 Nathan Rd, Yau Ma Tei, Kowloon; and the District Survey Office, 3/F, Sai Kung Government Offices, 34 Chan Man St, Sai Kung. Several Hong Kong **hiking guide books** (see "Contexts", p.329) include detailed maps of trails too.

In **Macau**, free maps from the MGTO cover the entire SAR, though they're a bit vague on street names. If you're serious about exploring, pick up the *Macau Touring Map* (HK$20), published by Universal Publications, available from bookshops in Hong Kong: it's clear, accurate and detailed, with all streets labelled in Chinese characters, many with Portuguese names too, plus bus routes and tourist attractions labelled in English and Chinese.

Money

Hong Kong's currency is the **Hong Kong dollar**, written as HK$ or just $, and divided into 100 cents (written as c). **Notes** come in HK$20, 50, 100, 500 and 1000 denominations; there's a nickel-and-bronze HK$10 coin; **silver coins** come as HK$1, 2 and 5; and **bronze coins** as 10c, 20c and 50c. Many businesses won't accept HK$1000 bills; change them for something smaller at the nearest bank.

At the time of writing the **rate of exchange** was HK$11 to the British pound, HK$10 to the euro and HK$7.7 to the US dollar – check the latest rates at ⓦwww.xe.com. There's no black market and money, in any amount, can be freely taken in and out of the territory.

Macau uses the **pataca**, made up of 100 avos. You'll see prices written as M$, ptcs or MOP$ (as in this book), all of which mean the same thing. **Coins** come as 10, 20 and 50 avos, and MOP$1, 2, 5 and 10; **notes** in denominations of MOP$10, 20, 50, 100, 500 and 1000.

The pataca is pegged to the Hong Kong dollar, though is officially worth roughly three percent less. In practice, **you can use Hong Kong dollars throughout Macau** to pay for anything, on a one-for-one basis – and should be given Hong Kong dollars in change if you do. You can't use patacas in Hong Kong, however, so spend them all before you leave Macau.

Accessing money

It's a good idea to buy at least a few Hong Kong dollars from a bank at home before you go; that way you don't have to use the airport exchange desk (which has poor rates) when you arrive. However, probably the most convenient way to bring money to Hong Kong or Macau is by using a **debit/bank card** issued by your bank to draw funds directly from your home account through the ubiquitous **automatic teller machines** (ATMs) scattered around the two SARs. Your card needs to be marked with the "Cirrus-Maestro" logo, and your PIN number must be compatible with ATMs here – check with your bank in both instances. One of the best features of this method is that you pay official exchange rates, without having to haggle or shop around for the best deals. **Charges** are either a set fee per transaction, or a percentage of the amount you withdraw, or both – check with your bank.

Traveller's cheques are the safest way to carry funds, as cheques can be cancelled and reissued to you if lost or stolen – make sure you keep the purchase agreement and a record of cheque serial numbers safe and separate from the cheques themselves. However, it's expensive: you pay a fee to buy the cheques, and then pay **commission** every time you cash them at either a bank or currency exchange counter.

There are **banks** of every nationality and description throughout Hong Kong, seemingly on every street corner. Opening hours are Monday to Friday 9am to 4.30pm, Saturday 9am to 12.30pm, with small fluctuations – half an hour each side – from branch to branch. You can also change money and cheques at a **licensed moneychanger** – there are many in Tsim Sha Tsui and Causeway Bay – which stay open late daily. They generally don't charge commission, but their exchange rates are worse – up to 5 percent lower than the banks'; if you're changing large amounts, you're better off using a bank. Big hotels also offer exchange services, but again the rates are lower.

In **Macau**, banks are generally open Monday to Friday 9am to 5pm, Saturday 9am to noon. Most banks change traveller's cheques; ATMs can provide either MOP$ or HK$ as requested. The main clutch of banks (all with ATMs) is around the junction of Av. de Almeida Ribeiro and Av. da Praia Grande in central Macau, including Banco Nacional Ultramarino (Av. de Almeida Ribeiro 2); Banco Comercial de Macau (Av. da Praia Grande 22 and Av. Sidónio Pais 69A); Bank of China (Av. Dr Mario Soares); Standard Chartered Bank (Av. do Infante D. Henrique 60–64); and HSBC (Av. da Praia Grande 639 and Av. Horta e Costa 122–124), which gives cash advances on Visa. There are licensed moneychangers (*casas de cambio*), including one at the Jetfoil Terminal and a 24hr service in the *Hotel Lisboa* – as always, shop around for the best rates.

You can use all major **credit cards** in Hong Kong; they're most useful for hotels and high-end purchases though many restaurants don't accept them. Watch out for the **three-percent commission** that many places try to add to the price. American Express, MasterCard and Visa cardholders can also use regional ATMs to withdraw funds, though these are considered cash advances, with interest accruing daily from the date of withdrawal.

Having **money wired** from home is never convenient or cheap, and should be considered a last resort. Travelers Express/ MoneyGram (🌐www.moneygram.com) or Western Union (🌐www.westernunion.com) typically charge eight to ten percent of the sum transferred. Alternatively, you can go to one of the major international banks and get them to have your bank telex the money to a specific branch in Hong Kong. This will take a couple of working days, and will cost about £25/$40 per transaction.

Opening hours and public holidays

In **Hong Kong**, offices are generally open Monday to Friday 9am to 5pm, and some open Saturday 9am to 1pm; banks Monday to Friday 9am to 4.30pm, Saturday 9am to 12.30pm; shops daily 10am to 7/8pm, though later in tourist areas; and post offices Monday to Friday 9.30am to 5pm, Saturday 9.30am to 1pm. Museums tend to close one day a week; check the text for exact details. Temples often have no set hours, though they are usually open from early morning to early evening; produce markets tend to kick off at dawn (when they're busiest) and peter out during the afternoon, though other markets (such as Kowloon's Temple Street Night Market and Jade Market) have varying opening times, which are given in the text.

In **Macau**, opening hours are more limited, with government and official offices open Monday to Friday 8.30/9am to 1pm and 3 to 5/5.30pm, Saturday 8.30/9am to 1pm. Shops and businesses are usually open throughout the day and have slightly longer hours.

On **public holidays** and some religious festivals most shops and all government offices in both Hong Kong and Macau are closed. See p.33 for details of festivals.

Phones

Local calls from a private phone are free in Hong Kong. Public **coin phones** cost HK$1 for five minutes, while there are also credit card phones and **card phones**. You'll find phones at MTR stations, ferry terminals, in shopping centres and hotel lobbies. You can buy **phonecards** from PCCW–HKT outlets, tourist offices and 7-Eleven stores; they come in units of HK$50, HK$100, HK$200 and HK$300. However, for overseas calls it's much cheaper to buy **discount phonecards** where you dial an access number, enter a PIN supplied with the card, and then dial the overseas phone number; costs to the UK, US or Australia are just a dollar or two per minute. Different cards give discounts for specific regions only, so you might have to shop around until you find the right one – Worldwide House in Central and Chungking Mansions in Tsim Sha Tsui have dozens of places selling them.

In **Macau**, local phone calls are also free from private phones, or MOP$1 from a

---

Public holidays in Hong Kong and Macau

January 1 New Year.
January/February Three days' holiday for Chinese New Year.
March/April Easter (holidays on Good Friday, Easter Saturday and Easter Monday).
April Ching Ming Festival (Cleaning Ancestors' Graves).
May Labour Day, Buddha's Birthday.
June Dragon Boat Festival.
July 1 HKSAR Establishment Day (Hong Kong only).
September Mid-Autumn Festival (special mooncake pastries are eaten).
October 1 Chinese National Day.
October Cheung Yeung Festival (hill-climbing events).
November 2 All Souls' Day (Macau only).
December 8 Feast of Immaculate Conception (Macau only).
December 20 Macau SAR Establishment Day (Macau only).
December 22 Winter Solstice (Macau only).
December 25 and 26 Christmas.

Lucky numbers

The Hong Kong Chinese consider certain **numbers** to be unlucky, principally because the words for some of the numbers sound like more ominous words – 4 (*sei*), for example, which sounds like the Cantonese word for "death". Lots of people won't accept the private telephone numbers they're allocated for this reason, and there's a continuous struggle to change numbers. Conversely, the numbers 3, 8 and 9 are considered intrinsically lucky and people will pay to have these included in their telephone number. The same applies, incidentally, to car number plates: each year there's a government auction of the best ones, some of which fetch exorbitant sums – the record so far being US$2.1 million paid in 2008 for the license plate "18".

payphone (there are groups of payphones around the Largo do Senado and at the Jetfoil Terminal). Hotels, however, may charge up to MOP$3 for each local call – check before you dial. For **international calls**, you'll want to buy a **phonecard** from the telephone office at the back of the main post office, the Jetfoil Terminal, the airport, the *Fortuna*, *Lisboa* and *Grandeur* hotels or CTM shops around town. They come in denominations of MOP$50, MOP$100 and MOP$150, and can be used in most public phones.

All telephone numbers in Hong Kong and Macau contain eight digits, with no area codes. For a list of useful numbers, see box on p.50.

Mobile phones

If your mobile phone is GSM-compatible then the cheapest way to use it is to buy a **pre-paid SIM** card, to replace the one you use in your home country (giving you a new number). Simply slot the HK$300 stored-value cards into your phone to make local and overseas calls to more than two hundred countries (apart from the US and Canada). You pay for both outgoing and incoming calls; recharge vouchers are available to top up the value. Pre-paid SIM cards are available from any shop selling mobile phones, as well as booths in Worldwide House in Central and Chungking Mansions in Tsim Sha Tsui – most will work in Macau and China, too.

The alternative is to set up **auto-roaming** with your mobile company before leaving home, though this is usually much more expensive – check with your provider for details.

Photography

Cameras and camera gear are big business in Hong Kong and Macau, and there's no model or accessory that you can't get hold of – see "Shopping", p.236 (Hong Kong) and p.306 (Macau). The run of subjects is endless: Hong Kong's harbour at night; festival activity; temple courtyards (photography **inside temples** is usually forbidden); market streets; hi-tech buildings in Central and the view from The Peak; the New Territories' mountains, beaches and Hakka homes; old stores; a Cantonese *dim sum* breakfast; the unbelievable crowds; and Portuguese colonial churches and ostentatious casinos in Macau. When **taking pictures**, avoid the harsh tropical lighting around the middle of the day – you'll get better pictures before about 10am and after 4pm.

Images can be **downloaded** onto disc or printed at any photo store – but as with paying for anything in Hong Kong and Macau, shop around first to establish prices and get a good deal.

Time

Hong Kong and Macau (and all of mainland China) share the same time zone, GMT +8 hours (thirteen hours ahead of New York, sixteen hours ahead of Los Angeles, and two hours behind Sydney). There is no daylight saving.

Toilets

You'll find **free public toilets** at all shopping plazas, though they're often discreetly hidden away and you might have to ask at the nearest information desk. Upmarket hotel lobbies are another good bet; the finest (and most intimidating) toilet experiences are those in the

Useful telephone numbers

Hong Kong
Collect calls ☎10010
Directory enquiries (English) ☎1081
Emergencies (ambulance, police or fire) ☎999
IDD and cardphone enquiries ☎10013
International operator assistance for foreign credit card calls ☎10011
Time and temperature ☎18501
Tourist information (multilingual) ☎2508 1234
Weather (English) ☎187 8200
Calling Macau from Hong Kong ☎001 + 853 + number.

Macau
Directory enquiries (Chinese and English) ☎181
Emergencies ☎999
Time (English) ☎140
Tourist information ☎2833 3000
Calling Hong Kong from Macau ☎00 + 852 + number.

Calling Hong Kong and Macau from home
Hong Kong Dial the international access code + ☎852 + number.
Macau Dial the international access code + ☎853 + number.
International access codes UK, Ireland and New Zealand ☎00; US and Canada ☎011; Australia ☎0011.

Calling home from Hong Kong and Macau
Note that the initial zero is omitted from the area code when dialling the UK, Ireland, Australia and New Zealand from abroad.
Australia international access code + 61
China international access code + 86
New Zealand international access code + 64
UK international access code + 44
US and Canada international access code +1
Republic of Ireland international access code + 353
South Africa international access code + 27
International access codes Hong Kong ☎001; Macau ☎00.

---

arcade of the *Peninsula Hotel* (men should go up to the *Felix* restaurant) or the *Mandarin* on Hong Kong Island. Amid brass and marble elegance, attendants turn on the taps, hand over the soap and retrieve the towels; there's talc, eau de toilette and hairbrushes, and when you've finished you can sit on the chaise longue and make phone calls all afternoon. Needless to say, you're expected to tip. Most beaches have toilets, too.

Tourist information

The **Hong Kong Tourism Board** (HKTB; daily 9am–6pm; ☎2508 1234; @www.hktb.com)

are well informed, helpful and hand out free **maps**, brochures and advice on restaurants, accommodation, sights, tours and activities, including transport schedules across the SAR. In addition, they organize free courses on tai chi, Cantonese opera, tea appreciation, pearl grading, and more, for which you need to sign up for a day in advance. Their **five** offices, all staffed by English-speakers, are located at the airport's arrival hall (daily 7am–11pm); at the Lo Wu border crossing arrival hall (8am–6pm daily); at the Tsim Sha Tsui Star Ferry Pier, Kowloon (8am–8pm daily); near Exit F, Causeway Bay MTR, Hong

Kong Island (8am–8pm daily); and in an old rail carriage at The Peak, Hong Kong Island (9am–9pm daily).

The **Macau Government Tourist Office** (MGTO; daily 8am–7pm; ☎2833 3000, ⓦwww.macautourism.gov.mo) is more laid-back than its Hong Kong counterpart, but still has plenty of brochures and advice on offer. The main offices are at the Jetfoil Terminal (daily 9am–10pm) and in the middle of Macau at Largo do Senado 9 (daily 9am–8pm); there are also useful counters at the Portas do Cerco (9am–6pm), and the airport (9am–1.30pm, 2.15–7.30pm & 8.15–10pm). The **Hong Kong office** is at the Macau Ferry Terminal, Shun Tak Tower, Connaught Road, Central (9am–1pm & 2.15–5.30pm; ☎2857 2287); you can usually get discounted rates for mid-range hotels here prior to departure.

Tourist offices abroad

Hong Kong Tourism Board (HKTB)

Australia Level 4, Hong Kong House, 80 Druitt St, Sydney, NSW 2000 ☎02/9283 3083, ⓔsydwwo @hktb.com.
Canada 3rd Floor, 9 Temperance St, Toronto, ON M5H 1Y6 ☎416-366-2389, ⓔyyzwwo @hktb.com.
UK 6 Grafton St, London W1S 4EQ ☎020/7533 7100, ⓔlonwwo@hktb.com.
US Suite 2050, 10940 Wilshire Blvd, Los Angeles, CA90024-3915 ☎310-208-4582, ⓔlaxwwo @hktb.com; 115 East 54th St, New York, NY 10022-4512 ☎212-421-3382, ⓔnycwwo @hktb.com.

Macau Government Tourist Office (MGTO)

Australia Level 17, Town Hall House, 456 Kent St, Sydney NSW 2000 ☎02/9264 1488, ⓔmacau @worldtradetravel.com.
New Zealand Level 5, Ballantyne House, 101 Customs St East, PO Box 3779, Auckland ☎09/308 5206, ⓔmacau@aviationandtourism.co.nz.
UK Parkshot House, 5 Kew Rd, Richmond TW9 2PR ☎20/8334 7026.
US 1334 Parkview Ave, Suite 300, Manhattan Beach, CA 90266 ☎310-545-3464, ⓔmacau @myriadmarketing.com; 501 5th Ave, Suite 1101, New York NY 10017 ☎646-277-0690, ⓔmacau @myriadmarketing.com.

Useful websites

ⓦ**www.afcd.gov.hk** The Hong Kong Agriculture, Fisheries and Conservation Department website, covering the official side for everything outdoors, including country parks, marine parks, hiking and mountain biking trails, campsites etc. Fantastic photos.

ⓦ**www.asiaexpat.com** Essential information (with a business slant) for any foreigner living, or planning to live, in Hong Kong or Macau – includes web-zine articles, news and classifieds, plus job and accommodation listings.

ⓦ**www.batgung.com** Two grumpy old expats with good eyes and a sense of humour writing about daily life, history and culture in Hong Kong. Also links and articles about visiting, living and working in Hong Kong.

ⓦ**www.cityguide.gov.mo** Well-laid-out site, with lots of illustrations of Macau, transport timetables and phone numbers. Also good ideas for walking tours.

ⓦ**www.gohk.gov.hk/eng/index.html** Thumbnails and highlights on Hong Kong's "eighteen districts", covering everything from the downtown to New Territories villages.

ⓦ**www.hkcrystal.com/hiking/Trails.htm** Essential hiking information for all major – and many minor – trails in Hong Kong, plus advice on conditions, weather etc.

ⓦ**www.hkoutdoors.com** Hong Kong's wilder corners, historic sights and walking trails covered in detail.

ⓦ**hong-kong-blogs-review.com** Even-handed rundown of blogs about Hong Kong, many of them written by (and for) Western expats.

ⓦ**orientalsweetlips.spaces.live.com** Excellent, informative blog about culture, history and obscure local places in Hong Kong (with a little bit on Macau, too). Also includes museum directory and many other interesting snippets.

ⓦ**www.scmp.com**. The online edition of *The South China Morning Post*, Hong Kong's English-language daily, with a useful careers page, classified listings and news rundown. However, you can't read more than a snippet of the articles unless you subscribe.

Government websites

Australian Department of Foreign Affairs
ⓦ www.dfat.gov.au, ⓦ www.smartraveller.gov.au.
British Foreign & Commonwealth Office
ⓦ www.fco.gov.uk.
Canadian Department of Foreign Affairs
ⓦ www.international.gc.ca.

Irish Department of Foreign Affairs ⓦwww
.foreignaffairs.gov.ie.
New Zealand Ministry of Foreign Affairs
ⓦwww.mft.govt.nz.
South African Department of Foreign Affairs
ⓦwww.dfa.gov.za.
US State Department ⓦwww.travel.state.gov.

Travellers with disabilities

Physically disabled travellers, especially those reliant on wheelchairs, will find Hong Kong easier to manage than they might have imagined, despite the steep streets and busy intersections. There are special access and toilet facilities at the airport, as well as on the main train stations. The Airport Express and MTR have carriages with wheelchair spaces and waist-level poles, though other forms of public transport are not so accessible – some buses have wheelchair access but trams are virtually out of bounds. Wheelchairs are able to gain access to the lower deck of cross-harbour and outlying island ferries, and taxis are usually obliging.

There are fewer facilities for **visually disabled** visitors, though assistance is offered by braille signage in rail station lifts and clicking poles at the top and bottom of escalators.

The HKTB's website includes a Disabled Traveller page (ⓦwww.discoverhongkong .com/eng/trip-planner/hongkong-disabled -traveller.html) with links to Hong Kong websites for disabled travellers.

Macau is far less easy to negotiate for physically disabled travellers. The streets are older, narrower, rougher and steeper, and it lacks the overhead ramps, wide, modern elevators etc, that make Hong Kong relatively approachable. Contact the Macau Tourist Office (ⓦwww.macautourism.gov.mo) before you travel for details of accommodation and transport facilities.

Hong Kong

Hong Kong

1

Hong Kong Island

To many people – visitors and residents alike – **Hong Kong Island** *is* Hong Kong. After the island was ceded to the British following the First Opium War in 1841, it was here, overlooking **Victoria Harbour** along the **North Shore**'s steep slopes, that the rich, industrious and influential colonists first settled down. Today, their warehouses and businesses have blossomed into an organic mass of concrete expressways and glass towers, an area so frenetically crowded that there's hardly room to drive or even walk at street level, and the only possible direction to build is upwards – or use **landfill** to deepen the shoreline. You can't help but be impressed at the sheer brash, unashamed striving for wealth and all its symbols here, though among the bars, boutiques and banks you'll find evidence of far more traditional ways of life and, incredibly, some refreshingly green spaces – notably on and around **The Peak** (formerly known as "Victoria Peak"). The pace slows slightly a short bus ride away on Hong Kong Island's **South Coast** – the entire island is only 15km wide by 11km deep – in a string of small bays and beaches, not all of them busy. If you're pushed for time, then the island can give you a taste of just about everything that Hong Kong has to offer: top shopping and nightlife, excellent dining, a glimpse of old China, plus outstanding cityscapes and views.

▲ Views over Hong Kong from The Peak

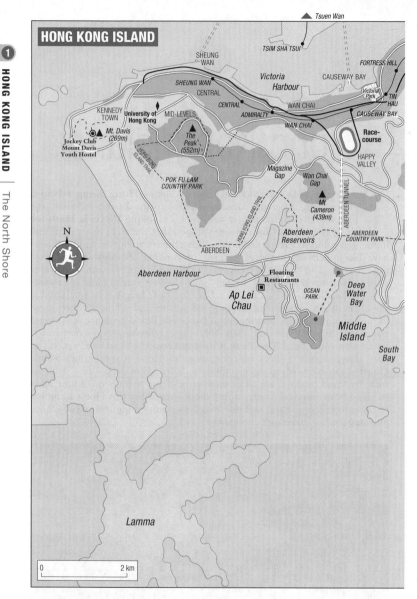

HONG KONG ISLAND

Tsuen Wan

TSIM SHA TSUI

SHEUNG WAN

FORTRESS HILL

Victoria
Harbour

CAUSEWAY BAY

SHEUNG WAN

CENTRAL

Victoria
Park

TIN
HAU

CENTRAL

WAN CHAI

CAUSEWAY BAY

KENNEDY
TOWN

University of
Hong Kong

MID-LEVELS

ADMIRALTY

WAN CHAI

Mt. Davis
(269m)

Jockey Club
Mount Davis
Youth Hostel

The
Peak
(552m)

Race-
course

HONG KONG ISLAND TRAIL

HAPPY
VALLEY

POK FU LAM
COUNTRY PARK

Magazine
Gap

Wan Chai
Gap

HONG KONG ISLAND TRAIL

Mt
Cameron
(439m)

ABERDEEN TUNNEL

Aberdeen
Reservoirs

ABERDEEN
COUNTRY PARK

ABERDEEN

Aberdeen Harbour

Floating
Restaurants

Deep
Water
Bay

Ap Lei
Chau

OCEAN
PARK

Middle
Island

South
Bay

N

Lamma

0   2 km

The North Shore

Hong Kong Island's **North Shore**, facing Kowloon across busy Victoria
Harbour, forms a virtually continuous ten-kilometre-long financial, commercial
and entertainment district. Most of the obvious attractions here are contemporary, especially **Central**'s soaring, cutting-edge architecture and the mass of

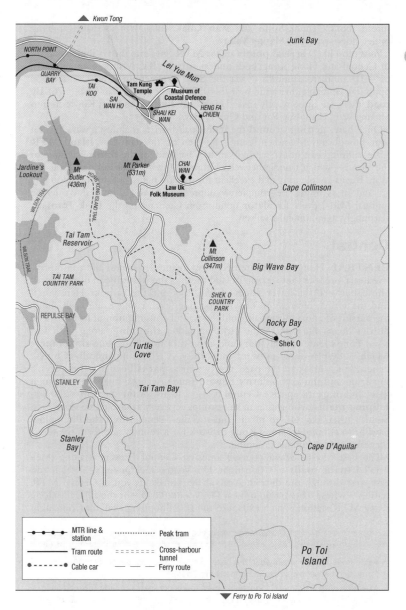

•━•━•	MTR line & station	··········	Peak tram
━━━	Tram route	=======	Cross-harbour tunnel
•·····●	Cable car	— —	Ferry route

▼ *Ferry to Po Toi Island*

shopping malls east at **Causeway Bay**. But you never seem too far away from Hong Kong's more traditional face – shops specializing in Chinese teas and medicines just west of Central in **Sheung Wan**, busy street markets and smoky old temples all over the place and even the occasional grand colonial building. The harbour's ever-present expanse and several attractive **parks** – not to mention views from skyscrapers or **The Peak** – also add a welcome sense of space, especially during the torrid summers. Hong Kong's core **nightlife** is spread about Central, **Soho** and **Wan Chai**, along with its main gambling outlet: horse-racing in **Happy Valley**.

Your most likely **arrival points** are via **MTR** lines into the co-joined stations of Central and Hong Kong, both underneath the IFC Mall in Central (p.61); or – far more romantically – via the **Star Ferry** from Kowloon (see box opposite), landing either again near the IFC Mall or east at Wan Chai (p.76). By **road**, there are three widely spaced cross-harbour tunnels from Kowloon into Sheung Wan, Causeway Bay and Quarry Bay.

Once here, **getting around** the individual districts is almost always best on foot, though travel between them is quickest on the dark blue **Island MTR Line**, running east from Sheung Wan to Chai Wan, or the **trams** – unique to the island – which trundle between Kennedy Town in the east and Shau Kei Wan. **Buses** are plentiful and excellent for specific sights, but don't hop on one at random as routes are completely unpredictable. You should also ride the unusual **Mid-Levels Escalator** uphill from Central, and the **Peak Tram**, an alarmingly steep funicular railway.

Central

CENTRAL, Hong Kong's intensely busy financial, business and administrative heart, is packed into a strip of land towards the western end of the North Shore, between the lower slopes of The Peak and the harbour. Here you'll find the visible incarnation of what, on one level, Hong Kong is all about: the pursuit of enormous wealth and the willful consumption of its fruits. The district boasts the best of the city's upmarket **shopping**, along with Lan Kwai Fong's knot of lively **bars** and a forest of mind-boggling **skyscrapers** which – despite their outward modernity – reflect intrinsically Chinese beliefs. For a break in the pace, the two local **parks** boast floral displays, a small zoo and the extraordinary Edward Youde Aviary, a huge walk-through space full of exotic species. Central is also a focus for the territory's 200,000 **Filipina maids**, who gather in vast groups on every available free space each Sunday (their day off) to picnic and socialize. People from the Philippines have been coming to Hong Kong to work for a century and form the territory's largest immigrant grouping.

The best way to orient yourself amongst Central's towers is along three parallel **main roads** – Connaught, Des Voeux and Queen's – which run east-west through the district. **Arrival** by train lands you at Central MTR station – whose exits are on or near Des Voeux Road – or the adjacent Hong Kong MTR station, which exits into the IFC Shopping Mall on Connaught

---

Useful North Shore bus routes

Aside from others mentioned in the text, these are the most generally useful buses for getting between districts along the North Shore:

#1 – runs daily 6.10am–11.15pm along main roads between Kennedy Town, Sheung Wan, Central and Wan Chai, then heads down to Happy Valley and the racecourse.

#2 – runs daily 5.45am–midnight from the Shun Tak Centre in Sheung Wan east along shoreline expressways to Causeway Bay, then follows the south side of Victoria Park to Tin Hau, North Point and Shau Kei Wan (see p.86 for more).

#15 – runs daily 6.15am–12.15am from Central Bus Station to The Peak via Central Star Ferry Pier (after 10am), Queen's Road East in Wan Chai, Bowen Road and the Police Museum (see pp.80–82 for more).

The Star Ferry

The **Star Ferry** began carrying passengers across the harbour between Kowloon and Hong Kong Island in 1898, and still provides a wonderfully dated, slow-paced journey, providing thrilling images of marine traffic and Central's skyscrapers framed by the looming hills behind. The broad, open-sided, two-decked vessels are all named after a star – "Morning Star", "Evening Star" etc – and run a handful of **routes**, the most popular being from **Tsim Sha Tsui to Central** (daily 6.30am–10.30pm), landing below the IFC2 tower and right next to the Outer Island Ferry Piers; and from **Tsim Sha Tsui to Wan Chai** (daily approximately 7.20am–11pm), arriving next to the Convention and Exhibition Centre. Either route is absurdly cheap – the most you'll pay is HK$2.20 – and takes around ten minutes. Star Ferry also offers hour-long **harbour tours** (daily 11am–9pm), costing HK$50–140; book at the Tsim Sha Tsui, Central or Wan Chai offices, or try ℡2367 7065, ⓦwww.starferry .com.hk for more info.

Road. Arriving by **Star Ferry from Kowloon** (see box above), follow the long, elevated walkway from the pier south past the unmistakably tall IFC2 tower to Connaught Road and beyond.

Aside from exploring Central at street level, make sure you use the extensive network of two-storey high **elevated walkways** linking the skyscrapers with civic buildings and shopping malls. They provide an entirely different view of the city, besides allowing you to get almost right across the district without having to touch the ground. **Trams** and **bus #1** run right through the district down Des Voeux Road and via Queensway into Wan Chai.

IFC2 and around

IFC2 – International Finance Centre, Tower 2 – is Central's most obvious landmark, an 88-storey, 420m-high waterfront monolith visible from just about any clear space along the North Shore. Until 2008 this was the tallest building in Hong Kong (now superseded by the International Commerce Centre across

▲ Elevated walkway in Central

the harbour in Kowloon), but is so beautifully proportioned that it's not until you see the top brushing the clouds that you realize it stands half as high again as anything else in the area, higher even than the Peak Tram's upper terminus. It is home to the Hong Kong Monetary Authority and while you can't ride the lift up for views there's a virtual 360-degree version on their website (Ⓦ www.ifc.com.hk/english). The tower and its much smaller sibling, IFC1, sit either end of the **IFC Mall**, which aside from shopping opportunities serves

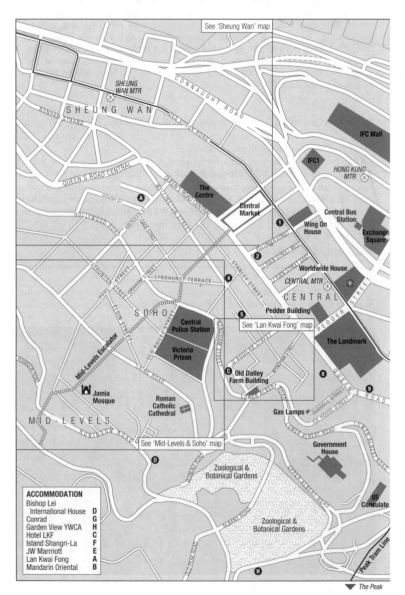

See 'Sheung Wan' map

SHEUNG WAN MTR

CONNAUGHT ROAD

BONHAM STRAND

SHEUNG WAN

DES VOEUX ROAD

IFC Mall

IFC1

HONG KONG MTR

QUEEN'S ROAD CENTRAL

GOUGH ST

QUEEN'S ROAD CENTRAL

The Centre

Central Market

Central Bus Station

Wing On House

Exchange Square

HOLLYWOOD ROAD

ABERDEEN ST

GAGE STREET

WELLINGTON STREET

POTTINGER STREET

LYNDHURST TERRACE

STAUNTON STREET

GRAHAM STREET

PEEL STREET

E. GRAHAM STREET

ELGIN STREET

STANLEY STREET

LYNDHURST STREET WEST

Worldwide House

CENTRAL MTR

CENTRAL

SOHO

Mid-Levels Escalator

Central Police Station

Victoria Prison

Pedder Building

See 'Lan Kwai Fong' map

Old Dalley Farm Building

PEDDER STREET

The Landmark

QUEEN'S ROAD

CAINE ROAD

OLD BAILEY STREET

WYNDHAM STREET

Jamia Mosque

Roman Catholic Cathedral

WYNDHAM STREET

ARBUTHNOT ROAD

LOWER ALBERT ROAD

Gas Lamps

ICE HOUSE STREET

DUDDELL STREET

MID-LEVELS

ROBINSON ROAD

See 'Mid-Levels & Soho' map

Government House

UPPER ALBERT ROAD

LOWER ALBERT ROAD

US Consulate

Zoological & Botanical Gardens

Zoological & Botanical Gardens

ALBANY ROAD

GARDEN ROAD

Peak Tram Line

ACCOMMODATION

Bishop Lei	
International House	D
Conrad	G
Garden View YWCA	H
Hotel LKF	C
Island Shangri-La	F
JW Marriott	E
Lan Kwai Fong	A
Mandarin Oriental	B

▼ The Peak

as a sort of arrivals hub: the **Central Star Ferry Pier** and **Outlying Islands Ferry Piers** are on the shore in front and connected to the IFC Mall by a pedestrian walkway; the mall sits above **Hong Kong MTR station** and next to **Central Bus Station** (located underneath Exchange Square), and is linked by tunnels to nearby **Central MTR station**.

The **pedestrian walkway** from the ferry piers passes south along IFC Mall's eastern side. From it, look east before you reach the **General Post**

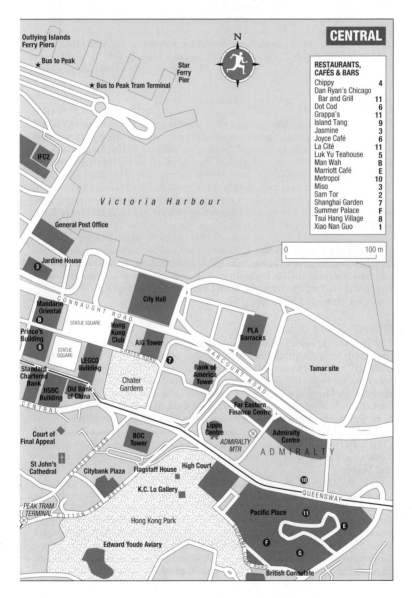

CENTRAL

Outlying Islands Ferry Piers
★ Bus to Peak
★ Bus to Peak Tram Terminal
Star Ferry Pier
N

IFC2

Victoria Harbour

General Post Office

Jardine House ❸

Mandarin Oriental ❽
CONNAUGHT ROAD
City Hall
STATUE SQUARE
Hong Kong Club
Prince's Building ❻
STATUE SQUARE
AIG Tower
PLA Barracks
Standard Chartered Bank
LEGCO Building
Chater Gardens
❼
Bank of America Tower
HARCOURT ROAD
Tamar site
CHATER ROAD
HSBC Building
Old Bank of China
CENTRAL
Far Eastern Finance Centre
Court of Final Appeal
BOC Tower
Lippo Centre
ADMIRALTY MTR
Admiralty Centre
ADMIRALTY
St John's Cathedral
Citybank Plaza
Flagstaff House
High Court
❿
K.C. Lo Gallery
QUEENSWAY
PEAK TRAM TERMINAL
COTTON TREE DRIVE
Hong Kong Park
Pacific Place
⓫
❻
Edward Youde Aviary
❻
❻
British Consulate

0   100 m

RESTAURANTS, CAFÉS & BARS

Chippy	4
Dan Ryan's Chicago Bar and Grill	11
Dot Cod	6
Grappa's	11
Island Tang	9
Jasmine	3
Joyce Café	6
La Cité	11
Luk Yu Teahouse	5
Man Wah	B
Marriott Café	E
Metropol	10
Miso	3
Sam Tor	2
Shanghai Garden	7
Summer Palace	F
Tsui Hang Village	8
Xiao Nan Guo	1

Office and you'll see a belt of **land reclamation** stretching up to Wan Chai, the latest development in a process which has seen the shoreline creep steadily north over the years – incredibly, Victoria Harbour is a whole kilometre narrower than when the British first arrived here. South of the post office, **Jardine House** stands out for its porthole windows and aluminium casing, and was the tallest building in Asia on its completion in 1972, showing just how far Hong Kong's skyline has changed since then. Opposite, west of the walkway, **Exchange Square** is an open-air, red-granite terrace fronting Hong Kong's stock exchange and decorated with sculptures by Henry Moore and Elizabeth Frink – a popular place with office workers to sit out at lunchtime. From here, the walkway branches west past Exchange Square and off along Connaught Road towards Sheung Wan, or south over Connaught Road to join a network of footbridges and overpasses reaching deep into Central.

Des Voeux Road

Des Voeux Road – easily recognized from its tram lines – and Queen's Road cut right across Central, between them taking in some of the territory's most exclusive shops and malls. One of the smartest of these is **The Landmark**, on the corner of Des Voeux and Pedder Street, which comes complete with a fountain atrium, though the best known is probably **Shanghai Tang** on Theatre Lane (right next to Exit D2 from Central MTR), specializing in pricey, classical-Chinese inspired designer garments in bright colours. Continuing west along Des Voeux takes you past **Li Yuen Street West** and **Li Yuen Street East**, small lanes crowded with stalls selling bags, cheap souvenir clothing and fabrics – you can get good deals on bolt silk here – to **Central Market**. Once a confronting testament to the Cantonese demand for fresh food, where you could watch livestock being selected, slaughtered, sectioned and sold to shoppers, today the market is an empty shell used only as a pedestrian thorough-fare at the start of the open-air **Mid-Levels Escalator**, which climbs uphill through Central and Soho (see p.67).

Queen's Road and around

For its part, **Queen's Road** marked the 1840s waterfront, when it was described by contemporaries as a "grand boulevard". Its eastern end is dissected by **Ice House Street**, named after a building that once stored blocks of ice imported from the United States before there were ice-making facilities in Hong Kong. Parallel and west with Ice House, tiny **Duddell Street** sports a colonial granite staircase lit 6pm to 6am by Hong Kong's last four **gas street lamps**, installed in the 1920s. There's another colonial survival up from here along Lower Albert Road, the brown-brick **Old Dairy Farm Building**, now housing the *Fringe Club* (see p.229) and the *Foreign Correspondents' Club*, a members-only retreat for journalists, diplomats and lawyers.

Back on Queen's Road, the two Li Yuen streets face more upmarket shopping at **Lane Crawford**, one of the city's top – and most staid – department stores, with a smart café at the top and aisles full of charge-card queens. Further along on the same side of the street, **Pottinger Street** climbs in an uneven succession of stone steps up to Wellington Street and Hollywood Road, lined with small stalls selling ribbons, flowers, locks and other minor household items. Beyond here, Queen's Road passes under the Mid-Levels Escalator and architect Denis Lau's **The Centre** – a black slab by day, but glowing in horizontal coloured bars at night – and so continues westwards into Sheung Wan.

Lan Kwai Fong and around

South off Queen's Road up D'Aguilar Street lies a sloping L-shaped lane known as **Lan Kwai Fong**. Once a flower market, "the Fong" has become Hong Kong's premier **bar district**, with so many pubs, bars, restaurants and clubs that they now overflow into D'Aguilar and Wing Wah Lane (known locally as "Rat Alley"), so that the name refers to the whole area. They're all late-opening – you can eat and drink here from noon until dawn – and mostly frequented by expats and Chinese yuppies. Even the local 7–Eleven store is a popular hangout, at least with the younger Hong Kongers who use it as a cheap place to buy a few beers before hitting the Fong's clubs.

The steep network of narrow streets north of Lan Kwai Fong has a far more local flavour. **Stanley Street** and **Wellington Street** together host a surprising concentration of eminently Chinese canteens and restaurants – including the *Tsui Wah*, *Yung Kee*, *Luk Yu* and *Lin Heung Teahouse* (see "Eating", p.206) – while immediately west of the Mid-Levels Escalator on Stanley Street is one of the last group of **dai pai dong** foodstalls in Hong Kong (see p.200). Gage, Peel and Graham streets are smaller but also packed with open-air markets and shop-houses, not at all touristy. **Gage Street** is especially busy, full of stalls selling fresh produce, dried foods, small household appliances, flowers, cheap clothes and accessories, temple incense and **spirit offerings**. These are paper models of all sorts of consumer goods – cars, houses, clothes, food, TVs and even "king of hell" banknotes – which are burned to provide departed relatives with comforts in the afterlife; you'll find places selling them all over Hong Kong.

RESTAURANTS, BARS & CLUBS	
Agave	10
Al's Diner	15
Arc Brasserie	2
Ashoka	3
Bit Point	9
Bulldog	18
C Bar	11
Club 97	20
D26	8
Dublin Jack	19
Fong's	13
Fringe Club	22
Indochine 1929	11
Insomnia	16
Jimmy's Kitchen	12
Kyoto Joe's	6
La Dolce Vita	17
Le Jardin	5
Post 97	20
Schnurrbart	7
Tsui Wah	1
Wooloo Mooloo	21
Yung Kee	4
Zinc	14

▲ The LEGCO Building on Statue Square

Statue Square and around

Des Voeux Road's eastern end cuts past **Statue Square**, a rectangle of dull paving and lawn bisected by Chater Road. The northern piece is bounded to the east by a bow-fronted **Hong Kong Club**, and to the west by the **Mandarin Oriental Hotel**, which hides an opulent interior inside an unassuming, box-like casing. Taking tea or having a drink is one way for the riff-raff to get a glimpse of the inside, or you can march in and use the toilet facilities, which, as well as being the last word in urinary comfort, offer telephones, grooming facilities and chaise longues.

Across Chater Road in the southern part of Statue Square is the **statue** itself: that of Sir Thomas Jackson, a nineteenth-century manager of the Hongkong and Shanghai Bank. But far more impressive is the **LEGCO Building**, the beautiful Neoclassical structure to the east; domed and collonaded, it's the grandest colonial structure in Hong Kong, and so it should be – built as the Supreme Court in 1898, it now houses the **Legislative Council**, Hong Kong's local government assembly.

North over Connaught Road and on the harbour, the concrete hulk of **City Hall** is a mean exercise in 1960s civic architecture, though you might visit to make use of the theatre or concert hall. East of here, a blocky white tower with undercut corners marks the **PLA Barracks**, housing the local Chinese military forces (the British Army was stationed here before 1997); next door is the **Tamar site**, named after the supply ship that once served as the British Royal Navy's administrative HQ, now another military area used as a local landmark.

The HSBC and BOC towers

Not far from Statue Square are the local headquarters of the **Hong Kong Shanghai Banking Corporation** (HSBC) and **Bank of China** (BOC), two rivals engaged in a very Chinese form of warfare: **feng shui**. Briefly, this involves creating a building which is sympathetic to the local landscape, thereby promoting your own fortunes – and spoiling your opponent's. The best place to view them both at once is from the glass-panelled office lobby of the **AIG Tower**, which sits on the north side of **Chater Garden**.

The Sir Norman Foster-designed **HSBC Building**, built in 1986, stands immediately south of Statue Square. In front are two **bronze lions** named Stephen and Stitt, after managers at the bank's original Shanghai office; lion statues often guard important buildings in China to scare away bad luck. Stephen was damaged by shrapnel in World War II and the pair are the sole remnants of the previous HSBC headquarters, knocked down to build this one. The battle-ship-grey building is supported off the ground by **eight** groups of pillars (eight being a "lucky" number) and it's possible to walk right through underneath. According to *feng shui*, this was necessary because the centre of power on the island, Government House, needs to be accessible in a straight line on foot to the main point of arrival on the island, the Star Ferry Pier – **water** is believed to carry along luck and good fortune with it. (When the pier was shifted in 2006, care was taken to keep the alignment.) From underneath, the bank's insides are transparent, so you can look up into its heart through the colossal glass atrium – and ride the escalators up to use the ATMs on the first floor.

Over on the south side of Chater Garden, I.M. Pei's **BOC tower** opened in 1990. While the HSBC employs inoffensive *feng shui*, the BOC's is immediately aggressive, with the pointed, 315-metre-high knife-like tower stabbing the heavens to draw all the good luck down before any can reach its shorter rival. At the same time, its sharp corners cut towards Government House – a good indication of how Beijing viewed Hong Kong's British administration. It's also rumoured that the tower was designed to be so much taller than the HSBC so that the BOC directors could – metaphorically at least – spit down on their opponents' heads. You can get a taste of their sense of superiority from the **public viewing window** on the 43rd floor (open Mon–Fri 9am–7pm and Sat 9am–1pm; free), which offers grand vistas of the harbour.

Incidentally, the much shorter **Old Bank of China** still stands next to the HSBC. Housing the exclusive, members-only **China Club**, the stone Art Deco structure today looks like a fossilized ancestor of the towers surrounding it – you can almost see an architectural evolution in progress.

To Government House and the Zoological Gardens

A leafy path directly behind the HSBC building off the eastern tail of Queen's Road ascends Central's upper slopes. Almost immediately you reach the nineteenth-century redbrick **Court of Final Appeal**, once the French Mission Building, past which is **St John's Cathedral**, founded in 1847 and supposedly the oldest Anglican church in the Far East. It's the only freehold building in Hong Kong, as opposed to standing on land leased from the government – presumably, the colonial administrators felt God would accept nothing less than perpetuity.

Uphill again from here on Upper Albert Road, **Government House** was the official residence of Hong Kong's colonial governors from 1855 to 1997. It's a strange conglomeration of styles, oddest of which is the tower with flared eaves added during the World War II Japanese occupation. Now officially the SAR Government HQ, the house is off-limits though the **gardens**, famous for their rhododendrons and azaleas, are opened to the public for a few days every year in spring. Note that the **Peak Tram Terminal** is just east across Cotton Tree Drive (see p.74).

Directly above Government House, the low-key **Zoological and Botanical Gardens** first opened in 1864 (entrances on Upper Albert, Garden, Albany and Glenealy roads; daily 6am–10pm; free). It's peaceful and airy here, with a nice mix of shrubs, trees and paved paths, though the main draws are the aviaries, home to cages of rare cranes, songbirds, and pheasants; and the collection of apes, including orang-utans and gibbons. **Bus #12** from outside Central's Star Ferry Pier stops nearby on Upper Albert Road.

Exit the gardens west onto Glenealy Road, followed by a left up a driveway, and you'll reach the city's **Roman Catholic Cathedral**. Finished in 1888 and financed largely by Portuguese Catholics from Macau, it's now sunken among surrounding residential towers and is worth a look for the stained-glass west windows, made in Toulouse.

Hong Kong Park

Right at Central's eastern edge, **Hong Kong Park** (daily 6am–11pm; free) is a splendid example of what Chinese landscapers can do with a steep, rocky hillside: plant it with trees and shrubs, put in lotus ponds and paths, and open it up to the public as a refuge from the noise and bustle outside. Not that the park is exactly quiet – it's too popular for that, especially with **wedding parties** being photographed (there's a registry office here) – but it's a beautiful spot, the greenery oddly framed by offices towering above the perimeter.

Arranged in tiers, the park contains a **conservatory** with dry and humid habitats for its orchids, cacti and trees, as well as the superb **Edward Youde Aviary** (daily 9am–5pm; free). This enormous mesh tent encloses a tropical canopy, through which raised wooden walkways put you within touching distance of scores of colourful tropical birds, all busy swooping about, nesting and breeding. Most are Southeast Asian and Australasian species – such as the unlikely New Guinea Pigeon, as large as a goose – and can be surprisingly hard to spot among the foliage, despite their bright colours.

At the park's northern tip, **Flagstaff House** dates to 1846, when this cool, white, shuttered building was the office and residence of the Commander of the British Forces in Hong Kong. Today it houses the **Museum of Teaware** (Mon & Wed–Sun 10am–5pm; free), although the elegant high-ceilinged rooms and polished wooden floors perhaps outstrip the collection of teapots, bowls and

▲ Edward Youde Aviary in Hong Kong Park

cups, some of which date to the Song dynasty (960–1279). Back then **powdered green tea** was the favoured brew, whisked up with hot water in a bowl; successive centuries saw the shift towards the **leaf teas** favoured today, along with the teapots and cups needed to serve them. You can sample some of these next door inside the **K.C. Lo Gallery** at the pricey but stylish *Lock Cha Teahouse* (daily 10am–10pm; see p.206), which also runs free tea-appreciation classes (Mon, Wed, Fri 4pm; book in advance on ☎ 2801 7177). The gallery itself displays a collection of antique **seal stones**, which the Chinese traditionally use, engraved with their names, to sign documents and artworks. A whole culture of appreciation exists around both the skill of the name engraving and the quality of the stone itself.

Hong Kong Park's **main entrances** are on Cotton Tree Drive near the Peak Tram Terminal and the BOC tower, and off Queensway, close to the **Admiralty MTR station**. **Bus** #12 from Central's Star Ferry Pier stops outside on Cotton Tree Drive, while #1 and the **tram** pass by along Queensway. From the Zoological Gardens, exit east across the pedestrian bridge over Garden Road, and head downhill for fifteen minutes past the Peak Tram Terminal.

Admiralty

Besides Hong Kong Park, Central's eastern boundaries are marked by a clutch of striking buildings along **Queensway**, the section of Queen's Road that links Central to Wan Chai. This is **ADMIRALTY**, easily accessed from elsewhere via walkways, Admiralty MTR station and by tram or bus #1 along Queensway.

The most obvious building here – unmissable even if you're just whipping past along the road – is the **Lippo Centre**, at the junction of Cotton Tree Drive. The mirrored, segmented hexagonal towers, designed by American architect Paul Rudolph, are supported on huge grey pillars; interlocking steel and glass spurs trace their way up the centre's twin towers, while in the central lobby a ten-metre-high stone relief of a dragon and junk dominates. Behind it, the **Far Eastern Finance Centre**'s gold-plated windows make it another eye-catching, if less inspired, architectural landmark.

Walkways connect the Lippo Centre to other office and retail buildings, including the Queensway Plaza and Hutchison House, from where you can cross over Queensway to the **High Court** building. This again merges seamlessly with **Pacific Place**, a giant shopping mall which includes a cinema, luxury hotels and an external escalator up to Hong Kong Park.

Soho and the Mid-Levels

From Central, cross south over Hollywood Road and you're in **SOHO**, above which again you're halfway up The Peak and so – reasonably enough – will find yourself in the **MID-LEVELS**. Together these form a swanky, if dull, residential enclave favoured by expats who want the kudos of looking down on Central's attractions without the costs of living on The Peak. But over-development threatens, and long-term locals complain about the escalating forest of new apartment buildings cutting out their sunlight and airflow.

Sights are thin on the ground here but Soho boasts an extraordinary density of **restaurants**, even for Hong Kong, while a ride on the **Mid-Levels Escalator** is another good reason to pass through. This eight-hundred-metre-long series of elevated walkways, escalators and travelators cuts up the hillside from Central Market on Des Voeux Road (see p.62) along Cochrane Street and across Hollywood Road, Caine Road and Robinson Road, ending at Conduit Road. It carries thirty thousand people daily and changes direction according

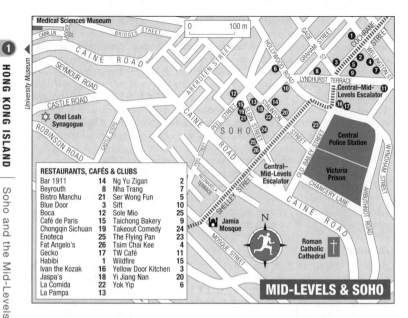

RESTAURANTS, CAFÉS & CLUBS

Bar 1911	14	Ng Yu Zigan	2
Beyrouth	8	Nha Trang	7
Bistro Manchu	21	Ser Wong Fun	5
Blue Door	3	Sift	10
Boca	12	Sole Mio	25
Café de Paris	15	Taichong Bakery	9
Chongqin Sichuan	19	Takeout Comedy	24
Enoteca	25	The Flying Pan	23
Fat Angelo's	26	Tsim Chai Kee	4
Gecko	17	TW Café	11
Habibi	1	Wildfire	15
Ivan the Kozak	16	Yellow Door Kitchen	3
Jaspa's	18	Yi Jiang Nan	20
La Comida	22	Yok Yip	6
La Pampa	13		

to workers' needs: **downhill** from 6am to 10am, **uphill** from 10am to midnight. The whole ride takes around twenty minutes, and you can get off and descend to street level every hundred metres or so.

Soho

The eastern stretch of **Hollywood Road** marks the boundary between Central and Soho – "Soho" stands for "South of Hollywood" – and is notable for its upmarket **art galleries** catering to the booming demand for works by Mainland Chinese artists. The galleries are good for a browse – though prices will probably leave you stunned – with works displaying a diversity of modernist styles. While you're in the area, have a look at the grey colonial facade of the old **Central Police Station** at 10 Hollywood Rd and the high walls of **Victoria Prison** behind it, built in 1841 as Hong Kong's first jail. Closed since 2005, the buildings are occasionally opened to the public and fortunately – given the government's enthusiasm for demolishing any structure over ten years old – enjoy protective heritage listing.

The rest of Soho is a mesh of old streets and shop-houses, formerly preserved from redevelopment by the steepness of the hills but now steadily being gentrified into florists, estate agents and interior decorators. The main thrust, however, is towards **restaurants**, with dozens lining **Elgin Street**, **Staunton Street** and below the escalator on **Shelley Street**. Most of these places are aimed at expat residents and have higher than average prices, but the choice is truly cosmopolitan, from pasta joints through to South American and regional Chinese – see p.199 for reviews.

The Mid-Levels

The Mid-Levels begin above **Caine Road**, though frankly there's very little reason to get off the escalator unless you live here. In passing, look out for

Jamia Mosque at 30 Shelley St; Hong Kong has fifty thousand Muslims and a mosque has stood on this site since the 1850s, though the present pale-green structure building dates from 1915. A nearby curiosity is **Rednaxela Terrace**, an unlikely name even for Hong Kong until you reverse the letters – it's actually a misspelling of "Alexandra" and named after the wife of the British king Edward VII.

Continue up Shelley Street and you'll come out on busy **Robinson Road**. Head west along here, and at no. 70 stairs lead down to the whitewashed **Ohel Leah Synagogue** (the name means "Tent of Leah"), lurking in its own quiet leafy hollow below the main road. The territory's best-known synagogue, it was built by the wealthy Sassoon family in memory of their mother and finished in 1902. From here, it's a short walk downhill via Castle and Seymour roads to the Medical Sciences Museum (p.72) off **Caine Road**, from where you can also pick up buses west to the University of Hong Kong (p.72).

Sheung Wan

SHEUNG WAN is only a few hundred metres west of Central's financial institutions, but the sudden thinning of office workers and tourists, the narrower streets and predominance of small, very Chinese businesses all create a distinctly

SHEUNG WAN

N

0   100 m

Sheung Wan MTR station
Tram route

RESTAURANTS
Bonheur   5
Fung Shing   1
Golden China   7
Leung Hing   2
Lin Heung Teahouse 8
Lok Cha Teashop   6
Sammy's Kitchen   3
Tim's Kitchen   4

ACCOMMODATION
Bridal Teahouse   C
Hua Tai   B
Lan Kwai Fong Hotel D
Ramada   A

Macau Ferry Terminal

Shun Tak Centre

CONNAUGHT ROAD WEST

Outlying Islands Ferry Piers

Car Park

NEW MARKET ST

Western Market

TUNG LOI LANE

WING LOK STREET

West Exchange Tower

DES VOEUX ROAD

Wing On Centre

PIER ROAD

BONHAM STRAND WEST

Sheung Wan Market

WING LOK STREET

Pang Yue Tai Teastore

SHEUNG WAN MTR

MAIN WA

LANE

Vicwood Plaza

CONNAUGHT ROAD

Harbour Building

CENTRAL

POSSESSION ST

QUEEN'S ROAD WEST

MORRISON ST

BONHAM STRAND EAST

MERCER ST

HILLIER ST

CTS House

Grand Millenium Plaza

GILMAN ST

TUNG STREET

UPPER STATION ST

SAI ST

LOK KU RD

UPPER LASCAR ROW

CLEVERLY ST

JERVOIS ST

BURD ST

QUEEN'S ROAD CENTRAL

QUEEN'S ROAD CENTRAL

WING KUT ST

MAN WA LANE

BONHAM STRAND

The Centre

TUNG LING ST

ROUND LN

TAI PING SHAN ST

HOLLYWOOD RD

SQUARE ST

KAU U FONG

GOUGH ST

WELLINGTON ST

Central Market

JUBILEE ST

PO TUNG FONG

TAI PING SHAN

LADDER ST

Man Mo Temple

HOLLYWOOD ROAD

ABERDEEN ST

Medical Sciences Museum

BRIDGES STREET

SHING WONG ST

PEEL STREET

GRAHAM ST

Central–Mid-Levels Escalator

CAINE ROAD

Mid-Levels ▼

Kennedy Town

Ko Shing St & A

Tai Ping Shan Temples

C & 3

University Museum & Art Gallery

VICTORIA ST

Central

different, neighbourhood feel. There are some good **markets** and traditional stores down near the waterfront here, while uphill on Hollywood Road, **Man Mo Temple** is one of the most famous and atmospheric on the island. The nearby **Tai Ping Shan** area conceals a sad history and the **Medical Sciences Museum**, from where you can catch a bus around to the **University of Hong Kong**, whose own museum hosts a fine collection of Chinese art.

The most useful thoroughfares here are **Des Voeux Road** and its trams, and **Queen's Road West**, served by plenty of buses. **Sheung Wan MTR** station currently marks the end of the Island Line, though there are plans to extend this out to Kennedy Town.

The Shun Tak Centre and nearby markets

Dominating Sheung Wan's waterfront is the **Shun Tak Centre** on Connaught Road, it's twin towers encased in a distinctive red framework. The **MTR station** is below and elevated walkways run here all the way from Central, making the Star Ferry Pier just thirty minutes away on foot. Inside is the **Macau Ferry Terminal**, departure point for helicopters and turbocats heading to Macau (see p.265 for more details).

Across Connaught Road – trams along Des Voeux stop just before a sharp bend – **Western Market**'s (daily 10am–7pm) fine Edwardian brick shell houses an uninspiring two-floor tourist complex, though the upstairs fabric shops can be reasonable value if you bargain hard. For a better experience, head up Morrison Street: the large white building on the right is the **Sheung Wan Indoor Market**, packed full of meat, fish, fruit and vegetable stalls – as usual, the cooked food centre is an inexpensive place to grab a bowl of noodle soup or plate of rice.

East of here is **Bonham Strand**, where Pang Yue Tai – an old **tea-trading store** at number 113 – is an incredibly ramshackle, archaic wooden establishment, its interior literally buried under blocks, bags and packets of tea. Past here, little **Man Wa Lane** is lined with booths specializing in carving **seals**, or "chops" as these name stamps are also called (see p.67 for more). The carvers here are used to tourists, and you can select a souvenir-quality stone – or even a block of perspex – onto which the craftsmen will engrave your name or message translated into Chinese. The process takes around an hour, making it possible to look around the rest of Sheung Wan while you're waiting.

Bonham Strand West and around

The area west of Sheung Wan Indoor Market is locally known as **Nam Pak Hong** – "North–South Trading Houses" – full of stores specializing in **dried foodstuffs** and **Traditional Chinese Medicine** products. A wander through the area will turn up dozens of dealers in dried mushrooms, salted and preserved fish, dried squid, oysters, sea slugs, seahorses, sharks' fins, scallops and seaweed. There's a fine line between food and medicine in China, but the best way of telling the difference here is seeing what is displayed in tiny red-and-gold gift packages (rare medicines), and what is shifted by the sackful (usually food).

One speciality of stores in **Bonham Strand West** and parallel **Wing Lok Street** is **ginseng**, the rhizome of a flat-leafed shrub found in northeast China, Korea and the US. Ginseng has an astringent taste and a reputation for curing everything from hangovers to impotence, and is even said to delay death by illness for three days. The most valuable pieces resemble a human body and must have all the trailing, hair-thin rootlets intact; trading companies here display examples in the window, while lesser roots are chopped up for sale by weight out the back. Many stores also sell **bird nests**, actually the salivary "cement" that holds together the nests of cave-roosting swiftlets. These little cups come in red and white varieties and are used to make **bird's nest soup**, a Hong Kong restaurant favourite said to promote longevity. As the nest is tasteless, however, the dish's quality rests in the soup itself.

Ko Shing Street, at the western end of Bonham Strand West, is devoted to the wholesale trade. Great sacks and wicker baskets arrive by truck and are dumped on the pavements to be sorted and packed by their contents. The shops here, open to the street, display deer antlers, crushed pearls, dried seahorses and all the assorted paraphernalia of Chinese herbalists.

From eastern end of Bonham Strand West, you can also head uphill to **Possession Street**, where the British claimed the island on 26 January, 1841. Though there's nothing of interest in the street itself, its inland location is another reminder of how completely Hong Kong's shoreline has been altered over the years.

To Hollywood Road and the Man Mo Temple

From Sheung Wan Indoor Market, follow **Morrison Street** up to Queen's Road, turn east and you'll soon see **Ladder Street**, a set of steep, broad stone steps heading uphill. This is one of many such stairways scattered between here and Central, a relic of the sedan-chair carriers who used them to get their loads up the hillsides. Near the top of the first section, **Upper Lascar Row** off to the west has hosted a busy **flea market** since the nineteenth century, when Europeans called the lane **Cat Street** – either after the number of brothels or the cat burglars who offloaded their wares here. Today it's wall-to-wall with stalls selling Mao badges and fun, antique-style trinkets alongside more substantial establishments dealing in reproduction porcelain, Tang statues and traditional paintings.

Ladder Street emerges onto **Hollywood Road**, which runs here from the Central–Soho border (see p.67) past a slew of **antique dealers**, ranging from upmarket galleries with the genuine articles (and prices to match), to shops selling low-budget curios. But the main draw is the 1840s **Man Mo Temple** (daily 8am–5pm), a lively example of southern Chinese temple design. Built of solid granite blocks and grey brick, with ornate wooden roof beams, it's dedicated to the complementary attributes of Man ("culture") and Mo ("martial"). Ahead as you enter the main hall, a gilt **spirit screen** carved with dragons and landscapes blocks bad luck from entering, while to the left are glass cases housing two ornate **wooden thrones**, once used to carry the temple's statues through the streets at festivals. Inside, below a canopy of red silk banners and huge hanging coils of smoking incense, are statues of the twin deities **Man Cheung**, the god of literature, and the red-faced god of war **Kuan Ti**. Either side are smaller altars to the protective city god Shing Wong and to Pao Kung, a judge in the afterlife.

Moving on, Hollywood Road is one-way to traffic, and the only bus along it is the #26, which runs east down to Queensway, then right out through Wan Chai to Causeway Bay.

Tai Ping Shan

Up Ladder Street from the Man Mo Temple lies the district of **TAI PING SHAN**, or "Peaceful Mountain". One of the earliest areas of Chinese settlement after the colony was founded, it belied its name by becoming a haunt of the early Hong Kong Triad societies, and a place whose overcrowded slums were notorious for outbreaks of **plague**. After a particularly virulent epidemic in 1894 killed 2500 people, the slums were levelled and a Pathalogical Institute built on the site; and it was here that French researcher **Alexandre Yersin** discovered that plague was spread to humans by fleas that had previously bitten infected rats (and so had the bacteria responsible, *Yersinia pestis*, named after him). The attractive Edwardian institute is now the **Medical Sciences Museum** (Tues–Sat 10am–5pm, Sun 1–5pm; HK$10), to the right off the top of Ladder Street and full of period medical equipment, photos and disturbing displays on the flu, plague and SARS pandemics which have bedevilled Hong Kong's history. There's a touch of humour, too, in the life-sized diorama of scientists injecting a buffalo calf with cowpox to farm smallpox vaccine; the Chinese are believed to have **innoculated** people against smallpox as early as the tenth century, and the vaccine used to be produced at the institute.

Down below, **Tai Ping Shan Street** runs back towards the western end of Hollywood Road, a walk which passes a cluster of old neighbourhood shrines raised above the street. The most interesting is the green-tiled **Shui Yuat Temple**, dedicated to the plague-quelling "Pacifying General" whose statue was set up here during the 1894 plague outbreak. A side hall is lined with statuettes of the **Tai Sui** – a series of sixty different gods, each one related to a specific year in the sixty-year cycle of the Chinese calendar. In times of strife, or to avert trouble, people come to pray and make offerings to the god associated with their year of birth. Further down the street, the **Kwung Fuk ancestral hall** holds little wooden memorial tablets for over 3000 people, many who died during the plague years far from their true ancestral homes in China.

The University of Hong Kong

Above the Museum of Medical Sciences, buses #3B, #23, #40 or #103 head west along Caine Road to the **University of Hong Kong** – after ten minutes, look for the red brick and white columns of Kings College and get out at the next stop. This lands you outside the **University Museum and Art Gallery** at 94 Bonham Rd (Mon–Sat 9.30am–6pm, Sun 1.30–5.30pm; Ⓦ www.hku .hk/hkumag; free), whose ever-changing display of Chinese artworks makes it well worth a visit.

You enter through the **Fung Ping Shan Building**, which houses a gallery for visiting exhibitions, plus a collection of antique **ceramics** showing classic designs from each period: wavy figurines of court ladies from the Han; Tang statuettes of horses and hook-nosed, bearded foreigners streaked in orange, brown and green glazes; and beautifully proportioned, purple-blotched *jun* ware from the Song and Yuan dynasties. The Song also produced exquisite brown-black hare's fur glaze, and pale-green *qinghai* ware, gently patterned with incised or moulded clouds, plants and animals. This contrasts with the bolder blue-and-white Ming dynasty glazes, which steadily decline into the vulgar, overcoloured and crowded designs which clutter up late-nineteenth century Qing porcelain. The connected **T.T. Tsui Building** has more in the way of **woodwork**, from temple statues to domestic furniture and elaborate carved screens depicting moral and historical tales, with traditional **scroll paintings** hung up alongside featuring landscapes and caligraphy.

Moving on from the museum, buses #3B, #23, #40 and #103 run east through the Mid-Levels and down Cotton Tree Drive between the Zoological Gardens and Hong Kong Park, the #23 and #103 continuing on through Wan Chai to Causeway Bay. **For Kennedy Town**, you'll need to walk west along Bonham Road, and then downhill via Pok Fu Lam Road to Queen's Road

West and Des Voeux Road, where you can pick up a tram – about twenty minutes in all.

Kennedy Town and Mount Davis

Marking Hong Kong Island's westernmost point, waterfront **Kennedy Town** is a low-key spot at the end of the **tram line**, and most visitors only wind up here because they've ridden the tram down from Central for the experience. Things are set to change, however, with talk of an **MTR extension** out this way already leading to a number of tourist hotels opening up, doubtless to be followed by an increase in appartment blocks and malls. The hill above, **Mount Davis**, is probably of most interest for its youth hostel, though some war relics might make it worth the effort of getting up here.

Kennedy Town

KENNEDY TOWN is a small grid of residential blocks, with a number of trade businesses and shopping complexes spread along central **Kennedy Town Praya**, down which the trams run to terminate outside *The Merton* complex on Catchick Street. Kennedy Town's main employment has always been shifting cargoes between the warehouses, wharfs and ships lining **Belcher Bay** and, though there's not a huge amount to see by way of activity, there's a definite maritime feel to the place.

For the town's one sight, get off the tram opposite **Belcher Bay Park** – it's hard to miss the trees – head uphill to Belcher's Street, and then ascend the broad steps on Li Po Lung Street to leafy **Ching Ling Terrace**. The building in front of you, its front decked out in garish figures depicting scenes from Cantonese opera, is a gem of a temple (daily 8am–5pm) dedicated to **Lo Pan**, patron saint of carpenters and engineers. Like many folk deities, Lo Pan – also known as Kungshu Pan – is believed to have been a real person, born in northeast China around 500 BC, and his birthday is celebrated here by construction workers every thirteenth day of the sixth moon (see "Festivals", p.35). The temple's interior is unassuming, but make sure you walk up to the little terrace above for views of the roofline, with its ear-like fire baffles and frolicking porcelain dragons, fish and lions.

Mount Davis

Mount Davis only rises to 269m, but it's quite a slog up here in the summer heat; no buses come this way and taxis are reluctant to take you as they won't get a return fare. Most visitors are budget travellers staying at the **youth hostel** (see p.196), the only one on Hong Kong Island, though the trek up is fun in an off-the-beaten-track sort of way. To **walk** from Kennedy Town, follow **Victoria Road** west from the tram terminus for about ten minutes, until you see a gully lined with steep concrete steps going up to the left. Climb these for twenty minutes through rank woodland and scrub – you'll think you're on the wrong track – to **Mount Davis Road**, then bear left and follow a signed path for another ten minutes up to the youth hostel. Alternatively, catch **bus #5** west from Victoria Road in Kennedy Town to its terminus at the bottom of Mount Davis Road, and walk for forty minutes up the road to the hostel.

The track continues for a short way past the hostel to Mount Davis' level **summit**, where aside from a picnic area and handful of transmitter masts you'll find a network of overgrown **concrete bunkers**. These date from World War II, when the mountain was part of a chain of gun batteries designed to defend the harbour, before Hong Kong fell in December 1941. There are good views over the western side of the island from here, while the bunkers are popular with war game enthusiasts, who come up here to play paintball.

The Peak

Rearing up above Central, the 552-metre heights of **THE PEAK** give you the only perspective that matters in Hong Kong: down. Since you're coming up primarily for the spectacular **views** of the cityscape and harbour, try to do so on a clear day, though even when the smog gathers below The Peak is worth the journey. It's cooler up here, the humidity is more bearable and there's a choice of shady, airy **walks** – little wonder that this has long been *the* place to live in the territory. Bring a picnic lunch (restaurants up here are expensive), or visit at **night** – transport runs late – to see the city aflame with neon.

The first path up to The Peak was made in 1859, and within twenty years it was a popular retreat from the summer heat only. Access was by sedan chair only, though things changed in 1888 with the opening of the **Peak Tram**, and the first road connection was made in 1924. Initially, the Chinese weren't allowed on The Peak except to carry up Europeans and supplies on their backs: now, of course, **money** is the only qualification for tenancy and the upper slopes are peppered with elite homes and apartments, all competing for phenomenal views and rental values.

Ascending The Peak

Half the fun of The Peak is the journey up, with all routes converging below the summit at **Victoria Gap**. For the fit, **walking** up is an option, following the **Old Peak Road** from the southern side of Central's Zoological Gardens at the corner of Albany and Robinson roads. The road is extremely steep but properly surfaced the whole way, leading first up around some dizzying residential towers, then into thick forest, where it becomes open to pedestrians only. It takes around an hour from the gardens to the roadhead beside the Peak Tower. You can also hike up from Aberdeen, though this takes far longer (see box opposite).

Catching a double-decker **bus** up doesn't sound very exciting, but is actually quite an adventure: the bus lurches from side to side as it negotiates tight bends and low-hanging branches, and you only have to sit upstairs at the front to enjoy a ride that rivals anything Disney or Ocean Park can provide. **Bus #15** departs Central Bus Station daily every 10 to 15 minutes, 6.15am to 12.15am (HK$9.80); from 10am it also travels via Central's Star Ferry Pier. The journey takes half an hour, though you could stop off along the way at Queen's Road East, Bowen Road and the Police Museum (see pp.80–82). On public holidays, you can also catch **bus #15B** (every 20min; noon–7pm; HK$9.10) from behind Tin Hau MTR, or from Leighton Road in Causeway Bay.

The most popular way to the top, however, is the eight-minute ride aboard the **Peak Tram** (daily 7am–midnight, every 10–15min; HK$32 return, HK$22 one-way). This 1.4-kilometre-long funicular railway climbs at a severe 27-degree angle, providing an odd perspective of the tall buildings of Central and Mid-Levels, which appear to lean inwards overhead as you sink back on angled wooden benches. The tram departs from the **Lower Peak Tram Terminal** on Garden Road, near Hong Kong Park in Central; you can get here direct from outside the Star Ferry Pier on **bus #15C** (6am–midnight). Be warned that the **queues** for the tram can be enormous, especially at weekends and public holidays: get here early.

Victoria Gap

However you got here, you'll wind up at a small saddle known as **Victoria Gap**, dominated by two huge buildings facing each other across an open square. Foremost is the **Peak Tower**, an ugly, wok-shaped eyesore designed to block everybody else's outlook, where they meanly charge HK$20 to use the **Sky Terrace** viewing platform. The **views** from here are stupendous, however, down over Hong Kong Island's bristling, intensely crowded north shore (incredibly, you're almost level with the top of IFC2), across the busy harbour to a generally lower-rise, unspectacular Kowloon, and the New Territories' moody green peaks. Inside the tower is the **Upper Peak Tram Terminal** with departures back to Central, and **Madame Tussaud's** (daily 10am–10pm; HK$140), where wax re-creations of kung fu hero Jackie Chan and Chinese President Hu Jintao rub shoulders with basketball star Yao Ming and actor-singers Andy Lau, Aaron Kwok and Joey Yung.

Across the square – where there's a dancing fountain, the excellent *Peak Lookout Restaurant* (see p.219) and a branch of the **Hong Kong Tourist Board** inside an old tram carriage (daily 9am–9pm) – the **Peak Galleria** is a touristy shopping mall offering little that you couldn't buy in Tsim Sha Tsui. It does have some virtues, however: a **free viewing terrace** on level 3, not as good as the Peak Tower's but also taking in the scenery south over Pok Fu Lam Reservoir; a useful Park N Shop **supermarket** on level 2, for drinks and picnic snacks; and more top views at *Café Deco* (if only average food, see p.218). **Buses and taxis** stop at ranks underneath the Galleria.

Walks around The Peak

Aside from the fact that Victoria Gap is not actually at the top of The Peak and you might want to reach the summit, there are some excellent **walks** to be made around the area. Easiest is simply to stroll east from the square for 100m along **Findlay Road** to a small pavilion, where you can enjoy much the same views as from the the Peak Tower, but for free. You can also zigzag downhill from Findlay onto the Old Peak Road and so back to Central in about forty minutes.

The Peak to Aberdeen hike

On a fine day, it takes around 3 hours 30 minutes to hike along signposted tracks from **The Peak to Aberdeen**, with some great views of the island's south and west coasts. Most of the way is shaded, but you'll need to carry drinking water as there are no shops along the way.

Start from Victoria Gap by following Harlech Road right to its end, by which time you're already on Section 1 of the **Hong Kong Island Trail**. This runs along the hillside through scrubby forest and grassland – look west over high-rises to Mount Davis – and then drops to little **Pok Fu Lam Reservoir**, around ninety minutes from your starting point. You walk east along the reservoir and past some cascades, then head steeply uphill, turning south about 500m along onto Section 2 of the Hong Kong Island Trail, where signposts indicate "Peel Rise". From here you slalom through a dry woodland of tea trees, with orange-patched bark and frail white flowers, until you suddenly emerge above the south coast, with Lamma Island (look for the power station towers) and narrow **Aberdeen harbour** spread out below. The descent is first down steps, then on a path alongside a concrete stormwater channel to where the Hong Kong Island Trail intersects with a small vehicle access road. Follow this road down, through the **Chinese cemetery**, and so on to **Peel Rise**, which enters Aberdeen town beside the **Tin Hau Temple** (see p.89).

Otherwise, the *Peak Lookout Restaurant* marks the start of all the other trails. For **The Peak itself**, make the stiff walk up **Mount Austin Road** to the landscaped **Peak Garden** – all that remains of the old governor's residence except for the miniature Georgian-style **Gate Lodge** you pass by the roadside on the way here. A service track continues past radio towers to The Peak's very top and yet more vistas of the territory. Allow ninety minutes for the return journey.

Most popular is the **Peak Circuit**, a level four-kilometre stroll via **Harlech Road** to a picnic area about halfway around, from where **Lugard Road** heads back to complete the circuit. Along the way is some shady forest, possibly the most expensive residences in the territory, and an evolving panorama of the island encompassing Aberdeen, Mount Davis, Sheung Wan, Victoria Harbour and Central.

Alternatively, follow Harlech Road as far as the junction with Lugard, and then either continue down along Harlech towards Pok Fu Lam Reservoir and Aberdeen (see box, p.75) or bear off along **Hatton Road**, which soon brings you to **Pinewood Battery**. This group of abandoned gun emplacements, concrete platforms and underground barracks overlooks Sheung Wan from the summit of **Lung Fu Shan**; built in 1905 as a naval barrage, it was later converted for anti-aircraft purposes but, like most of Hong Kong's defences, didn't survive World War II. Today it's another popular picnic site, with lawn, toilets, pavilion and a barbecue area.

Wan Chai

WAN CHAI spreads east for a couple of kilometres between Admiralty and the overhead expressway of Canal Road, beyond which is Causeway Bay. The harbour area here is modern in a functional way, dominated by the **Convention and Exhibition Centre** and some busy east–west arteries. Things get livelier a couple of streets back, where a knot of **bars**, clubs and pick-up joints recall the days when Wan Chai was a famous red-light district, immortalized in Richard Mason's novel, *The World of Suzie Wong*, whose heroine was a local prostitute. But Wan Chai is not all civic buildings and nightlife; as the rents have increased in Central, ordinary businesses have shifted into the area and there's good deal of workaday character to soak up – and some quirky antique corners – especially along **Queen's Road East**.

Wan Chai's **main roads** are **Gloucester** – a massive, multi-lane expressway – **Lockhart** and **Hennessy** (an extension of Queensway), all of which run right through the district from Admiralty and into Causeway Bay. Further inland, **trams** enter from Queensway in Admiralty, detour along **Johnston Road** and then move up onto Hennessy. **Wan Chai MTR station** sits right in the middle of the district on Hennessy Road; the **Star Ferry** from Kowloon (see p.59) docks at the pier just east of the Convention Centre, from where you can reach Johnston Road via the MTR station along a small network of pedestrian walkways.

The Convention and Exhibition Centre

The huge **Convention and Exhibition Centre** looms over the Wan Chai waterfront, though it's the curved-roofed **CEC New Wing** – looking vaguely like a giant manta ray – which most impresses as it juts out into the harbour. This was where the British formally handed Hong Kong back to the Chinese on 1 July, 1997, and so marks the spot where the **Hong Kong Special Administrative Region** (HKSAR) was founded. The event is commemorated in the harbourside square outside by the glum, black obelisk of the **Reunification Monument** – adorned with former Chinese President Zhang Zemin's calligraphy – and the far more cheerful **Golden Bauhinia Sculpture**. The five-petalled bauhinia flower is Hong Kong's regional emblem, and the site's patriotic associations means that this sculpture is a massive draw for visiting Mainland Chinese, who pose by the busload to have their photo taken. The bauhinia flower also appears on the red HKSAR **flag**, which – along with a neighbouring Chinese flag – is raised here in a daily cermony at 7.50am, and lowered at 6pm.

Aside from getting here on foot via the walkways between Wan Chai Ferry Pier and Wan Chai MTR on Hennessy Road, **bus #961** (daily 5.30am–11pm) runs direct to the Convention Centre from Sheung Wan, via Connaught Road in Central.

Central Plaza and around

Immediately south of the Convention and Exhibition Centre, **Central Plaza** stands 374m high, a triangular-sectioned tower topped by a glass pyramid and swathed in luminous panels that change colour every fifteen minutes between 6pm and 6am. There's a **public viewing bay** on the 46th floor (Mon–Fri 8am–8pm; free), which is sided in continuous glass panels so that you can enjoy a 360-degree view of adjacent high-rises, buildings scaffolded in bamboo, an extraordinary number of taxis far below on Gloucester Road and Victoria Harbour clogged with all types of vessels. Central Plaza is plugged into the local **elevated walkway** network about halfway between the Wan Chai Ferry Pier and MTR station.

Back at street level and east of Central Plaza – again, you can get here via the walkways – the **China Resources Building** contains (among other things) the Mainland's visa-issuing office, with an impressive, twenty-metre long **Nine Dragons Screen** in an outside courtyard. This brick and coloured ceramic-tile wall is a replica of a Ming dynasty example in Beijing's Forbidden City, and illustrates the legend of Buddha being washed by dragons at birth.

▲ The Convention and Exhibition Centre, Wan Chai

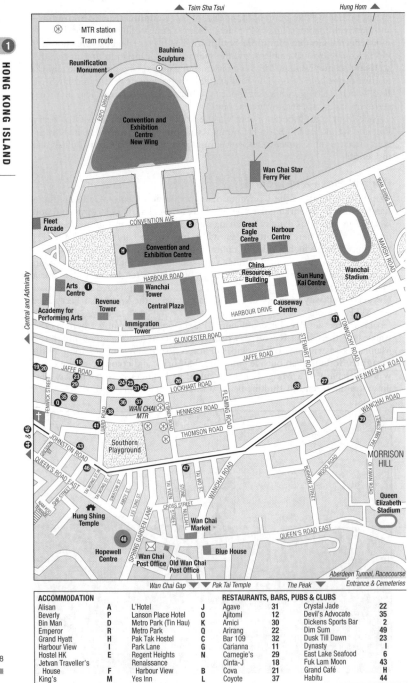

ACCOMMODATION				RESTAURANTS, BARS, PUBS & CLUBS			
Alisan	A	L'Hotel	J	Agave	31	Crystal Jade	22
Beverly	P	Lanson Place Hotel	O	Ajitomi	12	Devil's Advocate	35
Bin Man	D	Metro Park (Tin Hau)	K	Amici	30	Dickens Sports Bar	2
Emperor	R	Metro Park	Q	Arirang	22	Dim Sum	49
Grand Hyatt	H	Pak Tak Hostel	C	Bar 109	32	Dusk Till Dawn	23
Harbour View	I	Park Lane	G	Carianna	11	Dynasty	I
Hostel HK	E	Regent Heights	N	Carnegie's	29	East Lake Seafood	6
Jetvan Traveller's		Renaissance		Cinta-J	18	Fuk Lam Moon	43
House	F	Harbour View	B	Cova	21	Grand Café	H
King's	M	Yes Inn	L	Coyote	37	Habitu	44

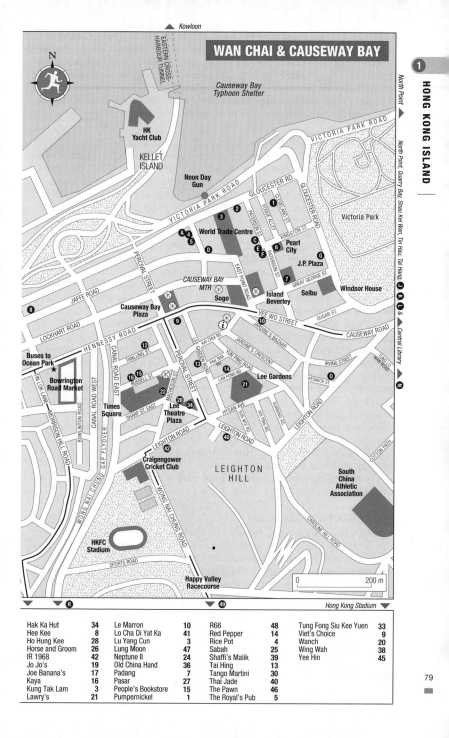

WAN CHAI & CAUSEWAY BAY

N

Causeway Bay Typhoon Shelter

EASTERN CROSS-HARBOUR TUNNEL

HK Yacht Club

KELLET ISLAND

Noon Day Gun

VICTORIA PARK ROAD

VICTORIA PARK ROAD

Victoria Park

GLOUCESTER RD.

GLOUCESTER ROAD

VICTORIA PARK ROAD

②
❶
CLEVELAND ST.
VOGUE ALLEY
③
PATERSON ST.
KINGSTON ST.
Ⓐ ④
⑤
World Trade Centre
Ⓒ
Ⓔ ⑥ Pearl City
Ⓓ
Ⓕ
PATERSON ST.
EAST POINT ROAD
Ⓖ
J.P. Plaza
GREAT GEORGE ST.
⑦

PERCIVAL STREET

CAUSEWAY BAY MTR
CAUSEWAY BAY MTR
Sogo
Island Beverley
Seibu
Windsor House

JAFFE ROAD

❽

LOCKHART ROAD

Causeway Bay Plaza

⑨
ⓘ
YEE WO STREET
SUGAR ST.
JARDINE'S BAZAAR
⑩
CAUSEWAY ROAD
IRVING STREET
TUNG LO WAN ROAD

HENNESSY ROAD

CANAL ROAD EAST

Buses to Ocean Park

Bowrington Road Market

TIN LOK LANE
MORRISON HILL ROAD

⑫
TANG LUNG ST.
⑯ ⑮
RUSSELL ST.
⑬
LEE GARDEN ROAD
KAI CHIU RD.
PAK SHA RD.
YUN PING ROAD
⑭
LAN FONG RD.
Lee Gardens
KESWICK ST.
Ⓞ

⑳①

BOWRINGTON ROAD
CANAL ROAD WEST

Times Square

㉒
MATHESON ST.
SHARP ST. EAST
Lee Theatre Plaza
㉘ ㉞

PERCIVAL STREET

HYSAN AVE.
SUN WUI RD.
HO PING RD.
SUNNING RD.
LEIGHTON ROAD

WONG NAI CHUNG GAP FLYOVER

㊷

LEIGHTON ROAD

Craigengower Cricket Club

⑩

LEIGHTON ROAD

LEIGHTON HILL

South China Athletic Association

COTTON PATH

WONG NAI CHUNG ROAD

HKFC Stadium

SPORTS ROAD

CAROLINE HILL ROAD

Happy Valley Racecourse

0   200 m

▼ ▼ Ⓡ   ▼ ㊾   Hong Kong Stadium ▼

West of Central Plaza on Harbour Road, **Hong Kong Arts Centre** is a leading venue for drama, film screenings and cultural events. It also houses the Goethe Institute and, on the fifth floor, the Pao Sui Loong Galleries (daily 10am–8pm; free), which hosts contemporary art exhibitions. Close by on Fenwick Street, the building with the triangular windows is Hong Kong's **Academy for Performing Arts** (APA), whose students regularly put on music and dance productions. For more on both venues, see p.229.

South to Johnston Road

The stretch of busy parallel drags running east through Wan Chai – **Jaffe Road**, **Lockhart Road** and **Hennessy Road** – are of most appeal for their **bars**, some of which are a mite sleazy but nothing like during their Korean and Vietnam war heydays, when Wan Chai was a thriving brothel district catering to US troops on leave. Many of the places here today are party-rowdy rather than confronting, with the biggest concentration down around the intersection with Luard Road (see p.226).

Hennessy Road is pretty much a border between this part of Wan Chai and the older, busier, more crowded areas south. The emphasis along **Johnston Road** – reached along the tram lines – is shopping for daily necessities, with a dash of history provided by *The Pawn* at no. 62 (p.227), a traditional **Chinese pawnbroker's** now restored and turned into a smart bar – an unusual example in Hong Kong of sympathetic urban redevelopment. East at no. 120, the huge *Lung Moon Restaurant* (see p.207) looks like something out of a 1950s film, all golden dragons, dim lighting and worn splendour, from where you can cut south to Queen's Road East through the Tai Yuen Street markets. In between the two, and occupying an entire block between Johnston and Hennessy roads, open-air **Southorn Playground** is an unexpected sight given its value as a piece of prime real estate. The story goes that the original owner couldn't be found after World War II, so the government built a public sports ground here to avoid legal problems.

Finally, if you're heading to Causeway Bay, follow **Wanchai Road** – which branches off Johnston – to its end, cross over Morrison Hill Road's tram lines and you'll be at **Bowrington Road Market**, a full-blown affair full of chunks of meat on hooks and endless barrowfulls of dried food, fruit and veggies. If you're hungry, the upstairs **cooked food area** is the cheapest place to eat in Wan Chai.

Along Queen's Road East

Queen's Road East, which branches off Queensway in Admiralty and runs due east to Happy Valley, offers an atmospheric walk along what was Wan Chai's original nineteenth-century shoreline. Get here from Central Bus Station aboard **bus #6** (to Stanley) or **#15** (to The Peak), or on foot from other arrival points in Wan Chai; allow an hour for a good stroll and a look around the sights.

Moving eastwards from Admiralty, the first thing you'll notice are the number of **furniture stores**, many dealing in classic Chinese designs with chairs, carved screens and tables all made from dark, fine-grained wood. Around halfway down on the south side of the road, **Ship Street**'s scruffy stone steps lead up to **Nam Koo Terrace**, where an abandoned nineteenth-century mansion, ancient fig trees, crumbling walls and skulking cats all lend credence to this being the most **haunted** place in Hong Kong.

A few doors along, where a steep granite slope pushes out into the road, tiny **Hung Shing Temple** (daily 8am–5.30pm) dates from 1840 and is nominally dedicated to Hung Shing, a Tang dynasty official revered by fishermen for his skill in forecasting the weather. Despite a cramped interior, the temple also manages to squeeze in a handful of shrines dedicated to Pao Kung, Kwun Yam and **Kam Fa**, a sea goddess with her main temple on Peng Chau island (see p.169).

Another few minutes walk brings you to the cylindrical **Hopewell Centre**, topped by a revolving restaurant on the 62nd floor (see p.203), and then the **Old Wan Chai Post Office**, a little whitewashed building opened in 1915 and now the Environmental Resources Agency. A steep lane beside it heads up to Wan Chai Gap (see below). Opposite, **Tai Yuen Street** cuts north to Johnston Road through a bustling **local market**, full of food, cheap clothes and plasticware; a great – if frustratingly crowded – place for a browse.

Back on Queen's Road East you reach **Stone Nullah Lane**, marked on the corner by **The Blue House**. This 1920s structure is one of the last tong lau residential blocks in Hong Kong, built in a mix of European and Chinese styles with wooden interior staircases and lightweight iron balconies. It was once a Traditional Chinese Medicine clinic and martial arts school founded by a follower of the famous master Wong Fei Hong; today it's being targeted for "revitalization" by the government. Further up at the top of Stone Nullah Lane, the beautiful **Pak Tai Temple** (daily 8am–5pm) is overhung by huge trees and sports a riot of pottery figurines along its roof. Pak Tai, Emperor of the North, is responsible for regulating water and preventing flooding, and there's a bearded copper statue of him inside dating from 1604 – the snake and tortoise underfoot represent him overpowering evil forces. From here, it's possible to follow a path behind the temple up to Wan Chai Gap – see below.

To Wan Chai Gap

The steep wooded hillsides between Wan Chai and **Wan Chai Gap** offer a remarkable contrast – over a very short distance – between the North Shore's cityscape and a more natural environment. Aside from scenery, there are a couple of peculiar sights to take in, after which you can catch a bus onwards to The Peak.

It's a stiff **walk** up here off Queen's Road East via the Old Wan Chai Post Office or the Pak Tai Temple. From either place, you'll shortly find yourself on Kennedy Road, which you cross and then continue uphill along pedestrian **Wan Chai Gap Road**. After about fifteen minutes you reach a terrace at the junction with Bowen Road; turn left here for Lover's Rock, or continue up Wan Chai Gap Road for another twenty minutes – it's exceedingly steep – to Stubb's Road near the Police Museum. If all this sounds like

Hiking Hong Kong Island

Hong Kong Island's coastal development gives way to some well-wooded areas inland, though come prepared for steep gradients on even the **short walks** around Lover's Rock (p.82) and The Peak (p.74). For a north–south traverse, you can follow the **Wilson Trail** (p.92) between Quarry Bay and Stanley, or take the Old Peak Road (p.74) from the Zoological Gardens to The Peak, then drop down the far side via various trails to Aberdeen (p.75) – about five hours in all. Part of this route follows the well-signposted **Hong Kong Island Trail**, which runs eastwards for 50km from The Peak to Big Wave Bay, just north of Shek O. Of the eight stages, the final section down to Big Wave Bay – known as the **Dragon's Back** (p.94) – is one of the most popular, crossing a high ridge with splendid sea views before descending to the beach. For more about maps and **hiking information**, see p.252.

too much hard work, catch the **#15 bus** towards The Peak (see p.58) and get off as described below.

Bowen Road and Lover's Rock

The first place to aim for on the way to Wan Chai Gap is **Bowen Road**, a concrete pedestrian pathway doubling as a jogging track, which runs level along the hillside through a forest of fig trees, bamboo, fan palms and red-flowering kapok trees. Either **walk up** from Queen's Road East as described above, or catch the #15 bus to the "Adventist Hospital" stop, immediately after it makes a severe hairpin turn to the right on a roundabout; Bowen Road emerges opposite. The walk up here places you west of Lover's Rock; the bus ride to the east of it.

Bowen Road is very pleasant, with views through the forest over Wan Chai and Happy Valley, and the path is dotted with red-daubed **shrines** to various deities. Whichever side you started from, after about fifteen minutes you'll reach the most impressive shrine, Yan Yuen Sek or **Lover's Rock**, an unabashed monument to fertility: steps climb from the path past a grotto surrounded by statuettes and religous paraphernalia, to where a nine-metre-high granite boulder points rudely towards the heavens, all painted red and hung with bright banners and ribbons. It's a focus of the Maidens' Festival (see p.35), held in mid-August, when unmarried women, wives and widows visit to pray for husbands and sons.

Wan Chai Gap and the Police Museum

Walking up Wan Chai Gap Road from Bowen Road, you eventually emerge gasping onto **Stubbs Road**, the main road up to The Peak; if you caught the #15 bus, get out at the "Wan Chai Gap Road" stop. Either way you're now at **WAN CHAI GAP** itself, a level terrace with a picnic area, small kiosk and large car park, with the **Police Museum** (Tues 2–5pm, Wed–Sun 9am–5pm; free) perched on the hill to the right. Inside, exhibits chart the history of the Royal Hong Kong Police Force from its earliest beginnings in 1841, with heaps of of old photos, uniforms and guns, as well as seized counterfeit cash presses and a tiger's head (a huge beast shot in Sheung Shui in 1915). Another room displays every kind of drug you've ever heard of and, perversely, shows you exactly how to smuggle them – hollowed-out Bibles and bras stuffed with heroin are just some of the more obvious methods. There's also a mock-up of a heroin factory and a Triad room, complete with ceremonial uniforms and some very offensive weapons retrieved by the police.

Moving on, you can catch the #15 bus up to The Peak or back towards Central or, of course, descend back down Wan Chai Gap Road into Wan Chai.

Causeway Bay

Midway along the island's North Shore, **CAUSEWAY BAY** was once just that – a large, natural bay around which the British built company warehouses and wharfs during the nineteenth century. But extensive **reclamation** in the 1950s buried all this under landfill, and now the "bay" exists in name only. Today it's one of Hong Kong's busiest **shopping districts**, a densely congested rectangle of plazas and streets bordered to the east by spacious **Victoria Park**. Shopping really is the mainstay, and about the only other reason to visit is for the small enclave of **budget accommodation** (see p.187), though the area is also thick with **restaurants**.

Causeway Bay is hemmed in on three sides by expressways, one of them serving the insanely busy Eastern Cross-Harbour Tunnel to Kowloon. The main through road is **Yee Wo Street**, an extension of Wan Chai's Hennessy Road, which in turn becomes **Causeway Road** as it runs out along Victoria Park's southern edge. The **Causeway Bay MTR station** is on Yee Wo Street, with a branch of the **Hong Kong Tourist Bureau** inside at Exit F (daily 8am–8pm). **Trams** run east–west along Yee Wo Street and Causeway Road, or branch off south down Percival Street and into Happy Valley.

The Noon Day Gun

Causeway Bay's sole sight as such is the **Noon Day Gun**, an eccentric survival from colonial days which points north over the harbour on Victoria Park Road. The story is vague, but it's said that this small ship's canon was once fired by a Jardine employee to salute one of the company's ships, an action that so outraged the governor – whose prerogative it was to fire off salutes – that he ordered the event to be repeated every day at noon for evermore. The tale was later enshrined in Noel Coward's ditty *Mad Dogs and Englishmen*:

In Hong Kong
They strike a gong
And fire off a noonday gun
To reprimand each inmate
Who's in late

from *Mad Dogs and Englishmen*

And so the tradition continues: at around 11.50am every day, two smartly dressed naval officers turn up, remove the gun's awning, load a shell and then, precisely at midday, fire it. Some of the harbour cruises catch the action (see "Organized Tours", p.29) and there's a more elaborate ceremony every New Year's Eve, when the gun is fired at midnight. At other times, don't expect to see anything except a gun under wraps in a railed-off garden. The easiest way to reach here is from the **car park** next to the *Excelsior Hotel* opposite; a tunnel runs under Victoria Park Road and emerges right next to the gun.

Shopping in Causeway Bay

Despite Causeway Bay's cachet in Hong Kong as one of the best places for a **shopping** spree, the truth is that it's neither as upmarket as Central, nor as inexpensive as Tsim Sha Tsui. Even so, you can spend a good few hours splitting your time between some monumental vertical malls and intimate – not to say seething – side streets.

Your first stop should be **south of Yee Wo Street** at the beige blockbuster of a building that is **Times Square**, on Matheson and Russell streets. Spearing skywards from a small square at ground level, it resembles nothing less than a cathedral, complete with a long cathedral-style window and – breaking the mood slightly – a giant video advertising screen. From the massive open-plan lobby, silver bullet-lifts whizz up to the various themed shopping floors, and there's even an elegant curved escalator to carry you downstairs. At ground level there's a cinema and access to Causeway Bay MTR station. Similar behemoths in the vicinity include **Lee Theatre Plaza**, a strangely narrow, sharp-ribbed spurt of steel and glass at the end of Percival Street; and **Lee Gardens**, a whopping great new plaza full of shiny upmarket boutiques that makes the other two look distinctly shabby. By contrast, nearby **Jardine's Bazaar** and pedestrianized **Jardine's Crescent** are two narrow, parallel lanes which have contained street markets since the earliest days of the colony. They're great places to poke around: cheap clothes abound, while deeper in you'll find the noisy little **Tang Lung Chau produce market** and all manner of shops and stalls selling herbs and provisions.

North of Yee Wo Street the pace is a little less frantic, the tail-ends of Jaffe and Lockhart roads full of low-cost places to eat and pet emporiums, trendy hairdressers and countless boutiques. There's a large Japanese department store – **Sogo** – stuffed with hi-tech, high-fashion articles; while the **World Trade Centre**, with a few more restaurants and aspiring stores, has yet to make its mark.

Victoria Park and Central Library

The eastern side of Causeway Bay comprises the large, green expanse of **Victoria Park**. It's busy all day, from the crack-of-dawn martial arts practitioners and old men strolling with their songbirds in little cages along the paths, to evening soccer matches on the lawns. Amid the paved areas and groves of trees and flowers, there's also a swimming pool, childrens' playground, jogging track and a pebbled path that people walk on in socks to massage their feet. You can catch some explosive **festival** celebrations here, including a flower market at Chinese New Year, a lantern display for the Mid-Autumn Festival and the annual candle-lit vigil for the victims of Tiananmen Square on June 4.

South across Causeway Road, Hong Kong's **Central Library** (Mon & Tues and Thurs–Sat 10am–9pm, Wed 1–9pm, Sun 10am–6pm) is a massive twelve-storey affair, with some 1.2 million books and a reading room with journals and papers from around the globe. There are also more than five hundred computer terminals with free internet access and wi-fi, plus a children's toy library on the second floor. It's all very user-friendly and aside from queues for the lifts, you shouldn't have trouble accessing the facilities. There's a small gift shop and a branch of *Delifrance* on the ground floor.

Note that from Victoria Park or the library, it's only a short walk or tram-ride east to Tin Hau and Tai Hang (p.86).

Happy Valley

Travel south from Causeway Bay and you're soon in **HAPPY VALLEY**, which occupies a small, flat plain below Wong Nai Chung Gap. The early colonial settlers should have known better, but it took them a couple of years to come to grips with the fact that every wet season the place turned into a boggy swamp rife with malaria. They eventually moved out, established **cemeteries** on the western slopes and turned the plain into a **racecourse** in 1846 – hence Happy Valley's Cantonese name, *Pau Ma Dei* or "Horse Racetrack". As Hong Kong's only legal outlet for **gambling** – a pastime dear to many Chinese people's hearts – a visit trackside is a must, when you can witness Hong Kong at its rawest and most gleefully grasping.

The racetrack is almost encircled by **Wong Nai Chung Road**, south of which Happy Valley township spreads up the hill along **Sing Woo Road**. Causeway Bay has the closest **MTR** station; **trams** from Causeway Bay run south down Percival Street, then circuit clockwise around to terminate at the racetrack's southern end on Wong Nai Chung Road, not far from the spectator entrances. **Bus #1** also runs all the way here from Kennedy Town via Sheung Wan, Central and Wan Chai, passing the tram stop and itself terminating up along Sing Woo Road.

Happy Valley Racecourse

Happy Valley Racecourse is the centre for Hong Kong's racing industry (with a second track at Sha Tin in the New Territories), and events are held here almost every **Wednesday night** during the **September–June racing season**. Each season some two million punters bet a staggering HK$65 billion, and a percentage of the profits are distributed to social and charitable causes all over the territory by the **Hong Kong Jockey Club** – hence their name appearing on everything from parks to schools and hospitals.

Races at Happy Valley begin after 7pm, with **entrance gates** (HK$10 for public area and upwards of HK$20 for the stands) down along the west side of the stadium, opposite the cemeteries on Wong Nai Chung Road. The atmosphere inside is animated, with high stands facing huge trackside TV screens so that you can follow the distant action. In the **public enclosure** you can mix with a beery expat crowd, watch the horses being paraded before each race and pump the bilingual staff to make sense of the intricate accumulator bets that Hong Kong specializes in. Other options include joining hard-bitten Hong Kong punters up in the **stands**, mostly watching the action on TV (with all the cigarette smoke and Cantonese swearing you can handle), or signing up for the **HKTB's Come Horseracing Tour** (HK$690–1260 depending on the event). This gets you a coach transfer and entry to the **Members' Enclosure** for a buffet meal with unlimited drinks; you need to be over 18 and to have been in Hong Kong for less than three weeks – take your passport to any HKTB office (see p.51) at least a day before the race.

Outside race meetings, the only part of the racecourse which is accessible is the **Hong Kong Racing Museum** (Tues–Sun 10am–5pm; free), at the northwest end of the building below the expressway at the western side of the track. The coverage of Hong Kong's racing history includes photos from the early days and accounts of famous thoroughbreds and the charitable projects funded by the Jockey Club.

The cemeteries

It's tempting to think that the series of **cemeteries** staggered up the valley west of the racecourse is full of failed punters. In fact, they provide a snapshot of the territory's ethnic and religious mix, with the **five separate areas** for Muslim, Catholic, Protestant, Parsee and Jewish remains dating back to the colony's earliest days. The **Protestant cemetery** is probably the most interesting, a bit wild and overgrown near the edges and full of ponderous granite monuments and sombre headstones haphazardly arranged in clusters around a small chapel. Many predate the twentieth century, with separate areas for the military and Chinese Christians. One striking thing is how almost everyone prior to the 1950s seems to have died from illness or disaster, starting with 103 members of the 95th regiment who were caught by an epidemic between June 1 and September 30, 1848.

You'll get a glimpse of the cemeteries in passing from various buses (such as the #15 to The Peak, or the #6 to Stanley), but for a closer look, head to the **entrances** off Wong Nai Chung Road, west of the racetrack. They all have separate **opening hours** but you should be able to get in daily 8.30am to 5pm.

Tin Hau to Chai Wan

East of Victoria Park, the north shore continues for another 5km between **Tin Hau** and **Chai Wan**, a string of residential districts full of towering estate blocks but nowhere near as built up as the Sheung Wan–Causeway Bay stretch. Attractions here are minor and spread out – though there are also a few hotels – with the pick being the **Museum of Coastal Defence** at Shau Kei Wan. If you're here during the Mid-Autumn Festival, don't miss the spectacular festivities at Tai Hang.

The main route through all this leaves Causeway Bay as **Causeway Road**, then becomes **King's Road** as far as Shau Kei Wan, after which it transforms into **Chai Wan Road**.

Both **MTR Island Line** and **tram** continue out this way, the tram terminating at Shau Kei Wan and the MTR winding up at Chai Wan, with stops close to all points of interest. **Bus #2** is useful as well, running from Causeway Road through the heart of the district to end up on the waterfront at Shau Kei Wan. Out along the shoreline – actually built out over the water in places – the **Eastern Island Corridor** expressway is a quick way to bypass the whole area and get directly to Chai Wan aboard **bus #8** from outside the Wan Chai Ferry Pier.

Tin Hau and Tai Hang

Just a stone's throw from Victoria Park, **TIN HAU** is named after its **Tin Hau Temple** (daily 8am–5pm), which sits at the bottom of a well of high-rises across from Tin Hau MTR station. Patron deity of sailors, **Tin Hau** is widely worshipped in Hong Kong and Macau (where she's known as A-Ma) as she has a reputation of appearing at sea during storms and leading mariners to safety. There are temples to her everywhere and while this one is nothing exceptional – the usual smoky, granite and brick halls hung with red drapes, with a pair of dragons facing off across the roof – it's worth a look if your itinerary doesn't include any larger affairs (such as Jordan's, see p.111). Tin Hau temples are traditionally sited on the sea though nowadays – as here – they're often marooned far inshore by land reclamation.

From the temple, walk back towards the MTR station and then turn south down **Tung Lo Wan Road**, and you'll soon see signs pointing you to the unusual **Lin Fa Kung Temple** (daily 7am–5pm). The front breaks with Southern Chinese design by bowing out in a huge curve, designed to accommodate a boulder in the main hall dedicated to **Kwun Yam**, the Boddhisatva of Mercy, who women pray to for children and an easy childbirth. The temple's beautiful decorations are worth a look, from the oddly Taoist cranes and peaches on the outside (both symbols of longevity), to the many **lotus flower** designs inside – "Lin Fa Kung" means "Lotus Flower Palace".

Continue south down Tung Lo Wan Road and you're immediately in **TAI HANG**, an ordinary grid of apartment blocks famous for its annual **Fire Dragon Dance**, held over three nights during the Mid-Autumn Festival (usually in Sept; see p.35). In 1880, this Hakka community was struck by plague following the killing of a large python, so locals organized a dragon dance to placate the snake's vengeful spirit. The narrow streets pack to capacity from 7.30pm onwards, as the dancers assemble with the 67-metre-long "dragon" made out of a thick rope of tightly bound rushes. It all looks unimpressive until the dragon's body is bulked out with thousands of burning **incense sticks**, hauled up by the dancers and run, glowing red, through the streets amidst shouting, drums and clouds of pungent smoke. The only drawback are the endless speeches by local dignataries before everything gets going – come early and grab something to eat while you wait for the action to start.

North Point

NORTH POINT, a couple of stations past Tin Hau on the MTR, is of most interest for the **Sun Kwong Theatre** (423 King's Rd, diagonally across from MTR exit B2), one of the few regular venues for **Cantonese Opera** in Hong

Kong – check with the HKTB for performance schedules before coming out here. Two streets back towards the water, opposite MTR exit A1, **Java Road Market** has an excellent and cheap cooked food court upstairs, with even a menu or two in English. Near the market, **ferries** (daily 7.23am–7.23pm; HK$4.50) cross north over the harbour to Hung Hom in East Kowloon, from where you can catch bus #2E to Jordan Road in Tsim Sha Tsui (see p.109). North Point's MTR is also an interchange station for the **Tseung Kwan O Line** across the harbour to Lam Tin, within striking distance of Lei Yue Mun (p.119).

Shau Kei Wan

SHAU KEI WAN is a tight grouping of narrow old streets overshadowed by the elevated Eastern Corridor expressway. If you're on the **#2 bus**, get out at **Shau Kei Wan MTR station**, from where you can follow signposts via a network of underpasses to reach the sights; from the **tram terminus**, head north up Shau Kei Wan Main Street. Either way, you'll soon arrive under the expressway near waterfront **Tam Kung temple**, a rather splendid hall to Tam Kung, yet another benevolent maritime deity. The temple is decked in bright gold and red trim, with especially complex interlocking roof brackets, quite a setting for Tam Kung's **birthday celebrations** on the eighth day of the fourth lunar month, which feature a Drunken Dragon parade similar to the one in Macau (see p.272). Next door, the little **A Kung Ngam Shipyards** are finding it hard to make ends meet nowadays by boatbuilding, and supplement their incomes by fixing cars and trucks.

Another 250m up the road and you're at the **Museum of Coastal Defence** (Mon–Wed & Fri–Sun 10am–5pm; HK$10, free on Wed; ⓦ www.lcsd.gov .hk/ce/museum/coastal). The museum, under its distinctive tent-like roof, fills the subterranean brick chambers of **Lei Yue Mun Fort**, constructed by the British in 1887 to defend the eastern approach to Victoria Harbour. The extensive exhibition covers Hong Kong's maritime history from the fourteenth century to the present, with excellent use of maps, models, dioramas and period weapons, but is so comprehensive that it challenges all but the most enthusiastic attention span. If so, just exploring the fort's tunnels is interesting enough, and there are fantastic views from outside over the narrow channel to Lei Yue Mun in Kowloon (p.119) – look for the settlement's untidy tin shacks and tiny Tin Hau temple.

Incidentally, note that **bus #9 to Shek O** on the Island's South Coast departs from outside Shau Kei Wan's MTR station – see p.95 for more.

Chai Wan and Law Uk Folk Museum

Right at the eastern end of MTR Island Line, **CHAI WAN** is a purely residential area whose **Law Uk Folk Museum** (Mon–Wed and Fri–Sat 10am–6pm, Sun 1–6pm; free) is only worth a special visit if you can't get out to see more extensive examples of **Hakka dwellings** in the New Territories. To reach the museum, take exit B from Chai Wan MTR and follow the signs for 150m.

The area was settled by Hakka migrants from southern China in the eighteenth century, and they built a small village of compact, whitewashed **brick houses** with tiled roofs, laid out so that the side wings enclose an atrium just inside the front door. The museum occupies the last surviving house, filled with rustic wooden furniture as it might have been when the place was finally vacated during the 1960s. What makes Law Uk extraordinary is its location: it is completely surrounded by modern, towering apartment blocks, where the villagers' descendants live today.

The South Coast

A short bus ride from the North Shore, Hong Kong Island's **South Coast** forms a long, fragmented coastline punctured by bays and inlets. The handful of settlements here are small and distinct from each other, and the emphasis is definitely towards relaxation rather than work. If you have children in tow, then **Ocean Park** – Hong Kong's original adventure park – is a great outing, as are the numerous sandy **beaches** and **Stanley Market**, a top place to pick up a tourist souvenir. The South Coast's main town, **Aberdeen**, offers Hong Kong's famous floating restaurants and tours around its harbour, while there's also a good hike to be made over to beautiful **Big Wave Bay** and **Shek O** at the island's southeastern corner.

There's **no MTR** to the South Coast yet – though a line is planned for the near future – but **buses** are plentiful and run until after dark, with direct services from the North Shore and Kowloon to Aberdeen, Stanley and Shek O. Note that, as with all recreational areas in Hong Kong, things can get **very busy** here at the weekends and on public holidays.

Aberdeen

ABERDEEN – or *Heung Gong Tsai*, "Little Hong Kong" in Cantonese – is the largest separate town on Hong Kong Island, with a population of over sixty thousand living in tower blocks around the sheltered **harbour**. Originally, many of them lived in the harbour on their fishing boats, and Aberdeen is still an important **fishing port**, its fleet of trawlers providing around a third of Hong Kong's fish and prawn catch. You can appreciate the fleet's size during the fishing **moratorium** (June–July), when the harbour is packed to capacity with freshly cleaned vessels. The harbour is also the venue for the annual **Dragon Boat Festival** held on the fifth day of the fifth lunar month (usually in June), one of the biggest in Hong Kong.

Aberdeen is a small grid of a place, only 500m across, facing the harbour to the south over busy **Aberdeen Praya Road**. On **arrival**, bus #70 and #75 from Central Bus Station, and the #973 from Kowloon, set down on Aberdeen Praya Road, while bus #7 from outside Central's Star Ferry Pier and #76 from behind the Central Library in Causeway Bay end up at the small backstreet **bus station** on the east side of town.

Moving on, buses #73 and #973 from Aberdeen Praya Road, and green minibus #52 from the bus station, link Aberdeen to Repulse Bay, Deep Water Bay

---

South Coast buses

Aside from others mentioned in the text, the following bus routes are useful for reaching and touring Hong Kong Island's South Coast:

#6 – runs daily 6am to 1am from Central Bus Station (Exchange Square), via Queen's Road East in Wan Chai, to Repulse Bay and Stanley.

#73 – runs from the Cyberport on Hong Kong Island's west coast, out along the south coast daily 6am to 11pm, passing Aberdeen, Deep Water Bay and Repulse Bay, terminating in Stanley.

#973 – runs daily 8.30am to 10.05pm from Concordia Plaza, behind the Science Museum in Kowloon, to Aberdeen, Deep Water Bay and Repulse Bay, terminating at Stanley.

Green minibus #52 also runs along the south coast from Aberdeen's back-street bus station, passing Deep Water Bay and Repulse Bay and terminating in Stanley.

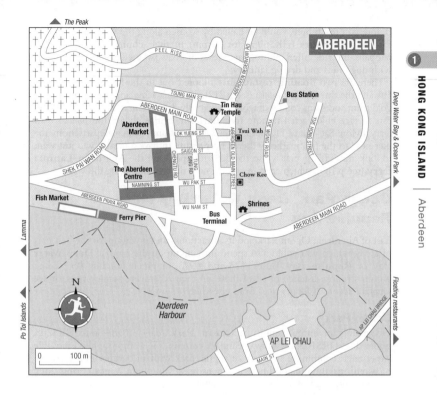

Map labels: The Peak; ABERDEEN; PEEL RISE; ABERDEEN RESERVOIR RD; Bus Station; TSUNG MAN ST; ABERDEEN MAIN ROAD; Tin Hau Temple; Aberdeen Market; LOK YUENG ST; Tsui Wah; YUE WONG ROAD; YUE HONG STREET; SAIGON ST; CHENGTU RD; TUNG SING RD; ABERDEEN OLD MAIN STREET; The Aberdeen Centre; SHEK PAI WAN ROAD; NAMNING ST; WU PAK ST; Chow Kee; Fish Market; ABERDEEN PRAYA ROAD; WU NAM ST; Shrines; Ferry Pier; Bus Terminal; ABERDEEN MAIN ROAD; Lamma; Po Toi Islands; N; Aberdeen Harbour; 0 100 m; AP LEI CHAU; MAIN ST; AP LEI CHAU BRIDGE; Deep Water Bay & Ocean Park; Floating restaurants

and Stanley, and stop near Ocean Park. There are also **ferries** from beside Aberdeen's fish market to Lamma Island (see p.162) and Po Toi island (see p.94).

The town and harbour

Aberdeen is a good place to wander for half an hour and simply take in street activity, but sooner or later you'll stumble across its two old corners. On the slope above the junction of Aberdeen Praya Road and the Old Main Street is a jumble of lean-to **shrines**, one of which is actually built into the branches of a **fig tree** like a tree house. The complete impartiality with which Buddhist, Taoist and folk deities are crowded together here nicely illustrates how the Chinese like to hedge their bets with religion. It's as if the area itself is holy – who exactly you pray to doesn't matter.

There's more of this at the town's strikingly clean **Tin Hau temple** (daily 8am– 5pm) back on the corner of the main street and **Aberdeen Reservoir Road**, with memorials to Tin Hau, Wong Tai Sin, Kwun Yam, Kuan Ti and the earth god inside. From the temple, it's a steep walk up Aberdeen Reservoir Road and then left along **Peel Rise**, which climbs up over the town to the terraces of an immense **cemetery**, offering fine views back over the harbour – the **trail to The Peak** carries on from here (p.75). Back in town, grab a light meal at the local branch of *Tsui Wah* or some *yum cha* at the scruffy, cheerful *Chow Kee* nearby (see map).

Over Aberdeen Praya Road, the harbour's huge **fish market** is chaos when morning catches are being loaded into lorries and the place is knee-deep in water and every kind of live seafood thrashing or scuttling about in plastic tubs.

Before you reach here, you'll be hailed by women along the waterfront touting for **harbour tours** (HK$60pp for 30min) in their chunky, wooden-hulled sampans; the ride offers photogenic views of boats jammed together, complete with dogs, nets and drying laundry.

There are two **floating restaurants** moored out in the harbour too, the *Tai Pak* and the three-storey *Jumbo* (see p.212), the latter being an ostentatious riot of gold paint and giant coiling dragons, ludicrously flamboyant at night. Cheapskates can, in fact, enjoy a ten-minute **free harbour cruise** aboard the *Jumbo's* own ferry (Mon–Sat 11am–11.30pm, Sun 7am–11.30pm), which departs from the pier next to the fish market – there's no pressure to have a meal if you just want to look around. The pier is also the departure point for the **Aberdeen–Lamma ferry** (see p.165), which again passes through the harbour along the way.

Ocean Park, Deep Water Bay and Repulse Bay

East of Aberdeen, Ocean Park and its attractions can tie you up for the best part of a day, which you could also spend unwinding on the sand at **Deep Water Bay** or **Repulse Bay**. Buses #73 and #973, or green minibus #52, come within striking distance of all of these on their Aberdeen–Stanley runs, or see separate accounts for services from elsewhere.

Ocean Park

Occupying an entire peninsula, **Ocean Park** (daily 10am–6pm; HK$208, under-11s HK$103; @www.oceanpark.com.hk) is a thoroughly enjoyable experience, combining an open-air theme park with an oceanarium. A couple of **warnings**, though: food here is expensive, so you might want to bring along a picnic (although officially you're not allowed to); and – what with the crowds and amount on offer – you'll need to go early to get your money's worth. If you can, avoid going on Sundays and public holidays, when the place is heaving.

The park's main focus is on wildlife and the natural world, and the first section, the **Lowland** area, is landscaped with gardens and greenhouses, a butterfly house, kiddies' adventure playground and a dinosaur discovery trail with full-size moving models (there's also a 3D film simulator for rainy days). The star attraction here, however, are four **giant pandas**, two of them recent presents from the Mainland to celebrate the tenth anniversary of Hong Kong's handover. Their two-thousand-square-metre complex includes misting machines, mountain slopes and all the bamboo they can eat; there's also a special clinic and kitchen at their disposal.

After this, catch the **cable car** 1.5km along the peninsula – with views over Deep Water Bay – to the **Headland** section. Here, you'll find a mix of

---

Bus routes to Ocean Park

The only direct daily services to Ocean Park are bus #629 (9am–4pm; HK$10.60, or all-inclusive bus and entry) from Drake Street behind Admiralty MTR station (exit B); and green minibus #6 (8am–6.40pm; HK$10.50) from the Central Star Ferry Pier.

The following daily services also stop nearby on Wong Chuk Hang Road: the #73 and #973 between Aberdeen and Stanley; and the #6x and #260 from Central Bus Station under Exchange Square.

At weekends and public holidays many more buses stop off at Ocean Park – check the Ocean Park website for details.

rides including the self-explanatory Abyss Turbo Drop; a walk-through aquarium, where you can view sharks nose-to-nose through glass; the **Ocean Theatre**, where trained dolphins and sea lions perform; plus the Atoll Reef, a coral-reef aquarium that contains more than five thousand fish. Lengthy **outdoor escalators** take you from here back to ground level at the western **Tai Shue Wan** area, where the Raging River ride is somewhere to enjoy a final soaking.

Deep Water Bay and Repulse Bay

The next stop along, **Deep Water Bay**, is a beautiful stretch of sand right by the roadside, where you can lounge under a fringe of trees and watch yachts, cruisers and gin palaces floating in the bay. During the week the bay's main customers are taxi drivers, who pull up to wash their cars and have a nap on the sand. Facilities include changing rooms, barbecue pits and the *Coco Thai Restaurant* (p.222), a great venue for an evening meal.

Over the adjacent headland, **REPULSE BAY** is a far larger place, a ribbon of modern high-rises spreading for a kilometre along a steep headland. Once known for its pirates, the coast became a popular resort in the 1920s, when the grand *Repulse Bay Hotel* was built, a celebrity hangout until being turned into a shopping mall in 1982. The most notable building here today is **The Repulse Bay**, a curvy, baby-blue residential block with a square, *feng shui*-inspired hole right through the middle. The broad **beach** below is always busy – the weekend record is seventy thousand people – with changing rooms, life-guards, a shopping complex and a barbecue area, though the water quality isn't great.

Connoisseurs of kitsch may want to amble down to the beach's western end, where a fifteen-metre-high **Kwun Yan statue** is just one of a multitude of brightly coloured, concrete-and-tile figures arranged along the seafront. They're all to do with snaring good fortune, including two fifteenth-century stone horses (inscribed with characters implying "As long-living as heaven, as prosperous as the sea"), and a statue of the god of matrimony, all decked in red ribbons.

Buses serving both Deep Water Bay and Repulse Bay include the #6X and #260 (from Central Bus Station under Exchange Square), and the #973, #73 and green minibus #52. Bus #6 from Central Bus Station and #63 from behind North Point MTR station also run over the island to Repulse Bay, then carry on to Stanley.

Stanley

Not far beyond Repulse Bay, the small beachfront town of **STANLEY** is a favourite with expats and tourists, who throng the waterfront **restaurants** and **tourist market** before heading for the local beaches or Po Toi island. There are also a few relics of the pre-colonial days when Stanley was a fishing village called *Chek Chue* (literally "Red Pillar"), either a reference to the red-flowering kapok trees growing along the coast or a euphemism for "robber's lair", after the pirates who once used the village as a base. The town also sits at one end of the **Wilson Trail**, which runs all the way north to the New Territories (see box, p.92).

The town is focused around the neck of a peninsula on **Stanley Village Road**, which forks south to become **Wong Ma Kok Road** and **Tung Tau Wan Road** (which runs 1km south to the prison on the peninsula's southern end). **Buses** stop at the town or 500m south on Tung Tau Wan Road; Stanley

The Wilson Trail

The 78-kilometre-long **Wilson Trail** starts just north of Stanley on steep Stanley Gap Road – bus #6, #73 or #260 pass the **sign**. The trail winds north over Hong Kong Island to Quarry Bay MTR station, where you catch the train across the harbour and resume the hike at **Yau Tong** (p.120), heading up past Lei Yue Mun village to **Amah Rock** (p.137) and over **Smugglers Ridge** to **Shing Mun Reservoir** (p.129). From here, the trail continues north via Tai Po Market to **Pat Sin Leng** (p.147), before winding down to where coastal **Luk Keng** (p.148) overlooks China.

Each of the trail's **ten sections** can be covered individually in less than a day, ranging from easy family walks (such as around wooded Shing Mun Reservoir) to fairly tough hikes along steep, exposed ridges (Pat Sin Leng). There are also several **campsites** along the way; for more about **maps and hiking information**, see p.252.

is the **terminus** for routes #6, #6X and #260 from Central Bus Station; the #63 from North Point MTR; bus #73 and green minibus #52 from Aberdeen; and bus #973 from Kowloon.

Around the town

Stanley is set on a tiny bay, with the peninsula stretching away to the south. Between the road and waterfront, **Stanley Market** (daily 10.30am–6.30pm) fills a small maze of back lanes with a shamelessly touristy selection of clothing, paintings and souvenirs; nothing is especially cheap, but it's a fun place to browse for a while. Emerging onto the seafront, there's a string of good **restaurants** and **pubs** (see pp.216–228) targeting *gweilo* wallets – and a couple of basic noodle joints – beyond which you'll see the Victorian-style ironwork of **Blake Pier**, departure point for Po Toi Island. The pier springs off a terrace in front of **Murray House**, a grand colonial edifice built in 1843 for the British Army and moved stone by stone in 1982 from its previous site in Central, where the Bank of China now stands. The ground floor is taken up with the **Maritime Museum** (Tues–Fri & Sun 10am–6pm, Sat 10am–7pm; HK$20), full of models, mementoes and maps; balcony restaurants upstairs are good for taking in sea views over a drink. Outside, the twelve stone columns marked with Chinese calligraphy were dug up from Shanghai Street in Yau Ma Tei.

Behind Murray House, walk past **Stanley Plaza** (with a supermarket, ATMs and a post office) and you'll find a cheery **Tin Hau Temple**, built in 1767 and of interest for the darkened pelt of a large tiger bagged nearby in 1942 – the last ever shot in Hong Kong. The temple itself is bright and airy and, as elsewhere, Tin Hau generously shares her space with many other deities including the Safe Wind Spirit (represented by a large model junk).

To St Stephen's Beach and Stanley Prison

From the town, follow Stanley Village Road south into Wong Ma Kok Road, and after about fifteen minutes you'll see signposted steps leading down to **St Stephen's Beach**, a nice stretch of clean sand with a short pier, a water-sports centre, barbecue pits, showers and decent swimming. Continue on past the beach, and the road terminates at a fenced-off headland containing **Stanley Fort**, a formerly British military base. The area is closed to the public; signs here say "Caution – Troops Marching".

Alternatively, bear left from Stanley Village Road down Tung Tau Wan Road and it's just a short walk to the gates of **Stanley Prison**, where

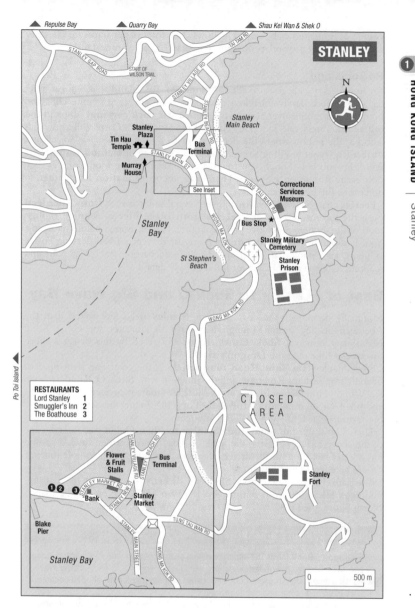

▲ Repulse Bay   ▲ Quarry Bay   ▲ Shau Kei Wan & Shek O

STANLEY

Stanley Village Rd
Tai Tam Rd
Stanley Gap Road
START OF WILSON TRAIL
Stanley Beach Rd

Stanley Main Beach

Stanley Plaza
Tin Hau Temple
Murray House
STANLEY MAIN ST
Bus Terminal
See Inset

Tung Tau Wan Rd
Correctional Services Museum

Stanley Bay

Bus Stop ★
Stanley Military Cemetery

St Stephen's Beach
Stanley Prison

Wong Ma Kok Rd

Po Toi Island

CLOSED AREA

RESTAURANTS
Lord Stanley   1
Smuggler's Inn   2
The Boathouse   3

Flower & Fruit Stalls
Stanley Village Rd
Stanley Beach Rd
Bus Terminal
❶❷ ❸ Stanley Market Rd
Bank
Stanley Market
Stanley Main Street
Tung Tau Wan Rd
Wong Ma Kok Rd
Blake Pier
Stanley Bay

Stanley Fort

0   500 m

hundreds of civilians were interned in dire conditions by the Japanese during World War II. Nowadays it's a maximum-security prison, housing (among others) convicted murderers who were on Hong Kong's death row until 1993, when capital punishment was abolished. Nobody had in fact been executed since 1966, but the fear was that China would have carried out the penalty after 1997 if it had remained in law. Before you reach the prison, the small **Correctional Services Museum** (Tues–Sun 10am–5pm; free) has a couple of simulated cells, a mock gallows and scores of apparatus for chastisement (including a wooden flogging frame and a cat-o'-nine-tails).

Po Toi island

An hour's ferry-ride south of Stanley, little **Po Toi island** makes for a quiet day's excursion. Barely inhabited nowadays, there are steep granite cliffs and boulders to scramble over, along with **prehistoric rock carvings** of spirals and fish and the inevitable Tin Hau temple. Fans of John Le Carré will know this island as the setting where the denouement to his *The Honourable Schoolboy*, a thriller largely set in Hong Kong, takes place. A spread of **seafood restaurants** will keep you fed, though you might want to bring some food along as they only really fire up on a Sunday. There's **no accommodation** here, either, so don't miss the boat back.

Ferries charge HK$40 return and run several times a week **from Aberdeen** (near the fish market) and at weekends **from Blake Pier in Stanley**, though most of the services don't give you much time to look around before returning. Your best bets are Sunday departures from Aberdeen at 8.15am (leaving Po Toi at 6pm), and Stanley at 10am and 11.30am (departing Po Toi at 3pm and 4.30pm). Contact the HKTB for full timetable details.

East of Stanley to Shek O and Big Wave Bay

Minimally developed, the coast **east of Stanley** is far less visited than the Aberdeen–Stanley stretch, though it's worth the journey for Hong Kong Island's top beach at **Shek O**, which you can reach by bus or on a short, spectacular hike over the **Dragon's Back**.

From Stanley, **Tai Tam Road** runs east along the coast and then up, past Turtle Cove, Tai Tam Reservoir and the junction with **Shek O Road**, to Shau Kei Wan on Hong Kong Island's north shore; this route is covered by **buses** #14 and #314. Green minibuses #16A, #16M or #16X follow much the same route but terminate at Chai Wan's MTR station.

There's no single bus route **from Stanley to Shek O,** but you can take any of the above services as far as the Shek O Road junction, then catch a passing bus #9 to Shek O – ask the driver where to change buses. The whole journey should take less than 30 minutes.

Alternatively, you can **reach Shek O directly** on bus #9 (daily 6am–midnight; HK$6.50) from outside Sha Kei Wan MTR station on the island's North Shore – see p.87.

see p.87

Hiking the Dragon's Back

The **Dragon's Back** forms the eighth and final section of the Hong Kong Island Trail, a two-hour walk with wonderful scenery which ends north of Shek O at Big Wave Bay. It's a little rough in places but signposted and easy to follow; shade is scarce, however, so take a hat and plenty of water.

Start by catching bus #9 towards Shek O, and ask the driver to set you down on Shek O Road at **To Tei Wan Tsuen**, where there's small parking bay with toilets and an information board showing the route. From here you climb out of the protective woodland and up onto undulating **Lung Chek** (Dragon's Back). This runs north, through open scrub and around granite boulders, to vistas taking in tropically green hills, Stanley, Tai Tam Reservoir and Shek O's headlands. Skirting around the back of **Mount Collison**, you enter a narrow pass and descend through woodland down to **Big Wave Bay's** beach and jumble of buildings, where it's time to have a picnic or carry on to Shek O.

Turtle Cove and Tai Tam Reservoir

All buses heading east from Stanley pass **Turtle Cove**, a small horseshoe of a beach with all the usual facilities. It's very quiet during the week, when you could well have the place to yourself.

Just north of here, the road passes alongside the lower overflow of **Tai Tam Reservoir**, the first in Hong Kong and starting point for several excellent **hill walks**. Get out straight after the reservoir and you can pick up the signposted Hong Kong Trail sections 6 and 5, which you then abandon for the Tai Tam Country Trail to **Wong Nai Chung Gap**, above Happy Valley – around two hours in all (walk on to Stubbs Road from here to pick up bus #15 into Central). A longer walk (4hr) leaves section 5 of the Hong Kong Island Trail for the Wilson Trail, which you can follow up to Quarry Bay for the MTR or trams along the North Shore.

Shek O

The isolated seafront village of **SHEK O**, right down at Hong Kong Island's southeastern edge, has an almost Mediterranean flavour in its narrow lanes and flat-roofed houses. A strong surf beats on the wide **beach** – one of the best in all Hong Kong – which is more or less deserted during the week but always busy at weekends. There are shade trees, changing rooms and a shark net; nearby **shops** such as the Tung Lok Beachside Store sell beachwear, inflatable floats, plastic buckets and so on, and have storage lockers for valuables. Come for sunbathing and a barbecue, or lunch at one of the local **restaurants**, which serve good-value Vietnamese–Thai fare.

The bucket-and-spade shops don't give the game away, but Shek O is actually one of the swankiest addresses in Hong Kong, with some opulent houses in the area. You can get a flavour of things by walking through the village and following the path up to **Shek O Headland**, where you'll be faced with yet more sweeping panoramas. To the right is **Cape D'Aguilar**; to the left, **Rocky Bay**, a nice beach, though with heavily polluted water – which means the sand is generally empty.

Bus #9 from Shau Kei Wan MTR station sets down at the edge of Shek O village, just 50m from the beach. On Sunday afternoons only, you can also get here direct from Central Bus Station on bus #309, which runs hourly 2.10 to 6.10pm (returning from Shek O hourly 3–7pm). Heading back to Shau Kei Wan from Shek O, you could also take a **red minibus** from the beachside car park: they're more frequent and a little quicker.

Big Wave Bay

For more space and fewer people, head 2km north of Shek O to **Big Wave Bay**, terminus of the Dragon's Back and Hong Kong Island Trail (see p.81). The bay's Cantonese name, **Tai Long Wan**, is a common one in Hong Kong for any bit of coast that catches some **surf**, though the waves here are usually only big enough for boogie boards. The beach is good, with changing rooms, toilets, a fringe of shady cotton trees and a couple of restaurants dishing out cold beers and steak sandwiches. You can also **rent surf gear** from the Tong Kee Store. To get here from Shek O, walk back past the bus stop and out of town, then turn right and follow this road alongside the **golf course** for twenty minutes.

Places

Aberdeen	香港仔
Admiralty	金鐘
Big Wave Bay	大浪灣
Causeway Bay	銅鑼灣
Central	中環
Chai Wan	柴灣
Deep Water Bay	深水灣
Happy Valley	跑馬地
Hong Kong	香港
Hong Kong Island	香港島
Kennedy Town	堅尼地城
Mid-Levels	半山區
Mount Davis	摩星嶺
North Point	北角
Repulse Bay	淺水灣
Shau Kei Wan	筲箕灣
Shek O	石澳
Sheung Wan	上環
Stanley	赤柱
Tai Hang	大坑
Tai Ping Shan	太平山
Tin Hau	天后
Wan Chai	灣仔

Sights

Bank of China tower	中國銀行大廈
Central Library	中央圖書館
Central Plaza	中環廣場
Central Police Station	前中環警署
Convention and Exhibition Centre	香港會議展覽中心
Correctional Services Museum	懲教博物館
Exchange Square	交易廣場
Government House	香港禮賓府
Happy Valley Racecourse	跑馬地馬場
Hong Kong Park	香港公園
HSBC	香港上海總豐銀行大廈
Hung Shing Temple	洪聖廟
IFC2	國際金融中心二期
International Finance Centre	國際金融中心
Java Road Market	渣華道市大廈
Kwung Fuk Ancestral Hall	廣福義祠
Law Uk Folk Museum	羅屋民俗館
LEGCO building	立法會大樓
Lin Fa Temple	連花廟
Lo Ban Temple	魯班廟
Lover's Rock	姻緣石
Man Mo Temple	文武廟
Medical Sciences Museum	香港醫學博物館
Museum of Coastal Defence	香港海防博物館
Nam Koo Terrace	南固台
Noon Day Gun	午炮
Ocean Park	香港海洋公園
Pak Tai Temple	北帝廟
The Peak	山頂

Pinewood Battery	廢堡
Police Museum	警隊博物館
Po Toi Island	蒲台島
Sheung Wan Market	上環市大廈
Shui Yuat Temple	水月宮
Shun Tak Centre	信德中心
Statue Square	皇后像廣場
Tai Tam Reservoir	大潭水塘
Tam Kung Temple	譚公廟
Times Square	時代廣場
Tin Hau Temple	天后宮
Turtle Cove	龜背灣
University of Hong Kong (Museum)	香港大學
Victoria Park	維多利亞公園
Western Market	西港城
Zoological Gardens	香港動植博公園

Transport

Bus stop	巴士站
Central Star Ferry Pier	天星碼頭
Ferry Pier	碼頭
Lower Peak Tram Terminal	纜車總站
Macau Ferry Terminal	香澳碼頭
Mid-Levels Escalator	半山行人電勤樓梯
MTR station	地下鐵車站
Outlying Islands Ferry Piers	香外線碼頭

Kowloon

The broad, five-kilometre-long peninsula jutting south into the harbour opposite Hong Kong Island is called **Kowloon**, an English transliteration of the Cantonese *gau lung*, "nine dragons". One explanation of the name is that the last boy-emperor of the Song Dynasty, fleeing the thirteenth-century Mongol invasion, counted eight hills here, purported to hide eight dragons – a figure that was rounded up to nine by sycophantic servants who pointed out that an emperor is himself a dragon.

At the turn of the nineteenth century, Kowloon was a farming district whose main settlement was a walled garrison town. Then in 1860, the tip of the peninsula as far as modern **Boundary Street** was ceded to Britain in perpetuity to add to their island over the harbour, and so was developed with gusto and confidence. Today, it forms an unmitigatedly built-up, intensely crowded commercial district whose main appeal is in the sheer density of **shopping** opportunities – from high-end jewellery to cutting-edge electronic goods and outright tourist tack – especially in the waterfront area of **Tsim Sha Tsui**. To the north, **Yau Ma Tei**, **Jordan** and **Mong Kok** are less obviously touristy – though no less populated – districts of tenement blocks and local markets, some of which sell modern daily necessities, others with a distinctly Chinese twist. Many visitors end up staying in the area between Tsim Sha Tsui and Mong Kok, as it's here you'll find many of Hong Kong's best hotels – and almost all of its **budget accommodation**.

After the New Territories were added to the colony in 1898, Kowloon's border was extended north from Boundary Street up to where the **Kowloon Hills** – the steep ridges which cut east–west right across the peninsula – form a very physical barrier between here and the New Territories on the far side. The emphasis is in towering **residential estates**, each clustered around shopping plazas, parks and other amenities, but visitors ride up this way for some bargain-basement shopping, historical relics and a few unusual temples – plus an extraordinarily beautiful Tang-style garden at **Diamond Hill**.

The two main ways to reach Kowloon are on the **Star Ferry** (see p.59), or along various **MTR** lines. Almost everything of interest south of Boundary Street lies on or within spitting distance of **Nathan Road**, Kowloon's monster north–south artery, with stations on the red **Tsuen Wan MTR Line** from Central dotted at regular intervals along its length. Beyond Boundary Street, you'll also find yourself using the green **Kwun Tong MTR Line** and buses to reach sights.

Tsim Sha Tsui

TSIM SHA TSUI revolves around its reputation as the best place in all Hong Kong for tourists to spend their money: in the kilometre or so from the waterfront to the boundary with Jordan along Austin Road, a devoted **shopper** could find every bauble, gadget and designer label known to man – either genuine or pirated by the locals for good measure. And if you can't make up your own mind about what to buy, there's no lack of hustlers to offer suggestions, hissing out "copy watch?", "a nice suit sir?" or "handbag for the lady?" as you try to push past them through the crowds. It's all gruesomely commercial and overwhelming but, for a while at least, a lot of fun too, and it's backed up by an equally lively choice of **restaurants** and **bars**.

As it was once in the flight path of Hong Kong's old airport at Kai Tak, Tsim Sha Tsui lacks Central's outrageous skyline, though there are dazzling views of the Island's North Shore from harbourside, particularly at night. A handful of good **museums** and the ornamental **Kowloon Park** also offer an escape from all the brash commercial activity elsewhere.

Tsim Sha Tsui's prime **arrival points** are the **Star Ferry Pier**, right on the southwestern tip of the peninsula, and **Tsim Sha Tsui MTR station**, located in the vicinity of Nathan Road. Coming in from the Airport or Lantau Island, you might wind up west at the **Kowloon Station** on the Tung Chung MTR/Airport Express lines (from where you can take a free hotel shuttle; see p.23); arriving from the New Territories on the East Rail Line will land you at **East Tsim Sha Tsui station**, down near the waterfront.

North from the Star Ferry

Star Ferries from Wan Chai and Central dock at Tsim Sha Tsui's **Star Ferry Pier**, where you'll find a branch of the **Hong Kong Tourist Board** (daily 8am–8pm) and, out front, a major bus terminal and taxi rank. You can walk east along Salisbury Road and the waterfront from here (see p.102), or head north, across a small square and up the escalators, into a kilometre-long complex of gleaming, air-conditioned **malls**, full of marble, swish shops and bright lights. The first section, **Ocean Terminal**, which juts out into the water, is where cruise liners dock; this merges with the adjacent **Ocean Centre**, and, the next block up, **Harbour City** – more shops, a couple of swanky hotels, and shoes the price of a small country's defence budget.

If you want to get back down to street level, signs everywhere will direct you out onto parallel **Canton Road**. East off it, just down Peking Road, **One Peking Road** is one of Tsim Sha Tsui's rare examples of modern boutique architecture, a 160-metre-high, glassy, bow-fronted edifice whose upper floors are mostly restaurants (including the renowned *Aqua*; see p.218), all with excellent harbour views. Back on Canton Road, continue north past Haiphong Road – which cuts east along Kowloon Park's southern edge – and you'll pass the **China Ferry Terminal**, a block of shops and restaurants around the ticket offices and departure lounges for ferry and hydrofoil trips to China and Macau (p.30).

Beyond the ferry terminal, land reclamation is causing Tsim Sha Tsui to gradually expand west, though at present the area is a no-man's-land of expressways and isolated, self-contained blocks. One of these, **Union Square**, houses Kowloon Station and the truly enormous **International Commerce Centre**, which at 484m and 112 storeys will be Hong Kong's tallest building on its completion in 2010. There are also plans to develop the nearby waterfront into

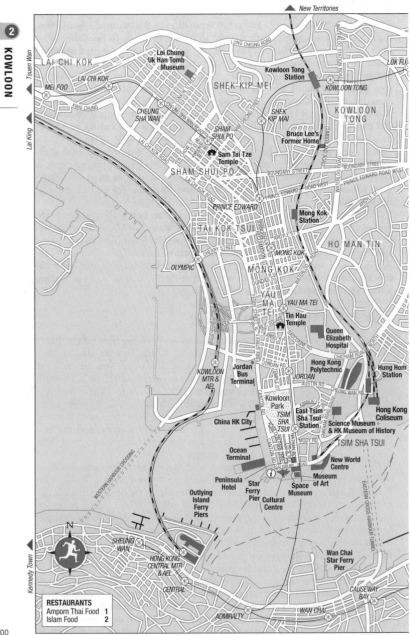

New Territories

LAI CHI KOK

Lei Chung Uk Han Tomb Museum

LAI CHI KOK

MEI FOO

SHEK-KIP MEI

Kowloon Tong Station

KOWLOON TONG

LOK FU

KWAI CHUNG

CHEUNG SHA WAN

SHEK KIP MAI

KOWLOON TONG

SHAM SHUI PO

Bruce Lee's Former Home

Sam Tai Tze Temple

SHAM SHUI PO

BOUNDARY STREET

PRINCE EDWARD

Mong Kok Station

TAI KOK TSUI

HO MAN TIN

CHERRY STREET

MONG KOK

MONG KOK

OLYMPIC

YAU MA TEI

YAU MA TEI

Tin Hau Temple

Queen Elizabeth Hospital

KOWLOON MTR & AEL

Jordan Bus Terminal

Hong Kong Polytechnic

JORDAN

Hung Hom Station

Kowloon Park

TSIM SHA TSUI

East Tsim Sha Tsui Station

Hong Kong Coliseum

China HK City

Science Museum & HK Museum of History

TSIM SHA TSUI

Ocean Terminal

New World Centre

Peninsula Hotel

Star Ferry Pier

Museum of Art

Space Museum

Outlying Island Ferry Piers

Cultural Centre

N

SHEUNG WAN

Wan Chai Star Ferry Pier

HONG KONG CENTRAL MTR & AEL

WESTERN HARBOUR CROSSING

EASTERN CROSS HARBOUR TUNNEL

CENTRAL

CAUSEWAY BAY

WAN CHAI

ADMIRALTY

Tsuen Wan

Lai King

Kennedy Town

RESTAURANTS

| Amporn Thai Food | 1 |
| Islam Food | 2 |

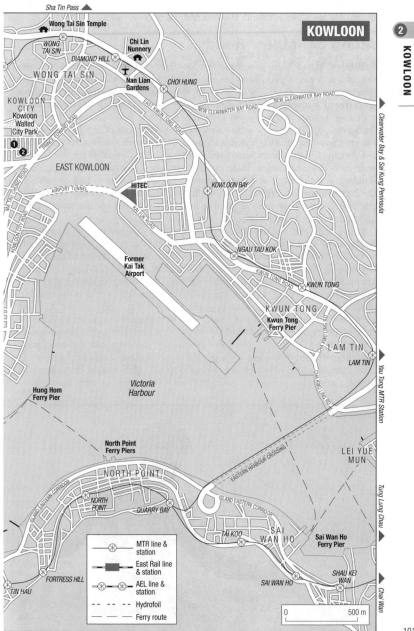

Sha Tin Pass

Wong Tai Sin Temple

Chi Lin Nunnery

WONG TAI SIN

DIAMOND HILL

WONG TAI SIN

Nan Lian Gardens

CHOI HUNG

KOWLOON CITY
Kowloon Walled City Park

EAST KWUN TONG ROAD

NEW CLEARWATER BAY ROAD

NEW CLEARWATER BAY ROAD

PRINCE EDWARD ROAD

❶ ❷

EAST KOWLOON

AIRPORT TUNNEL

HITEC

KOWLOON BAY

KAI FUK ROAD

MA TAU CHUNG ROAD

KOWLOON CITY ROAD

Former
Kai Tak
Airport

NGAU TAU KOK

KWUN TONG ROAD

KWUN TONG

KWUN TONG

Kwun Tong
Ferry Pier

LAM TIN

LAM TIN

CHA KWO LING ROAD

Hung Hom
Ferry Pier

Victoria
Harbour

North Point
Ferry Piers

LEI YUE
MUN

EASTERN HARBOUR CROSSING

NORTH POINT

ISLAND EASTERN CORRIDOR

ISLAND EASTERN CORRIDOR

NORTH
POINT

QUARRY BAY

TAI KOO

SAI
WAN HO

Sai Wan Ho
Ferry Pier

FORTRESS HILL

SHAU KEI
WAN

TIN HAU

SAI WAN HO

	MTR line & station
	East Rail line & station
	AEL line & station
- - -	Hydrofoil
	Ferry route

0   500 m

the **West Kowloon Cultural District**, though exactly what this will entail is the subject of hot debate – either another collection of oversized shopping malls, or a spread of parkland, theatres and galleries.

Along Salisbury Road

Salisbury Road runs east from the Star Ferry Pier along Tsim Sha Tsui's waterfront. A paved plaza between the road and the harbour contains a couple of museums, but it's the views over to Hong Kong Island from the adjacent **waterfront promenade** that dominate everything. During the daytime just watching marine traffic – tiny wooden sampans, ferries, cruise liners and dredgers – fills in time, or come after 7pm, when many of the North Shore's towers fire up in multicoloured splendour: The Centre, which changes colour continually; IFC2's plain white massif; gold panels on Central Plaza; the HSBC's restrained red and white patterns; the rainbow-coloured wall of the AIG building; and the Bank of China's geometric tracery. All these join together in the **Symphony of Lights** (daily 8pm; free; English commentary Mon, Wed and Fri), a supremely tacky, enjoyable half-hour show where the towers pulse and flash to an electronic beat.

As you walk east, the promenade bows out over the water as the **Avenue of Stars**, a spiritless tribute to Hong Kong's film industry (for more on which, see p.232). Brass plaques set in the pavement name local acting and directorial talent such as Raymond Chow, Chow Yun Fat, Andy Lau, Maggie Cheung, Wong Kar Wai and Tsui Hark, some with accompanying signatures and palm prints. The one magnetic draw here is a larger-than-life statue of martial arts star **Bruce Lee**, the man who brought Hong Kong cinema – and Chinese kung fu – to world attention in the 1970s; join the crowds of young Chinese striking poses alongside for photos.

Overlooking the water behind the promenade, the *Intercontinental* hotel has a glass-fronted **lobby lounge** with ground-floor harbour views where you can take afternoon tea, or watch the Symphony of Lights over a drink (though there's a minimum per person charge of HK$200 per person after 8pm).

▲ Bruce Lee statue, Tsim Sha Tsui waterfront

The Clock Tower and Hong Kong Cultural Centre

Some 50m east from the Star Ferry Pier, the slender, 45-metre-high **Clock Tower** dates from 1921 and once adorned the old Kowloon Railway Station, from where you could take a train all the way back to Europe, via Mongolia and Russia. The station was demolished in 1978 to make way for a new waterfront development, whose focal point is the astonishingly drab **Hong Kong Cultural Centre**. Given that it faces one of the greatest harbour views on earth, the most extraordinary thing about the brown-tiled, wedge-shaped design is that it has no windows – which, given the six hundred million Hong Kong dollar price tag, perhaps proves that money doesn't always buy style. Inside, the centre contains three separate venues – a **concert hall**, **grand theatre** and **studio theatre** – and its foyer hosts free exhibitions and events most days (see p.230 for full details).

The Museum of Art

The **Museum of Art** (Mon–Wed & Fri–Sun 10am–6pm; HK$10, Wed free; extra charge for special exhibitions; ☎2721 0116, ⓦhk.art.museum), on the waterfront east of the Cultural Centre, packs an outstanding collection of antique Chinese calligraphy, porcelain, paintings and fine art into four floors. A recorded **audio tour** (HK$10) of Curator's Picks is available, and there are frequent **touring exhibitions**, often featuring masterpieces from collections on the Mainland and Taiwan. A well-stocked **bookshop** sells art tomes and former exhibition catalogues and there is, incidentally, a great view of the harbour from any of the upper floors.

The first-floor **Chinese Antiquities Gallery** has an ever-changing exhibition of gold, jade and bronzes, many dating back to the semi-mythical Shang, Xia and Zhou dynasties, which predated the unification of China under the Qin in 220 BC. The second floor's **Xubaizhai Gallery** concentrates on classical silk scroll painting and calligraphy; the latter is interesting for the way it evolved over the centuries, from characters neatly incised on metal vessels or carved into stone monuments, to the much freer, livelier writing made possible by ink, paper and brush. The adjacent **Contemporary Art Gallery** features post-1950s work by mostly Hong Kong artists, but – as on the Mainland – in so many styles and going in so many directions that it's hard to tell what is important and what is just whimsy.

There's another **Antiquities Gallery** on the third floor, where a staid but informative display describes the evolution of **pottery**: Neolithic clay pots with black patterns; lively Han figurines and tomb models of houses and watch-towers; and the use of glazes that, artistically at least, peaked with the Tang's abstract colours and the Song's nature-inspired patterns. Also on the third floor, the **Historical Pictures Gallery** has a rotating selection of paintings, drawings and prints that trace the eighteenth- and nineteenth-century development of Hong Kong, Macau and Guangzhou as trading centres, as seen by both Western and local artists. The museum ends on the fourth floor with the **Chinese Fine Art Gallery**, which shows exhibits from a collection of three thousand works, including modern Chinese art and animal and bird paintings.

The Space Museum

Under a tiled dome in front of the Museum of Art, the **Space Museum** (Mon & Wed–Fri 1–9pm, Sat & Sun 10am–9pm; HK$10, Wed free; ☎2721 0226, ⓦhk.space.museum) was undergoing extensive refurbishment at the time of writing. The new display will probably focus on the Chinese view of space, from

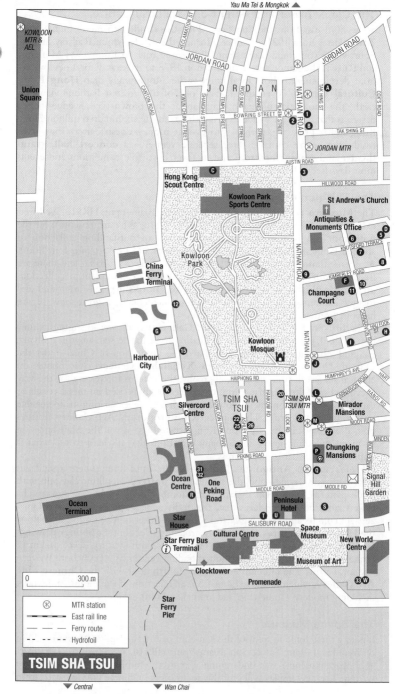

Yau Ma Tei & Mongkok ▲

KOWLOON MTR & AEL

Union Square

JORDAN ROAD

RECLAMATION ST

JORDAN ROAD

J O R D A N

CANTON ROAD

KWUN CHUNG STREET

SHANGHAI STREET

TEMPLE STREET

WOO SUNG STREET

PARKES STREET

PILEM STREET

BOWRING STREET

NATHAN ROAD

TAK HING ST

COX'S ROAD

Ⓐ

❶
Ⓑ

TAK SHING ST

JORDAN MTR

AUSTIN ROAD

❸

HILLWOOD ROAD

Hong Kong Scout Centre Ⓒ

St Andrew's Church

Kowloon Park Sports Centre

Antiquities & Monuments Office

❻
KNUTSFORD TERRACE
❼

Ⓓ
❺

❽

Kowloon Park

NATHAN ROAD

❾

KIMBERLEY ROAD

Ⓕ
❿
⓫

Champagne Court

CARNARVON ROAD

HAU FOOK ST

⓭

Ⓘ

Ⓗ

China Ferry Terminal

❿

Ⓖ

❶❺

Harbour City

Kowloon Mosque

Ⓐ

Ⓙ

HAIPHONG RD

HUMPHREY'S AVE

HART

Ⓚ

❿❾

HANKOW RD

TSIM SHA TSUI

⓴
TSIM SHA TSUI MTR

LOOK RD

Ⓛ

CARNARVON RD

HANOI RD

MODY ROAD

Mirador Mansions

Silvercord Centre

㉒
㉕ ㉖
㉙

ASHLEY RD

㉓

Ⓜ
㉗

MINDEN

CANTON ROAD

KOWLOON PARK DRIVE

㉚

㉘

PEKING ROAD

Ⓟ
㉔

Chungking Mansions

Ⓠ

Signal Hill Garden

Ocean Centre

㉛
㉜

One Peking Road

MIDDLE ROAD

MIDDLE RD

Ⓡ

Ⓢ

Ocean Terminal

Star House

Peninsula Hotel

SALISBURY ROAD

Ⓣ
Ⓤ

Space Museum

New World Centre

Cultural Centre

Star Ferry Bus ⓘ Terminal

Museum of Art

Clocktower

Promenade

㉝ Ⓦ

0   300 m

⊛ MTR station
      East rail line
--   -- Ferry route
-- -- -- Hydrofoil

Star Ferry Pier

TSIM SHA TSUI

▼ Central   ▼ Wan Chai

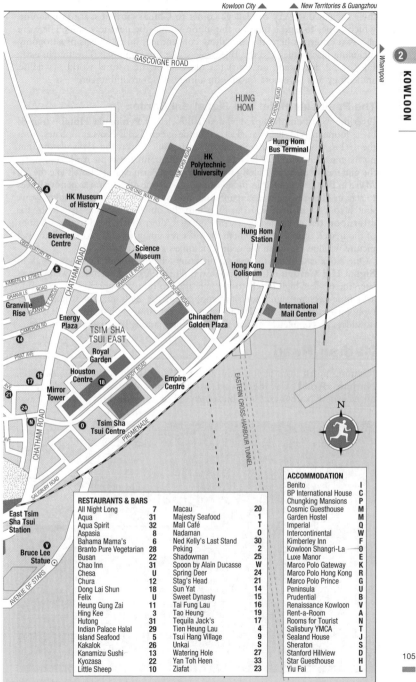

their ancient discovery of Halley's comet to China's current space programme, which hopes to land a man on the moon within the next few years. There are also two **cinemas** here: the Sky Show concentrates on all aspects of astronomy, including black holes and the Big Bang; while the Omnimax Theatre (an extra HK$24–32 depending on seats) has films about the natural world – wildlife, archeology and adventure travel – on a huge, wrap-around screen.

The Peninsula Hotel and Signal Hill Garden

Over the road from the Space Museum, the elegant **Peninsula Hotel** – fronted by a fountain and its own fleet of bottle-green Rolls-Royces – dates from the 1920s, when it stood right on the waterfront. It was the *Peninsula* that put up the travellers who had disembarked from the trains across the road; for decades the glitterati frequented it along with other grand Asian colonial hotels like the *Taj Mahal* in Bombay and *Raffles* in Singapore. It's still one of the most expensive places to stay in Hong Kong and certainly the most stylish by far; if your budget won't stretch to a room here, you can drop into the opulent, Baroque-style lobby for **afternoon tea**, serenaded by a string quartet. Alternatively, head to the top floor of the newer, central tower, where the *Felix* restaurant (p.218) boasts wall-to-wall picture windows (even in the gents) and mixes a mean martini.

One block east of the *Peninsula*, a final tiny relic of colonial Kowloon stands in **Signal Hill Garden** off Minden Row. Built in 1907 and extended twenty years later, the 62-feet-high **brick tower** here used to drop a copper ball at 1pm daily as a time-keeping signal for ships moored in the harbour, and would display typhoon warning signals. Radio rendered the tower obsolete in 1932, and nowadays it's completely hidden from the water among high-rise development.

Nathan Road

Running north from its junction with Salisbury Road at the *Peninsula* hotel, **Nathan Road** was developed as a mighty boulevard by Governor Sir Matthew Nathan in 1904, but remained so underused that for years it was

▲ Busy Nathan Road

Buses that head along **Nathan Road** from the Star Ferry Pier right through to Mong Kok include the #1, #1A, #2, #6, #6A, and #9. The **MTR** is also useful for short hops; the five stops on Nathan Road are Tsim Sha Tsui (for Chungking Mansions and Kowloon Park), Jordan (for Jordan Rd), Yau Ma Tei (Waterloo Rd), Mongkok (Argyle St) and Prince Edward (Prince Edward Rd) – with around 3km between the first and last.

known laughingly as "Nathan's Folly". Nobody laughs at it today though: this is Kowloon's main thoroughfare, roaring with traffic and crowds from dawn until late at night, the shops and hotels crammed in as tightly as possible, all overhung with bright, competing neon signs.

By no means a beautiful street, Nathan Road nonetheless houses a staggeringly concentrated collection of electronics shops, tailors, jewellery stores and fashion boutiques, and is an essential place to experience the commercial spirit that really drives Hong Kong. Actually spending money here is not always such a good idea, however – for more details, see p.236.

Along Nathan Road

Today, other than eating and drinking in the surrounding streets, most pedestrians on Nathan Road are intent on trawling the **shops** that have provided the road with its modern tag, the "Golden Mile". It's not just the signs here that glitter, but the windows, too – full of gold and silver, precious stones, hi-fis and cameras, watches and mobile phones, MP3 players, clothes, shoes and accessories. Less spectacular are a couple of fairly grim mansion blocks, whose ground floors contain numerous stalls selling cheap electrical goods, clothes and luggage. The biggest is **Chungking Mansions**, on the east side at nos. 36–44, where immigrants from the Indian subcontinent rub elbows with Western tourists, businessmen from central and southeastern Asia, and African entrepreneurs. It's also known for its many **Indian restaurants**, internet bars, and seemingly endless supply of **budget guesthouses**, where many backpackers choose to stay. Other, smaller blocks in the area such as **Mirador Mansions**, further up on the same side of the road (nos. 56–58), have more of the same.

The streets off Nathan Road are also alive with possibilities. On the east side, **Granville Road** in particular is famous for its bargain clothes shops, some of them showcasing the work of new, young designers, though you'll also find clothes, accessories and jewellery stores all the way along **Carnarvon**, **Cameron** and **Kimberley** roads. Parallel and above Kimberley, a string of **restaurant-bars** along **Knutsford Terrace** are popular with expats, and make a good focus for a night out.

Finally, there's a small historical corner here behind the fig trees at no. 136 Nathan Road, in the form of the colonnaded, red-brick **Antiquities and Monuments Office**, built in 1902 as the Kowloon British School. Up on the hill behind, **St Andrew's Church** is another vintage Victorian piece, in dark brick with white trim.

Kowloon Park

There's breathing space immediately west of Nathan Road at **Kowloon Park** (daily 5am–11pm), which stretches between Haiphong Road and Austin Road. It's not actually at ground level, but reached up steps at various points along Nathan Road, with ramps off Haiphong and Austin. Parts of it have been landscaped with fountains, rest areas, children's playground, and two **bird collections** – the wildfowl (including flamingos and mandarin ducks) outside in ponds, the parrots and others contained in a small aviary. There's also an outdoor and indoor **swimming complex** (Mon & Wed–Sun 6.30am–noon, 1–5pm & 6–10pm; Tues 6.30–10am, 6–10pm; free), an indoor games hall and a sculpture walk featuring work by local artists.

The southeastern corner of the park is taken up with an open terrace known as the **Kung Fu Corner**. Full of practitioners from about 6am every morning, it also hosts free displays of various martial arts and lion dances between 2.30pm and 4.30pm every Sunday. Below it, at 105 Nathan Rd, is **Kowloon Mosque**, built in the mid-1980s to serve the territory's fifty thousand Muslims (of whom about half are Chinese). It replaced a mosque originally built in 1894 for the British Army's Muslim troops from India, and retains its classic design, with a central white marble dome and minarets.

Tsim Sha Tsui East

Standing on land reclaimed during the 1980s, the area east of Chatham Road – **TSIM SHA TSUI EAST** – forms a badly thought-out wedge of concrete paving, large hotels and shopping centres. Two adjacent **museums** make excellent refuges on a rainy day, however, and can be reached from Tsim Sha Tsui on a pedestrian footbridge over Chatham Road off the end of Granville Road, or aboard **bus** #5, #5C, #8 or #28 from the Star Ferry Pier.

There are also two **East Rail train stations** in the area – East Tsim Sha Tsui and Hung Hom – though these are of less use for the museums and more for heading up through the New Territories towards the Chinese border (see p.123).

Hong Kong Science Museum

You could happily spend an hour or two with children at the **Hong Kong Science Museum**, 2 Science Museum Rd (Mon–Wed & Fri 1–9pm, Sat & Sun 10am–9pm; HK$25, Wed free; Ⓦhk.science.museum), as almost everything here is designed to be poked, prodded or taken apart. Each of the four floors has themed displays – optical illusions, electricity, engineering, structures – explored in fun ways: a virtual reality game; a flight simulator where you can attempt to land at Hong Kong's famously dangerous old Kai Tak airport; 3-D puzzles which seem obvious when completed but impossible while you're trying; and a simple hall of mirrors. Pick of the show are realistic, pull-apart models of a pig, not here to illustrate biology but rather food (a very Chinese perspective); and the giant **Energy Machine**, a maze of tracks, buckets, pulleys, kettle drums and gongs which stretches around the entire museum, through which wooden balls race several times a day – ask at the desk for the next performance time.

Hong Kong Museum of History

Opposite the Science Museum, the **Hong Kong Museum of History** (Mon & Wed–Sat 10am–6pm, Sun 10am–7pm; HK$10, free on Wed; Ⓦhk.history .museum) features colourful walk-through dioramas, the first of which reaches back four million years to when Hong Kong was covered in rainforest. There's a lot to take in here, from Neolithic pottery and stone axes, reconstructed Han tombs like the one at Lei Cheng Uk (p.116) and photographs illustrating archeological sites from the times when salt production was a major industry and pirates roamed the sea lanes. All this is topped, however, by a full-scale model junk, complete with sails, that you can enter and ponder what it was like to spend your whole life living aboard – as people did as recently as the 1990s (after which the government insisted that they settled ashore). There are also full-size reconstructions of temples, theatre stages and shops, and a "bun tower" from Cheung Chau's Tai Chiu Festival (p.166) along with extensive cases of traditional clothing worn by Hakka, Hoklo and Punti, who comprise a fair slice of Hong Kong's ethnic Chinese mix. One of the most impressive things about the museum are the authentic smells – from the sea-dwellers, sun-dried fish and fermented shrimp paste to fragrant tea shops, and a herbalist's niche filled with a bitter, pungent aroma.

Jordan to Mong Kok

Nathan Road continues its relentless journey north through the districts of **Jordan**, **Yau Ma Tei** and **Mong Kok**, areas which, like Tsim Sha Tsui, are unashamedly dedicated to shopping. The emphasis here is far more towards local needs, however: businesses sell everything you saw further south, but without the hustlers and – if you're careful – at better prices. You'll still see plenty of tourists up this way, especially at the many entertaining **street markets** dealing in everything from flowers to goldfish, but attractions are seldom laid on specifically for them. Impossible as it seems, the **crowds** get steadily worse as you go, until they reach a crescendo around Mong Kok – this is, in fact, reputedly the most densely populated place in the world, not too bad in the morning but terminal after dark, when everybody hits the streets for food and a window shop.

Jordan, Yau Ma Tei and Mong Kok all have **MTR stations**, or you can catch **buses** #1, #1A, #2, #6, #6A, #7 or #9 from the Star Ferry Pier up along Nathan Road.

Jordan and Yau Ma Tei

From Tsim Sha Tsui, cross north over **Austin Road** and you're in **JORDAN**, which merges around 700m further north with **YAU MA TEI**. The main area to concentrate on here are the narrow, parallel roads **west of Nathan Road**, concealing a wealth of traditional shops, businesses, markets and even a temple of some repute. In particular, Yau Ma Tei is the site of the popular **Temple Street Night Market**, which – while blatantly touristy – also sports some very Chinese goings-on around its fringes.

If you're simply passing through along Nathan Road, take the time to detour briefly east up broad **Waterloo Road** in Yau Ma Tei where, at no. 25, you'll find the **Kwung Wah Hospital**. This Traditional Chinese Medicine clinic treats the poor for free and was the first hospital specifically for Chinese in Hong Kong, with roots dating back to the 1870s, when practitioners operated out of the Hollywood Road Man Mo Temple on Hong Kong Island (see p.71). At the rear of the hospital, an open-fronted ancestral hall dating to 1911 is now the **Tung Hwa Museum** (Mon–Sat 10am–6pm; free), commemorating the hospital's founders.

The streets

Though the following streets mostly kick off from Austin Road, they only really get going a block north across **Jordan Road** – reach any of them by taking exit A from **Jordan MTR** and turning west along Jordan Road for a couple of minutes.

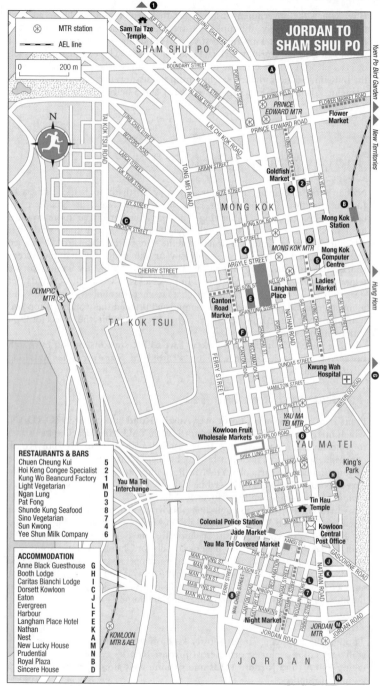

JORDAN TO
SHAM SHUI PO

⊛ MTR station
╾╾ AEL line

0   200 m

N

Sam Tai Tze
Temple

SHAM SHUI PO

AP LIU STREET
CHEUNG SHA WAN ROAD
BOUNDARY STREET
KI LUNG STREET
TAI NAM STREET
PORTLAND STREET
PLAYING FIELD ROAD
PRINCE
EDWARD MTR
LAI CHI KOK ROAD
PRINCE EDWARD ROAD
TUNG CHOI ST
SAI YEE ST

FLOWER MARKET ROAD
Flower
Market

Yuen Po Bird Garden
New Territories

A

TAI KOK TSUI ROAD
TONG CHAU STREET
BEDFORD ROAD
LARCH STREET
FUK TSUN STREET
TONG MEI ROAD

ARRAN STREET
BUTE STREET
IVY STREET
ANCHOR STREET
C

Goldfish
Market
3 2
MONG KOK
PAK TOI ST
SAI TEE ST

B
Mong Kok
Station

FIFE STREET
4
MONG KOK MTR
D
Mong Kok
Computer
Centre
5

MONG KOK ROAD

CHERRY STREET
ARGYLE STREET
NELSON ST
NELSON ST
Langham
Place
SAI YEUNG CHOI STREET
TUNG CHOI STREET
FA YUEN STREET
SAI YEE STREET
Ladies'
Market

OLYMPIC
MTR

TAI KOK TSUI

Canton
Road
Market
SHANTUNG STREET
E
F
SOY STREET
NATHAN ROAD
PORTLAND ROAD

FERRY STREET
CANTON ROAD
RECLAMATION ST
SHANGHAI ST
DUNDAS STREET
HAMILTON STREET
Kwung Wah
Hospital
G

Hung Hom

PITT STREET
YAU MA
TEI MTR
6
SHEK LUNG STREET
WATERLOO ROAD
WATERLOO ROAD
YAU MA TEI

Kowloon Fruit
Wholesale Markets

Yau Ma Tei
Interchange

MAN MING LANE
TONG LANE
WING SING LANE
LUNG KUN ST

King's
Park

H I
FIT RD

Tin Hau
Temple
PUBLIC SQUARE STREET
Colonial Police Station
Jade Market
MARKET STREET
Yau Ma Tei Covered Market
KANSU ST

Kowloon
Central
Post Office
GASCOIGNE ROAD

J

MAN CHONG ST
MAN WAI ST
MAN YUEN ST
MAN YING ST
MAN WUI ST
WAI CHING STREET
CANTON ROAD
BATTERY STREET
SAIGON ST
NINGPO RD
NANKING ST
PAK HOI ST
RECLAMATION STREET
SHANGHAI STREET
TEMPLE STREET
WOOSUNG STREET
PARKES STREET
NATHAN ROAD
L
K
7
Night Market
JORDAN ROAD
JORDAN
MTR
M
JORDAN ROAD

KOWLOON
MTR & AEL

J O R D A N

N

Tsim Sha Tsui ▽

RESTAURANTS & BARS

Chuen Cheung Kui	5
Hoi Keng Congee Specialist	2
Kung Wo Beancurd Factory	1
Light Vegetarian	M
Ngan Lung	D
Pat Fong	3
Shunde Kung Seafood	8
Sino Vegetarian	7
Sun Kwong	4
Yee Shun Milk Company	6

ACCOMMODATION

Anne Black Guesthouse	G
Booth Lodge	H
Caritas Bianchi Lodge	I
Dorsett Kowloon	C
Eaton	J
Evergreen	L
Harbour	F
Langham Place Hotel	E
Nathan	K
Nest	A
New Lucky House	M
Prudential	N
Royal Plaza	B
Sincere House	D

Shanghai Street is easily the pick of roads to follow north, full of all sorts of unexpected treats. At no. 194 (between Saigon and Pak Hoi sts) you'll find one of the last **tailors** specializing in the gorgeously embroidered traditional Chinese wedding dresses that Shanghai Street was once famous for. Further on are all manner of **esoteric stores**: medicines at no. 212, temple accessories at no. 216, dried seafood at no. 228 and then, north of Public Square Street, a string of Chinese **kitchen suppliers** – woks, chopping boards, wooden cake moulds and pastry cutters shaped as auspicious characters. A **smith** at no. 297 turns out razor-sharp cleavers in a range of styles, from heavy monsters designed to hack through bones to delicate kitchen blades. Cross over **Waterloo Road** – past the expanse of rickety 1930s sheds housing **Kowloon Fruit Wholesale Markets** – and there's another traditional bridal shop at 409 Shanghai St. Incidentally, the clacking noise coming out from doorways as you walk past them indicate **mahjong clubs**, full of cigarette smoke, bright lights, gold trim and illegal gambling.

Another street worth homing in on is **Reclamation Street**, immediately west of Shanghai; the whole lower stretch between Nanking and Kansu is an intense produce market with piles of just about every fruit and vegetable imaginable, and some that aren't, stacked up on stalls, while meat, fowl and fish are dispatched inside the covered section between Kansu and Pak Hoi streets. North of **Kansu Street**, underneath a flyover between a sports court and Battery Street, is the Jade Market (see p.112); pushing up past this you'll rejoin Reclamation Street to find another huge **temple accessory shop** at no. 158, with metal incense burners and thousands of statuettes.

The next street to the west, **Canton Road**, is another old thoroughfare. At the southern end, near the junction with Public Square Street, are **jade and ivory shops** (mahjong sets a speciality), with an old colonial **police station**, still in service, on the corner at 627 Public Square St. Canton Road's middle section from Waterloo Road as far as Dundas Street is yet another produce market, less stomach-turning than the one in Reclamation Street. The wholesale market trade is encamped around the Pitt Street junction, while the section around Dundas Street has twitching fish and shrimps in shallow plastic buckets. The northern section, from Dundas Street to Soy Street in Mong Kok, is devoted to **mechanical and electrical shops** – hardware, engines and engineering works piled high at the side of the road. Look out for the **medicinal tea shops** with their copper and brass urns decorated with dragons – you can stand on the street and drink a bowlful for around HK$5 (see p.202 for more).

Tin Hau Temple and Temple Street Night Market

One of the main sights in the area is Yau Ma Tei's **Tin Hau Temple** (daily 8am–5pm), just off Nathan Road on Public Square Street (about midway between Jordan and Yau Ma Tei MTR stations). It's a fair-sized complex, railed off at the back of a paved **square**, with the main hall dedicated to the sea goddess Tin Hau and side rooms for Shea Tan, protector of the local community; Shing Wong, the city god; and Fook Tak, an earth god. The square outside is usually teeming with men sitting around playing backgammon and mahjong, and people may ask for alms as you go in.

Though the temple is closed then, the best time to visit the area is after 7.30pm, when **Temple Street Night Market** fires up, filling the whole length of Temple Street between Jordan Road and Man Ming Lane with street stalls, bright lights and activity. Vendors sell clothes (for men particularly), Bruce Lee dolls, household goods, watches, pirated DVDs and tourist souvenirs with a Chinese flavour – scroll paintings, fake old coins and jade, Little Red Books and antique-style trinkets and jewellery. Check out nearby lanes immediately south of the temple, too, for singers belting out folk songs at open-mike **karaoke tents**, and **fortune telling booths** where you can have your palm or face read, check the prognosis with a tarot reading and, if you're still not satisfied, let a caged finch pick out a card inscribed with your future.

There's plenty of **food** available around the Night Market, either at nearby restaurants or the atmospheric, open-air **foodstalls** along Temple Street itself. A couple of plates of sea snails, prawns, mussels or clams, with a beer or two, won't be too expensive – just make sure you know the price of a dish before ordering it. There are established clusters of these stalls catering to foreigners south of Kansu Street, with locals tending to gravitate to cheaper, less-regulated affairs north of the temple.

The Jade Market

Just southwest of the Tin Hau temple, the **Jade Market** (daily 10am–5pm) sits underneath the Gascoigne Road flyover on Kansu Street. **Jade** is an extremely hard stone that has held a great fascination for the Chinese since prehistoric times, when it was used for ornamental knives, ritual objects and holed discs known as bi. It was later believed to prevent decay, and several Chinese rulers were buried in suits made out of thousands of jade tiles held together with gold thread, hoping to preserve their remains for eternity. Even today, many southern Chinese – both men and women – wear jade pendants or rings; older women also frequently wear jade bangles on their wrists.

Around four hundred stalls here display an enormous selection of stones, from earrings and jewellery to statues, and it's a lot of fun just to poke around. Basically, there are two kinds of jade: inexpensive **nephrite,** which can be varying shades of green and the rarer **jadeite**, which can be green, white or rusty brown. The best jade is a deep, dark green and comes from Burma; a rough guide to quality is that the jade should be cold to the touch and with a pure colour that remains constant all the way through – coloured tinges or blemishes can reduce the value. The HKTB runs **free jade appreciation classes** (see p.51), but if you don't know what you're doing, stick to small trinkets – rings, pendants, paperweights, earrings – if all you want is a souvenir.

Mong Kok

Beyond Yau Ma Tei, **MONG KOK** is a ludicrously busy area stretching north from around Dundas Street to **Boundary Street** which, prior to 1898, marked the border with China. Noisy, packed to the gills and full of mildewed apartment buildings, the atmosphere is down at heel in places but the main thrust is up and coming, with much **urban renewal** planned. Things have certainly changed from the mid-1980s, when Mong Kok was rife with drugs, prostitutes and **Triad gangs**, a situation that spawned a whole genre of gangster films like John Woo's *Hard Boiled*. Now most of the sleaze has gone and, while its reputation lingers, big businesses – the HSBC included – are shifting their headquarters to the area, attracted by relatively cheap real estate prices (at least compared with Hong Kong Island's). Mong Kok is somewhere to experience several excellent markets, **shop** for sportswear and electronic goods, and generally soak up some street life; just note that most businesses up this way don't get going before 11am, and stay open until 9pm or later.

Architecture

Hong Kong can be a wilfully contemporary place, where the past is abandoned – and usually built over – without regret. At the same time, however, Hong Kongers can also display a surprisingly conservative streak: buildings are still designed according to traditional *feng shui* principles, and the SAR's architectural heritage – from temples to New Towns – is in fact fairly diverse. Macau, on the other hand, doesn't have such a contemporary cityscape, but its extensive collection of colonial buildings far better illustrates its Portuguese heritage.

Feng shui

Whatever the scale of a building project, the Chinese consider **feng shui** (literally "wind and water") an essential part of the planning. *Feng shui* is a form of **geomancy**, which assesses how buildings must be positioned so as not to disturb the spiritual attributes of the surrounding landscape, which in a city includes other buildings. This reflects Taoist cosmology, which believes that all components of the universe exist in balance with one another, and thus the disruption of a single element can cause dangerous alterations to the whole. It is vital that structures are favourably oriented according to points on the compass and protected from local **"unlucky directions"** (features that drain or block the flow of good fortune) by the immediate arrangement of other buildings, walls, hills or water. Geomancy also proposes ideal forms for particular types of structure, and carefully arranges spaces and components within a building – even the angle of the escalators in the HSBC building was fixed according to *feng shui*. It's not difficult to spot smaller manifestations of *feng shui* around buildings in Hong Kong, such as mirrors hung above doors or woks placed outside windows to deflect bad influences. Water features also create positive *feng shui* – it is believed that wealth is borne along by the water.

Feng shui compass ▲

Traditional gateway, on the Ping Shan Heritage Trail ▼

Early buildings and temples

Before the British arrived, Hong Kong's settlements comprised fishing villages and self-contained, clan-based farming villages. The **Tanka village** of **Tai O** on Lantau Island (see p.175) gives an idea of how fishing villages would have looked, its stilt houses perched above the water. More substantial examples of traditional farming settlements survive in **Hakka walled villages**, such as **Sam Tung Uk** at Tsuen Wan in the New Territories (see p.128). The rectangular houses are arranged in a grid pattern inside a protective wall, with both house doors and village entrance facing south, a "lucky direction". Entering the village, the way ahead is blocked, and you have to turn sharp right or left into the narrow streets: in *feng shui* terms this stops evil spirits entering (they can't turn corners), while in practical terms it slows down anyone forcing their way in. Inside, the layout is confusing in its regularity, with the village's ancestral shrine tucked away towards the rear.

Temple design also has roots in *feng shui*. Southern Chinese temples are almost all built to the same plan: a walled compound surrounding an open-fronted hall (or halls). The halls are divided by wooden screens with statues of the temple deity at the back – usually the only clue as to denomination, the most blazing example being Po Lin Monastery's **Big Buddha** (see p.175). Colour is only present on the tiled roofs, which are often covered in models of dragons, heroic figures or historical scenes. The region's sole major deviation from standard temple design is the 1990s Tang dynasty-style **Chi Lin Nunnery** at Diamond Hill (see p.119), whose timber halls allow for broader, more gracefully proportioned roofs.

Colonial times

Both Hong Kong and Macau owe their first urban developments to their **colonial** eras, which in Macau date back to the sixteenth century, and in Hong Kong to the nineteenth. In both cases, residential and office buildings defended against

▲ Temple at Tai O, Lantau Island

▼ Buildings at Senado Square

The Lippo Centre in Central, Hong Kong ▲

High-rise apartments at Sha Tin ▼

the tropical heat and humidity with shady wrap-around balconies, thick stone walls, high-ceilinged rooms and shuttered windows; the finest examples survive around Macau's **Largo do Senado**, with Flagstaff House in Hong Kong Park and the Museum of Medical Sciences on Taiping Shan among the best of Hong Kong's more limited selection. Macau is also the best spot to see defensive stone **forts** and flamboyant Baroque **churches** – all executed in Portuguese taste.

Modern architecture

Hong Kong owes its modern appearance to a **population explosion** through the 1950s. Planners, faced with a shortage of both housing and space, had to build upwards, at the same time initiating land reclamation schemes and shifting the population away from the densely inhabited city centre into **New Towns**. These were designed to alleviate overcrowding with modern high-rise blocks, carefully designed open spaces and shopping centres, and are fairly successful, if soulless, conurbations.

Most of Hong Kong's signature **modern architecture** is located on the north shore of Hong Kong Island. **Central** is an almost organically complex maze of basements, atriums and lobbies interlinked by elevated walkways and overpasses and escalators, some of which are architecturally striking in their own right. Three of Hong Kong's greatest buildings are here: the **International Finance Centre**, with its perfectly proportioned tower, IFC2; Norman Foster's **HSBC** building, raised off the ground and partially hollow; and I.M. Pei's **Bank of China** tower, which offends just about every facet of *feng shui* with its razor-edged, pointy design.

▲ Street market, Mong Kok

West of Nathan Road

The most obvious landmark **west of Nathan Road** – in fact, one the biggest in all Kowloon – is **Langham Place**, at 555 Shanghai St (Mong Kok MTR Exit C3). Completed in 2004, this was the first Central-sized tower in Mong Kok, housing the inevitable shopping mall and the *Langham Place* hotel (see p.195), with a massive indoor escalator running from the fourth-floor food court up to the cinema. Touted as Hong Kong's largest urban renewal project, building Langham Place actually involved knocking down a historic block of markets, teahouses and homes housing six thousand people. Not surprisingly, Hong Kongers have since become very sceptical of similar projects across the territory, not least just north over Argyle Street at 598 Shanghai St, where a block of old 1930s shophouses await similar "renewal". Nearby at 625 Shanghai, **Mee Wah Embroidery** is another old establishment specializing in traditional Chinese bridal wear.

West of Shanghai Street, **Canton Road** hosts the local produce market, especially busy around the junction with Argyle Street. As usual, you can get all sorts of fresh, dried and preserved food here, along with **roast meats** – barbequed pork, duck and goose – hanging glistening on hooks at the front of specialist shops. As few Chinese homes have an oven, it's quite normal to buy cooked meats at markets.

East of Nathan Road

Streets **east of Nathan Road** form the core of Mong Kok's speciality: shopping for inexpensive clothes and **electronic goods**. Stores display acres of mobile phones, MP3 players and photographic gear, while anything to do with computers is taken care of inside the **Mongkok Computer Centre**, occupying the entire block south of Nelson Street between Tung Choi and Fa Yuen streets. Prices everywhere are geared towards locals, not tourists, so you're less likely to be ripped off here than in Tsim Sha Tsui – see p.236 for more. The whole area also has a good reputation for **snacking**, with inexpensive restaurants and food stalls all over the place.

For **clothes**, work north through the streets between **Dundas Street** – closest to Yau Ma Tei MTR (Exit A2) – and mighty **Argyle Street** (Mong Kok MTR exits D2 or D3). In particular, **Tung Choi Street** is completely filled by the lively **Ladies' Market** (daily noon–10.30pm), originally a locals' hangout but now definitely edging towards the tourist dollar. Bargain hard, however, and it's still a good place to pick up skirts, dresses, T-shirts and children's clothes – and if you can't find what you want here, head to Sham Shui Po (see opposite). Shops on parallel **Fa Yuen Street** are where you can get the latest brand-label sports shoes and clothing at good – but not cheap – prices.

Over Argyle Street, Tung Choi transforms into the **Goldfish Market**, its shop fronts festooned with plastic bags containing thousands of ornamental and tropical fish. Goldfish are especially popular as a symbol of good fortune; the Chinese for "fish" sounds similar to the word for "surplus", so "gold fish" has an auspicious ring to it. There are also more generalized pets shops here selling puppies, kittens, rabbits and all sorts of accessories.

The Flower Market and Yuen Po Bird Garden

From the top of Tung Choi Street, cross over **Prince Edward Road** and it's a short walk east to the **Flower Market** on Flower Market Road (Prince Edward MTR, exit B1). Shop interiors, shop fronts and even the pavement are bursting with bright seasonal sprays of gingers, orchids, lilies, chrysanthemums and roses, along with yuccas, cordelines, stone cactus and more. It's busy all the time, but especially around Chinese New Year, when many people come to buy narcissi, orange trees and plum blossom to decorate their apartments.

Off the eastern end of the flower market, Mong Kok's **Yuen Po Bird Garden** (daily 7am–8pm) occupies a flagstoned walk in Yuen Po Street shaded by old trees. Keeping songbirds is a popular pastime for older Chinese men, who put them in beautiful wicker cages, talk to them and take them to parks for an airing, where they hang up the cages alongside their friends' birds and listen while they sing to each other. The sizeable **market** here sells finches, mynahs, white-eyes, parrots, lorikeets, laughing thrushes and many others; one section is dedicated to cages (from HK$150), another to live crickets tied up in plastic bags (they're fed to the birds with chopsticks). Note that from here, it's only a short walk to Kowloon Tong – see below.

North of Boundary Street

North of Boundary Street, Kowloon quickly loses its intensity; the streets spread out, the buildings are not so packed and even the crowds thin a little. Of the places to head for this way, all accessible by MTR, the pick is probably **Sham Shui Po**: you might feel you've had enough of trawling Kowloon's markets by this point, but Sham Shui Po's stalls really are worth a visit to buy cheap clothes and browse through bric-a-brac. Otherwise, **Kowloon Tong**'s quiet, upmarket streets are a real contrast to elsewhere in Kowloon, while the **Lei Cheng Uk Han Tomb Museum** preserves one of the oldest dynastic sites in Hong Kong.

Kowloon Tong

Northeast of Mong Kok beyond Boundary Street, **KOWLOON TONG** is a wealthy residential area favoured by film stars, dotted with foreign kindergartens and religious institutions' headquarters. It's also noted for its euphemistically tagged "love hotels", though these aren't all as seedy as they might sound: many cater to ordinary couples wanting to get away from tiny apartments and the rest of the family.

Waterloo Road is the main north–south highway through Kowloon Tong, but it's too busy for a stroll; aim instead for **Cumberland Road**, which runs alongside Waterloo to the west. The most startling things here are the lack of people and tall buildings; there are no apartments at all and many houses are detached and even have their own gardens – an almost unheard-of luxury in Hong Kong. On the west side of the street, no. 41 **Cumberland Road** was Bruce Lee's residence until his death in 1973; today it's a love hotel, though there is talk of turning it into a museum. Some very splendid **Buddhist headquarters** lurk nearby, all gilt signs, orange tiles and red trim; religion is obviously big business in Hong Kong.

You can reach Cumberland Road by **walking** through Mong Kok's Yuen Po Bird Garden onto Boundary Street, turning east under the railway and continuing 100m to the road's southern end. Alternatively, catch the **East Rail** or green **Kwun Tong MTR line** to Kowloon Tong station, take Exit B1 and walk south down past the taxi rank onto To Fuk Road; Cumberland Road is a continuation. It's only about 1.5km from the Bird Garden to Kowloon Tong Station.

Sham Shui Po

Immediately across Boundary Street, Nathan Road veers northwest and becomes **Cheung Sha Wan Road** as it cuts through the heart of shabby **SHAM SHUI PO** – reached via Sham Shui Po station on the red **Kwun Tong MTR line**. This district was notorious for its prison during World War II, where British, Canadian and Indian servicemen were interned by the Japanese. Today, **wholesale fashion warehouses** are a good reason to visit: they line Cheung Sha Wan Road for several blocks between Wong Kuk Street and Yen Chow Street (MTR exits A1 and B1) and prices, styles and quantity easily outcompete anything Mongkok's Ladies' Market can offer. Shops in surrounding streets stock all manner of haberdashery – fabrics, buttons, ribbon, lace – while **Fuk Wa Street** (MTR Exit B2) has more clothing, along with toys and handbags in leather and plastic.

South and parallel with Cheung Sha Wan Road, **Ap Liu Street flea market** (MTR Exit A2; noon until after dark) is where to find everything from second-hand cameras, power tools and mobile phones to old records from the 1930s, fishing rods, used furniture and general household junk. More permanent stalls deal in household electrical appliances. This is somewhere to keep an eye open for completely unexpected things – even genuine antiques occasionally turn up.

The market extends south past some old colonnaded shops down **Kweilin Street** (MTR Exit C2), where at no. 38D you'll find **Leung Choi Shun**, a family-run, traditional "bonesetting" apothecary founded in the early twentieth century. The clinic's open front room is usually full of patients; you can buy their special **medicinal oil** here too. A block further down Kweilin on the corner of Ki Lung Street, the huge *Shun Hing Teahouse Restaurant* has no English sign but its green and red tiling are unmistakable; inside, it was last decorated around 1950 and has the atmosphere of a local's club, full of old men reading newspapers and enjoying *dim sum* with tea.

While you're here, duck around the corner of Kweilin Street down **Yu Chau Street**, where at no. 198 you'll find the **Sam Tai Tze Temple** (daily 8am–5pm). This dates to the 1890s, when local Hakkas paraded a statue of the unruly boy-god **Na Cha** – also known as Third Prince, or Sam Tai Tze – through Sham Shui Po to cure an outbreak of plague, and later built the temple in his honour. Inside, Na Cha is depicted holding a sword and fiery rings, flanked by Pao Kung, the god of justice, and Kwun Yam. An adjacent hall is dedicated to Pak Tai (see p.81).

Lei Cheng Uk Han Tomb Museum

CHEUNG SHA WAN, an otherwise ordinary residential district some 2.5km northwest of Boundary Street, is notable for the little **Lei Cheng Uk Han Tomb Museum**, at 41 Tonkin St (Mon–Wed & Fri–Sat 10am–6pm, Sun 1–6pm; free). To get here, ride to **Cheung Sha Wan MTR station** – the next stop past Sham Shui Po – take exit A3 and walk north for ten minutes up Tonkin Street.

Discovered in 1957 during construction of a housing estate, the tomb's cross-shaped, brick burial chamber dates to the Eastern Han period (25–220 AD) and provided archeologists with sound evidence that the region was then governed by **Panyu**, a town near modern day Guangzhou in southern China. The museum shows an informative **video** outlining the contemporary **Nam Yue culture** – a local version of mainstream Chinese beliefs – and events surrounding the excavation of the tomb; from here you pass cases of pottery and fragments of bronze ware unearthed at the site to reach the **tomb itself**, which has been preserved *in situ*. You can't go in, but a glass window gives you a peek at the low-ceilinged, interlocked brickwork. The tomb is assumed to have been built for a local official, but no trace of a body was ever found here – the museum provides several theories as to why this might have been.

Northeast Kowloon

Kowloon's northeastern corner, right up against the steep ridge of the **Kowloon Hills**, hides a string of attractions which can be tied into a satisfying half-day circuit using buses and the green **Kwun Tong MTR line**. Alternatively, you could stop off at any of the places below en route to catch a bus to Sai Kung or Clearwater Bay from **Diamond Hill** (see p.118). In addition to a pair of greatly contrasting **temples** – one engagingly lively, the other sublimely calm – there's an unusual historical relic in **Kowloon Walled City Park**, once the most notorious place in all Hong Kong. But if you've got time for only one thing, head for the **Nan Lian Gardens**, a truly splendid, unique example of traditional Chinese landscaping.

Kowloon Walled City Park

After the British took Hong Kong Island in the 1840s, the Chinese government built a line of defences on the mainland opposite, including a **walled garrison town** on a hillock in what is now northern Kowloon. The stone fortifications, dotted with watchtowers and gates, enclosed a small but well-defended community of about five hundred soldiers, along with their families, camp followers and staff, and the **Walled City** became an important administrative post, with a **yamen** – government quarters – headed by the military commander.

When the New Territories were leased to Britain in 1898, the garrison commanders refused to cede sovereignity, and the extraordinary consequence was that for nearly a century the city became a self-governing enclave. The east wall was **dismantled** by the Japanese in World War II and used to extend the nearby airstrip at Kai Tak, but following the war refugees from the Chinese mainland moved in and made the city their own. It grew into a high-rise shanty town, full of shabby tenement blocks crowded together and strung with drying laundry, the haunt of Triad gangs and a no-go area for the police. It took until 1991 to negotiate the Walled City's **closure**, after which the residents were resettled and the site was levelled, landscaped and turned into **Kowloon Walled City Park** (daily 6.30am–6pm). The restored *yamen* building now houses a collection of photos of the Walled City, from it's original regimental appearance to its final days; while the only other relic of the times are two stone blocks carved with the characters for "**south gate**", set into an ornamental wall. The rest of the park is very attractive, with ponds, waterfalls and angled galleries linking various terraces.

The Walled City Park lies in the suburb of **Kowloon City**, with its entrance south off **Tung Tau Tsuen Road**. The easiest way to get here is on **bus #1** from the Tsim Sha Tsui Star Ferry Pier, which runs the entire length of Nathan Road, turns east along Boundary Street and then passes the park gates on Tung Tau Tsuen Road – a thirty-minute journey in all. You can also catch the Kwun Tong MTR Line to **Lok Fu**, turn left out of Exit B and walk 100m to the intersection with Junction Road; turn left again and the corner with Tung Tau Tsuen Road is a ten-minute walk.

Wong Tai Sin

WONG TAI SIN is a bright, modern town on the Kwun Tong MTR line with a huge shopping centre surrounded by a wall of residential estates – a pattern of urban design you'll get to know well if you spend much time up in the New Territories (p.123). The town is named after its massive and colourful

▲ Wong Tai Sin Temple

Wong Tai Sin Temple (daily 7am–5.30pm; free), right next to the MTR station (exits B2 or B3). Wong Tai Sin – literally, the Yellow Immortal – was a mythical shepherd turned folk god whose temple here was founded in the 1920s. Over three million people now come to pay their respects every year, a popularity down to Wong Tai Sin's ability to cure illness and bring good luck to gamblers – two vital concerns among the Hong Kong Chinese.

The temple focuses on an open-air **courtyard** fronting the **main hall**. The hall itself is closed to the public, but you can often see in through the screened front to the altar and rich decoration inside. In any case, it's the courtyard where all the action takes place: people pack in here to kneel down and kowtow towards the hall with sticks of incense, or rattle a can full of numbered **bamboo sticks** until one drops out – this stick is then exchanged for a piece of paper bearing the same number, which has a **prediction** written on it. In keeping with Wong Tai Sin's skills, there's also a small clinic here, the upper floor of which offers **Chinese herbal medicine**.

Off to one side of the temple grounds, a covered street of booths houses **fortune-tellers**, who read palms, bumps, feet and faces. Many display testimonials of success for the sceptical, and some speak English (there's a map at the end of the building that indicates the English-speakers with a red dot), so if you want to find out whether or not you're going to win at the races, this is the place to ask.

The temple is always busy – even during the blazing summers – but if you want to experience absolute chaos, come here at Chinese New Year, when you'll be battered and bruised by the crowds seeking protection and good luck for the future. There are similar scenes too at **Wong Tai Sin's birthday** celebrations, on the twenty-third day of the eighth lunar month (usually in Sept).

Sha Tin Pass

Wong Tai Sin sits under the steep slope of the Kowloon Hills, from where there are fantastic views south at the **Sha Tin Pass**. To get there, turn left out of MTR Exit E and it's 50m around the corner to **green minibus #18**, which takes ten minutes to reach its terminus just past the intersection with **Sha Tin Pass Road**. Take Sha Tin Pass Road uphill, past the gaudy Fazang Temple, for the stiff, forty-minute ascent to the pass – popular with locals at the weekend – and once at the wooded top you'll find toilets, a pavilion and a small drinks kiosk (closes at 5pm).

Despite the name, the Sha Tin Pass – or the road, at any rate – doesn't run on to Sha Tin in the New Territories, though there is a footpath in that direction which lands you near Tsang Tai Uk (see p.136). Both the Wilson and MacLehose trails pass through here, however, the latter providing a marked 1.8-kilometre trail to **Lion Rock** from the top of Sha Tin Pass Road – see p.137 for more.

Diamond Hill

One reason to visit **DIAMOND HILL**, the next MTR stop east of Wong Tai Sin, is to see the superb **Nan Lian Gardens** and adjacent **Chi Lin Nunnery** – in which case, take Exit C2 from the MTR station and follow the signs for five minutes. The town is also a useful transport nexus: above the MTR is the **bus station** where transport to Sai Kung and Clearwater Bay departs from (pp.150–152), so you might find yourself passing through several times. If so, **Plaza Hollywood**, a glittering multistorey shopping centre right outside the stations, has a Park' N' Shop supermarket on the second floor for picnic supplies, along with a food court and several restaurants.

The Nan Lian Gardens and Chi Lin Nunnery

The **Nan Lian Gardens** (daily 7am–9pm) don't look too promising at first, sited as they are in the centre of a huge ring of busy traffic overpasses. But once through the gates you may as well have stepped back over a thousand years: screened by trees which block the traffic noise and the sight of soaring apartment blocks outside, a circuit of paths lead between groves of contorted pine trees, dwarf bougainvillea and crepe myrtles, all laid out in the classical Chinese style dating back to the **Tang dynasty** (618–907 AD). Large, oddly -shaped *taihu* rocks evoke landscapes in miniature, while **ponds** – one full of giant carp, another graced by a stunning gold-painted pavilion, reached across gently arched vermilion bridges – add a sense of space. Several **wooden halls** around the perimeter are also built to Tang designs; one contains a gift shop, another a gallery, a third displays models of the intricate wooden brackets needed to support the roofs. The gardens are not especially large, but the layout makes it feel bigger and it's not hard to spend an hour strolling around.

From the north side of the gardens, there's a pedestrian overpass across the main road outside and straight into the forecourt of the **Chi Lin Nunnery** (daily 7am–7pm; free). Again built in the Tang style, this is another oasis of calm, with more beautifully proportioned, dark timber buildings arranged around spacious central courtyards. Giant gilded representations of Buddha as the sage Sakyamuni, Manjusri (the incarnation of wisdom) and Samantabadhra (virtue) fill the **main hall**, whose roof sprouts two upright "horns", a structural necessity to give a gentle curve to the roofline. Side wings contain more statues of Buddhist deities in gold and precious wood – look for a very languid one of Avalokitesvara, the original Indian source for Kwun Yam, the Chinese goddess of mercy.

East Kowloon

East Kowloon stretches for about 5km out along Victoria Harbour, a residential district whose clusters of 1950s tower blocks, housing thousands of families in minute, badly serviced apartments, are steadily being replaced. **Salt panning** was once big business here: in the 1860s, the Hong Kong government decided that salt production wouldn't be taxed – unlike in China where the trade was rigidly controlled – which created a new industry in smuggling salt to the mainland where higher prices were paid. A century later, the construction of a full-sized runway out into the harbour turned local **Kai Tak Airport** into Hong Kong's main international arrival point, and right on into the 1990s many visitors got their first look at the SAR from a plane coming in disturbingly low over East Kowloon's high-rises. The opening of the current airport off Lantau put an end to all that, and now the vacant site at Kai Tak is awaiting decontamination so that it can be turned into a cruise-ship terminal.

None of this makes East Kowloon an essential destination, but you'll pass through the area if you head out to the quirky settlement of **Lei Yue Mun**, a famous place to eat seafood and departure point for one of Hong Kong's less-visited islands, **Tung Lung Chau**.

Lei Yue Mun

LEI YUE MUN village overlooks the easternmost end of Victoria Harbour across its narrowest point (also called Lei Yue Mun). It's a ramshackle settlement of low plaster buildings topped with corrugated iron roofs, an unexpected sight so close to such a sophisticated city, and for that alone is worth a wander through its small maze of narrow, covered lanes. At the far side of the village, a tiny, two-hundred-year-old **Tin Hau Temple** sits on a rock shelf just above the water among some large granite boulders, each inscribed with Taoist couplets. Two rusting canons point south over the harbour's narrow neck towards Shau Kei Wan and the Museum of Coastal Defence; you can follow signposts marking the **Wilson Trail** (p.92) up to the headland above for views.

Most people visit Lei Yue Mun to **eat seafood**, despite the fact that nowadays very little – if anything – is caught locally. It's a great experience, however, and there are stacks of fresh-fish shops and **restaurants** in the village, their slabs and tanks full of live reef fish, clams, snails, crayfish, cuttlefish and shrimps. The recognized procedure is to make your choice from a shop, where it will be weighed and priced, and then take it (or you'll be taken) to a restaurant, where it's cooked to your instructions. You generally pay the bill at the end – one to the fishmonger and one to the restaurant for cooking your dinner. The strongest possible warnings about **rip-offs** apply: fix the price of your fish before it's bashed on the head or you're just inviting someone to choose the most expensive creature in the tank for you. Restaurants vary from fairly basic to quite flash (some even offer imported wines) and most open for lunch at the earliest, though evenings are the liveliest time to come.

Getting there

The easiest way to reach Lei Yue Mun is aboard the MTR to **Yau Tong** (on both the green Kwun Tong line and the purple Tseng Kwan O line from North Point on Hong Kong Island). Take Exit A2, then turn left up Cha Kwo Ling Road and into Shung Shun Street, which leads down to the waterfront – all in all, a ten- to fifteen-minute walk. At the waterfront you'll find the **Sam Ka Tsuen** typhoon shelter, worth a visit in its own right if there's a storm on the way as you'll find it packed to bursting with all sorts of vessels. The adjacent pier is the departure point for **ferries** to **Tung Lung Chau** (see below). From here, bear left along the waterfront and you're at the village.

Tung Lung Chau

A thirty-minute boat ride from Lei Yue Mun, the small island of **TUNG LUNG CHAU** sits just south of Joss House Bay on the Clearwater Bay Peninsula (p.151). The island's eastern cliffs are popular with **rock climbers**, and there are a couple of historical sites to check out, but it's also a good spot if you're just trying to escape from the downtown for a few hours.

Ferries dock halfway along the north shore. The island's northeast corner – about a kilometre from the ferry – has a **campsite** with toilets, tap water and barbecue pits, along with a store open on weekends only. The restored, eighteenth-century **Tung Lung Fort** nearby, complete with stone walls, was built to keep an eye on pirates in the area. The same distance west from the ferry is Hong Kong's largest **rock carving**, a prehistoric representation of a dragon some two metres tall.

Despite the island's proximity to the Clearwater Bay Peninsula, it's reached from the **Sam Ka Tsuen ferry pier** at Lei Yue Mun on **weekends only**. There are five departures on Saturday between 9am and 4.30pm, and six departures on Sunday between 8.30am and 4.30pm; it costs HK$30 return. For more information, call Coral Sea Ferry on ☎2513 1103, or contact the HKTB.

Places

Cheung Sha Wan	長沙灣
Diamond Hill	鑽石山
Jordan	佐敦
Kowloon	九龍
Kowloon City	九龍城
Kowloon Tong	九龍塘
Lei Yue Mun	鯉魚門
Lok Fu	樂富
Mong Kok	旺角
Prince Edward	太子
Sham Shui Po	深水埗
Tsim Sha Tsui	尖沙咀
Tsim Sha Tsui East	尖沙咀東
Wong Tai Sin	黃大仙
Yau Ma Tei	油麻地

Sights

Avenue of Stars	星光大道
Chi Lin Nunnery	志蓮淨苑
Chungking Mansions	重慶大廈
Clock Tower	鐘樓
Flower Market	花墟
Goldfish Market	金魚街
Harbour City	香港城
Hong Kong Cultural Centre	香港文化中心
Hong Kong Museum of History	香港歷史博物館
Hong Kong Science Museum	香港科學館
International Commerce Centre	環球貿易廣場
Jade Market	玉器市場
Kowloon Park	九龍公園
Kowloon Walled City Park	九龍寨城公園
Kwung Wah Hospital	廣華醫院
Ladies' Market	女人街
Langham Place	朗豪坊
Lei Cheng Uk Han Tomb Museum	李鄭屋古墓
Museum of Art	香港藝術館
Nan Lian Gardens	南連公園
Ocean Centre	海洋中心
Ocean Terminal	海運大廈
The Peninsula Hotel	半島酒店
Sam Tai Tze Temple	三太子宮
Sha Tin Pass	沙田坳
Signal Hill Garden	訊號山
Space Museum	香港太空館
Temple Street Night Market	廟街夜市
Tin Hau Temple	天后宮
Tung Wah Museum	東華三院文物館
Wong Tai Sin Temple	黃大仙廟
Yuen Po Bird Garden	園圃街雀鳥花園

Streets

Ap Liu Street	鴨寮街
Argyle Street	亞皆老街
Boundary Street	界限街
Canton Road	廣東道

Cheung Sha Wan Road	長沙灣道
Cumberland Road	金巴倫道
Dundas Street	登打士街
Fa Yuen Street	花園街
Granville Road	加連威老道
Kansu Street	甘肅街
Kweilin Street	桂林街
Nathan Road	彌敦道
Prince Edward Road	太子道
Reclamation Street	新填地街
Salisbury Road	梳士巴利道
Shanghai Street	上海街
Sha Tin Pass Road	沙田坳道
Tung Choi Street	通菜街
Tung Lung Chau	東龍洲
Tung Tau Tsuen Road	東頭村道
Waterloo Road	窩打老道

Transport

China Ferry Terminal	中港碼頭
East Rail station	東鐵車站
MTR station	地下鐵車站
Sam Ka Tsuen Ferry Pier	三家村碼頭
Star Ferry Pier	天星碼頭

3

The New Territories

While Hong Kong's popular image is of a crowded harbourside city full of futuristic buildings, frantic businessmen and shoppers chasing the latest high-tech baubles, the **New Territories** – the 740 square kilometres between Kowloon and the Chinese border – offers a very different picture. Where Hong Kong Island and Kowloon were taken as permanent possessions by Britain, the New Territories was only **leased** from the Chinese for 99 years in 1898, and so was never developed to the same degree. However, as the source of much of Hong Kong's drinking water and food, the region had become so vital to the running of Hong Kong that – when the New Territories' lease expired in June 1997 – Britain had no choice but to hand all of Hong Kong back to China.

Around half of Hong Kong's citizens live in the New Territories, many of them settled in modern, purpose-built **New Towns** that have sprung up since the 1970s in an effort to ease the downtown areas' population density. These New Towns are self-contained cities in miniature, featuring local employment opportunities, cultural, civic and leisure services, shops and markets, and the better ones – such as **Tai Po** – are worth a look in themselves for their community-oriented urban planning. But what is really surprising about the New Territories is just how **rural** it can be: although it's not as easy as it once was to encounter water buffalo lumbering along the

The New Territories in one day

You'll need to start early. Kick off by catching the West Rail Line to Kam Sheung Road, for the **old Hakka buildings** at Kam Tin (p.131). From here, hop on the **#64K bus** east towards Tai Po, stopping off along the way to stretch your legs at **Kadoorie Farm** or **Ng Tung Chai waterfalls** (p.144), either of which could tie you up for a good couple of hours. Get back on the #64K, pausing briefly for at look at the **Lam Tsuen Wishing Trees** (p.144), then ride the bus to its terminus at **Tai Po** (p.141). Grab lunch in Tai Po, perhaps taking in the old market and Man Mo Temple, before catching **green minibus #26** eastwards from Tai Po's main street, Kwong Fuk Road. This takes you on a magnificent fifteen-minute spin along expressways lining the southern edge of Tolo Harbour and across the Shing Mun River to **Ma On Shan town**, with views of the harbour, New Towns and mountain ranges stretching down to Sha Tin. Stay on until the end of the run outside Ma On Shan train station, then pick up **bus #299** to **Sai Kung Town**, another twenty-minute run around a forested headland and down to Sai Kung's bus terminus. Have a stroll around Sai Kung (p.152) and a feed at one of the restaurants, before catching **bus #92** back south to Diamond Hill and the MTR line.

roads, a good number of **villages** and hamlets inhabited by **Hakka** families (see box, p.126) still have their century-old temples and meeting halls intact. What's more, over half the New Territories is designated as **Country Park** – in places containing some very rugged landscape indeed – and offering excellent outdoor escapes, such as **hiking** along the Wilson or MacLehose trails (p.92 & p.155).

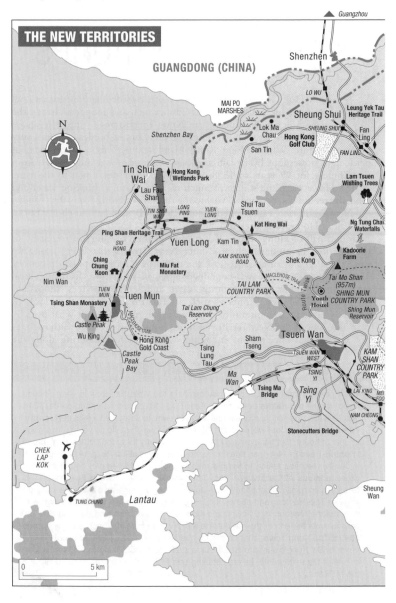

The New Territories splits into three regions. In the **west**, the countryside includes **Tai Mo Shan**, Hong Kong's highest peak; there's some well-preserved Hakka architecture to check out, along with the easily accessibly **Hong Kong Wetland Park**, an enjoyable spot to spy on birdlife. Heading **north** towards the Chinese border, either **Sha Tin** or Tai Po could occupy a full day or more, with their markets, temples and range of outdoor

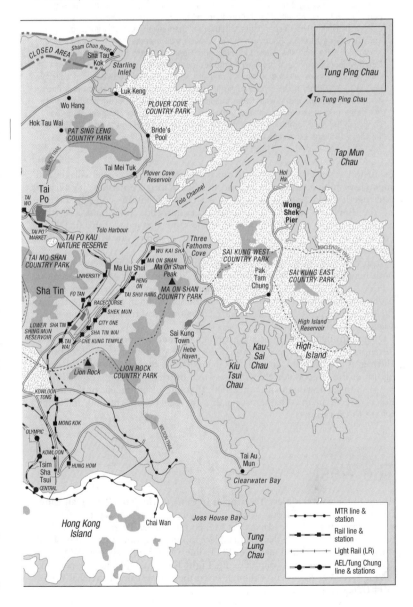

The Hakkas

The **Hakkas** – concentrated today in Hong Kong and the nearby Mainland – were dislodged from their homelands in central China by warfare milennia ago, and have never been sure of their welcome in places they subsequently settled. Indeed, *hakka* translates as "guest family", indicating their status as outsiders.

Hakkas are believed to have arrived by the New Territories before the thirteenth century, when the ancestor of the ubiquitous **Tang clan** moved here from China's Jiangxi province. His descendants established themselves around Fan Ling, Kam Tin, Yuen Long and Ping Shan, eventually spreading all over the New Territories. They were later joined by the Man, Liu, Hau and Pangs to form the **five clans**, who together founded many of the New Territories' settlements.

Traditional Hakka villages in Hong Kong are self-contained, fortified units called **wai**, with individual houses packed tightly together around an **ancestral hall** and enclosed by a thick stone wall. Older buildings often have flamboyant rooflines and fire-baffle end walls drawn up into **wok yee**, or "wok handle" shapes. Many *wai* survive in the New Territories, with the best examples at Kat Hing Wai (p.131), Tsang Tai Uk (p.136) and Lo Wai (p.148).

excursions nearby; while the **east coast** features beaches, coastal villages and superlative hiking, especially around the **Sai Kung Peninsula**. It's all best tied together on a number of trips – a day taking in antique buildings on one of the **heritage trails**, another on a countryside hike, and a further excursion to the coast for a sprawl on the sand. But if you can't fit this in, either concentrate on a single area, or try the **one day circuit** described in the box on p.123.

Both west and north regions are covered by **train lines**, with plenty of **buses** both here and around the east coast, though some remoter areas get a regular service only at weekends. Even so, it's impressive to see how well every corner of the New Territories is served by public transport, and in terms of travel time there's no one place that you couldn't cover on a day trip from Hong Kong Island or Kowloon.

Disappointingly, there's not a great range of **accommodation** in the New Territories: just a few pricey hotels, isolated youth hostels and campsites. **Eating** is no problem around the main towns, though you should carry plenty of food and water elsewhere as rural districts are poorly catered to as far as shops or restaurants is concerned. If you're planning any of the longer hikes covered in this chapter, see p.252 for general information, including where to find **maps**.

The West

Access to the **western New Territories** is primarily along the **West Rail Line**, best joined at Nam Cheong station on the orange Tung Chung line if you're coming from Hong Kong Island; or at Mei Foo on the red Tsuen Wan MTR line from Kowloon. Also note that the first place of interest out this way, **Tsuen Wan**, is itself at the end of the Tsuen Wan MTR line. Once here, aside from West Rail and buses, you might find yourself on the **Light Rail** system, a tram-like network linking several of the towns – though given the choice, parallel stretches of the West Rail are faster.

While the West's New Towns – Tsuen Wan, **Yuen Long**, **Tin Shui Wai** and **Tuen Mun** – don't offer much from a touristic viewpoint, they're interesting enough for a brief wander and useful for reaching other sights. Tsuen Wan is close to Hong Kong's apex, **Tai Mo Shan**, with a straightforward walk to the summit; and also to two nearby **country parks**, featuring lots of monkeys, an easy track around a wooded reservoir, or a harder trail up over the narrow ridge above. Similarly, Tin Shui Wai is an access point for the **Hong Kong Wetland Park** – an excellent place to take children – and a varied string of old buildings lining the **Ping Shan Heritage Trail**. Alternatively, you could head to **Kam Tin** for a look at the most famous Hakka village in Hong Kong, **Kat Hing Wai**.

Tsuen Wan

A stack of grey high-rises nestling between the hills, **TSUEN WAN** overlooks a brace of enormous **suspension bridges** leapfrogging Tsing Yi island as they carry expressways and trains between the mainland and Lantau. Tsuen Wan took off after **tungsten ore** was discovered up in the hills during the 1950s; today it's an industrial New Town of around a million people, with concrete-bound flyovers and walkways spinning off in all directions, and signposts pointing into interlinking malls and gardens. A small **museum** and a busy market area could fill in an hour or so, perhaps in transit to nearby Tai Mo Shan or the Shing Mun-Kam Shan country parks.

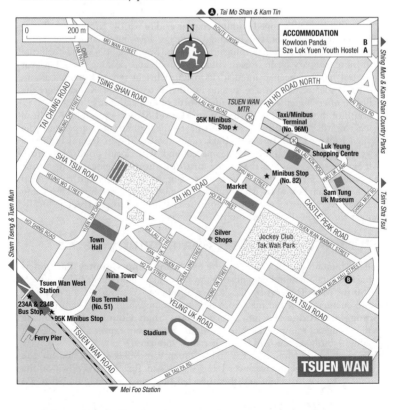

Tsuen Wan MTR station – terminus for the red Tsuen Wan MTR Line from Central and Kowloon – is up on the northern side of town. You can also get here on the West Rail to **Tsuen Wan West station**, located about a kilometre southwest from the MTR on the waterfront – green minibus #95K runs between the two. **Leaving**, Tsuen Wan West Station is where to catch a train via Kam Tin (p.131) to the rest of the western New Territories, or bus #51 via Tai Mo Shan to Kam Tin – a beautiful ride even if you don't get out to climb the mountain. For the country parks, catch minibus #82 from near Tsuen Wan MTR – see accounts for more details.

Tsuen Wan has one of the New Territories' few **hotels**, the *Kowloon Panda* (see p.195 for review). Inside on the second floor, the highly rated *Yuet Loy Heen* restaurant serves *dim sum* from 7am to 2.30pm; the seafood choices are especially good. You could also catch **bus #234A** or **#234B** from Tsuen Wan West Station for the fifteen-minute ride west along the coast to **Sham Tseng**, famous for its **goose restaurants** – see p.213.

Sam Tung Uk Museum and around

The older, more interesting part of Tsuen Wan sits on the northern side of town around Tsuen Wan MTR station. Take Exit B3, turn left and it's about 200m along Sai Lau Kok Road to **Sam Tung Uk Museum** (Mon & Wed–Sun 9am–5pm; free). This little Hakka walled village was lived in until the New Town went up around it in the 1970s, when it was cleaned out and renovated to its original eighteenth-century condition. As a museum it's unnaturally clean and uncluttered, making it easy to appreciate the village's layout, with the long, rectangular houses arranged within a regular grid of narrow lanes. The walls are whitewashed and cool, the buildings sporting low lintels and well-crafted beamed roofs; inside are farming implements, beautiful blackwood furniture and more ordinary chairs, tables, cooking utensils and cleaning tools. The rear ancestral hall has been painted in its original bright red and green colours, giving an idea of what you're missing in other parts of Hong Kong, where the halls are often ingrained with decades' worth of dust and dirt.

South of the museum on **Tsuen Wan Market Street** – you'll have to head back towards the station then take one of the pedestrian overpasses – the walled **Jockey Club Tak Wah Park** (daily 6.30am–11pm; free) is built in a sort of traditional Chinese style, paved and with lotus ponds, big trees, decorative rocks and a few more **antique houses** relocated from the now-defunct Hoi Pa village. Walk west along Market Street and you'll soon reach the **market area** itself, full of activity, stalls, roast meat shops and inexpensive places to eat; south from here, **Chuen Lung Street** is locally famed for its jewellers, gold shops and silversmiths.

Shing Mun and Kam Shan country parks

Fifteen minutes east of Tsuen Wan by bus, **Shing Mun Country Park** offers attractive rural surroundings and an enjoyable walk around the deep blue waters of **Shing Mun Reservoir** (also known as Jubilee Reservoir). If you're a little more energetic, you can hike from here past some World War II remains over **Smuggler's Ridge** and into adjacent **Kam Shan Country Park**, landing within range of transport back to Kowloon. Either way, expect to see a dash of wildlife – birds, reptiles and almost certainly monkeys.

To reach Shing Mun, take Exit B1 at Tsuen Wan MTR station and use the **pedestrian bridge** to cross over Tsing Shan Road. Turn left and down off the bridge, take the first right and then first left turnings and you're on **Shiu Wo**

Street, from where **green minibus #82** (daily 6.45am–11.45pm; HK$3.90) runs to the reservoir at **Pineapple Dam**. On arrival, steps on the left head up to a **visitors' centre** (Sat & Sun 9am–5pm), kiosk and toilet block; steps on the right follow around to the dam wall itself and the trailhead for Smugglers' Ridge and Kam Shan.

Around Shing Mun Reservoir

A signposted circuit from the visitors' centre runs clockwise **around Shing Mun Reservoir**, a beautiful two-hour walk through shady forest on an easy track. For the first few minutes you follow the water's edge, then climb steps onto a small concrete road heading off through the trees. The best **picnic ground** is about forty minutes along at the site of **Cheung Uk Tsuen**, a village that was abandoned when the dam was built in 1928. The overgrown remains of rice-terrace walls can still be seen amongst the trees, though it's hard to imagine this having once been an open hillside.

After here the road crosses the **Wilson Trail**, which heads northwest uphill towards **Lead Mine Pass** (see p.131) and Tai Mo Shan; follow it in the opposite direction along the road, which climbs steeply for 200m at the tail end of the reservoir. The Wilson Trail then drops down off the road into thinner, patchier woodland around the lakeshore; it's an hour or so along it to the reservoir's huge **dam wall**, set above a deep gorge. Another **picnic area** with benches, tables and barbecue pits on the far side marks the start of routes into Kam Shan, or it's just fifteen minutes back to the bus stop.

Over Smugglers' Ridge into Kam Shan Country Park

The following hike from Shing Mun Reservoir into **Kam Shan Country Park** should take around two hours. It's a hot, exposed hike with some steep stretches, so take plenty of water and a hat.

Begin at the **picnic area** at the dam wall, and walk through it to where steps descend into the gorge – signs point to "Kowloon Reservoir". A short way down, turn right, off the steps, and onto an unpaved walking track. About ten minutes along, the forest hides the **Shing Mun Redoubt**, a twelve-acre underground fortification built by the British in 1939 as part of the New Territories' defence (known as the "Gin Drinker's Line") against possible Japanese invasion. Based on a series of tunnels – each named after a London street or area – the line was over-run by the Japanese after a short but bloody battle in 1941. Large parts of the system still remain intact, covered by undergrowth: if you're intent on exploring, take a flashlight and be very careful, since the tunnels aren't maintained.

If you don't detour, it takes about twenty minutes to climb through the forest to **Smugglers' Ridge**, a razor-edged crest running southeast with brilliant views back over Shing Mun Reservoir, the dam wall and gorge below. Follow along the ridge and then down onto **Kam Shan Road**; take this uphill for 100m to a viewing pavilion, where you can either continue down along the road, or bear left onto the "Family Trail" through the forest. Head this way and you'll see plenty of **macaque monkeys** – so many, in fact, that the government is thinking of ways to cull their numbers. Whichever route you take, you'll end up on the **Tai Po Road**, where you can pick up **bus #81** (daily 5.30am–11.30pm; HK$5.50) to Jordan in Kowloon.

Tai Mo Shan

Around 4km north of Tsuen Wan, **Tai Mo Shan** rises 957m above sea level, its top usually obscured by a smudge of cloud (*tai mo shan* means "Big Hat

▲ Tai Mo Shan

Mountain"). Though this is Hong Kong's **highest peak**, it's by no means the hardest to climb, with a vehicle road all the way up the mountain's west face to the weather stations on top; people come here on cold winter mornings hoping to see **frost**. At other times, the two- or three-hour hike to the summit offers some wonderful panoramas, especially at dawn or sunset – there's the **Sze Lok Yuen Youth Hostel** (see p.197) partway up if you want to stay the night. The ascent follows section 8 of the **MacLehose Trail** (p.155), and it's possible to extend your walk east off the back of the mountain to either Shing Mun Reservoir or Tai Po (see opposite). Note that the walk is very exposed, with **no shade** at all for most of the way; and that ideally you want to choose a clear day with a southerly wind, which pushes the air pollution back into China.

To get here, ride the West Rail to **Tsuen Wan West station**, take Exit D, cross the road, turn left, and the **#51 bus** (daily 5.40am–10.50pm; HK$7.60) departs the concrete block of a station 150m down. The ride takes about twenty minutes along winding **Route Twisk**; get out at the "Country Park" stop at Tsuen Kam Au, where there's a **Visitors' Centre** (Sat & Sun 9.30am–4pm) and toilets, with a couple of campsites nearby. Incidentally, bus #51 continues on past the mountain to terminate among Kam Tin's Hakka monuments – see opposite.

To the summit and beyond

From the Visitors' Centre, either take the road uphill, or follow the **picnic ground trail** from the toilet block up steps through dry woodland onto a grassy hillside dotted with huge granite boulders. On the way you'll see docile **wild cattle** – the descendants of farmed herds – then the intermittent path joins the road at a picnic ground, near where a side track leads over to the **youth hostel**. Keep to the main road as it zigzags up, up and up again, the scenery getting better with every bend, until you finally reach the **summit area**. Unfortunately, you can't stand on the very top – the weather station is surrounded by razor wire – but the **views** are just stupendous: all of Hong Kong is spread out at your feet, from the Sai Kung Peninsula to

Lantau Island, and from Hong Kong Island to the border with China (clearly visible as a sudden, dense band of high-rises and smog to the north).

At this point, either retrace your steps back down to the Visitors' Centre, or follow the vehicle road around the summit to a locked gateway into the weather station compound. An old, disused road bends east off here, marked "Tai Mo Shan Forest Track", descending steeply to a hillside scarred in the chevron pattern of old tea terraces. A **signpost** here marks a trail north to **Ng Tung Chai waterfalls** (p.144; about two hours), though this doesn't actually take you past the falls themselves; or stay on the open ridge top until it dips through dry forest to **Lead Mine Pass**. There's a toilet block here, where the **Wilson Trail** heads south to Shing Mun Reservoir (and a bus to Tsuen Wan; see p.129) in about an hour, or north towards Tai Po (p.141). To reach **Tai Po**, follow the rough, rocky track down for an hour between cane breaks to a road, and then down again until you hit houses and the **green minibus #23K** stop (daily 5.30am–11pm; HK$4.20), which will have you at **Tai Po Market station** in ten minutes. In all, allow five hours for the walk from the Visitors' Centre to Tai Po.

Kam Tin

Around 8km northwest of Tsuen Wan, the small hamlet of **KAM TIN** is famous for its old buildings at **Kat Hing Wai** and **Shui Tau Tsuen**. Actually, even the modern, tiled, low-rise housing estates around town perfectly illustrate Hakka sentiment, their tightly clustered compounds surrounded by walls presenting a blank, fortified face to the world.

Kam Tin's high street is a 250-metre-long stretch of **Kam Tin Road**, whose shops and services include hardware stores, grocers, an ATM, a post office and several **places to eat** offering roast meat and rice dishes. **Bus #51** from Tsuen Wan terminates east outside the post office; the **#64K** between Tai Po and Yuen Long passes through the western side of town; while West Rail trains stop at **Kam Sheung Road station**, 500m south.

Kat Hing Wai

Kat Hing Wai (daily 9am–5pm; HK$3) is a large, old-style fortified Hakka village right in the middle of Kam Tin along Kam Tin Road, which pulls in bus-loads of visitors. It was founded in the fifteenth century by the **Tangs** (p.133) and today is most impressive from the outside, surrounded by a fetid moat and high stone walls, each corner guarded by a watchtower. The defences were originally intended to deter bandits and pirates, but also played their part when the British took over the New Territories in 1898. After villagers here pelted visiting officials with rotten eggs and organized an uprising against the colonial government, the British carted off Kat Hing Wai's **iron gates**, which were shipped to a country estate in Ireland before being returned in a goodwill gesture in 1925. Inside the walls things are not so interesting: the original grid layout of narrow alleys remains but most of the buildings are modern and old Hakka ladies in traditional hats pester visitors with cameras for donations.

Buses set down near Kat Hing Wai on Kam Tin Road; from **Kam Sheung Road station**, take Exit B, cross the bridge over the storm-water canal, and follow signs for 250m.

Shui Tau Tsuen

Off in the countryside about a kilometre north of Kam Tin, **SHUI TAU TSUEN** is another Hakka hamlet founded by the Tangs in the twelfth century, the surrounding fields still grazed by water buffalo. Though from the outside it looks like a modern estate, in among it all are a number of halls and houses from the eighteenth century, and the overall lack of tourists means that you get a good sense of ordinary village life. Most of the old buildings are open only on **Saturday and Sunday** (9am–1pm & 2–5pm; free), when you could spend an hour exploring.

From Kam Tin Road, look for the Mung Yeung Public School and follow narrow Kam Tin Shi Street north from here, over the Kam Tin Bypass and Kam Hing Road bridge, and straight on until you cross a second, bright yellow bridge – the village is right in front of you. Bear around to the right and you'll soon see a cluster of old buildings and bilingual signposts directing you off to others. It's hard to navigate the complex laneways, but wandering at random is part of the fun; pick of the buildings are the unpretentious **Tang Kwong Ancestral Hall**; the **Lik Wing Tong Study Hall**, whose decorative mouldings of pomegranates, peaches and scholars (all representing wisdom) were meant to inspire literary students; and the larger **Yi Tai Study Hall**, whose roof is alive with elaborate eaves and bright decorations. There's a lot of restoration going on at the moment, but look too for ruined compounds with decaying walls covered in trees and shrubs.

Yuen Long

One stop up the West Rail line from Kam Sheung Road, **YUEN LONG** is a scruffy, lively New Town where you might need to change transport. **Castle Peak Road** runs through as the east–west main street, with **Yuen Long station** to the east and **Long Ping station** – also on the West Rail line – to the north. **Bus #64K** from Tai Po and Kam Tin terminates just off Castle Peak Road in the centre of town (closest to Long Ping station); while **bus #K65** to Lau Fau Shan and the **Light Rail** – with connections to almost everywhere westwards of here – both begin from Yuen Long train station. If you're in Yuen Long at lunch time, try the famous and atmospheric *Tai Wing Wah* **restaurant** on On Ning Road, southeast of Long Ping Station (see p.213 for review).

Tin Shui Wai and around

The New Territories' northwestern corner faces China over **Shenzhen Bay**, an outer edge of the Pearl River Delta. The coast here is flat and muddy, fringed with mangroves, arranged into fish farms and overlooked by the oval conurbation of **TIN SHUI WAI**. Unfortunately, this New Town shows just how badly city planning can go wrong if it leaves out the human element: with no central focus, it's an alienating, depressing forest of anonymous concrete high-rises and main roads, all life and activity hidden away inside bland, faceless shopping malls. There are two excellent reasons to visit though: the **Ping Shan Heritage Trail** immediately south of town, with its host of antique buildings; and **Hong Kong Wetland Park**, a sort of compromise between an educational facility and a wildlife refuge. With time to spare, coastal **Lau Fau Shan** makes for a quirky side-trip and offers the chance to eat seafood.

Ping Shan Heritage Trail

The kilometre-long **Ping Shan Heritage Trail** follows signposts south from Tin Shui Wai train station, weaving through the most varied and accessible collection of the New Territories' old buildings. From the station, Exit E3 brings you straight to the **Tsui Sing Lau Pagoda** (Wed–Mon 9am–1pm &

2–5pm; free), a three-storeyed hexagonal tower built in grey brick during the fifteenth century – four more stories were destroyed long ago by lightning. It's the only old pagoda in Hong Kong, originally positioned on the "unlucky" north side of the village to ward off bad luck. From here you follow the road south to a pond and lorry park, where there's a chunky **earth god shrine**, then turn away from the water along a lane marked **Sheung Cheung Wai**. This is actually the name of the walled Hakka village 50m along, whose wooden-barred gateway leads into the usual narrow net of alleys guarding an old ancestor shrine at the back. Outside, the trail continues past a **well**, with the open-air **Yeung Hau Temple** up the slope behind dedicated to the protective deities Hau Wong, To Tei and Kam Fa (for more on whom, see p.169).

Duck back into the lanes here and head downhill for 150m and you're in an open square beside the twinned **Tang and Yu Kiu ancestral halls** (daily 9am–1pm & 2–5pm; free). These grand structures date to the nineteenth century, though the sites are far older, built of granite columns and wooden beams around a set of open courtyards. The elevated platform outside the Tang's hall possibly indicates Imperial favour: the clan's founder **Tang Wai-kap** is said to have married a Song princess, so his descendants can claim connections with the throne. Both halls are still used for important social events. Further down the lane from here, **Kung Ting Study Hall** (daily 9am–1pm & 2–5pm; free) forms a beautiful complex of tiny courtyards and terraces, linked to the elegant **Ching Shu Hin** – a nineteenth-century guesthouse – through a round gateway.

Past here you reach busy **Ping Ha Road**; cross straight over and it's a short way to the immense, stone-built **Shut Hing Study Hall Gate**, carved with scenes from the popular historical novels *Water Margin* and *Romance of the Three Kingdoms*. Sadly, this is the only surviving part of the hall, now fronting a block of 1980s flats. Back at the road, you can catch **bus #K65** west to Lau Fau Shan (see below).

Lau Fau Shan

LAU FAU SHAN is an old fishing village out on the coast a few kilometres northwest of Tin Shui Wai. It's a curious, ramshackle settlement literally built on sea shells, with a clutch of seafood restaurants as the main attraction. To get there, catch the **#K65 bus** (daily 6am–11.15pm; HK$3.70) from **Yuen Long train station** or pick it up en route on Ping Ha Road (see above).

The twenty-minute ride passes through an unplanned wasteland piled high in every direction with **shipping containers** – some have even been turned into prefab homes and offices. The road ends at a small traffic circle and you're immediately greeted by signs directing you to places to eat. Not that you can miss them; Lau Fau Shan's single "street" turns out to be a covered alley running down to the sea between a gauntlet of restaurants and stalls selling marine products. Walk to the end and you emerge onto a shore littered in millions of **oyster shells**, piled into middens, crushed to make lime and incorporated directly into house walls. The smell and colour of the water, however, make it obvious that nowadays all of Lau Fau Shan's seafood is imported – the only part of a local oyster you'd want to touch would be a pearl. Still, the surreal atmosphere and views across the bay to China make it well worth the journey and if you do stay for a meal, all the **restaurants** are pretty reliable: try fish at *Lung Yu*, which has been going since the 1960s; or head to *Siu Tao Yuen* for a mean crab-roe omelette. As usual – whatever you order – it's essential to fix prices first.

Hong Kong Wetland Park

Hong Kong Wetland Park (Wed–Mon 10am–5pm; HK$30; ⓦwww
.wetlandpark.com) covers 61 hectares of saltwater marsh along the Chinese
border north of Tin Shui Wai. Though full of natural attractions, in one way it
shows how the Chinese like nature to be tidy and accessible: there are paths,
landscaped ponds and gardens, and the place is so crammed with noisy, cheerful
crowds that it's unlikely you'll see much wildlife. It's a great place, however, if
you have children and are after an enjoyable half-day excursion; for serious
bird-watching, Mai Po Marshes (p.149) might be a better target. To **get here**,
take Exit E3 from Tin Shui Wai train station and catch the **Light Rail #706** to
the Wetland Park stop, from where it's a five-minute signposted walk. The entire
journey from downtown Hong Kong takes around 1hr 30min.

The park's paths and boardwalks weave over shallow ponds – look for
swimming snakes, fish and wildfowl – to a set of **bird hides**, with telescopes
trained over the mudflats. You'll certainly see herons and egrets; in November
waders, ducks, cryptically camouflaged snipe and – if you're exceedingly
lucky – rare **black-faced spoonbills** (see p.150) drop in. Other highlights
include the **mangrove boardwalk**, where you can watch mudskippers and
fiddler crabs scooting over the mud; and the **butterfly garden**, full of bright
flowers and pretty insects. Back inside, the informative **Visitors' Centre** has
a glassed-in observation deck overlooking ponds, an aquarium with estuarine
fish and gharial **crocodiles**, and tanks full of insects and amphibians. A branch
of *Café de Coral* here serves inexpensive lunches and drinks.

Tuen Mun

Around 9km south of Tin Shui Wai, at the end of the Light Rail and West Rail
lines, **TUEN MUN** was once an important defensive post, guarding the eastern
approaches to the Pearl River estuary below the five-hundred-metre-high
Castle Peak. These days it's a straggling New Town of half a million people
spreading 3km south to the coast along the **Tuen Mun River**, and the only
time you're likely to find yourself in town is for one of Hong Kong's bigger
Dragon Boat Festivals in June. Film buffs might also be interested in **Tsing
Shan Monastery**, halfway up Castle Peak, which – aside from being founded
by the fifth-century Buddhist monk **Beidu** – featured in the opening scenes of
the Bruce Lee film *Enter the Dragon*. From Tuen Mun station, catch the Light
Rail three stops west to **Tsing Shan Tsuen** and then follow the footpath uphill
from near the open-air platform to Yeung Tsing Road. Tsing Shan Monastery
Road is right ahead of you, with a stiff twenty-minute walk up to the monastery
itself. This is a mass of peeling primrose plaster and 1960s concrete all being
renovated to a smarter brick and granite finish, with fine views down over
the town; patchy forest makes it feel quite rural, and gives you an idea of the
temple's former isolation.

The **West Rail station** and adjacent main **Light Rail station** are on the
riverside in the centre of town; from here, the Light Rail and **bus #K52** run
south to **Tuen Mun Port**, where you can catch **ferries** to Tung Chung or Tai
O on Lantau Island (see timetables on p.176). There's also **accommodation**
3km east along the coast at the isolated and not-very-convincing **Hong Kong
Gold Coast** development – **bus #53** from east of the main station on
Castle Peak Road passes by as it runs east along the coast to Tsuen Wan and
the MTR line.

Heading north

The bulk of the New Territories spreads **north** from the Kowloon Hills to the border with China, easily explored along the **East Rail Line** from its terminus at East Tsim Sha Tsui. The route passes through a string of New Towns, all far more characterful than those further west: **Tai Wai** and neighbouring **Sha Tin** offer a clutch of temples and short hikes up minor peaks; **Tai Po** has more of the same plus waterfalls and nature reserves; while the market towns of **Fan Ling** and **Sheung Shui** – the furthest north you can go by train without a Chinese visa – are access points for a couple of heritage trails. From Tai Po or Fan Ling, it's only a short bus ride into some beautiful countryside around easterly **Plover Cove** and **Starling Inlet**; while it's also possible to catch a ferry from the region out to remote **Tung Ping Chau island**.

For more information about crossing the border beyond Sheung Shui at Lo Wu or Lok Ma Chau, see p.30.

Tai Wai

The first stop after the train tunnels under the Kowloon Hills, **TAI WAI** sits at a bend in the **Shing Mun River**, and merges pretty seamlessly with larger Sha Tin to the east. The bulk of Tai Wai comprises spread-out satellite estates below busy **Che Kung Miu Road**, which runs northeast along the south side of the river. It's along Che Kung Miu Road that you'll find Tai Wai's two **temples** and the well-preserved Hakka village of **Tsang Tai Uk**, after which you'll be close to Sha Tin's Heritage Museum (see p.139). Tai Wai is also the start for hikes into nearby Amah and Lion Rock **country parks**.

Tai Wai train station is just north of Che Kung Miu Road; in addition to the East Rail, the **Ma On Shan line** heads up the south side of the Shing Mun River, useful for reaching a couple of the sights. Note that **cycle paths** run from Tai Wai to Sha Tin, then around Tolo Harbour all the way to Tai Po and Plover Cove – some 18km in all. Bikes can be rented from outside Tai Wai station from around HK$10 an hour (or HK$50 a day), though the price rises at the weekend. You'll need to leave your passport or a cash deposit. Some bike outlets have a sister-shop in Tai Po and allow you to return the bicycle there, if you don't want to cycle all the way back.

Che Kung Temple

Just south of the river on Che Kung Miu Road, the imposing **Che Kung Temple** (daily 7am–6pm; free) is dedicated to the deified Song dynasty general Che Kung. **From Tai Wai station**, take Exit B through the bus station onto Che Kung Miu Road, turn left and follow the road until you see a signed underpass to the temple. Alternatively, ride the Ma On Shan Line one stop from Tai Wai to **Che Kung Temple station**, take Exit B and follow the signs – either way takes five minutes.

The temple was founded in the seventeenth century after locals dreamt of Che Kung driving away a plague which was sweeping their valley. The current high-roofed buildings date from 1993, an austere mix of white walls and black slate tiles, with a paved courtyard out front. Inside the spacious main hall, a snarling statue of the general, hand on his sword pommel, towers ten metres up to the roof, surrounded by guardian figures and racks of spiky military weapons. People spin the **brass fans** on his altar for luck – the courtyard walls are also covered in bright plastic pinwheels powered by the wind. Take a

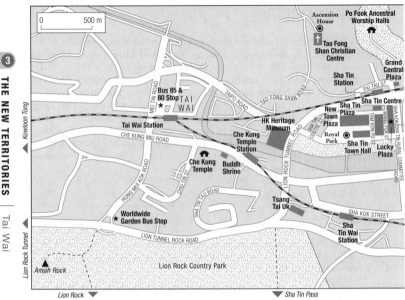

moment to check out the worried couples consulting **fortune tellers** around the main entrance, and the tiny **old temple** hidden away behind the new (it's usually locked, however). There are no fewer than four **festivals** to Che Kung each year, but the biggest by far is held on the second day of Chinese New Year, when the temple is packed with rowdy crowds coming here to pray for good luck.

To Tsang Tai Uk

Exit the temple and turn right (east) along Che Kung Miu Road, and it's not far to the **Four-Faced Buddha Shrine** (daily 7am–5pm; free) – the entrance, marked with a black and gold sign in Chinese, is down some steps overhung with red lanterns. This eccentric little garden, full of potted plants and colourful porcelain figurines, focuses on a Thai form of the Buddha with four faces, housed under a small pavilion sparkling in mirrored tiles. People come here seeking luck at the races (Hong Kong's second horse track is in nearby Sha Tin), and you're supposed to pray to each face in turn, moving around the shrine in an anticlockwise direction. The brick **main hall** behind has five hundred gilt statuettes of *luohans* – Buddhist saints – arranged up the walls, each with unique (and faintly absurd) postures and expressions.

East again, it's only a ten-minute walk following signposts to **TSANG TAI UK**, off Che Kung Miu Road behind some tennis courts. This **walled Hakka village**, built in the 1870s by a wealthy stonemason of the Tsang clan, looks very lost among nearby high-rises and expressways. Each corner of the outer wall sports a square watchtower, adorned with faded stone decoration, and a triple gateway leads into the village and its network of lanes choked with bicycles, gas canisters, discarded furniture and drying washing. What is surprising – especially if you've been out to better-known examples such as Kat Hing Wai (p.131) – is how many **old structures** still survive here, including traditional courtyard homes with *wok yee* baffles, an ancestral hall,

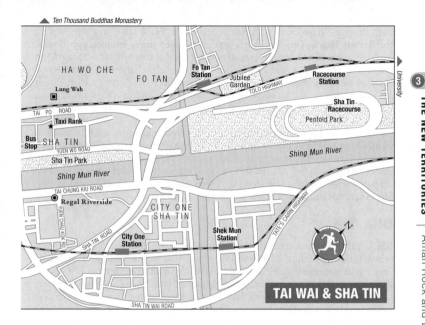

TAI WAI & SHA TIN

and two wells. Tsang Tai Uk's design, incidentally, is closer to Hakka villages found in southern China than to others in Hong Kong.

Walk back to the main road from Tsang Tai Uk and you're within a few minutes' of Che Kung Temple train station or the bridge over the river to Sha Tin's Heritage Museum – see p.139.

Amah Rock and Lion Rock

South of Tai Wai, trails climb wooded hills to **Amah Rock** and **Lion Rock**, whose reclining bulk is one of the most distinctive peaks on the ridges overlooking Kowloon. The walk up along marked paths has fantastic scenery as its reward and, while Lion Rock is a bit of a steep slog, Amah Rock should present no great problems – just take some water along.

The **trail starts** about a kilometre south of Tai Wai train station, where Hung Mui Kok Road runs onto Lion Rock Tunnel Road. It's a pain to get here though: pavements run out partway and you have to cut through housing estates and vegetable plots; and though plenty of buses pass by – take the **#80** or **#85** from outside the station (Exit C) on Mei Tin Road to the "World Wide Garden" stop – if you miss the stop you're on an expressway for the next 5km. It's best then, to catch a **taxi** from Tai Wai (HK$16), though it can be hard explaining where you want to go; try "Amah Rock path" (see p.158 for the Chinese characters). Note that the **MacLehose and Wilson trails** pass through the area, and you can also reach Lion Rock from Wong Tai Sin in Kowloon via the Sha Tin Pass – see p.118.

To the rocks

Once you've made it to the start of the trail, you'll find a toilet block and steps heading up through unexpectedly dense woods – look for monkeys. After about ten minutes you cross a concrete access road with signposts indicating an "Easy Trail" to Amah Rock and a "Hard Trail" to Lion. Aiming for **Amah Rock**, you'll find it a straightforward thirty-minute uphill walk to the cluster of tall granite boulders marking the top, with the Shing Mun River and Sha Tin's tower blocks laid out below. In Cantonese, Amah Rock is called *Mong Fu Shek* or "Yearning for Husband Rock", after a story about a woman who turned to stone waiting for her husband to return home from the sea. Young women make the pilgrimage up here during the annual Maiden's Festival (see p.35).

The trail to **Lion Rock** is also easy enough until you reach a pavilion overlooking Kowloon, from where it's an increasingly rough scramble to the open summits forming the lion's "head" and "rump" – allow two hours for the return climb. At the top, give yourself time to pick a good perch and admire the steep drop down to Kowloon, the views back over Amah Rock to Tai Wai, and Tai Mo Shan's summit rising high to the northwest.

Sha Tin

SHA TIN's name – meaning "sandy fields" – is a distant echo of the days when the surrounding narrow valley either side of the **Shing Mun River** was a patchwork of arable land dotted with small communities. In recent times the entire valley has disappeared under New Towns, all linked by busy roads and train lines, of which Sha Tin was the first and remains the largest, home to half a million people. The setting is impressive, though, with modern development balanced by the high, wild mountains looming to the east. There's a museum here and one of Hong Kong's brightest **temples**, and a quick sniff around will give you an idea of what makes up a typical New Town.

▲ Typical New Town cityscape, Sha Tin

Start out from **Sha Tin train station** on the East Rail line, whose lobby is joined to the air-conditioned leviathan that is **New Town Plaza**, which quite literally covers the entire town centre by linking into smaller, adjoining malls. The shops here are a reproduction of what you'd find in Tsim Sha Tsui or Central: floors dedicated to sportswear, electronics and upmarket clothing, with a sprinkle of cafés and restaurants – the best value ones are above the station in the **Citylink Plaza**. Follow signs through the centre to the **Town Hall** – a theatre venue – and you can exit into riverside **Sha Tin Park** (daily 6.30am–11pm; free), full of bamboo groves, trees and ponds. Head west along the river and it's about ten minutes to the Heritage Museum.

Sha Tin is also home to the **Sha Tin Racecourse**, Hong Kong's second track after Happy Valley. Races take place here most **Saturdays** in season; the biggest event is the Hong Kong Derby each March, a two-kilometre race for four-year-olds and one of the richest horse races in the world. On race days only, East Rail trains stop at Racecourse station, two stops after Sha Tin; for more on Hong Kong's racing scene, see p.253.

There are two business **hotels** in Sha Tin: the *Royal Park*, attached to New Town Plaza; and *Regal Riverside*, across the Shing Mun River and closer to City One station on the Ma On Shan line. You can also stay at the *Ascension House* **hostel** at Tao Fong Shan; see p.189 for details of all of these. As for **restaurants**, you should definitely visit – if not actually eat at – the eccentric *Lung Wah* (p.213), famous for its roast pigeon.

Hong Kong Heritage Museum

The orange-roofed **Hong Kong Heritage Museum** (Mon & Wed–Sat 10am–6pm, Sun 10am–7pm; HK$10, Wed free; ⓦwww.heritagemuseum.gov .hk) sits on the riverside just west of Sha Tin's centre. It's actually closest to Che Kung Temple station on the Ma On Shan line – follow the signs out of the station and over the bridge – or a fifteen-minute walk from Sha Tin station via New Town Plaza and Sha Tin Park. This is Hong Kong's largest museum but, frankly, not one of its best – it's too unfocused, with similar content to the History Museum in Tsim Sha Tsui East (p.108). The highlight is the **Cantonese Opera Heritage Hall**, where you can admire the flamboyant costumes, embroidered shoes, stage props, mock-ups of traditional stage sets and artists' dressing rooms, accompanied by the crashing cymbals of Chinese opera. Other permanent exhibitions include the **T.T. Tsui Gallery of Chinese Art** featuring fine Chinese ceramics, bronze, jade, laquerware and stone sculptures, as well as Tibetan Buddhist statues and thangka paintings; while **The New Territories Heritage Hall** has archeological remains dating back to 4000 BC, accounts of Hong Kong's various Chinese ethnic groups, plus mock-ups of early hardware and medicine shops, and explanations of ancestral worship, feasts and festivals.

The Ten Thousand Buddhas Monastery

Up on the hillside north of Sha Tin, the **Ten Thousand Buddhas Monastery** (daily 10am–5pm; free) is a brightly decorated, appealingly shabby temple dating from the 1960s. **From Sha Tin train station**, take Exit A2 and bear left down the ramp onto the road, which you follow towards the modern Grand Central Plaza building. Turn left again here and after about 50m you reach the entrance to the **Po Fook Ancestral Worship Halls**, comprising a complex of buildings full of memorial plaques and ashes of different families. Bear right, past a public car park and through a mesh fence, and you're on the path. A long,

▲ Statues of Buddhist saints, Ten Thousand Buddhas Monastery

steep flight of steps lead up to the monastery from here, flanked by five hundred life-sized, gold-painted **statues** of Buddhist saints. You emerge onto a terrace beside the main temple, which has an undistinguished exterior but houses around thirteen thousand black-and-gold **Buddha statuettes**, each about a foot high and sculpted in a different posture, lining the walls to a height of thirty feet or more. Outside on the terrace there's a small pagoda, along with floridly painted, shoddy concrete statues of Chinese deities, including a lion and elephant (representing the Buddhist gods of Wisdom and Benevolence). You can buy **vegetarian** lunches here, either off the menu or from a basic, better-value canteen selection.

Tao Fong Shan

Up on a ridge just north of Sha Tin, the **Tao Fong Shan Christian Centre** (Mon–Fri 9am–5pm, Sat & Sun 1.30–5pm) was built in the 1930s in a Chinese style. Tao Fong Shan's founder, the Norwegian evangelist Karl Ludwig Reichelt (1877–1952), wanted to convert Buddhist monks to Christianity and hoped that the buildings would dupe wandering monks seeking sanctuary. Aside from the novelty of seeing a church inside what appears to be a Chinese temple, the centre's workshops sell **artworks** with a Christian theme in various media, including tapestries, porcelain and paper-cuts. You can **stay here** too, at the excellent-value *Ascension House* hostel (p.189).

To get there, take the ramp from Sha Tin train station, but instead of walking straight on for the Ten Thousand Buddhas Monastery, turn back sharp left, parallel to the rail tracks, through Pai Tau village. You'll see a wooden post in front of a large tree, with a green arrow and logo. The path on the right leads up above the village, and, after about ten minutes' climb, brings you out on the main Tao Fong Shan Road, where it joins Pak Lok Path. Keep on up the road for another fifteen minutes or so and you can't miss the centre.

University and Tung Ping Chau

Up from Sha Tin at the mouth of the Shing Mun River, the **Chinese University of Hong Kong** looks northeast up the long, blue expanse of **Tolo Harbour**. The reason to get off the train here at **University station** is to catch a ferry up through Tolo Harbour, a beautiful trip on a sunny day between wild, isolated coastlines. For the **Ma Liu Shui ferry pier**, exit University station into the bus park, take Chak Cheung Street downhill, and then the pedestrian overpass across the Tolo Highway to the waterfront, and the pier is 250m up on the left.

The quickest option here is simply to ride up through the channel to **Wong Shek** on the Sai Kung Peninsula (p.157), taking in the scenery and catching a bus on from Wong Shek to Sai Kung Town. This ferry leaves daily at 8.30am, costs HK$16 during the week and HK$25 at weekends, and takes around two hours.

Alternatively, you can make a round-trip to banana-shaped **Tung Ping Chau**, a fantastically remote island by Hong Kong standards, right up against the Chinese border. It has no permanent residents and is a **marine park**, with a good snorkelling beach and unusually clean surrounding waters. There's a **campsite** at easterly Kang Lau Shek with pit toilets and a barbecue area, but otherwise few facilities – and only seasonal fresh water – so bring everything you'll need for a pleasant stay. It is, however, a popular trip with Hong Kongers: **ferries** only run at **weekends**, leaving Ma Liu Shui at 9am (Sat & Sun) and 3.30pm (Sat only), returning at about 5.15pm; the journey takes ninety minutes and costs HK$80 return.

Tai Po

TAI PO, around a headland from the university at the western end of Tolo Harbour, has been settled for a very long time. In the ninth century, government inspectors were sent to keep and eye on the local **salt** and **pearl** industries, and the Tang clan established a **market** on the north bank of the **Lam Tsuen River** here around 1670. Three hundred years later, the rival Man clan broke their monopoly on prices by setting up a **new market** south of the river, around which a town soon sprang up. By the time the British took over in 1898, Tai Po was the New Territories' de facto capital, and soon had its own **Colonial Office** and **train station**. Though no longer so important to the region, Tai Po is perhaps the most liveable place in all the New Territories, retaining the community feel and town centre of the older settlement, but with added modern amenities and infrastructure. A scattering of old buildings, markets, good food and a **railway museum** make for a couple of hours' exploration, after which there are buses out to scenic spots around Tai Po and at Plover Cove.

Tai Po is split either side of the river, with the older part of town and most of the sights to the south around **Tai Po Market station**, and the newer housing estates north of the river served by **Tai Wo station** – it takes about fifteen minutes to walk between the two. The town's major **bus depot** – useful for reaching outlying attractions – is right next to Tai Po Market station. Tai Po is

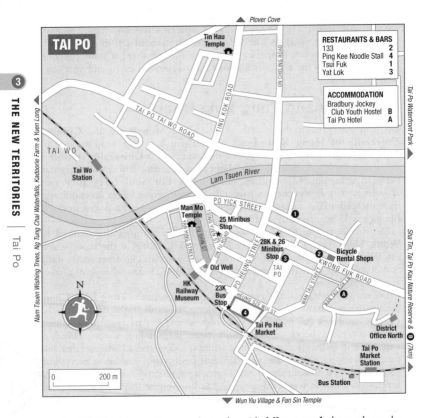

on the Tai Wai–Plover Cove cycle track, with **bike rental** shops along the eastern end of Kwong Fuk Road (see map above) charging HK$40–50 a day.

Sadly – given that Tai Po makes a perfect base for exploring the area – the town's one **hotel** is disappointing, though the youth hostel at Tai Mei Tuk is only a short bus ride away (see p.197 for reviews). **Restaurants** include the excellent *Tsui Fuk* (see p.208) and there are even several **bars** along Kwong Fuk Road such as the *133*, offering happy hours nightly from about 5pm.

The Town

Tai Po is all about markets, and the first place you should head is **Tai Po Hui Market** on Heung Sze Wui Street – turn right as you leave Tai Po Market station, follow the covered walkway alongside the track until you reach the road, turn right again under the railway bridge and it's the huge modern building to your left. It's the usual mix of meat, seafood, vegetables and fruit, with a **cooked food centre** on the second floor serving inexpensive meals – check out the *Ping Kee* noodle stall here, where the dough is kneaded with a bamboo pole. Over the road, Tai Kwong Lane is also full of market stalls and leads into the **old town square**, now a paved area with children's playground surrounded by restaurants.

West of here over On Fu Road, **Fu Shin Street** was the **new market** founded by the Man clan, still busy with shoppers picking through piles of fresh produce, dried seafood and herbs. There's an **old well** at the junction with On Fu Road, hidden behind a low wall under a star-fruit tree (the Chinese characters read "well spirit"); while the granite **Man Mo Temple** halfway down Fu Shin Street was built to mark the market's foundation in 1892, full of smoke, red brocade and carved wooden altars. Uphill at the southern end of On Fu Road, the **Hong Kong Railway Museum** (Mon & Wed–Sun 9am–5pm; free) occupies the unique Chinese-style old station, built in 1913, and is full of wooden furnishings, model trains and photographs documenting the construction of the original Kowloon-to-Canton Railway (KCR). Out the back are coaches and engines from the 1920s to 1950s.

Fifteen minutes' walk away on the eastern side of town – it's most easily reached on a footpath off Kwong Fuk Road – the former **District Office North** once housed the New Territories' colonial administration. This neat brick building currently sits empty at the top of a small hill, but you can admire the high ceilings, shutters and colonnades, all designed to make the tropical summers bearable.

Tin Hau Temple, Waterfront Park and Fan Sin Temple

North of the river, Tai Po's oldest building is the **Tin Hau Temple** on Ting Kok Road, a ten-minute walk from Fu Shin Street via Kwung Fu Bridge; **bus #71K** or **#75K** from Tai Po Market station also run past. The main hall – being heavily renovated at the time of writing – dates to 1691, and is particularly busy during the annual Tin Hau festival (late April/May), when the whole place is decorated with streamers, banners and little windmills.

A kilometre east of here along Tai Po Tai Wo Road, at the mouth of the river, **Tai Po Waterfront Park** offers a great line of sight up the Tolo Channel, which divides the New Territories' two most rural and rugged areas: Plover Cove to the north and southerly Sai Kung. The park itself is fairly new and full of colourful flowerbeds and attractive trees, very much a garden rather than just a park. There's an area for **kite-flying** – banned in most of Hong Kong's public spaces – and a spiral **viewing tower** overlooking the Tolo Harbour to distant Ma On Shan peak and the built-up Shing Mun River. If you don't fancy the walk here, catch **bus #275R** or **#275S** from Tai Po Market station; the park is also on the Tai Wai–Plover Cove cycle track.

There's one last, offbeat attraction a kilometre south of town at **Wun Yiu** village. The easiest way to get here is to catch **green minibus #23K** from Po Heung Street behind Tai Po Hui Market, and get off after you pass under the huge flyover just outside town. Walk along the little canal and cross the footbridge, where you'll see a **sign** pointing up steps to the **Fan Sin Temple** (Mon & Wed–Sun 9am–1pm & 2–5pm; free). The slope is littered with **pottery** shards and there were already kilns here when this temple was founded in the eighteenth century to the three **Fan brothers**, collectively the patron saints of potters. Local kilns were put out of business by mass production in the 1930s, and the temple's interior is new after a fire destroyed the original fittings, but it's an interesting spot to ponder the New Territory's traditions.

Around Tai Po

Tai Po sits below **Tai Mo Shan**'s forested northern slopes (see p.129), which you can explore in varying degrees of comfort. **Tai Po Kau Nature Reserve** and **Kadoorie Farm** are the most accessible places, with well-laid paths and a small zoo at Kadoorie, and make for good excursions with children; **Ng Tung Chai waterfalls** are a steeper proposition, even if you don't continue all the way up onto Tai Mo Shan. There's also a quick, fun trip from Tai Po out to the **Lam Tsuen Wishing Trees**, which you could tie in on the bus ride to the waterfalls and Kadoorie Farm.

Tai Po Kau Nature Reserve

Around 2.5km southeast of Tai Po, the **Tai Po Kau Nature Reserve** is a pleasant, thickly wooded area riddled with walking trails – **green minibus #28K** from Kwong Fuk Road in Tai Po can have you at the pavilion marking the entrance in five minutes (let the driver know where you're going). Walk 100m up the road behind to a **notice board** marking paths into the forest; the colour-coded circuits take from thirty minutes to over three hours to complete. On the way you'll pass streams, boulders and, of course, lots of trees – including Chinese red pine and Australian species introduced prior to 1946, when this was a timber plantation. There are butterflies, too, and monkeys, and the park is also known for its **birdlife**, especially sunbirds and minivets, otherwise rare in Hong Kong. Picnic sites at the reserve makes this a nice place for an outdoor lunch.

The Wishing Trees, Ng Tung Chai waterfalls and Kadoorie Farm

Starting at Tai Po Market station, **bus #64K** (daily 5.40am–12.10am; HK$6.90) runs west past the Wishing Trees, Ng Tung Chai waterfalls and Kadoorie Farm, and then on to the old Hakka settlements at **Kam Tin** (p.131) – though you'd have to be very energetic to cover all of these in a single trip. Note that you can also reach the trees and waterfalls aboard **green minibus #25K** (daily 4.40am–11.30pm; HK$4.80) from Tsing Yuen Street, near Tai Po's Man Mo Temple – see the Tai Po map.

Your first stop is some ten minutes from Tai Po at the **Lam Tsuen Wishing Trees** on Lam Kan Road, where a gnarled old fig near the roadside is propped up with poles against collapse. People used to write their wishes on paper slips, attach them to a weighted string and hurl them into the branches; but branches eventually broke off under the accumulated offerings and now wishes are pinned to a nearby notice board. Back behind here is a newer wishing tree, a pretty **Tin Hau temple** dating to 1736, and an astounding **toilet block**, surgically clean and full of piped music and potted orchids. The grounds are packed at Chinese New Year.

Back on Lam Kan Road and heading west, it's another ten minutes to bus #64K's "Ng Tung Chai" stop for the trail to **Ng Tung Chai waterfalls**. Walk up the sealed side road here (marked "Man Tak Yuen" in Chinese) for ten minutes to **Ng Tung Chai village** – or, if you're on green minibus #25K, just stay aboard the whole way to its terminus at the village. Head uphill again onto a paved path, and it's another fifteen minutes to **Man Tak Yuen**, a private Buddhist retreat. Immediately afterwards the path degenerates into a small, uneven, rocky track through the forest and – finally – there's a signpost for the falls, and a separate trail up to Tai Mo Shan (p.129). Stay on the falls track for ten minutes to the **Bottom Falls**, a tight, rocky canyon shaded by trees and cliffs; not much further, **Middle Falls** is a thin cascade tracing the rocks in foam, rather like a Chinese scroll painting. The track becomes much steeper and rougher after this for the final half-hour ascent to the **Main Falls**, where a fifty-metre-high ribbon of water drops into a plunge-pool wrapped in forest.

Back down below on Lam Kan Road aboard bus #64K, the next stop is a kilometre west at **Kadoorie Farm** (daily 9.30am–5pm; HK$10; check opening hours – it's closed for even minor holidays – on Ⓦ www.kfbg.org.hk or ☎ 2483 7200). Beautifully located among forest on a steep hillside, this working farm experiments with organic and sustainable agriculture, the results arranged in terraces up the slopes. You can get a look by following paths up through a forested gully, emerging high up with views north. The farm also serves as a **sanctuary** for injured and orphaned animals, with muntjac deer, leopard cats, birds of prey and wild boar on show – probably your one chance to see any of these shy, usually nocturnal animals at close range.

Tai Mei Tuk and Plover Cove

Northeast around Tolo Harbour from Tai Po, **Plover Cove** fronts for some attractive coastline and rugged countryside within **Plover Cove Country Park**. This was once a remote, marginal farming area, though nowadays most of the population have migrated to town and left the landscape to the weekend recreational crowd, here to picnic or hike along the host of walking trails – not all of them arduous. Access is via the little service centre of **Tai Mei Tuk**, 7km from Tai Po Market station on **bus #75K** (daily 5.30am–11.35pm; HK$4.70) or **green minibus #20C** (daily 5.30am–1am; HK$6) – it's also on the cycle route from Tai Wai, via Sha Tin and Tai Po.

Tai Mei Tuk

The bus terminates at **TAI MEI TUK**, which comprises an enormous car park and small village at the edge of the **Plover Cove Reservoir**. This was once a bay on the sea, but in 1967 it was blocked off by a dam wall and flooded with fresh water to provide a drinking supply for Hong Kong. The little peninsula before the dam shelters a barbecue site, watersports centre and the *Bradbury Jockey Club Youth Hostel* (p.197), the only accommodation nearby aside from a **campsite** two kilometres north along the road.

Across the main road from the bus stop, the **village** offers a string of **restaurants**, popular at weekends with expats, along with drink stalls and a line of **bike rental places** (HK$30–65 a day). Walk on up the road 250m, and you'll find a **Country Park Visitors' Centre** (Sat & Sun 9.30am–4.30pm) with useful information boards on local flora, fauna and geology, plus the start of **walking trails** north to Bride's Pool (see below) and west along the high ridges of the **Pat Sin Leng** range (p.147).

Plover Cove Country Park

The only road heads north from Tai Mei Tuk along the western edge of **Plover Cove Country Park**, past endless barbecue sites overlooking the reservoir. Follow it, and it's an hour or so to **Bride's Pool**, where you'll find a patch of forest just off the road hiding a series of **waterfalls** and lots of picnickers. You can also get here in two hours on the marked **Pat Sin Leng Nature Trail** from the Visitors' Centre, following a steep, rocky track through Pat Sin Leng's wooded foothills.

There are plenty of walks from Bride's Pool – make sure you stock up with refreshments at Tai Mei Tuk as there's nothing available along the way. The most obvious is to circuit clockwise all the way around Plover Cove Reservoir and back to Tai Mei Tuk along **Plover Cove Reservoir Country Trail** – a straightforward walk with excellent coastal scenery, but hot and long (8hr). Another good – and shorter – hike takes you east through the centre of the

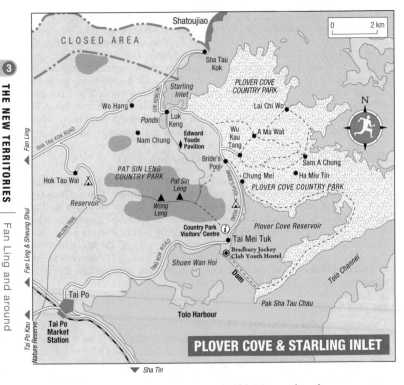

PLOVER COVE & STARLING INLET

country park and out to the coast at **Lai Chi Wo**, rated as the most remote inhabited village in Hong Kong, though actually most of the houses have been abandoned. From Bride's Pool, take paths upstream to open fields at **Wu Kau Tang**. Follow signposts here towards Sam A Chung and then **Sam A Tsuen**, from where you climb over a small ridge to the coast at Lai Chi Wo – about 2 hours 30 minutes in all. Lai Chi Wo's encircling **Feng Shui Wood** – so-called because it was planted to improve the luck of the village – has some mighty old trees, while views from slopes above take in a beautiful, isle-studded bay. For the return journey, head for **A Ma Wat**, and then back to Bride's Pool via San Uk Ha village – a further two hours.

Incidentally, the main road continues north past Bride's Pool for another hour to **Luk Keng** on Starling Inlet, where you can pick up a minibus to Fan Ling – see p.148.

Fan Ling and around

FAN LING – the next stop up the East Rail line from Tai Wo – is itself an unexceptional residential New Town, though a good **heritage trail** on the eastern outskirts showcases the region's long Hakka history. You'll also need the **green minibus terminus** in the train station's forecourt (Exit A) to reach more distant sights, including the **Pat Sin Leng trail** (see box opposite) and Starling Inlet.

If you have time, drop into Fan Ling's large, modern **Fung Ying Seen Koon** Taoist temple (daily 8am–5pm) – take Exit B from the train station and it's two minutes' walk. The central **main hall** contains statues of the Three Purities, each representing different aspects of the elusive Tao, and flying cranes painted on the ceiling symbolize the Taoist quest for immortality. If you're here in the early morning you can watch people practising tai chi – itself related to Taoism – around the complex's terraces. In keeping with many large temples in Hong Kong, other buildings here are mostly **ancestral halls**, housing remains of the deceased – a very profitable business (see p.326). You can also get lunch at the temple's **vegetarian restaurant** (daily 11am–5pm); they have English menus and their generously sized "prawn", "beef" and mushroom dishes work out around HK$50 each.

Lung Yeuk Tau Heritage Trail

The kilometre-long **Lung Yeuk Tau Heritage Trail** features several Hakka hamlets settled by the Tang clan during the fourteenth century – though the oldest buildings here date only to the eighteenth century. It's all relatively low-key, but definitely worth a look if you haven't seen the more comprehensive trails at Ping Shan or Kam Tin.

From Fan Ling train station, catch **green minibus #54K** and get out, after crossing a canal east of town, by the **Shung Him Church**, built in 1951. From here, follow purple trail markers past the **Shek Lo mansion** – a 1920s

---

Hiking Pat Sin Leng

The ten-kilometre-long trail between Hok Tau Wai and Tai Mei Tuk, along the serrated heights of **Pat Sin Leng** – the Eight Immortals' Ridge – is one of the most satisfying day-hikes that the New Territories can offer, with continually excellent scenery. Most of the route follows stage 9 of the **Wilson Trail**, and you can start at either end, though the advantages to hiking east from Hok Tau Wai – as described below – is that the bus knocks the first few hundred metres off the ascent, plus you'll finish among Tai Mei Tuk's restaurants and drink stalls. Be aware that there are many steep sections, and that most of the hike is spent in open country with no shade; read the **hiking information** on p.252 before setting out. Allow six hours walking time for the trip.

Start by catching **green minibus #52B** (daily 6am–8.20pm; HK$4.50) east from Fan Ling train station to its terminus at **Hok Tau Wai**, a scattering of houses out in the countryside. With a Chinese cemetery on your right, follow the sealed road for twenty minutes past **Hok Tau campsite** – an excellent place with trees, a toilet block, tables and barbecue pits – to **Hok Tau Reservoir**, Hong Kong's smallest. The path runs clockwise around the edge to more picnic spots, where you'll see signs for the Wilson Trail pointing up through pine woods; not much further on, you bear left into the open and begin the increasingly rough ascent. Around forty minutes later you'll be up on the ridge top, in the midst of undulating heath, patches of dwarf bamboo, grassland, gullies full of tea trees and wide, wide vistas encompassing Tai Po, Starling Inlet, the Chinese border and Tolo Harbour. From here it's an easy walk east along the crest to the trail's apex and halfway point at **Wong Leng** ridge – the 639-metre-high triangulation marker is a great spot to sit and eat lunch. After here the trail constantly climbs and descends, eventually reaching the rocky outcrop of **Shun Yeung Fung**, the first of the eight little summits named after the Taoist Immortals. The ups and downs now become extreme, though short, until you reach the last peak, **Hsien Ku Fung**, which sits right above Tai Mei Tuk and Plover Cove. From here it's all downhill through forest to join the Tai Mei Tuk–Bride's Pool trail – turn right onto it and you'll be at the Tai Mei Tuk Visitors' Centre (p.145) in half an hour.

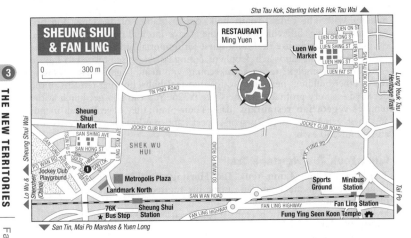

SHEUNG SHUI & FAN LING

0   300 m

RESTAURANT
Ming Yuen   **1**

LUEN ON ST
LUEN CHEONG ST
LUEN SHING ST
Luen Wo
Market
LUEN HING ST
LUEN FAT ST
SHA TAU KOK ROAD

Lung Yeuk Tau
Heritage Trail

TIN PING ROAD

Sheung
Shui
Market

JOCKEY CLUB ROAD

JOCKEY CLUB ROAD

SAN SHING AVE
SAN HONG ST

SHEK WU
HUI

PIK FUNG RD

SO KWUN PO ROAD

Jockey Club
Playground

Metropolis Plaza

Sports
Ground

Minibus
Station

Landmark North

SAN WAN ROAD

Tai Po

76K
Bus Stop

Sheung Shui
Station

Fan Ling Station

FAN LING HIGHWAY

FAN LING HIGHWAY

Fung Ying Seen Koon Temple

Shenzhen
(China)

Lo Wu &

Sheung Shui Wai

THE NEW TERRITORIES | Fan Ling and around

3

Chinese–European affair, half overgrown in a field – to **Ma Wat Wai**. This former fortified village has now lost its walls and overflows its original boundaries, but the arched stone entrance and gates made from interlinked iron rings remain. The worn sandstone inscription over the door reads *wat chung*, literally "flourishing onions" – a reference to the village's fertile fields.

Past here, turn right at a little earth god shrine and follow the road to **Lo Wai**, Lung Yeuk Tau's original settlement, whose ancient, 4.5-metre-high stone walls remain an insurmountable barrier: the village is closed to tourists. Around the corner, the splendidly decorated **Tang Chung Ling Ancestral Hall** (Mon & Wed–Sun 9am–1pm & 2–5pm; free) is dedicated to the Tang clan's founder; look for two dragon-headed memorial tablets in the main hall, that of the founder and his Song princess wife. After this it's a ten-minute walk north, across busy Shau Tau Kok Road, to **Kun Lung Wai** (also known as San Wai), whose imposing walls, watchtowers and iron gates surround modern buildings. You can catch **green minibus #56K** back to Fan Ling station from here.

Starling Inlet (Sha Tau Kok Hoi)

Starling Inlet, also known as **Sha Tau Kok Hoi**, is a nicely low-key, rural district facing over the water into China 8km northeast of Fan Ling. Villages up this way used to celebrate the Mid-Autumn festival by releasing little candle-powered **hot air balloons** made of rice paper, which would drift off into the night sky; a practice now banned for causing hill fires. **Green minibus #56K** from Fan Ling train station runs out here to **Luk Keng**, a peaceful village right on the foreshore, with a few kiosks and snack stalls near the bus stop. This unpretentious place marks the end of the **Wilson Trail**, which originated 78km away on southern Hong Kong Island (see p.92), and it's also a good spot to watch **birds** – there are mangroves fringing the muddy shore and a set of **freshwater ponds** in the low-lying marshes inland at Nam Chung. To reach these, walk back towards Fan Ling for about a kilometre until you reach a road heading south; this runs alongside the ponds, then climbs the gentle slope behind to the **Edward Youde Memorial Pavilion**.

East along the road from Luk Keng's bus stop, you soon come to a notice board indicating a half-hour "Family Walk" up onto the headland, which looks across the inlet to the Mainland settlement of **Sha Tau Kok** (or **Shatoujiao** in Mandarin Chinese) and its massive industrial wharves. Stay on the main road instead, and it's about an hour's walk southeast to **Bride's Pool** (see p.145).

Sheung Shui

A few minutes by train beyond Fan Ling and only 3km from the border, **SHEUNG SHUI** is a workaday market town with some antique corners; you'll need to stop here to catch a **bus** for the **Mai Po marshes** and old villages around **San Tin**. Note that Sheung Shui is as far as you are allowed to go by train without a Chinese visa: if you don't have one, you must get out here.

From the train station, take Exit B2 onto a walkway past the town's major shopping centre, **Landmark North**, skirt around it to the left and descend to the corner of Lung Sim Avenue and **San Fat Street**. Walk up the latter for 150m and you're facing a large **fig tree** – social focus for villages all over Asia – and an earth god shrine, surrounded by buildings long past their prime. There's no shortage of **restaurants** nearby: for a plate of roast meat and rice, or bowl of noodles, try the *Ming Yuen* on the corner of San Fat and Fu Hing streets. Turn right here and then left onto narrow **San Hong Street**, site of the old produce market before it shifted to an indoor facility in the east of town; the street retains a "village" feel, full of small, family-run shops selling clothes and dried goods – altogether unlike the average New Town.

Continue to the end of San Hong Street, cross San Fung Avenue and follow purple heritage signposts for fifteen minutes up **Po Wan Road** to **Sheung Shui Wai** (aka **Po Sheung Tsuen**). As usual, a seemingly modern estate conceals plenty of old buildings from Sheung Shui's original Hakka settlement, including stone gateways and the eighteenth-century **Liu Man Shek Tong** (Wed & Thurs, Sat & Sun, 9am–1pm & 2–5pm; free), an ancestral hall to the Liu clan from Fujian province. Though the hall is the usual courtyard design – rectangular, built in grey brick and with colourful roof ridges – few foreign visitors make it out here, and the atmosphere is a lifetime away from Tsim Sha Tsui.

Along the border: San Tin and the Mai Po Marshes

The **border with China** follows the course of the Sham Chun River, with two official crossing points at **Lo Wu** (the main one for tourists) and **Lok Ma Chau**. Without a visa you're not allowed to cross into the buffer zone before the border, but you can get within spitting distance of it around Hakka monuments at **San Tin**; and at the **Mai Po Marshes**, an international wetlands sanctuary for wildfowl. Both lie west from Sheung Shui on the **#76K bus** route (6am–10pm; HK$4.30) from Choi Yuen Road, behind Sheung Shui train station. Note that the bus also continues on **to Yuen Long** (p.132), passing Yuen Long station and terminating one block south of Long Ping station, both on West Rail line.

San Tin

SAN TIN hamlet is 5km west of Sheung Shui down the Fanling–Yuen Long road, via the huge **Hong Kong Golf Course**. Get off the #76K bus at the

"San Tin" stop, where a couple of small stores and a fuel station mark the village entrance. Tucked away behind the bus stop, the small **Tung Shan Temple** is mostly set aside for Tin Hau, with an unlikely painting of a European square-rigged ship inside the door.

Walk up the street away from the main road, and within five minutes you'll be at **Tai Fu Tai** (Mon & Wed–Sun 9am–1pm, 2–5pm; free), a beautiful study hall built for the wealthy Man clan in 1865 to encourage family scholarship. It's set at the back of a spacious lawn – a certain sign of wealth in Hong Kong – and there are some excellent murals inside, carved wooden panels and glazed friezes in high relief on the rooftops. From here, press on through the maze of quiet streets and you'll wind up in a long square at **Fan Tin Tsuen**, where three large and ragged **ancestral halls** lurk among car parks and nondescript old buildings co-opted into workshops. The best of these, the **Man Lun Fung Ancestral Hall**, was built in the mid-seventeenth century in honour of the clan founder, **Man Lung-fung**, who had migrated here from Jiangxi province two hundred years earlier and claimed connections to the Song dynasty general Man Tin-cheung. Despite a wobbly state of repair, the hall is in regular use as a meeting place, and faces north to China across the village's muddy cabbage fields.

Mai Po Marshes

The shallow, swampy coast west from San Tin has, since the 1940s, been divided into fish-farming ponds known as **gei wai**. These are filled during the fishing season and then allowed to drain in winter, exposing a 1500 hectare area of mudflats and embankments known as the **Mai Po Marshes**, a designated site of international importance for migratory waterfowl. About a quarter of the world's entire population of **black-faced spoonbills** turn up here each November, along with rare **Saunder's Gull** and various ducks and waders, making it the best place in all Hong Kong for some serious bird-watching.

For the marshes, get of the #76K bus at the "Mai Po" stop, cross the road and walk back 100m, then take the side road off across the marshes for twenty minutes to where the WWF (World Wildlife Fund) maintains an **information centre**. They run three-hour **guided tours** every Saturday and Sunday (HK$70 per person; more info and bookings at ⓦwww.wwf.org.hk/eng /maipo or ☏2471 3480); at other times you still need to contact them for advice as the reserve butts right up against the no-go border zone, and you don't want to cross it by accident.

The east coast

The New Territories' **east coast** splits into two main regions. The southernmost is a small peninsula around **Clearwater Bay**, where you can spend a day between beaches, a hiking track and an old Tin Hau temple. North of here, the much larger **Sai Kung Peninsula** has tremendous outdoor appeal, with enough to tie you up for several trips: the best beaches in Hong Kong, some beautiful hiking trails and a couple of little islands, all reached through the laid-back resort town of **Sai Kung**.

Access to Clearwater Bay and Sai Kung Town is by bus from **Diamond Hill**, reached on the Kwun Tong MTR line: the bus station is right outside the MTR exit (see p.118). For the Sai Kung Peninsula, you'll need additional transport from Sai Kung Town.

Clearwater Bay

Bus #91 (daily 6am–10.25pm; HK$6.10) from Diamond Hill runs east and then south along Clearwater Bay Road, a pleasant half-hour's ride through striking countryside, dotted with expensive villas overlooking the coast below. About halfway to Clearwater Bay you'll pass the old **Shaw Brothers' film studios**, where countless martial arts movies were churned out between 1934 and the 1980s, when the company abandoned cinema for TV. Now the site is

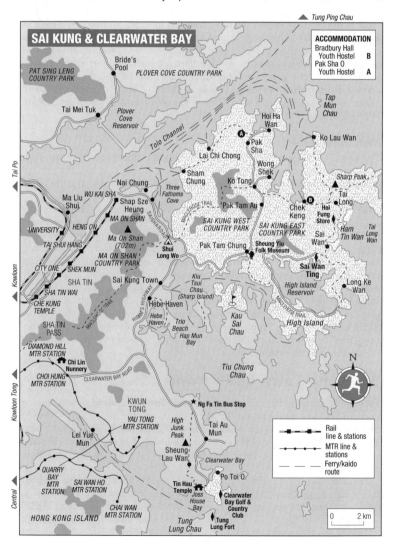

SAI KUNG & CLEARWATER BAY

ACCOMMODATION	
Bradbury Hall Youth Hostel	**B**
Pak Sha O Youth Hostel	**A**

occupied by Celestial Pictures, who own the rights to the Shaws' back catalogue and are busily remastering this gold mine on to DVD.

Eventually the bus reaches **Clearwater Bay** itself; get off at **Tai Au Mun** for the first, smaller **beach** (known as #1 beach), or continue down the hill to the bus terminus at the much bigger #2 beach. Count on this being packed on a sunny weekend, despite its size, and take your own food if you've come for the day, as there's only a snack kiosk here. A path connects the two beaches if you want to check on space at either one.

South from Clearwater Bay, the road continues for a final 1500m to the gates of the members-only **Clearwater Bay Golf and Country Club** – catch green minibus #16 from Clearwater Bay to its terminus by the gates. From here, a short flight of steps descend to where a beautifully sited **Tin Hau Temple** (daily 8am–5pm; free), founded in 1266, overlooks the coast at **Joss House Bay**. This is *the* major site for Hong Kong's annual Tin Hau celebrations, and there's a long pier below the temple where thousands of passengers disembark from the special chartered junks and ferries to come to pay homage to the goddess of the sea. A small track behind the hall leads to a **rock inscription** recording a visit made by a Song dynasty official in charge of salt administration in 1274 – the oldest-known dated inscription in Hong Kong.

High Junk Peak

The whole Clearwater Bay peninsula is overlooked by the spiky, 344-metre-high tip of **High Junk Peak**, with an excellent 6.5km hiking trail over the top and down to Joss House Bay. This is best made on an overcast day, as there's little cover en route.

For the start, you need to get off the #91 bus shortly before Clearwater Bay at the "Ng Fa Tin" stop, where there's a concrete pavilion with a green roof, a trail map, and signs pointing to "Tai Miu". Follow these up onto the open ridge, and then walk along the obvious dirt track. Around forty minutes along the path splits, with the partially barricaded left-hand fork heading up through thick undergrowth towards the crest, culminating in a short, very steep scramble to the top. Hong Kong Island, Sai Kung, a wild seascape and some incredible building projects are spread below; the hunchbacked island just off the peninsula's tip is **Tung Lung Chau**, reached by ferry from Kowloon (see p.120). From here it's a precipitous, slippery and potentially dangerous descent back to the main path, with a further hour or so to Joss House Bay and the temple.

Sai Kung Town and around

Facing east across an attractive bay, **Sai Kung Town** is a blend of local fishing port and low-key tourist retreat, set where the skirt of the mountainous **Ma On Shan Country Park** drops down to the sea. There are buses northeast onto the Sai Kung Peninsula and ferries to nearby islands, but the town itself is also a mellow place just to hang out over lunch at one of the waterfront restaurants.

Bus #92 from Diamond Hill (daily 6am–11pm; HK$5.50) takes half an hour to get here along Hiram's Highway via a marina full of yachts, cruisers and fishing boats at **Hebe Haven**. Alternatively, **bus #299** (daily 6am–midnight; HK$9) from New Town Plaza in Sha Tin takes about the same time via the south side of Tolo Harbour, a beautiful run past cityscape and sea views.

▲ Catch of the day, Sai Kung Town waterfront

The Town

SAI KUNG TOWN is a handful of streets between the highway and the sea, with the open-air **bus station** on the seafront just to the north. The paved **waterfront promenade** with its two long jetties is where to find small boats selling their catches of prawns, squid and fish; you point to what you want, negotiate the price and it's banged on the head, scaled and gutted and passed up to you in a long-handled net. A string of Chinese **seafood restaurants** along the water will cook it for you, or you can choose your meal straight out of their tanks; the best is probably the *Chuen Kee* (which also serves *yum cha* until early afternoon), though many cheaper places are just as appealing.

There's a strong expat presence in town, too, and in the streets back from the water you'll come across a few **pubs**, including the *Duke of York*, at 42–56 Fuk Man Rd, as well as several **café-restaurants** such as *Jaspa's* (13 Sha Tsui Path) and *Cru* (18 Wan King Path), offering breakfasts, coffee and meals at Lan Kwai Fong prices – see p.213 for reviews of these and others. There's a **supermarket** for picnic supplies if you're heading out to one of the beaches or the country parks, and heaps of small stores selling beach gear – trunks, plastic buckets, inflatable rings and the like. Sai Kung has no **accommodation** – the nearest places to stay are the **Shui Long Wo** campsite (p.154) and the Sai Kung Peninsula's two youth hostels.

Nearby islands and beaches

Along the Sai Kung Town quayside you'll be accosted by people selling tickets for *kaidos*, which run across to **islands and beaches** in the vicinity. It's sometimes a bit tricky to work out exactly where the boats are going, as there are no signs and few people speak English, but if you don't really mind and just want to hit a beach, take off with the first that offers itself – they leave and return at regular intervals all day, so you shouldn't get stuck anywhere you don't want to.

A popular trip is the short run across to **Kiu Tsui Chau** (also known as Sharp Island). Most of the island's rocky coast is inaccessible, and the main destination is the beach at **Hap Mun Bay**, at the island's southern tip, though it's small and can get mobbed at weekends. There are barbecue pits and a snack bar, and a rough trail up through thick vegetation to the island's highest point. Be warned that getting back to Sai Kung Town from Hap Mun Bay can be a bit of a scrum: you have to leave on a boat with the same coloured flag as the one that you came on, and, as there's no such thing as a queue in Hong Kong, it can be a fight to get aboard. *Kaidos* also run from Sai Kung Town to **Kiu Tsui**, a small bay to the northwest side of the island.

The island past Kiu Tsui Chau is larger **Kau Sai Chau**, with a regular **ferry** (Mon–Thurs 6.40am–7pm & Fri-Sun 6.40am–9pm; every 20min; HK$60 return) from its own jetty on the Sai Kung Town waterfront. Most people come out here to play **golf** at the **Jockey Club KSC Public Golf Course** (Ⓦwww.kscgolf.org.hk for fees and information) covering the north half of the island, the only public course in Hong Kong. There's also a **prehistoric stone carving** on the west shore, and a three-kilometre trail down to a splendidly decorated **Hung Shing Temple** at the island's southern end.

Other *kaidos* from Sai Kung Town head out past Kau Sai Chau to bays at **High Island**, now actually part of the mainland since the creation of the High Island Reservoir (see p.156). You can also catch *kaidos* from the yachting centre of **Hebe Haven** (Pak Sha Wan) south of Sai Kung Town, across to little **Trio Beach**, stuck at the end of a narrow peninsula opposite.

Ma On Shan Country Park

The high plateau running southwest behind Sai Kung Town forms **Ma On Shan Country Park**, traversed by some excellent – and demanding – sections of the MacLehose Trail. The most obvious target is 702-metre-high Ma On Shan peak, but you can also hike all the way back to Wong Tai Sin in Kowloon in around eight hours – after which you'll feel you've really achieved something. Neither options are a gentle stroll: you'll need good weather, water, food and a **map** – see p.252 for more information on hiking in Hong Kong.

For **Ma On Shan peak**, catch **bus #99** or **#299** from Sai Kung Town north to the "O Tau New Village" stop (about 10min), then walk 100m on up the road to where toilets, barbecue sites and an Agriculture & Fisheries depot mark where the **MacLehose Trail** crosses the road. Head west up the trail (section 4), which initially follows a concrete track through forest, and after about ten minutes you reach **Shui Long Wo campsite**, a flat glade with fire pits, stone benches and toilets. Another couple of hours along the signposted trail takes you up through forest and bamboo thickets to emerge below the seemingly impossible peak; press on and ever upwards and you'll arrive at a pass, with an undulating plateau and the main trail stretching away to the southwest. Ma On Shan's rocky **summit** is immediately north, needing one final burst of energy up an unmaintained, slippery side-track, and the truly spectacular views – south to Lion Rock, east over Sai Kung's coast, and west to Tai Po – are worth whatever it has taken you to get up here. Give yourself four or five hours for the return trip from the main road.

If you haven't had enough, descend back onto the MacLehose trail, which continues southwest along the **Ngong Ping Plateau** – a straightforward and largely downhill few hours through light woodland and open grassland to **Buffalo Hill**. You pass over this, then up again to the **Gilwell Camp** which marks the start of section 5. There's a road here but no transport: you need to cross it and spend another forty minutes tramping through woods, past World War II trenches and bunkers, to where the MacLehose and Wilson trails converge at a roadside pavilion overlooking Kowloon. Follow this road west for a further half hour and you're at **Sha Tin Pass** (p.118), with a short descent down to Wong Tai Sin's MTR station.

The Sai Kung Peninsula

Northeast of Sai Kung Town, the **Sai Kung Peninsula** comprises a 7500-hectare expanse of rugged, forested interior and a coastline twisted into supremely isolated headlands, coves and beaches. As with Plover Cove, this remote area was never widely populated and today all the peninsula's villages have been virtually abandoned, the few residents hanging on to provide services to the day-trippers who flock here each weekend for a breath of unpolluted country air. Away from the crowded picnic grounds, there's a marvellous stretch of sand at **Tai Long Wan**; the grassy island of **Tap Mun Chau**; and endless **hiking** opportunities on a network of paths spreading out from the first stages of the **MacLehose Trail**.

The peninsula is bisected by a single road running from Sai Kung Town, via a Visitors' Centre at **Pak Tam Chung**, to the tiny settlement of **Hoi Ha Wan** on the north coast. To the left of the road lies **Sai Kung West Country Park**, with **Sai Kung East Country Park** to the right. The area is served daily by a handful of **buses and minibuses**, most originating in Sai Kung Town – see accounts for details. The peninsula is well supplied with **campsites**, and two of Hong Kong's remoter **youth hostels** are out this way, too; just make sure you bring supplies as there are few places to eat and no shops to speak of.

All the hikes described below are along marked paths, but for serious exploration you'll need to pick up the relevant **maps** – see p.46 for details. **Tour operators** specializing in Sai Kung's outdoor attractions include Explore Sai Kung (Ⓦwww .exploresaikung.com) and Kayak-and-Hike (Ⓦwww.kayak-and-hike.com), along with a host of scuba operators – see p.251.

The MacLehose Trail

The hundred-kilometre-long **MacLehose Trail** stretches right across the New Territories from east to west. Starting at **Pak Tam Chung** near Sai Kung Town (p.156), it crosses the Sai Kung Peninsula, climbs **Ma On Shan** (p.154), cuts southwest to Sha Tin Pass and **Lion Rock** (p.138), veers up past **Shing Mun Reservoir** (p.129) and **Tai Mo Shan** (p.129), then follows the hills along the western coastline and so down to **Tuen Mun** (p.134). The trail is divided into ten signposted sections, most of which connect with public transport and so can be done individually – none take longer than a day. You could manage the whole trail in four or five days, but most people take it slower, particularly in the summer, when the going is hot; there are several **campsites** and one **youth hostel** along the route. An annual charity race sets teams a 48-hour target for the course; the winners usually manage it in well under 24, while the record (set by Gurkha troops) is just 13.

For more **information** about hiking in Hong Kong – including websites, trail guides and maps – see p.252.

Pak Tam Chung

Some 6km from Sai Kung Town, **Pak Tam Chung** is the Sai Kung Peninsula's "gateway", reached daily from Sai Kung Town on **bus #94** (6am–9pm; HK$5.50) or **green minibuses #9** (6.30am–9pm; HK$5.50) or **#7** (7.55am–6.25pm; HK$10). On Sundays you can also get here direct from Diamond Hill on **bus #96R** (7.30am–6.20pm; HK$15.60). Don't come to Pak Tam Chung expecting a town: there are shaded picnic areas, a large car park and bus stop, a kiosk, and the **Sai Kung Country Park Visitors' Centre** (Mon & Wed–Sun 9.30am–4.30pm), whose staff can provide hiking and access information.

Of the many short walks around Pak Tam Chung, the most interesting follows a fifteen-minute concrete track to **Sheung Yiu village**. This turns southeast off the main road along a small inlet lined with mangrove, long'an and pandanus trees, passing a **lime kiln** where seashells were once processed for whitewash and fertilizer. The village itself is now **Sheung Yiu Folk Museum** (Mon & Wed–Sun 9am–4pm; free), a modest Hakka fortress which grew from a roadside teahouse during the nineteenth century. It's more a family compound than a "village", with a single long building divided into separate kitchens, lofts and living spaces, all filled with old furniture and farm tools. The thick defensive wall is impressive, built to deter the pirates and bandits who roamed these parts at the time. After the lime industry collapsed in the 1950s, Sheung Yiu's inhabitants were left without an income and had to move out, and the family's descendants now all live overseas.

To High Island Reservoir

Walk a few minutes north along the main road from Pak Tam Chung – past the trail to Sheung Yiu – and you're at an intersection marking the start of the mighty **MacLehose Trail** (see box, p.155). The first section runs southeast for 10km along the southern side of **High Island Reservoir**, created in 1978 by actually welding an island onto the adjacent coastline, thereby turning a former marine channel into a freshwater catchment area. The trail follows a level service road for almost the whole way, popular with joggers, and ends around three hours later at **Long Ke Wan**, a coastal bay with a **campsite** and fine beach.

From Long Ke Wan, you could also pick up **section two** of the MacLehose trail and follow it north over Sai Wan Hill, up the coast to Tai Long Wan beach and then inland to the road at Pak Tam Au (see opposite). Give yourself a further five hours to complete this section, making for a full – but not too strenuous – day's walk.

Tai Long Wan

If you're looking for a beach with your walk, then aim for the long stretches of yellow sand at **Tai Long Wan** (Big Wave Bay). Although swimming isn't always safe due to strong undercurrents, the scenery is vivid, with a peacock-blue sea backed by steep headlands and high, deep green hills. You won't be the only one here, but crowds are minimized by the fact that you have to walk there – either along section two of the MacLehose trail, or more easily from **Sai Wan Ting**, a small pavilion at the end of a nearby service road. **Minibus #29R** to Sai Wan Ting departs daily from outside *McDonald's* on Chan Man Street, Sai Kung Town (Mon–Sat 9.15am, 11.30am and 3.30pm; Sun eleven services 8.30am–4.30pm; HK$15); it's a special service which seats 28 people and doesn't stop along the way. A **taxi** to Sai Wan Ting costs HK$85.

From Sai Wan Ting, follow a marked concrete track for forty minutes and you'll be at the southern end of Tai Long Wan at **Sai Wan village**, a knot of restaurant shacks (open weekends) overlooking a steep-sided, rocky inlet. The beach here is OK, with a campsite at its northern end, but press on over the next headland – following the MacLehose Trail – and down to **Ham Tin Wan**, a deep, open beach with the *Hoi Fung Store* (☎2328 2315) providing cold drinks and simple stir-fried dishes under the awnings. They can also sell you beach towels and mosquito repellent, and even rent out surfboards, camping gear and very basic **bungalows** – contact them in advance. Immediately north of here is an even better, longer beach at **Tai Wan**.

From Ham Tin Wan, the MacLehose trail turns west and inland to **Tai Long village** – perhaps the closest thing Hong Kong has to an unimproved old Hakka settlement, with a handful of unpretentious walled houses. The path then climbs to a saddle, from where a side-track heads northeast along the ridge and up the slippery summit of appropriately named **Sharp Peak**. Stay on the MacLehose Trail, however, and it's another ninety minutes, past the splendidly located *Bradbury Hall* **youth hostel** (p.196), to the main road at **Pak Tam Au** and buses back to Sai Kung Town.

Pak Tam Au and Wong Shek

Just over 2km up the road from Pak Tam Chung, **Pak Tam Au** is simply a **stop** for the #94 or #96R buses and green minibus #7, where the MacLehose trail crosses the road. You can walk east from here along section two, past *Bradbury Hall* youth hostel, to Tai Long Wan (see above), or west along **section three**. This takes a tough four hours with a serious uphill stretch at the start, but the reward is in crossing the whole of Sai Kung West Country Park. You wind up on the road at the start of the Ma On Shan hike (p.154), from where you can catch bus #99 or #299 south to Sai Kung Town.

A short way north of Pak Tam Au, the road splits, with the left branch and green minibus #7 running to its end at Hoi Ha Wan, while the #94 and #96R buses bear right for a final kilometre to **Wong Shek**. This comprises the bus stop, a clutch of barbecue pits and a long pier facing north up the narrow bay, where you can catch a **ferry to Tap Mun Chau** (Mon–Fri seven daily 8.30am–6.30pm, HK$8; Sat & Sun twelve daily 8.30am–6.35pm, HK$12), and arrange *kaitos* to *Bradbury Hall* youth hostel. There's also a ferry south to **Ma Liu Shui Pier** near Sha Tin (see p.141; daily 10.35am and 4.55pm; HK$16–25).

Tap Mun Chau

Ferries to **Tap Mun Chau** dock in a sheltered inlet on the island's west side that contains the only **village** – a single line of crumbling houses and small shops overlooking the fish farms that constitute the only industry. It's a run-down, ramshackle kind of place, nice and quiet, with the houses on the only street open to the pavement. There's a Tin Hau temple along here, too (to the left of the pier), the venue for a large annual festival, while to the right of the pier a fishermen's quarter straddles the low hill – nets and tackle stacked and stored in the huts and houses, many built on stilts over the water.

A couple of paths spread across the 2.5-kilometre-long island, which is surprisingly green, leading to its English name of "Grass Island". After you've ambled around, the only thing to do is to head back to the main street and its one good **restaurant**, the *New Hon Kee*; left from the ferry pier, and it's on the first corner. There's no English sign, but there is an English menu, which offers reasonable seafood, fried rice and beer in a room overlooking the water.

Don't miss the last ferry whatever you do – be at the pier in plenty of time. There's no accommodation on Tap Mun Chau, and even the restaurant owners don't live on the island but back in the New Territories.

Hoi Ha Wan

HOI HA WAN, a small village formerly known as **Jones' Cove**, sits just east of Sai Kung's northernmost tip, overlooking the Tolo Channel. It's a very quiet place with a long but gritty beach, well sited for shore walks – many people follow the two-hour **Tai Tan Country Trail** eastwards down the coast to Wong Shek. Just east past the village, large dry-stone cylinders are the remains of former **lime kilns**, a profitable business at one time. Now that shells are no longer harvested, the **bay** out front has been designated a **marine park** known for its hard corals, whose staff provide free ninety-minute **tours** on Sundays at 10.30am and 2.15pm – you have to book in person on the day at the warden post in the village. Despite marine park status – and a **WWF research centre** built out over the water beyond the lime kilns – it's not unusual to see people fishing here; this is quite legal and shows that Hong Kong's environmental protection legislation has some way to go.

Green minibus #7 from Sai Kung Town terminates at the village; it runs two or three times an hour, but crowds mean it can be a bit of a wait to get on at the weekends. The village has a stack of **restaurant shacks** above the beach, where you can sit under awnings with a beer and eat fried rice, noodles and basic seafood dishes; some places also rent out snorkelling gear. For **accommodation** nearby, head about a kilometre back down the road to the *Pak Sha O Youth Hostel* (see p.197) – you'll need to book in advance.

Places	
Amah Rock path	望夫石徑
Bride's Pool	新娘潭
Clearwater Bay	清水灣
Fan Ling	粉嶺
Hebe Haven	白沙灣
High Island Reservoir	萬宜水庫
High Junk Peak	釣魚翁
Hoi Ha Wan	海下灣
Hok Tau	鶴藪
Joss House Bay	大廟灣
Kam Shan Country Park	金山郊野公園
Kam Tin	錦田
Kau Sai Chau	滘西洲
Kiu Tsui Chau	橋咀洲
Lai Chi Wo	荔枝窩
Lau Fau Shan	流浮山
Luk Keng	鹿頸
Lung Yeuk Tau Heritage Trail	龍躍頭文物徑
Mai Po Marshes	米埔濕地
Ma On Shan Country Park	馬鞍山郊野公園
New Territories	新界
Pak Tam Chung	北潭涌
Ping Shan Heritage Trail	屏山文博徑
Plover Cove Country Park	船灣郊野公園
Sai Kung	西貢
San Tin	新田

Sham Tseng	深井
Sha Tin	沙田
Sheung Shui	上水
Shing Mun Country Park	城門 郊野公園
Starling Inlet	沙頭角海
Tai Long Wan	大浪灣
Tai Mei Tuk	大尾督
Tai Mo Shan Country Park	大帽山郊野公園
Tai Po	大埔
Tai Po Kau Nature Reserve	大埔滘自然護理區
Tai Wai	大圍
Tap Mun Chau	塔門洲
Tin Shui Wai	天水圍
Tsuen Wan	荃灣
Tuen Mun	屯門
Tung Lung Chau	東龍洲
Tung Ping Chau	東坪洲
Wong Shek	黃石
Wun Yiu village	碗窰村
Yuen Long	元朗香港中文大學

Sights

Amah Rock	望夫石
Che Kung Temple	車公廟
Chinese University	香港中文大學
Clearwater Bay Country Club	清水灣鄉村俱樂部
District Office North	舊北區理民府
Fan Sin Temple	樊仙宮
Four-Faced Buddha Shrine	四面佛廟
Fung Ying Seen Koon	蓬瀛仙館
Fu Shin Street	富喜街
Hong Kong Heritage Museum	香港文化博物館
Hong Kong Railway Museum	香港鐵路博物館
Hong Kong Wetland Park	香港濕地公園
Jockey Club Tak Wah Park	賽馬會 德華公園
Kadoorie Farm	嘉道理農場
Kat Hing Wai	吉慶圍圍村
Lam Tsuen Wishing Tree	林村許願樹
Lion Rock	獅子石
Liu Man Shek Tong Ancestral Hall	廖萬石堂
Man Mo Temple	文武廟
Man Tak Yuen	萬德苑
New Town Plaza	新城市廣場
Ng Tung Chai waterfalls	梧桐寨瀑布
Pat Sin Leng	八仙嶺
Pineapple Dam	菠蘿壩
Po Fook Ancestral Worship Halls	寶福社堂
Sam Tung Uk Museum	三棟屋博物館
Sha Tin Racecourse	沙田跑馬場
Sheung Yiu Folk Museum	上窰民俗文物館
Shing Mun Reservoir	城門水塘
Shui Tau Tsuen	水頭村圍村
Tai Fu Tai	大夫第
Tai Po Hui Market	大埔綜合大廈
Tai Po Waterfront Park	大埔海濱公園

Tao Fong Shan	道風山
Ten Thousand Buddhas Monastery	萬佛寺
Tin Hau Temple	天后宮
Tsang Tai Uk	曾大屋圍村
Tsing Shan Monastery	青山禪院

Transport

Bus stop	巴士站
East Rail station	東鐵綫 車站
Light Rail station	輕便鐵車站
Ma Liu Shui ferry pier	馬料水渡輪碼頭
Ma On Shan line station	馬鞍山綫 車站
MacLehose Trail	麥理浩徑
MTR station	地下鐵車站
West Rail station	西鐵綫車站
Wilson Trail	衞奕信徑

4

The outlying islands

Hong Kong's 260-odd **outlying islands** were part of the package that Britain leased from China in 1898 along with the New Territories. While many are tiny, uninhabited specks of land scattered about in the South China Sea, a southwesterly group of four – **Lamma**, **Cheung Chau**, **Peng Chau** and **Lantau** – stand out for their mix of easy accessibility, beaches, scenery, good food and distinctive island communities. None are exactly uncharted territory, and all have been developed to some extent – indeed, these islands have been settled since the Stone Age – but the pace of life here is positively rural compared with Central or Kowloon.

If you have time only for one island, it's hard to pass over Lantau, whose cultural diversions, practically deserted hiking trails and excellent beaches are enough to tie you up for a couple of days. Otherwise, at least make a quick trip to either Lamma, Cheung Chau or – to a lesser extent – Peng Chau for some great **seafood**; Cheng Chau's extraordinary **bun festival** in June is not to be missed either. Lantau, Cheung Chau and Lamma all offer a range of **accommodation**, too, at lower rates than the downtown, though just about within commuter distance – expect price hikes and room shortages on Friday and Saturday nights, however.

For other **minor islands**, accessible from various points on Hong Kong Island and in the New Territories, see: Tung Ping Chau p.141; Po Toi islands p.94; Tap Mun Chau p.157; and Tung Lung Chau p.120.

▲ The Lamma ferry departing from Central

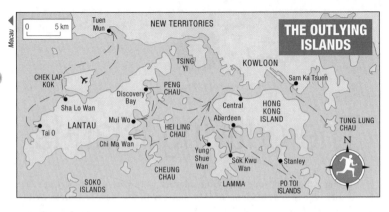

Getting there

The main **ferries** to Lamma, Cheung Chau, Peng Chau and Lantau all depart from the **Outlying Islands Ferry Piers** on Hong Kong Island, just west of the Star Ferry Pier in Central. There's a mix of ordinary and fast ferries, and they run pretty well around the clock, though services thin out between midnight and 6am. **Fares** range from about HK$11.50–32 each way; children under 12 pay half price. You can't reserve seats, and you pay or use your Octopus Card (see p.25) at the gate. Services are busier (and, in some cases, more frequent and more expensive) on **Sunday**, with enormous queues at the piers. None of the journeys is very long – around an hour maximum – and if you can't get a seat, you can always lounge on deck; coming back into Hong Kong, especially, the views are fabulous. Some of the ferries have a small **bar** selling coffee, sandwiches, hot noodles, cold drinks and beer. You can pick up **timetables** at ticket offices or from the HKTB, though schedule outlines are given in the island accounts below, along with **other ferries** and *kaido* services from elsewhere.

Note that major disruption to timetables can occur during the **typhoon season** (June–Oct), when ferry services can be abandoned at very short notice – contact the ferry companies direct using the details at the end of each island account.

If you don't mind splashing out, arranging a **charter boat** is possible: enquire at ferry piers on the islands, look in the classified sections of the newspapers or *HK Magazine*, or contact the HKTB for information. **Restaurant cruises** (see p.217) also often visit island beaches.

Finally, Lantau Island is also accessible by **rail** along the **Tung Chung MTR Line** from Central – see p.26 for further details.

Lamma

The closest inhabited island to Hong Kong – Aberdeen is only 3km from its northern point – **LAMMA** is an elongated fourteen square kilometres of land with some five thousand residents. It's a peaceful place: motorized traffic is limited to four-wheel bikes carting trailers, and the only downsides are views of the three massive chimneys rising above Lamma's coal-fired

power station. This supplies Hong Kong Island with most of its electricity, recently supplemented by a greener – if no less obvious – hilltop **wind turbine**, Hong Kong's first.

Well-marked paths link the main settlement, **Yung Shue Wan**, with small beaches, green hillsides and pleasant seascapes, and you can round off an easy couple of hours' walking with a meal at the tiny village of **Sok Kwu Wan**, famed for its seafood restaurants. **Ferries** run from Central to both Yung Shue Wan and Sok Kwu Wan, with additional services between the latter and Aberdeen, so whichever one you arrive at there's no need to retrace your steps. There's also **accommodation** (see p.189) on the island if you'd like to stay over.

Yung Shue Wan

YUNG SHUE WAN ("Banyan Bay") is a pretty, tree-shaded village at the northwestern end of the island where the bulk of Lamma's population lives. A good number of them are expats with distinctly New Age views, seeking a more mellow existence than that offered by city life – check out their take on the island at ⓦ www.lamma.com.hk.

If you've come to Lamma for a walk, there's nothing much to stop you heading off straight away, though Yung Shue Wan itself is worth a quick look:

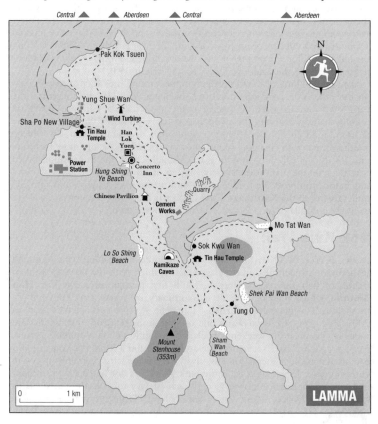

the seafront esplanade is **Yung Shue Wan Main Street**, at the end of which a typically gloomy, century-old **Tin Hau temple** overlooks the water. There are several **places to stay**, some small grocery stores, a **bank** with an ATM (though there's often no cash available after Saturday afternoon) and a **post office**. The current pick of several **seafood restaurants** are waterfront tables at *Lamma Seaview Man Fung Restaurant* (☎2982 0719) and *Sampan Seafood* (☎2982 2388), both near the pier and offering fresh crab, abalone, prawns and fish from live tanks, which will set you up nicely for an afternoon's walk. Lamma's expat scene focuses around the nearby *Island Bar* and the *Bookworm Café*, the latter 150m around the bay on Main Street, which offers organic vegetarian meals – including mighty breakfasts – along with **internet**.

The walk to Sok Kwu Wan

It's about an hour on foot southeast across the island to Sok Kwu Wan. In Yung Shue Wan, take the turning just after 64 Main Street into Yung Shue Wan Back Street, and follow the signs to "Hung Shing Yeh". If you want to **rent bicycles** for the journey, though the route is quite hilly, you can get them from the Hoi Nam Bicycle Shop just after Yung Shue Wan in Sha Po New Village, which charges HK$50 for a day.

It's a twenty-minute walk along a concrete path to **Hung Shing Ye**, where there's a tiny, shaded sand beach with unfortunately close views of the power station. It's nice enough when it's empty, however, and there are barbecue pits and a shower block. Nearby places to eat include the *Han Lok Yuen* (☎2982 0608) up the hill, known for its roast pigeon; and the beachside *Concerto Inn*, whose outdoor terrace overlooks the sand – you can also stay here (p.195).

From Hung Shing Ye, the footpath continues around the beach and up the hill on the other side, now signposted to "Sok Kwu Wan". It's not long until the path levels out to reach a viewing point marked by a **Chinese pavilion**, roughly halfway between the two villages. Carry on down the hill, and at the bottom, amid the houses, there's a signposted diversion to **Lo So Shing**, another beach with changing rooms, showers, a snack kiosk and more barbecue pits. It's usually OK for swimming, too, though check the information board first. Back on the main path, it's only another fifteen minutes to Sok Kwu Wan. Just before you cross the bridge at the end of the inlet a sign points into the undergrowth to the **Kamikaze Caves**, constructed by the Japanese in 1944–45 to house a flotilla of suicide motor boats, but never used.

Sok Kwu Wan

SOK KWU WAN is literally one hundred-metre-long lane jammed in-between a small hill and the bay, which is thick with the floating wooden frames of **fish farms**. Walking in, you'll first pass an attractive **Tin Hau Temple**, whose interior is made extraordinary by a glass tank containing a preserved, 2.75-metre-long **oarfish**, a rare deep-sea species trawled by locals in 2001. Past here, Sok Kwu Wan's line of waterfront **seafood restaurants** are sociably chaotic at the weekends, packed to the gills with face-stuffing patrons. Most restaurants have set menus averaging HK$200 a head, but you can also eat off the normal menu for less; always fix prices first, certainly if you're choosing your fish straight from the tank. As there's not much between them in terms of appearance and service, the easiest way to pick a restaurant is to look for the busiest. More entrepreneurial establishments such as *Rainbow Seafood* (☎2982 8100, ⓦwww.rainbowrest.com.hk) have set up a **free ferry**

Lamma ferries

Services **from Central** are run by Hong Kong and Kowloon Ferry Ltd (☎2815 6063, ⓦwww.hkkf.com.hk); Yung Shue Wan is 35 minutes by ordinary ferry and 20 minutes by fast, ferry, while it takes 25 minutes (fast ferry only) to Sok Kwu Wan. Services **from Aberdeen** are run by Chuen Kee Ferry Ltd (☎2375 7883, ⓦwww.ferry.com.hk) and take 30 minutes to Sok Kwu Wan via Mo Tat Wan.

Outlying Islands Ferry Piers to: Yung Shue Wan (Mon–Sat 31 daily, every 20–30min, 6.30am–12.30am; Sun 30 daily, 7.30am–12.30am); Sok Kwu Wan (Mon–Sat 11 daily, Sun 16 daily; 7.20am–11.30pm).

Aberdeen to: Mo Tat Wan then on to Sok Kwu Wan (Mon–Sat 13 daily, Sun 19 daily; 6.40am–10.50pm).

Yung Shue Wan to: Outlying Islands Ferry Piers (Mon–Sat 30 daily, 6.20am–11.30am; Sun 27 daily, 6.40am–11.30pm).

Sok Kwu Wan to: Outlying Islands Ferry Piers (Mon–Sat 11 daily, Sun 16 daily; 6.45am–10.40pm); Mo Tat Wan and then on to Aberdeen (Mon–Sat 13 daily, Sun 19 daily; 6am–10.10pm).

service for customers between Sok Kwu Wan and Central or the Tsim Sha Tsui waterfront; check the website for timetables and booking information. **Leaving** Sok Kwu Wan, there are regular ferries to both Central and Aberdeen – see box above for details.

Mo Tat Wan, Tung O and Mount Stenhouse

If you arrive early enough, there are a couple of other targets around Sok Kwu Wan to occupy the time before dinner. It's a 25-minute walk (left as you step off the ferry pier) to **Mo Tat Wan**, another small beach village, quieter than the others on the island – the Aberdeen–Sok Kwu Wan ferry stops here. The path continues from here for a kilometre or so to the bigger beach at **Shek Pai Wan** on the southeastern coast, and then to **Tung O**, a minute settlement famous as the childhood home of Hong Kong action star **Chow Yun-fat**. Past Tung O, smaller **Sham Wan beach** is perhaps the remotest on the island, and worth heading to if only for that reason.

Cast around a bit, either in Sok Kwu Wan or at Shek Pai Wan and Sham Wan, and it's not difficult to find one of the paths that lead eventually to the summit of **Mount Stenhouse** (also known as Shan Tei Tong), 353m up in the middle of the island's southwestern bulge. It's quite a climb, particularly since the paths aren't wonderful, but you'll be rewarded with some fine views. It should take around two hours from Sok Kwu Wan to climb up and down again; take plenty of water.

Cheung Chau

A fifty-minute ferry-ride southwest of Hong Kong Island, **CHEUNG CHAU** is the most densely populated of the outlying islands: thirty thousand people live here, the central waist of its dumb-bell shape is crammed with buildings, and its harbour is busy around the clock. Life here is in many ways independent of the fortunes of Hong Kong, with a prosperity based on

Tai Chiu Bun Festival

Every year, in late April/early May, Pak Tai Temple hosts the four-day **Tai Chiu Bun Festival,** held to appease the vengeful spirits of those killed by Cheung Chau's pirates. The action centres around the square in front of the Pak Tai Temple, where a set of twenty-metre-high, conical bamboo scaffolds are set up and completely studded in **steamed buns** dyed pink and painted with auspicious symbols. Temporary halls and shrines fill the rest of the square; there are martial arts displays, lion dances and Pak Tai's sword and chair are carried through the town. Around noon on the penultimate day, a float of **children**, all dressed up as historical characters and balancing atop of special poles, are paraded along the main streets; and then, at midnight, there's a race to scale the towers and grab as many buns as possible, which are later distributed among the crowds.

The island is packed to capacity during the festival – extra ferries are laid on from Hong Kong – and you'll need to book long in advance if you want to stay (and expect to pay well above standard rates). But it's a fascinating time to come: as well as the displays, there is a host of religious services, Chinese opera performances and all the noise and bustle that the Cantonese bring to any celebration. Note that **only vegetarian food** is eaten on the island during the festival.

fishing, supplemented in the past with smuggling and piracy, and Cheung Chau's strong local culture is manifest in one of Hong Kong's best annual events, the **Tai Chiu Bun Festival** (see box above). Concrete **paths** cover the entire island and, despite the name (meaning "long island"), you can whip around the place fairly quickly. Cheung Chau's two or three **beaches** are regularly crowded, but the island is a great place to wander around backstreets, watch waterfront activity, grab a meal and perhaps stay overnight for a glimpse into village life. Like Lamma, no cars are allowed, though look out for **bicycles** speeding through the narrow, crowded streets.

Cheung Chau Village

The ferry from Central picks its way through the breakwaters and junks to dock at **CHEUNG CHAU VILLAGE**, where the island's population and activity is concentrated. The waterfront road, or **Praya** (the full name is Pak She Praya Rd) is a good place for a walk and view of the harbour, packed with ferries, *kaido*, trawlers and ancient and modern sampans and junks, some with families living on them. The main **market** is south from the ferry pier inside a modern building, understandably excellent for seafood; opposite the pier, **Tung Wan Road** leads across the island's waist to Tung Wan Beach (see opposite) past an ancient **banyan tree** surrounded by little porcelain statuettes of Kwan Ti, and whose branches are garlanded in red ribbons. The Japanese are said to have executed prisoners here during World War II.

One block in from the water, the main thoroughfare, **San Hing Street**, leads up about 500m north to the **Pak Tai Temple** (daily 7am–5pm; donation requested), built in 1788 and today facing basketball courts. Not surprisingly for an island so dependent on the sea, the inhabitants deemed it prudent to dedicate a temple to Pak Tai, whose abilities include being able to control waters. It's a compact, beautifully decorated place with a beardless statue of Pak Tai behind the carved main altar. A room off a courtyard to the left holds an eight-hundred-year-old **iron sword**, fished out of the sea, and a gilded nineteenth-century sedan chair, made to carry the god's image during festivals.

Around the island

There are a number of places to head for **around the island**, none of them taking you more than thirty minutes from town. Most people aim for east-coast **Tung Wan Beach**: nearly 800m of fine sand and as popular as anywhere in Hong Kong at the weekend. At the southern end, below the *Warwick Hotel*, a glassed-in shed protects a three thousand-year-old **rock carving**, though it's impossible to say what these squiggles and lines represent. Just past here, around the little headland, there's another sweep of sand, **Kwun Yam Wan Beach** (aka Afternoon Beach), probably the best on the island.

If you've got a couple of hours, the **southern** part of the island offers a good **circular walk**, much of it along tree-shaded paths. From the ferry pier, either head south along the shore for twenty minutes or jump in a *kaido* (5min; HK$3) to **Sai Wan** at Cheung Chau's southwestern tip. A path up the hill here leads to

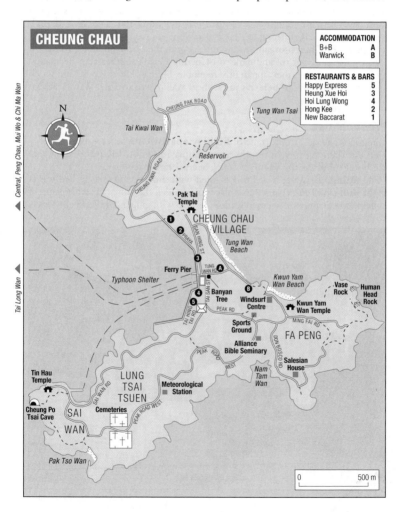

a rocky bluff where a nicely positioned **Tin Hau Temple** stares out to sea; carry on and you'll reach steps down to **Cheung Po Tsai Cave**. Cheung Po Tsai was a nineteenth-century pirate whose small armada of boats harassed shipping in the area, much to the embarrassment of the local authorities, who failed to defeat him in battle. In the end, the government negotiated Cheung Po Tsai's "surrender" in return for an official title. This cave is said to have been his hideout on Cheung Chau, and the agile can climb through the underground passage here: you'll need a flashlight, and the scramble is fairly hard going, though faint hearts will be shamed by the queue of elderly women risking the drop into the abyss with their grandchildren.

Back on the main path – here called **Peak Road West** – there's a **barbecue area** with covered seating and toilets, from where you can take a side-path down between the rocks onto a small rocky beach – though you might have to wade at this point if the tide is in – and back up to another headland covered in large, rounded granite boulders with some superb views over the sea on a calm day. The path continues down to small and sandy **Pak Tso Wan**, though it's a little grubby. Returning to Peak Road West, you pass a series of **cemeteries** and clutch of Church organizations and schools, then bear off along Ming Fai Road. This leads out to landmarks on Cheung Chau's southeastern headlands, all named after what they apparently resemble: Human Head Rock, Vase Rock and Loofa Rock. From here, it's just a short walk down to Tung Wan Beach or back to town.

Practicalities

Cheung Chau has no shortage of **holiday apartments** to let – exit the ferry pier and there's a row of booths ahead displaying photo albums – and there are hotel rooms at the *Warwick Hotel*. See p.195 for reviews.

For **eating**, the waterfront Praya is lined with small restaurants, decked out at night with tables and chairs. Most places offer much the same fare, with plates of delicious garlic prawns, steamed scallops or crab with ginger at HK$75–100 each.

▲ Bicycle rental, Cheung Chau

Cheung Chau ferries

Ordinary ferries (55min) run alternately with fast ferries (40min) between Central and Cheung Chau, while all sailings from Tsim Sha Tsui use fast ferries. For up-to-date ferry information, contact the New World First Ferry Company (℡2131 8181, ⓦwww .nwff.com.hk).

Ferries and fast ferries

Outlying Islands Ferry Piers to: Cheung Chau (daily, every 30min around the clock except for reduced sailings between 12.30am and 6.10am).

Cheung Chau to: Outlying Islands Ferry Piers (daily, every 30min around the clock, except for reduced service between 11.45pm and 5.10am).

Inter-island ferries

Cheung Chau to: Chi Ma Wan and Mui Wo (both on Lantau) and on to Peng Chau (daily, roughly every 2hr, first at 6am, last at 10.50pm; not every departure calls at every stop, so check the timetable at the pier).

North from the ferry pier, *New Baccarat* and the *Hong Kee* are typical and good, while *Heung Xue Hoi* is a popular *dim sum* place serving steamers until late afternoon. South from the ferry pier, the *Hoi Lung Wong* has no English sign but is unmissable for its size and tanks of live seafood outside; *Happy Express* (aka *Tin Yin Dessert*) specializes in all sorts of sweet desserts − banana splits, fruit salads, mango, sago and durian confections. To stock up on **picnic** food, head to the market for fruit and roast meats; there's also a Wellcome supermarket on the seafront and a Park N Shop near the banyan tree.

There are **bike rental** stands charging HK$10 an hour on the Praya, up north from the ferry pier. To rent a **kaido** for a tour around Cheung Chau's waters (roughly HK$150 an hour), head to the small pier just south of where the main ferries dock. The HSBC **bank**, at the northern end of the Praya, opens on Saturday mornings in addition to normal banking hours, and there are several ATMs around town.

Leaving Cheung Chau, there are regular daily ferries both back to Central and onwards to Lantau − see box above for details.

Peng Chau

PENG CHAU is a tiny horseshoe-shaped blob of land forty minutes from Hong Kong. Though pleasant in a very laid-back way there are no obvious attractions, but you can drop in en route to Cheung Chau or Lantau and spend a couple of hours exploring the place.

Wing On Street, just back from the pier, is a typical island street: part market, part residential, with a few noodle shops, Chinese herbalists and no traffic. A Qing dynasty proclamation carved on a stone tablet outside the **Tin Hau Temple** (7am−5pm) here cancels government orders allowing troops to borrow fishing boats in order to fight pirates; the temple itself dates to 1792 and has some splendidly carved wooden screens. Nearby, a large roadside shrine covered in coiled dragons and flower tiles is dedicated to **Kam Fa**, literally "Golden Flower". Originally a minor deity whom fisherman prayed to for bountiful catches, today she's also taken over helping women in childbirth and her cult is enjoying a surge of popularity.

Peng Chau travel details

Ferries and fast ferries

Ordinary ferries (40min) and fast ferries (25min) run roughly alternately. For up-to-date ferry information, contact the New World First Ferry Company (℡2131 8181, ⓦwww .nwff.com.hk).

Outlying Islands Ferry Piers to: Peng Chau (daily, at least hourly, 7am–12.30am, plus one service at 3am).

Peng Chau to: Outlying Islands Ferry Piers (daily, at least hourly, 6.15am–11.30pm, with one service at 3.25am).

Inter-island ferries

Peng Chau to: Mui Wo, Lantau (daily, roughly every 2hr, 5.40am–11.40pm). Most services also call in at Chi Ma Wan (Lantau) and then continue to Cheung Chau; check the timetable at the pier.

Kaidos

Kaidos depart from the small jetty next to the main ferry pier.

Peng Chau to: Discovery Bay, Lantau (daily, 20 services 6.30am–10pm); services between 8am and 5pm travel via the Trappist Dairy jetty (Lantau).

Don't bother with **Tung Wan**, the island's only beach, which is gritty and strewn with flotsam; but the walk up to **Finger Hill**, Peng Chau's 95-metre apex, provides some excellent views over to Lantau. If you want a **feed**, try the *Hoi King*, tucked a way next to the waterfront, a friendly and inexpensive place offering *yum cha*, seafood and fried rice dishes.

Lantau

By far the biggest island in the territory at around 25 kilometres across, **LANTAU** and its charms could occupy several days. Its beaches are some of Hong Kong's best and cultural attractions include the unusual fishing village of **Tai O** – from where you might see **pink dolphins** – and the **cable car ride** up to the world's largest seated outdoor **bronze Buddha** statue at **Po Lin Monastery**.

Lantau enjoys a venerable history, with archeological remains dating back to the stone age found on the southwest peninsula. It seems that even these earliest settlers farmed **salt**, which by the Song dynasty had become a major source of income for the islanders. This put them at odds with the Chinese government, which was trying to regulate the trade, and in 1197 salt producers staged an **uprising** on Lantau, put down with great brutality by the regional governor. The first of the island's **forts** were built then, and it was here that the last vestiges of the Song dynasty court sought sanctuary, while fleeing the invading Mongols in 1277. Both the Portuguese and British tried to set up trading posts on Lantau during the sixteenth and seventeenth centuries, which led to a revival of the island's coastal fortifications, later strengthened again to keep an eye on piracy. But by the twentieth century these had again been abandoned, and Lantau's population was confined to a handful of scattered fishing villages.

All this changed in 1998 with the opening of Hong Kong's **new airport** at Chek Lap Kok island, just off Lantau's **north coast**. The nearby sleepy settlement of **Tung Chung** has since transformed into a busy transport hub and ever-expanding New Town, while Hong Kong's **Disneyland** has set up to the east. Elsewhere the island retains a more rural feel: central Po Lin Monastery sits part-way up **Lantau Peak**, one of the highest in Hong Kong, whose summit can be reached along part of the lengthy **Lantau Trail**. The island's **south coast** is lined with long, empty stretches of sand, while the easterly small town of **Mui Wo** is a nice place to pull up for a couple of days' relaxation.

The easiest way to **reach Lantau** is by **train** aboard the orange **Tung Chung MTR Line**, which runs parallel with the Airport Express along Lantau's north coast to Disneyland and Tung Chung. You can pick it up at its terminus at Hong Kong Island station in Central, at Kowloon Station in Kowloon, or Olympic station, west of Mong Kok. There's also an interchange with the red Tsuen Wan MTR line at Lai King station. **Ferries from Central** head to the east coast at Mui Wo and Discovery Bay.

Once here, **local buses** cover most of the island – though bear in mind that they put their prices up at the weekends – as do Lantau's pale blue **taxis**. Many people turn their Lantau trip into a **circuit**, starting off in Tung Chung, riding the cable car to Po Lin, taking a bus to Tai O, then heading east along the south coast to pick up a ferry back to Central from Mui Wo. If you want to stay longer, there's a clutch of beachside **hotels** at Mui Wo, two **youth hostels** – one near the monastery below Lantau Peak – and a handful of **campsites**, along the south coast in particular.

The north coast

The Tung Chung MTR line runs southwest down Lantau's **north coast**, taking in the bayside scenery across to Castle Peak and Tuen Mun in the New Territories. Change trains at **Sunny Bay** for Disneyland, or stay aboard to the **Tung Chung terminus**, from where you can catch the cable car to Po Lin Monastery, or a bus to anywhere on the island.

Disneyland

Hong Kong Disneyland (daily 10am–7pm; adults HK$295, children aged 3–11 HK$210, special events HK$350/250; ⓦ www.hongkongdisneyland .com) is the smallest of this entertainment superpower's five franchises. Attractions include "Main Street USA", a shopping mall dolled up to resemble a typical Midwest Town around 1900; "Tomorrowland", featuring a spaceship flight-simulator and giant rollercoaster; "Adventureland", where you ride a jungle boat through Lion King country to Tarzan's treehouse; and "Fantasyland", filled by a bevy of familiar Disney cartoon characters.

The Lantau Trail

More than half of Lantau is designated country park, and the **Lantau Trail** loops for 70km across the island, beginning at Mui Wo. The twelve-stage trail is quite a tough hike, crossing Sunset Peak and Lantau Peak, the two highest points on the island, and circuiting the isolated southwestern peninsula before turning back east along the south coast. It passes both of Lantau's youth hostels and several campsites, though most sections can be covered individually if you don't have the time or inclination for the lot. You'll need to check the AFCD website (ⓦ www .afcd.gov.hk) to make sure the section you plan to tackle is accessible, however, as **landslips** are a common problem on Lantau. See p.252 for more information on hiking in Hong Kong.

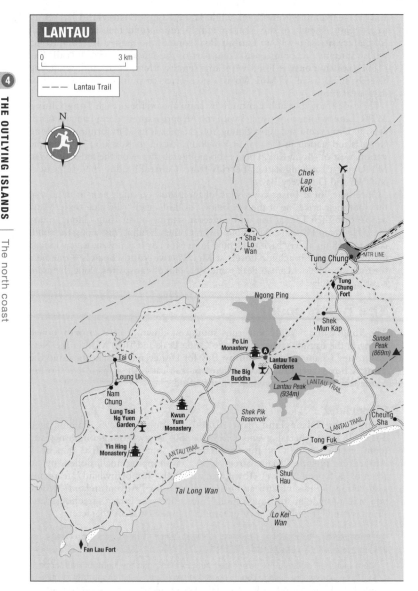

LANTAU

0 ——————— 3 km

— — — Lantau Trail

N

Chek Lap Kok

Sha Lo Wan

Tung Chung — MTR LINE

Tung Chung Fort

Ngong Ping

Shek Mun Kap

Sunset Peak (869m)

Po Lin Monastery Ⓐ

Lantau Tea Gardens

Tai O

The Big Buddha

Lantau Peak (934m) LANTAU TRAIL

Leung Uk

Nam Chung

Shek Pik Reservoir

LANTAU TRAIL

Cheung Sha

Lung Tsai Ng Yuen Garden

Kwun Yum Monastery

Yin Hing Monastery

LANTAU TRAIL

Tong Fuk

Shui Hau

Tai Long Wan

Lo Kei Wan

▼ **Fan Lau Fort**

Despite a string of controversies and lower-than-projected visitor numbers, if you're after a day's entertainment with youngsters in tow, Disneyland will certainly keep you busy, though don't expect to find much in the way of local content (Disney's one Chinese character, Mulan, has yet to be sighted). The park is especially good during festivals such as Christmas and Chinese New Year, when huge firework displays add to the fairground atmosphere.

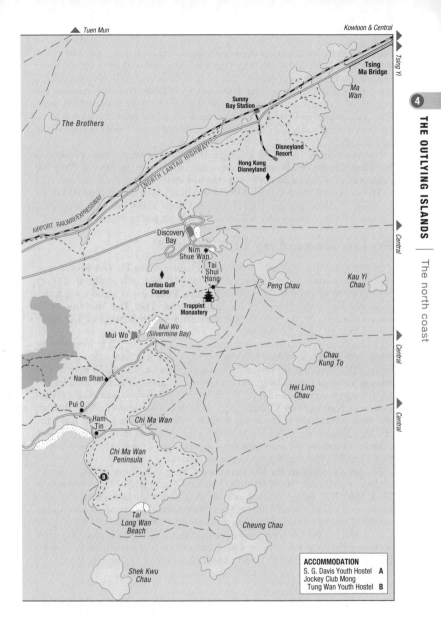

Tsing Yi

Tsing
Ma Bridge

Ma
Wan

Sunny
Bay Station

Disneyland
Resort

Hong Kong
Disneyland ◆

NORTH LANTAU HIGHWAY

The Brothers

AIRPORT RAILWAY/EXPRESSWAY

Discovery
Bay

Nim
Shue Wan

Tai
Shui
Hang

Lantau Golf
Course

Trappist
Monastery

Mui Wo
(Silvermine Bay)

Mui Wo

Peng Chau

Kau Yi
Chau

Central

Nam Shan

Pui O

Ham
Tin

Chi Ma Wan

Chi Ma Wan
Peninsula

Ⓑ

Tai
Long Wan
Beach

Chau
Kung To

Hei Ling
Chau

Central

Cheung Chau

Central

Shek Kwu
Chau

ACCOMMODATION
S. G. Davis Youth Hostel **A**
Jockey Club Mong
    Tung Wan Youth Hostel **B**

Tung Chung

TUNG CHUNG, just a stone's throw away from the airport on Chek Lap
Kok island, is a modern, booming New Town, home to almost half of Lantau's
45,000 inhabitants. Although now of most interest for its huge **transit centre**
– where island buses, the rail line and cable car to Po Lin converge – Tung
Chung started life as a fishing village around a Qing dynasty (1644–1912)

fort, which still stands a couple of kilometres south. You can **walk** here in fifteen minutes by following signs from the transit centre, or catch **bus** #3M, #11, #23 or #34 to the "Sheung Ling Pei" stop and walk 50m uphill. There was some sort of defence post here as early as the seventeenth century, though the present **Tung Chung Fort** dates only to 1817, built on the orders of the viceroy of Guangdong (Canton province) to defend Lantau's northern coast. The six cannons and crenellated stone walls currently protect a school; if the guns were fired today they'd take out some large tower blocks between here and the sea.

The transit centre focuses on a shopping mall with restaurants and cafés next to the **Tung Chung MTR station**. Follow signs for 50m to the **Ngong Ping 360 cable car**, or walk straight out front to the **bus station**. Here you'll find **bus #23** to Po Lin (daily 8.10am–7.10pm; HK$16 or HK$25 at weekends), **bus #11** to Tai O (daily 6.20am–1.20am; HK$11/18) and **bus #3M** to Mui Wo (daily 7.05am–11.50pm; HK$9.80/15). The #A35 will get you to the airport.

Po Lin Monastery and around

The one place that everyone makes for in Lantau is the **Po Lin Monastery**, up on the island's central Ngong Ping plateau. Not only is the monastery beautifully sited right at the base of **Lantau Peak**, it has a good vegetarian restaurant and is overlooked by the huge, beatific **Tian Tan Buddha** statue. Hikers often plan to stay overnight at the nearby **youth hostel** and then climb Lantau Peak to catch the sunrise.

The best way to reach Po Lin is from Tung Chung on the 5.7km-long **Ngong Ping 360 cable car** (Mon–Fri 10am–6pm, Sat & Sun 9am–6.30pm; HK$58 single, HK$88 return; ⓦwww.np360.com.hk). The astounding 25 minute ride takes in views of Tung Chung and the airport, Lantau's peaks, bare hillsides and lushly vegetated ravines and then, at the end, the big Buddha. The cable car exits into tacky **Ngong Ping Village**, a lame corridor of souvenir shops; get through and walk 50m up the road towards Buddha, whose head can be seen above the tree tops. **Buses** pull up below the Buddha: the #23 from Tung Chung, the #21 from Tai O and the #2 from Mui Wo. Come prepared for some massive queues to get on the cable car or buses at the weekends.

You can also **walk to Po Lin** from Tung Chung in a couple of hours, though it's best to first catch bus #34 (daily 7.30am–9.45pm; HK$4) to its terminus at **Shek Mun Kap** village, which knocks off the dull first few kilometres along main roads – a cab costs around HK$16. From Shek Mun Kap, a concrete path climbs steeply up through woodland, passing a scattering of houses and minor temples, the best of which is **Po Lam Sei**, a nunnery surrounded by vegetable plots. You arrive at Ngong Ping near the campsite below Lantau Peak, just a few minutes from Po Lin Monastery via the youth hostel and tea gardens – see opposite for more.

Po Lin Monastery

Hidden behind an ornamental *paifong* stone archway, the **Po Lin Monastery** was founded in 1906 by Buddhist monks from mainland China, and has grown to be one of the largest Chan (Zen) temples in Hong Kong – and a major tourist attraction. The grounds are full of potted plants and trees, and the **main hall** is notable for its roof-ridge sculptures of phoenixes and outer stone pillars carved into dynamic coiled dragons. Inside, a gilded Buddhist trinity sits isolated in the otherwise empty room; check out the multi-armed Kwun Yam painting behind, her eighteen limbs each holding a weapon and her thousands of hands fanned out behind her like a peacock's tail, each with an eye in the centre of the palm. Impressive though this hall is, it will eventually just be the entranceway to a **Ten Thousand Buddhas Hall** under construction out the back.

Inside the temple courtyard and to the left, there's a huge **vegetarian dining hall** (11.30am–4.30pm), where you can get a filling meal of fairly straightforward vegetarian food, orthodox enough to avoid the use of garlic, ginger or onions. Buy **meal tickets** (HK$60, or the "deluxe" meal, served in air-conditioned surroundings, for HK$100) just beside the restaurant's entrance. In the covered area outside, there's a long counter selling much cheaper takeaway **vegetarian dim sum** – mostly sweet dishes – which you can eat at the adjacent tables.

Tian Tan Big Buddha

The gigantic but serene **Tian Tan Big Buddha** statue (daily 10am–5.30pm), sits in a ring of outsized lotus petals on top of a flight of 268 steps up the hillside in front of the monastery. The 34-metre-high figure is cast in bronze and weighs 250 tonnes – roughly the same as a jumbo jet – and is unmissable except on days when low cloud up here can make it hard to see two steps ahead.

Before you climb up, stand right in the centre of the circular **stone platform** near the monastery's gate, facing the staircase; there's an odd harmonic effect created if you speak, which sounds as if you're standing inside some echoing building, not out in the open. The steps themselves can be slow going when they're crowded but there are supreme views at the top, from the base of the Buddha, of the surrounding hills and temple complex. If you've bought a meal ticket (see above), you'll also be allowed into the (dull) exhibition galleries underneath the statue.

Lantau Tea Gardens and beyond

Just to the left of the steps for the statue, a path leads the few hundred metres up to the **Lantau Tea Gardens**, once Hong Kong's only tea-producing estate. It contains the little *Tea Gardens Restaurant*, a slightly shabby place in woodland where you can sit outside, eat fried rice and drink a beer – the tea is good, too. Despite its proximity to the monastery, it's usually fairly peaceful. Past here the path forks: take the right hand branch for the Lantau Peak trail or the **Wisdom Path** – a set of giant wooden posts carved with the text of the Heart Sutra, favoured by Zen Buddhists – or bear left for the **S.G. Davis Youth Hostel** (see p.197 for essential advance bookings). Beyond the hostel it's another 700m along a concrete track to the exposed **Ngong Ping Campsite** – there's nothing here but some terraced tent pitches – and another *paifong*-style gateway (marked "East Mountain Gate" in Chinese) where the path heads down to Shek Mun Kap village and Tung Chung (see p.173).

A very steep path leads up from the Tea Gardens to 934-metre-high **Lantau Peak** (or Fung Wong Shan, as it is properly known), the second highest in Hong Kong after Tai Mo Shan. The two-kilometere-long trail takes over an hour and the views – as far as Macau on a clear day – are justly famous. The peak is on the Lantau Trail, which continues east from here for about 5km to the slightly lower **Tai Tung Shan**, or "Sunset Peak" and then, via a sharpish two-hour descent, to the road at Nam Shan, within shouting distance of Mui Wo (see p.179).

Tai O and the southwest

Set out on the western coast, **TAI O**, one of Hong Kong's oldest fishing settlements, was originally the centre of a thriving **salt trade** with China. The saltpans are still visible, though locals have converted them into ponds where they raise fish and tiny **shrimps**, used to make the fermented *har kau ham ha* shrimp paste that the village has become famous for. It's an interesting place, built either side of a tidal channel with a good smattering of old streets, antique temples and unique **stilt houses**; it's also possible to make a quick trip out to sea from here in the quest for elusive **pink dolphins**, an endangered species found only in Hong Kong. Below Tai O, walking tracks circuit Lantau's remote **southwestern peninsula**, a wild area with a few beaches, isolated temples and remains of a **fort** at its southernmost tip.

You can catch **buses to Tai O** from Tung Chung (#11; daily 6.20am–1.20am; HK$11, or HK$18 at weekends), Po Lin (#21; daily 7.45am–4.45pm; HK$6.30/13) and Mui Wo (#1; daily 6am–1.10am; HK$10/16.50). The bus stop is right at the village gates. **Ferries** also run here four times a day from Tuen Mun in the New Territories (see p.134), landing on the jetty west of town – phone ⓣ 2994 8155 or contact the HKTB for details.

Tai O

Tai O village is a compact few lanes either side of a narrow channel. From the bus stop, you walk into the village along **Wing On Street**, lined with stalls selling shrimp paste, salted whole fish with their heads wrapped in paper, preserved kumquats, a refreshing red drink made from begonias called *jee boi tin kwai* and all manner of dried seafood. Drop into the **Rural Committee Historic Showroom** (Tues–Sun 12.30–5pm; free), actually a small museum showcasing everyday artefacts such as fishing nets, vases, a threshing machine and some antique bits and pieces (including a cutlass).

A substantial, if short, **bridge** crosses the channel to the rest of the village, which is actually on an island. Right ahead at the top of the main street and surrounded by market stalls, Tai O's **Kwan Ti temple** was built around 1500 to the deity of war and righteousness and looks as if it hasn't been restored much since. Turn right here, and you'll soon find yourself among a clutch of **stilt houses**, made of tin and connected by boardwalks, sitting over the tidal mudflats at the edge of the village. After a fire burned down the older quarter

▲ Houses on stilts, Tai O

The pink dolphins

The waters around the western end of Lantau are where Hong Kong's few **pink dolphins** (the Indo-Pacific humpback dolphin) are most likely to be found. These rose-coloured creatures are beautiful but rare: the WWF (World Wildlife Fund) estimates that around 120 are now left, the remainder having been killed by a combination of polluted waters, disturbance by fishermen and, arguably, various developments around Lantau. Aside from short trips out of Tai O, you can visit the dolphins with Hong Kong Dolphinwatch (℡2984 1414; ⓦwww.hkdolphinwatch.com; trips last five hours and cost HK$360 for adults, HK$180 for children aged 3–11), who also raise money to help protect these threatened creatures. The WWF does not support the tour, arguing that frequent motorboat trips out to view the dolphins are harmful to the animals; Dolphinwatch does not dispute this, though the tours form only a tiny amount of the marine traffic using these extremely busy waters, and hopefully increase awareness about these endangered animals.

in 2000, the government planned to resettle the villagers in modern apartments; but there was such an outcry that they rebuilt their stilt homes instead. Continue through the village and along the shore and you eventually reach the **Yeung Hau Temple** from 1699, dedicated to Hau Wong, which houses the local dragon-racing boat, some sharks' bones, a whale's head found by Tai O's fishermen and a carved roof-frieze displaying two roaring dragons.

Turn left at the Kwan Ti temple, and you walk out of the main village along Shek Tsai Po Street. After about fifteen minutes the path bends out along the seafront past evil-smelling trays of purple shrimp paste drying in the sun, and down to the **jetty** where the Tuen Mun ferry docks. Up on the wooded hillside here is the former **Tai O Police Station**, a colonial building due to be restored and opened as a museum.

The other thing to do in Tai O is take a **boat tour** – operators sit at the village entrance and on the bridge, charging HK$25 per head for a half-hour spin. Tours take in the stilt village and then head out to sea looking for **pink dolphins**; it's not the most eco-friendly way of spotting these beasts, but at least the villagers now have an economic incentive to protect the dolphins and boat operators do keep a respectful distance if any are sighted.

Inevitably, Tai O also offers plenty of places to **eat seafood**, which is some of the best and freshest in Hong Kong. Try the *Relax* or *Good View Seafood* restaurants on the land side, or cross to the island where, next to the Kwan Ti temple, the *Fook Moon Lam* (11am–9.30pm; ℡2985 7071) has a short English-language menu featuring good scallop and prawn dishes from HK$90 a serving. Many snack places here also serve *toufu fa*, chilled soft tofu in a sweet syrup – very refreshing on a hot day. There's a small HSBC **minibank** (Mon & Thurs 9.15am–4pm) with an ATM, just after the bridge on the island side. At present, the YWCA at 61 Wing On Street (℡2985 6310, ⓦwww.ywca.org.hk) also organizes **stilt house rentals** at HK$800 a night for the whole house, which sleeps eight people – contact them for more information.

The southwestern peninsula

South of Tai O, Lantau's **southwestern peninsula** is one of the wildest parts of the island, and to see any of it you'll have to hike in. The route described below follows sections 5, 6, 7 and 8 of the Lantau Trail (see box, p.171) and takes around nine hours in total, though parts are not very far from main roads and either the first or last two sections make excellent walks in themselves.

Sections 5 and 6 begin just east of the crest marking the Tai O road and Po Lin road intersection – there's a trail notice board by the roadside. The signposted track heads southwest to Keung Shan peak, then down and up again to Ling Wui Shan (490m) before turning north to Man Cheung Po, where the isolated **Yin Hing Monastery** is guarded by a six-metre-long stone dragon. You're about 2 hours 30 minutes from your starting point here, and it's another ninety minutes downhill, past the classically styled **Ng Yuen gardens** (usually closed to the public), to the coast at **Nam Chung** and **Leung Uk** villages, just a kilometre south of Tai O.

Sections 7 and 8 run anticlockwise from Nam Chung along the coast, a fairly easy, flat walk though long – four hours if you don't stop. The first part brings you down to **Fan Lau**, a rounded peninsula with the solid ramparts of the old **Fan Lau Fort**, built in 1729, standing at the southernmost tip. Part of a line guarding the Pearl River Delta, the fort was originally manned by a garrison of thirty soldiers and armed with eight cannons. It wasn't entirely successful – at one point the fort was captured by the pirates it was meant to be defending against – and was abandoned altogether after the British government took over Lantau in 1898. Today the five-metre-high outer walls have been restored, and you can climb them at one point for views of ferries speeding past to Macau. East below the fort, **Fan Lau Tung Wan beach** would be beautiful if it didn't attract so much rubbish – there are times when you have to wade knee deep through piles of washed-up polystyrene to get onto the sand. From here the path soon joins a concrete access road, and another ninety minutes brings you – past the track to pleasant **Tai Long Wan beach** (see below) – back to the main road near the Shek Pik Reservoir.

The south coast

Lantau's best beaches are all on the **south coast**, accessible off the **South Lantau Road**. Buses #1 (Tai O–Mui Wo) and #2 (Po Lin–Mui Wo) pass all of them, while #3M (Tung Chung–Mui Wo) cover beaches east of Cheung Sha, while #11 (Tung Chung–Tai O) and #23 (Tung Chung–Po Lin) pass beaches west of Cheung Sha.

Coming from Tai O or Po Lin, the first place to get off the bus is at the **Shek Pik Reservoir**, the third largest in Hong Kong. There's a stop where the road drops steeply to the dam wall across the reservoir's southern end, and from here you can pick up the Lantau Trail towards Fan Lau. About twenty minutes along, a side road descends to **Tai Long Wan**, a small village and beach with a secluded, narrow crescent of sand – there are toilets and a drink stall in the village, but nowhere to eat.

Back on the main road and heading east, the next place to get off is at the tiny hamlet of **Shui Hau**, where a twenty-minute track leads down to the sea at **Lo Kei Wan**, another isolated little bay with a pretty beach and **campsite**; there's seasonal water, barbecue pits and a basic toilet, but no other facilities.

After Shui Hau the road runs right along the seafront. **Tong Fuk** is the first village here, with some cheap Chinese cafés, *The Gallery* (an English-style pub with Mediterranean food; ℡2980 2582 for bookings) and a swimming beach across the road. Then, past the junction with the Tung Chung road, you're at **Cheung Sha**, the best beach on the island; there are more **cafés** serving simple Chinese food, *The Stoep* for South African cuisine (bookings essential, ℡2980 2699), the *News Bistro* (Thurs–Mon; ℡2980 2233 for bookings), and another **campsite**.

The final stop is at **Pui O**, another small beachside village famed for its small herd of semi-wild, docile **water buffalo**. It's an excellent spot (if you can overlook the piles of rubbish on the way to the beach) and popular with the expat population, with barbecue pits, a **campsite** at its eastern end and, back on the main road, the *JK Club*, which has Sunday barbecues and is a friendly place for a quiet drink in the evening. From here, walking tracks head south to the **Chi Ma Wan Peninsula** (see below), or it's about fifteen minutes by bus to Mui Wo.

Chi Ma Wan Peninsula

The **Chi Ma Wan Peninsula**, a foot of land southeast of Pui O village, is another good place for a walk, with the added attraction of having Lantau's second **youth hostel**. From the bus stop on the main road at Pui O, follow the signpost to **Ham Tin**. A concrete footpath leads you across the fields and alongside the river to a small temple, from where another signpost points up towards **Mong Tung Wan**, a quiet bay reached in just under an hour's walk, with lovely views over Pui O beach. The *Jockey Club Mong Tung Wan Hostel* (see p.197) is here, made up of white bungalows set back from the harbour – a nice, clean place, though packed to the gills on Saturday nights from June to August. You can camp, too, and there are barbecue pits outside. The path from the hostel leads down to a tiny harbour, from where you can travel direct to Cheung Chau by *kaido* at around HK$100 for the boat.

The east coast

There are two settlements on Lantau's **east coast**: **Mui Wo**, the island's main **ferry port** and a pleasant place to stay overnight, sit idle on the beach or attempt some easy walks into the hills; and **Discovery Bay**, a modern expat residential settlement also linked to Central by a ferry service. The two are not connected by road, but there are buses from Mui Wo to the rest of the island, and from Discovery Bay to Tung Chung.

Mui Wo

MUI WO is where **ferries from Central** arrive on Lantau and most people never see the village, piling straight off the boats and onto buses waiting outside

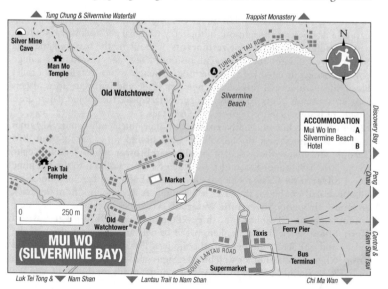

Tung Chung & Silvermine Waterfall   Trappist Monastery

N

Silver Mine Cave

Man Mo Temple

TUNG WAN TAU RD

Old Watchtower

Silvermine Beach

Discovery Bay

ACCOMMODATION
Mui Wo Inn   A
Silvermine Beach Hotel   B

Peng Chau

Pak Tai Temple

Market

0   250 m

Old Watchtower

Taxis

Ferry Pier

Central & Tsim Sha Tsui

MUI WO (SILVERMINE BAY)

SOUTH LANTAU ROAD

Bus Terminal

Supermarket

Luk Tei Tong & Nam Shan   Lantau Trail to Nam Shan   Chi Ma Wan

Lantau ferries

Ferries and fast ferries

Between Central and Mui Wo, roughly every third sailing is by ordinary ferry (about 55min), while the rest are fast ferries (40min); between Tsim Sha Tsui and Mui Wo, the two services alternate.

For up-to-date ferry information, contact the New World First Ferry Company (☎2131 8181, ⓦwww.nwff.com.hk), which runs the Central–Mui Wo ferry and inter-island ferries via Peng Chau and Cheung Chau.

For Discovery Bay ferry service, call Discovery Bay Transportation Services Ltd (☎2987 7351, ⓦwww.discoverybay.com.hk).

For ferries between Tai O and Tuen Mun, call Lee Tat Ferry Company (☎2984 8155); no English spoken.

Outlying Islands Ferry Piers to: Mui Wo (roughly every 30min, first at 6.10am, last at 11.50pm); Discovery Bay (24hr service; every 20–30min at peak times).

Mui Wo to: Outlying Islands Ferry Piers (roughly every 30min, first at 5.55am, last at 11.30pm).

Tai O to: Tuen Mun, New Territories (Mon–Sat 9.40am, 1.45pm & 4.15pm; Sun 9.40am, 11.40am, 1.45pm & 4.15pm).

Tuen Mun to: Tai O (Mon–Sat 8.40am, 12.40pm, 3pm & 6.15pm; Sun 8.40am, 10.40am, 12.40pm, 3pm & 6.15pm).

Discovery Bay to: Outlying Islands Ferry Piers, Central (24hr service; every 20–30min at peak times).

Inter-island ferries

Mui Wo to: Peng Chau (11 daily, first at 6.35am, last at 11.59pm); Chi Ma Wan then on to Cheung Chau (10 daily, first at 6am, last at 10.50pm).

Discovery Bay to: Mui Wo (Mon–Fri 7.25am, 11am, 3pm, 4.10pm & 6.10pm; Sat & Sun 7.25am, 8.40am, 10.35am, 1.10pm, 3pm, 4.10pm, 6.10pm & 7.50pm).

Mui Wo to: Discovery Bay (Mon–Fri 7.45am, 11.20am, 3.20pm, 4.30pm & 6.30pm; Sat & Sun 7.45am, 9am, 10.55am, 1.30pm, 3.20pm, 4.30pm, 6.30pm & 8.10pm).

to take them to beaches, Po Lin or Tai O. However, it's easy to spend the best part of a day here: turn right out of the ferry terminal and follow the seafront, past a handful of small Chinese **restaurants** overlooking the bay, cross the little **Silver River** and into the village. This is simply a few lanes surrounding a huge covered market, fronted by a kilometre-long **beach** where you'll find a toilet block, lifeguard, several drink stalls, trees for shade and barbecue areas; it gets busy at weekends but is otherwise a superbly lazy place to unwind. There are a couple of **hotels** here too – see p.196 for details.

Mui Wo is also known as **Silvermine Bay** after nineteenth-century diggings around 2km northwest of the village. Cast around for signs to **Man Mo Temple** and follow the path, past an **old watchtower** made of stone blocks, to the little hall, founded around 1600. It's just a short walk on to the old mine site at **Silvermine Cave**; it's closed off for safety but a sign here mentions that mining ceased in 1896 as the silver had run out. A separate fork from this track ends up at the pretty **Silvermine Waterfalls**, a two-tier cascade set is the forest.

Another good walk follows the three-kilometre-long "**Old Village Path to Nam Shan**". Pick up the trail from the bridge, and follow it through the village and out across the fields to the modern Hakka settlement of **Luk Tei Tong**, where there's another watchtower. Signs guide you between the houses and up over the hill behind to **Nam Shan**, just a point southwest of Mui Wo on the main road where the **Lantau Trail** heads west up towards Sunset Peak. For a longer hike from Mui Wo **to Discovery Bay**, walk to the far end of the beach, climb the hill – there are superb views back over the bay – and follow the path north for about ninety minutes, via a **Trappist Monastery**, to Discovery Bay. From here, you can catch a ferry back to Central or a bus to Tung Chung.

Mui Wo has a **bank** with an ATM, a post office and no shortage of places **to eat** – though these are mostly straightforward Chinese affairs. The **bus terminus** outside the ferry terminal has departures to Tung Chung (#3M; daily 7.05am–11.50pm; HK$9.80 or HK$15 at weekends), Po Lin (#2; daily 8am–4.30pm; HK$10/16.50) and Tai O (#1; daily 6am–1.10am; HK$10/16.50). The #A35 runs to the **airport** via Tung Chung.

Discovery Bay

Up the east coast around 5km from Mui Wo, **DISCOVERY BAY** ("Disco Bay" to the *gweilo* locals) is a fast-growing New Town popular with young families, with its own artificial beach, restaurants, shops, markets, banks and watersports facilities. The atmosphere is nightmarish, a too-perfect copy of idealized middle-American suburbia, with happy blonde families zipping about in golf carts, and very few Chinese faces. The main attraction is the 24-hour **hydrofoil** back to Hong Kong (every 20min during peak hours), which delivers you next to the Star Ferry Pier in Central in half an hour. There's also a high-speed ferry service that shuttles between Discovery Bay and Mui Wo, and **bus links** to Tung Chung (#DB01R) and the airport (#DB02R).

Places	
Cheung Chau	長洲
Cheung Sha	長沙
Chi Ma Wan	芝麻灣
Discovery Bay	愉景灣
Lamma Island	南丫島
Lantau Island	大嶼山
Lo Kei Wan	籮箕灣
Mong Tung Wan	望東灣
Mo Tat Wan	模達灣
Mount Stenhouse	山地塘
Mui Wo	梅窩
Nam Shan	南山
Peng Chau	坪洲
Pui O	貝澳
Shek Mun Kap village	石門甲
Shui Hau	水口
Sok Kwu Wan	索罟灣
Tai Long Wan	大浪灣
Tai O	大澳
Tong Fuk	塘福
Tung Chung	東涌
Tung O	東澳
Yung Shue Wan	榕樹灣
Sights	
Cheung Po Tsai Cave	張保仔洞
Disneyland	輕鈇)士尼樂園

Fan Lau Fort	分流炮台
Kam Fa Temple	金花廟
Kwan Ti Temple	關帝廟
Lantau Peak	鳳凰山
Man Mo Temple	文武廟
Ng Yuen Gardens	悟園
Pak Tai Temple	北帝廟
Po Lin Monastery	寶蓮寺
Shek Pik Reservoir	石壁水塘
Silvermine Cave	銀礦洞
Silvermine Waterfall	銀礦瀑布
Tai O Police Station	大澳警署
Tian Tan Big Buddha	天壇大佛
Tin Hau Temple	天后宮
Trappist Monastery	修道院
Tung Chung Fort	東涌炮台
Yeung Hau Temple	楊侯古廟
Yin Hing Monastery	慈興寺

Transport

Bus stop	巴士站
Ferry pier	碼頭
Lantau Trail	鳳凰徑
Ngong Ping 360 cable car	昂坪360

Listings

Listings

Accommodation

D espite Hong Kong's reputation for high living costs, **accommodation** here doesn't have to be a major expense. The downtown areas are swarming with **guesthouses** offering dorms and basic doubles from HK$100 a person, while for twice this you can get a perfectly decent room with shower and air conditioning. **Hotels** kick off at HK$500 a night for a functional room with no frills, though a good tourist-class hotel will cost upwards of the HK$1500 mark. Of course, if your budget will stretch to it, Hong Kong can provide some of the best hotels in the world, their rooms illuminated with views of the harbour and filled with costly Chinese antiques. There are a several options in the New Territories, too – always better value for money compared with similar places in town – along with a few **youth hostels** and plenty of **free campsites**.

One thing that ties all guesthouse and hotel accommodation together is **space**, and just how little of it Hong Kong has to spare. Until you reach the upper price echelons, there's really not a great deal of difference in how rooms are furnished: a bed, desk, somewhere to hang your clothes, perhaps a fridge. The space between these is essentially the only major difference between what your money gets you in a better guesthouse and a standard mid-range hotel room.

While it's unthinkable that you might arrive in Hong Kong and not be able to find a room of any sort, **booking ahead** is wise as popular places fill up early. You'll get the best deals **online** through accommodation websites, or the dedicated booking websites given below. At the very least, try phoning first and asking for their best rate, though if all else fails, haggling at the front desk can also pay off.

Guesthouses

In Hong Kong, the term **guesthouse** usually means a family-run hostel. At the bottom end, a few places offer **dormitories** from HK$100 a night, where you pay per bed in a room sleeping upwards of four people; bathrooms are always shared. In the **mid-range** – say HK$250–400 a night – you'll get a single or double room with a toilet/shower cubicle the size of a broom cupboard and with hardly enough space to get out of bed without shifting your luggage. There will always be a TV, sometimes a fridge and, if you're lucky, hooks or a rail to hang clothes on. While turnover at these places is fast and furious (qualities shared by many of the owners), they're not necessarily dives and there are at least a lot of them – if one doesn't appeal, an alternative will be just a short walk away. At the **top end**, you get a little more space and facilities begin to edge into the budget hotel bracket.

The vast majority of guesthouses are in **Kowloon**, with a smaller enclave in **Causeway Bay** on Hong Kong Island, and a scattering of similar "resorts" out

Long-term rentals and serviced apartments

If you're in town for a month or more, check whether your accommodation offers **long-term rates**, which often amount to only ten or twelve days of the nightly room price; guesthouse rates, for instance, start from HK$3500 or so. However, spending this long in such cramped quarters isn't much fun and you'll get slightly more room renting a **serviced apartment**. These range from about 200-square-foot (18-square-metre) furnished flats with bathroom, air conditioning and perhaps a rudimentary food preparation area for HK$9000 a month, to suites with hotel-style amenities such as gyms, pools and the like from HK$25,000 and up. You'll have to pay a month's rent up front as a deposit and utility bills might be extra. In additon to the following, check **listings** in the *South China Morning Post* or *HK* magazine:

Regent Heights 11 Tung Lo Wan Rd, Causeway Bay, Hong Kong Island ☎2895 2555, Ⓦwww.regentheights.com.hk. Suites HK$9000–25,000, plus utility charges of HK$1000–1500.

Rent-A-Room 2nd Floor, Flat A, Knight Garden, 7–8 Tak Hing St, Jordan ☎2366 3011, Ⓦwww.rentaroomhk.com. No sign; look for "Knight Garden" about halfway down street. Big choice of rooms in large apartment block, so ask to see a few as they vary a lot in size, brightness and general appeal. HK$9000

WStudios Ⓦwww.wstudios.com.hk. Set of modern studio apartments in Sheung Wan, Causeway Bay, and North Point, Hong Kong Island. Includes fridge, phone, microwave and ADSL/wi-fi. HK$8500

Yes Inn Ⓦwww.yesinn.com. Newish serviced apartments in Causeway Bay, Fortress Hill and Mong Kok; rooms have desk, ADSL, air-con, TV and phone, plus a basic kitchenette with fridge. HK$5000–12,000 plus HK$400 a month for power.

on **Lamma** and Cheung Chau islands. Most are located in residential or commercial multistorey blocks known as **mansions**, the largest and best-known being *Chungking Mansions* in Tsim Sha Tsui. Mansions are sometimes drab, sleazy and a fire risk, though the guesthouses themselves are generally clean and well run, if not always very secure. There might be dozens of independent guesthouses scattered over many floors: check out the options by taking a lift to the top floor and working down.

When **renting** your room, always ask to see it first, and don't be afraid to try and bargain the price down. There's not much price difference between **single or double rooms** and everywhere offers **weekly and monthly rates** (see box above). If you're not sure about a place, don't pay too much up front: you'll have a hard job getting your money back if you want to leave early. Check that the **air-conditioning** unit works and isn't too noisy; some places make an extra charge (HK$10–20 per night) for its use. Some places also offer **luggage storage** if, for instance, you wanted to head to Macau for a few days with minimal gear. There's always a charge, and you want to check that the storage area is secure before using it.

Booking websites for guesthouses include Ⓦwww.hostelbookers.com and Ⓦhkhostels.com, both of which are worth checking for discounts if the place of your choice doesn't offer any on its own website.

Hong Kong Island

Causeway Bay's guesthouses offer budget travellers a smaller, alternative version of Tsim Sha Tsui. All are close to Causeway Bay MTR station; see map on pp.78–79. Fortress Hill is two stops east from Causeway Bay on the MTR.

Causeway Bay

Alisan Flat A, 5th Floor, Hoi To Court, 275 Gloucester Rd ☎2838 0762, 🖰home .hkstar.com/~alisangh. Tidy guesthouse with helpful owners; rooms are the usual compromise between space and cost, but all come with a/c, shower and phone and a few even have limited sea views. HK$400

Bin Man & Clean 1st Floor, Central Building, 531 Jaffe Rd ☎2833 2063, 📠2838 5651. Two small, clean and slightly scruffy guesthouses run by the same management. Rooms are tiny, with attached bathrooms. HK$350

Hostel HK 3rd floor, Paterson Building, 47 Paterson St ☎2392 6868, 🖰www.hotel.hk. No sign at the entrance. Hospitable, efficient, bright and clean place with slightly more elbow room than most, a free laundry service and multilingual manager. HK$380

Jetvan Traveller's House 4th Floor, 4a Fairview Mansions, 51 Paterson St ☎2890 8133, 🖰www.jetvan.com. Eight rooms, all with telephone, air-con, TV and bathroom. A friendly place, though rooms are rather cramped and a little worn; some are also windowless. HK$400

Pak Tak Hostel 7th Floor, Block A, Hyde Park Mansions, 53 Paterson St ☎2890 2955. This fourteen-roomed guesthouse has a range of doubles and twins all with attached bath, a/c, telephone and TV. The rooms are bright and clean, with larger windows than most other budget choices. HK$380

Fortress Hill

Yes Inn Flat B, 5th Floor, Front Block, Continental Mansion, 294 King's Rd ☎2881 7077, 🖰www.yesinn.com. Fortress Hill MTR station Exit A, turn right and it's 200m. A bright, cheerful and popular hostel with dorms, singles and doubles. Also runs serviced apartments (minimum 28-day rental, HK$5000–12,000) in Causeway Bay, Mong Kok and Fortress Hill. Dorms HK$110, doubles with en-suite bathroom HK$350

Kowloon

Most budget travellers make a bee-line for Tsim Sha Tsui's guesthouses – especially inside *Chungking Mansions* – though you'll get a slightly better deal further north in Jordan and Mong Kok. All the following are very close to MTR stations; for locations see maps on pp.104–110.

Tsim Sha Tsui

Cosmic Guesthouse 12th Floor, Mirador Mansions, 56–58 Nathan Rd ☎2369 6669, 🖰www.cosmicguesthouse.com. English-speaking staff on hand around the clock and rooms ranging from basic singles to deluxe doubles with bathroom and good-sized windows. HK$240

Garden Hostel 3rd Floor, Mirador Mansions, 56–58 Nathan Rd ☎2311 1183, 🖰gardenhostel.com.hk. Friendly place with a large sofa-filled and pot-planted garden to chill out in with some secondhand books. They have more than fifty beds, and their eight-bed dorms are split into male- and female-only. The individual rooms are white-tiled to the ceiling and fairly spartan, which makes them clinical but clean. A *wing chun* martial arts school train here Tues and Thurs evenings too. Dorms HK$70 per person, rooms HK$220

Kimberley Inn 1st Floor, Champagne Court, 18–20 Kimberley Rd ☎2723 9280, 📠2723 6870. The furnishings are a bit dated but rooms are exceptionally clean, with good mattresses and proper bathrooms, and are larger than in other guesthouses – hence the higher-than-average room rate. Management staff don't speak much English. HK$500

Rooms for Tourist 6th Floor, Lyton House Building, 36 Mody Rd ☎9083 3300, 🖰www .roomsfortourist.com. A friendly and stylish hostel with a deadpan manager, and fresh orchids in the bathroom. The en-suite rooms are well sized, clean and simple. HK$300

Sealand House Flat D, 8th Floor, Majestic House, 80 Nathan Rd (the entrance is on Cameron Rd) ☎2368 2522, 🖰www .sealandhouse.com.hk. Spotless place with a cheerful manageress and bright rooms which, while not large, at least have decent elbow room and storage space for bags under the bed. HK$400

Star Guesthouse Flat B, 6th Floor, 21 Cameron Rd ☎2723 8951, 🖰www.starguesthouse .com.hk. A range of comfortable singles, doubles and triples in two locations along the road. While extremely secure, clean and friendly, rooms are small for the price – try negotiating or consider other options. HK$450

Yiu Fai 6th Floor, Golden Crown Court, 66–70 Nathan Rd ☎ 2739 0021, ⓦ www .yiufaiguesthouse.com. Another bright, clean shoebox with helpful staff, firm beds and tiny shower nooks. HK$350

Chungking Mansions, 36–44 Nathan Rd, Tsim Sha Tsui

Chungking Mansions (see p.107) is a monster of a building, with scores of cheap – and largely decent – guesthouses on its upper floors. There are five sets of **lifts**, labelled A to E, two for each block – one for the even floors, one for the odd floors. Notice boards tell you which guesthouses are on each floor: the numbers, A3, B4, etc, are the address on that floor for each guesthouse. Lifts are tiny and queues invariably large, so if you haven't booked in advance or want to inspect a few places first, try to leave one person downstairs with the luggage. A few owners run more than one place, so don't worry if you're packed off to another block or another floor when you try to check in: just make sure to

▲ Chungking Mansions

see the room first and fix the price. The list below is a fraction of the total available.

🏃 **Dragon Inn** Block B, 3rd Floor ☎ 2368 2007, ⓕ 2724 2841. Well-organized, hostel-cum-travel agent, with 21 clean and basic rooms including singles with shared bathroom and en-suite triples. Security cameras, no-nonsense manager and ever-present staff make this place feel safe. HK$240

🏃 **Hawaii Guesthouse** Block A, 14th Floor ☎ 2366 6127. One of the real bargains in the mansion, with standard singles, large singles and doubles, some with en suites. Popular and always full. Singles with shared bathroom HK$90, a/c use HK$10 extra. HK$160

Park Guesthouse Block A, 15th Floor, A1 ☎ 2368 1689, ⓕ 2367 7889. This long-established guesthouse has tidy box-like singles and doubles, some with fridges and shower. Management are brusque but efficient; there's a tiny communal kitchen too. Doubles HK$250–300 depending on size.

Pay Less Block A, 7th Floor ☎ 2369 5525, ⓕ 3119 2666. Well-equipped new guest-house with relatively spacious doubles and decent single rooms, though not all have windows. HK$220

Peking (New Peking) Guesthouse Block A, 12th Floor, A2 ☎ 2723 8320, ⓔ pekhotel @hotmail.com. The newer block boasts large rooms with tiled floor, fridge and big windows. The old block has smaller and older, but still presentable, rooms. A secure place with a welcoming manager. HK$250

Welcome Guesthouse Block A, 7th Floor, A5 ☎ 2721 7793 or 2367 1598. A/c doubles with and without shower, and some singles. Nice clean rooms, luggage storage and laundry service. Very friendly owners who sometimes run tai chi lessons in Kowloon Park in the morning. HK$180

Yan Yan Guesthouse Block E, 8th & 12th Floors ☎ 2366 8930, ⓕ 2721 0840. Reception on 8th floor. Singles, doubles, triples and four-person rooms with all facilities. It's a bit more relaxed and quieter than most and, all in all, good value for money. A/c charged at discretion of management – if used sparingly free, if used constantly HK$20 per day. HK$250

Jordan

Jordan has a slew of places to stay inside the huge corner block of **New Lucky House**, 300–306 Nathan Rd, though the entrance is on Jordan Road right by Jordan MTR station Exit B1. The building is elderly and a bit scruffy, but not at all squalid, and hostels here are a good alternative to *Chungking Mansions*.

Hakka's 3rd Floor ☎2771 3656 or 2770 1470. This place offers huge double rooms with bathroom, at least by guesthouse standards, with smaller doubles and singles also available. Staff are helpful. HK$400

Ocean 11th Floor ☎2385 0125, ⓔocean -guesthouse@hotmail.com. Owner tries hard to make this unpretentious place welcoming; all rooms are small but have windows, bar fridges and bathrooms. HK$250

Overseas 9th Floor ☎2384 5079. Very plain and somewhat elderly rooms inside a private home; doubles come with or without bathrooms and their "family room" sleeps four and looks out over the street. HK$280

Mong Kok

Most of Mong Kok's budget options lurk upstairs inside **Sincere House**, occupying an entire block at 83 Argyle Street. There's no sign on Argyle, but walk around the corner into Fa Yuen Street and you'll see a little English name plaque and doorway on the left, with lifts inside.

Dragon Hostel Room 707, 7th Floor ☎2395 0577, ⓦwww.dragonhostel.com. Guesthouse with helpful management and comparatively large doubles with and without bathrooms. They also specialize in getting visas for Vietnam and Laos, useful if you're heading that way, and offer long-term luggage storage. HK$240

Dragon Inn Ah Shan Room 1406, 14th Floor ☎2395 0577, ⓦwww.dragoninnhk .com. Exceptionally clean and friendly hostel; rooms are simple but well furnished and a very good deal for what you get. Not much English spoken. HK$280

King Wah 10th Floor ☎9770 5972, ⓦwww .kingwahhostel.com. Another plain, good value-for-money establishment with tiny en-suite rooms whose staff do their best to make you feel at home. HK$260

The New Territories

Aside from youth hostels, there's just one budget choice in the New Territories, at Sha Tin.

Ascension House 33 Tao Fong Shan Rd, Sha Tin ☎2691 4196, ⓦwww.achouse.com. See p.140 or website for directions. Backpacker hostel with dorm beds run by the Lutheran Church; price includes meals and laundry. Accommodation must be booked in advance. Dorm beds HK$125

The Outlying Islands

Prices for island "resorts" vary hugely depending on the size of the room, whether it's en suite, has a kitchenette or a balcony with/without sea views, etc. Standard rooms tend to be very ordinary; it's better to get something larger with a bathroom and sea views. The *Bali* on Lamma and Cheung Chau's *B&B* are more upmarket, closer to budget hotels. Wherever you stay, book in advance, though you might be able to walk in mid-week. Add fifty percent to the rates below for Friday and Saturday nights. See maps on p.163 and p.167.

Lamma

Bali Holiday Resort Yung Shue Wan, on the left just as you reach the main street from the ferry dock ☎2982 4580, ⓦwww.lammabali.com. Spacious rooms in apartment block, with or without views and kitchenettes – more modern than *Man Lai Wah* but further back from the water. There's also a garden patio, rooftop barbecue area and free wi-fi. Weekly and monthly rates. HK$380

Katmandhu Guesthouse 39 Main St, Yung Shue Wan ☎&ⓕ2982 0028. Attached to Bubbles Laundry. Rooms are no-frills, dark little cells with hard mattresses but are all self-contained with shower unit, microwave and TV. Little natural light inside, but a cheap, cleanish bed for the night; the only island accommodation with dorms. Dorm beds HK$100; HK$300

Man Lai Wah Hotel Yung Shue Wan ☎2982 0220, ⓔmanlaiwahhotel@yahoo.com. Right by the ferry pier, overlooking the harbour, this charming place has nine compact en-suite rooms stocked with ageing furniture, and beds with squeaky mattresses. Seaview rooms are usually booked up long in advance. HK$450

Cheung Chau

B&B 12–14 Tung Wan Rd, between the town and Tung Wan beach ☎ 2986 9990, Ⓦ www.bbcheungchau.com.hk. Little gem of a place – a genuine bed and breakfast with modern, boutique-style rooms which make up in comfort what they lack in size. There's also a tiny roof-top patio and restaurant. HK$520

Bella Vista Miami Resort ☎ 2981 7299, Ⓦ www .miamicheungchau.com.hk. Huge permutation of rooms in a residential estate at the northern end of Tung Wan beach; the website has photos of them all, so have a look and then reserve with a phone call according to your needs. Impossible to find without a map, which you can get from their booth opposite Cheung Chau's ferry pier. HK$380

Fuk Kee ☎ 2981 0093, mobile 6091 0434. Similar to *Miami* though rooms are perhaps a bit larger and better maintained on average. HK$300

Hotels

At the bottom end of Hong Kong's hotel scene, **budget hotels** – charging around HK$500–800 a night for a double – overlap with guesthouses: you'll get a double with attached bathroom and not much wasted space. A TV, air conditioning and perhaps a bar fridge complete the facilities, and most have windows – if not outstanding views. Go **mid-range**, paying HK$1000–2000, and things improve: while the actual facilities aren't much different they'll be better quality and more modern, and the room will be larger. Gyms, pools, restaurants and business centres begin to become part of the equation too. Above HK$2500 and you're bumping into the **upper range**, with plush furnishings, decadent empty spaces between the furniture and the option of harbour views; top in this class are the *Peninsula*, *Conrad* and *Mandarin Oriental*. There are also a growing number of **boutique hotels** in the HK$900–2500 range, with a touch more character than comparable hotel rooms; and several **religious organizations** offering accommodation with prices and facilities towards the lower end of the hotel spectrum.

All of Hong Kong's best – and most expensive – hotels are within sight of Victoria Harbour in Central and Tsim Sha Tsui; the moment you move away from these areas, prices begin to drop and the range of options improves. Almost everywhere, however, is near the downtown, either along Hong Kong Island's North Shore or over the water in Kowloon. For a change of pace, there are also a few places out in the New Territories and a couple of Outlying Islands – none of them too far if you fancy a day-trip into town.

Room rates as quoted by the hotels are given below, but you'll seldom need to pay them: look online for deals or packages which can slash prices enormously. Add an extra twenty percent for **harbour views** (if available), and always count on a ten-percent **service charge**. The **high seasons** – when you can pay thirty percent or more above standard rates – are all of November, and mid-March through to the end of April.

The **Hong Kong Hotels Association** (Ⓦ www.hkha.com) provides a list of hotels which measure up to the association's standards, though this doesn't of course mean that other hotels are necessarily bad. Dedicated **booking websites** include Ⓦ www.hong-kong-hotels.ws, which gives listings, photos and descriptions; Ⓦ www.asiarooms.com, which focuses on mid-range options; and Ⓦ www.hotel.hk, again netting decent discounts for mid-range rooms.

Hong Kong Island

Hong Kong Island doesn't have much in the budget hotel range, but there's a good choice of mid- and upper-level options aimed at the business community and upmarket package tours, all superbly placed to take advantage of the North Shore's attractions. The MTR, buses and trams come close to most hotels.

Central

For the accommodation listed below, see map on pp.60–61.

Conrad Pacific Place, 88 Queensway ☎2521 3838, ⊛www.conrad.com.hk. Spiffy modern hotel with large, well-equipped rooms that suffer from a lack of character despite all their comforts. But the hotel takes full advantage of its position on the upper floors of one of the Pacific Place towers with great views from all rooms, and superb restaurants. HK$4200

Hotel LKF 33 Wyndham St ☎3518 9688, ⊛www.hotel-lkf.com.hk. Much larger than average rooms, stylish interior design, luxury furnishings and attentive service make this a popular – but expensive – boutique option. Top location, too, close to Central's nightlife and restaurants. HK$2500

Island Shangri-La Pacific Place, Supreme Court Rd ☎2877 3838, ⊛www.shangri-la.com. Classy hotel at Pacific Place, with the best Peak or harbour views of the lot, particularly from the top-floor Cyrano's bar. Rooms are set around a central atrium holding a magnificent Chinese landscape painting spanning more than forty floors. HK$4200

JW Marriott Pacific Place, 88 Queensway ☎2810 8366, ⊛www.marriott.com. Flash Pacific Place complex, exuding Hong Kong luxury. The 602 rooms are on the small side but bright and comfortable, and all with views of the city, harbour or hills. HK$4100

🏃 **Mandarin Oriental** 5 Connaught Rd ☎2522 0111, ⊛www.mandarinoriental .com. The Mandarin is considered by many to be the best hotel in the world: there's no faulting the service (the staff run into hundreds), facilities (the rooms have antiques and balconies, the corridors eighteenth-century Chinese textiles) or location. You don't need to stay here to appreciate its atmosphere – people-watching in the lobby

▲ Room at the Mandarin Oriental

is a great way to see Hong Kong's finest at work and play. The café is a favourite lunch spot, the Chinnery Bar is where bankers come to unwind, and the Mandarin Grill is where government officials have their power lunches. HK$4500

Mid-Levels

These two options are just a fifteen-minute walk south of Central; contact them for bus routes or catch a cab. See map on pp.60–61.

Bishop Lei International House 4 Robinson Rd ☎2868 0828, ⊛www.bishopleihtl.com.hk. Ride the Mid-Levels Escalator to Robinson Rd, turn left and it's five minutes' walk. Being comprehensively upgraded at the time of writing, this church-run hotel offers similar amenities to the Garden View YWCA – though given the distance from the sea, charging extra for "harbour view" rooms is a bit cheeky. HK$1500

Garden View YWCA 1 Macdonnell Rd ☎2877 3737, ⊛www.ywca.org.hk. Po-faced staff and slightly high rates can be off-putting, but this is a secure place in a great location, close to Hong Kong Park, the Botanical Gardens and Peak Tram. Rooms are spacious and suites have kitchenettes. HK$1550

Sheung Wan

A workaday area with plenty of character, beginning to attract hotel construction as rents in Central skyrocket. See map on p.69.

Bridal Tea House 385–387 Queens Rd West ☎3188 6699, ⊛www.hkchhotel.com. Hong Kong-wide budget hotel chain with cutesy

5

ACCOMMODATION | Hotels

191

neon love-hearts and decorative frills around the lobby. Rooms have tiny en suites and are bright, plain and almost filled by the bed, a bit pricey for what you get. Downstairs cake shop serves afternoon teas. Near the tram lines but on arrival probably easiest to catch a taxi from Central. HK$650

Hua Tai 30–32 New Market St ☎ 2853 9488, ⓕ 2854 0921. Bright orange building west of Western Market, close to Sheung Wan MTR and Shun Tak Centre. A Mainland Chinese-run budget hotel which offers few frills and plenty of botched-up plaster and uneven floors, but larger rooms are not bad value given the location. HK$550

🛬 **Lan Kwai Fong Hotel** 3 Kau U Fong ☎ 3650 0000, ⓦ www.lankwaifonghotel.com.hk. Though not particularly close to Lan Kwai Fong, this well-run, smart boutique hotel has rooms furnished with antique-style Chinese furniture and is atmospherically located near old market streets along the Central-Sheung Wan border. If you're after a cosy, mid-range place with character, this is it. HK$1700

Ramada 308 Des Voeux Rd ☎ 3410 3333, ⓦ www.ramadahongkong.com. International mid-range hotel chain offering decent, run-of-the-mill comforts. On tram lines but best to catch a taxi from Central on arrival. HK$1600

Kennedy Town

While a little distant from Central, this atmospheric old harbour area is earmarked for expansion, with an MTR extension planned (see p.73). At the moment, you need to catch a tram, bus or taxi from Central.

Cosco 20–21 Kennedy Town Praya Rd ☎ 2816 2878, ⓕ 2816 5698. A basic but tidy Chinese hotel in a low-rise overlooking the seafront. No English is spoken and prices see-saw all over the place depending on what the manager thinks you'd pay, so come prepared to bargain. Trams stop outside; if you see Belcher Bay Park, get off and walk back 100m. HK$600

🛬 **Jen** 508 Queens Rd West ☎ 2974 1234, ⓦ www.hoteljen.com. Rather Nordic look to this trim boutique hotel, with lots of white furnishings, straight lines and pine flooring in the rooms. They run a shuttle bus from the Shun Tak Centre, Outlying Island Ferries Pier and Airport Express terminus, so call for pick-up times. HK$1400

Wan Chai

For the accommodation listed below, see map on pp.78–79.

Beverley Floor 4, 175–191 Lockhart Rd ☎ 2507 2026, ⓦ www.bchkhotel.hk. Down-to-earth budget hotel that's been around forever. Rooms are reasonably spacious and clean, though the lurid pink wallpaper and tacky, bed trim might put you off. Management amenable to a little bargaining. HK$800

Grand Hyatt 1 Harbour Rd ☎ 2588 1234, ⓦ www.hongkong.grand.hyatt.com. Part of the Convention and Exhibition Centre complex and bulging with harbour views. Aimed mainly at business trade, it's luxurious rather than tasteful, and houses the largest hotel swimming pool in Hong Kong. HK$2800

Harbourview 4 Harbour Rd ☎ 2802 0111, ⓦ www.theharbourview.com.hk. Excellent location close to the Convention Centre, and most rooms do indeed come with harbour views. Doubles are comfortable if bland – and the bathrooms are a bit of a squeeze – but altogether a bargain. No sports centre or swimming pool, but guests can use the facilities of the Tsim Sha Tsui YMCA across the harbour. HK$1500

King's 11th Floor, 303 Jaffe Rd ☎ 3188 2277, ⓦ www.kingshotelhk.com. Quirky boutique hotel with a "cyber" theme resulting in a sort of minimalist sci-fi decor with lots of moody black marble and chrome. Rooms come with IDD computers and plasma-screen TVs. HK$900

Metro Park 41–49 Hennessy Rd ☎ 2861 1166, ⓦ www.metroparkhotels.com. Bright, modern chic place although, if you look beyond the furnishings, the design and layout of the rooms is standard: bed, desk, bathroom, TV and exactly enough floor space to navigate between them. HK$900

Renaissance Harbour View 1 Harbour Rd ☎ 2802 8888, ⓦ www.renaissancehotels.com/hkghv. Splendid views and the same expense-account business clientele as the Grand Hyatt – you get to use the Grand Hyatt's facilities, too. A favourite with aircrews. HK$3500

Causeway Bay and Happy Valley

For the accommodation listed below, see map on pp.78–79.

Emperor 1 Wang Tak St, Happy Valley ☎ 2893 3693, ⓦ www.holidaycity.com/emperor-hong -kong. Value for money in a peaceful location away from the crushing crowds of Causeway Bay. The medium-sized rooms are nothing special but cheery and comfortable, with all the standard hotel facilities. It's a ten-minute walk from Causeway Bay MTR, or you can take the Happy Valley tram up Tin Lok Lane. HK$1000

Lanson Place Hotel 133 Leighton Rd, Causeway Bay ☎3477 6888, ⓦwww .lansonplace.com. A suave, upmarket boutique place with a stone facade modelled along the lines of a Victorian bank and genuinely airy, comfortable rooms. HK$2500

Park Lane 310 Gloucester Rd, Causeway Bay ☎2293 8888, ⓦwww.parklane.com.hk. Smart business or upmarket traveller option overlooking Victoria Park; well placed for MTR. HK$2700

Tin Hau

Tin Hau MTR station is one stop east of Causeway Bay close to Victoria Park; these two hotels are diagonally across the road from the station.

L'Hotel 18 Kings Rd ☎3553 2898, ⓦwww .lhotelcausewaybayhv.com. Popular business hotel near the Tin Hau temple. Rooms feature bathtubs – fairly uncommon in Hong Kong – and there's a rooftop pool. HK$1500

Metro Park 148 Tung Lo Wan Rd ☎2600 1000, ⓦwww.metroparkhotel.com. A stylish modern hotel with harbour views and another rooftop pool. HK$1900

Kowloon

Kowloon has the highest density of hotels in Hong Kong, especially down near the harbour side shopping district of Tsim Sha Tsui. While the emphasis is top-end, there are also some surprisingly good bargains to be had, though you start to get a lot more for your money the moment you cross north into Jordan, Yau Ma Tei and Mong Kok. Nowhere in Kowloon is far from either MTR stations or bus routes.

Tsim Sha Tsui

For the accommodation listed below, see map on pp.104–105.

Benito 7–7B Cameron Rd (entrance in Cameron Lane) ☎3653 0388, ⓦwww .hotelbenito.com. Small, modern boutique

hotel with guesthouse-sized rooms but better furnishings and hotel-quality service. HK$850

BP International House 8 Austin Rd ☎2376 1111, ⓦwww.bpih.com.hk. Run by the Scouting organization, this tidy mid-range place has smartly-furnished doubles facing Kowloon Park, along with excellent-value triples and quads. Doubles HK$1550, triples HK$1350, quads HK$1450

Imperial 32–34 Nathan Rd ☎2366 2201, ⓦwww.imperialhotel.com.hk. Rooms are small but modern and tidy, and a very good deal given the location within sight of the harbour. Popular, so definitely need to book ahead. HK$1400

Luxe Manor 39 Kimberley Rd ☎3763 8888, ⓦwww.theluxemanor.com. The themed rooms at this boutique hotel range from tasteful ordinary to downright Baroque, with flared chandeliers, mosaic tiling, fake animal skin rugs and ornate Chinese furnishings. Definitely somewhere to feel special and escape the mass-market crowd. HK$2400

Marco Polo Hongkong, Marco Polo Gateway, Marco Polo Prince Harbour City, Canton Rd ⓦwww.marcopolohotels.com. The massive Harbour City complex houses three different hotels under the same Marco Polo umbrella. They're all fairly fancy, if not overwhelming, and you can use each hotel's facilities at will. Only the *Hongkong* (the largest) has harbour views. HK$2050

Peninsula Salisbury Rd ☎2920 2888, ⓦwww.peninsula.com. The *Peninsula* has been putting visitors up in unrivalled, opulent style since the late 1920s. The original colonial wings lack the harbour

▲ Bathroom at the Peninsula

views of the newer central tower, but otherwise even the least expensive rooms here excel the best that almost any other luxury hotel in Hong Kong can provide. Afternoon tea in the lobby or a drink at top-floor *Felix* restaurant are two "to do" things for any visitor to the city. See p.106 for the hotel's history. HK$3600

Salisbury YMCA 41 Salisbury Rd ☎2268 7000, ⓦwww.ymcahk.org.hk. While the rooms themselves are nothing extraordinary, in terms of value for money they offer one of the best deals in Hong Kong, especially if you pay a touch extra for harbour views. Rather pricey dorm bunks are available, too, though these do also get you access to the hotel's pool, climbing wall, sauna and gym. Dorms HK$240, doubles HK$950

Sheraton 20 Nathan Rd ☎2317 3388, ⓦwww.sheraton.com/hongkong. Surprisingly friendly for such a big international chain, with the usual complement of chic restaurants and conference rooms, a pool with harbour views, and even a ballroom. Bathrooms in harbour view rooms are panelled in glass so you can watch the ferries while showering. HK$3600

Stanford Hillview Observatory Rd ☎2722 7822, ⓦwww.stanfordhillview.com. Well-maintained older building with tidy, smallish rooms tucked away in a relatively quiet bit of Tsim Sha Tsui, though close to Knutsford Terrace's restaurants and bars. HK$1480

Tsim Sha Tsui East

A knot of harbour front luxury business hotels where stunning views across to HK Island, top level of service, rooftop pools and cutting-edge restaurants are all taken for granted. See map on pp.104–105.

Intercontinental 18 Salisbury Rd ☎2721 1211, ⓦwww.ichotelsgroup.com. Top-notch hotel, preferred by some tycoons to nearby rival the *Peninsula*. The glassed-in harbour side lobby (open for afternoon teas and evening cocktails) and renowned *Yan Toh Heen* and *Spoon* restaurants make it popular with the resident business elite too. HK$3300

Kowloon Shangri-La 64 Mody Rd ☎2721 2111, ⓦwww.shangri-la.com. This huge, opulent hotel has 725 luxurious rooms, all with wall-to-ceiling bay windows for harbour views. HK$2500

Renaissance Kowloon 22 Salisbury Rd ☎2369 4111, ⓦrenaissancehotels.com/hkgnw.

Probably the most ordinary of the local bunch, though the sprawling red-brick building has all the services and facilities you'd expect. HK$2500

Jordan and Yau Ma Tei

See map on p.110.

Booth Lodge 7th Floor, 11 Wing Sing Lane, Yau Ma Tei ☎2771 9266, ⓦboothlodge.salvation.org.hk. A Salvation Army hotel just off Nathan Rd, whose functional rooms are on the small side. There's also a pleasant restaurant and outdoor café terrace. Breakfast buffet included. HK$840

Caritas Bianchi Lodge 4 Cliff Rd, Yau Ma Tei ☎2388 1111, ⓦwww.bianchi-lodge.com. Housed inside a well-maintained 1980s building, this Roman Catholic-run hotel is a bit friendlier than neighbouring *Booth Lodge*. Continental breakfast is included, and there's a restaurant serving cheap lunches and dinners. HK$820

Eaton 380 Nathan Rd (entrance in Pak Hoi St), Jordan ☎2782 1818, ⓦwww.eaton-hotel.com. Friendly staff, cheerful furnishings and rooms with comfy beds make this a pleasant place to stay. There's also a bar and terrace looking down from a few storeys over the busy shopping streets. HK$1000

Evergreen 48 Woo Sung St, Jordan ☎2780 4222, ⓦwww.evergreenhotel.com. Rooms here are slightly bigger than you'd get in a guesthouse, and some are windowless, but it's clean and tidy and everything works – bathrooms also have baths. Internet and breakfast included in rate. HK$980

Nathan 378 Nathan Rd (entrance in Pak Hoi St), Jordan ☎2388 5141, ⓦwww.nathanhotel.com. Very similar to adjacent Eaton with a bit more styling but, somehow, less character – though again, staff and services are good. HK$1080

Prudential 222 Nathan Rd, Jordan ☎2311 8222, ⓦwww.prudentialhotel.com. A lot of grey, black and red trim make rooms here feel neat rather than bright, but they are comfortable and a bit bigger than average, and most have city views. HK$1800

Mong Kok

For the accommodation listed below, see map on p.110.

Anne Black Guesthouse (YWCA) 5 Man Fuk Rd ☎2713 9211, ⓦwww.ywca.org.hk. Simple singles and doubles with shower at pretty good rates; men can stay here, too. From Jordan MTR, turn right out of Exit D and follow Waterloo Road for fifteen minutes, crossing under the train line, until you reach Pui Ching Road. Turn right onto Pui Ching, then take the first left – Man Fuk Road – and the hostel is 150m. HK$900

Dorsett Kowloon 48 Anchor St, Tai Kok Tsui ☎2380 2223, ☒www.dorsettkowloon.com.hk. Clean, modern hotel with broadband connections in all rooms. The area is busy residential, not very attractive but close to Mong Kok's markets and Olympic train station. HK$900

Harbour 968 Canton Rd ☎2771 3300, ☒www .harbourhotel.com.hk. Guesthouse-hotel off in Mong Kok's backstreets, but with above-average – if small – rooms. They unexpectedly speak English too. HK$600.

Langham Place 555 Shanghai St ☎3552 3322, ☒hongkong.langhamplacehotels.com. Adjoining a massive new shopping complex housed above the MTR station in Mong Kok's tallest building, this modern hotel has large rooms with equally spacious beds, baths and views. HK$2000

Royal Plaza 193 Prince Edward Rd West, ☎2928 8822, ☒www.royalplaza.com.hk. This smart tourist hotel sits on top of Mong Kok East Rail Line station with an entrance in the Grand Century Place shopping plaza. The rooms come with all the usual amenities and prices are good for a hotel that offers fountain-and-piano-in-the-lobby opulence, a forty-metre swimming pool, gym, an enormous ballroom and a library. HK$1800

Prince Edward

One stop north of Mong Kok on the MTR – see map on p.110.

🏃 **Nest 4th Floor, 209A–B Tung Choi St, near the corner with Boundary Rd** ☎2391 8060, ☒www.thenest.com.hk. This modern, cute place has many guesthouse features, but the furnishings and rates nudge it into hotel status. All rooms are en suite with a/c; there's free internet and a roof-garden café. HK$600

The New Territories

Kowloon Panda 3 Tsuen Wah St, Tsuen Wan ☎2409 1111, ☒www.pandahotel.com.hk. See map, p.127. Easily accessed on the MTR or the #A31 Airbus, this huge, one-thousand-roomed hotel has plenty of space, some rooms with water views, and masses of facilities (including a pool and two good restaurants), and offers the chance to see a bit of New Town life at first hand. HK$1600

Regal Riverside Tai Chung Kiu Rd, Sha Tin ☎2649 7878, ☒www.regalhotel.com. See map, pp.136–137. A comfortable conference-style hotel, rather isolated alongside the Shing Mun River, close to Sha Tin Wai station but a fifteen-minute walk to Sha Tin centre. The large rooms and bathrooms are a steal compared with the price you'd pay in Tsim Sha Tsui or Central. HK$900

Royal Park 8 Pak Hok Ting St, Sha Tin ☎2601 2111, ☒www.royalpark.com.hk. See map, pp.136–137. A red-brick tower that desperately lacks style on the outside, though rooms are well appointed and facilities include a gym, swimming pool and sauna. Connected to the rail station through New Town Plaza, though you can get lost walking here; there's also a shuttle bus to Tsim Sha Tsui. HK$1400

Tai Po Hotel 2nd Floor, 6 Wun Tau Kok Lane, Tai Po ☎2658 6121. See map, p.142. Nothing to write home about, with worn furnishings and a smoky, tired lobby. However, rooms are clean enough, if basic, with attached bathrooms, and Tai Po town itself is worth a stay. HK$400

The Outlying Islands

Outlying Islands' accommodation rates go up by fifty percent on Friday and Saturday nights, when half of Hong Kong seems to descend.

Lamma

🏃 **Concerto Inn Hung Shing Yeh** ☎2982 1668, ☒www.concertoinn.com.hk. See map, p.163. Lamma's best hotel, offering rooms with balconies overlooking the beach, satellite TV and a video and fridge in every room – some have kitchens, too. The restaurant is sited on a nice garden terrace. HK$600

Cheung Chau

Warwick East Bay ☎2981 0081, ☒www .warwickhotel.com.hk. See map, p.167. Overlooking Tung Wan Beach, this is the obvious – if most expensive – place to stay: a concrete box whose rooms all have sea views, balconies, baths and cable TV. There's also a terrace café and a swimming pool. HK$700

Lantau

For the accommodation listed below, see map on p.172 & p.179.

Mui Wo Inn Mui Wo ☎ 2984 7725, ⓕ 2984 1916. A short walk beyond the *Silvermine Beach*, this eccentric little hotel has a mob of statues out the front and fairly plain rooms; the front ones have balconies and sea views, while the rooms at the back are cheaper but not so nice. HK$480

Novotel Citygate 51 Man Tung Rd, Tung Chung ☎ 3602 8888, ⓦ www.novotel.com. The closest hotel to Hong Kong airport – just five minutes away – and also convenient for the Ngong Ping 360 cable car and trains to Kowloon and Hong Kong Island. HK$1400

🏃 **Silvermine Beach Hotel Mui Wo** ☎ 2984 8295, ⓦ www.resort.com.hk. Overlooking the beach at Silvermine Bay, this comfortable, laid-back hotel was being upgraded at the time of writing. Facilities include a swimming pool, gym, sauna and tennis courts. HK$1080

Youth hostels

The **Hong Kong Youth Hostel Association** (ⓦ www.yha.org.hk) operates a total of seven **youth hostels** on Hong Kong Island, Lantau and in the New Territories. While inexpensive and excellently placed to take advantage of Hong Kong's wilder corners, they are – with one exception – fairly remote and so can't be used as a base for exploring the whole of the SAR. The buildings tend to be a bit spartan and regimental if well maintained, with **self-catering kitchens** and communal toilets, bathrooms and washing facilities. **Rooms** range from single-sex dormitories HK$90–130 depending on the hostel) through to doubles (HK$230–340) and family rooms sleeping up to six (HK$880), though not all of these are available at all hostels.

You must **book in advance**, either through the Hong Kong Youth Hostel Association or the Hostelling International website (ⓦ www.hihostels.com /dba/country-HK.en.htm). International Youth Hostel Association **members** get a discount of up to thirty percent. The hostels are extremely popular so book as far ahead as possible.

The hostels are **closed** between 10am and 4pm on weekdays, and between 1 and 2pm at weekends. You'll also need a sheet **sleeping bag**, which you can rent at the hostel for a few dollars, and **food** – all are far from shops.

Hong Kong Island

For this hostel, see map on p.56.

🏃 **Jockey Club Mount Davis Youth Hostel Mount Davis** ☎ 2817 5715. Hong Kong's most popular hostel, above Kennedy Town on top of Mount Davis, with superb views. Facilities include TV, a/c, 92 bunks in dormitories, plus double, four- and six-person rooms. No camping. Getting here is a slog unless you catch one of the free hostel shuttles from the Shun Tak Centre in Sheung Wan (contact the hostel for pick-up times). Otherwise, ride bus #5 from Admiralty or minibus #54 from the Outlying Islands Ferry Piers in Central and get off near the junction of Victoria Rd and Mount Davis Path; walk back 100m from the bus stop and you'll see Mt Davis Path branching off up the hill – the hostel is a 35min walk. If you have a lot of luggage, a taxi from Kennedy Town costs around HK$50 (plus HK$5 per item of luggage), though drivers are reluctant to come up here as they won't get a return fare.

New Territories

For New Territories hostels, see map on pp.124–125.

Bradbury Hall Chek Keng, Sai Kung Peninsula ☎ 2328 2458. Beautifully located overlooking a small bay, with nearby walking tracks to Sharp Peak and Tai Long Wan beach. 48 bunks in dorms, plus 4–8 bedrooms and a campsite for up to 60 tents. From Sai Kung Town, catch bus #94 and either get off at Pak Tam Au and walk for an hour

Youth Hostel Associations

Australia Youth Hostels Association Australia Ⓦ www.yha.com.au.
Canada Canadian Hostelling Association Ⓦ www.hostellingintl.ca.
England and Wales Youth Hostel Association (YHA) Ⓦ www.yha.org.uk
International Ⓦ www.hihostels.com
Ireland An Oige Ⓦ www.irelandyha.org.
New Zealand Youth Hostels Association of New Zealand Ⓦ www.yha.co.nz.
Northern Ireland Hostelling International Northern Ireland Ⓦ www.hini.org.uk.
Scotland Scottish Youth Hostel Association Ⓦ www.syha.org.uk.
USA Hostelling International USA Ⓦ www.hiusa.org.

(see p.157), or continue to Wong Shek Pier and organize a *kaido* boat to the hostel.
Bradbury Jockey Club Youth Hostel Tai Mei Tuk, Tai Po ☎ 2662 5123. TV room, huge barbecue area and outdoor terrace, with nearby walks to Pat Sin Leng, Bride's Pool and Plover Cove. 72 beds in two- to eight-bed rooms. The only hostel within easy walking distance of restaurants. Catch bus #75K or green minibus #20C from Tai Po Market train station to the terminus at Tai Mei Tuk.
Pak Sha O Hoi Ha Rd, Sai Kung Peninsula ☎ 2328 2327. Close to Hoi Ha Wan Marine Park and a bevy of coastal walks. 112 beds in several dorms, plus space for 40 tents. Simple meals available during the day at Hoi Ha Wan village. From Sai Kung Town, catch green minibus #7 to Pak Sha O (tell the driver where you're going).
Sze Lok Yuen Tai Mo Shan, Tsuen Wan ☎ 2488 8188. Located halfway up Tai Mo Shan, Hong Kong's highest peak, with an easy walking track to the top. 88 bunk beds, plus camping for 50 tents. From Tsuen Wan West train station, catch bus #51 to Tsuen Kam Au and walk uphill for an hour to the hostel – see p.130.

Lantau

For Lantau hostels, see map on pp.172–173.

Hong Kong Bank Foundation S.G. Davis Ngong Ping ☎ 2985 5610. A basic lodge close to the Big Buddha, Po Lin Monastery and Lantau Peak. 38 beds in dorms only, with space for 25 tents. Catch a bus to Po Lin from Mui Wo or Tung Chung, or cable car from Tung Chung, and then walk for 10min to the hostel – see p.175 for more details.
Jockey Club Mong Tung Wan Chi Ma Wan peninsula ☎ 2984 1389. Island scenery, walking trails and a swimming beach nearby. 88 beds in dorms only, with camping facilities available. A 45min walk from Pui O village, near Mui Wo (see p.179 or the HKYHA website for more details).

Camping

The Agriculture, Fisheries and Conservation Department (AFCD; Ⓦ www.afcd.gov.hk) maintains 37 **campsites** in country parks across the New Territories and Lantau Island, with one more each on Tung Ping Chau Island (p.141) and Tung Lung Chau island (p.120). These are **free** and available only on a first come, first served basis, so you need to get in early for weekends and holidays, especially at popular spots like the Sai Kung Peninsula. Facilities include tent sites, benches, fire pits and **water**; this always needs to be boiled before drinking and supply can be an issue in dry years. Toilets are often just a long-drop, though busier sites will have modern amenities blocks with flushing toilets, hand basins and showers. Most campsites are a long way from shops, so bring everything in with you, including food and charcoal or a fuel stove. Several useful campsites are mentioned in area accounts throughout the Guide; check the **AFCD website** for full listings, plus regulations and current low-water warnings. Some

youth hostels also allow you to camp and use the hostel's facilities – see p.196 for details. Note that in Hong Kong camping is **prohibited** except in designated campsites.

Between May and October Hong Kong's **weather** is very hot and humid, with occasional tropical storms, so check forecasts before setting out and always use a flysheet with guy ropes on your tent. Conversely, night-time temperatures in January and February can drop surprisingly low, and you'll need a sleeping bag. The best place to pick up **camping gear** – everything from gas canisters to outdoor equipment – is RC Outfitters, 163 Johnston Rd, Wan Chai, and 5/F, Oriental House, 24–26 Argyle St, Mong Kok, Kowloon; Ⓦ www.alink.com.hk.

Eating

on't underestimate the importance of food in Chinese culture. Meals are a shared, family affair, informal but always full of opportunities to show respect for others by the way the food and drink is served, accepted and eaten. As a visitor the nuances might pass you by, but it will soon become apparent that the Hong Kong Chinese live to eat and – with most people living in tiny, kitchenless flats – almost everyone dines out on a regular basis.

Food needn't be too costly, certainly if you stick to bedrock Chinese restaurants. The very **cheapest** places charge around HK$20 for a bowl of soup, or HK$35 for a plate of rice seasoned with roast meat and bits of greens. An inexpensive **restaurant meal** will cost around HK$150 for two, though at top end places you can pay a thousand dollars or more per head. What's important is to make use of the enormous **variety** of culinary opportunities that the city offers: even just sticking to local **Cantonese** food, eating a bowl of wonton noodles at a cheap market stall, is as much part of an "authentic" Hong Kong experience as *dim sum* breakfasts, a seafood dinner on Lamma Island or being sneered at by the staff over an elegant Cantonese blow-out at *Fook Lam Moon*. There's also a host of **regional Chinese** restaurants, along with curry houses, sushi bars, British pub-style food,

Southeast Asian, American and European restaurants, hotel lunchtime buffets, pizzerias and all manner of fast food.

Opening hours are long overall and you'll seldom have a problem finding somewhere to eat between dawn and midnight. Cooked food markets and cheap diners open early and close late, while **dim sum** is served from 7am, though proper restaurants keep shorter hours between late morning and around 10pm. Once through the door you'll be seated quickly enough, but in many Chinese establishments you have to be quite **assertive** to catch the waiter's attention for menus and ordering. Count yourself lucky if you get a smile from anyone; staff are not necessarily rude but they are always very, very busy. **Ambience** will be bright, noisy and, except at the poshest venues, extremely **crowded** – cheaper places tend to cram in as much seating as physically possible and you often have to share tables with strangers. Don't count on being able to use **credit cards** as many places (pricier restaurants aside) will only take cash.

While the listings below are a good starting point, Hong Kong's dining scene is highly **volatile**: trends, health scares and stock market wobbles have all been responsible for widescale restaurant closures in the recent past. The free weekly **magazines** *BC* and *HK* review places of the moment, as does *Time Out Hong Kong* (ⓦ www.timeout.com.hk); or you can fork out HK$100 or so for annual **restaurant guides** – *Word Of Mouth* (*WOM*) is the best.

Street food and snacks

In Hong Kong, **street food** takes the form of myriad little nibbles – fishballs, radish cake, chicken wings, grilled octopus, *dim sum* dumplings and the like – impaled on skewers and cooked at open-fronted shop-stalls; they're also available warmed at branches of 7-Eleven stores. Other places specialize in **steamed buns** stuffed with fried meat, barbecued pork or vegetables, **sticky rice rolls** with peanuts, fried stuffed vegetables, and ravioli-like dumplings called *kaozai*. You can fill up on this stuff for HK$15–20.

There are also plenty of **cake shops** around – *Maxim's* and *Saint Honore* are the most widespread – selling custard tartlets, peanut biscuits, brightly coloured and insubstantial cream cakes and all manner of stuffed, sweetened bread buns. Any busy business or residential area – Central's backstreets, Mong Kok, lanes either side of Nathan Road in Tsim Sha Tsui – will have scores of these places.

Moving up a notch, **dai pai dongs** are streetside cooked-food stalls with open kitchens and low wobbly furniture, selling bowls of noodle soups and simple stir-fries. They used to fill the downtown back lanes, but new licences haven't been issued for years and now there are just 28 left. One, the *Yok Yip*, is reviewed below,

▲ Outdoor tables, Temple Street Night Market

but today your best bet for this sort of eating experience is at the **cooked food centres** – also listed below – on the upper floors of covered markets across Hong Kong. Here you'll find a sea of tables surrounded by competing stalls; they seldom have menus but it's usually obvious what each place offers. Food is often very good indeed: cooked by experts and freshly prepared in front of you, it seldom costs more than HK$30 a dish. Another, more touristy and expensive, place to try al fresco dining is at **Temple Street Night Market** in Kowloon (see p.111).

Bowrington Road Market Wan Chai, Hong Kong Island. See p.80.

Java Road Market North Point, Hong Kong Island. See p.87.

Kung Wo Beancurd Factory 118 Pei Ho St, Sham Shui Po, Kowloon. There's no English sign, but you'll see it just behind the market stalls diametrically opposite Sham Shui Po MTR exit B2. This simple traditional canteen is famous for its very cheap home-made bean curd, dished up hot and fried and stuffed with meat or fish. Daily 7.15am–8pm.

Reclamation Street Market Jordan, Kowloon. See p.111.

Sheung Wan Market Morrison St, Sheung Wan, Hong Kong Island. See p.70.

Taichong Bakery 32 Lyndhurst Terrace, Central, Hong Kong Island. See map, p.60. Takeaway Cantonese roast pork buns

and custard tarts, so popular that long queues form as each batch is removed from the oven.

Tai Po Hui Market Tai Po, New Territories. See p.142.

Temple Street Yau Ma Tei, Kowloon. Reliable seafood-based street food at the Temple St Night Market, full of noisy Chinese youths and groups of nervous-looking tourists – establish prices when you order, and check your change carefully to avoid rip-offs. Daily 7–11pm; see p.111.

Yok Yip corner of Hollywood and Peel sts, Soho, Hong Kong Island. See map, p.60. One of the very last street *dai pai dongs* in downtown Hong Kong, serving rice noodles, fish and beef balls, pork knuckle and wonton soups, with the Chinese-only menu tacked up in front. Point, pay, sit, slurp and go. HK$7–10 a serve.

Cafés, breakfasts and cha chaan tengs

Hong Kong has plenty of **Western-style cafés**, ranging from international chains with the usual run of oversize paper cups, unnecessarily complex lists of americano, espresso, cappuccino, mocha and latte and sticky muffins, to stylish hotel affairs with napkins and silverware. They tend to open from 8am and are popular places to have **breakfast**, though a good handful of proper restaurants – including in hotels – also open early for breakfast specials of muesli, fry-ups and coffee. The highest concentrations of cafés are around the downtown areas, but any big shopping plaza in Hong Kong will have a branch of *Pacific Coffee* somewhere. Note that many cafés also offer **free internet access** for their customers, either with terminals or wi-fi.

Chinese breakfasts are altogether different: either a **dim sum** session (see p.205) or something simple to line the stomach for a few hours – rice-porridge **congee** (called *juk* in Cantonese) flavoured with pickles, or a bowl of sweet bean curd milk with a doughnut stick (*yau char kwai*). The best place to try one is at a **cha chaan teng**, a cheap café-style restaurant, often open round the clock. They're a real Hong Kong institution, with surly staff and often distinctly seedy clientele, especially after the clubs close around 3am. The name translates as "tea restaurant", and the moment you sit down a plastic tumbler of weak black tea will be plonked on the table by the waiter. Menus are usually bilingual, extensive, and set under the glass table top; the waiter scrawls down your order on a slip of paper and slides it under the glass too. At the end you retrieve your

Tea, coffee and soft drinks

Tea is to China what wines are to France, and specialist tea shops stock a truly bewildering variety of leaves from famous tea-growing districts around the mainland, costing from a few dollars per 100g to several hundred. Stores will often let you taste before you buy, or try the free **tea appreciation course** run by the HKTB (see p.67). At *dim sum* joints the staff should ask what sort of tea you'd like (though foreigners are automatically brought a pot of *heung pin*, jasmine); and at more formal meals tea might be served before or after the meal, but very rarely with it.

Along with **medicinal teas** (see the *Cantonese cuisine* colour section), other types of teas served in Hong Kong cafés, snack bars and restaurants include Western-style tea, cold lemon tea, Taiwanese-style bubble tea (sweetened cold tea shaken to form a frothy top layer), pearl milk tea (sweet milk tea with tapioca balls, also originally from Taiwan) and Hong Kong-style milk tea, made with evaporated milk. For the real thing, venture into one of the big hotels for afternoon tea (see box opposite), something that is well worth doing at least once for the atmosphere alone. Coffee is also widely available in cafés, though not overly popular with the Chinese. The one exception is a local blend of tea, instant coffe and milk called yuanyang coffee, which frankly does nothing for the tastebuds.

For quick **drinks**, you can get all the usual soft pop at 7–Eleven stores and supermarkets. Around street market areas, look for stalls selling fresh mango, coconut milk, watermelon and sago drinks; and you could also try the local soft drinks: Vitamilk is a plain or flavoured soya milk drink – a few dollars a carton – while lemon tea, chocolate milk, iced teas and lots of other infusions all come cold and in cartons. Regular milk isn't drunk very much by the Cantonese, but there are, surprisingly, several milk bars around town, or you can buy it in supermarkets.

bill and take it to the front counter to pay the cashier. Aside from the above breakfasts, *cha chaan tengs* serve basic one-plate meals such as sandpot rice, barbecue pork on rice, stir-fried noodles, wonton or fishball soups and weird Chinese versions of Western dishes; you'll pay around HK$35 a helping.

Hong Kong-wide

Café de Coral Over a hundred branches around Hong Kong with bright, plastic interiors and a daily turnover of 300,000 customers seeking Chinese fast food. Noodles, chicken wings, fried rice, radish cakes, salads and sandwiches at low prices. Generally daily 8am–8pm.

Délifrance Pseudo-French deli-cafés selling croissants, baguettes, cakes and coffee from seventeen outlets strung between The Peak; Central and north Hong Kong Island; Kowloon; Sha Tin, Tsuen Wan and Kwai Fung in the New Territories; and Tung Chung on Lantau. Those in business areas might only operate Mon–Fri 8am–6pm, others generally daily 8am–8pm.

Fairwood Pretty well a clone of the *Café de Coral* chain, though a bit more variable in quality between local branches.

Häagen-Dazs Ice cream, cakes and drinks.

Branches (among others) at Central; The Peak; Times Square, Causeway Bay; and the *Hyatt Regency Hotel*, Tsim Sha Tsui. Daily 10am–8pm.

Hui Lau Shan Citywide chain specializing in cold mango-sago-coconut-aloe jelly drinks, incredibly refreshing on a hot day. Shop signs are not always in English – look for three gold characters on a red background.

Maxim's Larger branches are restaurants selling barbecued chicken legs, hamburgers, salads, roast-meat dishes, drinks and sandwiches. Smaller stalls concentrate on garish and synthetic-tasting cakes. At most train stations and many malls and shopping plazas. Generally daily 9am–8pm.

Oliver's Super Sandwiches Reliable but crowded deli and sandwich shop chain, also serving breakfast, afternoon tea and baked potatoes. Avoid the insipid pasta dishes. Branches around Central, Wan Chai,

Causeway Bay and Kowloon. Mon–Sat 8am–6pm.

Pacific Coffee Company Local generic-coffee chain with reasonable brews, comfy sofas, the usual range of sweet pastries and muffins, free internet for customers (terminals and wi-fi) plus local newspapers. Opening hours vary depending on the locality (Mon–Sat 8am–6pm in Central) but roughly daily 8am–9pm.

Saint's Alp In a few shopping centre food courts, especially in the New Territories. A cute, bright Taiwanese teahouse chain popular with teenagers and young couples, serving tea, pearl milk drinks, bubble tea and light snacks. They have bilingual menus.

Starbucks Coffee The international coffee imperialists are here to compete against the local *Pacific Coffee Company*. Opening hours vary depending on the branch, but generally daily 8am–8pm.

Central and Soho

Unless otherwise stated, the places listed below are marked on the map on pp.60–61.

Dan Ryan's Chicago Bar and Grill The Mall, One Pacific Place, 88 Queensway, Central. American restaurant serving classic breakfasts at weekends – eggs, pancakes and all the trimmings. Very good for children. Served Sat & Sun 7.30–11am.

Flying Pan 9 Old Bailey St, Soho. See map, p.68. Open round the clock for pots of coffee and pancakes, waffles, bagels and eggs cooked just about any way you can imagine them – benedict, rancheros, Spanish omelette or just a classic fry-up with sausages, bacon, mushroom and tomatoes. Some of the bigger options would feed two. HK$60–100 a head.

Jaspa's 28–30 Staunton St, Soho. See map, p.68. Chunky breakfasts served daily 7–11am including doorstopper toast, big bowls of muesli, and grilled Turkish bread with strawberries.

Joyce Café The Galleria, 9 Queen's Rd, Central. In a league of its own for stylish café surroundings, and expensive, although there are set breakfast menus (7.30am–noon). The menu is mostly soups, sandwiches, pastas and salads, with East–West fusion and health-food overtones. Mon–Sat 10am–9pm.

La Cité Basement, The Mall, One Pacific Place, 88 Queensway, Central. Smart bistro-cum-café that pushes all the right buttons – soup, snacks and set lunches, or just teas and coffees while you take the weight off your shopping feet. Daily 11am–11pm.

Mandarin Oriental Hotel 5 Connaught Rd, Central. For coffee, all-day snacks and light meals, and lunch or dinner buffet, the *Clipper Lounge* (7am–1am) is the favoured see-and-be-seen haunt, although its breakfast gets mixed reviews.

Marriott Café JW Marriott Hotel, One Pacific Place, 88 Queensway, Central. Western/Asian snacks and meals in an elegant hotel coffee shop whose long hours are a boon in this district. Daily 7am–1am.

Sift 46 Graham St, Soho. See map, p.68. Understated café and takeaway specializing in sweet pastry confections. Tues–Sun 3–11pm.

Tsui Wah 15–19 Wellington St, Central. See map, p.63. Original of ever-expanding

Afternoon tea

Sipping a cup of British-style tea, with proper milk and all the trimmings, especially in one of the SAR's most splendid hotels, has become something of a Hong Kong institution. The lobby lounges are generally the places to head for, among which the **Peninsula** (see p.106) is the most magnificent – all gilt and soaring pillars, and a string quartet playing as you drink tea and munch scones. Other marvellous venues for afternoon tea are the **Intercontinental** (see p.102), the **Island Shangri-La** (p.191) and the **Mandarin Oriental** (p.191). At all these places, expect to pay around HK$180 upwards per person for a set tea. Dress code is "smart casual": no sports-wear, no open shoes for men or T-shirts. For a less formal afternoon tea experience with 360° views, head to **R66** (62nd Floor, Hopewell Centre, 183 Queens Rd East, Wan Chai; ☎2862 6166), Hong Kong's only revolving restaurant – though the scenery outperforms the food.

cha chaan teng chain; a warehouse-sized place with a big range of inexpensive single-dish meals. It's always crammed full, a popularity down to them doing everything just a bit better than average. Fishball soups are excellent, as is the Hoi Nam chicken with rice. Around HK$30 a dish.

T.W. Café 12 Lyndhurst Terrace, Central. Not only fine coffee, but also large set breakfasts of egg and toast, fried fillet of sole, or chicken steaks for around HK$32. Window bar for people watching.

Wan Chai and Causeway Bay

The places listed below are marked on the map on pp.78–79.

Cova Ground Floor, Lee Gardens, 33 Hysan Rd, Causeway Bay ☎2832 9008. Branch of the Milanese restaurant, this upmarket café also offers pasta lunches and focaccia, but is best-known for its home-made *gelato* and sorbets (around HK$70 a serve).

Grand Café Grand Hyatt, 1 Harbour Rd. Hotel coffee shop with some of the finest window seats in the SAR and stylish, elegant surroundings. The food matches these step for step – always pricey, but top quality. Daily 6.30am–1am.

Habitu 8 Queens Rd East, Wan Chai. Classy but laid-back café with the best coffee for miles around and inexpensive light lunches (grilled sandwiches, pizza, salads etc), making it popular with local junior executives. Free wi-fi too.

Lo Cha Di Yat Ka Corner of Luard and Hennessy rds, Wan Chai. No English sign but easy to recognize this open-fronted Medicinal Chinese Tea counter, charging HK$7 a drink. Unique in that it labels all its brews in English as well as Chinese.

People's Bookstore 1st Floor, 18 Russell St, Causeway Bay (opposite Times Square). Hip, small café with Maoist themes (the menus are inside "Little Red Books"), plenty of books and newspapers, low tables and furniture to sprawl in. Coffee and light meals, including excellent cheesecake. Expensive though, at HK$35 a cup. 9am–11pm.

Pumpernickel 13 Cleveland St, Causeway Bay. Friendly café-restaurant with fresh-baked wholemeal bread, pasta, salads and risottos. Set lunches 11.30am–3pm for HK$70.

Renaissance Harbour View Hotel 1 Harbour Rd. This harbour-front hotel's coffee shop offers equally spectacular views to that in the nearby *Grand Hyatt*, at slightly cheaper prices. Daily 7am–10.30pm.

Tsim Sha Tsui, Yau Ma Tei and Mong Kok

Chungking Mansions 36–44 Nathan Rd, Tsim Sha Tsui. See map, p.104. Take your pick from Nepalese, Indian or Pakistani cuisine – cheap curried breakfasts for those with cast-iron constitutions. Daily 8am–10pm.

Hoi Keng Congee Specialist 72 Bute St, Mong Kok. See map, p.110. Great place for basic Chinese breakfast, including fresh soy milk and huge, crispy doughnut sticks – you'll see the latter displayed at the shop front if you're here early enough.

Langham Mall 555 Shanghai St, Mong Kok. See map, p.110. Third-floor atrium has a handful of cafés with outside seating on good days – on wet ones you can sit inside and watch sheets of rain hammering into the glassed-in roof.

Mall Café Ground Floor, YMCA, 41 Salisbury Rd, Tsim Sha Tsui. See map, p.104. Favourite Tsim Sha Tsui spot for a leisurely breakfast – Continental, English or Chinese for HK$60 – set lunch or sandwich. The Hong Kong daily papers are available. Daily 7am–midnight.

Shadowman 7 Lock Rd, Tsim Sha Tsui. See map, p.104. Convenient for all the back-packer's hostels, this café offers twenty free minutes on their high-speed Macs if you buy a drink or one of the light meals or snacks (halal food) – otherwise, it's about HK$1 per minute. Daily 8.30am–midnight.

Sun Yat 26–28 Cameron Rd, Tsim Sha Tsui. See map, p.104. Absolutely classic *cha chaan teng* with rapid turnover, an extensive menu and staff who, while not hostile, always seem too busy to take your order. They get a regular trickle of foreigners in here but prices are not tourist-inflated.

Yee Shun Milk Company 519 Nathan Rd, Yau Ma Tei. See map, p.110. Old *cha chaan teng* whose speciality is bowls of sweetened steamed milk, set and flavoured with ginger. You can also fill up on fruit or milk shakes, sandwiches, toast and steamed eggs. Daily 8am–9pm.

New Territories

Cru 18 Wan King Path, Sai Kung Town ☎2791 1792. Wine bar and grill that also opens for breakfast from 8am. Coffee is excellent.

EATING | Cafés, breakfasts and cha chaan tengs

6

204

Dim sum

Dim sum – a selection of small snacks served with tea – is the traditional Cantonese way to start the day. Nearly all regular Cantonese restaurants serve *dim sum* from 7am until lunch time or even 3pm, so just about every downtown area, shopping plaza or residential estate has a restaurant where you can grab a *dim sum* meal. Most dishes cost between HK$10 and HK$40 a serving, so even if you absolutely stuff yourself, it's hard to spend more than HK$90–120 a head in a group, perhaps rising to HK$150 if you eat in one of the fancier *dim sum* places. Some restaurants also offer discounts if you eat before 11am. A ten-percent service charge added to the bill is normal.

Central

Unless otherwise stated, the places listed below are marked on the map on pp.60–61.

Jasmine Shop 5, Lower Ground Floor, Jardine House, 1 Connaught Place ☎ 2524 5098. Dependable *dim sum* in upmarket surroundings served by staff who are used to novice visitors. Daily 11am–3pm & 6–11pm.

Dim sum restaurants

Most *dim sum* restaurants are enormous and noisy, often with tables on several floors; in the smarter places, staff with two-way radios check on space before letting you through. Decoration is often completely over-the-top: they're used for wedding receptions and parties and are covered in dragons, swirls, painted screens and ornate backgrounds.

Going in, you'll either be confronted by a maître d', who'll put your name on a list and tell you when there's space, or often you can just walk through and fight for a table yourself. It's busiest at lunchtime and on Sunday when families come out to eat, when you'll have to queue. This is not an orderly concept: just attach yourself to a likely looking table where people appear to be finishing up, and hover over the seats until they leave. Any hesitation and you'll lose your table, so keep an eye out. It's best to go in a **group** if you can, in order to share dishes. As all the tables seat about ten or more, you'll be surrounded by others anyway, which is fun if the experience is new to you.

How to order, how to pay

Once you've secured a table, you'll be asked what sort of tea you'd like or, more likely, brought a pot of jasmine by default (see box, p.202). There's usually no extra charge for a refill, and when you want a refill, just leave the lid off the teapot and it'll be topped up. At this stage, if you're Chinese, you'll have already started to wash your chopsticks and rinse your bowls in the hot tea or water: everything should be clean anyway, but it's almost a ritual with some people.

Traditionally, the *dim sum* selection is wheeled around the restaurant on trolleys stacked with bamboo steamers in which the dumplings are cooked; each steamer contains a small plate with three or four little dumplings, or a single serving of more substantial dishes. Only the more upmarket places still do this, however; usually you'll find an **order card** – looking like a little paper menu with blank boxes at the end of each dish – stacked in the centre of the table. Tick the box for every dish you want and then call over a waiter and give them the card. Often these cards are bilingual or even have photos of dishes, but otherwise ask for an English menu, try to find an English speaker, or use the *dim sum* **menu reader** box (p.207). Once you've sorted out your order, you'll be left with another piece of card marked up in rows denoting "small", "medium", "large", "special order" etc. The waiter delivering each dish will stamp this card accordingly and at the end you take it to the front desk to be charged for the number and size of dishes you've had.

Lok Cha Teahouse K.C. Lo Gallery, Hong Kong Park ☎2801 7177. Full of wooden screens and dark Chinese furniture, this is a pricey but very atmospheric place to try a selection of fine Chinese teas, with the lowdown on the importance of water temperature, aroma and taste explained by the staff as they serve you. Small selection of vegetarian *dim sum* to try, too. From HK$40 per person for the tea, HK$20 per *dim sum* serving. Bookings advised, especially at weekends. Daily 10am–10pm.

Luk Yu Teahouse 24–26 Stanley St ☎2523 1970. Famous as much for its 1930s vibe – heavy ceiling fans, dark wooden furniture, shell lamps, and *dim sum* carried around tables in tin trays by elderly staff – as for its food, whose quality is frankly not up to the hefty price tag (at least HK$150 a head). Even so, it's worth a trip to impress a business client or just for the ambience; you'll need to book at weekends. Daily 7am–6pm.

Metropol 4th Floor, United Centre, 95 Queensway ☎2865 1988. Seating for over a thousand, and they still use trolleys to wheel the selection around. The food is a cut above average – especially the flaky *cha siu* pastries and crunchy prawn dumplings. Tea is good too. Daily 8am–midnight.

Summer Palace 5th Floor, Island Shangri-La Hotel, Two Pacific Place, 88 Queensway ☎2820 8552. Superbly designed – but expensive – *dim sum*

in relaxed, stylish and reasonably quiet surroundings. Daily 11.30am–3pm.

Tsui Hang Village 2nd Floor, New World Tower, 16–18 Queen's Rd ☎2524 2012. Named after the home town of the 1920s revolutionary Dr Sun Yat-sen, the restaurant is well thought of – the food and decor are traditional and prices moderate for this part of the city.

Yung Kee 32–40 Wellington St ☎2522 1624. See map, p.63. Classic Cantonese restaurant that gets mobbed for its fine *dim sum*, in particular the roasted goose. Mon–Sat 2–5pm, Sun 10am–5.30pm.

Sheung Wan

The places listed below are marked on the map on p.69.

Fung Shing On Tai St, just behind Western Market, Sheung Wan. Underneath the much more ostentatious *Treasure Lake Golden Banquet* restaurant, this clean, friendly place doesn't get much foreign custom but the food is well above average – tissue-paper thin *sheung fun* rice noodles, crisp-fried prawn packets and fried mandarin fish rolls. The cuisine here is from Shunde, just across the border in China, and you might want to try local specials such as honey-roast meats and braised stuffed duck.

Lin Heung Teahouse 160–164 Wellington St ☎2544 4556. This place relocated here from Guangzhou (Canton) around 1950, and they've been so busy since that they haven't had time to change the furnishings or allow their ancient staff to retire. Decidedly brusque service and the menu is nothing unusual, but a fantastic atmosphere if you're after a traditional, crowded, lively venue. Daily from 7.30am.

Wan Chai and Causeway Bay

The places listed below are marked on the map on p.78.

Dim Sum 63 Sing Woo Rd, Happy Valley ☎2834 8893. Old-style wooden booths make this a nice, cosy place to experiment with *dim sum* – there are over eighty varieties on the menu, and staff are patient with foreigners. Daily 11am–4.30pm & 6–11pm.

Dynasty Renaissance Harbour View, 1 Harbour Rd ☎2802 8888. Harbour views and excellent, creative but pricey *dim sum*. Mon–Sat noon–3pm, Sun 11.30am–3pm.

▲ Selection of *dim sum*

Dim sum reader

Beef balls	san jook ngow yook	山竹牛肉
Beef rice roll	ngau yook cheung fun	牛肉腸粉
Beef tripe	ngau toe	牛肚
Chicken bun	gai bao	雞飽
Chicken feet	fung jow	鳳爪
Chive dumplings	jin gau choy bang	煎韭菜餅
Coconut jelly	yeh jup gau	椰汁糕
Congee	juk	粥
Crispy-fried squid tentacles	jar yo yu so	炸魷魚鬚
Crystal-skinned dumpling	chiu chao fun gwar	潮洲粉果
Custard tart	dan ta	蛋撻
Fried stuffed riceball	harm suey gok	咸水角
Fried taro ball	woo gok	芋角
Fried taro cake	woo tau gau	芋頭糕
Fried white radish cake	loh bok gau	蘿蔔糕
Fried wonton	jar won ton	炸雲吞
Lotus paste bun	lin yoong bao	蓮蓉飽
Mango pudding	mong gwar bo deen	芒果布甸
Pork dumpling	siu mai	燒賣
Prawn dumpling	har gau	蝦餃
Prawn rice roll	har cheung fun	蝦腸粉
Roast pork bun	char siu bao	叉燒飽
Roast pork rice roll	char siu cheung fun	叉燒腸粉
Sesame ball	jin dway	煎堆
"Shark fin" pork dumpling*	yu chee gau	魚翅餃
Spareribs	pai gwat	排骨
Spring roll	chun goon	春卷
Steamed chicken rice in lotus leaf	nor mai gai	糯米雞
Steamed fishballs	lang yu kau	鯪魚球
Stuffed beancurd-skin roll	seen jook goon	鮮竹卷
Stuffed green pepper	jin yong chang chiu	煎釀青椒
"Thousand year old" eggs	pay dan	皮蛋
Tofu in syrup	dao fa	豆花

*Named after their shape they don't contain shark's fin.

East Lake Seafood 4th Floor, Pearl City, 28 Paterson St, Causeway Bay ☎ 2504 3311. Cheerful, noisy placed packed with local Chinese daily from 7am to early afternoon.

Hak Ka Hut 21st Floor, Lee Theatre Plaza, Causeway Bay ☎ 2881 8578. *Dim sum* with a Chaozhou and Hakka twist, which means more rice rolls and clear-skinned dumplings than usual. You can also order classic Hakka dishes such as *kou rou* pork belly, stuffed tofu and salt-baked chicken. Excellent food, price and – if you get here early enough – views out over the Causeway Bay area.

Lung Moon 130–136 Johston Rd, Wan Chai. Massive, multi-floor old Cantonese restaurant of the kind that they really don't make any more, with gaudy trim that's slightly shabby round the edges. They do basic dishes like dry-fried beef noodles really well, and it's the only place in town that still roasts meat in a charcoal-burning oven.

Tsim Sha Tsui and Jordan

Majesty Seafood 3rd Floor, Prudential Centre, 216–228 Nathan Rd, Jordan ☎ 2723 2399. See map, p.110. Ride the lift to the third floor and settle down, surrounded by fish tanks, for tasty steamed beef balls, leek dumplings, *cha siu* puffs and egg custard tarts. The only drawback is that they can overkill with the a/c – you need a sweater to eat here.

🏃 **Tao Heung** Floor 3, Silvercord Centre, 30 Canton Rd (entrance on Haiphong Rd) ☎2375 9128. See map, pp.104–105. Come early for a window seat facing Kowloon Park. They have an English menu squirrelled away, and their selection is first-rate and inexpensive – try the white radish cake, roast pork *sheung fun* (stuffed rice noodles), and their beef rissoles with celery.

🏃 **Tsui Fuk** Upstairs in the Plover Cove Market building ☎2766 3788. See map, p.142. Vast interior with hundreds of people heading here every morning; you usually have to wait at the front desk and take a number. Top-notch *dim sum* at very reasonable prices; if this were in the downtown it would be famous. No English signs or speakers, but surprisingly the order card has an English translation.

Restaurants

There are **restaurants** absolutely everywhere in Hong Kong; aside from the very cheapest places (which open for breakfast), assume **opening times** of approximately 11am–3pm & 6–11pm unless otherwise specified in the text. Office **lunch hours** are between noon and 2pm, and if you're in downtown areas of Hong Kong Island or Kowloon, get in earlier or later if you don't want a long wait for a seat.

Most of the larger hotels put on self-service **buffets** for breakfast, lunch or afternoon tea, and sometimes for dinner, too; these cost HK$100–350 a head depending on the establishment and meal involved. You'll usually find a sign in hotel lobbies advertising times and costs, or phone for exact details. Expect to pay extra for drinks and a ten-percent service charge. Elsewhere, restaurants almost always offer good-value **set meals** through the day; and there's a group of places in Central with a **buy-one-get-one-free** deal on main courses Monday nights. Check ⓦ www.supermondays.com to buy a members' card (HK$50) and for the list of participating places (mostly in Soho and Lan Kwai Fong).

You'll find that many restaurants located in residential blocks – such as *Chungking Mansions*' Indian establishments – call themselves **clubs** or **kitchens**. This is to get around restaurant licensing laws, and technically you need to be a member to eat at them; though in all these places, entering the restaurant confers temporary membership. Real clubs, which do require you to be a member, or guest of a member, to eat there (such as the *Foreign Correspondents' Club*), are not covered in this guide.

Chinese

For the intricacies of **eating and ordering** in a Chinese restaurant, see the box on p.210. In addition to the following places, don't forget the **seafood restaurants** at Lei Yue Mun (see p.120) in Kowloon, Lau Fau Shan (p.133) in the New Territories, and Lamma and Cheung Chau islands (pp.162–169).

Central

Unless otherwise stated, the places listed below are marked on the map on pp.60–61.

Island Tang 222 The Galleria, 9 Queens Rd ☎2526 8798. Latest venture from David Tang, creator of Shanghai Tang and the China Club, this suavely designed restaurant sports a 1920s Chinese-colonial look that probably never existed but feels very authentic. Claims to be just a simple café but you'd be pushed to find another in Hong Kong offering bird's nest soup or abalone. Expensive.

Man Wah Mandarin Oriental Hotel, 5 Connaught Rd ☎2825 4003. If you've got the cash for one extravagantly priced Cantonese meal, blow it here on some beautiful food – the steamed crab with ginger shouldn't be missed – and spectacular views from the 25th floor. If they don't take your breath

Cantonese cuisine

Hong Kong's local cooking style is Cantonese, named after the nearby Chinese metropolis of Guangzhou (Canton). Emigrants from southern China have made Cantonese food broadly familiar to most Westerners, though you'll find that it has changed somewhat in translation, and dishes on the menu in Hong Kong often bear little resemblance to versions served up overseas. As with the other major branches of Chinese cuisine, the cornerstone of Cantonese cooking is creating a balance of flavour, texture and colour – for instance, sweet with sour, crispness with juiciness, dark with light.

Newly caught fish and seafood for sale, Sai Kung Town ▲

Vegetable market, Cheung Chau ▼

A fine balance

Unlike other parts of China, Hong Kong is blessed with good soil, access to fresh seafood, and a year-round growing season – factors that lend the Cantonese their obsession with **freshness** of taste. In markets you'll see meat from animals slaughtered that morning; fowl probably still alive in cages; and fish and shellfish moving around in buckets of water. Food's **natural qualities** are brought out by stir-frying over high heat to seal in flavour, or by gentle steaming or poaching.

There are famous exceptions of course, influenced by other Chinese and foreign styles. The Cantonese excel at **roasting** meat, specifically pigeon, duck, goose and pork. The meat is marinated in sugar, soy sauce and wine, and the end product is juicy with crispy skin. In one version, goose is flavoured with sour plum, a technique from Chiu Chow (Chaozhou) in southern China, where **sweet and sour** dishes with fruit also originated; the town's biggest contribution, however, is translucent *fun gwor* dumplings (popular in Hong Kong's *dim sum* restaurants). **Shunde** dishes (from another nearby town in China) include honey-roast pork, while **Hakka** food features preserved vegetables, chicken baked whole under a pile of crushed salt, and stewed tofu cubes stuffed with minced pork.

Taste and texture

Cantonese **seasoning** involves minimal use of sugar, soy sauce, rice wine and vinegar to tease out underlying fresh, sweet tastes; stronger spices such as chilli, salted black beans and five-spice powder are sparingly employed only to offer a contrast. The object is always to season without being obvious – any heavy-handedness and diners would immediately suspect that what they are eating is not fresh. Nothing illustrates this better than **seafood**; many restaurants allow diners to pick their own straight from the tank. Seafood is best eaten steamed, lightly seasoned with soy, ginger, spring onion and some fermented black soya beans. Any Cantonese restaurant will have a signature seafood dish – even if it's just a fishball soup – but for atmosphere, it's hard to beat the outdoor places on Lamma and Cheung Chau islands.

The Cantonese most enjoy well-defined **textures**, such as the crunchiness of a really fresh, lightly cooked prawn, or the smooth resilience of steamed beef balls with fresh coriander (which actually get their texture and juiciness from added fish paste). **Vegetables** also provide contrasting textures, with mushrooms, green beans, bean sprouts, taro, carrot, aubergine and especially *choi sum* (Chinese broccoli), served steamed with garlic or oyster sauce. Though most people eat a far greater quantity of vegetables than meat, the Chinese believe that only meat can provide essential energy. However, for both physical and spiritual reasons, people do eat vegetarian dishes regularly, and there is a sophisticated **vegetarian cuisine**, which uses gluten and tofu in all its forms to mimic meat. White steamed **rice** is the Cantonese staple, along with broad **rice noodles** (*hefen*); fried rice is considered a special dish.

Another source of texture are **preserved ingredients** such as birds' nests and sea cucumber, which are actually completely flavourless but are served in a slow-cooked meat **stock**, sieved and skimmed until all fat and residues are removed and only the requisite "fresh" flavour remains.

▲ Cantonese dish of scallops and broccoli

▼ Pressed meat, a speciality of Macau

Freshly steamed *dim sum* ▲

Medicinal tea shop ▼

Dim sum

The name **dim sum**, "little heart", refers to the dozens of types of small dumplings stuffed with vegetables, meat or seafood, and boiled, fried, baked or steamed – crunchy *har gau*, minced prawns wrapped in transparent rice-flour skins, are the hallmark of a good restaurant. These are backed up by spring rolls, prawn toast and other snacks, along with small servings of main-meal dishes such as squid with black beans, rice and cooked meats in lotus leaves, rissoles, curried squid, chicken feet, turnip cake and stuffed peppers. *Dim sum* meals also feature sweet **desserts**, such as coconut jelly, a very foreign concept in Chinese food. It is also known as **yum cha**, "with tea", as a pot always accompanies a meal.

Tea

Chinese **tea** falls into three broad categories: **green**, where the leaves are picked and dried straightaway, producing a green- or yellow-tinted brew; **black**, where the leaves are fermented before drying, for a dark red infusion; and **oolong**, where the leaves are part-fermented before drying, creating a yellow or light red brew. Famous varieties include *heung pin cha* (jasmine, a green tea scented by flowers), green *longjing* ("Dragon Well"), *tiet kwunyam* ("Iron Buddha", a popular type of *oolong*-style tea) and black *bolei* (*pu'er* tea), the favoured accompaniment to a *dim sum* meal for its supposed fat-reducing properties. Another integral brew is **medicinal tea**; concoctions made from various medicinally "cooling" astringent herbs (the Cantonese term, *lok cha*, translates as "cool tea"); two popular for driving off colds are *ng fa cha* (five-flower tea) and *ya sei mei* (twenty-four flavour tea).

away, the bill will. Reservations are essential.

Sam Tor 30 Pottinger St. An unusually friendly hole-in-the-wall known for its wonton soups and fried goose innards; extremely cheap and consequently marked by lunchtime queues trailing around the corner.

Ser Wong Fun 30 Cochrane St. See map, p.68. The name means "Snake King", and this long-time institution does indeed offer snake dishes from HK$65. They also do good fish head in bean curd and ginger sauce (HK$90) and the usual run of roast meat, noodle and congee dishes.

🏃 **Tsim Chai Kee Near the corner of Wellington and Cochrane sts. See map, p.68.** Tiny place serving just three things: beef ball soup, prawn wontons – jokingly known as "ping pong" wonton because of their huge size – and greens in oyster sauce. But it's all so tasty and cheap you'll have a wait to get seated at lunch. HK$16 a bowl.

🏃 **Yung Kee 32–40 Wellington St ☎2522 1624. See map, p.68.** Four-storey eating-house and a great Cantonese institution, known for its exceptional roast goose, *char siu* pork and pigeon – the best you will find anywhere. Very reasonable prices considering; expect HK$350 a head. Daily 11am–11.30pm.

Sheung Wan

Golden China 9 Jubilee St ☎2545 1472. See map, p.69. There's a small English sign, but don't expect any to be spoken inside – no problem, however, as this small,

▲ Tucking in to noodles, Sheung Wan

comfortable Cantonese diner has a limited menu along the lines of roast duck or roast pork and rice; portions HK$28–38. Has been catering to Central's office workers since 1963. Daily 8am–late afternoon.

Tim's Kitchen 93 Jervois St, Sheung Wan ☎2543 5919. See map, p.69. Informal, low-decor Cantonese place which doesn't look as if it runs to much more than barbequed pork, so the menu – featuring lashings of abalone, fish maw, bird nests and sea cucumber dishes – is a bit of a surprise. Not cheap, but not outrageous either given the ingredients; mains upwards of HK$150. Bookings essential.

Wan Chai and Causeway Bay

The places listed below are marked on the map on pp.78–79.

🏃 **Fook Lam Moon 35–45 Johnston Rd, Wan Chai ☎2866 0663.** Among Hong Kong's finest and most famous Cantonese restaurants, this is not the place to come if you're skimping on costs. House specialities include bird's nest soup, abalone, crispy piglet and crisp-skinned chicken. Service is snotty and offhand unless they already know you.

Hee Kee 392 Jaffe Rd, Wan Chai ☎2893 7565. A crab restaurant going since 1965 and recently refurbished, with a reputation as a celebrity hangout. Fried chilli crab is the way to go, at around HK$200 a head.

Ho Hung Kee 2 Sharp St East, near Times Square, Causeway Bay. Cramped, bustling place serving inexpensive wonton noodles, beef brisket soup and congee; the large Chinese neon sign edging into the street makes it hard to miss.

Kung Tak Lam 10th Floor, World Trade Centre, 280 Gloucester Rd, Causeway Bay ☎2881 9966. Famous vegetarian restaurant chain (the original is in Beijing) with a huge variety of "meat" dishes made out of potato, bean curd, mushrooms and gluten. The food can be a bit stodgy if you order the wrong mix of dishes but it's very attractively presented and views of the harbour are great. Mains from HK$90.

Tai Hing 49–57 Lee Garden Rd, Causeway Bay. Superlative roast meat restaurant – though perhaps a little fatty for some – where you can get a portion of barbecued or crispy-skinned pork, roast goose or soy-sauce chicken on rice for HK$31. A whole goose

Don't be intimidated by the prospect of eating in a Chinese restaurant in Hong Kong. The following tips will help smooth the way.

Chopsticks and other utensils

You eat, naturally enough, with **chopsticks**. If these are new to you, hold one midway along its length like a pencil, then slide the other underneath, and use them as extensions of your fingers to pick up the food. Don't worry too much about your skill – the important thing is to get the food into your mouth. If you can't manage, use the china **spoon** provided, or ask for a fork and spoon – many restaurants have them. You eat out of the little bowl in front of you (the smaller cup is for your tea), putting your rice in and plonking bits of food on top. Then, raise the bowl to your lips and shovel it in with the chopsticks (much easier than eating with chopsticks from a plate), chucking bones onto the small plate as you go (you can ask for clean ones as you go along). They'll change the cloth when you leave, so it's no problem if your table looks like culinary Armageddon.

Don't stick your chopsticks upright in your bowl when you're not eating (it's a Taoist death sign); place them across the top of the bowl, or on the chopstick rests.

Ordering food and drink

Most places have **menus** in English, though these are sometimes less extensive and exciting than the Chinese one: don't be afraid to ask for a missing favourite or even point at what other Chinese diners are eating if it looks interesting. To get the most out of a Chinese meal, you're best off in a group; as a rule of thumb, order one more dish than there are people. The idea is that you put together a **balanced meal**, including the "five tastes" – acid, hot, bitter, sweet and salty – achieved by balancing separate servings of meat, fish and vegetables, plus rice and soup. Soup – normally meat, fish or vegetable stock in a tureen – is drunk throughout the meal (or, in very old-fashioned restaurants, at the end) rather than as a starter. Rice with food is white and steamed; fried rice comes as a fancier dish as part of a large meal. It's bad manners to leave rice, so don't order too much. The food will either come with various sauces (such as plum sauce or chilli sauce), which are poured into the little dishes provided to be used as a dip, or you can add the soy sauce and sesame oil on the table to flavour your food. **Dessert** isn't always available, though you'll often get a sliced orange with which to cleanse the palate.

The classic drink with your meal is tea (see box, p.202), which will be brought as a matter of course. Beer also goes well with most Chinese food. Wine is generally expensive, and the stronger taste and higher alcohol content make it a less suitable accompaniment, although that hasn't stopped it becoming increasingly popular among Chinese diners (at the expense of the traditional drink of brandy or whisky), who increasingly regard wine (red, particularly) as healthy. Having a couple of bottles from an expensive, well-known French chateau on your table is also a way of indicating status when entertaining or celebrating (even if it is then diluted with Coke or Sprite to make it sweeter!). Westerners usually prefer a dry white so as not to kill the taste of the food.

To ask for the bill, you say *mai dan*, though – with the wrong intonation – this can also mean to "buy eggs". Sign language works just as well. Nearly all restaurants will add a ten-percent service charge to your bill, and if small plates of nuts and pickles

is just HK$140 if you wanted to order some greens and make a meal of it. Four-to-a-booth seating and you'll have to share at lunchtime. 7am–11pm.

Tung Fong Siu Kee Yuen 241 Hennessy Rd, Wan Chai ☎ 2507 4839. Classic 1905 vegetarian restaurant; there's a cake shop out front while upstairs is a comfortably dated dining room with helpful, English-speaking staff. Some of the dishes don't sound very appealing in translation but it's all good and portions are generous. Around HK$75 a head.

are brought with tea, you'll pay for them, too – wave them away if you don't want them. In places where there's no service charge, leaving ten percent or a few dollars from your change is fine. Even if you've paid service, the waiter may wave your change airily above your head in the leather wallet that the bill came in; if you want the change, make a move for it or that will be deemed a tip, too.

The cuisines

Cantonese cuisine is the most common cooking style found in Hong Kong, along with Chiu Chow and Hakka, which are essentially variations on the Cantonese theme. However, many types of regional Chinese food are also found here, either at specialist restaurants or as individual dishes in places that are otherwise firmly Cantonese – the waiter should always be able to point you towards the house speciality.

Beijing (Peking)

Beijing food is a northern, colder-climate style of cooking that relies more on pickles and meat, and favours wheat noodles and heavy dough dumplings instead of rice. One speciality is the Mongolian hotpot of sliced meat, vegetables and dumplings cooked and mixed together in a stock that's boiled at your table in a special stove; you dip the raw ingredients in, eat them once cooked and then drink the resulting soup at the end of the meal. The most famous Beijing food of all is Peking duck – slices of skin and meat from a barbecued duck, wrapped in a pancake with spring onion and radish and smeared with plum sauce. The local ducks are usually rather fattier than what you may be used to at home. If you order this, be sure to ask for the duck carcass to be taken away after carving and turned into soup with vegetables and mushrooms, which is then served later.

Shanghainese

Shanghainese is also a heavier cuisine than Cantonese, using more oil and spices, as well as preserved vegetables, pickles and steamed dumplings. Where the southern cuisines are interested in fresh flavours, Shanghai's is more concerned in emphasizing each ingredient's characteristic taste, with a bias towards sweetness. Meals often start with cold dishes such as smoked fish; and might include "drunken chicken" cooked in rice wine; or "red-cooked" pork stewed in an aromatic stock containing soy sauce, sugar and aniseed. Seafood is also widely used, particularly fried or braised eels, while the great speciality is the expensive hairy crab – sent from Shanghai in the autumn, it is steamed and accompanied by ginger tea; the roe is considered a delicacy.

Sichuan (Szechuan)

Totally at odds with the above regions, Sichuan food takes little interest in original tastes or freshness, instead constructing pungent flavours with a heavy use of garlic, chillies and aromatic Sichuan pepper. Salted bean paste is a common cooking agent. Marinades are widely used, and specialities include spicy tofu, smoked duck (marinaded in wine, highly seasoned and cooked over tea leaves), and "strange-flavoured" chicken (served with a soya-sesame-vinegar sauce). Other dishes you'll see are braised aubergine, pork with raw garlic purée, and braised beans. You'll get through a lot of beer with a Sichuan meal.

Wing Wah 89 Hennessy Rd, Corner of Luard Rd, Wan Chai (there's no English sign). Known for its wonton soup, this locally famous noodle house also does mostly inexpensive, unusual medicinal soups, beef tendon noodles, and minced shrimps on pomelo skins.

Yee Hin 2 Landale St, off Queens Rd East, Wan Chai. Congee, noodles and rice but best for its sweet desserts and iced Chinese teas.

Aberdeen

The places listed below are marked on the map on p.89.

Chow Kee 154 Old Main St. Well-known basic noodle and fishball restaurant, also serving *dim sum*. There are two separate entrances, which can be confusing. Daily 10.30am–6pm.

Jumbo Floating Restaurant Shum Wan, Wong Chuk Hang, free ferry from near Aberdeen fish market (see p.90) ℡2553 9111. Moored in Aberdeen Harbour, every inch of this three-storey floating palace is decked with festive red and gold, and the entrance is guarded by giant coiled dragons with lightbulb eyes. Once inside you'll find the food equally loud and not really up to the price tag, though set meals are not desperately expensive from (HK$200 a head). Locals avoid the place, but as a one-off experience it's a lot of fun. The *Top Deck* bar here also does Sun lunch buffets 11.30am–4.30pm with free champagne (HK$378 per person).

Tsim Sha Tsui

The places listed below are marked on the map on pp.104–105.

🏃 **Hing Kee 1st Floor, Bowa House, 180 Nathan Rd** ℡2722 0022. A little hard to find, and snappish staff give the impression that they'd rather you hadn't managed to do so, but the home-style Cantonese food is worth it: try the superb duck noodle soup for something inexpensive, or giant prawns, "fried gross crab" or a plate of clams to splash out a little. Dishes HK$48–185. Opens after 6pm.

Kakalok Corner of Ashley Rd and Ichang St. A fast-food joint to end them all: noodles, rice, chicken, fish, whatever, all fried. Has the distinction of serving the cheapest fish and chips in Hong Kong (HK$25), and has fed many hard-up backpackers over the years. No seats, but Kowloon Park is 100m away. Daily mid-morning–late.

Macau 40–46 Lock Rd ℡2628 1990. Come here to enjoy Macanese fast food with what seems like the rest of Hong Kong. It's all tasty, but some things – sardines, braised mussels, curry crab, baked seafood – are really good. Their pork cutlets in a bun (HK$19) make a quick snack. Mains HK$60 and up.

Sweet Dynasty 88 Canton Rd ℡2199 7799. A bustling restaurant specializing in sweet Chinese desserts packed with taro, sago, sweet sesame paste, coconut milk and fruit. They also do a range of noodle, *congee* and weird dishes including *hasma* (frog ovaries) with lotus seeds and red dates. Daily 8am–midnight.

Tsui Hang Village Ground Floor, Mira Shopping Centre, 132–134 Nathan Rd ℡2376 2882. Smart restaurant serving regional Chinese cuisine with a strong southern emphasis, including salt-baked chicken, goose with sour plum and rock sugar, sea bass and bird's nest, and tofu, crab and scrambled egg. Mains HK$120 and up.

🏃 **Yan Toh Heen Intercontinental Hotel, 18 Salisbury Rd** ℡2721 1211. Reckoned one of Hong Kong's best for cutting-edge Cantonese cooking – and for the excellent service and amazing harbour views. Count on HK$800 a head for the works, though a HK$600 set menu relieves the pain a little. Reservations essential.

Jordan, Yau Ma Tei and Mong Kok

See map on p.110 for the following restaurants.

Light Vegetarian Ground Floor, New Lucky House, 13 Jordan Rd, Jordan ℡2384 2833. Airy, busy place with a big selection of classic Cantonese and Shanghai vegetarian dishes: taro fish; a "bird's nest" basket with fried vegetables; pumpkin soup served in a pumpkin; "yin-yang" mushroom, corn and spinach soup; or vegetarian duck. Around HK$65 a dish.

Ngan Lung 118 Tung Choi St, near the corner with Fife, Mong Kok. Not worth crossing town for, just a good place to escape the market crowds outside for a plate of roast pork on rice or a bowl of noodles.

Pat Fong 171 Tung Choi St, up near the Goldfish Market. Taiwanese dumpling restaurant chain offering a simple choice of four types of dumplings, either steamed or fried, plus soup and a drink – circle your choice on a tear-off form at the table and give it to staff. Pretty unbeatable for just HK$30. There's no English sign outside, look for a narrow glass front with lots of bright orange trim inside.

Shunde Kung Seafood 26–30 Wai Ching St, Jordan ℡2332 0603. Don't be put off by the out-of-the-way location or the eccentric English translations on the menu ("boiled fried milk" and "mud carp"), the food here is excellent and even the wooden furnishings give a touch of antique glory – just. Most mains around HK\$60.

🏃 **Sino Vegetarian 131–135 Parkes St, Yau Ma Tei** ☎2771 2393. Whether or not you're a vegetarian, do yourself a favour and eat here: the "eel" in black vinegar, "tiger skin peppers", "prawn" and vegetable dumplings and plain vegetable dishes are all delicious. A photo-menu makes ordering easy. Mains around HK\$55.

New Territories

Chuen Kee 51–55 Hoi Pong St (waterfront), Sai Kung Town ☎2792 6938. The best seafood and *dim sum* in town, with seafront views. Popular, but not especially cheap at around HK\$150 a head.

🏃 **Honeymoon Dessert 9 Po Tung Rd (on the highway), Sai Kung Town.** The original of a citywide chain serving desserts made from sago, mango, grass jelly, coconut milk, fruit and ice cream in every conceivable combination; their mango puddings are justly famous. Separate area for durian dishes. Extremely popular with children so a bit lively around 4pm on school days.

Lung Wah 22 Wo Che St, Sha Tin ☎2691 1594. See map, pp.136–137. This mid-range place serves excellent greasy pigeon – a Cantonese speciality – and good bean curd and almond desserts. The restaurant itself seems to have bypassed hygiene regulations but makes for a fascinating wander past cages of peacocks and pigeons lining the entrance passageway. Bizarrely, there's no road access: exit Sha Tin station, walk down the ramp and then straight ahead until you're on a footpath following the train lines. After 5min you'll pass a footbridge, with the restaurant's red walls just ahead to the left.

Sham Tseng Village One-time "village" – now a clutch of buildings sunk below high-rises and surrounded by expressways – long famous for its roast goose restaurants. The *Yue Kee* (9 Main St, ☎2491 0105) has been going forever and serves all things goose, plus excellent salt and pepper squid – HK\$250 will buy enough for two. There are heaps of other places too, including the *Chan Kee* at 69 Main St (☎2491 0877). Ride the Tung Chung line to Tsuen Wan West station, then catch bus #234A or #234B west for 15min to Sham Tseng.

Tai Wing Wah 2–6 On Ning Rd, Yuen Long ☎2476 9888. Lively, friendly place to share tables with locals over *yum cha* and home-cooked Cantonese dishes. Famous for its *poon choi* (book ahead), a New Territories banquet speciality where a stack of ingredients are slow-simmered together. Downstairs shop sells cured meats and cakes made on the premises. Catch the West Rail to Long Ping station, take Exit E and turn left along On Lok Road for 300m until you reach Wang Chau Road; turn right down here for 150m and then left onto On Ning Road; the restaurant is just ahead on the bend.

Yat Lok Po Wah House, Tai Ming Lane, Tai Po. See map, p.142. There's a small English sign in the window and a fish tank inside this typical, clean roast meat restaurant that featured in American chef Anthony Bourdain's TV series – though to be honest, the food here is no better or worse than many other eateries in Hong Kong.

Hakka

Chuen Cheung Kui 91–95 Fa Yuen St, Mong Kok ☎2395 9370. See map, p.110. Large portions of family-style cooking and moderate prices make this a popular place with locals – weekends are always packed. Not much English spoken, but there's an English menu; try the Hakka specialities such as salt-baked chicken, stewed pork with preserved vegetables or tofu cubes stuffed with mince. Daily 11am–midnight.

Chiu Chow

Carianna 1st Floor, 151 Gloucester Rd (entrance around corner in Tonnochy Rd), Wan Chai ☎2511 1282. See map, pp.78–79. Rated as one of the better Chiu Chow places in Hong Kong, with a huge range of seafood and classics such as soy-roasted goose and stewed abalone and stuffed goose webs. The service won't impress though. Mains HK\$80–400 a dish.

🏃 **Chao Inn 7th Floor, One Peking Rd, Tsim Sha Tsui** ☎2369 8819. See map, pp.104–105. You'll need to book window tables for harbour views, and the moderately priced food – cuisine from Chaozhou in Guangdong province – is also a cut above average, especially the sliced soy goose, shrimp and crab paste rolls and pork with plum sauce. Mains around HK\$90. 10am–10pm.

Heung Gung Zai 40 Carnarvon Rd, Tsim Sha Tsui. See map, p.104. No English sign – the name means "Aberdeen" – but look for roast meats hanging up in the window. What this place does best are soups with Chiu Chow-style fish balls (called *yu dan*, "fish eggs", in Chinese thanks to their shape) and fish noodles, actually made with fish paste. Portions are generous and there's a limited English menu. Soups from HK$24.

Leung Hing 27 Queens Rd West ☎2850 6666. See map, p.69. There's no English sign, though the big green and red Chinese one with a fish is pretty distinctive. Roast and soy-braised goose, seafood such as stewed fish maw and crabmeat balls, and attractive dumplings. Mains from HK$60, HK$300 for more elaborate dishes.

Beijing (Peking)

Dong Lai Shun Basement 2, 69 Mody Rd, Tsim Sha Tsui East ☎2733 2020. See map, pp.104–105. Branch of the famous Beijing restaurant originally specializing in Mongolian hotpot, now branching out to include Peking duck and – rather pointlessly given the local competition – Cantonese dishes. Stick with the excellent duck (HK$320) or lamb hotpot with all the trimmings (HK$400, enough for two).

Hutong 28th Floor, One Peking Rd, Tsim Sha Tsui ☎3428 8342. See map, pp.104–105. Part of the *Aqua* chain, similarly smart, expensive, and gifted with stunning views. Minimalist chic takes on northern Chinese food (with a few Sichuan-inspired items); the house speciality is slow-cooked lamb ribs served on a wooden plate. HK$500 a head.

Peking 227 Nathan Rd, Jordan ☎2730 1315. See map, p.110. Don't be put off by the fairly glum decor and creaky, unsmiling staff; this moderately priced place serves wonderful Peking duck, cabbage and noodle soup, deep-fried prawn balls (not for calorie counters), fragrant chicken and cold spiced beef with cucumber. Expect to pay HK$150 a head in a group – the duck is HK$350 but most dishes are far less and you can order small portions. Gets very busy; reservations recommended.

Spring Deer 1st Floor, 42 Mody Rd, Tsim Sha Tsui ☎2366 4012. See map, pp.104–105. Long-established place; you can tell from the elderly, formal waiters and conservative

menu. But get over this and the food is excellent: Peking duck, of course, walnut cream dessert, steamed ham in honey sauce and chicken in wine-sediment paste – genuine, old-style dishes that many places don't bother with nowadays. Good value considering the quality and reasonably sized portions; you can order small portions for most dishes, too. Mains HK$200.

Tai Fung Lau 29–31 Chatham Rd, Tsim Sha Tsui ☎2366 2494. See map, pp.104–105. The gloomy furnishings will never win any awards, but the northeastern Chinese food is good. Copious lamb and beef dishes – including Mongolian hotpot (which you need to order a day in advance) – along with Peking duck, and Shandong preserved chicken. Most mains HK$100–150, though you can ask for half portions. Daily noon–11pm.

Shanghainese

Crystal Jade Basement 2, Times Square, Causeway Bay. See map, pp.78–79. One of a citywide chain specializing in light meals such as steamers of *xiaolongbao* or bowls of *lamian*, all made on the premises, though they also do more accomplished dishes such as smoked pigeon, crispy eel and vegetarian "duck". Top flavours and large portions will keep you happy; the slack service and lunchtime queues are less appealing. Soups around HK$40, mains HK$100 a head.

Lu Yang Cun (Green Willow Village) 11th Floor, World Trade Centre, 280 Gloucester Rd, Causeway Bay ☎2881 6669. See map, pp.78–79. Smart modern Shanghai restaurant serving classics such as Dongpo pork (cubes of fatty meat slow-braised in a soy stock), stewed pork knuckle and "crackling rice" (a seafood soup poured over crispy, deep-fried rice crusts). They also do some Sichuan dishes. Mains from around HK$100, but larger dishes HK$150 upwards.

Ng Yu Zigan 26 Cochrane St, Mid-Levels. See map, p.68. Small English sign over the doorway reads "Between Wu Yue". Great snacks and light meals, including spicy noodles, little dumplings and marinated cucumber slices; use of raw garlic and chillies may prove too pungent for some. Big soups for under HK$40, or order a selection to share at around HK$35 a dish. Daily 8am–9pm.

Shanghai Garden Hutchison House, 10 Harcourt Rd, Central ☎2524 8181.

Shark's fin

If there's one dish that epitomizes both the Chinese propensity for eating unlikely animal body parts and their willingness to pay through the nose for the privilege, it's shark's fin. Many Cantonese restaurants offer it up as thick, fibrous shark's fin soup, not so much an acquired taste as an outrageously expensive one: suffice to say that if there's a cheap bowl of shark's fin on the menu, it isn't the real thing.

Quite how and why it came to be eaten in the first place is unclear, though the Chinese claim medicinal properties for the fin – being high in cartilage, it's believed to reinforce bone and help arthritis sufferers. Whatever the truth of this, the wider concern is that eating shark's fin soup is putting many shark species at risk. Economic growth in Southeast Asia and the Pacific Rim has fuelled demand for shark's fin, and, consequently, shark fishing is now very big business. Numbers are declining rapidly and since the shark is an important part of the food chain, the destruction of large numbers of them has disturbing implications for the marine environment.

For this reason alone, there's a growing move to boycott the eating of shark's fin products. If you need any more convincing, it's worth noting that shark flesh is not usually eaten in the Far East, so the fish are killed just for their fins. These are cut off while the shark is still alive and then the fish is thrown back into the sea, where – without its fins to give it mobility – it drowns.

See map, pp.60–61. Not really so authentic, but the dishes are tasty enough and service is excellent. HK$200 a head should cover things.

Tien Heung Lau 18 Austin Ave, Tsim Sha Tsui ☎2366 2414. See map, pp.104–105. There's no English sign – look for the blue board with orange characters over the street and the same in gold over the entrance. Unimpressive from outside, this small place is famed for its Beggar's Chicken, baked in a clay parcel which is smashed open at the table to reveal the juicy, fragrant fowl inside. Not cheap, despite the unpretentious decor; count on HK$500 a head and book in advance.

Xiao Nan Guo 3rd Floor, Man Yee Building, 68 des Voeux Rd, Central ☎2259 9393. See map, pp.60–61. Good-value mid-range place which fills up through the evening. The menu includes lots of predictable old favourites – marinated aubergine, dumplings, steamed autumn crabs and light chicken and bean sheet dishes – and you should reserve room for the sticky rice desserts. Mains from HK$80.

Yi Jiang Nan 35 Staunton St, Soho ☎2136 0886. See map, p.68. Chinese food from the Yangtze river region, incorporating both Shanghai and Sichuanese dishes – twice-cooked pork, crisp-skinned lamb and Longjing tea prawns. Good food but overpriced, with most mains above HK$90.

Sichuan (Szechuan)

Chongqing Sichuan 29 Elgin St, Soho ☎2810 8868. See map, p.68. Highly-rated Sichuanese restaurant which does far more than just pour Tabasco over stir-fries: try the superb shredded smoked duck, orange-peel chicken, sliced beef in pungent sauce (volcanically hot), mapo tofu or dry-fried green beans. Mains upwards of HK$90.

Red Pepper 7 Lan Fong Rd, Causeway Bay ☎2577 3811. See map, pp.78–79. Sichuanese dishes toned down for local tastes, though there are a few more authentic offerings such as smoked duck. A favourite with expats, which means higher than warranted prices and overbearing staff. Best booked in advance. Count on HK$90 per main.

Yellow Door Kitchen 6th Floor, 37 Cochrane St, Central ☎2858 6555. See map, p.68. Entrance on Lyndhurst Terrace. Home-style Sichuanese cooking in a cheerful, low-key but slightly upmarket place. They do lunches for HK$100 a head, but set dinners at HK$220 are what everyone comes for, featuring a selection of little dishes – make sure you try their legendary "mouth-watering chicken". Bookings essential.

Other Chinese regions

Bistro Manchu 33 Elgin St, Soho ☎2536 9218. See map, p.68. Moderately priced Manchurian food of the hearty stew and dumpling variety – northern Chinese with a bit of Mongolian and Korean thrown in, served in stylish East-meets-West surroundings. Daily noon–2.30pm & 6–11pm.

Islam Food 1 Lung Kong Rd, Kowloon City ☎2382 2822. See map, pp.100–101. This excellent, friendly, no-frills restaurant focuses on the traditional food of China's Muslim minority peoples, but also serves some Beijing, Shanghainese and Sichuan dishes. The juicy beef-cakes are renowned locally. Daily 11am–11pm.

Little Sheep 1st Floor, 26 Kimberley Rd, Tsim Sha Tsui ☎2722 7633. See map, pp.104–105. Mainland Chinese chain loosely based on Mongolian hotpot, offering a range of thinly sliced meats, vegetables and noodles to cook yourself at the table in bubbling vats of stock – "white" is plain stock; "red" is very spicy. Not much English spoken. Around HK$110 a head.

African

The Stoep 32 Lower Cheung Sha Village, Lantau Island ☎2980 2699. A relaxed, moderately priced restaurant serving jugs of Pimms by the sea. Mediterranean and meaty South African cuisine, including the scary-sounding Boerewors – a home-made sausage. Reservations advisable. Daily 11am–11pm.

American

Al's Diner 37 D'Aguilar St, Central ☎2521 8714. See map, p.68. Straightforward diner serving average burgers, dogs, chilli and sandwiches, but late weekend hours makes it popular with ravenous clubbers. Mon–Thurs 11am–12.30am, Fri & Sat 11am–3.30am, Sun 6pm–12.30am.

Dan Ryan's Chicago Bar and Grill 114 The Mall, One Pacific Place, 88 Queensway, Central ☎2845 4600. See map, pp.60–61. Bumper American-size portions of ribs, burgers, steaks, salads and clam chowder. You'll get enough food to sink a battleship, but it doesn't come cheap at HK$220 for a steak. Daily 11am–midnight.

Lawry's 4th Floor, Lee Gardens, Causeway Bay ☎2907 2218. See map, pp.78–79. Prime grilled rib steaks and great seafood, including lobster tail platters. Excellent wine list too. Reservations essential. HK$500 and up per head.

Wildfire 21 Elgin St, on the corner with Peel St, Soho ☎2810 0670. See map, p.68. Well above average wood-fired pizzas with thin, crunchy crusts; the downside is a terribly cramped interior. HK$150 a head.

Australian

Ned Kelly's Last Stand 11a Ashley Rd, Tsim Sha Tsui ☎2376 0562. See map, pp.104–105. Laid-back, Aussie pub menu featuring pies, Irish stew, bangers and mash and steaks. They also do huge all-day breakfasts. Live Jazz 9.30pm–1am, too;.

Wooloo Mooloo 29 Wyndham St, Lan Kwai Fong, Central ☎2894 8010. See map, p.63. Popular Aussie barbecue restaurant-bar; slow-grilled ribeye steaks are the business. Downstairs can get very rowdy, especially at weekends; the upstairs restaurant is quieter.

British

For no-nonsense portions of fish and chips, steak-and-kidney pie or an all-day English breakfast, most pubs can do the honours; see the next chapter for full pub and bar listings.

Boathouse 88 Stanley Main St, Stanley ☎2813 4467. See map, p.93. Fish and chips, seafood platters, buckets of prawns or just a good old steak. Wash it down with a cold beer and enjoy views of Stanley's waterfront area. Mains HK$150 and up.

Chippy 51 Wellington St, Central. See map, pp.60–61. Tiny diner serving mushy peas, bangers and mash, and pie and chips, along with slightly classier items such as pasta and a glass of wine. Entrance facing the steps leading down to Stanley St. Plate of battered cod and fries costs HK$85.

Dot Cod Basement, Prince's Building, 10 Chater Rd, Central ☎2810 6988. See map, p.61. A busy Brit-style seafood restaurant and oyster bar, seething at lunchtime with city-types tucking into grilled cod and chips, seafood platters and, of course, oysters. Some of their supplies are from sustainable fisheries. They also do grilled kipper break-fasts. Mon–Sat 7.30am–midnight. Expensive at HK$228 for cod and chips.

Jimmy's Kitchen 1–3 Wyndham St, Central ☎2526 5293. See map, p.61. British-pub-like interior, complete with horse brasses and dark woodwork, and an upmarket pub menu – pan-fried cod, oyster chowder and

Food cruises

Jaspas (☎2792 6001, ⓦwww.jaspasjunk.com) have several **party junks** which spend a day cruising, boozing and feeding you around uninhabited beaches and islands at HK$600 a head, minimum of 14. Loads of room for sunbathing and dancing on top deck; make sure you have the next day free to recover.

lamb fillets. Also does great martinis. Pricey at HK$200 a head.

Sammy's Kitchen 204–206 Queens Rd West, Sheung Wan, ☎2548 8400. See map, p.69. Look for the huge cow-shaped sign jutting over the road. Perhaps "British" is stretching things a bit, though this Chinese-run place is locally renowned for its inexpensive, Western-style roast chicken and steak dishes. They also do picnic catering for groups of ten or more. Mains HK$65–110.

French

Arc Brasserie 8–13 Wo On Lane, Central ☎2234 9918. See map, p.61. Extensive menu of French bistro classics such as mussels, snails, baked wild mushrooms and roast duck breast, served in a laid-back lounge-like setting. The signature dish is goose liver, and the desserts are wonderful. Daily 11am–11pm. Around HK$500 per person for a full meal.

Bonheur 6th Floor, 22–26 Bonham Strand, Sheung Wan ☎2544 6333. See map, pp.60–61. Hard to find unless you know it's there, this pleasant, popular bistro has excellent lunchtime set menus and evening à la carte dining for around HK$350 a head.

Café de Paris 23 Elgin St, Soho. See map, p.68. Not really a café, when a bowl of onion soup costs HK$80, but this is a small, friendly place to spend an evening enjoying home-style French cooking. Mains HK$200.

Gaddi's 1st Floor, Peninsula Hotel, Salisbury Rd, Tsim Sha Tsui ☎2315 3171. See map, pp.104–105. Conservative and pretentious with extraordinary food at extraordinary prices (at HK$1000 per person for a full meal). Advance booking and smart dress essential. Noon–2.30pm & 7–11pm.

Le Marron 12th Floor, Ying Kong Mansion, 2–6 Yee Wo St, Causeway Bay. See map, pp.78–79. Small place with homely ambience that does first-rate escargot, frog legs, lamb and seafood dishes, and mouthwatering desserts (such as Grand Marnier soufflé). There's a small delicatessen at the front,

too, and a balcony bar. Count on HK$200 a head and book in advance.

Spoon by Alain Ducasse Intercontinental Hotel, 18 Salisbury Rd, Tsim Sha Tsui ☎2313 2256. See map, pp.104–105. Like most of Hong Kong's foodies, you'll either love or hate this cutting-edge restaurant serving extremely odd, intriguing dishes. You might find it safer to stick to the set menu (changes daily), though even this is expensive. Daily 6pm–midnight.

Indian and Pakistani

Hong Kong Island

Ashoka 57–59 Wyndham St, Central ☎2524 9623. See map, pp.60–61. Very popular northern Indian restaurant serving good-value set lunches and dinners, and several vegetarian choices, including large *thalis*. A much more elaborate affair than the Indian "clubs" in town. About HK$150 a head for a full meal. Daily 10am–10.30pm.

Jo Jo's 2nd Floor, David House 37–39 Lockhart Rd, Wan Chai ☎2527 3776. See map, pp.78–79. Comfortable surroundings, and a deservedly popular, inexpensive halal menu with tandoori specialities. Mains from HK$72.

Lord Stanley 92 Stanley Main St, Stanley ☎2899 0811. See map, p.93. Friendly restaurant with attached sports bar and decent Indian food from all regions. The set lunch is fair value, but you can't go wrong choosing à la carte either. Make sure you book at weekends. HK$250 a head.

Shaffi's Malik 185 Wanchai Rd, Wan Chai ☎2572 7474. See map, pp.78–79. Claims to be the oldest Indian restaurant in town – nothing spectacular, but good, tasty staples such as sheek kebabs, chicken tikka, *saag paneer* and naan. Also decent set lunches (HK$45), and set meal for two (HK$180).

Tsim Sha Tsui

There are a good number of Indian restaurants inside *Chungking Mansions*; touts waiting on the pavement outside after dark will try to drag you in. The places listed below are marked on the map on pp.104–105.

Branto Pure Vegetarian 1st Floor, 9 Lock Rd ☎2366 8161. Inexpensive south Indian and Punjabi vegetarian meals, with mains such as *dosa dhal*, *paneer palak* and jalfrezi at HK\$40–65. Their *thalis* are highly recommended. Portions are large so go in hungry; it gets very busy with Indian and Pakistani customers at lunchtime.

Delhi Club Block C, 3rd Floor, Chungking Mansions, 36–44 Nathan Rd ☎2368 1682. An Indian–Nepali curry-house *par excellence*, despite the spartan surroundings, slap-down service and slightly stingy portions. There's a good range of vegetarian dishes, mutton specialities and clay oven-cooked naan. Daily noon–2.30pm & 6–11.30pm, but book on Friday and Saturday nights or be prepared to queue. Mains from HK\$60.

Indian Palace Halal 1st Floor, 19–21 Hankow Rd ☎2736 6617. Somewhere to fill up fairly cheaply on basic curries, dhal and naan; or try the two-feet-long paper *masala dosa*. Window seats for street watching. Set lunches Mon–Fri noon–2.30pm, HK\$55; otherwise mains around HK\$50.

Khyber Pass Block E, 7th Floor, Chungking Mansions, 36–44 Nathan Rd ☎2721 2786. Mess-hall seating at long tables, good – if unoriginal – food such as chicken tikka and *saag paneer*, and low prices. HK\$45–60 a dish.

Indonesian, Malay and Singaporean

For the following places, see map on pp.78–79

IR 1968 28 Leighton Rd, Causeway Bay ☎2577 9981. A smart but overpriced restaurant serving excellent Indonesian staples such as char-grilled fish, curries and spicy aubergine. HK\$250 a head. Daily 11.30am–11pm.

Padang J.P. Plaza, 22–36 Paterson St, Causeway Bay ☎2881 5075. This unpretentious Indonesian place serves a run of *rendang*, satays, grilled seafood, mutton curry and – especially – durian-flavoured desserts. Mains from HK\$60.

Pasar 197 Johnston Rd, Wan Chai ☎3168 2057. Singaporean diner with lunch plates of *laksa*, tamarind fish curry, *kuay teow* or Hokkien noodles for HK\$55–70. They also do refreshing juices and *es*

kachang (shaved ice with peanuts, condensed milk and coloured syrups).

Sabah 98–102 Jaffe Rd, Wan Chai ☎2143 6626. Cheerful, inexpensive Malaysian place which does very tasty *otak* (fish grilled in banana leaves), pineapple-fried rice, fish head curry, *nonya* deep-fried pomfret and water spinach with prawn paste sauce – and, of course, *roti canai*. Also a few Indian and Thai staples. Mains HK\$70–120.

Sun Kwong 631–633 Shanghai St, Mong Kok. See p.110. Malay–Chinese curry house; HK\$45 gets you a bowl of *laksa* or satay beef on rice. It's all designed to be shovelled in, not savoured, but you can't complain about the taste or quantity. Save room for a bowl of sweet *cendol*, a sort of jelly noodle.

International

Aqua 29th Floor and Penthouse, One Peking Rd, Tsim Sha Tsui ☎3427 2288. See map, pp.104–105. Sunken slate tables and superlative harbour views are the setting for consuming an unexpectedly successful blend of Italian and Japanese dishes. The atmosphere is informal, and the prices high. Reservations essential.

Café Deco Levels 1 & 2, Peak Galleria, 118 Peak Rd, The Peak ☎2849 5111. Unrivalled views and a stylish Art Deco interior define this expensive, upmarket café serving pizzas, pastas, curries and grilled meats. Or just call in for a drink, or cake and coffee; at night, there's often live jazz. Mains above HK\$150. Mon–Sat 11.30am–midnight, Sun 9.30am–midnight.

Felix 28th Floor, Peninsula Hotel, Salisbury Rd, Tsim Sha Tsui ☎2315 3188. See map, pp.104–105. This restaurant was designed by Philippe Starck, and the incredible views of Hong Kong Island in themselves warrant a visit. The Eurasian menu, however, is not as good as it should be at over HK\$600 a head, but many people just come for a martini at the bar. Restaurant 6–11pm; bar 6pm–2am.

Island Seafood 10 Knutsford Terrace, Tsim Sha Tsui ☎2312 6663. See map, pp.104–105. Welcoming place whose mainstay are fresh oysters, though high prices might keep you away. HK\$400 a head.

M at the Fringe 2 Lower Albert Rd, Central ☎2877 4000. See map, pp.60–61. Stylish restaurant much favoured by the glitterati for its boldly flavoured, health-conscious dishes – meat, fish and veggie – whose influences span the world. Reservations advised. Mon–Sat noon–2.30pm & 7–10.30pm, Sun 7–10.30pm. Count on HK$500 a head for a three-course meal without drinks.

Peak Lookout 121 Peak Rd, The Peak ☎2531 **6274**. No longer true to the name, what with the adjacent Peak Tower blocking the views, but this low stone building with raked wooden ceiling still has more panache than anything else in the area – somewhere to dine, rather than just eat. Grills, seafood and burgers from about HK$160 up. Daily 10.30am–11.30pm.

Post '97 1st Floor, 9–11 Lan Kwai Fong, Central ☎2810 9333. **See map, p.63**. Relaxed brasserie surroundings and an eclectic, expensive menu of Mediterranean and American food, plus a daily vegetarian choice. There's also coffee and herbal teas, while brunch specials are served all day on Sunday. Sun–Thurs 9.30am–1.30am, Sat 9.30am–3am.

Roof Garden at the Fringe, 2 Lower Albert Rd, Central. See map, pp.60–61. Vegetarian lunchtime buffet Mon–Fri noon–2.30pm ($80), with weekend brunch – either a self-serve buffet or full breakfast – served Sat & Sun 10.30am–4pm (HK$99). All a very good deal; no bookings.

Italian

Aspasia 39 Kimberley Rd, Knutsford Terrace, Tsim Sha Tsui ☎3763 8800. **See map, pp.104–105**. Chic, pricey Italian: dishes like mascarpone ravioli with duck ragout, morel risotto and veal with chestnut purée all point to this being somewhere to linger over your meal, rather than just fill up. About HK$700 a head.

Enoteca 47 Elgin St, Soho ☎2525 9944. **See map, p.68**. Popular pizzeria with low prices for this part of town: thin-crust pizzas from HK$100, antipasti platter HK$198 and tapas-like sides for HK$60–80. Bookings essential.

Fat Angelo's 49 Elgin St, Soho ☎2973 6808. **See map, p.68**. Extremely popular, noisy Italian joint serving enormous pizzas and a range of pasta dishes. Two people can happily share one dish. Most expensive main course is lobster pasta for HK$150, and most are much cheaper. Lunch sets HK$80–130 a head. Daily noon–midnight.

Grappa's The Mall, One Pacific Place, 88 Queensway, Central ☎2868 0086. **See map, pp.60–61**. A good place to meet or eat, whether you want a glass of wine, a snack or

a full meal. Despite being fairly pricey the restaurant is usually full, but turnover is quick. Daily 11am–midnight. HK$200 a head.

Sole Mio 47A Elgin St, Soho ☎2869 6522. **See map, p.68**. Respected Italian restaurant with set lunches for HK$96 and mains such as osso bucco, grilled seabass and pepper steak from HK$155.

Japanese

Ajitomi 7th Floor, Circle Tower, 28 Tang Lung St, Causeway Bay ☎2836 0671. **See map, pp.78–79**. Elegant in a minimalist way, this small, smart restaurant is packed with Japanese at lunchtime and offers a mix of pure Japanese dishes and some with a Westernized twist. Around HK$140 a head.

Chura 100 Canton Rd, Toy House Basement ☎3105 8950. **See map, pp.104–105**. Discreet Okinawan Japanese place with low tables and cushions on the floor and a choice of sashimi, sushi and dishes such as bitter gourd with pork. In a building full of Japanese restaurants, this one is always popular. Mains HK$200 and up.

Kanamizu Sushi 8 Granville Rd, Tsim Sha Tsui. See map, pp.104–105. Looks upmarket, but pretty reasonable at HK$12–45 per colour-coded plate of an almost entirely raw seafood selection. You can also order off the menu and have it made directly. Daily 11.30am–midnight.

Kyoto Joe 21 D'Aguilar St, Central ☎2804 6800. **See map, p.63**. Modern Japanese restaurant with several dining areas and bars; very popular with the expat crowd and serving reliable (and a bit expensive) lightweight Japanese meals. Set lunches around HK$150, otherwise mains from HK$100.

Kyozasa 20 Ashley Rd, Tsim Sha Tsui ☎2376 **1888**. **See map, pp.104–105**. Homely Japanese country food such as soba noodles and tofu. Low prices and plain decor makes this a relaxing and unpretentious place to eat; the sushi is not good, however, but crowds of Japanese consistently pack out this tiny restaurant.

Miso Lower Ground Floor, Jardine House, Connaught Rd, Central ☎2521 8848. **See map, pp.60–61**. This ultramodern, ultra-cool restaurant will cook any Japanese delicacy you want (though not cheaply). The menu includes sushi standards such as rolls, cones and *nigiri*, and sake, lapped up by a business crowd. HK$300 a head.

Nadaman Basement 2, Kowloon Shangri-La, 64 Mody Rd, Tsim Sha Tsui ☎2733 8751. See map, pp.104–105. Traditional, minimalist Japanese dining room where most of the business clientele tucks in at the sushi bar or spends big on the other house specials, such as the *kaiseki*, a set dinner of various small, beautifully presented dishes. HK$800 a head.

Unkai 3rd Floor, Sheraton Hotel, 20 Nathan Rd, Tsim Sha Tsui ☎2369 1111. See map, pp.104–105. If you're going to blow your money on one expensive Japanese meal, this is the place to do it. The food here is authentic and beautifully presented. HK$800 a head.

Korean

Nearly all Korean restaurants in Hong Kong feature a "barbecue" (*bulgogi*) as part of the menu – the table contains a grill, over which you cook marinated slices of meat, fish or seafood; assorted pickles (including *kimchi* – spicy, pickled cabbage), rice and soup come with the meal.

Arirang 11th Floor, Times Square, Causeway Bay ☎2506 3298. See map, pp.78–79. Dependable, moderately priced restaurant offering the usual Korean specialities – barbecued meat platters, spicy cold noodles – plus one free Korean beer for each guest.

Busan 29 Ashley Rd, Tsim Sha Tsui ☎2376 3385. See map, pp.104–105. Highly popular barbecue place, which also does good ginseng chicken, cold noodles and seaweed soup. It's a little expensive, though; count on at least HK$160 a head.

Kaya 6th Floor, 8 Russell St, Causeway Bay ☎2577 5145. See map, pp.78–79. A roomy place that looks far more upmarket than it actually is: you can get a decent set lunch of beef rice pot, grilled mackerel, spicy bean curd or beef and ginseng soup for HK$70–100. A barbecue works out around HK$150 a head.

Mexican

Agave 33 D'Aguilar St, Central ☎2521 2010. See map, p.63. A fine selection of burritos, enchiladas and fajitas, plus more than a hundred types of tequila. This place is not cheap – you'll have to cough up HK$275 for some of the rarer shots of tequila – but the Mexican chef uses his imported ingredients well and generally pleases the punters.

Mon–Thurs 5.30pm–2am, Fri–Sat 5.30pm–4am.

Middle Eastern

Beyrouth 39 Lyndhurst Terrace, Central ☎2854 1872. See map, p.68. Take-away arm of adjacent *Assaf* Lebanese restaurant; also has a small sit-down counter inside. The menu of Middle-Eastern staples includes excellent kebabs (HK$55).

Habibi/Habibi Café 112 Wellington St, Central ☎2544 3886. See map, p.68. Top Egyptian restaurant; the café is great value for money but the restaurant has belly-dancing Friday and Saturday nights. Set dinners such as mezze platter from HK$95; otherwise try mains of kofta, kebabs or shawarma at HK$40–80, or delicious treats like chicken stuffed with apricots, figs and raisins for HK$155.

Ziafat 6th Floor, Harilela Mansion, 81 Nathan Rd, Tsim Sha Tsui ☎2312 1015. See map, pp.104–105. No signs on the building or inside, though sometimes they put a board out on the street nearby. Tasty halal Egyptian food with generous portions – the roast meat platter with sides of tabouleh, hummus and spiced rice is easily enough for two hungry people. They have two completely separate menus, "Indian" and "Egyptian". Note that the restaurant is alcohol-free. HK$100 a head.

Russian/Ukrainian

Ivan the Kozak Ground Floor, 46–48 Cochrane St, Mid-Levels ☎2851 1193. See map, p.68. Cold-weather food a bit out of place here in the tropics, but portions of dumplings with pork and potatoes, stuffed cabbage leaves, baked fish or ox tongue are huge and authentic. The *riba pod shuboy* – an appetizer of sole, potatoes, beetroot and mayonnaise – and a vodka chaser make a good light meal. The highlight here is donning a fur coat and walking into the huge freezer for a shot of vodka and a photo. Mains HK$130 and up. Mon–Fri noon–midnight, Sat & Sun 6pm–midnight.

South American

La Pampa 32 Staunton St, Soho ☎2868 6959. See map, p.68. Moderately expensive Argentinian restaurant that does what it does – barbecued steak – exceedingly well.

You order by weight (minimum 250g), it's grilled just how you want it and served with nominal quantities of vegetables. Make sure you try the red wine, too. Mains around HK$200, sides of vegetables HK$32.

Spanish

Boca 65 Peel St, Soho ☎2548 1717. See map, **p.68.** Tapas bar whose atmosphere gets steadily livelier through the night, especially at weekends. Mon–Fri 4pm–2am, Sat & Sun 11.30am–2am.

La Comida 22 Staunton St, Soho ☎2530 3118. See map, **p.68.** Relaxed restaurant, pleasant service and with tasty, good-value tapas, but not much else. The evening crowds are proof of its consistently good food. Daily 11am–11pm.

Swiss

Chesa 1st Floor, Peninsula Hotel, Salisbury Rd, Tsim Sha Tsui ☎2315 3169. See map, **pp.104–105.** The chalet-like wooden ceiling has been bemusing customers for the last forty years, but this unlikely Swiss restaurant serves superb fondue and meat dishes. Reservations essential. HK$800 a head.

Thai

Thai restaurants are spread all over Hong Kong, but the best places are in Kowloon City – take bus #1 from Tsim Sha Tsui Star Ferry Pier and get off on Grampian Road, near the junction with Nga Tsin Wai Road. Walk along Nga Tsin Wai Road and look down side streets to see dozens of restaurant signs.

Amporn Thai Food 3rd Floor, Cooked Food Hall, Kowloon City Market, 100 Nga Tsin Wai Rd, Kowloon City ☎2716 3689. See map, **pp.100–101.** Head to the third floor of the market, and *Amporn Thai Food* takes up most of the Cooked Food Hall. Don't be put off by the plastic stools and tables and the clattering din – this place is the real thing.

Vegetarian food

Most restaurants have vegetable, mushroom and beancurd (tofu) dishes on the menu, or you can order a regular noodle dish without the meat. Bear in mind, though, if you're a purist, that many Chinese dishes start off life with a meat stock; waiters will sometimes also insist that light meats, such as chicken, or fish are not really meat. If you really eat nothing of animal origin, it's better to say "I eat vegetarian food" (*ngor sik tzai*), or Buddhist monk's food as it's thought of, which is an accepted concept.

To avoid any problems, it's easiest to eat in one of the excellent **Chinese vegetarian restaurants**, where the food is based on tofu, yam, taro and gluten, which can be shaped into – and made to taste of – its meaty counterpart (you even call it by the same names). Some of these places also serve excellent vegetarian *dim sum*, which is fortunate, as you'll have a hard time getting meat-free items in a real *dim sum* restaurant.

Other than these places, you're best off in the SAR's **Indian and Pakistani restaurants** (p.218), which have lots of non-meat choices, or a hotel buffet, which will always have a good salad bar and other vegetarian options. A meal at one of the **Buddhist monasteries** in Hong Kong will also consist of strictly vegetarian food; see especially Lantau (chapter 4) and the various temples in the New Territories (chapter 3).

Vegetarian restaurants

The places listed below are completely vegetarian, and are reviewed elsewhere in this chapter.

Branto p.218.
Kung Tak Lam p.209.
Lok Cha Teahouse p.206.
Light Vegetarian p.212.
Sino-Vegetarian p.213.
Tung Fong Siu Kee Yuen p.210.

There's no English menu, but the staff are friendly and can speak a little English; the Thai steamboat and fresh prawns are recommended. Daily noon–midnight.

Coco Thai Island Rd, Deepwater Bay, Hong Kong Island, opposite the bus stop ☎2812 1826. Romantic place to sit under umbrellas on the terrace, look out over the beach, sip drinks and stuff yourself on tasty Thai food: starters like beef salad or pomelo and prawn salad cost HK$80, while mains of curries or seafood are upwards of HK$150.

Happy Garden Vietnamese Thai Near the bus stop, main corner, Shek O, Hong Kong Island. One of several laid-back places with outdoor tables, luridly coloured drinks and excellent food – try the morning glory with *blechan* beef, or huge Thai fish cakes. Mains around HK$60. Daily noon–10pm.

Thai Jade 50 Leighton Rd, Causeway Bay ☎2808 0734. See map, pp.78–79. Low-decor place packed to the rafters at lunchtime for set meals of *tom yam gung*, penang curry, fish cakes, etc, plus rice and soft drink for just HK$45. Evening menus run to more elaborate dishes including seafood, grilled pork shoulder and pineapple rice, but still very reasonably priced. The chilli quotient is perhaps toned down for local palates but otherwise authentic use of sour limes, *kaffir* leaves and lemongrass.

Vietnamese

Indochine 1929 2nd Floor, California Tower, 30–32 D'Aguilar St, Lan Kwai Fong, Central ☎2869 7399. See map, p.63. An elegant restaurant with a whiff of French colonial style about the place – stuffed snails feature on the menu – and every dish is a winner. Reservations advised. Mon–Sat noon–late, Sun 6pm–late. HK$200 a head.

Nha Trang 88–90 Wellington St, Central ☎2581 9992. See map, p.68. First-rate and inexpensively priced Vietnamese food, whose crisp, clean, and sharp flavours make a nice break from heavier Chinese fare. Their huge *pho* noodle soups are a meal in themselves, or choose a selection of rice cakes, beef grilled in pepper leaves, or prawn and pomelo salad. Around HK$100 a head.

Rice Pot 19 Cannon St, Causeway Bay. See map, pp.78–79. Bright, small place with minimal elbow room serving rice rolls or huge bowls of noodle soups from about HK$35, good for a quick, inexpensive lunch.

Viet's Choice 3rd Floor, 488 Hennessy Rd, Causeway Bay ☎2882 2569. See map, pp.78–79. One of a chain offering straightforward, tasty and inexpensive Vietnamese soups and stir-fries for HK$40 or so.

Markets, supermarkets and barbecues

With hot food and snacks so cheap in Hong Kong, there isn't much incentive to buy picnic food. There are, however, supermarkets right across Hong Kong that may be useful if you're going to use any of the hundreds of barbecue sites throughout the SAR. Be warned, though, that for anything recognizably Western, you'll pay a lot more than you would at home.

Markets

Cantonese markets are interesting places in themselves, and many are detailed in the text. A market is where the bulk of the population buys its fresh food, shopping at least once a day for meat, fish, fruit and vegetables. All the towns and residential buildings, especially in the developments in the New Territories, have a market hall.

They can look a bit intimidating at first, but no one minds you wandering around and checking out the produce. Prodding and handling **fruit and veg** is almost expected: just pick out the items you want and hand them over. They'll invariably be weighed on an ingenious set of hand-held scales and, although the metric system is in official use, will be priced according to traditional Chinese weights and measures – most food is sold by the **catty**, which equals 1.3lb or 600g. Some stallholders will let you sample some of the more obscure fruit: one to watch for is the durian, a yellow, spiky fruit shaped like a rugby ball, that is fairly pricey and decidedly smelly – very much an acquired taste.

Buying **meat and fish** is also straightforward, though if you're going by sight alone make sure that the pretty fish you're pointing at isn't extremely rare and very expensive. It's perfectly alright to have several things weighed until you find the piece you want. For the best fish, either get to the market early in the morning, or come back in the mid-afternoon when the second catch is delivered. Every market will also have a **cooked meat** stall selling roast pork, duck and chicken, which can perk up a picnic lunch no end.

Supermarkets

Hong Kong supermarkets sell broadly what any supermarket in the West would, though with a strong Chinese bias – real coffee might be hard to find but frozen dumplings are easy. All stock beer and spirits. **Opening hours** are daily roughly 8am–8pm, though individual stores vary their times.

Hong Kong-wide supermarkets

Park N Shop including branches at Ground Floor, Hang Seng Bank Building, Central; 1st Floor, Admiralty Centre MTR level; and Shop 5, Festival Walk, Kowloon Tong (this branch has a wider than average range of Western goods).

Wellcome including branches at 2nd Floor, The Forum, Exchange Square, Central; 84 Queen's Rd Central, Central; Shop 2b, Lower Basement, The Landmark, Central; and 78 Nathan Rd, Tsim Sha Tsui.

Specialist stores

City'super Times Square, 1 Matheson St, Causeway Bay. Large Western supermarket and delicatessen.

Great Basement One Pacific Place, 88 Queensway, Central. Upmarket Japanese food hall, selling top-quality fresh produce, alongside an enormous range of international foodstuffs including Harrods' teas.

Indian Provision Store Ground Floor, 65–68 Chungking Mansions, 36–44 Nathan Rd, Tsim Sha Tsui. Indian spices, sweets and pickles, as well as tins and dairy products.

Oliver's Delicatessen 2nd Floor, Prince's Building, Central. A Mecca for Hong Kong's expat community, stocking bread, wine, cheese, biscuits, meat and a huge range of other Western products.

Sogo East Point Centre, 555 Hennessy Rd, Causeway Bay. There's a Japanese supermarket inside the department store – takeaway Japanese snacks and food as well.

Barbecues

Almost everywhere of scenic interest you go in Hong Kong (and at some youth hostels and campsites) there are special barbecue pits provided in picnic areas. They're inordinately popular, and getting the ingredients together for a barbecue isn't difficult. Supermarkets sell fuel, barbecue forks, rubbish bags and all the food, as do kiosks at some of the more enterprising sites; either buy ready-made satay sticks, or pick up cuts of meat and fish from the market.

EATING | Markets, supermarkets and barbecues

Nightlife: bars, pubs and clubs

I f you're not making eating your sole evening's entertainment, you can easily while away the night in some of Hong Kong's many **bars, pubs and clubs**. The majority are American in style, with comfy seating, a huge range of alcohol and loud music, though there are also more casual places where conversations are possible without flash-cards, and even a few British-style pubs complete with homesick expats, horse brasses and dartboards. Most of the newer, trendier places are in Central, especially **Lan Kwai Fong** and **Soho**, with a thinner scattering around **Tsim Sha Tsui**; those in **Wan Chai** are slightly harder core, geared towards more serious barflies.

Most bars are **open** from around lunchtime until well after midnight; some, especially in Lan Kwai Fong and Wan Chai, stay open until breakfast, and a few keep serving drinks around the clock, particularly at the weekend. Many don't have a specific closing time at all – if it's busy, they stay open till 4 or 5am, if it's quiet, they shut at 1 or 2am: where this is the case, we have simply said "late" for the closing time. If there's a DJ or it's a **club night**, you might have to pay to get in: from around HK$60 at the smaller places up to HK$400 at the flash designer clubs (which will also require "smart casual" dress). Some include a drink or two in the entry price, and lots only charge an entrance fee on the busy Friday and Saturday nights. Many bars also put on **DJs** or **live music**, and while this usually means some singer-guitarist mangling *Yesterday*, a few places – notably *Blue Door Jazz*, *Cinta-J*, *Ned Kelly's Last Stand* and *The Wanch* – are well above average.

Drinking is a comparatively **expensive** hobby in Hong Kong, and you'll need a substantial budget to party every night. **Happy hours** take the edge off costs, where you'll get something like half-priced drinks or two-for-one deals. They generally last a lot more than an hour: sometime between 5pm and 8pm is usual, though some places sell cheap drinks all afternoon. Blackboards and notices in pubs and bars have details, or check the reviews below. In addition, many bars now feature a **ladies' night** in the week where women get in free and are either offered cheap or free drinks, while men are charged a (hefty) entrance fee. It may be a sad way to lure in extra male punters, but it dramatically cuts the cost of a night out for the girls: check adverts in the listings magazines. Finally, it's worth noting that in the newer, trendier bars you're expected to **tip the bar staff** – ten percent will cover it.

As with everything else in Hong Kong, the nightlife changes very quickly, and to keep up to speed with latest developments you'll need to check

Alcoholic drinks

Hong Kong's favourite alcoholic beverage is **beer** – lager-style and served ice cold. San Miguel and mainland-brand Tsingtao are the top contenders, though bars and restaurants (and lots of supermarkets) also sell British bitter, Guinness and untold other foreign beers, designer or otherwise, draught or bottled, Belgian to Venezuelan. In a supermarket, beer costs around HK$12–25 for a small can. In most restaurants, it's around HK$25–50 for the same can; while in bars and pubs, this can rise dramatically – anything from HK$40 upwards for a small bottle, HK$60–85 for a draught pint.

Drinking **wine** in a bar or restaurant is similarly expensive, starting at around HK$40 a glass, HK$200 a bottle for even the most average of wines – considerably more for anything halfway decent – though in a supermarket a bottle of European plonk will set you back as little as HK$30, with a decent tipple costing from HK$60 upwards. China also produces Dynasty and Great Wall wine, but it's pretty awful. Most internationally known spirits are available in bars and restaurants, again at a price; **Chinese grain spirits** (*bok jau*, literally translating as "white spirit") are incredibly popular on the mainland but most Westerners can't stomach the rough, raw flavours – Moutai is the most famous brand.

magazine **listings and reviews**. There are two free weeklies: *BC* is thorough but dry; *HK Magazine* livelier, trendier and more up to speed. *Time Out Hong Kong* ($18) is probably the most complete of the bunch, but only comes out alternate weeks; and it's also worth checking the *South China Morning Post's* 24/7 supplement each Friday.

Lan Kwai Fong

The places listed below are marked on the map on p.63.

Bit Point 31 D'Aguilar St ☎ 2523 7436. German theme-bar, concentrating on meals until around 10pm, after which the bar starts selling industrial quantities of lager and schnapps as the jukebox blares. Mon–Sat noon–late, Sun 4pm–late; happy hour 4–9pm.
Bulldog Ground Floor, 17 Lan Kwai Fong ☎ 2523 3528. Fourteen-metre-long bar, plasma screen TVs tuned to world sports, dartboard, plus heaps of private nooks and crannies – this bar and grill is for kicking back and getting rowdy over a game of soccer. Sun–Thurs noon–2am, Fri & Sat noon–4am; happy hour 5–8pm.
C Bar Ground Floor, California Tower, 30–32 D'Aguilar St ☎ 2530 3695. Tiny corner-bar, with just a few stools, whose big draw is frozen cocktails dispensed with a giant syringe. A fun and rowdy place with happy hour 5pm–9pm. Mon–Thurs 9am–1am, Fri–Sat 9am–late, Sun 3–midnight.
Club 97 9 Lan Kwai Fong ☎ 2186 1816. A disco downstairs and a vaguely arty, bohemian atmosphere in the bar upstairs, with a strong gay presence on Friday nights. DJs

Wed, Fri and Sat, with laid-back reggae on Sun. Happy hour Mon–Thurs 6pm–2am. Mon–Thurs 6pm–2am, Fri 6pm–4am, Sat–Sun 8pm–late.
D26 26 D'Aguilar St ☎ 2877 1610. Small, low-key bar; a good place for a warm-up drink or if you actually want a conversation with your companions. Happy hour 3–9pm.
Dublin Jack 17 Lan Kwai Fong ☎ 2543 0081. Lan Kwai Fong's biggest bar, serving draught Guinness, over a hundred different varieties of whiskey, big portions of Irish stew and char-grilled steaks; great views down over the street too. Daily noon–late; happy hour noon–8pm.
Fong's 34–36 D'Aguilar St ☎ 2801 4946. Open-fronted bar whose punters often spill out into the street as the night progresses and the crowds increase. Quieter lounge bar upstairs. Daily 5pm–late; happy hour 5–8pm.
Insomnia 38–44 D'Aguilar St ☎ 2525 0957. Street-side bar open from 8am–6am where, for part of the time at least, conversation is possible. Further in, the house band plays covers at maximum volume to an enthusiastic dance crowd.
La Dolce Vita 9 Lan Kwai Fong ☎ 2186 1888. Open-fronted bar known for its huge cocktail selection and weekend brunch. Occasional live music, too. Mon–Thurs noon–2am,

225

Friday noon–3am, Sat 2pm–3am, Sun 2pm–2am. Happy hour 4.30–8.30pm.

Le Jardin Top of Wing Wah Lane ☎2526 2717. There's no sign of this friendly, informal place until you're actually there – walk up Wing Wah Lane, turn left through the pavement tables, keeping to the right, and at the end go up the stairs through the plastic curtain to this covered terrace bar. Laid-back vibe, not as noisy as many, and popular for a warm-up gin or two before hitting the town.

Schnurrbart Ground Floor, Winner Building, 27 D'Aguilar St ☎2523 4700. Long-standing German bar with herring and sausage snacks, and some of the best beer around. Serious headaches are available courtesy of the 25 different kinds of schnapps – try the butterscotch. Mon–Thurs noon–12.30am, Fri & Sat noon–1.30am, Sun 6pm–12.30am.

Wooloo Mooloo 29 Wyndham St ☎2894 8010. Smart Aussie bar, more or less, with good, loud rock, 'n' roll, sports TV, and plenty of beers.

Zinc 35 D'Aguilar St ☎2868 3446. Very hip, unusually upmarket bar for Lan Kwai Fong, serving a huge list of cocktails with names that you wouldn't read to your mother. Fairly quiet early on, but gets clubbing after around 11pm.

Soho

The places listed below are marked on the map on p.68.

Bar 1911 27 Staunton St ☎2810 6681. Ignore the "members only" sign. This is one of Soho's longest-established joints, offering a sort of early twentieth-century ambience with lots of stained glass and heavy wooden furniture. Comfortable noise levels if you want to talk. Not a bargain, but nowhere in this area is. Happy hour 5–9pm. Mon–Sat 5pm–midnight, Sun 5–11pm.

Gecko Ezra Lane, Lower Hollywood Rd ☎2537 4680. A cool, stylish wine bar-lounge, somewhere to relax rather than party. Live jazz 10pm Tues–Thurs, DJ Fri & Sat.

The Globe 39 Hollywood Rd ☎2543 1941. Cosy, friendly bar serving snacks, with a great jukebox and the best beer in Soho, including British and European ales and Belgian wheat beer. Popular with locals after work – can get rowdier later on. Mon–Fri 7.30pm–late, Sat & Sun 10.30pm–late.

Takeout Comedy Basement, 34 Elgin St ☎6220 4436, ⊛www.takeoutcomedy.com. Blackboard outside with the week's events chalked up; Fri & Sat from 9.30pm, HK$150; also runs a free comedy workshop; open mic sessions most nights.

Central

Blue Door Floor 5, 37 Cochrane St, Central. See map, p.68. Tiny jazz club, with live music Saturday night 10.30pm–12.30am.

M Bar Mandarin Oriental Hotel, 5 Connaught Rd ☎2825 4002. See map, pp.60–61. Knowledge-able bar staff can provide you with every cocktail known to man, and the atmosphere is lively. Not cheap. Mon–Fri 11am–1am, Sat 5pm–1am, Sun 5pm–midnight.

Roof Garden 3rd Floor at the Fringe, 2 Lower Albert Rd ☎2521 7251. See map, pp.60–61. Realistically priced drinks at this quiet, chat-friendly bar; sit out on the excellent rooftop terrace with views of skyscrapers rising all around you.

Wan Chai

The places listed below are marked on the map on pp.78–79.

Agave 93–107 Lockhart Rd ☎2866 3228. Rowdy, popular restaurant-bar decked in rich red and orange, which claims to stock over 190 types of tequila. DJ Wed–Sat after 10pm. Happy hour 3–9pm. Sun–Thurs noon–2am, Fri–Sat noon–4am.

Amici 1st Floor, 81 Lockhart Rd (on the corner with Luard) ☎2866 1918. "Sport, vino, pizza" in that order, with happy hour noon–9pm. Sun–Thurs noon–1am, Fri–Sat noon–2am.

Bar 109 109 Lockhart Rd ☎2861 3336. Big party venue, with DJs Wed–Sat nights and Sun afternoon, and reggae Tuesday nights, though there's also a more laid-back upstairs lounge if you just want a drink. Happy hour 3–9pm.

Carnegie's 53–55 Lockhart Rd ☎2866 6289. Packed and noisy, with hordes of punters keen to revel the night away fighting for dancing space on the bar. Regular live music, DJ on Thursday night, occasional club nights. Daily 11am–3am, often later.

Cinta-J 69 Jaffe Rd, Wan Chai ☎2529 6622. Great Filipino restaurant-bar with live music provided by the house band from 7.15pm Mon–Sat and 4.30pm on Sundays.

Gay nightlife

In recent years, the gay scene has quietly expanded in Hong Kong, and there are a few clubs and bars geared specifically to a gay crowd. Longest running include **Propaganda**, 1 Hollywood Rd, Central (℡2868 1316; Mon–Thurs 9pm–3.30am, Fri & Sat 9pm–6am), which has a decent-sized dancefloor, adjacent chill-out bar quiet enough to have a conversation in, and a pricey cover charge of HK$200 most nights; and **Works**, 1st Floor, 30–32 Wyndham St, Central (℡2868 6102; Tues–Thurs 7pm–1.30am, Fri–Sun 9pm–late), an industrial-looking warehouse of a club with plenty of dark corners and a HK$60 cover charge. A couple of mainstream joints host gay nights, or have an obviously mixed crowd.

While the above venues are male-dominated, lesbian nightlife is a more local affair, restricted to karaoke-lounge-type bars or dimly lit clubs playing loud Canto-pop. A cover charge of around HK$120, which includes one drink, is standard. Try **The Temptation Lesbian Pub**, 21st Floor, Lamma Tower, 12–12A Hau Fook St, Tsim Sha Tsui, Kowloon (℡2332 1098); **Loft Bar De**, 2nd Floor, 126–128 Lockhart Rd, Wan Chai ℡2866 3268); and **No.2**, 2nd Floor, Universal House, 229–230 Gloucester Rd, Wan Chai (℡2577 7027).

For the latest gay and lesbian listings, check ⓦsqzm14.ust.hk/hkgay. See also p.41.

Coyote 114–120 Lockhart Rd ℡2861 2221. Competition for nearby Agave, with much the same TexMex atmosphere, menu and drinks list.

Devil's Advocate 48–50 Lockhart Rd ℡2865 7271. Hugely popular, especially with young office workers and expats – rotten jukebox selection, though. Beers HK$29 during 3–9pm happy hour. Daily 11am–late.

Dusk Till Dawn 76 Jaffe Rd ℡2528 4689. The colour scheme is vaguely Mediterranean, but this is not the place for a quiet drink – loud live music, raucous staff, and equally energetic punters. Daily afternoon–late; happy hour 5–11pm.

Horse and Groom 161 Lockhart Rd ℡2507 2517. Large, dark venue with wreaths of wrought iron and neon. The cheap drinks and Western pub food attract a good mixed crowd of expats and locals. Mon–Sat 11am–4.30am, Sun 7pm–4am; happy hour Sat 6–9pm, Sun 8–10pm.

Joe Banana's 23 Luard Rd ℡2529 1811. Lively, unsophisticated American bar with a late disco, fake palms, occasional live music, and marathon weekend opening hours; happy hour noon–8pm when beers are just HK$20. You need to be (or look) 21 and there's a strict door policy – men need a shirt with a collar. Mon–Thurs 11.30am–5am, Fri & Sat 11.30am–6am, Sun 5pm–late.

Neptune II 98–108 Jaffe Rd ℡2865 2238. Dingy but good-natured club, the backdrop for mostly Western pop, interspersed with bouts of the Filipino house band playing cover versions. The clientele is mainly Filipina, too – which means there are significant numbers of Western men on the prowl. Daily 6pm–7am.

Old China Hand 104 Lockhart Rd ℡2527 9174. Great pub for hard-core drinkers, hung-over clubbers (who come for breakfast), embittered, seedy expats acting the part, and those with a taste for loud music. Mon–Sat 24hr, Sun 9am–2am.

The Pawn 62 Johnston Rd, Wan Chai ℡2866 3444. Smart pub in restored old pawnbroker's building dating from 1888, façade and some old wooden fixtures still in place, with a balcony overlooking busy road. Extensive list of imported spirits, beers and wine, with pub-style fish and chips, ploughman's and English breakfasts at HK$100–200.

Tango Martini 3rd Floor, Empire Land Commercial Centre, 81–85 Lockhart Rd ℡2528 0855. This lounge-style bar and restaurant features comfy tiger-print couches and chairs and more than 201 martinis, setting it apart from most of Wan Chai's gritty establishments. Chic and expensive, you'll either love it or hate it. Mon–Fri noon–3pm & 6pm–2am, Sat & Sun 6pm–2am.

Wanch 54 Jaffe Rd ℡2861 1621. A Wan Chai institution, this tiny, unpretentious bar is jostling and friendly and has live music – usually folk and rock – every night. Also serves cheap chunky cheeseburgers and sandwiches. Mon–Sat 11am–2am, Sun noon–2am.

Bars with views

The places below all offer excellent views while you drink, mostly of the harbour, and most charge more than usual for the privilege.

Aqua Spirit Top of 1 Peking Rd, Tsim Sha Tsui. See p.218 for review.

Café Deco Levels 1 & 2, Peak Galleria, The Peak. See p.218 for review.

Felix 28th Floor, *Peninsula Hotel*, Salisbury Rd, Tsim Sha Tsui. See p.218 for review. Minimum spend of HK$200 per person (which might just get you two martinis), but the men's toilets have the best views in the SAR.

Oasis Lounge 8th Floor, *Renaissance Harbour View Hotel*, 1 Harbour Rd, Wan Chai ℡2721 5161.

Sky Lounge 18th Floor, *Sheraton Hotel*, 20 Nathan Rd, Tsim Sha Tsui ℡2369 1111.

Causeway Bay

The places listed below are marked on the map on pp.78–79.

Dickens Sports Bar Lower Ground Floor, Excelsior Hotel, 281 Gloucester Rd ℡2837 6782. This bar prides itself on re-creating an authentic British atmosphere: the kitchen dishes up genuine British pub grub, the TV airs British sitcoms, and there are English papers to read. Mon–Thurs & Sun 11am–2am, Fri & Sat 11am–3am.

The Royal's Pub 21 Cannon St ℡2832 7879. British pub furnishings but largely Chinese customers at this dark, rowdy bar, where you can watch the locals playing dice, accompanied by loud Canto-pop. Happy hour 11.30am–9pm. Daily 11am–2am.

Tsim Sha Tsui

The places listed below are marked on the map on pp.104–105.

All Night Long 9 Knutsford Terrace. Asian cover bands and DJs dishing up the 1980s–1990s mix available on your local radio station – cheesy but can be fun.

Aqua Spirit 30th Floor, 1 Peking Rd ℡3427 2288. Attached to the equally spiffy *Aqua* restaurant, this smart bar tempts with killer martinis and staggering views. Minimum HK$150pp for drinks; cocktails about HK$100 each. Sun–Thurs 5pm–2am, Fri–Sat 5pm–3am.

Bahama Mama's 4–5 Knutsford Terrace ℡2368 2121. Beach-bar theme and outdoor terrace that prompts party-crowd antics. Has one of Hong Kong's only football tables, and is one of the rare bars that is popular with both Westerners and local Chinese. For the best crack, stump up the cover charge and come along on club nights where a mixed music policy offers everything from garage to world. Mon–Thurs 5pm–3am, Fri & Sat 5pm–4am, Sun 6pm–2am.

Ned Kelly's Last Stand 11a Ashley Rd ℡2376 0562. Dark Australian bar with great live jazz from the house band after 9pm; good beer and meaty Aussie food served at the tables. It's a real favourite with travellers, and good fun. Daily 11.45am–1.45am.

Stag's Head 11 Hart Ave, Tsim Sha Tsui ℡2369 3142. Popular pub with good jukebox selection, attracting expats and tourists alike; almost always has beer, spirit and wine promotions during noon–10pm happy hours.

Tequila Jack's 33–35 Chatham Rd South ℡3428 5133. Best range of Mexican beers in Hong Kong at this popular little cantina, with a handful of pavement tables for people watching.

Watering Hole Basement, 1A Mody Rd ℡2312 2288. An enormous subterranean bar with darts and a small selection of beers. The decor is nondescript, but there's a good mix of locals, expats and tourists, and the bar staff are friendly. Daily 4pm–1pm.

Elsewhere

Café Deco Level 1 & 2, Peak Galleria, 118 Peak Rd, The Peak ℡2849 5111. Great views and regular live jazz make this a good spot for an evening drink on The Peak – even if the food isn't especially good. Mon–Thurs & Sun 10am–midnight, Fri & Sat 10am–1am.

Smuggler's Inn 90a Stanley Main St, Stanley ℡2813 8852. See map, p.93. A grungy little bar with cheap snacks and indifferent staff, but it's very popular with locals who shut themselves in after midnight to bop to loud music. Daily 10am–2am.

8

Arts and entertainment

Despite a certain amount of snobbery among the local population that Hong Kong is a repository of Chinese culture, having been largely unaffected by the various turmoils that beset mainland China during the twentieth century, "cultural events" here can be few and far between. This is not for want of trying: the **Cultural Centre** in Tsim Sha Tsui and the **Hong Kong Arts Centre** and adjacent **Academy for Performing Arts** in Wan Chai all host domestic and international dance, opera and music performances. Somehow, though, it all seems a bit artificial; the only art form that commands a mass audience in Hong Kong is **film**, with the cinemas packed for every new Hollywood or Chinese release. That's not to say that you can't experience **Chinese culture**, just that it tends to be at its best when it's informally presented: at the night markets, perhaps, or during religious holidays at temples and on the street.

Information, tickets and venues

Information about cultural events and performances can be picked up at any of the venues listed below. The best sources of detailed **listings** are the free weeklies *HK Magazine* and *BC Magazine*, available at most cafés, *Time Out Hong Kong* (HK$18) from any newsagent, or the *South China Morning Post's 24/7* magazine, which comes free with the Friday edition of the paper. It's also well worth scouring the **Leisure and Cultural Services Department**'s website (Ⓦwww.lcsd.gov.hk) to find out what's on at many of the more local venues everywhere from downtown districts to New Town city halls. Otherwise, contact the venues themselves for current performances.

Tickets for most events can be bought up to four weeks in advance through URBTIX (Ⓦwww.urbtix.hk) or purchased direct from venues. Many cultural events are subsidized; seats for local productions cost around HK$50–120, rising to HK$250–1000 for anything international.

Main venues

Academy for Performing Arts 1 Gloucester Rd, Wan Chai Ⓦwww.hkapa.edu. Six separate stages for local and international drama, and modern and classical dance. Box office daily 10am–6pm.

Alliance Française 2nd Floor, 123 Hennessy Rd, Wan Chai ☎2527 7825, Ⓦwww.alliancefrancaise .com.hk; Ho Kwan Building, 3rd Floor, 52 Jordan Rd, Kowloon ☎2730 3257. Films and culture at the French Cultural Institute. Box office daily 8.30am–9.30pm.

City Hall 1 Edinburgh Place, Central ☎2921 2840. Drama, concerts, recitals, exhibitions and lectures. Box office daily 10am–9.30pm.

Fringe Club 2 Lower Albert Rd, Central ☎2521 7251, Ⓦwww.hkfringeclub.com. Offbeat venue for cabaret, alternative theatre, jazz,

▲ The Fringe Club in Central

concerts and poetry, as well as exhibitions, classes and workshops. Pick up the schedule from the venue; temporary membership available. Box office Mon–Sat 10am–10pm.

Goethe Institute 14th Floor, Hong Kong Arts Centre, 2 Harbour Rd, Wan Chai ☎2802 0088, ⓦwww.goethe.de/hongkong. Films and events at the German Cultural Institute.

Hong Kong Arts Centre 2 Harbour Rd, Wan Chai ☎2582 0200, ⓦwww.hkac.org.hk. Local art, drama, concerts, film screenings, galleries and exhibitions. Box office daily 10am–6pm.

Hong Kong International Trade and Exhibition Centre (HITEC) 1 Trademart Drive, Kowloon Bay, Kowloon ⓦwww.hitec.com.hk. General event venue that every year hosts a couple of big bands, usually Southeast Asian or Chinese.

Hong Kong Coliseum 9 Cheong Wan Rd, Hung Hom ☎2355 7233. Hong Kong's largest venue (12,000 seats) for dance, sports and everything from major international rock bands to Cantonese operatic solos and lengthy concerts by Canto-pop superstars. Box office daily 10am–6.30pm.

Hong Kong Convention and Exhibition Centre Expo Drive, Wan Chai ☎2582 8888, ⓦwww.hkcec.com.hk. Major conventions, exhibitions, concerts and performances. Box office varies according to the promoter; check press for details.

Hong Kong Cultural Centre 10 Salisbury Rd, Tsim Sha Tsui ☎2734 2009. Dance, drama and concerts, drawing on local and international performers. Box office daily 10am–9.30pm.

Kwai Tsing Theatre 12 Hing Ning Rd, Kwai Chung ☎2406 7505. Hosts local dance and drama, including occasional Cantonese opera. Box office daily 10am–9.30pm.

Ngau Chi Wan Civic Centre 2nd Floor, Ngau Chi Wan Complex, 11 Clearwater Bay Rd, Kowloon (Choi Hung MTR) ☎2325 1970, ⓦwww.lcsd.gov .hk/ncwcc. Drama, dance and film. Box office daily 10am–6.30pm.

Queen Elizabeth Stadium 18 Oi Kwan Rd, Wan Chai ☎2591 1346. Stadium with a 3500 capacity for large concerts and sports events. Box office daily 10am–6.30pm.

Sha Tin Town Hall 1 Yuen Wo Rd, New Town Plaza, Sha Tin, New Territories ☎2694 2509. Drama, dance and concerts, with many internationally renowned troupes. Box office daily 10am–9.30pm.

Sheung Wan Civic Centre 345 Queen's Rd, Sheung Wan ☎2853 2678. Drama, concerts, lectures and exhibitions. Box office daily 10am–6.30pm.

Tsuen Wan Town Hall 72 Tai Ho Rd, Tsuen Wan, New Territories ☎2414 0144. Large venue for concerts, dance and drama. Box office daily 10am–9.30pm.

Tuen Mun Town Hall 3 Tuen Hi Rd, Tuen Mun, New Territories ☎2450 3680. Local venue for concerts, dance and drama. Box office daily 10am–9.30pm.

Free events

The Leisure and Cultural Services Department (ⓦwww.lcsd.gov.hk) arranges regular **free events**, from summertime jazz concerts to children's shadow-puppet theatre performances, in venues around the city. The Cultural Centre holds free concerts on Thursday afternoons, while the Academy for Performing Arts also has regular free concerts performed by its own students in its recital hall – phone first to reserve a ticket. There are also occasional lunchtime and afternoon recitals at St John's Cathedral, Garden Road, Central (☎2523 4157), usually on a Wednesday.

Chinese cultural performances

Chinese cultural performances are widespread in Hong Kong – every town and village has a hall, theatre or outdoor space where traditional opera and dance are put on. All performances are highly theatrical; coming across one by accident can be a real highlight of your stay.

The best known is **Chinese opera**, which you'll see performed locally at festivals, on religious holidays and in some of the larger venues by visiting and local troupes. In Hong Kong, the style is mostly Cantonese (though visiting mainland Chinese groups perform Beijing opera on occasion, too), a musical drama with mime, set songs and responses based on well-known legends and stories. The costumes and garish make-up are magnificent, and although the strident singing and percussion may test Western ears, it becomes compelling after a while – particularly as the story is interspersed with bouts of elaborate sword fighting and acrobatics. Performances often go on for three hours or more, but the ones held in or near temples at festivals are usually informal, with people walking about, chatting and eating right the way through. Only two places host regular **Cantonese opera performances**: the Sun Kwong Theatre, right behind North Point MTR station on King's Road, North Point, Hong Kong Island (T2856 0161 or 2856 0162), and Ko Shan Theatre, Ko Shan Road Park, To Kwa Wan, Kowloon (T9465 6823). It's best to check with HKTB for current programmes before heading out to either. Opera buffs may also want to visit the Cantonese opera exhibition on the first floor of the Heritage Museum in Sha Tin (see p.139).

Other cultural shows you might catch include traditional Chinese **music**, **puppet theatre**, **folk dancing**, **acrobatics**, **magic** and **martial arts** – all things that soon become evident if you're in Hong Kong for any length of time. Street markets and festivals are good places to look; or check in the local press for specific performances at some of the main venues.

Obviously, it's most rewarding to stumble on performances as you travel around the territory; religious festival events (see p.33) and cultural shows out in the New Territories (listed in the press) are put on for the locals and have few pretensions. For more information, contact any of the HKTB offices (see p.50).

Arts festivals

There are several main arts festivals in Hong Kong each year. More information about all of them can be obtained from the HKTB, but it's worth knowing that tickets for the best performances can be hard to come by; book well in advance, or be prepared to settle for what performances you can get into.

City Festival (Jan/Feb). An alternative arts festival organized by the Fringe Club, with street performances by local and international artists; check Ⓦ www.hkfringe.com.hk for information.

Hong Kong Arts Festival (Feb/Mar). Wide-ranging international arts festival bringing together leading artists from China and the West. Usually includes opera, theatre, ballet and concerts; check Ⓦ www.hk.artsfestival.org for information.

Hong Kong International Film Festival (April). A month of international films at various venues – very popular and imaginative with screenings of current releases as well as old-world cinema classics. City Hall has specific information if you want to book in advance, or check Ⓦ www.hkiff.org.hk.

International Arts Carnival (July/Aug). Six weeks of acrobatics, puppet shows, clown theatre, mime and magic, aimed at children and families; check Ⓦ www.hkiac .gov.hk for information.

Film

Cinemas in Hong Kong are multi-screen complexes showing a mixture of new Hollywood and local releases. Going to the movies is inexpensive (around HK$55 a ticket; half-price on Tues) and it's worth taking in one of the **Chinese-language films** if you can: most are the domestic product (see "Hong Kong cinema" box opposite), though films from the mainland are

Hong Kong cinema and the world

Hong Kong is traditionally ranked as the world's **third largest movie producer** (after India and the US), though output has slipped considerably since the glory days of the early 1990s. DVD is perhaps to blame, along with an erratic economy and mainland China's increasing dominance in the field, but there's still no denying local cinema's popular appeal, made easier by the content: generally easy-to-digest romances, comedies or high-speed action, with little interest in deeper meanings or the outside world – and certainly not in politics.

The boom started after World War II, when a slew of **wuxia** – kung fu – movies about the Cantonese folk-hero **Wong Fei Hung** proved a massive hit with the public. Studios like **Shaw Brothers** and **Golden Harvest** grew fat, but the rest of the world couldn't have cared less, until its interest was stirred in the early 1970s by martial arts prodigy **Bruce Lee**. Although better known overseas for the Hollywood-financed *Enter the Dragon*, the success in Hong Kong of his earlier film *Fist of Fury* launched a domestic **kung fu movie** explosion, off the back of which sprung **Jackie Chan** and a much-needed element of slapstick comedy – best seen in Chan's early works, such as *Drunken Master*. As the genre faltered in the 1980s, directors mixed in a supernatural aspect, pioneered by **Tsui Hark** in *Zu: Warriors from the Magic Mountain* and *Chinese Ghost Story*. The **wuxia** genre has again been revived in recent years following mainland-produced blockbusters such as *Crouching Tiger, Hidden Dragon*; **Stephen Chow**'s excellent *Shaolin Soccer* and *Kung Fu Hustle* sport uniquely surreal humour and visuals; while *Ip Man* is a largely fictional account of the life of Bruce Lee's main teacher.

The 1980s saw the rise of Hong Kong's modern **action movies**, typified by police thrillers like **John Woo**'s influential 1980s hits *A Better Tomorrow* and *Hard Boiled*, which feature Chow Yun Fat shooting his way through relentless scenes of orchestrated violence. Woo's immediate imitators generally only succeeded in making pointless, bloody movies which inevitably concluded with the massacre of the entire cast, until *Infernal Affairs* – remade as *The Departed* by US director Martin Scorsese – brought in stylish, moody, downbeat plots and characters. Incidentally, many of the *Infernal Affairs* cast – including Andy Lau, Tony Leung, Kelly Chen and Sammi Cheng – were moonlighting from successful Canto-pop careers.

In the meantime, Hong Kong's film industry has also churned out endless quantities of (usually tragic) romances, or domestic comedies using a Laurel and Hardy format. These often rely on a knowledge of the ins-and-outs of Chinese daily life and, as neither translate very well, are fairly inaccessible to a Western audience. The most recent trend seems to be in **historical dramas**, with movies like *Red Cliff* plundering the almost limitless, complex plots and characterization provided by Chinese historical novels.

At present, Hong Kong's only director interested in anything but light entertainment is **Wong Karwai**, whose early works such as *Chungking Express* depicted Hong Kong as a crowded, disjointed city where people, though forced together, seemed unable to communicate. His more recent films have added a European sense of style, which worked in the sensuous *In the Mood for Love* (whose 1960s Hong Kong scenes were shot in Macau's old backstreets) but overwhelmed the plot in the obscure, self-referential *2046*.

increasingly on view as well. Look for a showing with English subtitles. Current films are reviewed in the English-language daily newspapers, as well as *HK Magazine* and *BC Magazine*. All the major **English-language films** make it to Hong Kong soon after release, and are usually shown in their original language, with Chinese subtitles – but check the performance you want isn't a dubbed version.

All the major venues offer computerized booking systems, so you can either phone in advance and let the system select the best available seats, or go in person and pick your seat from those available, shown on the video monitor by the box office (the loge, incidentally, is equivalent to the dress circle). It's not uncommon for Chinese members of the audience

▲ Hong Kong film poster

to talk right through the show – sometimes on their mobile phones – and most cinemas have the air-conditioning turned up so high you'll need a jacket to stop your teeth chattering.

The **major cinemas**, and a few interesting minor ones, are listed below, but for a full rundown of what's on where, consult the local press. If you're just wandering and fancy a movie, the biggest concentration of cinemas is in Wan Chai and Causeway Bay. There are also regular film shows (often free) sponsored by the Alliance Française and Goethe Institute (see "Main venues" on p.230 for addresses), while occasional film shows are held in the Space Museum (see p.103) and Science Museum lecture halls (see p.108).

The best venues for **art-house cinema** are Broadway Cinematheque and the Cine-Art House (see below); film buffs will also want to try to coincide with the annual **film festival** (see the "Arts festivals" box on p.231), which always has an excellent and entertaining international programme, though it can be hard to get seats.

Finally, real fans of Hong Kong cinema should check out the **Hong Kong Film Archive** (Fri–Wed 10am–8pm; free; ⓦ www.filmarchive.gov.hk) on Lei King Road at Sai Wan Ho, east of Tin Hau on Hong Kong Island's North Shore – take the Island Line to Sai Wan Ho MTR station, take Exit A and follow the signs for ten minutes. Their regular local and international cinema screenings can be worth a look – especially if you like old Cantonese films – but check the website for programme details before heading out here.

AMC Festival Walk Upper Ground Floor, Festival Walk, Kowloon Tong ⓣ 2265 8595. A mammoth eleven-screen cinema showing everything from mainstream Hollywood through Hong Kong cinema to art house.
Broadway ⓦ www.cinema.com.hk. Eleven cinemas scattered through the SAR.
Broadway Cinematheque Prosperous Gardens, 3 Public Square St, Yau Ma Tei ⓦ bc.cinema.com.hk.

"Alternative" and art-house films, many from Europe and East Asia.
Chinachem Circuit ⓦ www.cel-cinemas.com. Two cinemas in Kowloon and the New Territories.
Cine-Art House Sun Hung Kai Centre, 30 Harbour Rd, Wan Chai ⓦ www.cityline.com.hk. Another art-house cinema, similar to Broadway Cinemateque.

Hong Kong Arts Centre 2 Harbour Rd, Wan Chai ☎2582 0200. Seasons of alternative and foreign films and Chinese cinema.
New York Cinema 463–483 Lockhart Rd, Plaza II, Causeway Bay ☎2838 7380. Plush cinema for new Western and Chinese releases.
UA ☎2317 6666. Eight cinemas in Kowloon and Hong Kong Island.

Live music

Hong Kong is never the first place that touring Western **rock and pop bands** think of, but there's a good deal of **Canto-pop** talent in town (see box below), not to mention visiting groups from Taiwan and Mainland China.

The main local exponent of **Western classical music** is the Hong Kong Philharmonic Orchestra (Ⓦ www.hkpo.com), whose season runs from September through to June, and which regularly employs excellent guest conductors and soloists. The Hong Kong Sinfonietta is another professional orchestra, although their performances can be rather ragged.

For **Chinese orchestral music**, watch for performances by the Hong Kong Chinese Orchestra (Ⓦ www.hkco.org), the territory's only professional Chinese music group. The orchestra plays one weekend every month at City Hall and the Cultural Centre, performing reworkings of Western classical music on traditional Chinese instruments – a combination not to everyone's taste, but certainly worth hearing.

Check the "Main Venues" list (p.229) for places to see all these things, though any major pop events will almost certainly be at either the Hong Kong Coliseum or the Queen Elizabeth Stadium. For other Chinese classical music, check with the HKTB, and look out for student concerts at the university and Academy of Performing Arts (APA), which regularly hosts free concerts (see p.229). For details of Chinese opera performances, see p.231.

Theatre and the performing arts

Hong Kong has a solid base of domestically produced **drama and perform-ance art**, alongside the usual international touring companies and artists who enliven the cultural year. Big musical productions are popular, although the lack of suitable venues limits their numbers. A rundown of **venues** is given on p.229, but check whether **productions** are in English or Cantonese.

Canto-pop

Canto-pop, a bland, Chinese-language blending of Western pop ballads and disco, is easily the most popular music in Hong Kong. Its origins lie in the Cantonese movie musicals of the 1950s and 1960s, whose soundtracks became enormously popular in post-war Hong Kong. Then Hong Kong-based artist **Sam Hui** mixed Cantonese lyrics with Western pop music in the mid-1970s, and Canto-pop was born. Output is phenomenal – many of the big names routinely record five or more albums per year – and its **stars** are accorded tremendous status: Tony Leung, the late Leslie Cheung, Andy Lau, Sammi Cheng, Beijing-born Faye Wong, and Kelly Chen are household names in the SAR, and can't appear in public without getting mobbed by fans. Live performances, where fans sit waving coloured light sticks and holding message boards for their heroes, sell out months in advance – try and book before you travel if you're hoping to catch one.

Other than straight drama, some of the most exciting local performances are of **dance**, which doesn't have the disadvantage of a language barrier and often mixes Western and Chinese forms very successfully. **Fringe events** are common, too; the Fringe Club (see p.229), especially, hosts its fair share of mime, magic, cabaret and comedy.

Some interesting **local companies** to watch out for, who perform at venues all over the territory, include:

City Contemporary Dance Company Ⓦwww .ccdc.com.hk. Very good, full-time professional company; they usually perform at the Hong Kong Arts Centre.

Hong Kong Ballet Company Ⓦwww.hkballet .com. Classical and contemporary ballet performances at various venues.

Hong Kong Dance Company Ⓦ www.hkdance .com. Modern and classical Chinese dance.

Hong Kong Singers Ⓦ www.hksingers.com. Musical comedy of the Gilbert and Sullivan variety.

Visual arts

Some of the main venues listed above have **gallery and exhibition space** that's worth checking for current displays. Otherwise, keep an eye on the SAR's **museums**, which host occasional lectures and exhibitions. Both the Heritage Museum (see p.139) and the Hong Kong Museum of Art (see p.103) host temporary art exhibitions, while the University of Hong Kong (see p.72) and the Chinese University near Sha Tin (see p.141) have free galleries open to the public. The Leisure and Cultural Services Department's district **libraries** also put on year-round lectures (sometimes in English) and exhibitions that might be of interest.

There are many **private art galleries** in Hong Kong. The *South China Morning Post* highlights a good selection of current exhibitions in its daily What's On section, as does the weekly *HK Magazine*. The places listed below are usually worth dropping in on, though most are closed on Sundays:

Alisan Fine Arts 315 Prince's Building, 10 Chater Rd, Central ℡2526 1091, Ⓦwww.alisan .com.hk. Mainly Chinese contemporary work of a not too challenging variety.

Altfield Gallery 248–49 Prince's Building, 10 Chater Rd, Central ℡2537 6370, Ⓦwww .altfield.com.hk. China trade paintings, maps, prints, Chinese furniture and Southeast Asian works of art. Open Sun.

The Fringe Club 2 Lower Albert Rd, Central ℡2521 7251, Ⓦwww.hkfringeclub.com. Currently houses two galleries, the Montblanc and Nokia Galleries, with the emphasis on local artists, though international multimedia works are also shown.

Galerie La Vong 13th Floor, One Lan Kwai Fong, Central ℡2869 6863. Leading modern Vietnamese painters.

Gallery On Old Bailey 17 Old Bailey St, Central ℡2869 7122, Ⓦwww.galleryonoldbailey.com.

Largely contemporary Chinese oil paintings, and small sculptures from around the world. Open Sun afternoon.

Hanart TZ Gallery 2nd Floor, Henley Building, 5 Queen's Rd, Central ℡2526 9019, Ⓦwww .hanart.com. Leading dealer of modern Chinese painters.

John Batten Gallery 64 Peel St, Central ℡2854 1018, Ⓦwww.johnbattengallery.com. Specializes in kooky, off-beat art.

Schoeni 27 Hollywood Rd, Central ℡2542 3143, and 21–31 Old Bailey St, Central ℡2869 8802, Ⓦwww.schoeni.com.hk. Exhibitions of international and Chinese contemporary artists.

Zee Stone Gallery Yu Yuet Lai Building, 43–55 Wyndham St, Central ℡2810 5895, Ⓦwww .zeestone.com. Modern Vietnamese, Chinese and Tibetan paintings and antique furniture. Open Sun 1–5pm.

Shopping

Hong Kong is an amazing place to **shop**, although stories about giveaway prices – especially for electronic goods – are no longer true, thanks to Hong Kong's high living costs and the advent of internet shopping. But what is incredible here is the **huge range of goods** crammed into such a small area and, as long as you keep your wits about you, you can still find plenty of good deals on clothing, mobile phones, MP3 players, cameras, computers, jewellery and Chinese arts and crafts.

If amazingly low prices are now a myth, stories about being spectacularly **ripped off** are only too true. The rule for buying anything in Hong Kong is to **know your subject**, especially the price you'd pay at home and the price you'd pay online for identical goods. There are no import or sales taxes in Hong Kong, so whatever you're looking at should at least be this much cheaper than the same item bought at home. Refunds are almost unknown (and being overcharged won't negate that), so it's absolutely essential to make sure you know what you're getting and that it's exactly what you want for the price. Ask for a **fully itemized receipt**.

Shop opening hours vary according to which part of Hong Kong you shop in, and most areas have late-night shopping once a week. Shops generally open seven days a week, though some smaller establishments close on Sunday. Otherwise, the only time shops close is for the first three days around Chinese New Year, and even then by no means all do so. Opening hours for street **markets** (apart from fresh-food markets) are even longer, usually daily until 11pm or midnight, though a couple of exceptions are mentioned in the text.

Shopping: a survival guide

Not everyone in Hong Kong is out to cheat you, but there are some things to be aware of before you part with any cash. Most importantly, **shop around** to get an idea of what things cost. For widely available items like jewellery, clothing and electronics, **chain stores** anywhere in the city will give you a baseline price which you can then compare with specialist stores or markets elsewhere. **Pirated and fake goods** (DVDs and clothes especially) are

Shopping hours

Central and Western: daily 10am–7pm.
Wan Chai and Causeway Bay: daily 10am–10pm.
Tsim Sha Tsui, Yau Ma Tei and Mongkok: daily 10am–10pm.
Tsim Sha Tsui East: daily 10am–7.30pm.

common, so keep this in mind if you encounter any unusually cheap prices. **Parallel imports** (imports which come via a third party, rather than directly from the manufacturer) can also be problematic, not in the goods themselves, but because the warranties may be invalid and the manufacturer unwilling to service them if something goes wrong. So, whatever you're after, **take your time**; find out exactly what's included, ask for demonstrations and – on principle – don't buy the first thing you see. If you're being unduly pressurized to buy, you're probably in the wrong shop.

Choosing a shop

For expensive items, consider using shops that are members of the **Quality Tourism Services** (QTS) Scheme, run by the Hong Kong Tourism Board (HKTB). All members display the QTS symbol in their window – a golden Q encircling the Chinese character for "excellence" – and are annually tested to make sure they display clear prices and give good customer service. Obviously, only a fraction of Hong Kong's shops and stores are in the QTS scheme and the others aren't necessarily villains, but it's a starting point if you're worried. You can get a list of member shops from the HKTB. Other places to look for shopping information include the free *HK* magazine and listings in the *South China Morning Post*.

For general complaints about goods made in Hong Kong, try the Consumer Council on ⓦ www .consumer.org.hk.

Guarantees

Always check the **guarantee** you're given for photographic, electronic or electrical goods. Some are **international**, in which case they should carry the name of the sole agent in Hong Kong for that product, but most are purely **local guarantees**, which are only valid in Hong Kong, usually for a period of twelve months. All guarantees should carry a description of the product, including a model number and serial number, as well as the date of purchase, the name and address of the shop you bought it from and the shop's official stamp.

Deposits and refunds

You don't need to put down a **deposit** on anything unless it's being made for you. For tailored clothes, expect to put down fifty percent of the price, or a little more. On other items, if the shop tries to insist (to "secure" the item, or to order a new one because they're "out of stock") go somewhere else – there are always plenty of alternatives. Generally, goods are **not returnable or refundable**, though if something is faulty or missing the better shops may replace your goods. It will help if you have your receipt itemized and go straight back to the shop if there's something wrong.

Compatibility

Check that **electronic goods** are compatible with your domestic mains voltage, and that television sets and DVD players are compatible with each other, and with your domestic broad-casting system. Beware of the "bait and switch" scam, when having paid for a certain product, you are then told it can't be used in your home country. The shop refuses to refund the trans-action, forcing you to pay more for a "better, compatible" model. Be aware, too, that legitimate DVD films bought in Hong Kong are regionally coded, and may not work in your machine at home – there are no such problems with pirated DVD films, audio CDs or computer software, however.

Customs, shipping and insurance

Before making large purchases, check with the relevant consulate (see p.40) or the HKTB about **customs**

regulations for the country you want to import the goods to. The shop may be able to arrange to have your purchase packed and sent overseas, but make sure you have it **insured** to cover damage in transit as well as loss (and of course also ensure that you keep the receipt). To send items home yourself, you need to go to a main post office, where you can also arrange insurance (though check first to see if you're covered by your own travel insurance). Parcels usually take about a month by surface mail and a week by airmail to reach Europe or North America.

Avoiding rip-offs

Having checked all the main points, you still need to be armed against the out-and-out bad guys – or simply against the shopkeepers who see their chance to make some extra profit from an unsuspecting visitor. Shops along the lower end of Nathan Road in Tsim Sha Tsui are especially bad for this.

Always ask the **price**, and what that price includes. Ask more than once to ensure a consistent answer.

Bargaining: for most large items in the bigger shops and department stores, the price will be fixed and you won't be able to bargain, though you might be able to wangle extra accessories and the like before completing the sale. However, it's almost mandatory to bargain in markets and smaller shops, especially for electronic goods. Decide the price you want to pay for an item and stick with it, and if you can't get them down to that, politely walk away. Often the staff will call you back and grudgingly agree to your price if it's a fair one. They are more likely to agree to a discount if you buy two or more items.

Switching goods: if you've paid for goods, don't let them out of your sight as it's not unknown for bits and pieces to have mysteriously vanished by the time you get home, or for cheaper or damaged gear to have

been substituted. Either pack your purchases yourself, or check everything before you leave the shop. If things like camera cases or electrical leads are part of the package, make sure they're there and itemized on the receipt: otherwise if you return later to complain you may be told that they're "extras" which you now have to pay for.

Fake and pirate gear: sometimes you know that goods are fakes or copies and it doesn't matter. Pirated DVDs, computer software and CDs, for instance, are available in many places. Copies of leading international jewellery brands' signature designs, by local jewellers (in gold and precious stones), are also good value. Fake designer-label gear from markets may also have a certain cachet. But if you want the real thing, don't buy anything from anyone on the street, and don't be tempted by stupid "bargains" – pay the going rate and get receipts and guarantees.

Boycotting products

There's almost nothing you can't buy in Hong Kong, which means that there is trade in several products you may not feel entirely happy about, including furs, leather and skin goods made from rare and exotic or endangered species, such as **ivory**. There are huge stocks of this in Hong Kong, one of the world's largest markets in the product, and it is still home to a big ivory-processing industry – you'll see the results in shop windows. However, both the Chinese government and the Hong Kong authorities are parties to CITES (the Convention on International Trade in Endangered Species), and since 1990 the Hong Kong authorities have abided more stringently by the rules of the worldwide ban.

There is also a growing trade in **shatoosh**, a fibre even finer than cashmere. It comes from Tibetan antelopes that are shot by poachers (the fur isn't gathered after being rubbed off on thorns, as vendors would have you believe). The shawls produced can go for US$10,000 or more.

The trade in endangered species also rears its head in **Traditional Chinese Medicine**, which often uses the body parts of critically endangered animals like tigers and rhinos. Surprisingly, many of the medicines carry bilingual ingredient lists – if you're going to buy anything, check first.

Antiques and art galleries

Hong Kong offers good opportunities to buy Chinese **antiques and arts**, although local buyers are very clued up and bargains are consequently rare. Most of the galleries dealing in the market are on **Hollywood Road** in Central; many also maintain larger **warehouses** elsewhere (including over the border), so if you're really interested, ask about visiting. The type of stock available changes from year to year, though the premium on really good pieces never changes. For interesting old bric-a-brac and the very occasional genuine antique, you could also visit **Sham Shui Po Market** (see p.115) in Kowloon. Hollywood Road is also home to several **contemporary art** dealers representing mainland Chinese painters – expect some astronomical prices for famous artists.

Most antiques come from China, usually by "unofficial" routes. There are no problems in re-exporting these items from Hong Kong, but if you're worried, pieces that have left China legitimately will have a small red seal on them. Art and antiques more than one hundred years old are usually allowed into most countries duty-free, though check first with your consulate (there's a list on p.40). As there couldn't possibly be such a huge supply of antique furniture, statuary, teapots, ceramics, embroideries, carvings and paintings in town, you'll need to assume that a certain proportion are reproductions – if you've paid for a genuine antique, the shop should provide the necessary **certificate of authenticity**.

Antique shops

The two main hotspots for antique hunting are Hollywood Road in Central and the third floor of Pacific Place in Admiralty. The shops below are all well established, and close on Sundays, unless otherwise stated.

Altfield Gallery 2nd Floor, Prince's Building, 10 Chater Rd, Central ☎ 2537 6370, ⓦ www .altfield.com.hk. Specializes in Southeast Asian furniture, textiles, Burmese Buddha figures and a good selection of Oriental prints, paintings and maps – all expensive but good quality. Hosts regular exhibitions, and has very helpful, unpushy staff. Open Sun 11am–5pm.

Archangel Antiques 53–55 Hollywood Rd, Central ☎ 2851 6848, ⓦ www.archangelgalleries .com. Antique porcelain, paintings and furniture, worth a visit just to browse the mighty collection.

Art Treasures Gallery 42 Hollywood Rd, Central ☎ 2543 0430, ⓦ www.art-treasures-gallery.com. Helpful small gallery with a warehouse in Zhu Hai in China. Core specializations are furniture – bargain hard on this – and burial items, but they're also branching out into other things.

▲ Antiques and bric-a-brac, Sheung Wan

Contemporary by Angela Li **90–92 Hollywood Rd, Central** T3571 8200, Wwww.cbal.com.hk. Modern Chinese painting and sculpture.

Dragon Culture **231 & 184 Hollywood Rd, Central** T2545 8098, Wwww.dragonculture .com.hk. Vast selection of burial ceramics and other items (including fossilized dinosaur eggs) in all price ranges.

Friendship Trading Co **105–107 Hollywood Rd** T2548 3830. Mostly outsize porcelain vases and reproduction antique furniture, somewhere to get ball-park prices or to shop in bulk.

Honeychurch Antiques **29 Hollywood Rd, Central** T2543 2433, Wwww.honeychurch.com/hong _kong.html. One of the longest-established galleries, offering a wide selection of small items from throughout Asia, including Japan. Silver, porcelain, books, prints and many other things. Expensive but interesting.

Joyce Gallery **123 Hollywood Rd**, T2545 1869, Wwww.joycegallery.com. Fine antiques and contemporary Chinese art.

Karin Weber Gallery **20 Aberdeen St, Central** T2544 5004, Wwww.karinwebergallery.com. International contemporary art, including many artists from Southeast Asia.

L&E **21st Floor, Remex Centre, 42 Wong Chuk Hang Rd, Aberdeen** T2656 1220,

Wwww.lneco.com. Warehouse stocked with new decorative porcelain and old-style Chinese furniture. Phone first for appointment. Packing and shipping can be arranged.

Low Price Shop **47 Hollywood Rd, Central**. A Hong Kong institution. More of a stall, really, selling bric-a-brac, old photos and general junk. Bargain hard.

Oi Ling **57 Hollywood Rd** T2815 9422, Wwww .oilingantiques.com. Fine antiques, including Tang statues, ancient bronzes and elegant Qing furniture.

Schoeni **27 Hollywood Rd** T2542 3143, Wwww.schoeni.com.hk. Excellent gallery that represents several contemporary Chinese artists.

Sundaram Tagore Gallery **57–59 Hollywood Rd** T2581 9678, Wwww.sundaramtagore.com. Internationally renowned dealer with a taste for contemporary fine art.

Teresa Coleman **79 Wyndham St, Central** T2526 2450, Wwww.teresacoleman.com. One of Hong Kong's best-known dealers, with an international reputation for dealing in Chinese textiles and a good selection of pictures and prints.

True Arts & Curios **91 Hollywood Rd**. Tiny place that has been going for ages, stocked with the latest run of antique-style trinkets, wooden figures and miniature bronzes.

Books and magazines

All the bookshops below sell **English–language books**, and many sell overseas newspapers and magazines too. There are, of course, hundreds of other bookshops selling Chinese–language books only. For **secondhand books**, head to Flow in Central or Leisure Book Shop in Sai Kung Town.

Angelo De Carpi **18 Wo On Lane, Central**. A range of gay and lesbian fiction, studies and joke books, and piles of male magazines.

Bookazine **Prince's Building, 10 Chater Rd, Central; Canton House, 54–56 Queens Rd, Central; Oterprise Square, 26 Nathan Rd, Tsim Sha Tsui**. Excellent selection of books on China and Hong Kong and about the only English-language bookshop with a decent range of Chinese cookbooks.

Chaip Coin Co. **Shop 233, 2nd Floor, World-Wide House, 19 Des Voeux Rd, Central**. A tiny shop selling all manner of foreign magazines, from *Viz* through motorcycle magazines to obscure food and fashion publications from the UK, US and Australia.

The Commercial Press **9 Yee Woo St, Causeway Bay; 395 King's Rd, North Point; Shop 213, Miramar Shopping Arcade, 118–130 Nathan Rd, Tsim Sha Tsui; 608 Nathan Rd, Mong Kok; and 2nd Floor, New Town Plaza, Sha Tin**. Largely Chinese-language books but very good for Chinese-learning texts (both Cantonese and Mandarin), and lots of contemporary nonfiction (in English) on China and Hong Kong.

Cosmos Books **1st Floor, 30 Johnston Rd, Wan Chai; and 2nd Floor, Mansion House 74–78 Nathan Rd, Tsim Sha Tsui**. A good stock of Chinese- and English-language novels, art, travel and history books.

Dymocks **Harbour Centre, 25 Harbour Rd, Wan Chai; Shop 307, Hopewell Centre, 183 Queens**

Rd East, Wan Chai; Shop 2007, Level 2, IFC Mall, Central; 46 Lyndhurst Terrace, Central; and others. Fine selection of English-language novels, travel guides, dictionaries, maps and books on Hong Kong and China, and foreign newspapers.

Flow 40 Lyndhurst Terrace (enter from around corner in Cochrane, underneath escalator) daily noon–7.30pm. A huge range of second-hand paperbacks including sci-fi, local authors, fiction, crime and gay plus DVDs.

Government Publications Centre Queensway Government Offices, Low Block, Ground Floor, 66 Queensway, Admiralty. Official government publications, Hong Kong maps, exhibition catalogues and books on local flora, fauna, politics, environment, industry and anything else you can think of.

Hong Kong Book Centre Basement On Lok Yuen Building, 25 Des Voeux Rd, Central. Cramped, library-like interior, but well stocked with novels and travel books, and good on Chinese history and politics. Also has foreign newspapers.

Leisure Book Shop Shop 6, Sai Kung Garden, Chan Man St, Sai Kung Town. A good selection of secondhand novels.

Page One 10th Floor, Times Square, Causeway Bay; Shop 3002, 3rd Floor, Harbour City, Canton Rd, Tsim Sha Tsui; and Shop 30, LG1, Festival Walk, Kowloon Tong. Perhaps the best bookshops in Hong Kong, selling a huge selection of English-language books and magazines from fiction through to archeology and computer manuals. They also stock a healthy number of gay and lesbian books and magazines. The vast Kowloon Tong branch has a café selling great cakes to munch while you read.

Swindon Book Co. Ltd 13–15 Lock Rd, Tsim Sha Tsui. A good general, English-language bookshop with a large section on travel, local interest and Chinese culture.

Times Bookshop Shop P315–316, 3rd Floor, World Trade Centre, 280 Gloucester Rd, Causeway Bay; and Basement, Golden Crown Court, 66–70 Nathan Rd, Tsim Sha Tsui. Fairly standard not-too-expensive bookshop with a reasonable section of books and some nice stationery.

CDs, VCDs and DVDs

Most mainstream **CDs** can be found in Hong Kong: prices are generally around twenty to thirty percent lower than in the UK (and slightly higher than in the US). Check out the locally produced Canto-pop releases, as well as recordings of mainland Chinese artists. Note that artists are almost always filed under first names. Also widely available are **VCDs** and **DVDs** of movies, from old Hollywood classics through Hong Kong mass-produced titles to newly released blockbusters. If you head for the independent outlets along **Hennessy Road** from Causeway Bay to Wan Chai, or along **Nathan Road** from Mong Kok to Jordan, you'll get VCDs for as little as HK$10 and DVDs for HK$50–150. Alternatively, you can pick up even cheaper bootlegs from stalls along Temple Street Night Market in Yau Ma Tei, Kowloon.

HMV Pacific Centre, 28 Hankow Rd, Tsim Sha Tsui; The Park Lane, Causeway Bay; and Central Building, 1–3 Pedder St, Central. Megastores with listening stations and a mammoth choice, as good for world and Canto-pop as for Western releases.

Hong Kong Records Shop 146, The Mall, Pacific Place, 88 Queensway, Admiralty. Good mixture of styles and prices; no vinyl in sight, despite the name.

Monitor Records 4–16 Tak Shing St, Jordan. The widest selection of CDs in Hong Kong, with titles going for HK$30 less than in high-street chains. As well as mainstream pop you'll find dance, funk and all kinds of club music, world music and even very select genres such as darkwave medieval, darkwave gothic to darkwave neofolk. Amazingly, there's also a good collection of vinyl.

White Noise Records 4 Canal Rd East, Causeway Bay. Vintage and independent music; some very unusual stuff.

Works Records 38 Hankow Rd, Tsim Sha Tsui. Scruffy shop selling a diverse range of bootleg CDs (mainly from Germany) from artists across the board; all kinds of musical genres from mainstream pop through drum'n'bass to thrash metal. Not cheap.

China and porcelain

Porcelain has been a traditional export of Hong Kong for hundreds of years, and is still a good buy. The available quality varies enormously – from the cheapest household blue and white (still very pretty) to museum-quality replicas of old patterns. Also see "Chinese products stores", below, and "Antiques", above.

Hing Cheung Fu Kee Chinaware Co. 17 Staunton St, Soho. A down-to-earth warehouse-style shop with piles of cheap Chinese teapots and plate ware.

Lee Fung Chinaware 18 Shelley St, Mid-Levels. Good-quality selection of china, well displayed.

Museum of Teaware Flagstaff House, Hong Kong Park, Central. Pretty reproduction antique cups and purple sandware teapots; the adjacent *Lok Cha Teahouse* also has a similar selection.

Wah Tung China Ltd 59 Hollywood Rd, Central. Very high-quality selection, representing all the major decorative trends in Chinese porcelain. They pack and dispatch worldwide.

Chinese products stores

These stores specialize in products **made in mainland China**: everything from foot spas to clothing, fabrics, reproduction porcelain (and a few genuine antiques), carved stone, jade and classical furniture and Chinese teas and medicines. They always seem to be having a sale of some sort on.

Chinese Arts and Crafts JD Mall, 233 Nathan Rd, Jordan; Star House, 3 Salisbury Rd, Tsim Sha Tsui; Asia Standard Tower, 59 Queens Rd Central; Shop 220, The Mall, Pacific Place, 88 Queensway; China Resources Building, 26 Harbour Rd, Wan Chai. Good quality, broad range of goods; the Wan Chai branch is largest.

Yue Hwa Chinese Products 301–309 Nathan Rd, Yau Ma Tei. Long-standing department store selling just about everything; sports goods, musical instruments and medical equipment (top floor) are surprisingly inexpensive.

Clothes

For the addresses of the **big-name designers** – from Armani to Valentino, as well as local Hong Kong whizz kids – look no further than the *HKTB Guide to Quality Merchants*, which lists them all in exhaustive detail. Otherwise, simply check out stores as you wend your way around the city. Western designer clothes are often significantly more expensive here than they are back home because of the extra cachet attached to foreign labels.

For cheaper clothes shopping, check out the main local **fashion chain stores** – Giordano, U2, Baleno, Bossini and the unfortunately named Wanko – for decent-quality, value-for-money casual wear, including shirts, chinos, jackets, skirts and socks. There are countless branches in all areas of the city. Alternatively, track down the factory and **warehouse outlets** (see p.244), whose bargain prices for designer shirts and jackets really start to save you money. For other ideas, visit the various **markets** (p.248) that specialize in clothes. The Chinese products stores are also worth checking for fabrics, silk clothing, cashmere and padded winter jackets.

For **local designers** and more off-beat designs, head to Island Beverley, 1 Great George St, Causeway Bay (the entrance is via an escalator above SOGO's supermarket); or Rise Commercial Building, 5–11 Granville Circuit, Tsim Sha Tsui (just off the eastern end of Granville Rd). Be aware that these

Clothing and shoe sizes

Women's clothing

American	4	6	8	10	12	14	16	18
British	6	8	10	12	14	16	18	20
Continental	34	36	38	40	42	44	46	48

Women's shoes

American	5	6	7	8	9	10	11	
British	3	4	5	6	7	8	9	
Continental	36	37	38	39	40	41	42	

Men's shirts

American	14	15	15.5	16	16.5	17	17.5	18
British	14	15	15.5	16	16.5	17	17.5	18
Continental	36	38	39	41	42	43	44	45

Men's shoes

American	7	7.5	8	8.5	9.5	10	10.5	11	11.5
British	6	7	7.5	8	9	9.5	10	11	12
Continental	39	40	41	42	43	44	44	45	46

Men's suits

American	34	36	38	40	42	44	46	48
British	34	36	38	40	42	44	46	48
Continental	44	46	48	50	52	54	56	58

clothes are made for the local market and larger Western figures might not find much to fit them here. Both open in the afternoon and close around 10pm.

Local designers

Blanc De Chine 2nd Floor, Pedder Building, 12 Pedder St, Central. Designs loosely based on traditional Chinese clothes, in silk and cashmere using muted colours.

▲ Chinese chic at Shanghai Tang

Joyce Ground Floor, New World Tower, Central; Shop 334, Pacific Place, 88 Queensway, Admiralty; and 23 Nathan Rd, Tsim Sha Tsui. Hong Kong's most fashionable boutique offers its own range of clothing, as well as many top overseas designer brands.

Shanghai Tang Pedder Building, 12 Pedder St, Central, and several smaller stores across the city. The store is beautifully done up in 1930s Shanghai style, making it a must to visit, if not to buy. It specializes in new takes on traditional Chinese designs – often in vibrant colours – and can also make things to order (see below). Some household items and gifts are available, too.

Vivienne Tam Shop 209, Pacific Place, 88 Queensway, Admiralty; Shop 219, Times Square, 1 Matheson St, Causeway Bay; Shop G310–311, Harbour City, Tsim Sha Tsui; and Shop 55, LG1, Festival Walk, Kowloon Tong. Funky shirts and dresses in David-Hockney-meets-Vivienne-Westwood style, often featuring Chairman Mao and other icons of the East.

Walter Ma 9 Queen's Rd Central, Central. Party clothes for Hong Kong's smart set.

Factory and warehouse outlets

One unusual aspect of shopping in Hong Kong is the chance to buy from a wide variety of factory and warehouse outlets. These are in commercial buildings, not shops, and sell clothes, fabrics and jewellery direct to the public. They can open and close very quickly – consult the HKTB brochure *Factory Outlets* for addresses, or pick up a locally published guide like *The Smart Shopper in Hong Kong* or *The Complete Guide to Hong Kong Factory Bargains*. Many outlets can be difficult to find if you don't have the exact address. Be sure to try things on before you buy – marked sizes mean nothing. Prices are competitive, either because there's a low mark-up or because you're buying samples, ends-of-lines or high-quality seconds.

If you just want to browse, **Granville Road** in Tsim Sha Tsui (off Nathan Rd) is a good place to look, as are the many stores along **Cheung Sha Wan Road** in Sham Shui Po, Kowloon – see p.115. In Central, look for signs in doorways along **Wyndham Street** and **D'Aguilar Street**, and don't forget the **Pedder Building** (12 Pedder St), which is full of discount outlets. In Aberdeen, check out the **Joyce Warehouse**, 21st Floor, Horizon Plaza, Ap Lei Chau, where Hong Kong's most fashionable shop puts all last season's stuff that didn't sell – with discounts of up to eighty percent. Finally, **Citygate Outlets**, 20 Tat Tung Rd, Tung Chung, Lantau (right by Tung Chung MTR station), has 28 factory outlet stores including Benetton, Esprit, Calvin Klein, Laura Ashley and Giordano.

Tailors

Hong Kong has long been known for the speed and value of its **tailors**. Whatever you're told, however, don't demand a suit to be made in 24 hours: it either won't fit, will fall apart, or both. Prices are good value, rather than cheap: a cashmere man's suit, with a couple of shirts and ties, will cost upwards of HK$1700, more likely twice this. Sales techniques are fairly high-pressure, but don't commit yourself without knowing exactly what's included. Expect at least two or three fittings over several days if you want a good result. You'll need to pay about fifty percent of the price as deposit.

When it comes to **style**, the easiest way is to bring the tailor something to copy, perhaps with some alterations. If that's not possible, a picture is useful – most shops have piles of magazines to help you choose. The best way to find a good tailor is personal recommendation – if you don't know anyone try asking in your hotel. Alternatively, look for a tailor who relies on regular clients, not passing tourists; the big hotels, shopping malls or areas around Mid-Levels, Happy Valley and Causeway Bay are promising locations. Ask to look at some of the garments they have under way. Women may want to choose a tailor with an established Western clientele, as they will be used to dealing with the rather different body shape. Some suggestions include:

Classic Fashion Shop 22, National Court, 242 Nathan Rd, Jordan. Good benchmark tailor with fairly fast, reliable work.

Italian Tailor 1st Floor, Prince's Building, 10 Chater Rd, Central. Upmarket men's tailor which makes suits for many local businessmen. Quality fabric selection.

Johnson & Co. 44 Hankow Rd, Tsim Sha Tsui. Does a lot of work for mostly male military and naval customers. Prices a bit higher than average, but the quality of their work is, too.

Linva Tailor 38 Cochrane St, Central. Well-established ladies' tailor, whose core business is making party clothes (*cheongsam*) for local ladies. Also does embroidery.

Margaret Court Tailoress Floor 8, Winner Building, 27 D'Aguilar St, Central. Lots of local Western female clients, and a solid reputation for good work, although it doesn't come cheaply. A shirt costs around HK$400, plus fabric.

Mee Wah Embroidery 625 Shanghai St, Mong Kok, Kowloon. Traditional Chinese clothing, especially ornate wedding assemblages.

Modern Tailor 207–209 Portland St, Mong Kok. A Chinese tailor with sound work and good prices.

Punjab House Shop J, Ground Floor, Golden Crown Court, 66–70 Nathan Rd, Tsim Sha Tsui. Founded in 1889 and a former favourite of the British Forces and firefighters; good quality male and female formal wear.

Sam's Tailors 94 Nathan Rd, Tsim Sha Tsui. A Hong Kong institution, as much for Sam's talent for self-publicity as for the quality of his clothes. A long list of distinguished clients.

Shanghai Tang 12 Pedder St, Central. This boutique's tailoring service specializes in modern adaptations of traditional Chinese styles for men and women, and has a fabulous selection of fabrics. They are very geared up to helping visitors and can arrange quick fittings and the posting of finished garments.

Fabrics

All tailors keep a selection of fabrics or samples, but if you want to choose your own, or don't have time to wait for theirs to arrive in stock, note that there are a number of **fabric shops** around town, particularly in Li Yuen streets East and West, at the junction of Queen's Road and Wellington Street, in D'Aguilar Street, and at Western Market in Sheung Wan.

Outdoor gear

Outdoor gear for **hiking** can be quite a good deal in Hong Kong; much of it is made over the border in China. As always, watch out for fakes – it's amazing how stitching a well-known logo onto an inferior imitation jacket makes it look like the real thing – and don't expect rock-bottom prices. Probably the best place to try is RC Outfitters (Ⓦ www.alink.com.hk), 163 Johnston Rd, Wan Chai, and 5/F, Oriental House, 24–26 Argyle St, Mong Kok, Kowloon.

Crafts

In addition to what's available in the Chinese products stores (see p.242), the shops below offer various types of modern arts-and-crafts products from throughout Asia. For more furniture, check out the shops along Queen's Road East, in Wan Chai (p.80).

G.O.D. 6th Floor, Horizon Plaza, Ap Lei Chau, Aberdeen; Shop 27, Festival Walk, Kowloon Tong; and Shop 2, 3rd Floor, Discovery Park, Tsuen Wan. Simple, modern household products and furniture for Chinese yuppies. Some very good designs and colours, in natural materials and at reasonable prices.

King and Country 3rd Floor, Pacific Place, 88 Queensway, Admiralty. An amazing shop which sells beautiful hand-painted lead soldiers and models. Many have military themes, but there are also wonderful sets showing Chinese life, the Qing Dynasty court and a traditional wedding.

Mountain Folkcraft 12 Wo On Lane (off D'Aguilar St), Central. Beautiful handmade folk arts and crafts from Southeast Asia and elsewhere.

Museum Shop Hong Kong Arts Centre, Cultural Centre, Salisbury Rd, Tsim Sha Tsui. Art books and supplies, calligraphy materials, prints, postcards, gifts and stationery.

Welfare Handicrafts Shops Shop 7, Lower Ground Floor, Jardine House, One Connaught Place, Central; and Salisbury Rd (opposite the Cultural Centre), Tsim Sha Tsui. Locally made arts and crafts sold on behalf of charities.

Department stores

There is a vast selection of mammoth, air-conditioned department stores, owned by parent companies from different countries; pick your culture and dive in. Most have cafés and coffee shops inside, too.

Local stores

Lane Crawford IFC Mall, Central; Pacific Place, 88 Queensway, Admiralty; Canton Rd, Tsim Sha Tsui; and Times Square, Causeway Bay. Hong Kong's oldest Western-style department store.

Sincere 173 Des Voeux Rd, Central; 83 Argyle St, Mong Kok; and Dragon Centre, 37K Yen Chow St, Sham Shui Po, Kowloon. A more down-market store; the Argyle St branch is good for shoes.

Wing On 211 Des Voeux Rd, Central; 345 Nathan Rd, Yau Ma Tei. Standard department store, good for everyday items.

Japanese stores

Mitsukoshi Hennessy Centre, 500 Hennessy Rd, Causeway Bay. A good place for upmarket labels, with an excellent Park N Shop supermarket in the basement selling a wide range of Western foodstuffs until late (10pm).

Seibu Pacific Place, 88 Queensway, Admiralty and Windsor House, 311 Gloucester Rd, Causeway Bay. Upmarket store, carrying a big proportion of European household goods and fashion.

Sogo East Point Centre, 555 Hennessy Rd, Causeway Bay; 12 Salisbury Rd, Tsim Sha Tsui (in the pedestrian underpass below Salisbury Rd). Japanese department store; the Causeway Bay branch includes a supermarket.

Electronic goods and software

Despite few astounding bargains, Hong Kong remains an excellent place to stock up on **electronic goods and software**. As locals want nothing but the very latest models, the best deals are to be had buying recently dated stock, which shop owners want to shift before it becomes unsaleable. This holds most true for mobile phones, computers and MP3 players; for other types of electronics, such as **cameras and DVD players**, expect less competitive prices.

Be warned, however, that you're almost guaranteed to be **ripped off** when buying electronics and software unless you've thoroughly researched prices and kept alert for scams (see p.238). In general, avoid hard-core tourist shopping areas such as Nathan Road: there are no bargains of any sort to be had from the scheming, glib dealers here.

▲ Camera shop, Tsim Sha Tsui

Chain stores with city-wide branches – such as Fortress, Broadway, Citicall and PCCW – are good places to get an idea of prices, but you'll get better deals at one of the stores listed below. **Computer centres** are warehouse-sized buildings with hundreds of booths on several floors selling all the hardware, software and accessories you can think of, plus MP3 players; some also have second-hand goods. More **second-hand cameras and mobile phones** can be found at Sham Shui Po market (see p.115) – though it's likely that most gear here is stolen. **Pirated computer software** is more elusive than it used to be: you'll possibly encounter dealers at the computer centres listed below, though you'll have to look carefully and be prepared for cloak-and-dagger antics with placing and collecting your order. For the best deals on **camera gear**, check ⓦwww.ygdragon.net/index.php?page=photo/cameraprice.htm, which compares models and prices across dozens of stores.

298 Computer Zone 298 Hennessy Rd, Wan Chai. Warren-like place, full of shops selling new, secondhand, official and pirated computer gear; also some repair shops.
Computer & Digital Mall 10th and 11th Floor, Windsor House, 311 Gloucester Rd (corner with Great George St), Causeway Bay. Over-the-counter prices for name brands and some good deals on Chinese clones, mostly hardware.
Golden Computer Centre 156 Fuk Wah St, Sham Shui Po, Kowloon. Famous for its supply of cheap computer goods, but also notorious as a centre for pirate software.
Mongkok Computer Centre 8 Nelson St, Mongkok. Similar to 298 and Golden centres.
Photo Scientific 6 Stanley St, Central. One of many photo specialist places in this street, and a good place to get a feel for prices.
Wing Shing Photo Supplies 55 Sai Yeung Choi St South, Mong Kok. Regular deals on all photo gear.

Food and drink

For a list of **bakeries**, **delicatessens**, **takeaways** and **supermarkets**, consult the relevant sections of chapter 6. You'll find accounts of **markets** where you can buy food throughout the book, including Sheung Wan and Java Road markets (p.70 & p.87), Canton Road market (p.113), and Tsuen Wan and Tai Po markets (p.128 & p.141).

When buying food in markets, you need to know that **Chinese weights and measures** are different from Western ones. Most things (vegetables, bean sprouts, rice, dried foods) are sold by the **catty**, which is the equivalent of 1.3lb or 600g; the smaller unit is the **tael**, equivalent to 1.3oz or 38g. That said, unless you can speak and read Chinese, you'll probably find that simply picking up the amount you want and handing it to the stallholder is the best way to go about things. Fruit is sold by the piece or the pound, meat and fish by the ounce.

Jewellery

Jewellery **prices** are low in Hong Kong and there are thousands of jewellers, reflecting the local population's love for glitter and sparkle. Most of their designs tend towards the flashy – this is a town where you wear your wealth on your sleeve, or your finger – although many also do pieces that are extremely close to the signature designs of some of the most famous international jewellers. Alternatively, given time they can make or copy to your requirements. As always, **shop around** the **citywide stores** first – Chow Tai Fuk, Chow Sang Sang and King Fuk – to get an idea of prices, before venturing into some den offering bargains along Nathan Road or Queen's Road Central. The HKTB arranges **free courses** in jade, pearl and diamond appreciation and, though these only last an hour or so, they might give you enough pointers to save yourself from buying a dud.

There's a special **Jade Market** in Kansu Street, Yau Ma Tei (p.112), but you'd better know what you're doing before buying anything more than a souvenir here. If you need help or information on buying **diamonds**, contact the Diamond Importers' Association Ltd, 7A Hong Kong Jewellery Building, 178–180 Queen's Rd Central, Central ⓦwww.jewelrynet.com. For **opals**, a fun place to visit is The Opal Mine (Burlington House, Ground Floor, 92 Nathan Rd, Tsim Sha Tsui), which also has an informative exhibition on the mining of opal in Australia, where ninety percent of the world's supply comes from.

Elissa Cohen Jewellery 209 Hankow Centre, 5–15 Hankow Rd, Tsim Sha Tsui. Individual designs, lots of pearls.
Gallery One 31–33 Hollywood Rd. A huge selection of semiprecious beads and necklaces – amber, amethyst, tiger's eye, crystal and much more. They will string any arrangement you want.
Johnson & Co. 1st Floor, 44 Hankow Rd, Tsim Sha Tsui. Straight, middle-of-the-road jeweller, not too pushy.
Just Gold Ground Floor, Shop 139, Pacific Place, 88 Queensway, Admiralty; 452 Hennessy Rd, Wan Chai; Shop A2, 27 Nathan Rd, Tsim Sha Tsui; and Unit UG14, Festival Walk, Kowloon Tong. Local chain specializing in fun, fashionable, cheapish designs for young women. They

have the licence for Mickey Mouse gold jewellery – very popular locally.
Kai-Yin Lo ⓦ www.kaiyinlo-design.com. Hong Kong's best-known jewellery designer, who also sells in New York. Makes interesting use of old jade, carvings and semiprecious stones. Expensive, but nice to look. Contact through website for a meeting.
New Universal Jewellery Company 10 Ice House St, Central. Reliable, quality jewellers with wide range of styles. Competitive prices.
President Jewellery and Gems G16, Holiday Inn Golden Mile Shopping Mall, 50 Nathan Rd, Kowloon. Good place to get advice on diamonds, jade and pearls; not too pushy and moderate prices.

Markets: clothes, fabrics and bric-a-brac

The cheapest clothes and fabrics can be found in markets, but shop around and haggle. You won't be able to try anything on and you'll never be able to take anything back, but be sensible and you shouldn't go too far wrong.

Ap Liu Street Sham Shui Po. Flea market; good for household electricals and second-hand mobile phones; p.115.
Jade Market Kansu St, Yau Ma Tei. Jade jewellery, artefacts and statues; p.112.
Jardine's Bazaar Causeway Bay. Clothes and household goods; p.83.
Li Yuen Street East and West Central. Women's and children's clothes; p.62.
Man Wa Lane Sheung Wan. Traditional Chinese seals; p.70.

Stanley Market Stanley Village. Silk, cashmere, and some fake designer labels a speciality; p.92.
Temple Street Yau Ma Tei. The SAR's best night market: clothes, CDs, watches, jewellery, and digital bits and pieces; p.111.
Tung Choi Street Mongkok. Women's and children's clothes and accessories; p.114.
Upper Lascar Row (Cat St) Central. Flea market; p.71.
Western Market Sheung Wan. Fabrics; p.70.

Secondhand

Bizarrely, Hong Kong is rather a good place to buy secondhand stuff, or – as it's coyly known locally – "pre-owned". The local population is so fashion- and brand-conscious that there is a lot of turnover, and apartments are so small people don't have room to keep last season's stuff.

Cameras Try the shops in Stanley St, Central; or David Chan Co, 15 Champagne Court, 16 Kimberley Rd, Tsim Sha Tsui; Tin Cheung Camera Co., 26 Tung Yung Building, 100 Nathan Rd, Tsim Sha Tsui; or Hing Lee Camera Co., 25 Lyndhurst Terrace, Central.

Clothes The Pedder Building, 12 Pedder St, Central, has some outlets such as La Place which deal in upmarket secondhand clothes. Oxfam (Shop 8, Lower Ground Floor, Jardine House, One Connaught Rd, Central) stocks everything from cast-off designer gear to shabby togs. Other options include Retrostone (1st Floor, 504 Lockhart Rd, Causeway Bay) for secondhand jeans and beaded accessories, and Beatniks (Shop A–C, Yuet Wah Ct, 19–21 Shelter St, Causeway Bay; Shop 1, Ground Floor, Rise Commercial Building, 5–11 Granville Circuit, Tsim Sha Tsui; and Shop 2, Ground Floor, 54C Granville Rd, Tsim Sha Tsui), selling pricey clothes, including denim, supposedly all imported from New York.

Computers Try outlets in 298 Computer Zone, 298 Hennessy Rd, Wan Chai; or Windsor House, 311 Gloucester Rd, Causeway Bay.

Watches Berne Horology (Kam On Building, 176A Queen's Rd, Central) sells everything from antique clocks and watches through to old egg-timers, gramophone players and sundials.

Shopping malls

Even if you hate shopping, it's impossible to avoid walking through a **shopping mall** sooner or later, since half the pedestrian overpasses and walkways in Central and Tsim Sha Tsui East pass straight through one or more of them. You may as well accept that you're going to see the inside of more shopping malls than you thought existed; you may even enjoy them when the weather is wet or hot since they're air-conditioned. The main concentrations are in **Central**, **Admiralty** and **Tsim Sha Tsui**, with a few in Causeway Bay and a couple of other major malls in the New Territories. Many are sights in themselves: gleaming, climate-controlled consumer paradises, serviced by state-of-the-art lifts, enlivened by galleries, lights and fountains, and sustained by bars, cafés and restaurants. All the important ones are covered in the main guide, but a quick checklist of the best includes:

Dragon Centre 37K Yen Chow St, Sham Shui Po. A down-market shopping plaza, whose top floor is ringed by a snaking rollercoaster above a popular ice rink. There's the usual run of inexpensive chain food outlets, clothes stores and electronics shops, while the ground floor often hosts free jazz concerts or ballroom dancing.

Festival Walk Kowloon Tong. Linked by underpass to Kowloon Tong MTR. One of the shiniest of the Hong Kong malls, designed by the super-trendy Miami architectural practice, Arquitechtonica. The design incorporates *feng shui* principles, so there are no pointed edges and lots of references to nature – water with the fountains, a glacier with the ice rink, a cave for the food court. There are also more than two hundred shops and an eleven-screen cinema.

Harbour City Tsim Sha Tsui, near the Kowloon Star Ferry Terminal. A warren-like building incorporating seven hundred shops, the Ocean Centre, Ocean Terminal and the Marco Polo Hong Kong Hotel Arcade. Includes a couple of posh antique shops, a good bookshop, Toys' R' Us, and a number of local jewellers, as well as the usual boutiques.

The Landmark Des Voeux Rd, Central. Central MTR. You're almost certain to pass through this mall, 5min walk from the Star Ferry Pier, as it's an intersection for Central's raised walkways. Check out the basement for local brands and a good bookshop. The designer boutiques on the upper floors are interesting in the sales.

Pacific Place 88 Queensway, Admiralty. Linked by underpass directly to Admiralty MTR. One of the swankiest malls around, but in addition to the designer outlets on the upper floors it also has a good range of ordinary shops and local boutiques on the lower ones.

Prince's Building 10 Chater Rd, Central. Next to Chater Square and 2min from the Star Ferry. Not really a mall, but it has become a second home for many of Hong Kong's expats because of the deli on the third floor, which stocks loads of foreign foods and wines. Also home to some interesting fashion accessory shops, jewellers and tailors, two good bookshops and stationers, and an expensive but totally genuine antique shop.

Times Square 1 Matheson St, Causeway Bay. Linked by walkway to Causeway Bay MTR; the

tram also runs nearby. The main mall in Causeway Bay, with the usual selection of local and international retailers, plus lots of restaurants, a cinema complex and a forum area often used for special exhibitions.

World-Wide House 19 Des Voeux Rd, Central. A lively, friendly and offbeat shopping mall, packed with inexpensive gold shops, boutiques and snack stalls selling Philippine rice-and-fish staples, plus a Delifrance on the first floor.

Chinese tea and medicines

Chinese tea in decorative tins and boxes makes a nice, portable souvenir, and can be bought from any of Hong Kong's numerous **specialist tea shops**, or in prepacked selections from **Chinese products shops** (see p.242). In traditional teashops, tea is treated like wine, with different vintages and producers. Some shops will let you taste before you make your choice. You buy in small amounts, since most tea loses its flavour after a while – except *bo lei*, which improves with age and so costs a small fortune for vintage leaves. Most shops stock teapots and cups, too, most often fine porcelain but also in **purple sandware**, often artistically shaped and said to retain the flavour of tea.

Shops dealing in **Chinese medicines** are also widespread, with the heart of the business in Sheung Wan, Hong Kong Island (see p.70). There are three **citywide stores** – Eu Yan Song, Tung Fong Hung and Tong Ren Tang – of which the latter is the most reputable, having been founded several hundred years ago in Beijing. Decked out on heavy, dark wooden furnishings, the shops make for an interesting browse but buying anything is best left to specialists.

Best Tea House Shop 136A, 2nd Floor, CKE Shopping Mall, 36–44 Nathan Rd, Tsim Sha Tsui; and Jumbo Floating Restaurant, Aberdeen.
Ki Chan Tea Co. 174 Johnston Rd, Wan Chai; and Shop C8, 1st Floor, Queensway Plaza, 93 Queensway, Central. Old men distribute the tea leaves from their red and gold cylinders in this no-nonsense, well-established shop.
Lok Cha Tea Shop 290A, Queen's Rd Central, Sheung Wan (bottom of Ladder St). Long-established place well used to dealing with foreigners. There's another branch in Hong Kong Park, see p.66.
Ying Kee 2–4 Hysan Ave, Causeway Bay; Times Square; The Peak; 151 Queen's Rd Central, Central; 170 Johnston Rd, Wan Chai; 21 Cameron Rd Tsim Sha Tsui; 192 Shanghai St, Yau Ma Tei; 719 Nathan Rd; and elsewhere. Huge selection of Chinese teas and teapots; another friendly choice for first-time buyers.

10

Sports and recreation

T he only drawback to Hong Kong's varied range of **sporting and recreation opportunities** is the inevitable lack of space for such things. One particularly good sports centre is the **South China Athletic Association** (88 Caroline Hill, Causeway Bay ☎2577 6932, Ⓦwww.scaa.org.hk), which offers one-month visitors' passes for HK$50 and has facilities for all kinds of sports and keep-fit activities including several swimming pools. The centre is next to the Hong Kong Stadium football ground, a fifteen-minute walk from exit F of Causeway Bay MTR Station. All **public sports centres**, where you can rent all manner of sports courts, are listed on the **Leisure and Cultural Services Department** website (Ⓦwww .lcsd.gov.hk).

There are **spectator sports** events throughout the year; the SAR's main sporting venue is the **Queen Elizabeth Stadium** (see below). The HKTB's website (Ⓦwww.discoverhongkong.com) gives details of forthcoming events, which are also usually listed in the *South China Morning Post*, the weekly freebies *HK Magazine* and *BC Magazine*, and *Time Out Hong Kong* (HK$18).

Badminton

You can rent badminton courts for around HK$60 an hour at any Leisure and Cultural Services Department indoor games hall see (Ⓦwww.lcsd.gov.hk). You'll need to book in advance and show your passport. More general information is available from the Hong Kong Badminton Association (☎2504 8318, Ⓦwww .hkbadmintonassn.org.hk).

Diving

Scuba diving is increasingly popular in Hong Kong; waters are relatively shallow and visibility generally poor, but you can still see everything from seahorses to sharks. The season runs from around April to October and an afternoon of diving including all equipment, boat trip and food should come to HK$500–800. Most of the following run out of Sai Kung, though offices might be elsewhere.

Asiatic Marine Ⓦwww.asiaticmarine.com. Harder-core diving around Hong Kong; also organizes South China Sea trips.
Diving Adventure Ⓦwww.divinghk.com. One of the most popular local operators, with six boats – all packed through the summer.

Diving Express Ⓦwww.divingexpress.com. Top live-aboard dive trips and training.
Mandarin Divers Ⓦwww.mandarin-divers.com. Based in Aberdeen, caters to technical divers.
Ocean Sky Diving Training Centre Ⓦwww .oceanskydiver.com. Mostly training courses; based in Tsim Sha Tsui.

Golf

Golf is a pricey sport in Hong Kong, and you'll have to be keen to play at any of the SAR's clubs. Most, if they are open to non-members at all, take them only during the week. You also have to be careful what you wear: tracksuits, T-shirts, collarless shirts, shorts more than four inches above the knee, jeans, vests and bathing gear are all specifically banned from the greens. Less serious golf is catered for by the mini-golf course at Shek O, right by the beach, and a similar set-up, with a driving range, at Sha Tin's New Town Plaza.

Clearwater Bay Golf and Country Club Sai Kung Peninsula ⓦ www.cwbgolf.org. Green fees on the 18-hole championship course starts at $1800.

Discovery Bay Lantau ⓣ 2987 7273, ⓦ www .dbgc.hk. Among the newest of Hong Kong's golf clubs, with a course spectacularly laid out on top of the island's hills. Non-members can play Mon–Fri 7.30am–sunset; Sat & Sun 7.30–9.30am & 11.50am–1.42pm by arrangement. Fees here are around $900 from Monday to Friday, and $1700 at weekends, plus extras.

Hong Kong Golf Club (HKGC) Fan Ling, New Territories ⓦ www.hkgolfclub.org. The SAR's major club, and home of the Hong Kong

Open, boasts three 18-hole courses at which visitors can play on weekdays for around HK$1400 per person, plus caddies and clubs. The HKGC also operates a course at Deep Water Bay on Hong Kong Island; visitors pay around HK$450 plus extras, again on weekdays only (8.30am–3pm). You should book well in advance for all these courses.

Kau Sai Chau Public Golf Course Kau Sai Chau Island, Sai Kung Peninsula ⓦ www.kscgolf.org .hk. Hong Kong's only public golf course (run by the Jockey Club) is a little bit out of the way – see p.154 for access information from Sai Kung Town. Depending on when you play, you'll pay between HK$300 and HK$900.

Hiking

Despite the density of its urban areas, there's some superlative **hiking** to be done in Hong Kong: nearly forty percent of the SAR is contained inside 24 undeveloped **country parks**, run by the **Agriculture, Fisheries and Conservation Department** or AFCD (ⓦ www.afcd.gov.hk). Most of the parks – and their interconnected **hiking trails** – are up in the New Territories, with others on Lantau and Hong Kong islands; many of them are covered in the text. The **landscape** varies from subtropical vegetation to pine forests and barren hillsides, remote coastline and steep mountains offering fantastic views. There's also plenty of **wildlife**: you'll probably encounter docile feral cattle and buffalo, monkeys, reptiles and hundreds of birds and butterflies, and with exceptional luck might spot tiny muntjac deer and leopard cat, and not-so-tiny wild boar. All the parks are easily **accessible** by public transport, and some have free, AFCD **campsites** – see the website and p.197 for more.

Don't be deceived, however, into thinking that because of their closeness to the city the country parks are easy or tame countryside. Much of the terrain is **mountainous and unshaded**, particularly exposed during the intensely humid, scorching summers: you need to take plenty of water, a hat, sunglasses and sunscreen. There's a lot of loose soil too, so **good footware** is equally essential. **Summer storms** – with torrential rain and lightning – can cause dangerous landslides; dry periods are known for their **hill fires**. Check the AFCD website for latest conditions, or ⓦ www.hko.gov.hk for **weather reports**. It's always wise **not to hike alone**, to carry a mobile phone and to leave your route and estimated time of arrival back with someone reliable, so they can contact emergency services in case you don't show. Be aware, too, that hikers are occasionally **mugged** – another good reason to go with friends.

The SAR's four **long-distance hikes** are covered in the text: the Lantau Trail (p.171), the one-hundred-kilometre MacLehose Trail (p.155), the cross-harbour Wilson Trail (p.92), and the Hong Kong Island Trail (p.81). None of these need to be attempted in their entirety, as individual sections make good **day hikes** in themselves. Pick of these are the easy walk around Shing Mun Reservoir (p.129); beachscapes at Tai Long Wan on the Sai Kung Peninsula (p.156); beautiful, steady views from the heights of Pat Sin Leng (p.147); and the exhausting ascent of Ma On Shan (p.154).

The best **maps** are the five *Countryside Series* sheets, which cover all of Hong Kong's outdoor areas (see Basics, p.46). For **hiking guides** – which generally have decent maps in themselves – try the bilingual *Hiking All in One* and *New Walker's Companion* (both published by the AFCD and sold through Cosmos Books and Commercial Press stores), and Pete Spurrier's *Leisurely Hiker's Guide to Hong Kong* and *Serious Hiker's Guide to Hong Kong* – all reviewed on p.329. Good **websites** include the AFCD's, which gives park descriptions and inspirational photos that will have you reaching for your boots; and ⓦwww.hkcrystal.com/hiking, which has stage-by-stage information on hiking trails and regular organized hikes to join.

Horseracing

The only sport in Hong Kong to command true mass appeal, horseracing is a spectating must if you're here during the season, which runs from September to mid-June. There are two courses, both run by the Hong Kong Jockey Club (☎2966 8397, ⓦwww.hkjc.com): the original one at Happy Valley (meetings every Wednesday evening during the season) and a much newer, state-of-the-art affair at Sha Tin in the New Territories, which stages races most weekends during the season. The HKTB can organize tours and tickets for the enclosures; for more on this, or just turning up and watching, see p.84.

Martial arts

If China has an indigenous "sport", it's the martial arts – not surprising, perhaps, in a country whose history is littered with long periods of civil conflict. Isolated communities often had to defend themselves against bands of marauders, and so developed their own systems of fighting, which were traditionally taught only to community members – meaning that today there are hundreds of Chinese martial arts styles. Most trace their origins back to the Shaolin Temple in China's Henan province, where it is said that Boddhidharma, the sixth-century originator of Zen Buddhism, taught the monks exercises based on animal movements to balance their long periods of inactivity while meditating. These exercises were then developed into fighting routines for defending the temple, and gradually disseminated into the rest of China.

Betting on the horses

Minimum bet at the racecourses is HK$10 and you can only bet in multiples of this sum. Aside from simply betting on a win or place, try betting a quinella (predicting first and second horse, in any order); a tierce (first, second and third horse in correct order); double or triple trio (first three horses, in any order, in two or three designated races); or a treble (winners of three designated races). Betting tax is 11.5 percent, rising to 17.5 percent on a more complicated bet.

Today, Chinese martial arts tend to be grouped into two types: "**external**" or hard styles, such as Shaolin kung fu, which concentrate on developing physical power; and "**internal**" or soft styles, such as tai chi, which concentrate on developing *qi* (chi), an internal force. Only experts can easily tell internal and external styles apart by just watching, despite the techniques being substantially at odds; both produce effective fighting systems, though internal arts tend to improve as you age (hence tai chi's popularity with the elderly), whereas the external styles are more effective for younger practitioners.

Get up early enough – around 7am – and you'll see many styles being practised in the nearest park, especially Kowloon Park in Tsim Sha Tsui (where experts also put on displays every Sun at 2.30pm), and Victoria Park on Hong Kong Island. The large groups moving slowly through their routines are doing **tai chi**; if you see people walking in endless tight circles they're practising **pa kwa**, another internal martial art. Specific southern Chinese styles include **wing chun**, which concentrates on very accurate handwork and became famous as being the first martial art Bruce Lee studied; southern forms of **praying mantis** and **white crane**, **choy li fut**; and **hung gar**, associated with the nineteenth-century master Wong Fei Hung.

The HKTB organizes free tai chi lessons in English, every Monday, Wednesday, Thursday and Friday at 8 to 9am, at the Avenue of Stars in Tsim Sha Tsui, but if you're serious about studying a Chinese martial art, try contacting one of the following (all speak English):

Hong Kong Chinese Martial Arts Association 687 Nathan Rd, Jordan ☎2394 4803. General advice and contacts.

C.S. Tang ☎9426 9253, ⓦcstang .www3.50megs.com. *Yiquan*, *xingyi*, tai chi and *pa kwa* taught by a long-time student of the late *pa kwa* master Ho Ho Choi. An excellent teacher with several foreign students.

Donald Mak ☎9132 8162, ⓦwww.hkwingchun .com. Good *wing chun* instructor.

William Wan ☎9885 8336, ⓦwww.kungfuwan .com. *Choy li fut* and Shaolin styles.

Mountain biking

Mountain biking is a developing sport in Hong Kong, and there are currently **trails** on Lantau Island, the Sai Kung Peninsula, Tai Lam Country Park, Shek O Country Park and Clearwater Bay Country Park (the latter closed on Sundays and public holidays). To ride on these, you'll need a **permit** from the Agriculture, Fisheries and Conservation Department (ⓦwww.afcd.gov.hk). For online maps and more information about the trails, check the Hong Kong Mountain Biking Association's website at ⓦwww .hkmba.org, or www.crosscountryhk.com.

Rock climbing

Away from central Hong Kong's office towers, the SAR's countryside offers some excellent rock climbing. Lion Rock (see p.138) near Sha Tin is probably the most popular site, but there are plenty of other recognized routes on rockfaces and crags everywhere from Clearwater Bay and the Sai Kung Peninsula to outlying parts of Kowloon and Hong Kong Island, as well as on Lamma and Lantau Islands.

The best source of **information** is ⓦwww.hongkongclimbing.com, which grades and provides practical details for a score of climbs around Hong Kong;

they also give links to local clubs and associations, as well as details of various **climbing walls** if you want some practice first.

Rugby

Rugby (Union, not League) is generally of a good standard and each Easter three days are devoted to a series of **Rugby Sevens** matches with international teams – the boisterous crowd is as entertaining as the matches themselves. The event is organized by the Hong Kong Rugby Football Union (Room 2001, Sports House, 1 Stadium Path, So Kon Po, Causeway Bay ☎2504 8311, ⓦwww.hkrugby.com), which can provide more information and tell you how to go about joining a team in Hong Kong. Tickets for the three-day event cost around HK$750.

Running

You'll see people jogging at dozens of places throughout the SAR, some of which have marked routes and exercise stops along the way. A few of the most popular spots are along **Bowen Road** in Mid-Levels; around the roads at the top of the Peak; along the **Tsim Sha Tsui waterfront**; and around **Victoria Park**. If you do run or jog, remember that the summer heat and humidity are crippling; run in the early morning or evening and take some water along.

An increasingly wide variety of **races** now take place for walkers and runners – traditional marathons, endurance events and adventure racing. Notable events include the **Standard Chartered Hong Kong Marathon** (ⓦwww .hkmarathon.com), held in February, the **MacLehose Trailwalker** in November and the **Action Asia Challenge** in December. You can get information, and entry forms for the Hong Kong Marathon, from the Hong Kong Amateur Athletic Association (ⓦwww.hkaaa.com); the HKTB can help with the others. All such events start early, because of the climate.

More offbeat running is provided by the **Orienteering Association of Hong Kong** (Room 1014, Sports House, 1 Stadium Path, So Kon Po, Causeway Bay ☎2504 8111, ⓦwww.oahk.org.hk), which maintains an orienteering course in Pokfulam Country Park on Hong Kong Island. Plans are in the pipeline for six more courses in country parks around the SAR, including two on Lantau Island, and one on Monkey Mountain, in Kam Shan Country Park. **Hashers** should check out ⓦwww.hashchina.com.

Soccer

Soccer is played widely throughout the SAR. In the old days, Hong Kong's First Division was kept keen through competition with British army teams; now it's littered with has-been or never-were players from other countries – teams are allowed five overseas players. Good local talent is fairly thin on the ground, but games can be entertaining, not least because the foreign players brought in tend to be strikers and consequently face local defences comprising people much shorter than themselves.

If you're sufficiently interested, teams to watch are Happy Valley, South China and Eastern. The "national team", such as it is, usually has a torrid time in the World Cup qualifying matches, making heavy weather against such footballing giants as Bahrain and Lebanon. The best advice for soccer fans is to find a TV on Saturday evenings during the English soccer season, when you get an hour's worth of the previous week's top English matches; most major cup and international matches are televised live, too.

Spas, gyms and massage

Health is a big issue in Chinese culture, and Hong Kong has no shortage of places to keep yourself trim. Most of the upmarket hotels – such as the *Peninsula* and *Langham* (see pp.106–113) – have luxurious **spas**, great for a pamper; just make sure your wallet can cope before signing up for a session. **Gyms** are more down-to-earth, and branches of popular chains California Fitness (ⓦwww .californiafitness.com) and Fitness First (ⓦwww.fitnessfirst.com.hk) offer day passes from HK$150 and up; Seasons Fitness at 3rd Floor, ICBC Tower, Citibank Plaza, Garden Rd, Central ⓦwww.seasonsfitness.com) offers a free trail and is a notch above the others, with sauna and pool as well as gym space.

Getting a **massage** in Hong Kong isn't necessarily the sleazy experience you'd expect. Golden Rock Acupressure and Massage Centre of the Blind, 8th Floor, Golden Swan Building, 438 Hennessy Rd, Causeway Bay, and Health Home Acupressure and Massage Centre of the Blind, 17th Floor, Eastern Commercial Building, 397 Hennessy Rd, Causeway Bay (both ⓦwww.yp.com .hk) charge HK$250 for the first hour, then HK$100 per thirty minutes to have your body pulled apart by a blind masseur. Alternatively, try a **foot massage**; you get approached for this every other step in Tsim Sha Tsui, and a recommended operator is Hong Wai, 7th Floor, Chung Fung Commercial Building, 12 Canton Rd, Tsim Sha Tsui, who charges around HK$100 for a half-hour reflexology session, or HK$150 with a shoulder massage included.

Squash

Squash is about the most popular indoor racket sport in Hong Kong. Book well in advance, and expect to pay around HK$60 an hour at the public courts listed below. Courts are generally open daily 7am–11pm.

Fa Yuen Street Complex Indoor Games Hall 13th Floor, 123a Fa Yuen St, Mong Kok ☏2395 1501.

Harbour Road Indoor Games Hall 27 Harbour Rd, Wan Chai, just in front of the Star Ferry Pier ☏2542 2852.

Hong Kong Squash Centre 23 Cotton Tree Drive, Central ☏2869 0611, ⓦwww.hksquash .org.hk.

Kowloon Park Indoor Games Hall 22 Austin Rd, Jordan ☏2724 3494.

Lockhart Road Indoor Games Hall 10th Floor, Lockhart Rd Complex, 225 Hennessy Rd, Wan Chai ☏2879 5521.

Queen Elizabeth Stadium 18 Oi Kwan Rd, Wan Chai ☏2591 1346.

Victoria Park Hing Fat St, Causeway Bay ☏2570 6186.

Surfing

Hong Kong will never be a world centre for surf, but during the summer typhoon season there can be decent swell, usually along east-facing beaches such as Big Wave Bay and Shek O on Hong Kong Island (p.95), and Tai Long Wan on the Sai Kung Peninsula (p.156) – *tai long wan*, incidentally, means "Big Wave Bay". For the lowdown – including details of the annual **Hong Kong Surf Cup** in November – contact X Game at 18–20 Lyndhurst Terrace, Central; 10 Pak Sha Rd, Causeway Bay; 32A Granville Rd, Tsim Sha Tsui; or Level 9, Langham Place, 555 Shanghai St, Mong Kok (ⓦwww.xgamehk.com).

Swimming

If you don't want to risk the water at any of the SAR's beaches – the best of which are covered in the text – then you'll have to take your dip in one of the eighteen crowded **swimming pools** operated by the Leisure and Cultural Services Department (Ⓦwww.lcsd.gov.hk/beach/en/swim-intro.php for details). These pools charge HK$19 for adults, HK$9 for children; they open daily (though some are closed Monday afternoons) approximately 6.30am–noon, 1–5pm & 6–10pm from April to December. Alternatively, some of the bigger hotels will let you use their modest-sized pools for a large fee – expect at least HK$250. Try the *Kowloon Shangri-La* (see p.194), the *Sheraton* (see p.194), the *Conrad* (see p.191), and *JW Marriott* (see p.191). Three useful Leisure and Cultural Services Department pools are:

Kowloon Park Nathan Rd, Tsim Sha Tsui
ⓉＴ2724 3577.
Morrison Hill 7 Oi Kwan Rd, Wan Chai
Ⓣ2575 3028.

Victoria Park Hing Fat St, Causeway Bay
Ⓣ2570 4682.

Tennis

Public tennis courts are often solidly booked, but if you can get a court you'll pay around HK$40 an hour during the day and up to HK$60 in the evening (after 7pm). The Queen Elizabeth Stadium (see p.230) also has facilities for table tennis, which costs about HK$20 per hour.

Hong Kong Tennis Centre Wong Nai Chung Gap Rd, Happy Valley Ⓦwww.tennishk.org. Daily 7am–11pm.
King's Park Tennis Courts 15 King's Park Rise,

King's Park, Yau Ma Tei Ⓣ2385 8985 or 2388 8154. Daily 7am–10pm.
Victoria Park Hing Fat St, Causeway Bay
Ⓣ2570 6186. Daily 7am–10pm.

Watersports

As you might expect, there's plenty of choice for watersports in a region of 230 islands. **Sailing** enthusiasts who are members of an overseas club can contact the prestigious Hong Kong Yacht Club on Kellet Island, Causeway Bay (Ⓦwww.rhkyc.org.hk), which has reciprocal arrangements with many foreign clubs. The Hong Kong Sailing Federation (Ⓦwww.sailing.org.hk) operates intensive instruction courses at Clearwater Bay. For plain **boating and pleasure cruising**, contact any of the tour companies listed under "Organized Tours", p.29, or ask the HKTB for recommendations.

You can rent **windsurfing** equipment at quite a few of Hong Kong's beaches: both the government-funded centre at Tei Mei Tuk near Tai Po (Ⓣ2665 2591) and Sai Kung's Chong Hing Windsurf Centre (Ⓣ2792 6810) offer classes where you can learn the basics fairly cheaply; or try the Windsurf Centre (Ⓣ2981 8316; daily 10am–7pm) on Kwun Yam Wan beach on Cheung Chau (p.167), which also offers courses and rental. The Windsurfing Association of Hong Kong (1 Stadium Path, So Kon Po, Causeway Bay Ⓣ2504 8255, Ⓦwww .windsurfing.org.hk) can help with other enquiries.

Some beachside operations also offer **water-skiing** and **canoeing** (particularly at the Cheung Chau Windsurf Centre); you can get more information from the Hong Kong Water-Skiing Association (Ⓦwww.waterski.org.hk).

Children's Hong Kong

Although Hong Kong doesn't have an enormous amount in the way of specialized children's activities and events, the place itself can be a playground – the transport, particularly the trams and ferries, is exciting; most of the views and walks more so; and there are several venues with a real family slant, such as Ocean Park and Disneyland. The sections below should give you some ideas for day-to-day activities, which are followed up in more detail in the guide.

Outings

You can base a day-trip around the places and activities below, all of which can occupy several hours with kids in tow. Some also offer a way to get out of the crowds – lunch times in Central and Causeway Bay can be frightening for small children.

Botanical Gardens **Central (see p.65).** A pleasant green area, housing tropical birds and some small mammals. The best-known inhabitant is a jaguar, but don't miss the lemurs, gibbons and orang-utans.

Disneyland **Lantau Island (see p.171).** No Chinese content here, but a host of cartoon favourites and a safari-park-style boat ride populating a middle-America amusement park.
Hong Kong Park **Central (see p.66).** Across the road from the Botanical Gardens. Enormous

Babysitting
Most large hotels can organize babysitting for you; the HKTB (see p.50) has a full list of those that will oblige, if you want to check before you leave.

Playgroups and information
Playgroups and parent-toddler groups are run by a variety of organizations, although most are aimed at residents rather than short-term visitors. Information is available from – among others – the Preschool Playgroups Association (Ⓦhkppa.org); St John's Cathedral, Garden Road, Central (Ⓦwww.stjohnscathedral.org.hk/playgroup .html); or the bilingual *Parent's Journal* magazine (Ⓦwww.parentsjournal.com.hk), available from children's clothes stores and toddler shops. See also Travelling with Children, p.37.

Clothes and supplies
Hong Kong has six branches of the specialist store Mothercare (Ⓦwww.mothercare .com.hk), of which the most central are Shop 303, Prince's Building, Chater Rd, Central; shop 304–307, 3rd Floor, Lee Gardens Two, Causeway Bay; and Ground Floor, Ocean Terminal, Harbour City, Canton Rd, Tsim Sha Tsui. There are also children's clothes and toy shops in most of the large shopping malls.

⑪

walk-in aviary, greenhouses, gardens, picnic areas and a restaurant. Also close to the pedestrian walkways that snake off into the hi-tech buildings of Central.

Hong Kong Wetland Park Near Tin Shui Wai, New Territories (see p.134). Short walks around landscaped wetlands, with bird hides looking out over tidal ponds and a butterfly garden. Indoors are live crocodiles, fish and a museum full of stuffed animals.

Kadoorie Farm Near Tai Po, New Territories (see p.145). Farm with a experimental breeding programme, lots of animals, abandoned and injured wildlife, walks, views and plants.

Ocean Park Deep Water Bay, Hong Kong Island (see p.90). Multi-ride amusement and theme park, with moving dinosaurs, marine animals, shows, gardens and giant pandas in their purpose-built home. Next door, Middle Kingdom re-creates life in ancient China, with acrobats, lion dancing and the chance to try skills such as calligraphy.

Outlying islands (see pp.161–182). Ferry rides to all the main islands, where there are beaches, walks, temples, watersports and – on Cheung Chau particularly – cycling trails.

Sea cruises (see "Organized tours", p.29). Cruises lasting anything from an hour to a whole day through the harbour and around the outlying islands; many include lunch. The Dolphinwatch trip to see the endangered pink dolphins is particularly good.

Shek O Hong Kong Island (see p.95). One of Hong Kong's nicest beaches, easy to reach and with plenty of restaurants and beach stores.

Shing Mun Reservoir Island (see p.129). Easy, flat walk with picnic areas and a chance to see wild monkeys.

Stanley Village Hong Kong Island (see p.91). Beaches, watersports, a covered market, some child-friendly restaurants and a good bus ride there and back.

The Peak (see p.74). A trip up on the Peak Tram or bus; easy flat walks around the top; the shops of The Peak Galleria; Madame Tussaud's; panoramic views and picnic areas.

Train to Sheung Shui New Territories (See p.135). Many possible stops at traditional markets, brand-new towns and shopping centres, and a railway museum.

Museums and temples

The following places will interest an inquisitive child. The museums are ones where participation is encouraged – operating robots, clambering on old train carriages, exploring a renovated village – and while nearly all the temples in Hong Kong are unusual enough for most visitors, the ones listed below are particularly large and colourful.

Heritage Museum Sha Tin (see p.139).
History Museum East Tsim Sha Tsui (see p.108).
Po Lin Monastery Lantau Island (see p.174).
Railway Museum Tai Po, New Territories (see p.143).
Sam Tung Uk Museum Tsuen Wan, New Territories (see p.128).

Science Museum Science Museum Rd, Tsim Sha Tsui East (see p.108).
Space Museum Salisbury Rd, Tsim Sha Tsui (see p.103).
Wong Tai Sin Temple Kowloon (see p.118).

Entertainment

Obvious ideas include cinemas, which show the latest films in English; the HKTB-organized cultural shows, with song, dance and mime in various venues; and a (brief) visit to a Chinese opera for the singing and costumes. Some places, like the Arts Centre and local libraries, organize special events for children throughout the school summer holiday: the HKTB will have current information, or call into City Hall and look at the notice boards.

Coinciding with one of Hong Kong's **festivals** is another way to expose kids to a bit of cultural entertainment. If they're happy with crowds and loud noise they'll particularly enjoy the Cheung Chau Bun Festival (see p.166), Tai Hang's Fire Dragon Dance (p.86), Dragon boat racing (see p.35) and any of the Tin Hau celebrations (see p.35) – not to mention the titanic **fireworks show** that ushers in the Chinese New Year (p.35). Suitable **arts events** include the **Arts Festival** in February and March, and the **International Arts Carnival** in July and August, aimed at families and children with puppets, clowns and acrobats.

Shopping

Shopping can keep children amused, too, especially when it's raining, since if you pick one of the huge **shopping malls** you don't have to set foot outside for hours on end, even to eat. There's a list of the main malls on p.249; while specific shops that you might want to take in include the enormous Toys' R' Us (Shop 003, Ground Floor, Ocean Terminal, Canton Rd, Tsim Sha Tsui; 7th Floor, Windsor House, 311 Gloucester Rd, Causeway Bay; and Man Yee Building, 67 Queen's Rd Central, Central); and Wise Kids (Shop 134, Pacific Place, 88 Queensway, Admiralty; Shop 301, Prince's Building, Central; Shop B223, New World Centre, 20–24 Salisbury Rd, Tsim Sha Tsui). Mitsukoshi and Sogo, the Japanese department stores in Causeway Bay (see p.84), are good, with games, toys, comics and cafés, as is the entire Festival Walk complex in Kowloon Tong (see p.114). Head to Tai Yuen Street, just off Johnston Rd, opposite Southorn Playground in Wan Chai, for Hong Kong's budget toy street, selling all manner of plastic goodies and old-fashioned Hong Kong toys.

Eating

Restaurants in Hong Kong (certainly Chinese restaurants) generally welcome children with open arms, and many have high chairs available. Eating is a family affair, as a trip to any *dim sum* restaurant shows, but if your children are unadventurous about their food, there are no problems getting fish and chips, pizzas, hamburgers and the usual more familiar meals – see chapter 6 for details.

Macau

Macau

Macau, Taipa and Coloane

L
ying 60km west from Hong Kong across the Pearl River delta, the former Portuguese enclave of **MACAU** occupies a peninsula and a pair of conjoined islands that together cover just 26 square kilo metres. As in Hong Kong, Macau's atmosphere has been shaped by the blending of European and Chinese culture, especially noticeable here in the antique colonial architecture and Portuguese-influenced **Macanese cooking** existing alongside a predominantly Cantonese-speaking population. While fairly laid-back compared with Hong Kong, Macau attracts millions of big-spending tourists each year – many from mainland China – who come to gamble frenetically at its many **casinos**, the only place in China where they have been legalized. Though economic downturn since 2008 has stalled things, the income generated has been colossal, funding all sorts of ambitious land reclamation and building projects that have turned Macau from a sleepy little colonial hollow into a bustling modern city in less than a decade.

The **peninsula** that the city of Macau itself occupies is about 4km by 2km at its widest points and easy to negotiate on foot – though the few hills can make for tiring climbing in the heat of the day. It's here that you'll find most of the casinos, restaurants and sights, including the ruined church of **São Paulo** and the adjacent **Fortaleza do Monte** with its informative museum. Other attractions include a couple of **temples** that equal any of the better-known ones in Hong Kong; a couple of interesting **markets**; an excellent **maritime museum**, which illuminates Macau's long association with fishing and trade; and a series of quiet and beautiful **gardens** and squares reflecting the enclave's relaxed approach to life. Many central streets retain a dated, decaying, slightly seedy charm, in particular **Rua da Felicidade**, with its whitewashed buildings, and the area north of the main **Avenida de Almeida Ribeiro**.

Three undulating, ribbon-like bridges link the peninsula with **Taipa** Island, from where a strip of reclaimed land – known as **Cotai** – runs across to the southernmost **Coloane** Island. Both islands are small, easily reached by **bus**, and feature more good restaurants and the odd church and temple; Coloane also has the enclave's only **beaches**.

The only trouble you're likely to have in Macau is one of **language**. English signs dry up quickly once you're out of the downtown area, and on

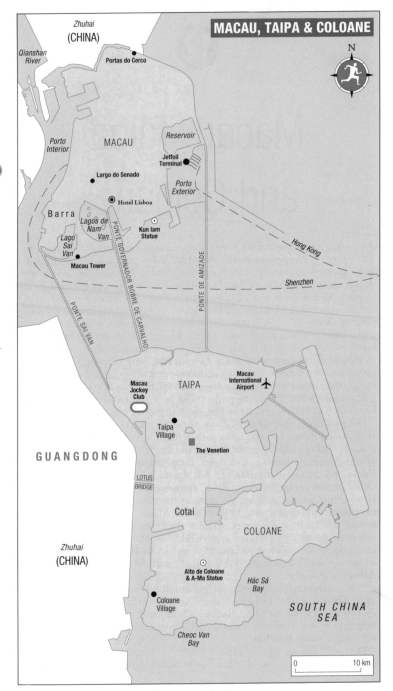

MACAU, TAIPA & COLOANE

N

Zhuhai
(CHINA)

Qianshan
River

Portas do Cerco

Porto
Interior

MACAU

Reservoir

Jetfoil
Terminal

Largo do Senado

Porto
Exterior

Hotel Lisboa

Barra

Lagos de
Nam Van

Kun Iam
Statue

Hong Kong

Lago
Sai Van

Macau Tower

PONTE GOVERNADOR BOBRE DE CARVALHO

PONTE DE AMIZADE

Shenzhen

PONTE SAI VAN

Macau
International
Airport

Macau
Jockey
Club

TAIPA

Taipa
Village

The Venetian

GUANGDONG

LOTUS
BRIDGE

Cotai

COLOANE

Zhuhai
(CHINA)

Alto de Coloane
& A-Ma Statue

Hác Sá
Bay

Coloane
Village

SOUTH CHINA
SEA

Cheoc Van
Bay

0   10 km

By sea

There are two departure points for ferries from Hong Kong to Macau. The **Macau Ferry Terminal** in the Shun Tak Centre, Central, Hong Kong Island, has departures round the clock to Macau's main **Porto Exterior Jetfoil Terminal** with Turbojet (Ⓦwww.turbojet.com.hk); and to **Cotai Temporary Pier**, on the northeast tip of Taipa Island, with Cotai Jet (Ⓦwww.cotaijet.com.mo; at least hourly 7am–1am). Alternatively, New World First Ferry (Ⓦwww.nwff.com.hk) departs from the **China Ferry Terminal** on Canton Road, Tsim Sha Tsui, Kowloon, around twice an hour between 7am and 10pm, for the Porto Exterior Jetfoil Terminal. All ferries are modern, take just over an hour, and cost around HK$135 one-way.

Buying a ticket is rarely a problem and you can often simply turn up and go; though it's advisable to **book in advance** at the weekend and on public holidays – you can book anything from same-day departure up to 28 days before you travel. Buying a **return ticket** is also recommended since it saves time at the other end. Aside from the terminals themselves, you can book tickets at the following MTR stations: Tsim Sha Tsui, Mongkok, Tsuen Wan, Kwun Tong, Causeway Bay, Central and Admiralty.

All tickets are for a specific departure time (though if you're early and there's room, you can usually catch an earlier ferry); be at the ferry terminal at least **thirty minutes before departure** to clear customs. You'll be allowed on with a suitcase or rucksack, but anything more and you'll have to check it in at the counter, again at least thirty minutes before departure, and you'll pay an extra HK$20–40, depending on weight. All services have drinks and snacks for sale on board.

For the **return journery**, all ferry tickets are sold at marked booths on the second floor of Macau's Jetfoil Terminal and at an outlet in the *Hotel Lisboa*'s shopping arcade. Departure frequencies are the same as from Hong Kong, as are the prices – though they're expressed in local patacas (MOP$).

By air

East Asia Airlines (3rd Floor, Shun Tak Centre in Hong Kong ☎2108 4838; Macau ☎727288, Ⓦwww.helihongkong.com) runs a **helicopter service** between Hong Kong and Macau, roughly every thirty minutes between 9am and 10.30pm. The sixteen-minute flight costs HK$2200 one-way. Departures are from the helipad at Hong Kong's Macau Ferry Terminal, where you can buy tickets from a window adjacent to the turbocat and catamaran ticket offices, and arrive at the helipad on top of Macau's Jetfoil Terminal. For the return journey, you can get tickets from marked booths on the second floor of the Jetfoil Terminal and at an outlet in the *Hotel Lisboa*'s shopping arcade.

Taipa and Coloane you'll probably only see written Portuguese and Chinese – though you'd be unlucky to be unable to locate an English-speaker if you needed one.

Around the peninsula

Macau's **PENINSULA** contains not just the remnants of its colonial past, but also a large and bustling modern quarter. The main artery, which cuts diagonally northwest across the peninsula, begins as Avenida do Infante D. Henrique, changing its name halfway along to **Avenida de Almeida Ribeiro**; it's north of here that you'll find the core of the **old city** and many of its major sights

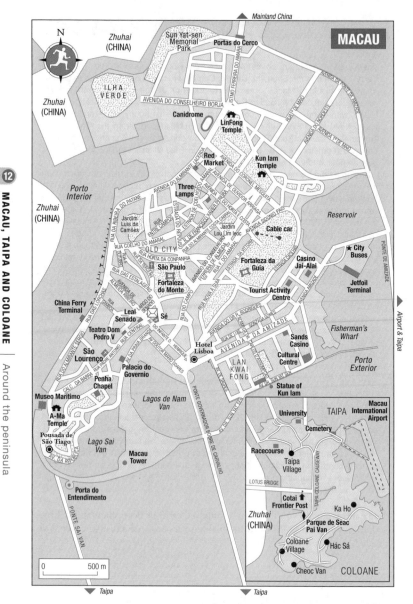

Mainland China

Zhuhai
(CHINA)

Sun Yat-sen
Memorial
Park

Portas do Cerco

MACAU

ILHA
VERDE

Zhuhai
(CHINA)

N

AVENIDA DO CONSELHEIRO BORJA

Canidrome

LinFong
Temple

Zhuhai
(CHINA)

Porto
Interior

Red
Market

Kun Iam
Temple

Three
Lamps

Jardim
Luis de
Camões

Jardim
Lou Lim Ieoc

Cable car

Reservoir

OLD CITY

São Paulo

Fortaleza
da Guia

Casino
Jai-Alai

City
Buses

Fortaleza
do Monte

Jetfoil
Terminal

China Ferry
Terminal

Leal
Senado

Sé

Tourist Activity
Centre

Teatro Dom
Pedro V

São
Lourenço

Hotel
Lisboa

Sands
Casino

Fisherman's
Wharf

Penha
Chapel

Palacio do
Governio

LAN
KWAI
FONG

Cultural
Centre

Porto
Exterior

Museo Maritimo

Lagos de Nam
Van

Statue of
Kun Iam

A-Ma
Temple

Pousada de
São Tiago

Lago Sai
Van

Macau
Tower

University

TAIPA

Macau
International
Airport

Porta do
Entendimento

Cemetery

Racecourse

Taipa
Village

LOTUS BRIDGE

Cotai
Frontier Post

Ka Ho

Zhuhai
(CHINA)

Parque de Seac
Pai Van

Coloane
Village

Hác Sá

Cheoc Van

COLOANE

0   500 m

Taipa

Taipa

Airport & Taipa

between **Largo do Senado** (Senate Square) and the **Guia** hilltop. East of here
are the bright lights and modern development of **Avenida da Amizade** and
associated casinos; while south of Avenida de Almeida Ribeiro there's more
historic architecture through the narrow lanes of the **southern peninsula**.
There are also a few sights in the otherwise nondescript north of **town** on the
way to the **Chinese border**. Just about everything is within walking distance

of most accommodation options, though you'll probably need a bus for the northernmost bits of town.

The old centre: Largo do Senado to the Fortaleza da Guia

The best place to start a tour of Macau is in **Largo do Senado**, the old city's main focus, usually full of sociable crowds out shopping during the day, or heading to restaurants in the evening. Just north is the iconic ruined facade of **São Paulo** and the nearby fortified hilltop, **Fortaleza do Monte**, beyond which the older-style streets fade out among a couple of city gardens and another defensive post, **Fortaleza da Guia**. You could make an easy circuit of these central sights in about four hours – long enough on a hot day – before heading back to Largo do Senado for a coffee.

Leal Senado and Largo do Senado

Begin a tour of the old town at the **Leal Senado** (Mon–Sun 9am–9pm; free) on Avenida de Almeida Ribeiro, the seat of Macau's early government. The name means "Loyal Senate", bestowed by a grateful Portuguese monarchy after Macau refused to fly the Castilian flag following the Spanish occupation of Portugal in 1580. Its elegant Portuguese design sports stone stairways and interior courtyard walls decorated with classic blue and white *azulejo* tiling, with an ornamental courtyard out the back. It's something of a civic centre today, housing a small **art gallery** on the ground floor with ever-changing exhibitions, and an upstairs **library** (Mon–Sat 1–7pm), whose wooden shelves are stacked with a large collection of books (many in English) about China, dating from the sixteenth century onwards – ask the librarians if you want to have a read. On the next level up, the **Senate Chamber** – a grand room with panelled walls and ceiling and excellent views over the square – is sometimes open to the public when not in use.

Directly over the road, **Largo do Senado** (Senate Square) is the city's public focus, cobbled and surrounded by elegant colonial buildings painted pale pink, yellow or white, whose shuttered upper storey and street-level colonnades exude a wonderful tropical charm. There's a small fountain in the middle, while west between the square and Rua dos Mercadores is the **San Domingos Covered Market**, three storeys of fresh produce (whose upper **cooked food market** is good for a cheap bowl of noodles) surrounded by a quadrangle of inexpensive clothes stalls. This has always been a market area; hunt carefully and you'll find the minute **San Kai Vui Kun**, literally the "Three Lanes Guildhall", where Macau's merchants used to meet.

Opposite on the east side of the square, **Santa Casa de Misericórdia** (Holy House of Mercy; Mon–Sat 10am–5.30pm; MOP$5) is Macau's oldest social institution, founded in 1569 by Dom Belchior Carneiro, the city's first Catholic bishop. His skull is displayed in a wood-panelled **museum** upstairs, along with porcelain marked with the Jesuit logo "JHS", and other religious artefacts.

Up from here you'll pass the mouth of **Travessa da Sé**, a lane leading east to the Sé cathedral (see p.268), along which you'll find **Casa de Lou Kau** (Lou Family Mansion; Tues–Sun 9am–7pm; free), a nineteenth-century merchant's house in fantastic condition, two storeys high and built in brick around cool interior atriums with wooden galleries upstairs. The open roof lets in light and air but keeps out the heat; the only lapse in balanced taste is in the

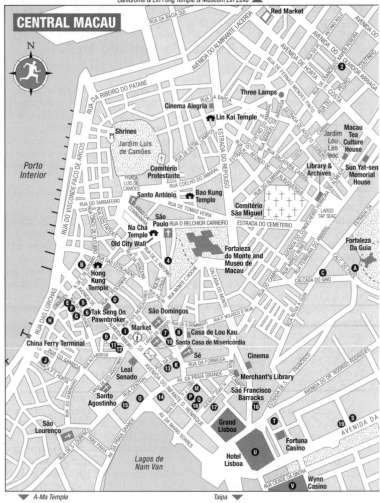

heavy and uncomfortable-looking wooden furniture favoured at the time. Incidentally, this was the home of the family who financed the Lou Lim Ieoc gardens (see p.273).

Sé and São Domingos

Two of Macau's most important churches are just off Largo do Senado. East at the top of Travessa da Sé, the squat **Sé**, Macau's cathedral, was founded in the sixteenth century, though the plain exterior dates only to 1937, impressive inside for its sense of space rather than any ornamentation. The adjacent **Bishop's House** (daily 10am–5.30pm; free) makes up for this austerity, however, filled with over-the-top Baroque statues and religious artefacts in gold and silver.

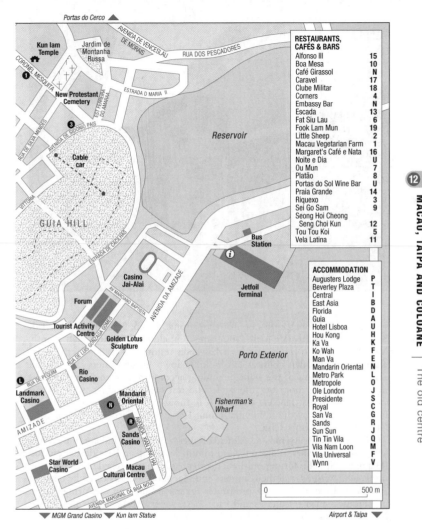

The map contains the following labels:

Portas do Cerco

AVENIDA DE VENCESLAU DE MORAIS

Kun Iam Temple

Jardim de Montanha Russa

RUA DOS PESCADORES

CORONEL MESQUITA

New Protestant Cemetery

EST FERREIRA DO AMARAL

ESTRADA D MARIA II

RUA DE SILVA MENDES

AVENIDA DE SIDONIO PAIS

Reservoir

Cable car

VITTORIA

GUIA HILL

ESTRADA DE CACILHAS

Bus Station

Casino Jai-Alai

AV MARCIANO BAPTISTA

AVENIDA DA AMIZADE

Jetfoil Terminal

Forum

Tourist Activity Centre

RUA DE LUIS GONZAGA GOMES

Golden Lotus Sculpture

Porto Exterior

Rio Casino

RUA DE PEQUIM

Landmark Casino

AMIZADE

Mandarin Oriental

Fisherman's Wharf

AVENIDA DO DR RODRIGO RODRIGUES

Sands Casino

AVENIDA DR SUN YAT SEN

Star World Casino

Macau Cultural Centre

AVENIDA MARGINAL DA BAIA NOVA

0   500 m

MGM Grand Casino   Kun Iam Statue

Airport & Taipa

RESTAURANTS, CAFÉS & BARS

Alfonso III	15
Boa Mesa	10
Café Girassol	N
Caravel	17
Clube Militar	18
Corners	4
Embassy Bar	N
Escada	13
Fat Siu Lau	6
Fook Lam Mun	19
Little Sheep	2
Macau Vegetarian Farm	1
Margaret's Café e Nata	16
Noite e Dia	U
Ou Mun	7
Platão	8
Portas do Sol Wine Bar	U
Praia Grande	14
Riquexo	3
Sei Go Sam	9
Seong Hoi Cheong Seng Choi Kun	12
Tou Tou Koi	5
Vela Latina	11

ACCOMMODATION

Augusters Lodge	P
Beverley Plaza	T
Central	I
East Asia	B
Florida	D
Guia	A
Hotel Lisboa	U
Hou Kong	H
Ka Va	K
Ko Wah	F
Man Va	E
Mandarin Oriental	N
Metro Park	L
Metropole	O
Ole London	J
Presidente	S
Royal	C
San Va	G
Sands	R
Sun Sun	J
Tin Tin Vila	Q
Vila Nam Loon	M
Vila Universal	F
Wynn	V

At the north end of Largo do Senado, the arcaded buildings peter out in the adjacent Largo São Domingos, which holds Macau's most beautiful church, the fine seventeenth-century **São Domingos**. Built for Macau's Dominicans, its restrained cream-and-stucco facade is echoed inside by the pastel colours on display on the pillars and walls, and on the statue of the Virgin and Child that sits on top of the altar. On May 13, every year, the church is the starting point for a major procession in honour of Our Lady of Fatima. The adjacent **Treasury of Sacred Art** is open daily 10am–6pm.

Avenida de Almeida Ribeiro and around

West from Leal Senado, colonnaded **Avenida de Almeida Ribeiro** runs for 700m to the Porto Interior past a succession of gold and jewellery shops, all

▲ Rua da Felicidade

still set behind nineteenth-century shop fronts. At no. 396, the former **Tak Seng On pawnbroker** (daily 10.30am–7pm; closed first Mon each month; MOP\$5) is now a museum which has been restored to its 1917 condition, with a high wooden counter for looking down on customers and a small display of the tools of the trade, including account books; you can also visit the caged strong room out the back. The rest of the building is a souvenir shop selling tourist trinkets and fine teas, though there's also – strangely – a library of works by the influential Hong Kong martial arts novelist Jin Yong (also known as **Louis Cha**).

Cross south over Avenida de Almeida Ribeiro from here and continue down any of the short lanes, and you'll almost immediately be on **Rua da Felicidade** (Happiness St). This former red-light district has been smartened up, its old shop fronts whitewashed, and their shutters and big wooden doors carefully restored and painted red; though the prostitutes remain it's now an endearing run of guesthouses, small restaurants and *pastelarias* (sweet shops) such as the popular **Koi Kei**, selling almond biscuits and cured pork.

São Paulo

A short walk north of Largo do Senado through a nest of cobbled lanes flanked by *pastelarias*, stands Macau's most enduring monument: the imposing facade of the church of **São Paulo**. Building began in 1602 on a Jesuit church here, attached to the Madre de Deus ("Mother of God") college, and its rich design reflected the precocious, cosmopolitan nature of early Macau. Designed by an Italian, it was built largely by Japanese craftsmen who produced a Spanish-style facade that took 25 years to complete. The church and adjacent Jesuit college became a noted centre of learning, while the building evoked rapture in those who saw it: "I have not seen anything that can equal it, even in all the beautiful churches of Italy, except St Peter's" wrote one visitor in the 1630s. However, following the expulsion of the Jesuits from Macau, the college did duty as an army barracks and on a fateful day in 1835, a fire, which had started in the kitchens, swept through the entire complex leaving just the carved stone façade and foundations.

Approaching up the impressive wide swathe of steps (floodlit at night, when locals come here to sit and chat), you can just about convince yourself that the church still stands, but then the lone **facade** is revealed, like a misplaced theatre backdrop, rising in four tiers and chipped and cracked with age and fire damage. The statues and reliefs have lost none of their power, however: a dove at the top (the Holy Spirit) is flanked by the sun and moon; below is Jesus, around whom reliefs show the implements of the Crucifixion – a ladder, manacles, a crown of thorns and a flail. Below are the Virgin Mary and angels, flowers representing China (a peony) and Japan (chrysanthemum), a griffin and a rigged galleon, while the bottom tier holds four Jesuit saints, and the crowning words "Mater Dei" above the central door.

Behind the facade, São Paulo's subterranean crypt also survived the fire and now houses a **museum of sacred art** (daily 9am–6pm; free), which displays religious paintings, sculptures and church regalia, including a rendition of the mass crucifixion of 23 Christians in Nagasaki, Japan, in 1597. Their remains – along with those of the college's founder, Father Alexandre Valignano – are stored in the former chancel of the church, which has been converted into a **crypt**.

Immediately west of São Paulo, there's a tiny temple to **Na Cha** (see p.325), built after the boy-god was believed to have put down a nineteenth-century plague. This joins onto the last surviving fragment of Macau's **Old City Wall**, a ten-metre-long stretch with an archway dating to 1569.

Fortaleza do Monte and the Museu de Macau

Immediately east of São Paulo, a path and steps lead up the few hundred metres to the solid **Fortaleza do Monte**, a fortress that was part of the Jesuit complex of São Paulo and dates from the same period. It saw action only once, when its cannons helped drive back the Dutch in 1622; like São Paulo, it fell into disuse after the Jesuits had gone. From the ramparts (made from a hardened mixture of earth, shells, straw and lime, packed in layers between strips of wood) you can appreciate its excellent defensive position, its solid iron cannons now with a line of sight on the *Grand Lisboa* (see p.274) and the parapets giving fine views around almost the whole peninsula.

The fort's main attraction is the **Museu de Macau** (Tues–Sun 10am–6pm; MOP\$15), which sets out to explain the origins and development of the enclave, with some excellent full-sized reconstructions of shops and streets. The first floor charts the arrival of the Portuguese and the heydays of the trading routes with displays of typical bartered goods – wooden casks, porcelainware, spices, silver and silk. The second floor has a more Chinese theme, with religious artefacts, house facades and interiors, as well as videos of customs and festivals and even a Chinese wedding where the scarlet-clad bride watches the ritual burning of all her possessions on her wedding morning. Look too for offbeat items such as the cricket-fighting display, complete with a tiny cricket coffin and grave headstone for expired, prized fighters, along with information about why Chinese babies are wrapped in red, and what the rice dumpling hawker used to cry to advertise his wares.

West from São Paulo

There's a fascinating maze of lanes spreading **west from São Paulo** to the seafront. Along **Rua das Estalagens** and **Rua da Tercena** you'll find smiths beating metal, jade carvers, carpenters working wood and various stores selling joss sticks, wedding dresses, antiques, blackwood furniture, medicines, silk and shoes. Further on things become more intense as the very old streets degenerate into a noisome wholesale market: wicker baskets full of vegetables and roots, chickens in coops waiting to be killed and plucked, and whole side alleys turned over to different trades – one full of ironmongers, another of street barbers. **Rua de Cinco de Outubro** is similar, with a remarkable decorated facade of the Farmacia Tai Neng Tong on the left at no. 146. Where Rua das Estalagens and Rua de Cinco de Outubro intersect, check out the **Hong Kung Temple**, dedicated to Kwan Tai, god of riches and war, and focus for the extraordinary **Drunken Dragon Festival**, held on the eighth day of the fourth lunar month (April/May). Organized by the Fish Retailers' Association, the festival features opera, religious ceremonies, martial arts performances and a drunken parade of men carrying large wooden dragon heads from here to the Porto Interior via all the local fish shops.

All these streets eventually intersect north with **Rua do Tarrafeiro**, just a short way from Jardim Luís de Camões (see below).

Jardim Luís de Camões and around

From São Paulo, Rua de São Paulo becomes Rua de Santo António as it runs northwest, past antique furniture shops, to the church of **Santo António**. This is rather plain in appearance, though given that it was wrecked by fire in 1809, 1874 and 1930 it's perhaps surprising that it survives at all. Each St Anthony's Day (June 13) the saint – a military figurehead – is presented with his wages by the president of the Senate, after which his image is paraded around the city to inspect the battlements.

Just beyond here is a square, the Praça Luís de Camões (buses #17 & #18 run past), at the head of which lies the **Jardim Luís de Camões** (Camões Garden; open daily 6am–8pm). This very tropical, laid-back spread of banyans, ferns, fan palms, paved terraces and flowers is always full of people pottering about, exercising, or just playing cards under the trees, and commemorates a sixteenth-century Portuguese poet who is supposed to have visited Macau and written part of his epic *Os Lusíadas* (about Vasco da Gama's voyages) here. Exit the rear of the gardens and steps take you down past a host of lively **shrines** built into the granite rock face, including one to the Tang dynasty Buddhist pilgrim **Xuan Zang** and his renowned – though wholly fictional – acolytes Monkey, Sandy and Pigsy.

To the right of the Camões Garden's main entrance, **Cemitério Protestante** (Old Protestant Cemetery; daily 8.30am–5.30pm) houses many of the non-Portuguese traders and visitors who expired in the enclave. The most famous resident is the artist **George Chinnery** (on the cemetery's upper tier), who spent his life painting much of the local Chinese coast; though the cemetery's most poignant graves are those belonging to ordinary **seamen**: Samuel Smith "died by a fall from aloft"; the cabin boy of ship's master Athson similarly met his end "through the effects of a fall into the hold"; while poor Oliver Mitchell "died of dysentery". There's also the grave of the missionary Robert Morrison, who translated the Bible into Chinese, and his wife who died in childbirth.

Several roads head east from Camões Garden to Estrada do Repouso (see p.280); the best is **Rua de Coelho do Amaral**, which passes a huge open-air earth god shrine on the corner with Rua do Potane and – south up Rua da Entena – a bright yellow temple to **Bao Kung**, the god of Justice.

Jardim Lou Lim Ieoc and around

East of Fortaleza do Monte, **Rua Do Campo** is a busy commercial street full of clothing and electronics stores. Walk north along it for ten minutes and you exit into **Largo Tap Seac**, a newly-created public square though cobbled in the "antique" manner and with a string of colonial mansions on its west side housing the **City Library** (Tues–Sun 2–8pm) and the **National Archives**. Just west along Estrada do Cemitério, **Cemitério São Miguel** (daily 8am–6pm) is Macau's largest cemetery and full of both European and Christian Chinese headstones, an interesting place to wander.

North from here, Avenida do Conselheiro Ferreira de Almeida runs past a high wall enclosing the beautiful **Jardim Lou Lim Ieoc** (daily 6am–9pm; free) a formal Chinese arrangement of pavilions, carp ponds, bamboo groves and frangipani trees where you might catch amateur opera performances on a Sunday. Built in the nineteenth century, it was modelled on the famous classical Chinese gardens of Suzhou, and typically manages to appear much more spacious than it really is. The garden is known locally as Lou Kau, after the Chinese family who funded its construction. On the garden's northeast side, the **Macau Tea Culture House** (Tues–Sun 9am–7pm; free) gives an insight into the many different types of Chinese teas, the ways of processing leaves to provide a particular brew, and the importance of regional varieties – there's a lot of text compared with exhibits but it's worth the read.

Just to the east, on Avenida de Sidonio Pais (at the junction with Rua de Silva Mendes), the granite, Moorish-style **Sun Yat-sen Memorial House** (Wed–Mon 10am–5pm; free) was built by the late revolutionary leader's family in the 1930s to house relics of his life. Sun Yat-sen lived in Macau for a few years in the 1890s, practising as a doctor and developing his republican beliefs, and while there's no massive interest in the period furniture and old photos, you could spend half an hour quite happily in this odd building, with its Arabesque arches and spiral columns. The top floor is used for occasional art exhibitions.

Guia Hill and Fortaleza da Guia

The steep ridge east of here is **Guia Hill**, Macau's apex and one-time defence headquarters, and now a landscaped park. The **entrance** is on Avenida de Sidonio Pais through a small botanic garden – housing an aviary and a sad collection of animals in bare steel and concrete cages – from where you can either ascend to the top of Guia Hill along a winding path, or take the **cable car** (Tues–Sun 8am–6pm; MOP$3 return, MOP$2 one-way). Either way, you'll end up on paths to the remains of **Fortaleza da Guia** (daily 9am–5.30pm; free) a fortress completed in 1638, and originally designed to defend the border with China – though given its extraordinary perch above the whole peninsula it's seen most service as an observation post. The main points of interest here are a network of short, disconnected **tunnels** used in the 1930s to store munitions; and a small seventeenth-century **chapel** within the walls dedicated to Our Lady of Guia, which contains an image of the Virgin that local legend says left the chapel and deflected enemy bullets with her robe during the Dutch attack of 1622. Inside are the recently uncovered original blue and pink frescoes, which combine Chinese elements with Christian religious images. The chapel's other function was to ring its bell to warn of storms, something now taken care of by the fortress's **lighthouse**, built in 1865. The best views from the fortress walls are southeast down over the modern Porto Exterior, and westwards towards Fortaleza do Monte and the old town.

Avenida da Amizade and the Porto Exterior

The area southeast of Guia Hill is entirely modern, built on land **reclaimed** from the **Porto Exterior**, the Outer Harbour, over the last few decades. The main artery here is **Avenida da Amizade**, a multi-laned carriageway that runs for around 1.5km between the gaudy *Hotel Lisboa* and the Jetfoil Terminal, where you probably arrived in town from Hong Kong. It's an area catering to big spenders, thick with upmarket hotels and **casinos** and the setting for the annual **Macau Grand Prix** race (see p.307) – though a couple of museums add a shot of culture too. **Buses** #3, #3A and #10A run from Avenida Almeida Ribeiro near Largo do Senado, via the *Hotel Lisboa*, and up to the Jetfoil Terminal, though not continually along Avenida da Amizade.

The Lisboa, Grand Lisboa and São Francisco barracks

Roads from all over the peninsula – and the bridge to Taipa – converge at a huge **roundabout** at the southern end of Avenida da Amizade, where you'll also find two of the most outrageous buildings in Macau: the **Hotel Lisboa** and the **Grand Lisboa**. Both are the product of the astoundingly wealthy **Stanley Ho**, who until the Chinese took over in 1999 had a monopoly on Macau's casino licences, and built the original *Lisboa* as a monument to the fact, its multistorey orange exterior crowned by a roulette wheel and lit to extravagant effect at night. No one should miss a venture into the hotel's 24-hour **casinos** – all pseudo-1930s decor and noisy, crowded tables – or a wander through the hotel's gilt and marble surroundings, past the gift shops, Stanley Ho's private art collection, and the ten restaurants and bars inside. The *Lisboa* is, however, absolutely dwarfed by the newer *Grand Lisboa* over the road; it's hard to describe but if you imagine a 58-storey, 258-metre-high gold-plated feather you won't be far off the mark. At night it flashes in rainbow colours, though the interior – while vast – is a bit disappointing, just the inevitable expanse of gaming tables with a vaguely naughty stage show in the background.

Just north from the *Lisboa*, on Avenida da Praia Grande, stands the area's one old colonial touch: **São Francisco barracks**, painted a deep pink highlighted with white trim (as are all of Macau's military buildings); you can eat in style here at the **Clube Militar** (see p.298). The building itself dates from 1864; before that, on the same site, stood the original São Francisco fortress, which guarded the edge of the old waterfront Praia Grande – giving you some idea of how far land reclamation has changed this part of the city. The fine round tower in the upper level of the ornate gardens behind the barracks was built to honour those from Macau who saw service in World War I.

Just west from the barracks, the squat octagonal building with a Chinese-style roof at the junction of Praia Grande and busy Rua do Campo houses a tiny **library** (Tues–Sun 9am–noon) funded by the Macau Merchants' Association.

Avenida da Amizade and around

Moving up Avenida de Amizade, both sides of road are lined with huge **casino complexes**, housing more shopping arcades, casinos, restaurants and hotels than you could ever want to experience in a single visit. Smaller side streets – especially **Avenida do Dr Rodrigo Rodrigues** and **Rua de Pequim** – are full of small restaurants, anonymous places to stay and an army of **pawnbrokers** feeding off the seedy, recently impoverished clusters of mainland Chinese tourists orbiting between them.

South across Amizade from the original *Lisboa*, **Wynn Macau** is a stylish upmarket casino with real panache, quite a rarity among the other brighter, glibber establishments nearby; the lobby is lined with international brand-name stores and looks through to an atrium pool, though the gaming tables here – and at the nearby **MGM Grand Casino** – are indistinguishable from most others in town. It's a similar story as you continue up Amizade past the *Landmark*, *Star World* and other casinos, though it's worth noting in passing the gold-plated, US-owned **Sands**, which opened in 2003 as Macau's first foreign-operated venture. Completely at odds with the home-grown brand of the time, whose crowds and dim lighting preserved anonymity, the *Sands'* vast lozenge-shaped interior provided Macau with its first taste of Las Vegas slickness, well lit with a live band and a high tier of balcony bars and restaurants from where you can spy down on the action.

Behind the *Sands*, the **Macau Cultural Centre**, on Avenida Xian Xing Hai (buses #8, #12, or #17), sits on the southeast edge of a grid of new streets jutting into the bay. Its highlight is the five-storey **Museum of Art** (Tues–Sun, 10am–6.30pm; MOP$5, free on Sunday) whose galleries contain a display of nineteenth-century paintings of Macau – including pieces by George Chinnery – as well as temporary exhibitions from overseas. The adjacent blue-grey block houses the auditoriums where international music, dance and theatre shows are staged. For **ticketing information**, see ⓦwww.ccm.gov.mo.

A five-minute walk along the waterfront on an artificial island joined to the mainland by a causeway is the captivating **Kun Iam Statue and Ecumenical Centre** (daily except Fri, 10.30am–6pm; free), designed and built by Portuguese artist, Christina Reiria. The twenty-metre bronze sculpture (whose sweeping garments are designed to withstand the strong offshore winds) had a mixed reception from the locals, many of whom feel that it looks more like Mary, mother of Jesus, than the Chinese goddess of mercy.

To the Jetfoil Terminal

Across Avenida de Amizade from the *Sands* casino, holidaying mainlanders pose in front of a **Golden Lotus Flower** sculpture – an attempt, perhaps, to rival Hong Kong's Golden Bauhinia – which rises up out of a concrete-paved square. Behind here on Rua de Luís Gonzaga Gomes is the **Tourist Activity Centre**, housing two subterranean museums. The **Museu da Grande Prémio** (Grand Prix Museum; daily 10am–6pm; MOP$10) displays vintage and modern racing cars with race videos and information boards. It's a rather dull display, rescued by the opportunity of spending a few minutes strapped into a race simulator experiencing the twists and turns of the Formula 3 circuit (MOP$20). The **Museu do Vinho** (Wine Museum; daily 10am–6pm; MOP$15) charts the history of Portuguese viniculture with maps, peasant costumes and hundreds of bottles; entry gets you a free sample, and the shop sells some interesting vintages – including much sought-after 1994, considered the twentieth century's finest year for Port. A couple of blocks north from here, the old **Jai-Alai Stadium** is now yet another casino, a down-market, dingy affair filled mainly with slot machines (or "Hungry Tigers" as they're known in Chinese).

Back over Avenida de Amizade between the *Sands* and the Jetfoil Terminal, **Fisherman's Wharf** is a themed open-air shopping plaza and entertainment complex incorporating a Chinese fort, a forty-metre-high man-made volcano, a Roman amphitheatre, re-creations of Chinese and European streets, and the usual restaurants and nightclubs. It's all rather lacklustre at the moment, with the air of a half-completed project that nobody really knows what to do with, though things perk up for specific events like the Grand Prix or Chinese New Year. From here, it's just a short walk on to the **Jetfoil Terminal**, outside of which you'll find a **bus terminal** (buses #3, #3A and #10A will get you back to *Hotel Lisboa* or Largo do Senado).

The southern peninsula

The hilly, narrow peninsula south of Avenida de Almeida Ribeiro and Largo do Senado was for centuries one of the busiest areas of Macau, faced to the west by its main harbour, to the east by its main promenade, and capped by elegant dwellings and churches. Today it's a mostly quiet, slightly seedy district, but remains an interesting place to roam twisting lanes between quietly mouldering buildings. The two main sights here are **A-Ma Temple**, the most famous in Macau, and the adjacent **maritime museum**. This is really an area to explore on foot, wandering down to the temple either past the old wharves of the Porto Interior or through the historic **Barra** district as described below, though **bus** #10A also runs from the Jetfoil Terminal, via *Hotel Lisboa* and Avenida de Almeida Ribeiro, down to the temple and museum.

The Porto Interior

The west side of the southern peninsula fronts the **Porto Interior** or Inner Harbour, Macau's main port until the new terminals were built over on the

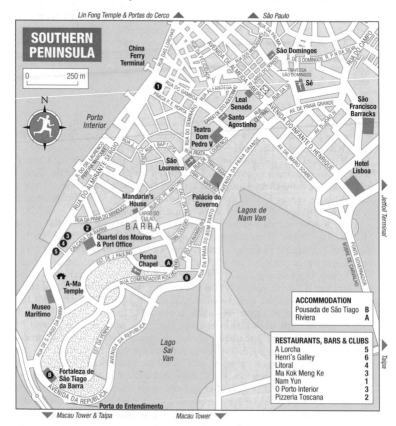

Porto Exterior. From Avenida de Almeida Ribeiro, the 1.5-kilometre-long waterfront strip is first known as **Rua das Lorchas**, its shabby 1950s facade undergoing some redevelopment at present, as it heads past old wharfs, warehouses, and the well-hidden **China Ferry Terminal**. A few hundred metres down it becomes **Rua do Almirante Sergio**, an arcaded stretch of chandlers and fishing-supply shops (selling nets and great steel hawsers), greasy electrical and hardware stores, pawnshops, incense sellers, pedlars with jade ornaments, vegetable sellers and *dai pai dongs* (see p.200). There's also a small temple at no. 131, while the side streets around conceal a tumbledown world of dark, tatty shops and houses. Down towards the southern end you pass a clutch of famous **restaurants**, including *O Porto Interior* and *A Lorcha* (see p.298), before arriving at the pedestrianized square outside the A-Ma Temple, with the maritime museum straight ahead.

The Barra

Alternatively, you can explore the southern peninsula on an excellent forty-minute walk to the A-Ma temple down through the **Barra district**. Start from the Leal Senado and head south along **Rua Central**; your first stop is a few minutes along at the peppermint-coloured **Teatro Dom Pedro V**, built in 1873 and still staging occasional performances, despite its main function as the members-only *Clube Macao*. Opposite is **Santo Agostinho**, a grand church with yellow and white fluted columns and a barrel vault over the altar. The church was founded in 1591, when the Chinese called it *long siu miu* or "Dragon Beard Temple", after the original ragged palm-frond roof; the current building dates from 1874.

By now you're on Rua de São Lourenço, and you'll soon pass the square-towered **São Lourenço**, a wonderfully tropical nineteenth-century church built on a terrace above the street, its bright exterior framed by palms and fig trees. This is one of the most elegant churches in town, whose interior balances lighting, colour and scale in a very pleasant way; the saint's life is depicted in stained glass and there are carved wooden wall panels documenting the Stations of the Cross.

Past here you'll see a sign for the detour up **Penha Hill**, a steep climb rewarded by the nineteenth-century Bishop's Palace and the rather drab **Penha Chapel** (daily 9am–5.30pm), with grand views south of the bridges snaking over to Taipa. Stay on the main road south, however – now called Rua do Padre Antonio – and it's another few minutes to pretty **Largo do Lilau** (Lilau Square), a clutch of shuttered, pastel-coloured homes surrounding a tiny, shaded square where a **spring** seeps out of a wall-fountain. This was one of the first areas of Macau to be settled, and older buildings here include the **Mandarin's House** on Travessa Antonio da Silva (being restored at the time of writing), the 1881 residence of merchant and social reformist Zheng Guanying. From here the main road becomes **Calçada da Barra**, and 500m south brings you to the yellow and white arched colonnade surrounding the **Quartel dos Mouros** (Moorish Barracks), built in 1874 to house a 200-strong Goan regiment and now home to the **Port Office**. You're allowed into the lobby, where you're met by a tiled floor and an unlikely collection of naval cannon and ceremonial pikestaffs. From here, it's only a couple of minutes downhill to the A-Ma Temple.

A-Ma Temple

Facing the water at the back of a large cobbled square, the **A-Ma Temple** is the oldest place of worship in Macau. The legend goes that A-Ma (known in Hong Kong as **Tin Hau**) was a girl from the mainland province of Fujian,

▲ A-Ma Temple on Macau's southern peninsula

whose spirit would appear to save people at sea. After one such apparition saved a group of Fujianese traders during a storm in the 1370s, they founded this temple in her honour at the spot where she had led them to shore. As this was also where the Portuguese later made landfall, they unintentionally named the whole territory after her ("Macau" being a corruption of *a ma kok*, the name of the headland).

The complex comprises a series of small stone halls and pavilions jumbled together on the hillside amongst granite boulders, all cluttered with incense spirals and red-draped wooden models of boats and statues of the goddess. Many of these rocks are also carved with symbols of the A-Ma story and poems in flowery Chinese, describing Macau and its religious associations. An array of fish tanks are full of turtles, onto whose shells people try to drop coins for good luck. The busiest time to visit is either around the Chinese New Year or for **A-Ma's festival** (late April/May; the 23rd day of the third moon), when alongside the devotions there's also Cantonese opera in a temporary theatre.

Museu Marítimo

Over the road from the A-Ma temple, in purpose-built premises designed to look like wharf buildings, is Macau's superb **Museu Marítimo** (Maritime

Museum; Wed–Mon 10am–5.30pm; MOP$10, MOP$5 on Sunday). Ranged across three storeys is an engaging and well-presented collection relating to local fishing techniques and festivals, Chinese and Portuguese maritime prowess, and boat building. Poke around and you'll discover navigational equipment, a scale model of seventeenth-century Macau, traditional local clothing used by the fishermen, a host of lovingly made models of both Chinese and Portuguese vessels, and even a small assembly of boats moored at the pier, including a traditional wooden *lorcha* – used for chasing pirate ships – and a dragon-racing boat. The whole collection is made eminently accessible with the help of explanatory English-language notes and video displays.

Fortaleza de São Tiago da Barra

Keep on past the museum and Rua São Tiago da Barra – a quiet, cobbled street – leads down to the tip of the peninsula and what was once Macau's most important fortress, the **Fortaleza de São Tiago da Barra**. The fortress, finished in 1629, was designed to protect the entrance to the Porto Interior, a function it achieved by hiding two dozen cannons within its ten-metre-high walls. Over the centuries, it fell into disrepair along with all Macau's other forts, and was rescued in 1976 when it was converted into the hotel **Pousada de São Tiago** (see p.293); with the old battlements covered in fig trees and ferns it's one of the most romantic – and most expensive – places to stay in either Hong Kong or Macau. No one will mind if you walk in through the old brick-lined tunnel and up to the reasonably priced terrace bar, which makes a good venue for a drink overlooking the water.

Around the lakes

The *Pousada de São Tiago* sits at the edge of **Lago Sai Van**, the more westerly of the lakes formed by the enclosing of the southern peninsula's eastern side with a causeway. An expressway follows this around the outside edge of the lake to the unintentionally bleak **Porta do Entendimento** ("Gate of Understanding") erected in 1993, where three interlocking black marble fingers, 40m high, supposedly symbolize the "spirit of Macau". Past here, the road continues to the 338-metre-high **Macau Tower**, with an outside walkway at 216m (MOP$100) for views as far as Hong Kong's islands on a clear day. Alternatively, you can just make use of the **revolving restaurant**, a great place for an evening drink with night views of the city. You can get direct from here to the *Hotel Lisboa* or Jetfoil Terminal on bus #32.

Alternatively, instead of following the outside edge of Lago Sai Van, you can walk back to town from *Pousada de São Tiago* along **Avenida da Republica**, a quiet tree-lined esplanade whose modern and colonial-era houses look out over the lake. The road in turn develops, via Avenida do Bom Parto, into **Avenida da Praia Grande**, once a grand promenade and, in its lower reaches at least, retaining something of that feel, with a further string of trees and European-style mansions culminating in the graceful pink mid-nineteenth century **Palácio do Governo** ("Government House"), now stamped with the five gold-starred emblem of the People's Republic of China. Past here, you're immediately thrown back into the modern world as the road becomes a highway on the concrete shore of **Lagos de Nam Van**, the Nam Van Lakes, bisected by the main Ponte Governador Bobre de Carvalho. This is the best place to watch the huge **midnight fireworks display** on the first night of the Chinese New Year – conveniently held not to compete with Hong Kong's bigger pyrotechnics show, which is on the third night.

North to the border

The peninsula's northern end comprises a bland concoction of grey apartment blocks and main roads, though there are a couple of interesting traditional corners worth investigating in the area between Forteleza do Monte and the **Chinese border** with Zhuhai. It's definitely something to do on foot if you have time; otherwise catch buses as mentioned below.

To the Three Lamps District and the Red Market

From Forteleza do Monte, **Estrada do Repouso** runs north between an initially unexciting stretch of ordinary apartment blocks. After ten minutes, however, look for the low-set walls of the large **Lin Kai Temple** on the left down Travessa da Corda; inside is a maze of small halls dedicated to the Heavenly Mother, Kam Fa (attended by eighteen handmaidens covered in children) and a host of male deities. The temple is old, shabby and in need of a little attention, but it oozes character and there's a small bric-a-brac **night market** outside on the weekends. Just a few doors up on Estrada do Repouso, the little green and white Art Deco **Cinema Alegria** still has all its original fittings, making it an atmospheric place to catch the latest Hollywood or Chinese blockbuster in Cantonese. What looks like another temple entrance next door is in fact a community **teahouse**, a tiny courtyard with pot plants and concrete tables populated by pensioners gossiping over mugs of *Liptons*; you can join in for MOP$5 a cup. Buses #8, #8A and #26 stop nearby.

Backtrack to the Lin Kai Temple, then take any of the streets opposite northeast through an area of open-fronted workshops and all manner of small industries, including those brewing Chinese spirits. After a few minutes you should be at the blue-tiled **Rotunda de Carlos da Maia**, a roundabout marking the centre of the pedestrianized **Three Lamps District** or Sam Jan Dang. The streets immediately north of here are packed with busy **market stalls** selling clothes, shoes, bedding, fabrics, fresh fruit and vegetables and dried goods. Hidden among it is another temple, the bizarre **Cheoc Lam Temple**, all walled with green tiles, planted with bamboo and again divided into a host of ancestral halls and shrines to an impartial mix of Buddhist and Taoist saints.

There's more activity just north again inside the **Red Market**, another Art Deco building at the intersection of Avenida de Horta e Costa and Avenida do Almirante Lacerda. Designed in 1936 by local architect Jio Alberto Basto, it houses a produce market full of slabs of meat and frozen seafood along with live chickens, pigeons, ducks, fish, frogs and turtles, all waiting to be carted off for dinner. Heaps of buses, including the #3, #5 and #9A pass by en route to the border.

Kun Iam Temple

A few blocks east of the Red Market on Avenida do Coronel Mesquita, the **Kun Iam Temple** (daily 7am–6pm; free) is dedicated to the Buddhist goddess of Mercy, Kun Iam (also known as Kwun Yum or Guan Yin). The complex dates back around four hundred years and is of the usual heavy stone courtyard design, the rooflines decked with elaborate and colourful porcelain tiles depicting folk tales and historical scenes. Inside the third hall are statues of Kun Iam herself, dressed in Chinese bridal robes and pearls, surrounded by eighteen **Boddhisatvas** (of which Kun Iam was also one), those who had attained the right to enter paradise but chose to stay on earth to help humanity. There's no sign, however, of the temple's historical significance – this is where the first ever **US–China treaty** was signed on July 3, 1844, by Viceroy Tai Yeng and the US Commissioner Caleb Cushing. Among other things this allowed Americans to buy land in China and conduct business at designated cities known as "Treaty Ports", in return for banning the opium trade. Directly opposite the temple are a handful of **vegetarian restaurants**, including *Macau Vegetarian Farm* (see p.299). Bus #17 stops outside.

Lin Fong Temple and Museu Lin Zexu

From the Red Market, it's a ten-minute walk north up Avenida do Almirante Lacerda, past Asia's only **canidrome** (dog track; see p.307) to the **Lin Fong Temple** (daily 7am–6pm; free). This is a splendid affair, established in 1592 to provide accommodation for travelling officials, full of gaudy woodwork painted gold and red, coloured wall mouldings of fantastic beasts and very fine stone carvings depicting moral operatic scenes above the entrances. The temple is dedicated to **Kwan Tai**, a loyal general during the turbulent Three Kingdoms period (around 184–280 AD), who chose to be executed rather than betray his oath brothers, the warlords Liu Bei and Zhang Fei (who are also represented in the temple). Check out the right hall, where a statue of a **horse** is a memorial to Kwan Tai's steed **Red Hare**, who pined away and died after his master's execution – people often place vegetables in the statue's mouth.

Off the temple's forecourt, **Museu Lin Zexu** (Tues–Sun 9am–5pm; MOP$5) commemorates another upstanding official, **Lin Zexu** (or Lam Kung), who tried to stamp out the nineteenth-century opium trade by destroying British supplies of the drug (see Contexts, p.313), only to be blamed for precipitating the first Opium War and exiled to China's northwest. The museum displays an overtly staid collection of documents and period artefacts, though read some of the translations and you'll find some astounding facts. The account books for 1830–39, for instance, show that the opium trade cost the Chinese treasury between seven and eight million silver pieces annually, amply illustrating why the Chinese court was keen to stop the trade – and why British traders and local Chinese merchants wanted to keep it going.

The border

Bus #5 from Lin Fong Temple runs the final kilometre to the border area, past an escalation of shops and backstreet **markets** selling all the things you might have forgotten to buy – or never even realized were for sale – during your stay. There's also a lot of contraband on show, having slipped over from the cheaper side of the border. The only historical monument of any sort is the old stone archway of the **Portas do Cerco** ("Siege Gate", though referred to in English as the Barrier Gate), which has stood in this spot, more or less, since 1849, though now made obsolete by the huge modern **border terminal** behind. There's not really any reason to be here unless you're **crossing into China** at Zhuhai, in which case – assuming you already have your visa (see p.30) – just follow the crowds into the terminal. If you're just arriving, join the similar hordes streaming south to waiting taxis and casino buses (the public bus station is underground).

Taipa

In the eighteenth century the island of **TAIPA** (*Tam Zai* in Cantonese) – just to the south of the Macau peninsula – was actually three adjacent islands, whose sheltered harbour was an important anchorage for trading ships unloading their China-bound cargo at the mouth of the Pearl River. Silting of the channels between the islands eventually caused them to merge, providing valuable farming land. With the emergence of Hong Kong and the development of the Macau peninsula, Taipa was left to get on as best it could, and for decades it was a quiet, laid-back sort of place, with little industry – just a couple of fireworks factories – and not much to it. That all changed once it was decided to build the **airport** off the island's east coast in the 1990s, and Taipa's centre is now a busy network of roads lined with residential and office tower blocks. The original **Taipa village** still holds some dated charms – and a couple of good **restaurants** – though it's the **Cotai** strip to the south and its casinos which is drawing the crowds today.

Across the bridges: western Taipa

Three bridges link Macau to Taipa: from east to west these are the four-kilometre-long Ponte de Amizade ("Friendship Bridge"), between the Jetfoil Terminal and eastern Taipa (a route used by the airport bus #AP1); the 2.5-kilometre Ponte Governador Bobre de Carvalho (also known in English as the Macau–Taipa Bridge), used by the other Macau–Taipa–Coloane buses; and the Ponte Sai Van ("Sai Van Bridge"), from the southernmost tip of the peninsula to western Taipa.

Once over the central Ponte Governador Bobre de Carvalho, the first bus stop on the island is on a lozenge-shaped roundabout by a group of hotels. Uphill overlooking the water from here is the **University of Macau**, just down from which is a small **Kun Iam Temple**, with an image of the goddess of mercy in a pink-tiled altar, where food is offered on tiny red plastic saucers with matching chopsticks. Around 500m west from the roundabout, on Estrada Lou Lim Eoc, is the more interesting **Pou Tai Un Monastery** (daily 8am–9pm; free), the largest temple complex on the island and still expanding. The central part is the three-storey Buddhist Palace, whose ground floor is given over to Kun Iam and sports an unusual statue of the goddess with 42 hands; the middle floor houses reading and meditation rooms for the resident monks; while on the top floor there's a 5.4-metre-high bronze Buddha. There's also a **vegetarian restaurant** open at lunchtime.

The next bus stop is the **racecourse**, operated by the Macau Jockey Club set in an otherwise drab and lifeless part of town. The season runs from September

---

Buses from Macau to Taipa and Coloane

For Taipa village, take bus #11 or #26A from Avenida de Almeida Ribeiro near Largo do Senado; bus #28A from the Jetfoil Terminal; or buses #22 or #33 from the *Hotel Lisboa*. All these drop off at a stop near the unmissable Taipa Stadium, just a short walk from the village. **For Coloane**, you need to catch bus #21 or #21A from the *Hotel Lisboa*; cutting straight across Taipa, these both travel down Coloane's west side to Coloane village, from where the #21A and #26 continue via Cheoc Van Beach through to Hác Sá Beach. If you're already at Taipa village, take bus #15, which runs around Coloane's east side via the *Westin Resort* and Hác Sá Beach, before terminating at Coloane village.

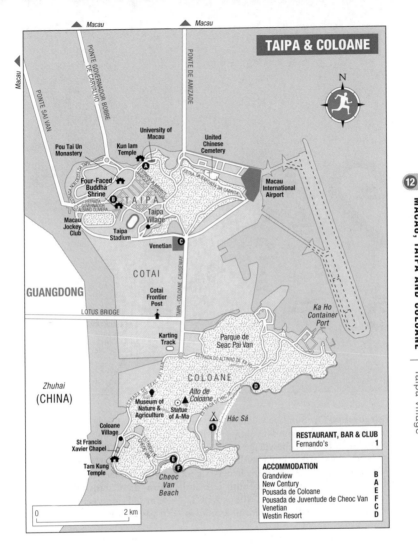

to the end of July and a satellite dish beams the racing to other Asian countries, giving Hong Kong a run for its money. The **Four-Faced Buddha Shrine** outside the stadium is meant to bring luck to the punters.

Taipa village

Taipa's main point of interest is old **TAIPA VILLAGE**, set on what would once have been the island's south coast but now overlooking the Cotai strip between Taipa and Coloane. The village is just a couple of lanes really, an isolated colonial fragment surrounded by ever-increasing modern development, but it's a good spot for an hour's wander, perhaps followed by a meal at one of the many nearby

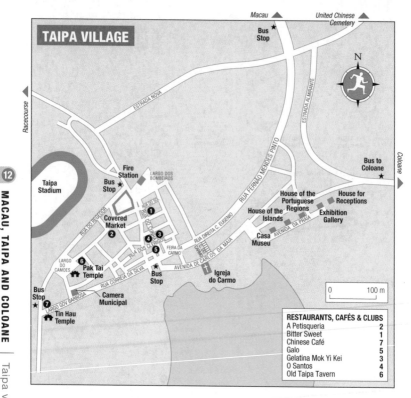

restaurants. On Sundays (11am–8pm) there's also a handicraft, souvenir and food market, while outdoor shows are held in the main square.

The main focus of the village is 150-metre-long Rua do Cunha, a narrow pedestrianized street lined with restaurants, *pastelarias*, and *Gelatina Mok Yi Kei*, whose menu of home-made desserts includes durian ice cream and fruit jellies. Rua do Cunha exits south into little Feira da Carmo, the village square at whose centre is the covered, colonnaded nineteenth-century marketplace, recently restored; all around are old pastel-coloured homes and more places to eat.

West off the end of Feira da Carmo it's 100m down Rua Correia da Silva, past the peppermint green Camera Municipal (Municipal Building), to the local Tin Hau Temple, a small grey-brick edifice whose doorway is lined with painted red paper. There's also a bus stop here, and a cheap Chinese-style café with outdoor tables dealing in noodle dishes, coffee and tea. In the lanes north of here, there's a large Pak Tai Temple dedicated to the eponymous water god. Inside, there's a carved altar whose figures are echoed in the impressive stone frieze above the entrance.

East from Feira da Carmo off Rua Diretta C. Eugeno, look for a flowing set of stairs lined with fig trees; at the top is the 100-year-old Igreja do Carmo ("Our Lady of Carmel Church"; daily except Tues 8am–5pm). East again on Avenida da Praia, are the five early twentieth-century mansions of Casa Museu ("Taipa House Museum"; Tues–Sun 10am–6pm; MOP$5, free Sunday), filled with period furnishings, costumed mannequins and exhibitions of photographs about the old days in what was once rural Macau. The terrace in front faces south over a tiny lagoon towards Cotai and the *Venetian* casino.

Cotai and the Venetian

South of Taipa village – reached on bus #15, #25, #26 and #26A – **Cotai** is a huge, flat expanse of **reclaimed land** joining Taipa to Coloane. Remarkably – given that it's traversed by a four-lane highway and dotted with huge construction projects – it was only laid down in 2004, before which Taipa and Coloane were separate islands. The area is targeted as a **casino strip**, though things have been on hold since gambling regulations and the financial crisis hit in 2008; even so, there's a direct border crossing from Zhuhai in China to attract mainland gamblers.

For now, Cotai's main sight is **the Venetian**, a full-sized re-creation of Venice's St Mark's Square, whose interior is an unabashed, surreal temple to Mammon: acres of upmarket shopping malls, restaurants and bars (including a *Moët & Chandon* champagne bar); a handful of **hotels**; a lobby covered in reproduction Italian murals; an inconceivably vast casino floor, approached down a magnificent staircase; its own **Cirque du Soleil** troupe; and even a canal through it all, flanked by artificial buildings under a fake sky, along which you can ride in a real gondola. Make sure you visit, but come prepared to be overwhelmed by the sheer audaciousness of the project which – despite the economic downturn – plans to expand still further.

Coloane

COLOANE island (*Lo Wan* in Cantonese) is around twice the size of Taipa, and was until the early twentieth century a base for pirates who hid out in the cliffs and caves, seizing the cargoes of trading ships passing between Macau and Guangzhou. Attractions here are low-key, but include a peaceful village with a mix of temples and colonial leftovers, along with a couple of good sand **beaches** for unwinding on – certainly the least crowded part of all Macau.

Parque de Seac Pai Van

On their way to southwestern Coloane village, buses pass the **Parque de Seac Pai Van** (Tues–Sun 9am–5.45pm; free), with gardens, ponds, pavilions, views out over the water, an aviary and the **Museum of Nature and Agriculture** (Tues–Sun 10am–4pm; free), whose most interesting feature is a display of medicinal herbs. Outdoors, you can clamber around some models of traditional farming equipment. Trails also provide good walking in the park, including one up to the heights of the **Alto de Coloane**, where the twenty-metre-high white marble statue of A-Ma is the tallest of this goddess in the world. To reach the statue, get off the bus at the Mobil petrol station and take the road marked Trilho do Coloane.

Coloane village

COLOANE VILLAGE comprises a little central square surrounded by shops and cafés; a small covered market stands to one side. Signs point off to the few local attractions down cobbled roads, chickens scratch around the potholes, and a ramshackle air hangs over the low-key Chinese houses, shrines and temples.

Right on the square you'll find three branches of *Lord Stow's Bakery* (see p.297), a must for all lovers of Portuguese custard tarts; otherwise, walk down to the bottom of the square and turn left along an alley of shops which winds around to the tiny, pale-yellow chapel of **St Francis Xavier** (dawn to dusk), set back a few metres from the waterfront. The chapel dates from 1928 and honours the eponymous sixteenth-century missionary who passed through Macau on his way to China and Japan. It reveals its Chinese influences with an unusual painting of Mary and Jesus depicted as a traditional Chinese goddess holding a plump oriental baby. Out front is **Largo Eduardo Marques**, facing China (look for the wind-farms on the hills opposite), with a couple of good restaurants hidden under the colonnades either side. By the waterfront, the **monument** with embedded cannons commemorates the repelling of the last pirate attack in Coloane, which took place on July 12–13, 1910.

Further along the waterfront (to the left), past the library, a **Kun Iam Temple** is set back among the houses, though the **Tam Kung Temple** at the end of the road is more interesting, facing China across the narrow channel. The prize piece here is a three-metre-long whalebone shaped into a dragon boat with oarsmen. There's a festival held here, with opera performances honouring Tam Kung, on the eighth day of the fourth lunar month (usually early May).

Heading the other way from the square, there's a very quiet lane of stone houses facing the waterfront, over which are built corrugated iron and wooden homes painted red, green and blue. Little shrines on the roadside are to Choi Shen, the god of wealth; there's a very Southeast Asian feel to the smell of dried fish, the clacking of mah jong tiles, and red good-luck posters stuck up on doorways. The road terminates 100m on at Largo do Cais, where there's a small police station and a jetty jutting out towards China, beside which a couple of shops sell dried and salted fish.

Beaches

Coloane's good **beaches** are all easily reached by **bus** – either the #21A, #25, #26A or #15 (which also continues past the beaches to the *Westin Resort*). Note, however, that swimming is not a good idea, as the water is contaminated by outflows from the heavily industrialized Pearl River Delta towns.

The closest sandy beach to the village is at **Cheoc Van**, just a couple of kilometres east. It's fairly well developed, featuring cafés, the *Pousada de Coloane* (see "Accommodation", p.294) and a swimming pool (daily 8am–9pm, Sun 8am–midnight; MOP$10). A few kilometres further east, however, **Hác Sá** is much the better choice. The grey-black sand beach (*hac sa* means "black sand") is very long and backed by a pine grove, with plenty of picnic places amid the trees, and a campsite. Around the bay, towards the *Westin Resort*, you can rent windsurfers and jet skis (MOP$250 for 30min), while if you don't fancy the sea or sands there's a **sports and recreation complex** behind the beach (Mon–Sat 8am–9pm, Sun 8am–midnight), where a dip in the Olympic-size pool costs MOP$15. On the sands there's a beach bar, as well as a couple of **restaurants** near the bus stop (including the popular *Fernando's*; see p.299), while at the northeastern end of the beach the upmarket *Westin Resort* complex and golf course sprawl across the headland. Just behind the recreation centre on Estrada de Hác Sá at the **Water Activities Centre** (daily 9am–6pm) you can hire paddle and rowing boats for a quick splash around the small Hác Sá Reservoir (MOP$20 for 20min). There's also a small outdoor café selling sandwiches, soft drinks and beer, and some pleasant walking trails that meander around the surrounding wooded hills.

Places

Barra	媽閣
Coloane	路環
Cotai	路氹城
Lago Sai Van	西灣湖
Lagos de Nam Van	南灣湖
Macau	澳門
Porto Exterior	外港
Porto Interior	內港
Taipa	氹仔
Zhuhai	珠海

Sights

A-Ma Temple	媽閣廟
Bao Kung Temple	包公廟
Casa de Lou Kau	盧家大屋
Casa Museu	龍環葡韻住宅式博物館
Cemitério Protestante	基督教墳場
Cemetério São Miguel	西洋墳場
Cheoc Lam Temple	竹林廟
Cheoc Van	竹灣
Coloane village	路環市區
Fisherman's Wharf	漁人碼頭
Fortaleza da Guia	東望洋炮台
Fortaleza de São Tiago da Barra	媽閣炮台
Fortaleza do Monte	大炮台
Guia Hill	東望洋山
Hác Sá beach	黑沙海灘
Hong Kung Temple	康公廟
Hotel Lisboa	葡京酒店
Igreja do Carmo	嘉模聖　母教堂
Jai-Alai Casino	回力球娛樂場
Jardim Lou Lim Ieoc	盧廉若公園
Jardim Luís de Camões	白鴿巢賈梅士公園
Kun Iam Statue and Ecumenical Centre	觀音像／佛教文化中心
Kun Iam Temple	觀音堂
Largo do Lilau	亞婆井前地
Largo do Senado	議事亭前地
Largo Tap Seac	塔石廣場
Leal Senado	議事亭
Lin Fong Temple	連峰廟
Lin Kai Temple	連溪廟
Macau Cultural Centre	澳門文化中心
Macau Tea Culture House	澳門茶文化館
Macau Tower	澳門觀光塔
Mandarin's House	鄭家大屋
Museu de Macau	澳門博物館
Museu Lin Zexu	林則徐紀館
Museu Maritimo	海事博物館
Na Cha Temple	哪吒廟
Pak Tai Temple	北帝廟
Palácio do Governo	政府總部
Parque de Seac Pai Van	石排灣郊野公園
Penha Chapel	主教山教堂
Portas do Cerco	關閘

Pou Tai Un Monastery	菩提禪院
Quartel dos Mouros	港局大樓
Racecourse	賽馬場
Red Market	紅街市
San Kai Vui Kun	三街會館
Santa Casa de Misericórdia	仁慈堂大摟
Santo Agostinho	聖澳斯定教堂
Santo Antonio	聖安多尼教堂
São Domingos	玫瑰堂
São Lourenço	聖老愣佐教堂
São Paulo	大三巴牌坊
Sé	大堂
St Francis Xavier Chapel	路環聖方濟各教堂
Sun Yat-sen Memorial House	國父紀念館
Taipa village	氹仔老城區
Tak Seng On pawnbroker museum	德成按文化館
Tam Kung Temple	譚公廟
Teatro Dom Pedro V	伯多祿五世劇院
Three Lamps District	三盞燈
Tin Hau Temple	天后古廟
Tourist Activity Centre	旅遊活動中心
University of Macau	澳門大學
Venetian	威尼斯人度假村
Water Activities Centre	水上活動中心

Streets

Avenida da Amizade	友誼大馬路
Avenida da Republica	民國大馬路
Avenida de Almeida Ribeiro	新馬路
Praia Grande	南灣大馬路
Rua Central	龍嵩正街
Rua da Felicidade	福隆新街
Rua das Estalagens	草堆街
Rua de Cinco de Outubro	十月初五街
Rua do Almirante Sergio	河邊新街
Rua do Cunha	宮也街
Rua Sul do Mercado de São Domingos	板樟堂街

Transport

Bus stop	巴士站
China Ferry terminal	蛇口碼頭
Jetfoil Terminal	港澳碼頭
Macau airport	澳門幾場

Macau
listings

Macau listings

13

Accommodation

T here's a huge number of places to stay in Macau, and you should always be able to find somewhere to stay outside of peak periods (such as Easter and during the Grand Prix). During major festivals such as Chinese New Year, hotels lose custom to Hong Kong's bright lights and might actually offer discounts.

Prices here are much better value than in Hong Kong – at the bottom end of the market you'll often be able to find a self-contained room for around the same price as a sweatbox in Kowloon. Note, however, that **weekend rates** are always around thirty percent higher than midweek. Prices below are for the **cheapest double in high season**, excluding the fifteen-percent tax added by top-end places.

Two things make **booking in advance** advisable: first, you'll generally get a discounted rate on mid- to upper-range hotel rooms this way; and weekends and public holidays are always busy with gamblers coming over from Hong Kong, when even the cheaper end of the market may be full. In Hong Kong, Beng Seng Travel are the Macau specialist, located at the Macau Ferry Terminal, Shun Tak Centre, Sheung Wan (see p.29). You can also try dealing directly with hotels and guesthouses themselves in Macau; many can be persuaded to drop their advertised rates a bit if you call in advance. If you've arrived without a booking, there are **courtesy phones** in the Jetfoil Terminal for the larger hotels.

Guesthouses and hotels

The bulk of Macau's **budget hotels** (called either a *vila*, *hospedaria* or *pensão*) lie around the **central peninsula** within easy walking distance of Largo do Senado – take buses #3, #3A or #10A from the Jetfoil Terminal. This is an atmospheric area, full of narrow lanes, cheap restaurants, and street markets, though the atmosphere can be a little sleazy too. Rooms – even within a single hotel – can vary between perfectly acceptable and dark, noisy, and grubby, so check a few out if the first one you're shown doesn't appeal. If you find yourself being waved away before you've even reached the reception, it's probably because none of the staff speak English and don't fancy the trouble of booking you in – you'll get around this if you can speak some Chinese (even Mandarin).

You'll have no such problems with **mid-range** and **top-of-the-range** places, especially midweek when there may be **discounts** of up to fifty percent available – always check websites for promotional deals. Most upmarket places operate airport shuttle buses, and often casino buses too. The biggest concentration is in **eastern Macau** between the Lagos de Nam Van and the Jetfoil Terminal, where many cater almost exclusively to mainland Chinese customers and have in-house casinos; there are also a few choices on the **southern peninsula** and the islands of **Taipa** and **Coloane**. Finally, there's a **free campsite** with toilets, payphone and barbecue area near the bus stop at Hác Sá beach in Coloane – see p.286.

East: Lagos Nam Van to the Jetfoil Terminal

The places listed below are marked on the map on pp.268–269.

Beverly Plaza Av. do Dr Rodrigo Rodrigues 70–106 ☎2878 2288, ⓦwww.beverlyplaza.com. Just a few doors down from the *Lisboa*, this China Travel Service-run hotel offers 300 good-sized but nondescript rooms, with all the usual facilities – bar a pool and casino. It has its own 24hr coffee shop and offers good midweek deals. MOP$1980

Guia Estrada do Eng. Trigo 1–5 ☎2851 3888, ⓕ2855 9822. A mid-range Chinese hotel with views (if your room's high enough), on the southern fringes of the Guia hill. Decently priced, though certainly not luxurious. MOP$650

🏃 **Lisboa** Av. de Lisboa 2–4 ☎2888 3888, ⓦwww.hotelisboa.com. A monstrous orange circular drum (with adjacent annexe) that has roughly 1000 rooms and a bundle of 24hr casinos, shops, bars and restaurants, outdoor pool and sauna – some people never set foot outside the front door. Cheaper rooms in the rear block don't have the same atmosphere as those at the front. MOP$2050

🏃 **Mandarin Oriental** Av. da Amizade ☎2856 7888, ⓦwww.mandarinoriental.com /macau. Outstanding comforts in a resort tailor-made for families (children's club, poolside restaurant), corporate groups (a team-building climbing wall and trapeze) and the more traditional Macau tourist (casino, popular bar). Guests are pampered with a staff to room ratio of 1:1, and a renowned spa. Although close to the jetfoil it's a fair distance to walk to the old part of town. MOP$3500

Metropark Rua de Pequim 199 ☎2878 1233, ⓦwww.hotelgrandeur.com. Another China Travel Service-run business hotel with a revolving restaurant, sauna, pool, gym and coffee shop, if no panache. At least a fifty-percent discount for booking online. MOP$1700

Metropole Av. da Praia Grande 493–501 ☎2838 8166, ⓦwww.mctshmi.com. This well-placed, central hotel is just back from the Praia Grande, and good value if you're looking for rooms with all the trimmings at a lowish cost. It also has a fast food centre, serving *dim sum*, roast meats and *congee* 8am–10.30pm. MOP$960

Presidente Av. da Amizade ☎2855 3888, ⓦwww.hotelpresident.com.mo. This ageing tower caters mostly to a business clientele, and is perfectly serviceable if not exactly plush. MOP$1050

Royal Estrada da Vitoria 2–4 ☎2855 2222, ⓦwww.hotelroyal.com.mo. Smart, efficiently run high-rise, close to the Fortaleza da Guia and a 10min walk from Largo do Senado. Facilities include a pool and a slew of Macanese, Portuguese and Chinese restaurants. MOP$2000

Sands Largo do Monte Carlo 23 (Av. da Amizade) ☎2888 3388, ⓦwww.sands.com.mo. The city's first foreign-owned casino offers a choice of luxury suites overlooking the city or the bay. MOP$3500

Wynn Rua Cidade da Sintra ☎2888 9966, ⓦwww.mynnmacau.com. Macau's most stylish upmarket casino-resort, and one of the few which balances opulence with taste. MOP$3000

The Centre

The places listed below are marked on the map on pp.268–269.

🏃 **Augusters Lodge** Rua do Dr Pedro José Lobo 24 ☎2871 3242, ⓦwww .augusters.de. Don't be put off by the dingy stairwell on the way up to the third-floor reception; this place is elderly and basic but well geared to foreign travellers, with the only dorm beds in the town centre. Dorms MOP$112, doubles MOP$256

Central Av. de Almeida Ribeiro 264–270 ☎2837 3888. Opened in 1928 it is now overdue for a facelift; the best thing to say about this noisy, indifferent place is that it has hundreds of rooms in all sorts of permutations – singles, doubles, with/

without bathrooms or a/c – and the location next to Largo do Senado couldn't be more convenient. MOP$180, or MOP$300 for en suite.

East Asia Rua da Madeira 1 ☎2892 2433. In the heart of old Macau, off Rua de Cinco de Outubro, this 1950s building has distinctive green and white, angular exterior, with balconies which now only face the blank walls of surrounding buildings. Inside there's a strangely tired, vacant atmosphere, though the rooms are tidy and reasonable value for money. MOP$340

Florida Beco Do Pa Ralelo 2 ☎2892 3198, ☏2892 3199. Decidedly seedy, with the lobby packed with mainland prostitutes every night, but the rooms are large and clean. MOP$300

Hou Kong Travessa das Virtudes 1 ☎2893 7555, ☏2833 8884. This basic 1950s hotel has plain but bright and clean, well-equipped rooms with attached bathrooms, some quite spacious. MOP$300

Ka Va Calçada de São João 5 ☎2832 3063 or 2832 9355. Good budget choice on lane running from the Sé to the upper end of Av. Praia Grande, with 28 plain rooms with wooden shutters, en-suite bathroom, a/c and TV. Rear rooms are preferable to streetside ones, which can be noisy; a few also prone to damp. MOP$200

🏃 **Ko Wah Floor 3 Rua da Felicidade 71,** ☎2893 0755 or 2837 5599. Low-end hotel accessed by lift from the cupboard-sized street lobby. There's a mix of recently renovated, larger rooms with modern furnishings, and older – but still perfectly presentable – doubles. All are en suite but some are windowless, so check first. Cheaper rooms are a good deal. MOP$300–500

🏃 **Man Va Rua da Felicidade** ☎2838 8655, ☏2834 2179. Well-run budget hotel with clean, modern rooms; the bathrooms are spacious and the management helpful, though they don't speak English. Excellent value for money, and usually booked out. MOP$300

🏃 **Ole London Praça Ponte e Horta 4–6** ☎2893 7761, ☏2893 7790. Smart little boutique hotel with modern rooms and ADSL available. Cheapest rooms are windowless; best pay a little extra for one looking onto the square outside. MOP$400

🏃 **San Va Rua da Felicidade 67** ☎8210 0193, ⊛www.sanvahotel.com. Genuine old guesthouse complete with painted wooden panelling, hard beds and ceiling fans, all spotlessly maintained and well cared for. Some rooms have balconies. Basic furnishings and only shared bathrooms, but the most characterful budget deal in Macau. MOP$160

Sun Sun Praça Ponte e Horta 14–16 ☎2893 9393, ⊛www.bestwestern.com. Part of an international motel chain, this smart, low-key business hotel has inoffensively furnished rooms with TV and bath, and plenty of marble and wood in the lobby. Bus #3A from the ferry terminal stops just outside. MOP$950

Tin Tin Vila Rua Do Comandante Mate E Oliveira 17 ☎2871 0064. A few doors down from the *Café Nata*, this small guesthouse offers cell-like but fairly clean, airy rooms with firm beds, some with their own bathroom and some with shared facilities. Cheap and well positioned, but no English spoken. A/c use costs an extra MOP$10 per night. MOP$200

Vila Nam Loon Rua do Dr Pedro José Lobo 30 ☎2871 2573. Very clean and bright budget hotel; rooms have attached bathrooms but are so small that the beds almost fill them. MOP$280

Vila Universal Rua Felicidade 73 ☎2857 3247 or 6684 8197. Clean, basic rooms in this elderly guesthouse, priced according to size. Management can be a bit brusque. MOP$150–190

Southern peninsula

The places listed below are marked on the map on p.276.

🏃 **Pousada de São Tiago Av. da República** ☎2837 8111, ⊛www.saotiago.com.mo. A gloriously preserved seventeenth-century fortress converted into an upmarket hotel complete with swimming pool and terrace bar – see p.279 for more. Unmatched in terms of location, ambiance, service and – unfortunately – cost. MOP$6800

Riviera Rua do Comendador Kou Ho Neng, Penha Hill ☎2833 9955, ⊛www .mctshmi.com. Rather glitzy for a CTS-managed hotel, this 163-room block has superb views from the terrace and some rooms, plus an indoor pool, billiards room, jacuzzi and mini-golf among other amenities. Usually has rooms at short notice. MOP$1800

Taipa

The places listed below are marked on the map on p.283.

Grandview Estrada Governador Albano de Oliveira ⊤837788, ⊛www.grandview-hotel .com. Diagonally across from the Jockey Club and Buddha statue, the only real downside of this otherwise excellent business hotel is a location in a soulless part of town, though it perks up on race days. MOP$950

New Century Av. Padre Tomás Pereira 889 ⊤2883 1111, ⊛www.newcenturyhotel-macau .com. Enormous five-star hotel with good views from rooms; also offers serviced apartments for longer stays. MOP$1850

Venetian Estrada da Baía de N. Senhora da Esperança, Cotai Strip ⊤2882 8877, ⊛www .venetianmacao.com. Definitely the most surreal, ludicrous place to stay in Macau, but certainly offers a superb level of service and facilities – see p.285 for more. Check the website for package deals, which can include substantial discounts on room plus tickets for Cirque du Soleil or pop concert performances. MOP$2000

Coloane

The places listed below are marked on the map on p.283.

Pousada de Coloane Praia de Cheoc Van ⊤2888 2143, ⊛www.hotelpcoloane.com .mo. An elegant, if quirky hotel with 22 rooms, each with their own terrace overlooking the beach tucked into Cheoc Van bay. The rooms on the top floor are enormous with sofa, table and king-sized bed. It's a bit remote as, apart from its own Portuguese restaurant and a stretch of sand, there's not much else here. Taxi (MOP$100) or buses #21A, #26A and #25 from Macau stop outside. MOP$750

Pousada de Juventude de Cheoc Van Cheoc Van ⊤2855 5533, ⊛www.dsej .gov.mo. Small hostel overlooking the sea, run by the Macau Education & Youth Affairs Bureau; IYHA card holders can stay here, but you need to book in advance through the website. Bring your own food for the large kitchen and barbecue area. It's functional rather than flash – dorms and doubles all have shared facilities – but you can't complain about the price. Catch buses #21A, #26A or #25 from Macau. Dorms MOP$30 per person, doubles MOP$100.

Westin Resort Estrada de Hác Sá ⊤2887 1111, ⊛www.westin.com/macau. The *Westin* lies at the far end of *Hác Sá's* narrow beach – a swathe of terraced rooms spread across the hillside. Midweek it's the terrain of corporate groups and fairly quiet, and at the weekend it fills up with Hong Kong families. The hotel offers Macau's only eighteen-hole golf course, two pools and a Jacuzzi. All the modern, spacious rooms have up-to-date technology, comfortable beds, a terrace and beach or sea views. You're a little stranded once the sun goes down, though *Fernando's* (see p.299) is just a 15min walk along the beach and the hotel has three restaurants. MOP$1500

14

Eating and drinking

Although most of the **food** eaten in Macau is Cantonese, the enclave also enjoys a unique **Macanese cuisine** – a blend of influences from China, Portugal and Portuguese colonies from Brazil to Goa. Sometimes this manifests itself as straightforward imported dishes, such as Portuguese *caldo verde* (cabbage and potato soup), *bacalhau* (dried salted cod), *pudim flán* (crème caramel), or grilled steak, sausages, chicken, or sardines; African-influenced spicy prawns and "African Chicken" (served in a peppery peanut sauce); or *feijoada* from Brazil, an elaborate meal made from meat, beans, sausage and vegetables. However, many cooks cross-fertilize these influences with **Cantonese** ingredients and dishes, creating pigeon, quail, duck and seafood dishes that are ostensibly "Chinese" but unlike anything you'll find elsewhere.

Other Portuguese culinary influences can be seen in the freshly baked **bread** served with meals, and **Portuguese wine** to wash it all down – fine, heavy reds, chilled whites and slightly sparkling *vinho verde*, as well as any number of **ports** and brandies; and you can get decent **coffee** too. In most places, the **menu** is in Portuguese and English as well as Chinese; check the lists overleaf for descriptions of food you don't recognize.

Vegetarians should do well for themselves. Every Portuguese restaurant serves excellent mixed salads; and most places will fry eggs and serve them up with some of the best French fries around. In addition, there are a few Chinese vegetarian eateries in town, too.

Macau also has a reputation for **cakes**, the most famous of which are Portuguese-style **custard tarts**, or *natas*, a light pastry cup filled with set baked custard and then briefly grilled to darken the top. There are also numerous **biscuit shops** – *pastelarias* – in the centre of town on Rua da Felicidade and around São Paulo; you'll find them by the crowds of Hong Kongers busy filling up on presents. Their best products are peanut or sesame toffee, and almond biscuits baked in a mould, but they also sell savouries such as bright red pressed sheets of baked pork.

▲ Grilled sardines and Portuguese wine

Basics and snacks

Arroz – Rice
Batatas fritas – French fries
Legumes – Vegetables
Manteiga – Butter
Omeleta – Omelette
Ovos – Eggs
Pimenta – Pepper
Prego – Steak roll
Sal – Salt
Salada mista – Mixed salad
Sandes – Sandwiches

Meat

Almondegas – Meatballs
Bife – Steak
Chouriço – Spicy sausage
Coelho – Rabbit
Cordoniz – Quail
Costeleta – Chop, cutlet
Dobrada – Tripe
Figado – Liver
Galinha – Chicken
Pombo – Pigeon
Porco – Pork
Salsicha – Sausage

Fish and seafood

Ameijoas – Clams
Bacalhau – Dried, salted cod
Camarões – Shrimp
Carangueijo – Crab
Gambas – Prawns
Linguado – Sole
Lulas – Squid
Meixilhões – Mussels
Pescada – Hake
Sardinhas – Sardines

Soups

Caldo verde – Green cabbage and potato soup, often served with spicy sausage
Sopa álentejana – Garlic and bread soup with a poached egg
Sopa de mariscos – Shellfish soup
Sopa de peixe – Fish soup

Cooking terms

Assado – Roasted
Cozido – Boiled, stewed
Frito – Fried
Grelhado – Grilled
No forno – Baked

Specialities

Arroz doce – Portuguese rice pudding
Camarões – Huge grilled prawns with chillies and peppers
Cataplana – Pressure-cooked seafood with bacon, sausage and peppers (named after the dish in which it's cooked)
Cozido á Portuguesa – Boiled casserole of mixed meats (including things like pig's trotters), rice and vegetables
Feijoada – Rich Brazilian stew of beans, pork, sausage and vegetables
Galinha á Africana (African chicken) – Chicken baked or grilled with peppers and chillies; either "dry", with spices baked in, or with a thick, spicy sauce made from crushed peanuts.
Galinha á Portuguesa – Chicken baked with eggs, potatoes, onion and saffron in a mild, creamy curry sauce
Pasteis de bacalhau – Cod fishcakes, deep-fried
Porco á álentejana – Pork and clams in a stew
Pudim flán – Crème caramel

Drinks

Água mineral – Mineral water
Café – Coffee
Cerveja – Beer
Chá – Tea
Sumo de laranja – Orange juice
Vinho – Wine (*tinto*, red; *branco*, white)
Vinho do Porto – Port (both red and white)
Vinho verde – Green wine, ie a young wine, slightly sparkling and very refreshing. It can be white, red or rosé in Portugal but in Macau it's usually white

Meals

Almoço – Lunch
Comidas – Meals
Jantar – Dinner
Prato dia/Menu do dia – Dish/menu of the day

14

EATING AND DRINKING

Finally, if you're after an **ice cream** on a hot day, there's only one serious choice: the Italian-style *Lemon Cello* on Travessa São Domingos (just off Largo do Senado), where a cone of peach, vanilla, tiramisù or mango sorbet will set you back MOP$15.

Though, thanks to the casinos, you can get fed around the clock in hotel cafés, **restaurant opening hours** are around 11am–3pm and 6–10pm. Unlike in Hong Kong, cheaper places rarely have English **menus**. In terms of **price**, a soup or salad plus a main course, with half a bottle of wine and coffee, comes to around MOP$250 almost everywhere. Dessert and a glass of port adds another MOP$70. Eating Macanese specialities – especially seafood – pushes the price up quite a bit. Look out for little **extra charges** levied by some devious places for bread, butter and water all brought to your table as if they were part of the meal, which can add up to a surprising amount. Also keep your eyes peeled for restaurants offering good-value **set meals** at lunchtime – usually only Monday to Friday – where you get a main course, soup and coffee for around MOP$100 or less. A fifteen-percent service charge is usually added to the bill except in the cheapest places. Be warned that many restaurants, bars and cafés **don't take credit cards**.

Cafés

You'll find small **cafés** all over Macau, many serving a mixture of local Cantonese food and Portuguese-style snacks – expect to pay around MOP$50 a head for coffee and a cake. Some are known as *Casa de Pasto*, a traditional Portuguese workers' dining room, though in Macau they're usually Chinese in cuisine and atmosphere. For late-night meals and snacks, many hotels have **24-hour coffee shops**, serving bleary-eyed gamblers.

Bitter Sweet Rua do Cunha, Taipa Village. See map, p.284. Café-restaurant specializing in desserts – *serradura*, herbal ice creams and tiramisù. Their set lunches are a fine deal at MOP$60 – plus MOP$15 for coffee – but even mains are good value as one portion is enough for two people. Daily noon–10pm.

Café Girassol Mandarin Oriental, Av. de Amizade. See map, pp.268–269. High-quality café with lots of choice on the menu, as well as a buffet on most days. Open 24hr, except on Thursday, when it closes at midnight.

Caravel Av. Dom João IV. See map, pp.268–269. Down an alley near the *Grand Lisboa*, this smart place serves top coffee, cakes and light meals through the day, and is very popular with Portuguese expats – expect to be glared at by whichever regular customer usually sits in the seat you've taken.

Lord Stow's Bakery Coloane Town Square, Coloane. Although British-owned, this is one of the best places to eat *natas*. The recipe is originally Portuguese, but this bakery claims to use a secret,

improved version without animal fat. Buy takeaways from the bakery itself, or sit down for coffee and a light meal at their two nearby cafés. Daily 7am–5pm.

Margeret's Café e Nata Rua Comandante Mata e Oliveira. See map, pp.268–269. On a small alley between Av. Dom João IV and Rua P.J. Lobo, just northwest of the *Lisboa*, this Macau institution has street-side benches for munching inexpensive chunky sandwiches, baguettes, home-baked quiches, muffins and some of the best *natas* in town. Also a whole range of iced teas, coffees and fruit juices. Mon–Sat 6.30am–8pm, Sun 10am–7pm.

Noite e Dia Hotel Lisboa, Av. de Lisboa 2–4. See map, pp.268–269. The *Lisboa's* splendid 24hr coffee shop, serving everything from *dim sum* and breakfast to snacks and meals.

Ou Mun Travessa de S. Domingos 12. See map, pp.268–269. Café-restaurant with excellent coffee, croissants and toasted sandwiches; also good light meals at lunchtime. Tues–Sun 9am–8pm.

Restaurants

The listings below concentrate on the enclave's excellent Portuguese and Macanese restaurants, but there are also many good Chinese places around. For other cuisines, you're best off heading to one of the large hotels. Inexpensive wine can be bought in all Macau's restaurants, Portuguese or not.

Macanese and Portuguese

Unless otherwise stated, all the places below are marked on the map on pp.268–269.

Alfonso III Rua Central 11A ☏2858 6272. Split-level café-restaurant specializing in Portuguese food. Provincial dishes feature, like a mammoth, oily serving of Álentejo pork with clams, drenched in fresh coriander. Check the daily list of specials to see what the mainly Portuguese clientele is eating; expect to pay MOP$85–150 per dish. Mon–Sat noon–3pm & 6.30–10.30pm.

A Lorcha Rua do Almirante Sergio 289 ☏2831 3193. **See map, p.276.** Near the Maritime Museum, this attractive wood-beamed restaurant serves outstanding, moderately priced Portuguese food, and is consequently always busy – it's best to reserve in advance for lunch when the Portuguese business community is out in force. There's a large menu of staples, including *serradura,* a spectacular cream and biscuit dessert. 12.30–3.30pm & 6.30–11pm; closed Tues.

Boa Mesa Travessa do S. Domingos 16A, between the Sé and Largo do Senado ☏2838 9453. A relaxed, friendly place that specializes in "black pork" dishes from farm-bred pigs. Excellent-value lunchtime specials at MOP$80, but even à la carte it's not too expensive – a plate of sardines and salad, a jug of house red and *serradura* with coffee shouldn't top MOP$200.

Clube Militar Av. da Praia Grande 975 ☏2871 4000. This private club within the São Francisco barracks has a dining room open to the public and offers an elegant colonial experience with formal staff and sparkling silver service. The Portuguese food is competent and expensive (mains from MOP$170), but the set-price lunchtime buffet – with a choice of soups, starters, mains and desserts – is ridiculously good value for what you get at MOP$120 a head. Alternatively, go for afternoon tea or a drink

– they have a large selection of ports. There's a "no sportswear" dress code. Daily noon–3pm & 7–11pm.

Escada Rua da Sé 6–8 (on the steps beside the Post Office) ☏2896 6900. Smart little place that draws an unusual number of Japanese tourists and offers lunchtime specials of soup and a main course for MOP$65. Otherwise a bit pricier than usual, but the food is good – best for stewed cod (MOP$138), baked duck rice (MOP$95) and beer-stewed pork hock (MOP$128).

Fat Siu Lau Rua da Felicidade 64 ☏9857 3585. One of Macau's oldest and most famous restaurants, with pigeon the speciality, best eaten with their excellent French fries. Relaxed atmosphere, but – pigeon apart – not the best food in Macau for the price. Around MOP$90 for mains. Daily 11am–midnight.

Henri's Galley Av. da República 4 ☏2855 6251. Unexciting decor, but try for an indoor window seat, or pavement table with waterfront view. They do very good spicy prawns, roast pigeon, curried crab and African chicken, but tend to be irritatingly familiar and charge you extra for everything they bring to the table, probably even the salt and napkins. Daily 11am–11pm.

Litoral Rua do Almirante Sergio 261 ☏2896 7878. **See map, p.276.** Rated by some as serving the best Portuguese and Macanese food in Macau, with a menu based on old family recipes including curried crab, stewed pork with shrimp paste and stuffed jumbo prawns. You'll need to book. Daily noon–3pm and 5.30–10.30pm. Mains from MOP$100.

O Porto Interior Rua do Almirante Sergio 259 ☏2896 7770. **See map, p.276.** Like the nearby *A Lorcha* and *Litoral,* this smart, relaxed place excels in mid-priced Portuguese and Macanese fare, served amid a mix of Chinese wooden screens and terracotta tiling. Wed–Mon noon–3pm & 7–11.30pm.

Platão Travessa do S. Domingos 3 ☏2833 1818. Set back in a street running between the Sé and Largo do Senado, this lively, pricey restaurant boasts a great sit-out courtyard in front, perfect for a beer. The menu is colonial Portuguese and includes cod soufflé, baked duck rice, and – with advance warning – suckling pig. Mains MOP$150–300. Tues–Sun noon–11pm.

Praia Grande Praça Lobo d'Avila 10, Av. da Praia Grande ☎2897 3022. One of Macau's best Portuguese restaurants, whose upstairs rooms have a good harbour view. The staff are pleasant and the food is excellent, featuring pan-fried clams in white wine sauce, baked onion soup and grilled codfish. Mains MOP$65 plus. Daily noon–11pm.

Riquexo Av. de Sidónio Pais 69. Self-service canteen with absolutely no frills, but the half-dozen offerings of Portuguese dishes such as *bacalhau*, *feijoada*, curry and fried rice from MOP$35 are tasty and filling, and it's a popular place at lunchtime with local office workers. Daily noon–10pm.

Vela Latina Av. Almeida Ribeiro 201 ☎2835 6888. Comfortable Macanese–Portuguese restaurant with views of Largo do Senado. Specialities include African Chicken and Cream of Cod, served inside a hollowed-out loaf of bread. Around MOP$300 for three courses with wine. Daily noon–3pm and 6.30–10pm.

Taipa Village

All the restaurants below are marked on the map on p.284.

Galo Rua do Cunha 45 ☎2882 7423. Decorated in Portuguese country style with the cock (*galo*) – the national emblem of Portugal – much in evidence. The photographic menu sports plenty of boiled meats and pig's trotters, but mainstream dishes include steaks, great grilled squid or crab, and large mixed salads; around MOP$80 a serving. Mon–Fri 10.30am–3.30pm & 5.30–10.30pm, Sat & Sun 10.30am–10.30pm.

A Petisqueira Rua de S. João 15 ☎2882 5354. With its relaxing green interior, this friendly, well-regarded Portuguese restaurant has all the usual favourites including their popular fresh cheese and whole grilled sea bass (the latter MOP$90). Mon–Fri noon–2.15pm & 7pm–10pm, Sat & Sun 12.30–2.30pm and 7–10pm.

O Santos Rua do Cunha ☎2882 7508. Huge helpings of seafood rice, pork and bean stew, rabbit, roast suckling pig and other Portuguese mainstays from MOP$85.

Coloane

Espaço Lisboa Off the main village square at Rua das Gaivotas 8 ☎2888 2226. Welcoming and deservedly popular two-storey restaurant with excellent daily specials and affordable prices – try their flambéed Portuguese sausage. Mon–Fri noon–3pm & 6.30–10pm, Sat & Sun noon–11.30pm. Bookings essential.

Fernando's Hác Sá Beach 9 ☎2888 2531. The sign is hidden, but this restaurant is very close to the bus stop, at the end of the car park, the nearest to the sea in a small line of cafés. There's a huge barn-like dining room; clams and crab are house specials, the grilled chicken is enormous and succulent. It's an institution with local expats, who fill it on Sundays with their large lunch parties. Slightly pricier than average. Daily noon–10.30pm.

Nga Tim Café Largo Eduardo Marques, in front of the Xavier Chapel, Coloane Village. A nice place to sit outside on a warm evening and enjoy a glass of Portuguese wine with hearty Macanese and Portuguese food – stewed rabbit, char-grilled prawns, baked crab, salt cod and potatoes, sardines and more. You can also pick from the Chinese seafood menu from the restaurant just behind it, *Chan Chi Mei*, which is run by the same owner. Daily noon–1am.

Chinese

Fook Lam Mun Av. Dr Mario Soares 259 ☎2878 6622. See map, pp.268–269. Next to the *President hotel*, this is the place to come for Cantonese seafood specialities. High prices (although more affordable in the morning and at lunchtime for *dim sum*) but considered one of the best in town. Mon–Fri 11am–3pm & 5.30–11pm, Sat & Sun 8.30am–3pm & 5.30–11pm.

Little Sheep Av. do Ouvidor Arriaga 59B ☎2852 6862. See map, pp.268–269. Popular Mongolian hotpot chain close to the Kun Iam Temple and Red Market, where you can stuff yourself from MOP$100 a head on thinly sliced lamb and vegetables which you cook for yourself at the table. Daily 11am–3pm and 5.30pm–late.

Macau Vegetarian Farm Av. do Cor. Mesquita 11 ☎2875 2824. See map, pp.268–269. No English sign, but it's the huge place opposite the Kun Iam Temple. Sophisticated Chinese food, which – despite dishes' appearances – is strictly vegetarian, with tofu, gluten and mushrooms prepared cunningly to resemble meat. The Chinese-only menu is illustrated with photographs, making ordering easy. Main dishes MOP$30–50, with set meals from MOP$60 a head. Daily 10am–3pm and 5.30–10pm.

Ma Kok Meng Ke Rua do Almirante Sergio 259. See map, p.276. Next to the *O Porto Interior* restaurant, this basic noodle house has no English sign or menu and serves simple one-dish Chinese meals for MOP$35 or less.

Nam Yun Rua Gamboa, near the Sun Sun hotel ☎2893 8288. **See map, p.276.** There's no English sign but you can't miss this place, just off Rua das Lorchas before an old stone archway. Daily *dim sum* sessions 7am–3pm, then reopens at 6pm as a hotpot restaurant. No English menu but staff are helpful.

Sei Go Sam Rua dos Mercadores 119, just off Av. Almeida Ribeiro. See map, pp.268–269. Northern Chinese light meals – steamed dumplings, dry-fried beans, mutton and spicy noodle soups – served in a cramped, fast-turnover interior. The food is tasty and portions are huge and cheap – with beer, two can fill to bursting for MOP$100. The small, black-and-red Chinese sign has a prominent "3" on the left.

Seong Hoi Cheong Seng Choi Kun Rua do Dr. Soares 1a, uphill and diagonally across from Largo do Senado ☎2832 3757. **See map, pp.268–269.** Main sign is in Chinese but for once the name is also spelled out below in tiny letters. A bright, popular place to eat tasty portions of Shanghai food – drunken chicken, five-spice beef shank, mushroom and bamboo shoots, crispy-fried duck – and you can watch them making classic *xiaolongbao* dumplings at the counter downstairs. Around MOP$75 a head.

Tou Tou Koi Travessa do Mastro 6, between Av. Almeida Ribeiro and Rua Felicidade. See map, pp.268–269. Good Cantonese food in a comfortable, noisy setting, popular for its roast meats, seafood and *dim sum*. There's a small English sign.

Other cuisines

Pizzeria Toscana Calçada da Barra 2A, opposite the Moorish Barracks ☎2872 6637. **See map, p.276.** A friendly, cheerful subterranean Italian restaurant with a deli, large selection of wines and desserts and, of course, pizza; count on MOP$100–150 a head for a thirty-centimetre-wide crust with wine and starters. Daily 11.30am–3.30pm and 6.30–11.30pm; closed first Tuesday of each month.

Drinking

Macau doesn't have the **bar scene** that there is in Hong Kong, and most drinking is done with meals. There are a few new bars in the chunk of reclaimed land south of Avenida de Amizade, known locally as Lan Kwai Fong, but these mainly cater to a Cantonese clientele, and tend to have deafening dance music, more deafening dice games and arctic air-conditioning. A few, such as the *Macau Jazz Club* are a bit more relaxing, with live music and alfresco seating, plus all the upmarket hotels have their own bars. Macau also lacks any good **nightclubs**, with the few there are tending to be sleazy joints packed with table dancers and call girls.

Most of Macau's **gay** community heads to Hong Kong for weekend nightlife, but in general gay couples shouldn't face any problem in any of Macau's bars.

Bars

Corners Travessa de São Paolo 3, just off the steps below São Paolo. Rooftop tapas bar with views across to São Paolo. Tapas from MOP$30, wine about MOP$200 a bottle. Daily 3pm–late, but you want to get there after dark when the cathedral facade is all lit up; happy hour Mon–Fri 3–8pm.

Embassy Bar Mandarin Oriental, Av. da Amizade. One of the better hotel bars and a regular expat haunt. Weekdays 5–9pm and weekends 11am–9pm there's big-screen sporting action. Happy hour 5–7pm.

Macau Jazz Club The Glasshouse, Macau Water-front. Very popular night spot on the harbourside near the Kun Iam statue. This small joint hosts regular jazz festivals: phone or check their website to see what's on. Live music every Friday and Saturday. Wed–Sun 6pm–2am. Cover charge MOP$180 for big events.

Moonwalker Av. Marginal da Baia Nova, Vista Magnifica Court. One of the better bars along the seafront, with outdoor seating, live music daily (except Tues) and some Mediterranean food. Daily noon–4am.

Old Taipa Tavern Rua de Negociantes 21, Taipa Village, near the Pak Tai Temple. Unexpected location for this popular expat sports/Irish bar, with beer on tap and pub lunches. Live band Friday and Saturday night.

Portas do Sol Wine Bar Hotel Lisboa. A brightly lit bar with a good selection of Portuguese wines by the glass. You can also enjoy the live Shanghai band (daily except Mon) playing swing and easy-listening numbers in the adjacent restaurant and join the dancing couples on the floor. Daily 11am–3am.

▲ Portuguese port

Buying your own food and wine

Apart from the market just off Largo do Senado on Rua do Mercado de São Domingos, where you can buy fruit and veg, there are branches of the **supermarket** Park N Shop at Av. Sidónio Pais 69 and Praça Ponte e Horta 11. Pavilions supermarket on Av. Praia Grande 417–425 (daily 10.30am–9.30pm) has a wine cellar with bottles for as little as MOP$30. There are also several markets and grocery stores selling snacks, fruit and wine on, and in the back lanes off, Avenida de Almeida Ribeiro, where a bottle of good port costs around MOP$75.

Casinos and other entertainment

Along with eating out, the main entertainment in Macau is **gambling** in various shapes and forms. Most people spend their evenings lurching between Macau's 29 **casinos**, and a couple of nights is all you need to get around the more interesting venues in which to lose your money – though in many cases, just people-watching is entertainment enough.

Cultural activities of any kind are thin on the ground, though a couple of annual music and arts festivals do their best to bridge the gap, along with the **Cultural Centre** (see p.275), which hosts regular international film, theatre and ballet performances, as well as free or inexpensive local productions and workshops.

Casinos

With few exceptions, Macau's **casinos** are noisy, frenetic places, nearly always packed, especially at the weekend, with a constant stream of people who leg it off the jetfoil and into the gaming rooms. In the old days – before 2006 – casinos

The games

There are an astounding number of **games** on offer in any of Macau's casinos. Many are familiar: you'll need no coaching to work the **one-armed bandits** or slot machines (called "hungry tigers" locally), which take either Hong Kong dollars or patacas (MOP$) and pay out accordingly. Many of the card games are also the ones you would expect, like **baccarat** and **blackjack**.

However, local variations and peculiarly **Chinese games** can make a casino trip more interesting. For more advice, ask at the tourist information centres where you can buy the A-O-A Macau Gambling Guide, which details all the games, rules and odds. **Boule** is like roulette but with a larger ball and fewer numbers (25) to bet on. **Pai kao** is Chinese dominoes and is utterly confusing for novices. **Fan tan** is easier to grasp, involving a cup being scooped through a pile of buttons which are then counted out in groups of four, bets being laid on how many are left at the end of the count – about as exciting as it sounds. In **dai-siu** ("big-small") you bet on the value of three dice, either having a small (3–9) or big (10–18) value – this is probably the easiest to pick up if you're new to the games. In all the games, the **minimum bet** is usually MOP$100 (MOP$200 on blackjack), though some of the games played in the VIP rooms have minimum bets of MOP$3000 or more.

provided little padding to the basic fact of being places to chance your life savings; but since the advent of foreign-owned ventures, there's a lot more over-the-top glitz around – just take a peek at the *Venetian, Sands* or *Wynn*.

Formerly, the vast majority of the **punters** were Hong Kong Chinese who flocked to Macau since there's no legal betting except horse racing in their own territory. Now, mainland Chinese account for seventy percent of casino customers, and an unforeseen embarrassment for the Chinese government was that mainland officials were caught gambling away billions of yuan of public funds during holidays in the SAR. This led to a **crackdown** on visas, which unfortunately coincided with the 2008 world economic meltdown and together caused Macau's five-year gambling boom to suddenly stall.

Given that the sole object of the casinos is to take money off ordinary people – amounting to US$500 million a year in Macau – there aren't the **dress restrictions** you might expect. **Cameras**, however, aren't allowed in any of the casinos; **passports** have to be shown at the door; and if you've got a bag you'll have to check it in, noting down the serial numbers of any valuable items on a pad provided.

Most of the casinos are located in a strip between the Jetfoil terminal and Avenida do Doutor Mario Soares. Each has its own character and variety of games; the following list is a pick of favourites. To get in, visitors officially need to be (or look) 18; there's no entry fee. All the casinos are open 24 hours a day.

Casino Fortuna Rua do Foshan. Known also as the Chinese Casino on account of the mainly Chinese card and dice games played here. Very popular and very intense.

Casino Jai-Alai Porto Exterior by the Jetfoil Terminal. One of the SAR's more down-market dens, with all-night table action in a stadium that used to host *jai-alai* games (a sort of high-speed Basque version of squash).

Grand Lisboa Av. da Amizade. Better on the outside than within, though the scale of the place is impressive and there are balconies for looking down on the gaming area.

Lisboa At the Hotel Lisboa, Av. da Amizade. A four-level extravaganza featuring every game possible. There are enough comings-and-goings here to entertain you without losing a cent. Bars, restaurants and shops are all within chip-flicking distance.

Mandarin Oriental Av. da Amizade. Upmarket hotel casino. Still no Las Vegas, but you'll need decent clothes to play the small range of games.

MGM Grand Avenida Marginal da Baia Nove. An impressive building layered in distinctive gold, silver and bronze sections, though inside it's a completely forgettable, walk-through run of pub carpets and slot machines.

Sands Av. da Amizade. The first foreign-owned casino in town, appropriately enough with

▲ The Grand Lisboa Casino, Macau

▲ The casino at the Venetian resort

gold-tinted glass facade and unusually bright and spacious.

Venetian Cotai strip. An insane place, and an essential stop in Macau – see p.285.

Wynn Av. da Amizade. Smartest of the larger casinos, with elegant, single-level gaming hall.

Arts and culture

The best place to find out **what's on in Macau** is the Macau Tourist Office website (ⓦ www.macautourism.gov.mo), or by calling in to the Macau Business Tourist Office in Largo do Senado, where they have a broadsheet of current events. Hong Kong's *South China Morning Post* also runs a Macau listing in its weekly *24/7* magazine, free with the Friday edition of the newspaper.

The main **venues** for art exhibitions, concerts, international ballet and theatre include the **Macau Cultural Centre** (ⓦ www.ccm.gov.mo/en/index .asp); the gallery in the **Leal Senado**, which puts on temporary art displays; the **University of Macau** (ⓦ www.umac.mo) on Taipa, whose auditorium is used for concerts; and – more rarely – the **Jardim Lou Lim Ieoc**, which also hosts recitals and concerts. Other occasional concerts are given in a couple of the central churches (like São Lourenço), the **Teatro Dom Pedro V**, and the **Venetian** on the Cotai strip (ⓦ www.venetianmacao.com), which has its own Cirque du Soleil troupe and sometimes hosts rock gigs. Tickets for events in Macau are usually cheaper than in Hong Kong.

Annual arts festivals

Annual arts events worth catching include the **International Music Festival**, in October, when Chinese and Western orchestras and performers put on theatre, opera and classical music at all the above venues over a two- or three-week period, and the annual **Macau International Jazz**

Festival in May, organized by the Macau Jazz Club, with concerts held in the Cultural Centre. There's also the two-week-long **Macau Arts Festival**, usually held in March, which features events and performances by local cultural and artistic groups. Check ⓦ www.icm.gov.mo for more information on all these events.

Every autumn Macau hosts an international **fireworks festival**, with teams competing to produce the biggest and brightest bangs over the Praia Grande and Lagos Nam Van. The festival usually lasts several weeks around November, with different competitors putting on displays each weekend, before a grand final between the best two. Check dates with the MGTO.

Chinese opera

The Macau Cultural Centre is the venue for regular travelling shows put on by mainland operatic troupes. Tickets are MOP$100–300.

Cinema

The **Cineteatro Macau**, Rua de Santa Clara (ⓣ2857 2050), near the junction with Rua do Campo, has three screens; there should usually be something in English. Tickets are MOP$50. There's also a **UA** cinema (ⓣ2871 2622) at the Jai-Alai Stadium, near the Jetfoil Terminal, which shows a few English-language films; and the Art Deco Cinema Alegria in the north of town (see p.280). The Macau Cultural Centre also has a small cinema, which hosts an annual **animation festival** and shows art-house releases from the mainland and Taiwan.

Shopping

L
ike in Hong Kong, Macau is a good place to **shop**, though there's not the same range and variety of goods. The best deals are on jewellery (especially gold), antique-style furniture and furnishings, electronic items, watches and clothes. Look for **Macau Consumer Council** "Certified Shop" stickers on business windows, which means that there have been no recent complaints about the store.

For **clothing**, head to Largo do Senado (p.267) for casual wear chains like Giordano, and a handful of tailors, fabric merchants and baby clothes shops west between the square and Rua dos Mercadores. North up Mercadores and then left, **Rua das Estalagens** is again good for fabric shops, especially silk. East between Largo do Senado and Rua do Campo, **Rua de Pedro Nolasco** is good for shoe shops. Otherwise, head up to the Three Lamps District (p.280), where there are whole streets of inexpensive clothing stalls, though you should ignore marked sizes – check garments will fit before handing money over as refunds are unheard of. Nearby Avenida Horta e Costa has several upmarket fashion stores.

For **electronics**, stores along Rua de Pedro Nolasco are a good place to start; prices are similar to Hong Kong but with less competition you don't have the same bargaining power. As ever, know what you're doing and check prices online first; always insist on a receipt and warranty. The best **jewellery shops** are on Avenida de Almeida Ribeiro (p.269), though pawnbrokers around town are worth checking out too if you can tell a fake gem or Rolex from the real thing.

The biggest selection of **furniture** – mostly reproduction antique Chinese – is in the lane leading up to São Paulo (p.270). Prices here are a good deal, though not cheap; you can get everything from carved screens to chairs, tables and cupboards of various sizes. Shops can usually arrange shipping overseas. For **antiques**, continue uphill from here and then bear left in front of São Paolo's steps along Rua de S. Antonio, which is lined all the way up to Santo Antonio (p.272) with stores selling old porcelain and bits and bobs – any genuine antiques should have a wax seal and come with a certificate of authenticity. There are also two **flea markets**, held after dark at weekends and worth checking for all sorts of junk, outside the Hou Kung temple (p.272) and the Lin Kai Temple (p.280).

The only **bookshop** in Macau with any selection in English (though most of its stock is in Portuguese or Chinese) is the excellent Livrari Portuguesa, Rua de São Domingos 18–22 (off Largo do Senado), which has titles on local history, cooking, culture and politics.

Finally, no Chinese tourist would leave Macau without a huge bag of biscuits, pressed meat, port and peanut nougat from a **pastelaria** such as *Koi Kei* – Rua de Felicidade (p.270) has the biggest choice.

Sports and recreation

A part from horse and dog racing, Macau's biggest sporting draw is the annual **Macau Grand Prix** (in Nov), which takes place on the enclave's streets. Accommodation and transport are mobbed over this weekend, and you'll need to book well in advance if you want to see it.

There are various other recreational **sports** on offer, too, from squash to horse riding, though most people will probably be content with a swim at one of the beaches on Coloane.

Spectator sports

Most **spectator sports** take place either at the **Forum** (Av. Marciano Baptista, near the Jetfoil Terminal ☎2870 2986) – which hosts things like volleyball, table tennis and indoor athletics meetings – or the **Taipa Stadium**, a 20,000-seater next to the racecourse, for soccer and track and field events.

Macau Grand Prix

Held on the third weekend in November, the **Macau Grand Prix** is a Formula 3 event (plus a motorbike race). **Tickets** in the stand run to around MOP$800 for two days' racing and are available from the MGTO or from overseas tourist representatives. Check the event website (Ⓦwww .macau.grandprix.gov.mo) for more information. Be sure to book well in advance.

Horseracing

Horseracing in Macau is as popular as in Hong Kong. The Macau Jockey Club hosts regular meets at the racecourse on Taipa several days a week from September to June (beginning at 12.35pm), and night races from June to August (beginning at around 7pm). Entrance to the ground and first floor stands is free, the second floor costs MOP$20, and the minimum bet is MOP$10. Contact the Macau Jockey Club (Ⓦwww.macauhorse.com) for exact times and dates of races. The buses to Taipa (#11, #22, #28A or #33) from close to the *Hotel Lisboa* all return via the racecourse.

Greyhound racing

Asia's only **greyhound racing** track is at the Yat Yuen Canidrome in Avenida General Castelo Branco, very close to the Lin Fong Temple; bus #5 from Avenida de Almeida Ribeiro, and buses #23 and #25 from outside the *Hotel Lisboa*, go right past it. The races are held on Monday, Thursday, Saturday and Sunday from 8pm until 12.20am, providing the weather is good. Entrance is MOP$10 which includes a MOP$10 bet (the minimum). You'll pay MOP$40 to get inside the Club VIP room with its bar and ringside view. Phone ⓣ2822 1199 for more details, or check ⓦwww.macauyydog.com if you read Chinese.

Participatory sports

The list of participatory sports include **squash** and **tennis**, which you can play at the *Mandarin Oriental* and the *Westin Resort* for around MOP$90 a session. Otherwise, head for the *Hotel Lisboa*, whose labyrinthine twists and turns conceal a **swimming pool** open to the public and a **snooker and billiards** room. There's also a swimming pool at Cheoc Van beach (p.286) on Coloane, while Hác Sá beach (p.286), also on Coloane, has a **recreation centre** (Mon–Sat 8am–9pm, Sun 8am–midnight) with a pool (MOP$15), roller-skating, mini-golf, children's playground and tennis courts. You can rent **windsurfing** equipment and **jet skis** further along the beach towards the *Westin Resort*, while the Macau Golf and Country Club runs a members-only championship **golf** course, just behind the *Westin* on the southeast tip of Coloane island, which *Westin Resort* guests can use at certain times. Paddle- and **rowing boats** can be hired at the Water Activities Centre (see p.286) on Estrada de Hác Sá, behind the recreation centre.

Walking/jogging trails crisscross the land around the Guia Fortress, the most popular being a 1700-metre trail reached from the lower car park, just up the hill from the *Guia Hotel*. There are also signposted walking trails on Coloane: the Trilho de Coloane and Trilho Nordeste de Coloane – the latter, a six-kilometre walk that begins and ends near Ká Ho beach, is the more accessible.

At the end of November or early December the **Macau Marathon** (ⓦwww.macaumarathon.com) clogs up the enclave's streets, the course running from Macau to Taipa and Coloane. Finally, the Macau **Horse-Riding** School, on Estrada de Cheoc Van 2H, Coloane (ⓣ2888 2303; Tues–Sun; around MOP$200 per hr), takes proficient riders around the hill trails on Coloane.

Contexts

Contexts

History

Western histories tend to assume that Hong Kong and Macau were little more than "barren lumps of rock" when the first foreign colonials arrived in the sixteenth century. But these fringes of southern China had, in fact, been settled long before by farmers, fishermen, merchants and pirates, and – now that the former colonists have departed – their thoroughly Chinese pasts are once again emerging. The following account is intended to set some context for the places and buildings you'll encounter while exploring the two SARs.

Early times

Neolithic sites across Hong Kong's New Territories and on Lantau and Lamma islands show that some six thousand years ago the area was inhabited by peoples who hunted, gathered and created pottery. The mountainous interior was originally covered in thick forest (there were still tigers here as recently as the 1940s) so people settled along the coast, rich in fish, and the fertile river valleys a short way inland. By the time of the Han dynasty (206 BC to AD 220), the region was under the administration of **Panyu**, near modern Guangzhou in southern China, as Hong Kong's Lei Cheng Uk tomb shows (p.116). During the later Tang dynasty (AD 618–907) **salt**, panned from the sea, became an important trade item – indeed, there was a Song dynasty uprising on Lantau in 1197 after the government attempted to restrict the industry.

The Song also saw the region's first major appearance in Chinese history, when the last prince of the dynasty fled to the Hong Kong area in 1279 to escape the Mongol invasions, only to be drowned off Lantau during a sea battle. After the restoration of Chinese rule under the Ming dynasty (1368–1644), the area saw its first big influx of **migrants** from elsewhere in China. These included the **Cantonese** from adjacent Guangdong province; the **Hoklo** from Fujian (Hokkien); the **Hakka**, a peripatetic grouping who had come down from the north (see p.126); and the **Tankas**, an outcast race who had lived on the water in boats. Villages were clan-based, self-contained and fortified with thick walls, and the inhabitants owned and worked their nearby lands. The elders maintained temples and ancestral halls within the villages, and daily life followed something of an ordained pattern, with activities and ceremonies mapped out by a geomancer, who interpreted social and religious ideas through the laws of **fung soi** (also known as *feng shui*) or "wind and water".

The first market towns also emerged during the Ming, and **porcelain kilns** were established near Tai Po, in Hong Kong: a huge dump of broken porcelain from the period found off the coast of Lantau – probably unwanted ship's ballast or broken cargoes – indicated that trading vessels stopped here while plying the "**maritime Silk Road**" between **southern China** and Europe. It's also probable that Hong Kong was first named at this time: the Cantonese name *Heung Gang*, or **Fragrant Harbour**, refers to the island being a source of the incense tree (*aquilaria sinensis*), whose wood is used for making incense sticks. The increase in trade was mirrored by growth in **piracy**, with the first of a string of defensive **coastal forts** built during this time. The situation had became so bad by the early Qing dynasty that in 1661 an edict was issued ordering the forced **evacuation** of all coastal areas so that the pirates would have no source of supply onshore; villages were burnt and the population shifted inland. When the edict was repealed eight years later, migrants again flocked back into the region, snapping up vacant land.

The first Westerners

Though largely concerned with its own affairs – and morally convinced of its own inherent superiority over other nations – the Chinese empire had never really been cut off from the rest of the world. **Trade** links with Europe were forged very early on indeed: the Romans dressed in Chinese silks, while Central Asia introduced glassware, cloth and horses into the country. However, trade goods were often described as "tribute" from other countries, and – although earlier dynasties such as the Tang had been incredibly cosmopolitan in outlook – by the time of the Ming dynasty foreigners were not allowed to settle within the borders of the empire or learn the Chinese language, and were generally treated with disdain by Chinese officials.

This relationship changed slightly when, in 1542, **Portuguese** traders persuaded Chinese officials to let them rent a remote peninsula of land at the very foot of the empire known as A-Ma-Kok or A-Ma Gao, transliterated by the settlers as "**Macau**". The Portuguese were looking for trading opportunities to add to their string of successes in India and the Malay peninsula; in particular, they needed a base from where they could coordinate their regional interests in Malacca and Japan.

To the Chinese, it was a concession of limited importance: the Portuguese were confined to the very edge of the country, far from any real power or influence. Initially, the sixteenth and early seventeenth centuries saw the new city of Macau thriving on trade and Christian **missionary activity**, pioneered in China and Japan by the **Jesuits**. It was their funding that established Macau's great Baroque churches, though from 1612 onwards the authorities were also forced to build fortifications on the city's hills to ward off attacks from a new regional power, the **Dutch**. Despite failing to capture Macau, the Dutch otherwise successfully destroyed Portugal's commercial interests in Southeast Asia by taking over Indonesia's wealthy spice trade from the Spanish, managing to get the Jesuits expelled from Japan in 1639, and finally occupying Malacca in 1641. With its trading links cut, Macau floundered – and the Chinese government seemed to have been correct in their belief that this remote foreign outpost would prove trivial and worthless.

The opium trade

But if Macau's failure had lulled the Chinese into thinking that Western powers were ineffectual compared with their own rulers, they were soon to be proved wrong. From 1714, other nations – the British, Dutch, Americans and French – were also allowed to establish trading posts on Chinese soil at **Canton**, at first in a very limited manner: their **warehouses** (called "factories") were set on the waterfront outside the city walls, which the foreigners were not allowed to enter. All trade was conducted through a group of Chinese merchants, who formed a guild known as a **Cohong**; and in summer, foreigners had to leave for Macau, where most of them kept houses.

The Westerners endured these restrictions because they saw this trade, however small, as the first step towards opening up China to foreign markets on a wider scale. But the Chinese viewed things entirely differently: they were happy enough if the Europeans wanted to pay for Chinese tea and silk, but saw nothing of value in any foreign goods. Casting around for any produce that might reverse this trade imbalance, the Europeans discovered **opium**, in demand in China but illegal and consequently little grown. The Portuguese had been smuggling it into Macau from their Indian territories for years, and other Western powers soon followed suit. Most energetic were the British, who began to channel opium – "foreign mud" as the Chinese called it – from Bengal to Canton, where it was sold to Chinese merchants and officials. Encouraged by the British government, traders such as **William Jardine** and **James Matheson**, both Scottish Calvinists who had no qualms about making fortunes from a Chinese reliance on drugs, were annually importing forty thousand chests of opium (worth some eight million weights of silver) into China by 1837.

Eventually, the scale of this new trade imbalance came to the attention of the Chinese emperor in Peking (Beijing), who also began to show concern for the adverse effect that opium was having on the health of his population. In 1839, the emperor appointed the upstanding governor **Lin Zexu** to end the import of opium: Lin went to Canton, forced the Europeans to hand over the twenty thousand chests of opium in their possession, and then publicly destroyed them. Furious at this treatment, the foreign traders withdrew to Macau, where – after Lin reminded the Portuguese of their official neutrality – their humiliation was compounded when they were refused permission to establish a new base.

The First Opium War

Unfortunately, Governor Lin's attempts to end the opium trade and cut the British down to size backfired disastrously. The Chinese destruction of British property – not to mention the potential danger to British personnel – fanned a mood of aggressive expansionism in London, championed by the foreign secretary, **Lord Palmerston**. Palmerston ordered an **expeditionary fleet** comprising four thousand men from India, which arrived off the Pearl River in June 1840 with the express purpose of demanding compensation for the lost opium chests, obtaining an apology from the Chinese, and – most importantly – acquiring a stronghold on the Chinese coast, which could be used to open up the country for free trade.

The British fleet promptly achieved its military objectives: it attacked coastal forts, ports and cities from Canton all the way up the Chinese coast, and when the fleet reached the Yangtze River, approaching Peking itself, the Chinese were forced to negotiate. Governor Lin was dismissed and, after the British again attacked forts around Canton, his successor Kishen capitulated and Britain **seized Hong Kong Island** on January 26, 1841. They soon wanted more, however, and after gunboats had once more raided along the coast, the Chinese government was forced to sign the **Treaty of Nanking** in 1842, which opened up Shanghai, Amoy (Xiamen), Fuzhou, Canton and other towns as "Treaty Ports" where foreigners would be allowed to reside and trade. The treaty also ceded Hong Kong Island to Britain in perpetuity, allowing them to establish their much-longed-for regional base.

The new colonies

Despite Hong Kong harbour's excellent anchorage, not everyone was thrilled with Britain's acquisition; it was initially felt in Britain that in accepting the island they had lost the chance to force better concessions from the Chinese. Nevertheless, the ownership of Hong Kong – which formally became a British Crown Colony in 1843 – gave a proper base for the opium trade, which became ever more profitable. By 1850 Britain was exporting 52,000 chests of opium a year to China through the colony.

Sir **Henry Pottinger** became the colony's **first governor**, a constitution was drawn up, and from 1844 onwards, a Legislative Council (later known as **LEGCO**) and a separate Executive Council were convened – though the governor retained a veto in all matters. In the British colonial fashion, government departments were created, the law administered and public works commissioned. The population of around fifteen thousand was mostly made up of Chinese; many sold land rights (that often they didn't own in the first place) to the newly arrived British, who began to build permanent houses, warehouses (called "**godowns**") and trading depots.

The first buildings to go up were around Possession Point, in today's Sheung Wan, though the area was abandoned after the first colonists discovered it to be malarial and moved to Happy Valley – which turned out to be even worse. Gradually though, sanitation was improved: Happy Valley was drained and turned into a racecourse; summer houses were built on The Peak; and a small but thriving town began to emerge called **Victoria**, on the site of today's Central. The number of Europeans living there was still comparatively small – just a few hundred in the mid-1840s – but they existed within a rigid colonial framework, segregated from the Chinese by early governors and buoyed by new colonial styles and comforts. Streets and settlements were named after Queen Victoria and her ministers: St John's Cathedral was opened in 1849; Government House finished in 1855; the first path up The Peak cut in 1859; and the Zoological and Botanical Gardens laid out in 1864. As Hong Kong began to come into its own as a trading port, the British merchants who lived there started to have more say in how the colony was run, and in 1850, two merchants were appointed to the Legislative Council.

Meanwhile, Hong Kong's free port status sealed Macau's fate as a backwater, as local traders immediately transferred their interests to the new colony and the opportunities it offered. Not that the Portuguese took this lying down. A new governor, João Ferreira do Amaral, arrived in 1846 and annexed the neighbouring island of **Taipa**, expelled the Chinese customs officials from Macau, built new roads and, in 1847, licensed **gambling** in an effort to garner some income for the territory. After much wrangling, the Chinese decided that they could do without this troublesome corner of their country, and **ceded sovereignty** of Macau to Portugal in 1887.

The Second Opium War and colonial growth

Conflict between Britain and China flared up again in 1856 when the Chinese authorities, ostensibly looking for pirates, boarded and arrested a Hong Kong-registered schooner, the *Arrow*. This incident gave Britain the chance to dispatch another fleet up the Pearl River to besiege Canton – instigating a series of events sometimes known as the **Second Opium War**. Joined by the French, the British continued the fighting for two years, and in 1858 an Anglo-French fleet captured more northern possessions. The proposed **Treaty of Tientsin** (Tianjin) gave foreigners the right to diplomatic representation in Peking, something that Palmerston and the traders saw as crucial to the future success of their enterprise. But with the Chinese refusing to ratify the treaty, the Anglo-French forces moved on Peking, occupying the capital in order to force Chinese concessions.

This second, more protracted series of military engagements finally ended in 1860 with the signing of the so-called **Convention of Peking**, which ceded more important territory to the British. The southern part of the Kowloon peninsula – as far north as Boundary Street – and the small Stonecutters Island were handed over in perpetuity, increasing the British territory to over ninety square kilometres. This enabled the British to establish control over the fairly lawless village that had grown up on the peninsula at Tsim Sha Tsui, while Victoria Harbour could now be more easily protected from both sides. Almost as a by-product of the agreement, the opium trade was legalized, too.

The period immediately after was one of **rapid growth** for Hong Kong. Commercial trade increased and Hong Kong became a stop for ships en route to other Far Eastern ports. They could easily be repaired and refitted in the colony, which began to sustain an important shipping industry of its own. As a result of the increased business, the **Hongkong and Shanghai Bank** was set up in 1864 and allowed to issue banknotes, later building the first of its famous office buildings. The large foreign trading companies, the **hongs**, established themselves in the colony: Jardine-Matheson was already there, but it was followed in the 1860s by Swire, which had started life as a shipping firm in Shanghai. The town of Victoria spread east and west along the harbour around its new City Hall, taking on all the trappings of a flourishing colonial town, a world away from the rather down-at-heel settlement of twenty years earlier. One of the major changes was in the size of the **population**: in a pattern that was to repeat many times in the future, turmoil in mainland China (on this occasion, the Taiping Uprising), saw swarms of **refugees** crossing the border, and by 1865 there were around 150,000 people in the colony. With Hong Kong soon handling roughly a third of China's foreign trade, the colony began to adopt the role it assumes today – as a broker in people and goods.

By **the 1880s**, Hong Kong's transformation was complete. Although the vast majority of the Chinese population were poor workers, the beginnings of today's meritocracy were apparent, as small numbers of Chinese businessmen and traders flourished. One enlightened governor, **Sir John Pope Hennessy**, advocated a change in attitude towards the Chinese that didn't go down at all well: he appointed Chinese people to government jobs, the judicial system, and even the Legislative Council. It was an inevitable move, but one that was resisted by the colonialists, who banned the Chinese from living in the plusher areas of Victoria and on The Peak.

1898: the leasing of the New Territories

Following Japan's victory in the **Sino-Japanese War** (1894–95), China became subject to some final land concessions. Russia, France and Germany had all pressed claims on Chinese territory in return for limiting Japanese demands after the war, and Britain followed suit by demanding a substantial lease on the land on the Kowloon peninsula, north of Boundary Street. Agreement was reached on an area stretching across from Mirs Bay in the east to Deep Bay in the west, including the water and islands in between, and this territory was **leased** from China for 99 years, from July 1, 1898. These **New Territories** became the legal focus for the return of Hong Kong to China in 1997, as they eventually became so vital to the functioning of the colony that it could never have survived as a viable entity without them; the British authorities had thus unwittingly provided a date for the abolition of what subsequently became one of their most dynamic colonies.

The colony of Hong Kong was now made up of just under 1100 square kilometres of islands, peninsula and water, but there was an indigenous Chinese population of around a hundred thousand in the newly acquired territory that resisted the change. Many villagers feared that their ancestral grounds would be disturbed and their traditional life interfered with, and local meetings were called in order to form militias to resist the British. There were clashes at **Tai Po** in April 1899, though British troops soon took control of the main roads and strategic points. Resistance in the New Territories eventually fizzled out and civil administration was established, but the villagers retained their distrust of the authorities. One further problem caused by the leasing agreement was the anomalous position of **Kowloon Walled City**, a Chinese garrison post beyond the original Boundary Street (see p.116). The leasing agreement didn't include the Walled City, and China continued to claim jurisdiction over it, hastening its degeneration over the years into an anarchic crime-ridden settlement and a flashpoint between the two sets of authorities.

The years to World War II

By the turn of the **twentieth century** the population of Hong Kong had increased to around a quarter of a million (with more pouring in after the fall of the Qing dynasty in China in 1911); the colony's trade showed an equally impressive performance, finally moving away from opium – which still accounted for nearly half of the Hong Kong government's finances in 1890. In 1907 Britain agreed to **end the opium trade**, and imports were cut over a ten-year period – though all that happened was that the cultivation of poppies shifted from India to China, and continued under the protection of local Chinese warlords. Opium smoking was not made illegal in Hong Kong until 1946, and three years later in China.

Alongside the trade and manufacturing booms came other improvements and developments: the **Kowloon Railway**, through the New Territories to the border, was opened in 1910 (and extended to Canton by the Chinese in 1912); the **University of Hong Kong** was founded in 1911; **land reclamation** in Victoria had begun; and the **Supreme Court** building was erected in the first decade of the new century (and still stands today, in Central, as the LEGCO building).

Despite this activity, events outside the colony's control were soon to have their effect, and the years following World War I saw a distinct economic shift away from Hong Kong. Shanghai overtook it in the 1920s as China's foremost trading city, and Hong Kong lost its pre-eminence for the next thirty years. Most of Hong Kong's Chinese were desperately poor and there had been the occasional riot over the years, culminating in 1926 in the total **economic boycott** of the colony, organized and led by the Chinese nationalists (the Kuomintang), based in Canton. There was no trade, few services and – more importantly – no food imports from China, a state of affairs that lasted for several months and did untold damage to manufacturing and commercial activity. Strike leaders in Hong Kong encouraged Chinese to leave the colony so as to press home their demands: a shorter working day; less discrimination against the local Chinese population; and a reduction in rent.

The strike didn't last, but the colony's confidence had been badly dented and was further rocked during the 1930s by the **Japanese occupation of southern China**. Hundreds of thousands more people fled into the colony, almost doubling the population, and many saw the eventual occupation of Hong Kong itself as inevitable.

1941–1945

The Japanese had been advancing across China from the north since 1933, seizing Manchuria and Beijing before establishing troops in Canton in 1939 – an advance that had temporarily halted the civil war then raging in China between Nationalist and Communist factions. What was clear was that any further move to take Hong Kong was bound to succeed: the colony only had a small defensive force of a few battalions and a couple of ships, and couldn't hope to resist the Japanese army.

Some thought that the Japanese wouldn't attack, and certainly, although Hong Kong had been prepared mentally for war since 1939, there was a feeling that old commercial links with the Japanese would save the colony. However, a line of pillboxes and guns was established across the New Territories (the so-called **Gin Drinkers Line**; see p.129), which it was hoped would delay any advancing army long enough for Kowloon to be evacuated and Hong Kong Island to be turned into a fortress from which the resistance could be directed.

On December 8, 1941, the **Japanese** army invaded, overran the border from Canton, bombed the airport and swept through the New Territories' defences. They took Kowloon within six days, the British forces retreating to Hong Kong Island where they were shelled and bombed from the other side of the harbour. The Japanese then moved across to the island, split the defence forces in hard fighting and finished them off. The **British surrender** came on Christmas Day, the first time a British Crown Colony had ever been surrendered to enemy forces. Casualties amounted to around six thousand military and civilian deaths, with nine thousand more men captured. The soldiers were held in prisoner-of-war camps in Kowloon – although some officers were held elsewhere, including camps in Japan itself – while those British civilians who had not previously been evacuated to Australia were interned in Stanley Prison on the island.

Although some Hong Kong Chinese collaborated with the Japanese during the occupation, many others smuggled in food and medicines to the European and Allied prisoners, and organized guerilla action through the New Territories. This wasn't necessarily a show of support for the British, but an indication of the loyalty Hong Kong Chinese felt towards China, which had suffered even worse under the Japanese. **Atrocities** faced the Allied prisoners too: during the short campaign, the Japanese had murdered hospital staff, patients and prisoners, and in prison, beatings, executions for escape attempts and torture were commonplace. Things were somewhat better in **Macau**, which had remained neutral, though after 1943 the Japanese were de facto rulers here, too, as the colony was too small – and too over-run with refugees – to support itself in isolation.

The Japanese meanwhile sent a military governor to Hong Kong to supervise the **occupation**, but found the colony to be much less use to them than they had imagined. It wasn't incorporated into the Japanese-run parts of China, and apart from changing the names of buildings and organizations – and adding a few Japanese architectural touches to Government House – nothing fruitful came of their time there. As the Japanese gradually lost the war elsewhere, Hong Kong became more and more of an irrelevance to them, and when the **Japanese surrendered to the Allies** in August 1945, colonial government re-established itself quickly.

Post-war reconstruction: the 1950s and 1960s

The prime concern after the war was getting business back on its feet. The economic boost for this came after 1949, when the ongoing civil war in mainland China ended in a Communist victory: China's former nationalist government fled to **Taiwan**, and those of their followers who were unable to leave with them poured over the borders into Hong Kong and Macau. By 1951, Hong Kong's population had grown to around two and a half million; new, lucrative industries – directly attributable to the recent refugees – included textiles and construction. A further incentive for a change in emphasis in the colony came with the American embargo on Chinese goods sold through Hong Kong during the **Korean War**, so that the territory was forced into manufacturing goods as a means of economic survival.

The new immigrants unleashed problems however, not least the fact that there was nowhere for them to live. In Hong Kong, **squatter settlements** mushroomed, and faced with a private housing sector that couldn't build new homes fast enough, the government established approved squatters' areas throughout the territory and instituted a vast programme of **land reclamation** and **urban redevelopment**. In addition, virtually all of the new immigrants were ardently anti-communist, and they took every opportunity during the 1950s to unsettle the relationship between Hong Kong and China.

This uneasy link with China was exploited by both sides throughout the 1960s, each action emphasizing Hong Kong and Macau's odd position as both foreign colonies and parts of China. In 1962, the point was made by the Chinese government in the so-called **trial run**, which allowed (and encouraged) upwards of sixty thousand people to leave China for Hong Kong. The border was flooded, and though the British authorities were determined to keep such an influx out, there was little they could do in the face of blatant provocation from the Chinese army, which was directing the flow of people.

Far more serious events were afoot, however, as the **Cultural Revolution** gained momentum on the mainland. This movement had begun in 1964 as a student protest against China's academic institutions' "old ways of thinking", but had escalated into an attempt to completely demolish traditional Chinese society. The result was near anarchy across China, as the movement's **Red Guard** assaulted academics, burned books and desecrated ancient monuments: tens of thousands of people were ostracized, imprisoned or simply murdered. Inevitably, the effects spilled over into the colonies: in Macau, a minor dispute in 1966 over building permits spiralled out of control and led to the death of eight Chinese protesters; while Hong Kong saw serious rioting fanned by pro-Red Guard factions in which Government House was besieged, Europeans were attacked and a bomb exploded on Hong Kong Island. However, it became clear that there was little support from the mainland for these local agitators – the Chinese leader, Chairman Mao, was keen to avoid destabilizing the colonies, as they were an important source of revenue – and the unrest fizzled out by late 1967.

The 1970s

As the Cultural Revolution petered out on the mainland in the early 1970s, Hong Kong and Macau's relationship with its neighbour improved dramatically. Cross-border trade increased, Chinese investment in Hong Kong became substantial – in Chinese-owned banks, hotels, businesses and shops – and Hong Kong was a ready market for Chinese food products. This shift in relationship was recognized in the mid-1970s, when the word "colony" was expunged from all official British titles in Hong Kong: in came the concept of Hong Kong as a "territory", which sounded much better to Chinese ears. While this was going on, the 1974 **revolution in Portugal** saw a new left-wing government in Lisbon, keen to disentangle itself from its colonial possessions, offer to withdraw unilaterally from Macau. Yet China refused to take the territory back: the gambling and organized crime that by this time had become Macau's lifeblood would have been an embarrassment to China's Communist government had they left it alone, yet cleaning it up would have killed a golden goose – after all, half of Macau's GDP and seventy percent of its government revenue (around half a billion US dollars annually) comes from gambling.

Meanwhile, Hong Kong's **population** continued to grow, bolstered by the ever-increasing number of immigrants from China alongside 65,000 **Vietnamese boat people** – fleeing their country after the North Vietnamese victory over America in 1972 – trying to enter Hong Kong. All this led to the development of **New Towns**, the first of which, Tuen Mun, opened in 1973 as the prototype of the concrete-towerblock cities that now sprawl across the New Territories, housing more than four million people and making the Hong Kong government the world's largest landlord. Roughly half the population lives in public housing, although one reason for this is the fact that the government owns all the land in Hong Kong and carefully controls how many new plot leases reach the market every year. This has enabled property developers to ensure incredibly high prices, something that has made buying even the smallest flat well beyond the means of many.

The other major problem during this period was that of **crime and corruption**, behind much of which were various Mafia-like **Triad** organizations. Established as anti-dynastic secret societies in seventeenth-century China, they moved into Hong Kong early in the colony's history, where they were able to organize among the new immigrants, splitting up into separate societies with their own elaborate initiation rites and ceremonies. Deeply involved in every level of business – from claiming protection money off shopkeepers to manipulation of Macau's gambling industry – their activities in Hong Kong were accompanied by an increase in **official and police corruption** – a state of affairs only partly redeemed by the setting up in 1974 of the **Independent Commission Against Corruption**.

The 1980s

Meanwhile, 1997 – and the expiration of Britain's 99-year lease over Hong Kong's New Territories – was fast approaching. It was clear by this time that the New Territories and the rest of Hong Kong (though technically owned in perpetuity by Britain) had become an indivisible entity, and there was no choice but to hand over the entire package to China when the lease expired. The question was only what Britain was going to get from the deal – it had, after all, invested vast wealth and time in Hong Kong, and would be losing one of the world's great financial centres.

The moves towards finding a solution began in 1982, with a trip to Beijing by the British prime minister Margaret Thatcher. After an initial bout of aggressive posturing, the **Sino–British Joint Declaration** was signed in September 1984, with Britain agreeing to hand back the entire territory to China in 1997. In return, Hong Kong would continue with the same legal and capitalistic system for at least the next fifty years, becoming a **Special Administrative Region** (SAR) of China, in which it would have virtual autonomy from Beijing – a concept the Chinese leader Deng Xiaoping famously described as "one country, two systems". **Macau's return** was also being negotiated at this time, with a similar agreement signed in 1987 between Portugal and China to return Macau to Chinese sovereignty in 1999.

After the signings, however, critics pointed out that with virtually no democratic institutions in either Hong Kong or Macau, the Chinese would effectively be able to do what they liked after regaining the territories: only the sense of maintaining any wealth-producing status would limit their actions. Confidence in China's future goodwill remained low even after the publication in 1988 of the **Basic Law**, a constitutional framework confirming the preservation of both Hong Kong and Macau's capitalist systems, along with freedoms of travel, speech, and the right to strike. There were also disturbingly vague references to clampdowns on "subversion" post-1997, which did nothing to relieve concerns.

The worst pessimist would hardly have predicted the events of 1989, however. On June 4, after student-dominated pro-democracy demonstrations in China, the Chinese leader Deng Xiaoping sent the tanks into **Tiananmen Square** in Beijing to crush the protest – an act that killed hundreds, possibly thousands, of people. The Hong Kong population's worst fears that Britain had sold them out to a murderous regime seemed confirmed: with the People's Liberation Army due to be stationed on Hong Kong territory after 1997, nobody doubted that critics of Chinese authoritarian rule would be violently suppressed, whatever the Basic Law said. Successive rallies in Hong Kong brought up to a million people out onto the streets to protest that without democratic institutions in place before 1997, the territory and its people would be entirely at the mercy of Beijing's whims.

The early 1990s in Hong Kong

At the turn of the decade Hong Kong's **economy** was booming: the territory ranked eighth in the world league of trading nations; it was the world's busiest container port; it had the third largest foreign exchange reserves; and was the fourth largest source of foreign direct investment in the world. Its economic growth averaged eight percent a year for more than a decade, and its citizens enjoyed virtually full employment and a GDP per capita of more than US$25,000 – higher than the United Kingdom and not far below that of the United States. In addition, more than half of all China's exports passed through Hong Kong, while the territory itself accounted for well over fifty percent of foreign investment in China – a formidable record for a place that had been founded just a century earlier.

However, despite Hong Kong's long association with Britain, the population had few of the **rights and privileges** that people in Britain enjoyed and expected, especially regarding the **right of abode** in the UK should the situation in Hong Kong deteriorate after the handover to China. It was argued that most people wanted to stay in Hong Kong and that, if forced to leave, wouldn't come to Britain anyway, the most popular destinations for Hong Kong Chinese emigrants being Canada and Australia. But **a British passport** – which would accompany right of abode in the UK – would give the residents of Hong Kong security, and thus lend the territory some stability.

The British government, however, balked at the spectre of a potential five million people flooding into Britain, and instead offered passports and space in Britain to just 225,000 of the territory's elite. This pleased nobody: neither the majority of the Hong Kong population; the UK voters who opposed letting any Hong Kong Chinese settle in Britain; nor the Chinese government, which argued that as Hong Kong would be Chinese after 1997, citizens would not be entitled to leave or enter the territory on "foreign" passports. This of course ignored those Hong Kongers not of ethnic Chinese origin, such as Indians or Filipinos. China, meanwhile, published the **final draft of the Basic Law** – which included Beijing's right to declare martial law, and cancelled the promise of eventual universal suffrage.

The response in Hong Kong was to found fledgling **political organizations**, including the left-wing Democratic Party and conservative, business-led Liberal Democratic Federation. The territory's **first direct elections** in September 1991 saw the Democratic Party winning sixteen of the eighteen seats on the sixty-seat Legislative Council (LEGCO) that were up for grabs (the twenty-one other candidates were appointed by the governor and interest groups). The pro-China candidates failed to win a single seat, making it clear to Beijing that Hong Kong people were dissatisfied with the Basic Law.

The approach of Hong Kong's handover

Into this volatile situation stepped **Chris Patten**, Hong Kong's 28th – and last – governor. Any thoughts that he would sit idly by until 1997 disappeared when he proposed **widening the voter franchise** by lowering the voting age from 21 to 18, increasing the number of indirectly elected council members and creating extra "functional constituencies". This would give the vote to 2.7 million Hong Kong people – as opposed to the two hundred thousand voters allowed by the previous system.

Elections in September 1995 marked the first time that each of LEGCO's sixty seats was contested and brought gains for the Democratic Party, which could, for the first time, count on the support of almost half of LEGCO's members. The main pro-Beijing grouping came a distant second, and Beijing announced that it would not recognize the sitting LEGCO. This was a major blow for Hong Kong's democracy activists, who had hoped that legislators elected in 1995 would see out their terms after the handover. Clearly, the Chinese government had no intention of allowing itself to be confronted by a robust democratic legislature that would turn the recovery of its prize into a political fiasco played out on worldwide television.

It's hard not to be cynical about Britain's behaviour in bestowing democracy at the very moment that it made no difference to itself, yet would cause maximum discomfort for the territory's new rulers. Nor did it help the population of Hong Kong: Beijing's counterstrike to Patten's scheming reduced the potential for post-handover democratic reforms even further, by creating a "provisional legislature" made up of compliant politicians and a **chief executive** appointed by Beijing, who would assume the governor's role in the new Special Administrative Region.

Post-handover Hong Kong

After the build-up, however, the **handover** was something of an anticlimax. The British sailed away on HMS *Britannia*, Beijing carried out its threat to disband the elected LEGCO and reduce the enfranchised population, and **Tung Chee-hwa**, a shipping billionaire, became the first chief executive of the Hong Kong SAR. But his highly unpopular tenure was doomed from the start: within days, the **Asian Financial Crisis** had begun, causing a recession and soaring unemployment as stock and property values crashed. Added to this were the recurrent outbreaks of **bird flu**, involving huge slaughter of chickens amid fears that humans might also contract the potentially deadly virus. Meanwhile, Tung stood unopposed for a second term in 2002, despite his inability to propose or see through any effective policy, alter the public's perception of increased government **corruption**, or improve a continuously sluggish economy – not helped by Shanghai's rising star as a place to do business. And the worst was yet come. Previous fears of bird flu soon proved nothing next to the global panic wrought by southern China's **SARS outbreak** of 2003 – some 299 people died and Hong Kong's tourist industry collapsed. Meanwhile, each June 4 (the anniversary of the Tiananmen Square crackdown) saw about half a million people turn out to **demonstrate** against Tung – and by extension, China's rule over the SAR.

It was these public displays of dissatisfaction that most annoyed the powers in Beijing, who wanted Hong Kong to showcase the benefits of the "One Country, Two Systems" approach to **Taiwan** – which, now that Hong Kong and Macau have been reclaimed, remains the last hurdle to China being reunited under one government. In March 2005 Tung was forced to **stand down** mid-term to be replaced as chief executive by career civil servant **Donald Tsang**. Re-elected for a full term in 2007, Tsang has not proved outstandingly popular despite early public confidence: many Hong Kongers see him as too dedicated to bureaucracy, completely ignoring public concerns about welfare and urban redevelopment, which has seen large swathes of Hong Kong's historic streets and buildings demolished to make way for ill-planned roads and ever-larger shopping malls.

Meanwhile, local politics seem more divided than ever along pro-Beijing and pro-democracy lines, with the latter continually pushing for **universal suffrage** – which Beijing has promised in part by 2017. The balance is against democratic reforms: half of LEGCO seats are reserved for "functional constituencies" – Chinese-government-approved interest groups – the other half chosen by popular vote; so that even if democrats win a majority of votes, they can't win a majority of LEGCO seats. Democratic factions have, in fact, polled over a third of the vote since the handover (most recently in 2008 when they won 23 of the 30 electable seats), meaning that they hold a power of veto over bills passed through LEGCO. But how all parties involved will pull together in the face of the world economic downturn of 2009 remains to be seen.

The return of Macau

In December 1999 China accepted the return of Macau as the **Macau Special Administrative Region** (MSAR), having dealt with a pre-handover spree of violence by Triad gangs. Their next step was to end the monopoly on casino licences in 2001, leading to an explosion of domestic and foreign-owned casinos. The economic success has been astounding – in 2008, Macau had 29 casinos (up from just six in 2001), with more than 4,300 gaming tables – but at the price of growing **social unrest**; as living costs rise, so many locals are finding it harder to make ends meet. In 2008 the former minister of public works, Ao Man-long, was convicted of **corruption** in the allocation of casino licenses and jailed for 27 years. The same year, Macau's Chief Executive **Edmund Ho** was also forced to freeze further expansion of the gambling industry, after Beijing – worried about a growing social divide – ordered the diversification of Macau's economy.

Officially, the **1983 Basic Law** means that Macau – like Hong Kong – will keep its capitalist structure intact for at least fifty years under the "one country, two systems model", with members of the executive council, legislative council and other key government posts now filled by Chinese permanent residents of the MSAR. In practice, though, Macau has always been far more under China's influence than Hong Kong. Local liberals and pro-democracy activists are in the minority and on the defensive, concerned that the enclave is rapidly losing its Portuguese heritage under the new system. The conservatives, for their part, talk of the need for "convergence" with China if Macau is to continue to be economically viable. And indeed, the MSAR looks determined to forge ever closer **economic ties with China**, as marked by some huge infrastructure projects that include new highways and rail lines linking it to cities in the adjacent mainland province of Guangdong (and, it is rumoured, a bridge to Hong Kong). Macau is also keen to be a major player in any move to create a Pearl River Delta economy, binding it further to Hong Kong and Guangdong in a super-regional partnership.

Religion

M ost major religions are represented in Hong Kong and Macau, though it's the three main Chinese ones – Taoism, Confucianism and Buddhism – that are of most interest to visitors. You'll come across temples and shrines everywhere, while many of the public holidays are connected with a particular religious occasion. There's a pragmatic flexibility within the Chinese belief system that often baffles outsiders – temples often share Buddhist and Taoist shrines, for instance – and the picture is also overlaid by the contemporary importance of superstition and ancestor worship.

The religions

The main belief system, **Taoism**, probably dates back in some form to prehistoric times, though it only became organized as a religion in response to the appearance of Buddhism in China around the first century AD. A philosophical movement, Taoism advocates that people follow the *Tao* or "The Way", which leads to an understanding of the natural order of things. This search for truth has often expressed itself in Taoism by way of superstition on the part of its devotees, who engage in fortune-telling and other similar activities. The Taoist gods are mainly folk heroes and legendary figures, with specific powers – protective or otherwise – that you can usually determine from their form as warriors, statesmen or scholars. Taoist temples are generally very colourful, hosting the rowdiest of the annual festivals.

Also represented in Hong Kong and, to a lesser extent, Macau, is **Buddhism**, which was originally brought from India to China in the first century AD. It recognizes that there is suffering in the world, which can be relieved only by attaining a state of personal enlightenment, *nirvana*, or extinction, at which point you will find true bliss. Buddhist temples are relaxed places, less common and less bright than Taoist, but often built in beautiful, out-of-the-way places and with resident monks and nuns.

Confucianism is less a religion and more a moral code or philosophy, first espoused by Confucius (or Kong Fu Zi) around 500 BC. The product of a feudal age, Confucianism demanded that children respect their parents, parents respect their ancestors, and everybody respect the nation's rulers: in short, be happy with your lot, and don't question your superiors. Confucius' ideas were slow to catch on – he spent his life orbiting between patrons, failing to get his views established in law – but they became popular after his death, and despite many attempts to cleanse his ideas from the national psyche (China's first emperor ordered a purge of Confucian values around 220 BC, as did Chairman Mao in the 1960s), they have come to permeate every aspect of Chinese life.

Inside a temple

Although the majority of temples and shrines in Hong Kong and Macau are nominally Taoist, there isn't really much difference between these and Buddhist temples – Chinese temple architecture is very conservative, irrespective of the religion involved. Temples are **open** approximately 8am–5pm or later, and

There are thousands of deities in the Chinese pantheon, some specific to just one place, some with overlapping roles, others the deified forms of historical characters. You'll find further information about the following in the Guide, usually under the entry for the main temple at which they're worshipped – also see "Festivals", p.33.

A-Ma see Tin Hau below.

Che Kung Protector against floods and plagues at Tai Wai, Hong Kong.

Choi Sin God of wealth; look for tiny pavement shrines with sticks of incense outside downtown businesses.

Earth God see To Tei below.

Hau Wong Deified form of the loyal general Yeung Leung-jit, who was a bodyguard for the last Song prince when the court fled to Kowloon to escape the Mongols.

Hung Shing Tang dynasty administrator and scientist, whose skills at forecasting the weather and natural disasters made him popular with fishermen.

Kam Fa Originally a Song dynasty warrior and Robin Hood-like character, she later became worshipped by fishermen who prayed to her for bountiful catches, and women wanting safe pregnancies.

Kwan Ti (also Kwan Tai or Kwan Kung) Deified version of the Han dynasty general Guan Yu, now the red-faced patron saint of pawnshops, policemen, secret societies and the military. Often portrayed holding a huge halberd.

Kwun Yam (or Kwun Yum/Kuan Yam/Kun Iam, etc) Buddhist goddess of mercy, with a shrine in almost every temple in Hong Kong and Macau, irrespective of religion, as she's prayed to for children and for help in childbirth.

Lung Mo The "Dragon Mother", who has a side-shrine in many temples. Her birthday is the eighth day of the fifth lunar month.

Lu Pan (or Lo Pan, or Ban) Builders' god, whose temple is at Kennedy Town, Hong Kong.

Man Cheung (or Man Cheong) Protector of Civil Servants, god of literature and learning.

Man Mo Paired deities of Culture (Man Cheung) and Warfare (Kwan Ti).

Na Cha Wild and unpredictable god, usually portrayed as a boy holding flaming rings. Also called "Sam Tai Tze", the "Third Prince".

Pak Tai God of order and protection, especially against flooding; the name means "Emperor of the North".

Pao Kung The Song dynasty administrator Lord Bao, famous for his impartial rulings; deified as a judge in the afterlife and often given his own shrine in larger temples. He's usually depicted as a portly figure with a "winged" hat and dark face.

Shing Wong A generalized city god, responsible for those living in certain areas.

Shui Yuat Pak A god who cures illness; also known as the "Pacifying General".

Tam Kung Another patron deity of fishermen.

Tin Hau Female patron saint of sailors, widely worshipped in Hong Kong and Macau, where she's called A-Ma. She's often depicted with two guardians – horned demons – standing either side of the front of her altar. Known elsewhere in southern China and Southeast Asia as Matzu.

To Tei Earth god whose low, open-air shrines – usually painted red and topped by a large stone – can be found throughout Hong Kong and Macau, sometimes shared with Choi Sin shrines. Also depicted as a smiling old man just inside the door of some temples.

Wong Tai Sin A god who cures illness and brings good fortune.

people go in when they like, to make offerings or to pray; there are no set prayer and service times except for resident monks.

Most temples are **built** of solid grey brick or granite blocks, their interiors divided up into separate halls, wings and courtyards. Outside the main entrance, look for good-luck stone lions, or **fu dogs** as they're sometimes called: the right-hand one is male and holds down a ball representing the world; while the left-hand one is female, with her paw holding down a puppy-sized male. The lions usually have round stones in their mouths: turn the stones three times for luck.

Temple **roofs** are usually decorated with colourful porcelain sculptures of mythological creatures and figures acting out moral or historical themes from Cantonese operas. The **threshold** is always built up; don't step on it or trip over it (as Margaret Thatcher did while discussing Hong Kong's return to China in the 1980s), as it's considered bad luck. Immediately inside the door will probably be a wooden screen known as a **spirit wall**, which blocks evil spirits from entering as they can't turn corners. Behind this will be the **main shrine**, usually under a ceiling hung with red and gold banners and smoking spirals of incense, and flanked by other, minor shrines to all sorts of gods; Chinese deities are very generous about sharing their space, even with gods of different religions.

Nowadays, side halls (especially in Buddhist temples) are often co-opted as **ancestral shrines**, with rooms full of name tablets and walls of little cupboards, each one with a photo of the deceased and containing their ashes. With land for burials – or anything else – at a premium in such a densely crowded part of the world, this is a very lucrative service for temples to provide, and even the smallest cupboards go for HK$50,000.

In Taoist temples there's almost always a room for **fortune-telling**, most commonly achieved by shaking sticks in a cylinder until one falls out: the number on the stick corresponds to a piece of fortune paper, which has to be paid for and interpreted by a fortune-teller at a stall. Go with a Chinese speaker if you want to try this, or visit Hong Kong's massive Wong Tai Sin temple in Kowloon (see p.117), where fortune-telling takes place on a much more elaborate scale: here you'll find lots of long-established fortune tellers, as well as palmists and phrenologists, who are used to foreign tourists, and lots of explanatory notes.

Obviously, coinciding with one of the main religious **festivals** (see Basics, p.34) is an invigorating experience, and this is when you'll see the various temples at their best: lavishly decorated and full of people. There'll be dances, Chinese opera displays, plenty of noise and a series of **offerings** left in the temples – food, and paper goods, which are burned as offerings to the dead.

Books

There's no shortage of books written about Hong Kong and Macau, many of which you can get in the two territories (see p.240 & p.306 for bookshop addresses). What there is a lack of – certainly in translation – is books about both territories written by Chinese authors. In the reviews below, the UK publisher is listed first, followed by the publisher in the US – unless the title is available in one country only, in which case we've specified the country; o/p signifies out of print; UP signifies University Press.

Hong Kong

History and politics

Jonathan Chamberlain *King Hui: The Man Who Owned All the Opium in Hong Kong* (Blacksmith Books, HK). Biography of the extraordinary Peter Hui: tailor, martial artist, playboy, gangster, horse breeder and CIA operative, who flourished in postwar Hong Kong.

Austin Coates *Myself a Mandarin* (Oxford UP East Asia, UK). Light-hearted account of the author's time as a magistrate in the colonial administration during the 1950s. For more from the prolific Mr Coates, see under "Macau" on p.330.

Maurice Collis *Foreign Mud* (Faber, o/p). Useful coverage of the opening up of China to trade and of the Opium Wars.

Jonathan Dimbleby *The Last Governor* (Little Brown & Co, UK & US). An insider's account of the battle for democracy between the last British governor and the Chinese government, with a dash of Whitehall treachery thrown in.

Colourful portraits of many of Hong Kong's leading figures.

E. J. Eitel *Europe in China* (Oxford UP China, o/p). First published in 1895, this is an out-and-out colonial history of early Hong Kong – lively, biased and interesting.

Jean Gittins *Stanley: Behind Barbed Wire* (HK UP). Well-written and moving eyewitness account of time spent behind bars at Stanley Prison during the internment of civilians by the Japanese in World War II.

Steve Tsang *A Modern History of Hong Kong 1841–1997* (IB Tauris, UK). Thorough account of Hong Kong's history up until the handover – written with hindsight in 2002 – including a Chinese perspective.

Arthur Waley *The Opium War Through Chinese Eyes* (Routledge, o/p). Rare insight into the Chinese side of the conflict, from official papers edited and translated by a noted China scholar.

Travel and contemporary life

Martin Booth *Gweilo: Memories of a Hong Kong Childhood* (Doubleday/Bantam).

Well-observed, moving and humourous account of a Westerner growing up in Hong Kong during the 1950s; trying to find the location of places mentioned in the text is a favourite pastime of long-term expats.

Susanna Hoe *The Private Life of Old Hong Kong* (Oxford UP East Asia, UK & US). A history of the lives of Western women in Hong Kong from 1841 to 1941, re-created from contemporary letters and diaries. A fine book, and telling of the hitherto neglected contribution of a whole range of people who had a hand in shaping modern Hong Kong.

Jan Morris *Hong Kong: Epilogue to an Empire* (Penguin/Vintage). A dated view of Hong Kong – historical, contem-porary and future – dealt with in typical Morris fashion, which means an engaging mix of anecdote, solid research, acute observation and lively opinion.

Kate Whitehead *Hong Kong Murders* (Oxford UP, UK & US). A local journalist's account of 14 homicides, covering the work of a serial killer, Triad brutality and a kidnapping gone awry. A coherent effort to make some sense of Hong Kong's hidden violence.

Fiction

John Burdett *The Last Six Million Seconds* (Coronet, UK). Lively cops-and-commissars thriller involving stolen nuclear fuel, Triad gangsters and headless corpses. Written with reeking authenticity from the girlie bars of Mongkok to the bloody roast beef at the Hong Kong Club.

Louis Cha *The Book and the Sword* (Oxford UP). Northwestern China becomes a battleground for secret societies, evil henchmen, Muslim warlords and sword-wielding Taoists as a quest to save a valuable copy of the Koran uncovers a secret which threatens to topple the Qing emperor. Written in the 1950s by Hong Kong's foremost martial-arts novelist, it has inspired numerous films and TV series.

James Clavell *Tai-Pan* (Coronet/Dell) and *Noble House* (Coronet/Dell). Big, thick bodice-rippers set respec-tively at the founding of the territory and in the 1960s, and dealing with the same one-dimensional pirates and businessmen. Unwittingly verging on parody in places.

Barry Eisler *Choke Point* (Penguin UK). Fast-paced CIA thriller set in Hong Kong and Macau, written by someone who clearly knows the territory – and the local streets – well.

John Le Carré *The Honourable Schoolboy* (Coronet/Bantam). Taut George Smiley novel, with spooks and moles chasing each other across Hong Kong and the Far East. Accurate and enthusiastic reflections on the territory, and the usual sharp eye trained on the intelligence world.

Richard Mason *The World of Suzie Wong* (Pegasus, UK). Classic 1950s romance between a down-and-out American author and a Wan Chai prostitute. Well told and touching, loosely based on the author's own experiences.

Timothy Mo *An Insular Posses-sion* (Pan/Random House, o/p). A splendid novel, re-creating the nineteenth-century foundation of Hong Kong, taking in the trading ports of Macau and Canton along the way. Mo's ear and eye for detail can also be glimpsed in *The Monkey King* (Vintage/Doubleday, o/p), his enter-taining first novel about the conflicts and manoeuvrings of family life in postwar Hong Kong, and his filmed novel *Sour Sweet* (Vintage/Random House, o/p) – an endearing tale of an immigrant Hong Kong family setting up business in 1960s London.

Nury Vittachi *The Feng Shui Detective* (Chameleon Press, HK). Whodunnit with a twist – C.F. Wong, the detective of the title, solves crimes using geomancy. Heaps of cultural background, and solid enough to win critical acclaim in Hong Kong itself.

Xu Xi *Unwalled City* (Chameleon Press, HK). A fluffy novel that whisks through the tangled lives of the central characters, including a young Canto-pop singer, up to the 1997 handover.

Reference and guides

AFCD *Hiking All in One and New Walker's Companion* (AFCD Hong Kong). Agriculture, Fisheries and Conservation Department's hiking guides, with text and maps: the first covers the lengthy Wilson, MacLehose, Hong Kong Island and Lantau Island trails; the second covers fifty shorter hikes of varying degrees of difficulty.

Frederick Dannen and Barry Long *Hong Kong Babylon* (Faber, UK & US, o/p). Subtitled "An Insider's Guide to the Hollywood of the East", this pacey book gets to grips with every facet of the Hong Kong movie scene, from plot summaries to interviews with stuntmen.

Leung Wai Shan *Dim Sum in Hong Kong* (Food Paradise Publishing, HK). If you've ever enjoyed a top *dim sum* meal, get yourself this excellent cookbook and try making exquisite dumplings and buns for yourself. It's bilingual, with restaurant histories included – look for it in branches of the Commercial Press (see p.240).

Patricia Lim *Discovering Hong Kong's Cultural Heritage* (Oxford UP). Two well-illustrated guides (one covering Hong Kong Island and Kowloon, the other the New

Territories) describing easy, thematic walks which fill in on heaps of background on history and culture. Includes maps.

Peter Moss *Skylines: Hong Kong* (Form Asia). Hong Kong's most famous buildings, ancient and modern, with good photographs and solid background text. Not quite up-to-the-moment, but then nothing could be, given the city's pace of change – and it is at least updated regularly.

🏃 **Pete Spurrier** *The Leisurely Hiker's Guide to Hong Kong* and *The Serious Hiker's Guide to Hong Kong* (Form Asia). Excellent text, photos and maps for hiking Hong Kong's four major country trails, plus a winning selection of easier walks.

🏃 **Jason Wordie** *Streets* (Hong Kong University Press). Two excellent guidebooks covering the historic side of Hong Kong Island and Kowloon through guided walks; a mine of well-researched, invaluable and often quirky information.

Rachel Wright *Living and Working in Hong Kong* (How To Books). Useful expat's guide to living, working and enjoying yourself in Hong Kong.

Language texts

Pocket Cantonese Dictionary (Periplus). Handy, basic dictionary designed for translating what you hear and answering back; not academic but good for travellers' needs.

Hugh Baker and Ho Pui-Kei *Teach Yourself Cantonese*. A good choice for getting a grounding in Cantonese on your own, comprising two CDs with a companion text. Far more direct and interesting than other similar courses, covering basic social interactions, travel and business. Concentrates on speaking and uses romanized text, not Chinese characters.

🏃 **Christopher Hutton and Kingsley Bolton** *A Dictionary of Cantonese Slang*. A fun book to have around at markets, Happy Valley Racecourse, *cha chaan teng* restaurants and, of course, during a Cantonese gangster movie, to help make sense of Hong Kong's more colourful expressions. It's not all swearing, though; recommended for anyone wanting to expand their colloquial vocabulary.

Macau

Steven Bailey *Strolling in Macau* (ThingsAsian Press). Series of guided walks through Macau's historic quarters, with plenty of photos and background historical and cultural information.

C.R. Boxer *Seventeenth Century Macau* (Heinemann US, o/p). Interesting survey of documents, engravings, inscriptions and maps of Macau culled from the years either side of the restoration of the Portuguese monarchy in 1640. An academic study, but accessible enough for some informative titbits about the enclave.

Daniel Carney *Macau* (Corgi/ Kensington). Improbable characterization in a Clavell-like thriller set in the enclave.

Austin Coates *Macao and the British* (Oxford UP East Asia, UK), *A Macao Narrative* (Oxford UP East Asia, UK), *City of Broken Promises* (Oxford UP East Asia, UK). Coates has written widely about the Far East, where he was Assistant Colonial Secretary in Hong Kong in the 1950s. *Macao and the British* follows the early years of Anglo–Chinese relations and underlines the importance of the Portuguese enclave as a staging post for other traders. *A Macao Narrative* is a short but more specific account of Macau's history up to the mid-1970s; *City of Broken Promises* is an entertaining historical novel set in Macau in the late eighteenth century.

Cesar Guillen-Nunez *Macau* (Oxford UP, UK & US). Decent, slim hardback history of Macau, worth a look for the insights it offers into the churches, buildings and gardens of the city.

Cecilia Jorge *Macanese Cooking* (Associação Promotora da Instrução dos Macaenses). Seemingly unavailable outside of Macau, this excellent cookbook includes many classic Macanese dishes, as well as a comprehensive history of the style (though, strangely, *natas* are omitted).

Books about China

Chen Guidi and Wu Chuntao *Will the Boat Sink the Water?* (Public Affairs, UK). Modern China was founded to improve the lot of its peasant majority, but the journalist authors show how – and how badly – the country's officials are failing them. Banned in China, it has since sold ten million copies on the black market.

🏃 **Rachel DeWoskin** *Foreign Babes in Beijing* (Granta UK). Wry, witty snapshot of 1990s Beijing as a place of untested, unexpected opportunities: the author arrives to manage a PR firm and ends up as a bohemian soap-opera star.

Tim Glissold *Mr China* (Constable and Robinson, UK). A cautionary tale about doing business in China, explaining how the author lost US$400 million of venture capital and suffered a heart attack. Essential reading for all budding entrepreneurs.

Duncan Hewitt *Getting Rich First* (Chatto & Windus). Written by a long-term foreign resident and journalist, this excellent book moves beyond commonplace Western views of China – all dynastic history, Cultural Revolution and economic boom – with an informed look at the major social themes shaping the nation.

Christopher Hibbert *The Dragon Wakes: China and the West 1793–1911* (Penguin/Viking Penguin). Superbly entertaining account of the opening up of China to Western trade and influence. Hibbert leaves you in no doubt about the cultural misunderstandings that bedevilled early missions to China – or about the morally dubious acquisition of Hong Kong and the other Treaty Ports by Western powers.

Karen Smith *Nine Lives: Birth of Avant-Garde Art in New China* (Thames & Hudson). Explores the development of the increasingly influential, confusing Chinese contemporary art scene, through dense studies of nine of its key players.

Arthur Waley *Three Ways of Thought in Ancient China* (Routledge/Stanford University Press). Translated extracts from the writings of three of the early philosophers – Zhuang Zi, Mencius and Han Feizi. A useful introduction.

Frances Wood *No Dogs and Not Many Chinese* (John Murray, UK). Historical snapshot of the Treaty Ports and the life lived within them – entertaining and instructive.

Language

Language

Cantonese

The language spoken by the overwhelming majority of Hong Kong and Macau's population is Cantonese, a southern Chinese dialect used in the province of Guangdong – and one spoken by millions of Chinese emigrants throughout the world. Unfortunately, Cantonese is a difficult language for Westerners to learn: it's tonal, meaning that the specific tone with which a word is spoken affects its meaning. Cantonese has nine tones, a huge number even by Chinese standards (Mandarin, the mainland's primary dialect, has just five tones). However, this is most often a problem when uttering individual words; set phrases provide their own context and you may be surprised how far your attempts at communication are understood, despite bad pronunciation.

Written Chinese is, in some ways, more accessible to the newcomer. Chinese characters embody meanings rather than pronunciation – rather like the symbol "2" meaning the same thing whether pronounced "two","yi" or "dos" – so it's not necessary to learn to speak Chinese in order to read it. However, unlike the 26 letters of the Roman alphabet, there are an estimated 10,000 Chinese characters, although relatively few are used in daily life – you need around 2500 to read a newspaper, for example. While this will be beyond the scope of a short stay, with a little curiosity you might learn to recognize enough to get the gist of dishes on a menu.

Most visitors get by without speaking or reading a word of Chinese. Hong Kong is officially **bilingual** in Cantonese and English, and all signs, public transport and utility notices and street names are supposed to be written in both scripts. Many of the people you'll have dealings with in Central, Tsim Sha Tsui and most other tourist destinations should speak at least some English, although it may be hard going, particularly in taxis, restaurants and on the telephone. In **Macau**, where Portuguese is the official second language, you may have a few more problems.

The basic guide below should help with pronouncing some everyday words and phrases in Cantonese. However, because the romanized versions don't convey the tone, you may find that people don't understand you. We've also provided Chinese characters for some of the most useful signs (see p.337) and place names (see box at the end of each chapter), as well as a menu reader to help you choose and order *dim sum* (see p.207). If you're having problems making yourself understood, simply show the waiter/taxi driver/passer-by the relevant Chinese character in the book.

Cantonese words and phrases

Pronunciation

oy as in **boy**
ai as in **fine**
i as in **see**
er as in **urn**
o as in **pot**

ow as in **now**
oe as in **oh**
or as in **law**
initial ng as **m'**

Countries

Hong Kong	herng gong	Britain	ying gwok
China	chung gwok	America	may gwok

Meeting someone

Good morning	joe sun	I am American	ngor hai may gwok yan
Hello/how are you?	lay hoe ma	I am a student	ngor hai hok sarng
Thank you/excuse me	m goy	What time is it?	ching mun, gay dim ah?
Goodnight	joe tow		
Goodbye	joy geen	Can you speak English?	lay sik m sik gong ying man?
I'm sorry	doy m joot		
What is your name?	lay gew mut yeh meng?	I'm sorry, I can't speak Cantonese	doy m joot, ngor m sik gong gong dong wa
My name is...	ngor gew...		
I am English	ngor hai ying gwok yan	I don't understand	ngor m ming bat

Asking directions

Where is this place? (while pointing to the place name or map)	ching mun, leedi day fong hai been do ah?	Taxi	dik-see
		Airport	fay gay cherng
		Hotel	jow deem
Where is the train station?	for chair tsam hai been do ah?	Hostel	loy gwun
		Restaurant	charn teng
Where is the bus stop?	ba-see tsam hai been doe ah?	Campsite	loe ying ying day
		Toilets	chee saw
Where is the ferry pier?	ma-tow hai been doe ah?	Where is the toilet?	chee saw hai been doe ah?
Train	for chair	Police	ging chat
Bus	ba-see	I want to go to...	ngor serng hoy...
Ferry	do lun schoon		

Shopping

1	yat	30	saam sap
2	yee	100	yat bat
3	saam	1000	yat cheen
4	say	How much is it?	ching mun, gay daw cheen?
5	mm		
6	lok	Do you have any...	lay yow mo...
7	chat	Too expensive!	Tai gwei le!
8	bat	I don't have any money	Ngor mo cheen
9	gow (to rhyme with "how")		
10	sap	Can you make it cheaper?	Peng dee, dat mm dat ah?
11	sap yat	Do you have any change?	Lay yow mo sarn zee?
12	sap yee		
20	yee sap		

Some signs

Entrance	入口	Danger	危險
Exit	出口	Customs	關稅
Toilets	廁所	Bus	公共汽車
Gentlemen	男廁	Ferry	渡船
Ladies	女廁	Train	火車
Open	營業中	Airport	飛幾場
Closed	休業	Police	警察
Arrivals	到達	Restaurant	飯店
Departures	出發	Hotel	賓館
Closed for holidays	休假	Campsite	野營位置
Out of order	出故障	Beach	海灘
Drinking/mineral water	礦泉水	No Swimming	禁止游永
No Smoking	請勿吸菸		

Eating

I'm vegetarian	ngor sik chai		Do you serve beer?	leedo yow mo bair
It's delicious!	ho may doe!			tsow yum ah, m goy?
Do you have an English menu?	lay yow mo ying man chan pie, m goy?		Yes, we have	yow ah!
			No, we don't have	mo ah!
			Bill, please!	m goy, mai dan!

Note that the number two changes when asking for two of something **lerng wei** (a table for two) or stating something other than counting **lerng mun** (two dollars).

Portuguese

Roughly 96 percent of the population of Macau is Chinese, with the remainder consisting of those of Portuguese descent, a large Philippine expat community and other ethnic minorities. Macau's two official languages are **Portuguese** and **Cantonese**, though in reality – other than the street and office signs – Portuguese is little used. A few Portuguese words are given below to help decipher signs and maps, though you won't need much Portuguese to get around; you may find the menu reader on p.296 useful, however. Although taught in schools, English is patchily spoken and understood – a few words of Cantonese will always help smooth the way.

Some useful Portuguese words

Alfandega	Customs	**Jardim**	Garden
Avenida	Avenue	**Largo**	Square
Baia	Bay	**Lavabos**	Toilets
Beco	Alley	**Mercado**	Market
Bilheteira	Ticket office	**Pensão**	Guesthouse
Calçada	Alley	**Ponte**	Bridge
Correios	Post office	**Pousada**	Inn/Hotel
Edificio	Building	**Praça**	Square
Estrada	Road	**Praia**	Beach
Farmácia	Pharmacy	**Rua**	Street
Farol	Lighthouse	**Sé**	Cathedral
Fortaleza	Fortress	**Travessa**	Lane
Hospedaria	Guesthouse	**Vila**	Guesthouse

Glossary of words and terms

Lots of strange words have entered the vocabulary of Hong Kong and Macau people, Chinese and Westerners alike, and you'll come across most of them during your time here. Some are derivations of Cantonese words, adapted by successive generations of European settlers; others come from the different foreign and colonial languages represented in Hong Kong and Macau from Chinese dialects to Anglo-Indian words. For words and terms specifically to do with Chinese food, see the chapter on "Eating", p.199.

AEL Airport Express.

AFCD Agriculture, Fisheries and Conservation Department.

Amah Female housekeeper/servant.

Ancestral hall Main room or hall in a temple complex where the ancestral records are kept, and where devotions take place.

Aye Ayes Illegal immigrants.

BOC Bank of China.

Cha chan teng A cheap indoor restaurant serving basic noodles, rice and European-inspired dishes such as toast and spaghetti.

CE Chief executive.

Cheongsam Chinese dress from the 1930s with a high collar and long slits up the sides.

Chop A personal seal or stamp of authority; also used by the illiterate instead of signatures.

Dai pai dong Street stall or modest café selling snacks and food.

EXCO Executive Council.

Expat Expatriate; a foreigner living in Hong Kong.

Feng shui Literally "wind and water", the Chinese art of geomancy.

Godown Warehouse.

Gweilo Literally "ghost man"; used by the Cantonese for all Westerners, male and female (also *gweipor* "ghost woman", *gwei mui* "ghost girl" and *gwei tsa*, "ghost boy"); originally derogatory, but now in accepted use.

HKTB Hong Kong Tourism Board.

Hong Major company.

HSBC Hong Kong & Shanghai Banking Corporation.

IFC (1 or 2) International Finance Centre (towers 1 or 2).

Junk Large flat-bottomed boat with a high deck and an overhanging stern; once distinguished by their trademark sails, all Hong Kong's junks nowadays are engine-powered.

Kaido A small ferry, or a boat used as a ferry; a sampan (also *kaito*).

LEGCO Legislative Council.

LR Light Rail.

Mah jong A Chinese gambling game with similar rules to Bridge, played with tiles by four people on a green-baize table.

MGTB Macau Government Tourist Board.

Miu The Cantonese word for temple.

MTR Mass Transit Railway.

Nullah Gully, ravine, or narrow waterway.

Praya The Portuguese word for waterfront promenade (in occasional use).

Sampan Small flat-bottomed boat.

SAR Special Administrative Region; so, HKSAR (Hong Kong SAR) and MSAR (Macau SAR).

SARS Severe Acute Respiratory Syndrome.

Shroff Cashier.

Soho South of Hollywood Road.

Tai chi A martial arts exercise.

Taipan Boss of a major company.

Tai tai Literally means "wife", but often used to describe rich ladies who lunch and shop.

Triad Organized crime syndicate or member.

Uk Village.

Wai A walled village.

Small print and
Index

A Rough Guide to Rough Guides

Published in 1982, the first Rough Guide – to Greece – was a student scheme that became a publishing phenomenon. Mark Ellingham, a recent graduate in English from Bristol University, had been travelling in Greece the previous summer and couldn't find the right guidebook. With a small group of friends he wrote his own guide, combining a highly contemporary, journalistic style with a thoroughly practical approach to travellers' needs.

The immediate success of the book spawned a series that rapidly covered dozens of destinations. And, in addition to impecunious backpackers, Rough Guides soon acquired a much broader and older readership that relished the guides' wit and inquisitiveness as much as their enthusiastic, critical approach and value-for-money ethos.

These days, Rough Guides include recommendations from shoestring to luxury and cover more than 200 destinations around the globe, including almost every country in the Americas and Europe, more than half of Africa and most of Asia and Australasia. Our ever-growing team of authors and photographers is spread all over the world, particularly in Europe, the US and Australia.

In the early 1990s, Rough Guides branched out of travel, with the publication of Rough Guides to World Music, Classical Music and the Internet. All three have become benchmark titles in their fields, spearheading the publication of a wide range of books under the Rough Guide name.

Including the travel series, Rough Guides now number more than 350 titles, covering: phrasebooks, waterproof maps, music guides from Opera to Heavy Metal, reference works as diverse as Conspiracy Theories and Shakespeare, and popular culture books from iPods to Poker. Rough Guides also produce a series of more than 120 World Music CDs in partnership with World Music Network.

Visit www.roughguides.com to see our latest publications.

Rough Guide travel images are available for commercial licensing at www.roughguidespictures.com

Rough Guide credits

Text editor: Anna Streiffert Limerick
Layout: Sachin Gupta
Cartography: Karobi Gogoi
Picture editor: Emily Taylor
Production: Rebecca Short
Proofreader: Susannah Wight
Cover design: Chloë Roberts
Photographer: Karen Trist
Editorial: Ruth Blackmore, Andy Turner, Keith
Drew, Edward Aves, Alice Park, Lucy White,
Jo Kirby, James Smart, Natasha Foges, Róisín
Cameron, Emma Traynor, Emma Gibbs, Kathryn
Lane, Christina Valhouli, Monica Woods, Mani
Ramaswamy, Harry Wilson, Lucy Cowie, Helen
Ochyra, Amanda Howard, Lara Kavanagh, Alison
Roberts, Joe Staines, Peter Buckley, Matthew
Milton, Tracy Hopkins, Ruth Tidball; **Delhi**
Madhavi Singh, Karen D'Souza, Lubna Shaheen
Design & Pictures: **London** Scott Stickland,
Dan May, Diana Jarvis, Mark Thomas, Nicole
Newman, Sarah Cummins, Emily Taylor;
Delhi Umesh Aggarwal, Ajay Verma, Jessica
Subramanian, Ankur Guha, Pradeep Thapliyal,
Sachin Tanwar, Anita Singh, Nikhil Agarwal
Production: Vicky Baldwin

Cartography: **London** Maxine Repath, Ed
Wright, Katie Lloyd-Jones; **Delhi** Rajesh
Chhibber, Ashutosh Bharti, Rajesh Mishra,
Animesh Pathak, Jasbir Sandhu, Alakananda
Bhattacharya, Swati Handoo, Deshpal Dabas
Online: **London** George Atwell, Faye Hellon,
Jeanette Angell, Fergus Day, Justine Bright, Clare
Bryson, Aine Fearon, Adrian Low, Ezgi Celebi,
Amber Bloomfield; **Delhi** Amit Verma, Rahul Kumar,
Narender Kumar, Ravi Yadav, Debojit Borah,
Rakesh Kumar, Ganesh Sharma, Shisir Basumatari
Marketing & Publicity: **London** Liz Statham,
Niki Hanmer, Louise Maher, Jess Carter, Vanessa
Godden, Vivienne Watton, Anna Paynton, Rachel
Sprackett, Libby Jellie, Laura Vipond, Vanessa
McDonald; **New York** Katy Ball, Judi Powers,
Nancy Lambert; **Delhi** Ragini Govind
Manager India: Punita Singh
Reference Director: Andrew Lockett
Operations Manager: Helen Phillips
PA to Publishing Director: Nicola Henderson
Publishing Director: Martin Dunford
Commercial Manager: Gino Magnotta
Managing Director: John Duhigg

ROUGH
GUIDES

SMALL PRINT

Publishing information

This seventh edition published October 2009 by
Rough Guides Ltd,
80 Strand, London WC2R 0RL
14 Local Shopping Centre, Panchsheel Park,
New Delhi 110017, India
Distributed by the Penguin Group
Penguin Books Ltd,
80 Strand, London WC2R 0RL
Penguin Group (USA)
375 Hudson Street, NY 10014, USA
Penguin Group (Australia)
250 Camberwell Road, Camberwell,
Victoria 3124, Australia
Penguin Group (Canada)
195 Harry Walker Parkway N, Newmarket, ON,
L3Y 7B3 Canada
Penguin Group (NZ)
67 Apollo Drive, Mairangi Bay, Auckland 1310,
New Zealand
Cover concept by Peter Dyer.

Typeset in Bembo and Helvetica to an original
design by Henry Iles.
Printed in Singapore
© Jules Brown and David Leffman, 2009
Maps © Rough Guides
No part of this book may be reproduced in any
form without permission from the publisher except
for the quotation of brief passages in reviews.
352pp includes index
A catalogue record for this book is available from
the British Library
ISBN: 978-1-84836-188-1
The publishers and authors have done their
best to ensure the accuracy and currency of all
the information in **The Rough Guide to Hong
Kong & Macau**, however, they can accept no
responsibility for any loss, injury, or inconvenience
sustained by any traveller as a result of
information or advice contained in the guide.

1   3   5   7   9   8   6   4   2

Help us update

We've gone to a lot of effort to ensure that
the seventh edition of **The Rough Guide to
Hong Kong & Macau** is accurate and up-to-
date. However, things change – places get
"discovered", opening hours are notoriously
fickle, restaurants and rooms raise prices or lower
standards. If you feel we've got it wrong or left
something out, we'd like to know, and if you can
remember the address, the price, the hours, the
phone number, so much the better.

Please send your comments with the subject
line "**Rough Guide Hong Kong & Macau
Update**" to ©mail@roughguides.com. We'll credit
all contributions and send a copy of the next
edition (or any other Rough Guide if you prefer)
for the very best emails.
Have your questions answered and tell others
about your trip at ⓦcommunity.roughguides.com

Acknowledgements

For Narrell, with love. Heartfelt thanks to
CS Tang, Philip Kenny, Winnie Chow, Mr Luk,
Mr Loi, Alex & Stuart, Michael Udel, Damian
Ryan and Richard in Hong Kong; and to Leaf,
Phil and Zander in Oz for a roof and a room. Sei
Hoi Yat Ka.

Readers' letters

Thanks to all the readers who have taken the time to write in with comments and suggestions (and apologies if we've inadvertently omitted or misspelt anyone's name):

Ted Bier, Jeremy Board, John Broughton, David
Burnett, Lily Chan, James Cotterill, Robbie Ho,
Ukirsari Manggalani-Brodjokaloso,
Alison Middleton, Simon Rowntree, Tom
Shortland, Danielle Stafford.

Photo credits

All photos © Rough Guides except the following:

Title page
Golden dragon © GeekPie

Fullpage
Hong Kong skyline at night © Amanda Hall/
  Photolibrary

Introduction
Dim sum at teahouse © Courtesy of Hong Kong
  Tourist Board
Clearwater Bay, New Territories © Fraser Hall/
  Jupiter Images
Burning incense at Wong Tai Sin Temple
  © Courtesy of Hong Kong Tourist Board

Things not to miss
01 Nan Lian Garden, Hong Kong © Nick Ledger/
  Alamy
04 Pink dolphin © Courtesy of Ken Fung/Hong
  Kong Dolphinwatch
08 Climber on Lion Rock, Hong Kong © Dan
  Morris/Alamy
10 São Paulo facade, Macau © Pictures Colour
  Library–PCL
11 Happy Valley Racecourse © David Lomax/
  Jupiter Images
18 Night view of Grand Lisboa © Courtesy of
  The Grand Lisboa Hotel
19 Buildings in Largo do Senado, Macao
  © Photolibrary

Architecture colour section
Bank of China Tower, Flagstaff House, Hong
  Kong Park © M. Winch/Axiom
Traditional gateway on the Ping Shan Heritage
  Trail © Courtesy of Hong Kong Tourist Board
Colonial buildings at Largo do Senado, Macao
  © Photolibrary

New skyscrapers and high-rise apartments, Sha
  Tin © Roger Hutchings/Alamy

Cantonese cuisine colour section
Fishing boat in Saikung, New Territories
  © Pictures Colour Library–PCL
Dim sum © Courtesy of Hong Kong Tourist Board
Chinese herbal tea shop © Courtesy of Hong
  Kong Tourist Board

Black and white photos
p.55 Lion Pavilion, The Peak © Courtesy of Hong
  Kong Tourist Board
p.64 Statue Square and skyscrapers © Reed
  Kaestner/PhotoLibrary
p.77 Junk in Hong Kong harbour © Courtesy of
  Hong Kong Tourist Board
p.102 Avenue of Stars, Bruce Lee © Steve Vidler/
  PhotoLibrary
p.117 Wong Tai Sin Temple © Courtesy of Hong
  Kong Tourist Board
p.130 Tai Mo Shan, New Territories © Matthew
  Wellings/Alamy
p.138 New Town Plaza in Central Park, Shatin
  © Martin Jones/Corbis
p.153 Waterfront seafood boats (Sai Kung Town)
  © Courtesy of Hong Kong Tourist Board
p.161 Sea Supreme hydrofoil, Lamma Island ferry
  © Doug Houghton
p.230 Fringe Club © Axiom
p.278 Barra Square, A-Ma Temple © Imagestate/
  Alamy
p.303 Grand Lisboa Hotel © Courtesy of Grand
  Lisboa Hotel
p.304 Venetian Hotel and Casino, Macau
  © Courtesy of Venetian Hotel

Index

Map entries are in colour.

INDEX

INDEX

INDEX

Map symbols

maps are listed in the full index using coloured text

– – – Chapter boundary

—··— Special admin. region boundary

═══ Major road

═══ Minor road

▬▬▬ Pedestrianized road

- - - - Tunnel

▥▥▥▥ Steps

- - - - - Path

——— River

— — Hydrofoil, *kaido* and ferry route

▬●▬ Railway

——— Tram route

●- - -● Cable car

▲ Mountain peak

⬭⬭ Rocks

🚿 Waterfall

⌓ Cave

🌳 Tree

⚇ Garden

⚐ Golf course

⊙ Statue

❦ Museum

✦ Point of interest

ⓘ Tourist information

@ Internet

⊠ Post office

⊞ Hospital

)(Bridge

⊛ MTR station

★ Bus/taxi stop

✈ Airport

Ⓐ Airbus stop

◉ Hotel

▣ Restaurant

⚠ Campsite

⚑ Mountain refuge

♦ Immigration post

⟲ Windmill

⚐ Monastery

♠ Temple

ᴨ Shrine

♨ Mosque

✡ Synagogue

⬭ Stadium

▭ Market

⊞ Church

▮ Building

⊡ Cemetery

▦ Park

▦ Beach

⋿ Marshland

▨ Reclaimed land

▬ High ground

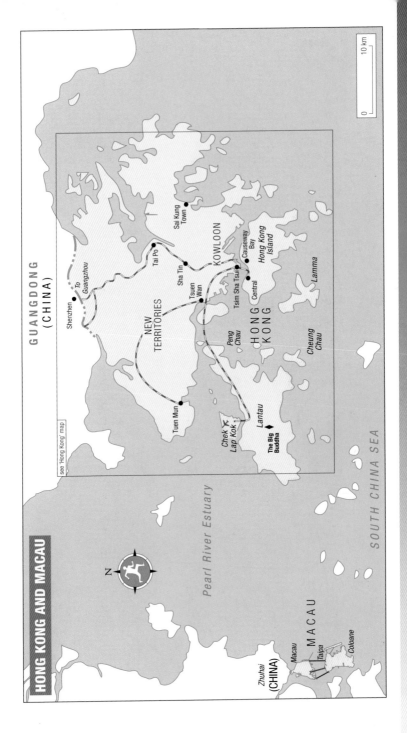

HONG KONG AND MACAU

GUANGDONG
(CHINA)

see 'Hong Kong' map

Shenzhen

To
Guangzhou

Tuen Mun

Tai Po

**NEW
TERRITORIES**

Sha Tin

Sai Kung
Town

KOWLOON

Tsuen
Wan

Causeway
Bay

Tsim Sha Tsui

Central

*Hong Kong
Island*

Peng
Chau

**H O N G
K O N G**

Lamma

*Cheung
Chau*

Chek
Lap Kok

Lantau

**The Big
Buddha**

Pearl River Estuary

N

SOUTH CHINA SEA

Zhuhai
(CHINA)

Macau

M A C A U

Taipa

Coloane

0   10 km

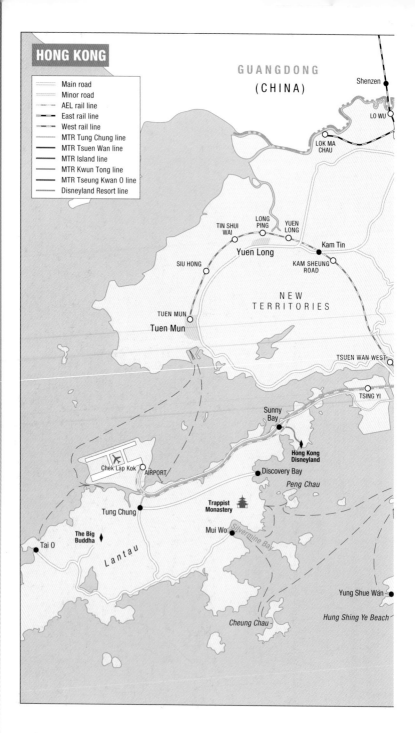

HONG KONG

Legend	
	Main road
	Minor road
	AEL rail line
	East rail line
	West rail line
	MTR Tung Chung line
	MTR Tsuen Wan line
	MTR Island line
	MTR Kwun Tong line
	MTR Tseung Kwan O line
	Disneyland Resort line

GUANGDONG
(CHINA)

Shenzen

LO WU

LOK MA CHAU

TIN SHUI WAI

LONG PING

YUEN LONG

Kam Tin

Yuen Long

SIU HONG

KAM SHEUNG ROAD

NEW TERRITORIES

TUEN MUN

Tuen Mun

TSUEN WAN WEST

TSING YI

Sunny Bay

Hong Kong Disneyland

Chek Lap Kok

AIRPORT

Discovery Bay

Peng Chau

Trappist Monastery

Tung Chung

Mui Wo

Silvermine Bay

The Big Buddha

Tai O

Lantau

Yung Shue Wan

Hung Shing Ye Beach

Cheung Chau

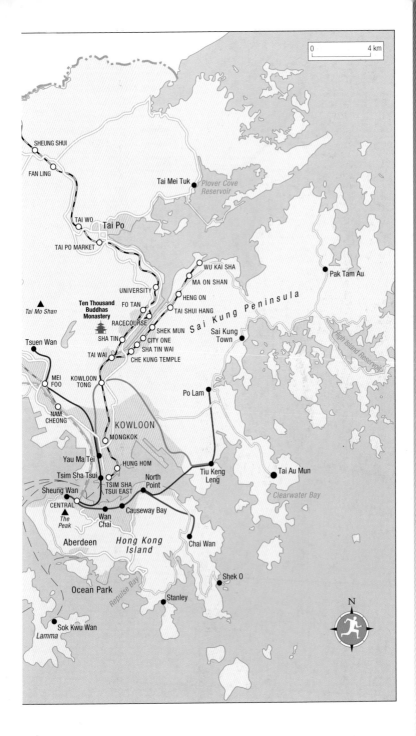

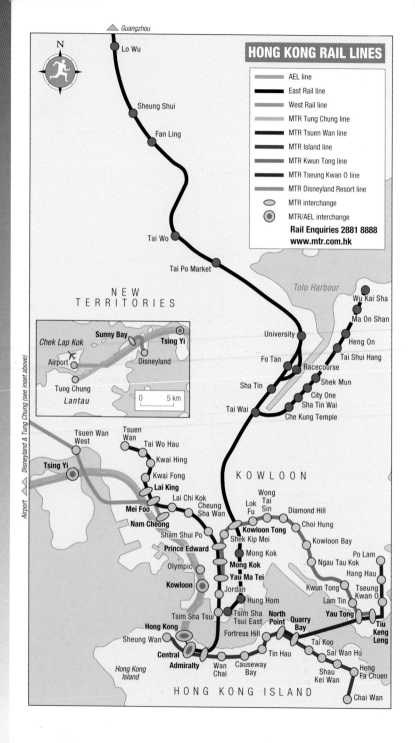

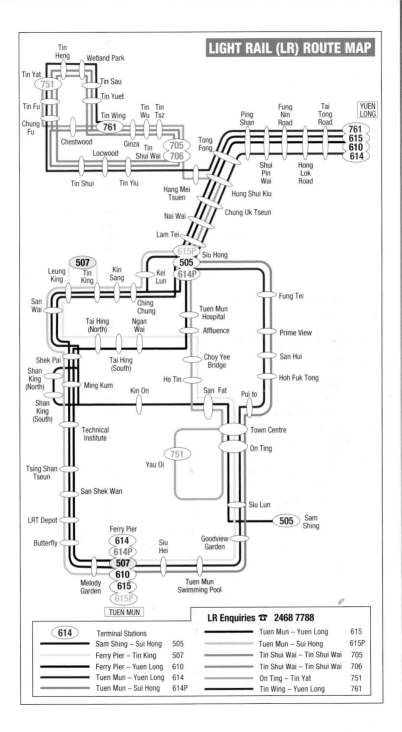

LIGHT RAIL (LR) ROUTE MAP

Tin Heng
Wetland Park
Tin Yat
751
Tin Sau
Tin Fu
Tin Yuet
Chung Fu
Tin Wing
761
Tin Wu Tin Tsz
Chestwood
Ginza
705
706
Locwood
Tin Shui Wai
Tin Shui
Tin Yiu
Hang Mei Tsuen
Nai Wai
Lam Tei
615P
505
614P
Siu Hong
Ping Shan
Fung Nin Road
Tai Tong Road
YUEN LONG
761
615
610
614
Shui Pin Wai
Hong Lok Road
Tong Fong
Hung Shui Kiu
Chung Uk Tseun

507
Tin King
Leung King
Kin Sang
Kei Lun
San Wai
Ching Chung
Fung Tei
Tai Hing (North)
Ngan Wai
Tuen Mun Hospital
Prime View
Affluence
San Hui
Shek Pai
Tai Hing (South)
Choy Yee Bridge
Hoh Fuk Tong
Shan King (North)
Ming Kum
Kin On
Ho Tin
San Fat
Pui to
Shan King (South)
Technical Institute
751
Yau Oi
Town Centre
On Ting
Tsing Shan Tseun
San Shek Wan
Siu Lun
LRT Depot
505
Sam Shing
Butterfly
Ferry Pier
614
614P
507
610
615
615P
Siu Hei
Goodview Garden
Melody Garden
Tuen Mun Swimming Pool
TUEN MUN

LR Enquiries ☎ 2468 7788

614	Terminal Stations	
	Sam Shing – Sui Hong	505
	Ferry Pier – Tin King	507
	Ferry Pier – Yuen Long	610
	Tuen Mun – Yuen Long	614
	Tuen Mun – Sui Hong	614P

Tuen Mun – Yuen Long	615
Tuen Mun – Sui Hong	615P
Tin Shui Wai – Tin Shui Wai	705
Tin Shui Wai – Tin Shui Wai	706
On Ting – Tin Yat	751
Tin Wing – Yuen Long	761

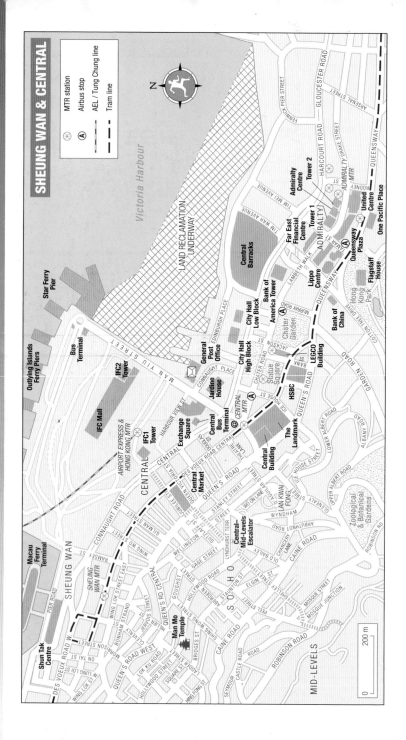

SHEUNG WAN & CENTRAL

Legend:
- ⊗ MTR station
- Ⓐ Airbus stop
- –––– AEL / Tung Chung line
- ––– Tram line

N

0 — 200 m

Victoria Harbour

LAND RECLAMATION UNDERWAY

Star Ferry Pier

Outlying Islands Ferry Piers

Bus Terminal

IFC2 Tower

IFC Mall

IFC1 Tower

AIRPORT EXPRESS & HONG KONG MTR

Exchange Square

HARBOUR VIEW ST

Central Bus Terminal

Jardine House

General Post Office

CONNAUGHT PLACE

EDINBURGH PLACE

City Hall Low Block

City Hall High Block

Bank of America Tower

Central Barracks

TIM MEI AVENUE

TIM WAH AVENUE

Far East Financial Centre

Admiralty Centre Tower 2

Admiralty Centre Tower 1

ADMIRALTY

HARCOURT ROAD

ARSENAL STREET

GLOUCESTER ROAD

QUEENSWAY

ADMIRALTY DRAKE STREET

United Centre

One Pacific Place

Queensway Plaza

Flagstaff House

Hong Kong Park

COTTON TREE DRIVE

Lippo Centre

Bank of China

MURRAY ROAD

JACKSON RD

Chater Garden

CHATER ROAD

Statue Square

HSBC

LEGCO Building

ICE HOUSE ST

BANK ST

QUEEN'S ROAD

The Landmark

Central Building

THEATRE LANE

D'AGUILAR STREET

WO ON LANE

LAN KWAI FONG

WYNDHAM STREET

ICE HOUSE STREET

LOWER ALBERT ROAD

ALBANY

GARDEN ROAD

Zoological & Botanical Gardens

UPPER ALBERT ROAD

ROBINSON RD

GLENEALY

CENTRAL

CENTRAL ST

DES VOEUX ROAD CENTRAL

Central Market

Queen's Road

STANLEY STREET

GRAHAM STREET

PEEL STREET

Central–Mid-Levels Escalator

WELLINGTON STREET

GAGE STREET

LYNDHURST TERR

COCHRANE STREET

SUTZA ST

GUTZLAFF ST

AGED ST

LYDHURST

OLD BAILEY

CHANCERY

SHELLEY STREET

ELGIN ST

STAUNTON ST

SOHO

ABERDEEN ST

PEEL ST

MOSQUE STREET

MOSQUE JUNCTION

CAINE ROAD

MID-LEVELS

ROBINSON ROAD

SEYMOUR RD

CASTLE ROAD

Man Mo Temple

HOLLYWOOD ROAD

LADDER STREET

SQUARE ST

SHING WONG STREET

BRIDGES ST

GOUGH ST

HING LUNG ST

TUNG ST

LOK KU ROAD

Queen's Rd Central

QUEEN'S ROAD WEST

JERVOIS STREET

WING LOK STREET

BONHAM STRAND

MORRISON STREET

CLEVERLY ST

WING LOK ROAD W.

ON TAI ST

LUNG LOI ST

DES VOEUX ROAD W.

PIER ROAD

Macau Ferry Terminal

Shun Tak Centre

SHEUNG WAN

SHEUNG WAN MTR

CONNAUGHT ROAD

WING WO STREET

GILMAN STREET

JUBILEE STREET

WING KUT ST

RUMSEY STREET

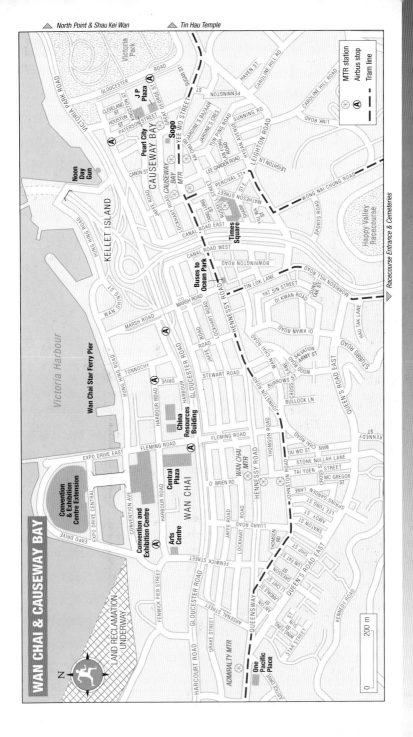

WAN CHAI & CAUSEWAY BAY

North Point & Shau Kei Wan

Tin Hau Temple

Victoria Harbour

Victoria Park

LAND RECLAMATION UNDERWAY

Convention & Exhibition Centre Extension

Convention and Exhibition Centre

Arts Centre

Central Plaza

China Resources Building

Wan Chai Star Ferry Pier

KELLET ISLAND

Noon Day Gun

Pearl City Plaza

J P Plaza

Sogo

CAUSEWAY BAY

Times Square

Buses to Ocean Park

WAN CHAI

One Pacific Place

ADMIRALTY MTR

WAN CHAI MTR

CAUSEWAY BAY MTR

Happy Valley Racecourse

Racecourse Entrance & Cemeteries

N

MTR station
Airbus stop
Tram line

200 m

0

VICTORIA PARK ROAD
GLOUCESTER ROAD
CLEVELAND ST
HOUSTON ST
KINGSTON ST
PATERSON STREET
GREAT GEORGE ST
SUGAR ST
PENNINGTON ST
HAVEN ST
CAROLINE HILL RD
CANAL ROAD
JAFFE ROAD
LOCKHART ROAD
GREAT WO STREET
YEE WO STREET
JARDINE'S BAZAAR
KAI CHIU RD
JARDINE'S CRES.
YUN PING ROAD
PAK SHA ROAD
LAN FONG ROAD
SUNNING RD
HYSAN AVENUE
LEE GARDEN ROAD
LEIGHTON ROAD
LEIGHTON LN
CAROLINE HILL RD
LINK ROAD
PERCIVAL ST
RUSSELL STREET
MATHESON STREET
SHARP ST E
YIU WA
KAI FUNG LUNG
WONG NAI CHUNG ROAD
SPORTS ROAD
CANAL ROAD EAST
CANAL ROAD WEST
BOWRINGTON ROAD
MORRISON HILL ROAD
TIN LOK LANE
YAT SIN STREET
OI KWAN ROAD
OI KWAN ROAD
SUNG TAK ST
HAU TAK LANE
STUBBS ROAD
QUEEN'S ROAD EAST
MARSH ROAD
WAN CHING ST
HING HING ROAD
TONNOCHY
HARBOUR DRIVE
HARBOUR ROAD
GLOUCESTER ROAD
JAFFE ROAD
STEWART ROAD
WAN CHAI ROAD
JOHNSTON ROAD
CROSS ST
WOOD ROAD
SALVATION ARMY ST
BURROWS ST
BULLOCK LN
FLEMING ROAD
THOMSON ROAD
TAI WO ST
STONE NULLAH LANE
TAI YUEN STREET
MC GREGOR ST
SPRING GARDEN LANE
LEE TUNG ST
AMOY ST
SWATOW ST
SHIP ST
GRESSON ST
THOMSON RD
QUEEN'S ROAD EAST
KENNEDY ST
KENNEDY ROAD
EXPO DRIVE EAST
CONVENTION AVE
EXPO DRIVE CENTRAL
EXPO DRIVE
HARBOUR ROAD
O' BRIEN RD
LUARD ROAD
LOCKHART ROAD
JAFFE ROAD
FENWICK STREET
FENWICK PIER STREET
GLOUCESTER ROAD
ARSENAL STREET
DRAKE STREET
HARCOURT ROAD
QUEENSWAY
AN TON ST
LI CHIT ST
LANDALE ST
WING FUNG ST
STAR STREET
SUN ST
HENNESSY ROAD
HENNESSY ROAD

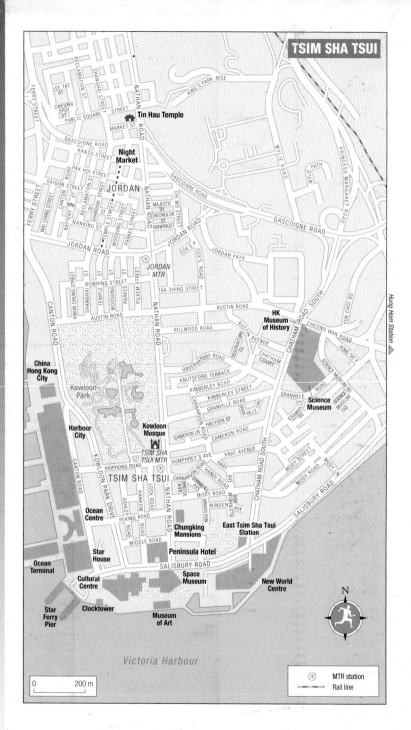

TSIM SHA TSUI

Tin Hau Temple

Night Market

JORDAN

JORDAN MTR

HK Museum of History

China Hong Kong City

Kowloon Park

Kowloon Mosque

TSIM SHA TSUI MTR

Harbour City

Science Museum

TSIM SHA TSUI

Ocean Centre

Chungking Mansions

East Tsim Sha Tsui Station

Star House

Peninsula Hotel

Ocean Terminal

Space Museum

New World Centre

Cultural Centre

Clocktower

Star Ferry Pier

Museum of Art

Victoria Harbour

Hung Hom Station ▷

Streets and labels

LEE TAT ST, CHEUNG SHUI ST, FERRY STREET, RECLAMATION STREET, SHANGHAI STREET, PUBLIC SQUARE STREET, MARKET ST, KING'S PARK RISE

GASCOIGNE ROAD, KANSU STREET, PAK HOI STREET, SAIGON STREET, CANTON ROAD, NING, NANKING ST, RECLAMATION STREET, SHANGHAI STREET, WOOSUNG STREET, TEMPLE STREET, PARKES STREET, WYLIE ROAD, WYLIE PATH, PRINCESS MARGARET ROAD

WAI CHING STREET, BATTERY, NATHAN ROAD, MAJESTIC TH, CHEONGLOK ST, NANKINGST, CHI WO ST, JORDAN ROAD

JORDAN ROAD, GASCOIGNE ROAD

COX'S P, COX'S ROAD, JORDAN PATH

KWUN CHUNG STREET, BOWRING STREET, SHANGHAI ST, TEMPLE ST, WOOSUNG ST, PILKEM ST, PILKEM STREET, TAK SHING STREET

AUSTIN ROAD, CANTON ROAD, HILLWOOD ROAD, AUSTIN ROAD, AUSTIN AVENUE, CHATHAM ROAD SOUTH, CHEONG WAN ROAD, YUK CHOI RD, HONG TAI P

OBSERVATORY ROAD, OBSERVATORY CL, CHATHAM COURT, SCIENCE MUSEUM RD, SCIENCE MUSEUM SQ

KNUTSFORD TERRACE, KIMBERLEY ROAD, KIMBERLEY STREET, CARNARVON ROAD, GRANVILLE ROAD, GRANVILLE CIRC, GRANVILLE SQ, GRANVILLE ROAD

HAU FOOK ST, CAMERON LN ROAD, CAMERON ROAD, HUMPHREY'S AVE, HART AVE, PRAT AVENUE, CHATHAM ROAD SOUTH

HAIPHONG ROAD, KOWLOON PARK DRIVE, CARNARVON ROAD, CORNWALL, HANOI ROAD, MODY ROAD, MODY STREET, MODY ROAD, MODY LN

ASHLEY ROAD, HANKOW ROAD, LOCK ROAD, BRISTOL AVE, MINDEN ROW, MINDEN AVE, BLENHEIM AVE, SALISBURY ROAD

PEKING ROAD, MIDDLE ROAD

SALISBURY ROAD

N

| 0 | 200 m |

Ⓚ MTR station
═══ Rail line